Data Visualization in R and Python

Data Visualization in R and Python

Marco Cremonini
University of Milan, Italy

WILEY

Published by John Wiley & Sons, Inc., Hoboken, New Jersey.
Published simultaneously in Canada.

Library of Congress Cataloging-in-Publication Data is applied for:

Hardback ISBN 9781394289486

Cover Design: Manuela Ruggeri
Cover Images: Courtesy of Marco Cremonini, © ulimi/Getty Images

Set in 9.5/12.5pt STIXTwoText by Straive, Chennai, India

Contents

Preface

The idea of this handbook came to me when I noticed something that made me pause and reflect. What I saw was that when I mentioned *data visualization* to a person who know just a little about it, perhaps adding that it involves representing data and the results of data analysis with *figures*, sometimes even *interactive one*, the reaction was often of curiosity with a shade of perplexity, the name sounded nice, but what is it, exactly? After all, if we have a table with data and we want to produce a graph, isn't it enough to search in a menu, choose the stylized figure of the graph you want to create and click? Is there so much to say to fill an entire book? When I also add that what I was talking about were completely different graphic tools from those of office automation and that, to tell the truth, it doesn't even stop at the graphics, even if they are interactive, but there are also *dashboards*, i.e. the latest evolution of data visualization, when real dynamic web applications are created, then the expression of the interlocutor was generally crossed by a shadow of concern. At that moment, I typically threw the ace up the sleeve by saying that in data visualization there are also maps, geographical maps – why not? – those are data too, they are spatial data, geographical data, and the maps are produced with the zoom, the flags, colored areas, and also cartographic maps, you may work with maps of New York, Tokyo, Paris, Rome, New Delhi, you name it.

At that point the interlocutors were usually looking puzzled, the references they had from the common experience were lost and doesn't really know what this data visualization is about, only that there actually seems to be a lot to say, enough to fill an entire book.

If anyone recognizes themselves in this interlocutor, be assured that you are in good company. Good in a literal not figurative sense, because data visualization is the Cinderella of data science that many admire but always from a certain distance, it arrives last and at the best moment it is forced to step back because there is no longer enough time to teach, study, or practice it. Yet, it frequently happens that those who, given the right opportunity to study and practice it, sense that it could be decidedly interesting, certainly prove useful and applicable in an infinite number of fields. This is due to a property that data visualization has and is instead absent in data analysis or code development: *it stimulates visual creativity together with logic*. Even statisticians and programmers use creativity, those who deny it have never been neither of them, but that is logical creativity. With data visualization, another dimension of otherwise neglected data science comes into play, *the visual language combined with computational logic*, meaning that data are represented with an expressive form that is no longer just logical and symbolic, but also perceptive, sensorial, shapes together with colors come into play, the once passive observer starts interacting, or projections of geographical areas suddenly become artifacts to use in a visual communication. Data visualization conveys different knowledge and logic for an expressive form that always has a double nature: computational for the data that feeds it, visual and sometimes interactive for the language it uses to communicate with the observer. There is enough to fill not a single book, in fact, what is contained in this book is a part of the discourse on data visualization, the one more practical and operative, other publications approach data visualization considering complementary aspects, such as the aesthetical composition of graphics, the storytelling behind a visual communication, and the syntax and semantic of a visual language together with the sensorial perception and psychology, and there is a lot to say for each one of these topics. All of them are essential for a complete understanding of the aim and extent of data visualization, but together they just don't fit in one single handbook, unless presented in a truly superficial fashion, for this reason almost every book on data visualization focuses more explicitly on a few of those aspects. This book is dedicated to the more operational and computational issues, because you have to know the low-level logic behind modern data visualization artifacts and you have to know and practice with tools, they are not all alike, "just pick the easiest to use and you're all set" is definitely not a good advice and, given the liveliness of the proprietary data visualization tools' market, it is easy to forget about open-source ones, which instead rival and often surpass what proprietary tools are able to offer; may be with a little more of initial efforts, but not much.

To conclude, data visualization probably deserves better consideration in educational programs and a recognition as a coherent and evolving discipline. It could be a lot of fun to study and practice it, it could make also you pause and reflect about tools for communicating data science results with a visual language, and it includes many different aspects from diverse disciplines, both theoretical and practical, all converging and enmeshing in a coherent body of knowledge. These are all good characteristics for curious persons. The Cinderella role of data visualization can be overcome by recognizing its educational and professional value and, no less important, its creative stimulus.

October 8, 2024

Marco Cremonini
University of Milan

Introduction

When you mention *data visualization* to a person who doesn't know it, perhaps adding that it involves data and the results of data analysis with *figures,* sometimes even *interactive ones,* the reaction you observe is often that the person in front of you looks intrigued but doesn't know exactly what it consists of. After all, if we have a table with data and we want to produce a graph, isn't it enough to open the usual application, go to a certain drop-down menu, choose the stylized figure of the graph you want to create and click? Is there so much to say to fill an entire book? At that moment, when you perceive that the interlocutor is thinking of the well-known spreadsheet product, you may add that those described in the book are graphic tools completely different from those of office automation and, to tell the truth, we don't even stop at the graphics, even if interactive, but there are also *dashboards*, namely the latest evolution of data visualization, when it is transformed into dynamic web applications, and to obtain dashboards it is not sufficient to click on menus but you have to go deeper into the inner logic and mechanisms. It's then that the expression of the interlocutor is generally crossed by a shadow of concern and you can play the ace up your sleeve by saying that in data visualization there are also *maps*, geographical maps, sure, those are made by data too: spatial data and geographical data, and the maps can be produced with the many available widgets such as zoom, flags, and colored areas; and we even go beyond simple maps, because there are also cartographic maps with layers of cartographic quality, such as maps of Rome, of Venice, of New York, of the most famous, and also not-so-famous cities and places, possibly with very detailed geographical information.

At that point the interlocutor has likely lost the references she or he had from the usual experience with office automation products and doesn't really know what this data visualization is, only that there seems to be a lot to say, enough to fill an entire book. If anyone recognizes themselves in this imaginary interlocutor (imaginary up to a certain point, to be honest), know that you are in good company. Good in a literal not figurative sense, because data visualization is a little like the Cinderella of data science that many admire from a certain distance, it arrives last in a project and sometimes it does not receive the attention it deserves. Yet there are many who, given the right opportunity to study and practice it, sense that it could be interesting and enjoyable, it could certainly prove useful and applicable in an infinite number of areas, situations, and results. This is due to a property that data visualization has and is instead absent in traditional data analysis or code development: *it stimulates visual creativity together with logic*. Even statisticians and programmers use creativity, those who deny it have never really practiced one of those disciplines, but that is logical creativity. With data visualization, another dimension of data science that is otherwise neglected comes into play, *the visual language combined with computational logic*, the data represented with an expressive form that is no longer just logical and formal, but also perceptive, and sensorial, comes into play with shapes, colors, use and projections of space, and it is always accompanied with meaning that the originator wish to convey and the observers will interpret, often subjectively. Data visualization conveys different knowledge and logic for an expressive form that always has a double soul: computational for the data that feeds it, visual and sometimes interactive for the language it uses to communicate with the observer. Data visualization has always a double nature: it is a key part of data science for its methods, techniques, and tools, and it is storytelling; who produces visual representations from data tells a story that may have different guises and may produce different reactions. There is enough to fill not just a single book.

Organization of the Work: Foundations and Advanced Contents

The text is divided into four parts already mentioned in the previous introduction. The ***first part*** presents the *fundamentals* of data visualization with Python and R, the two reference languages and environments for data science, employed to create *static graphs* as a direct result of a previous data wrangling (import, transformation) and analysis activity. The reference libraries for this first part are *Seaborn* for Python and *ggplot2* for R. They are both modern open-source graphics libraries and in constant evolution, both produced by the *core developers* and with the contributions of the respective *communities,* very large and lively in engaging in continuous innovations. *Seaborn* is the more recent of the two and partly represents an evolved interface of Python's traditional *matplotlib graphics library*, made more functional and enriched with features and graph types popular in modern data visualization. *Ggplot2* is the traditional graphic library for R, unanimously recognized as one of the best ever, both in the open-source and proprietary world. Ggplot is full of high-level features and constantly evolving, it receives contributions from researchers and developers from various scientific and application fields. A simply unavoidable tool for anyone approaching data visualization. The two have different settings, more traditional Seaborn, with a collection of functions and options for the different types of charts supported. Instead, ggplot is organized by overlapping graphic levels, according to a setting that goes by the name of *grammar of graphics,* shared by some of the most widespread digital graphics tools, and suitable for developing even unconventional types of graphics, thanks to the extreme flexibility it allows. This first part covers about a third of the work.

The ***second part*** introduces *Altair,* a Python library capable of producing interactive graphics in HTML and JSON format, as well as static versions in bitmap (PNG and JPG) and vector (SVG) formats. Altair is a young but solid graphic library because in all respects it represents a modern interface of *Vega-Lite,* a graphic library with an established tradition for web applications thanks to the declarative syntax in JSON format. Altair offers the same web-oriented functionality as Vega-Lite for typical data science use, with a syntax that supports the definition of overlapping graphical layers and aesthetics composed with a syntax that is easy to use and common to similar tools. This second part presents a higher level of difficulty than the first, but certainly within reach for those who have acquired the fundamental knowledge given by the first part. The first and second parts cover approximately half of the work.

The third and fourth parts represent ***advanced*** data visualization contents. The difficulty increases and so does the commitment required, on the other hand, we face two real worlds: that of *web dashboards* and of *spatial data* and *maps*. The term *dashboard* may be new to many, but dashboards are not. Whenever you access environments on the web that show menus and configurable graphic objects according to user's choices and content in the form of data or graphs, what you are using is most likely a dashboard. If you access Open Data of a large institution, such as the Organisation for Economic Co-operation and Development (OECD) or the United Nations, or even an internal company application that displays graphs and statistics, you are most likely using a dashboard. Numerous systems and products for creating dashboards with different technologies are available, it is a vast market. In data science environments with Python and R, there are two formidable tools, *Plotly/Dash* and *Shiny*, respectively. They are professional tools, and the list of relevant organizations using them is long. They are also irreplaceable teaching tools for learning the logic and basic mechanisms of a dashboard, which, in its final form, is a web application, therefore integrated with the typical technology of pages and websites. However, a Dash or Shiny dashboard is also something else, it is the terminal point of a *pipeline* that begins with the fundamentals of data science, data import, data wrangling, data analysis, and then static and dynamic graphs. The dashboard is the final end in which everything is concentrated and integrated: logic, mechanisms, requirements, and creativity. Technically they are challenging due to the presence of reactive logic which allows them to be dynamic and interactive and due to the integration of various components. The text discusses and develops examples of medium complexity, with different solutions, from web scraping of online content to the integration of Altair interactive graphics.

The second world that opens up, that of *geographical maps*, is undeniably fascinating. *Spatial data*, choropleth *maps*, the simplest ones with the colored areas (such as maps with areas colored according to the coalition that won the elections or the rate of unemployment by province, region, or nation), but also *maps* based on *cartography data* are the declination given by data science of a discipline that has very ancient roots and still constitutes an almost independent environment composed of high-resolution maps and geographic information systems (GIS), with its specializations and professional skills. Until a few years ago, data science tools could not even touch that world, but today they have come surprisingly close. This is thanks to extraordinary progress in open-source systems and tools, Python but above all R, which is now offering formidable tools capable of also using shape files from a technical cartography and geographic coordinate systems according to international standards. In the examples presented, geographic and cartographic files from Venice, Rome, and New York were used with the aim of showing the impressive potential offered by the Python and R tools.

Who is it Aimed at?

It is simple to specify to whom this text is addressed: it is addressed to everyone. Anyone who finds data visualization interesting, and images useful for their work, study, and the skills they are building, will find a learning path that starts from the fundamentals and goes up to cartography and web applications. Of course, saying "it's aimed at everyone" is simple, then doubts may arise in the reader, "but am I also part of those *everyone*?" Trying to make a list of those included in this "everyone" will inevitably leave out someone, but we could certainly mention students, researchers, and instructors of social, political, and economic sciences. In addition to many generic data, they may have spatial data to represent (e.g. movement of people and goods, global supply chains, logistics, spatial or ethnographic analyses). Next, students, researchers, and instructors of marketing, communication, public relations, journalism, media, and advertising, for whom interactive representations via the web and graphics in general are important, as products and skills. Also, students, researchers, and instructors of scientific and medical disciplines could be interested, they often deal with sophisticated graphic representations, for example in biology or epidemiology, without forgetting that the graphic contributions from the genomics and molecular biology community are among the most numerous. Students, researchers, and instructors of engineering, management, or bioengineering, for example, use data science tools and visualization as an integral part of their analyses. Historians, archaeologists, and paleontologists produce high-quality graphic representations, so the text can be useful for them too. Well, the list is already long, and I'm definitely forgetting someone who should be mentioned instead.

In general, undergraduate and graduate students, teachers, researchers, and Ph.D. students will find many examples and explanations to help them graphically present content and organize exercises. Likewise, professionals and companies, for their corporate and institutional communication and training, may enjoy the material presented in the text.

What I'm trying to say is that data visualization, like data science as a whole, is not a sectoral discipline for which you need to have a specific background, such as a statistician, computer scientist, engineer, or graphic designer. It is not necessary at all, in fact the opposite is needed, that is, that data visualization and data science be as transversal as possible, being studied and used by all those who, for their formation and work interests, in their specific field, from economics to paleontology, from psychology to molecular biology, find themselves working with data, whether numerical, textual, or spatial and find useful to obtain high-quality visual representations from those data, perhaps interactive or structured in dashboards.

What is Required and What is Learned

To follow and learn the contents of the text it is necessary to know the fundamentals of data science with Python and R, meaning those concerned with importing and reading operations of datasets and the typical data wrangling operations (sorting, aggregations, shape and type transformations, selections, and so on). Numerous examples are presented in the text which include the data wrangling part (the cases where it is longer can be found in the Supplementary Material), so to replicate a visualization all the necessary code is available, starting from reading the Open Data. Therefore, it is not required to independently produce the preliminary part of operations on the data, but it is necessary to be able to interpret the logic and the operations that are performed. Hence the need to know the fundamentals, as well as the possibility of producing variations of the examples.

Another aspect that may appear problematic is knowledge of the fundamentals of data science with both Python and R because often one only knows one of the two environments and languages. In this regard, I would like to reassure anyone who finds themselves in this situation. If you know data wrangling operations with R or Python, interpreting the logic of those carried out with the other language requires little effort, at most the details of the syntax will need some specific attention and learning efforts. But here a second consideration comes into play: knowledge of both Python and R is particularly useful in modern data science, those who know only one of the two probably just need a good opportunity to learn the second, discovering that the learning curve is much smoother than could have been imagined and the effort will be certainly reasonable. The advantage will be considerable in terms of new features and tools that will become available.

The organization into parts also suggests a progression and division in learning and teaching. The *first part* is also suitable for those who have just learned the fundamentals of data science and can be carried out in parallel with the study of those fundamentals. Most static graphs require basic data wrangling operations and generating graphs can be a great educational tool for demonstrating the logic and use of data wrangling operations. The presentation of the different types of static graphs follows an order of increasing complexity, from the first intuitive and easily modifiable in infinite variations, up to the last ones which require knowledge of some important properties of statistical analysis. The difficulty level of code is generally low. The *second part* is a natural continuation of the first. The Altair library has a linear and clear syntax, so the greater difficulty introduced by the interactive features, especially in terms of computational logic, is completely within reach for anyone who has learned the fundamentals contained in the first part. The result will be motivating, the Altair interactive graphics are of excellent quality, allowing various configurations and alternative solutions.

Between these two parts and the subsequent *third* and *fourth parts*, there is a gap in terms of what is required and what is learned, for this reason in the initial introductory part the last two parts were presented as *advanced content*. It is necessary to have acquired a good familiarity with the fundamentals, confidence in searching for information in the documentation of libraries, and knowing how to patiently and methodically manage errors. In other words, you need to have done a good number of exercises with the fundamental part.

For the *third part on dashboards,* it is necessary to have basic knowledge of HTML, CSS, and in general how a traditional web page is made. They are not difficult notions, but it may take some time to acquire them. You don't need more advanced knowledge, such as JavaScript or web application frameworks. You also need to have gained some confidence in writing scripts in Python and R. In both cases you learn the basic reactive mechanisms to manage interactivity, it is a different logic from the traditional one.

For the *fourth part on maps,* it is necessary to learn the fundamental notions of geographic coordinate systems, the form of geographic data with the typical organization in geometries, and the often-necessary coordinate transformations. The tools used are partly known, *ggplot* for R and *pandas* for Python, but many new ones will be encountered because in any case, not only in the world of cartography but also in that of data science, the logic, methods, and tools to use spatial data have specificities that distinguish them. As mentioned initially, there are some initial difficulties to overcome and it is required to go into the details of the shape of the spatial data, but the use of these data and the production of geographical maps is fascinating, right from the first and simple choropleth maps. However, it is right after those initial maps that there's the real beauty of working with spatial data and geographic maps.

What is Excluded

As always, or almost always, much remains excluded from the content of a book, sometimes simply due to the need not to exceed a certain number of pages, sometimes out of pure forgetfulness, and often due to a conscious choice by the Author. All three motifs also exist in this work. For the first, that is simply how a publisher works; for the second, other than apologizing I don't know what to say since those are things I've forgotten; for the third however, there is something to comment on, if for no other reason than to give some explanation of the motives for exclusions by choice.

The first obvious exclusion is the absence of proprietary technologies and tools. For data visualization there are many proprietary solutions, from very specialized ones produced by small companies to generalist ones produced by big players. Manufacturers of data visualization software will say that their tools are better than those presented in this book. For some aspects, it might be true, but almost always it is false and in general, to define itself as better than the open-source tools of Python and R would require several distinctions and clarifications that are rarely presented. One of the main reasons is the ease of use of the graphical interfaces of proprietary tools compared to the low-level programming of open-source ones. An old, worn out, and now out-of-date issue that is slowly, perhaps, starting to be overcome. It is obvious that learning to click sequences of buttons and menus or drag graphic icons is initially simpler than writing code with a programming language. The initial learning curve is different in the two cases. The point, however, lies in that adjective, "initial." What happens next? What is the purpose of learning to use these tools? If the purpose is educational, teaching and learning the fundamentals and advanced contents of data visualization, there is practically no choice, only the environments and tools that exhibit low-level details are teaching tools. The others simply aren't. They are suitable for professional training courses on that particular instrument, but not for basic teaching or learning. This is enough to exclude any proprietary instrument from this text. It should be noted that some of the most modern proprietary tools (or perhaps made by intelligent manufacturers) are integrating the open-source technologies of Python and R into their frameworks, with the idea of offering both possibilities.

Then there is a specific and perhaps surprising exclusion among the basic chart types, and not one of the exotic kind that very few use, on the contrary of the most widespread, very widespread indeed. The excluded is *pie charts* and reason is simply that *it is not useful* in the true sense of data visualization in data science. The statement will seem surprising, in what sense are pie charts, ubiquitous and used millions of times, not useful? I will briefly explain the reason, which is also shared by many who deal with data visualization. A graph is produced to visually represent the information contained in certain data and this representation is based on at least two conditions: (1) that the visual representation is clear and interpretable in an unambiguous way and (2) that with the graph, the information contained in the data is easier to understand than the tabular form (or at least of equal difficulty). Pie charts satisfy neither condition. They are ambiguous because the relative size of the slices is often unclear and above all they make it more difficult to interpret the data than the equivalent table. In other words, if the table with the values is presented instead of the pie chart, the reader has easier, clearer, and more understandable information. On the contrary, bar charts are one of the fundamental type of graphics, despite the fact that pie charts are simply the polar coordinate representation of a bar chart. So why this difference and why pie charts are so common? The reason for the difference is that visually evaluating angles is considerably more difficult than comparing linear heights. Pie charts are mostly used because they just give a touch of color to an otherwise monotonous text, not for their informative content. And what about the difficulty of evaluating the slice proportions? Well, the numerical values are often added to the slices, that is, in practice, to rewrite the data table right over the graphic.

To conclude, data visualization deserves more space in educational programs and clearer recognition as a coherent and evolving discipline and body of knowledge. The Cinderella role of data science can be overcome by recognizing its educational value and, no less importantly, its creative stimulus.

About the Companion Website

This book is accompanied by a companion website:

https://www.wiley.com/go/Cremonini/DataVisualization1e

This website includes:
- Codes
- Figures
- Datasets

Part I

Static Graphics with ggplot (R) and Seaborn (Python)

Grammar of Graphics

The grammar of graphics was cited in the Introduction and will continue to be mentioned in the rest of the text. We see a brief summary here. The concept of grammar of graphics was proposed by Leland Wilkinson in the early 2000s with the idea of creating grammatical, mathematical, and aesthetic rules to define the graphics that were produced by statistical analysis. The different approach, with respect to the fixed definition of chart types composed of stylized reference schemes, is that a graph's grammar would instead have allowed previously unknown flexibility. In Wilkinson's definition, seven fundamental components were identified, but the construction by overlapping layers was not yet highlighted. It is Hadley Wickham, core developer of R and ggplot, who in 2010 introduced the *layered* grammar of graphics, with which Wilkinson's approach was updated by reviewing the fundamental elements. The definition by levels provides the representation of the data, combining statistics and geometries, two of the fundamental elements, together with *positions*, *aesthetics*, *scales*, a *coordinate system*, and possibly *facets*. We will find all these elements in ggplot and Altair, the two graphic libraries organized according to the grammar of graphics considered in this book, as well as in the recent but still preliminary Seaborn Objects interface of Seaborn, the reference graphic library for Python.

Data Visualization in R and Python, First Edition. Marco Cremonini.

Companion website: www.wiley.com/go/Cremonini/DataVisualization1e

References

Leland Wilkinson, *The Grammar of Graphics*, 2nd Ed., Springer-Verlag New York 2005, https://doi.org/10.1007/0-387-28695-0.

Leland Wilkinson, The Grammar of Graphics, Chapter 13, *Handbook of Computational Statistics, Concepts and Methods*, 2nd Ed., Gentle J.E., Härdle W. K. and Mori Y. (eds.), Springer-Verlag Berlin Heidelberg 2012. https://doi.org/10.1007/978-3-642-21551-3.

Wickham, H. (2010). A Layered Grammar of Graphics. *Journal of Computational and Graphical Statistics* 19 (1): 3–28. http://dx.doi.org/10.1198/jcgs.2009.07098.

1

Scatterplots and Line Plots

Scatterplots, with the main variant represented by line plots, are the fundamental type of graphic for pairs of continuous variables or for a continuous variable and a categorical variable and, in addition to representing the most common type of graphic together with bar plots (or bar charts/bar graphs), form the basis for numerous variations. The logic that guides a scatterplot graphic is to represent with *markers* (e.g., dots or other symbols) the values that two quantities (variables and attributes) take on during a certain number of observations. The pairs of variables are conventionally associated with the Cartesian axes x and y, with scales ordered in ascending order, according to units of measurement, which may be different. By convention, the variable associated with the x-axis is said to be the *independent* variable and put in relation with the *dependent* variable on the y-axis, meaning that what is shown is implicitly a correlation between the two variables. This traditional interpretation of the meaning of the representation of variables on Cartesian axes must be put in the right context to avoid all too frequent errors. The result of a scatterplot graphic, in no case, demonstrates the existence of a cause–effect relationship between two variables. The cause–effect relationship must already be known in order to consider one variable as truly dependent on the other. Or it must be demonstrated, extending the graphic analysis with considerations about the phenomenon observed and the reasons in favor of the existence of such a cause–effect relationship. Conversely, a scatterplot simply shows how pairs of values from two variables are distributed for a sample of observations, nothing is said about the reasons. A typical example that is often presented considers the height and weight of a certain sample of people. Each person represents a single observation, the two quantities have different units of measurement and for each person, the intersection between the coordinates of height (x-axis) and weight (y-axis) is marked with a dot (or other marker). In this case, we know that there is a cause–effect relationship between the two physical characteristics: a greater height tends to correspond to a greater weight for purely

Data Visualization in R and Python, First Edition. Marco Cremonini.

Companion website: www.wiley.com/go/Cremonini/DataVisualization1e

physiological reasons regarding body size. This does not mean that a tall person always weighs more than a short one, which is obviously false, but only that this tends to be true, given a homogeneous sample of the population.

Dataset

Inflation, consumer prices (annual %), World Bank Open Data (https://data.worldbank.org/indicator/FP.CPI.TOTL.ZG).

Copyright: Creative Commons CC BY-4.0 (https://creativecommons.org/licenses/by/4.0/)

Compiled historical daily temperature and precipitation data for selected 210 U.S. cities, Yuchuan Lai and David Dzombak, Carnegie Mellon University, April 2022, DOI: 10.1184/R1/7890488.v5 (https://kilthub.cmu.edu/articles/dataset/Compiled_daily_temperature_and_precipitation_data_for_the_U_S_cities/7890488).

Copyright: Creative Commons CC0 1.0 DEED.

GDP growth (annual %), World Bank Open Data (https://data.worldbank.org/indicator/NY.GDP.MKTP.KD.ZG).*Copyright*: Creative Commons CC BY-4.0 (https://creativecommons.org/licenses/by/4.0/).

1.1 R: ggplot

1.1.1 Scatterplot

Let us start with the just mentioned relation between height and weight of a sample of people. For this, we can use the dataset *heights*, predefined into package *modelr*, which is part of the *tidyverse* package. For simplicity, we always assume to load the *tidyverse* package for all R examples. The dataset refers to a sample of US citizens collected in a 2012 study of the *U.S. Bureau of Labor Statistics*. Values are expressed as centimeters and kilograms, for readers familiar with the Imperial system, they could be visualized simply by omitting the two transformations into centimeters and kilograms with the conversion coefficients shown in the code.

```
library(tidyverse)

df= modelr::heights
df$height_cm= 2.54*df$height
df$weight_kg= 0.45359237*df$weight

df
# A tibble: 7,006 × 10
   income height weight   age marital  sex     height_cm weight_kg
    <int>  <dbl>  <int> <int> <fct>    <fct>   <dbl>         <dbl>
 1  19000     60    155    53 married  female  152.           70.3
```

```
2   35000         70      156     51 married  female  178.        70.8
3 105000          65      195     52 married  male    165.        88.5
4   40000         63      197     54 married  female  160.        89.4
5   75000         66      190     49 married  male    168.        86.2
# ... with 7,001 more rows
```

The dataset contains data of 7006 individuals, with information regarding sex, income, and marital status, in addition to height and weight.

We can create the scatterplot of height and weight by using *ggplot* (in the book, for simplicity, we generically refer to *ggplot* meaning the current *ggplot2* version of the R package). The main function is `ggplot()`, with the data frame to use as its first attribute, while the second attribute represents the *aesthetics* of the grammar of graphics, defined with function `aes()`. Aesthetics represent graphical elements whose *values are derived from data frame's variables/columns.* In other words, every graphical element that should depend on data must be defined into the `aes()` function and it is called an *aesthetic.* The main aesthetics are attributes `x` and `y` corresponding to the Cartesian axes. Figure 1.1 shows the result of executing just the *ggplot* function with *x* and *y* aesthetics.

```
ggplot(data= df, aes(x= height_cm, y= weight_kg))
```

We have obtained exactly what we specified: the Cartesian plan with the two variables associated to the axes and the scales defined according to data values. Consistent with the *grammar of graphics*, this represents the first layer of our graphic, now we could proceed by adding the following layers with graphical elements. If we want to draw a scatterplot, we should specify it by means of the corresponding function `geom_point()`. In this first example, we do not specify anything else, scatterplot aesthetics are inherited from those defined in the main ggplot function. The plus sign + concatenates the two layers: first the Cartesian plan is created, then, on top of it, the scatterplot markers are designed (Figure 1.2).

Figure 1.1 Output of the ggplot function with *x* and *y* aesthetics.

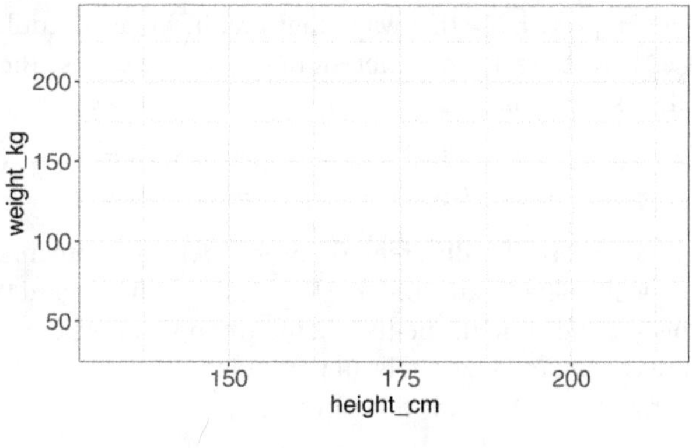

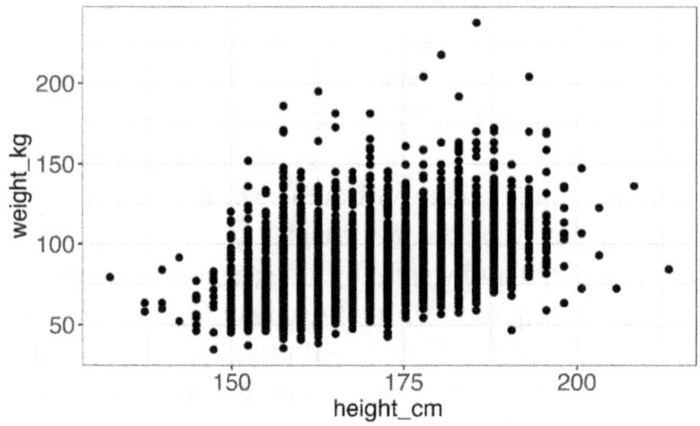

Figure 1.2 First ggplot's scatterplot.

```
ggplot(data= df, aes(x= height_cm, y= weight_kg)) +
  geom_point()
```

This is the scatterplot of our sample of citizens' heights and weights. The existing causal relation between height and weight is confirmed by the increasing trend, although the large variability represented by the dispersion of points should be noted. We make another step forward. The relation should be studied for homogeneous samples, for example, it would not be correct to mix infants with adults given the largely different body shapes and proportions, likewise, men and women have different body structures so it would be better to analyze them separately. A possibility is to divide the data frame into two subsets of data for men and for women and plot them separately. A better option is to visualize men and women differently in the same plot, for example, using colors to differentiate the two subsets. In this case, the color of the markers is an aesthetic that will depend on data values from the data frame variable *sex*. We should define it accordingly using `color=sex` in the `aes()` function. It could be done in two ways, either it is defined in the `ggplot()` function and inherited by all following elements (except for the case of explicitly denying inheritance through the parameter `inherit.aes=FALSE`), or set only for the specific layer defined by `geom_point()` (this way other graphical layers could associate the same color aesthetic to variables different than *sex*). We choose the second option. Figure 1.3 shows the result.

```
ggplot(data= df, aes(x= height_cm, y= weight_kg)) +
  geom_point(aes(color= sex))
```

Now we see the difference between men and women, with men, not surprisingly, typically taller than women. However, for what regard the causal relation between height and weight, the increasing trend result is less evident if men and women are considered separately, in particular for women, apparently exhibiting a larger variability, at least for this sample.

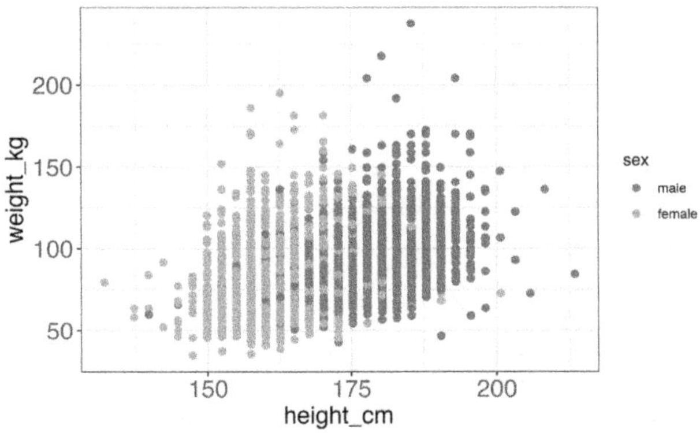

Figure 1.3 Scatterplot with color aesthetic.

If we try with a different variable to analyze homogeneous subsets in the population, for example, coloring points for marital status, the result changes, and in this case, it does not exhibit any apparent causal relation (Figure 1.4).

```
ggplot(data= df, aes(x= height_cm, y= weight_kg)) +
  geom_point(aes(color= marital))
```

We could consider another relation, here between height and income, which sometimes is pretended to carry some truth, with tall people supposedly earning more than short ones (Figure 1.5).

```
ggplot(data= df, aes(x= height_cm, y= income)) +
  geom_point(aes(color= sex))
```

Again, at first sight, no causal relation seems to emerge for this sample of citizens, except that women appear to earn less than men, and that among the

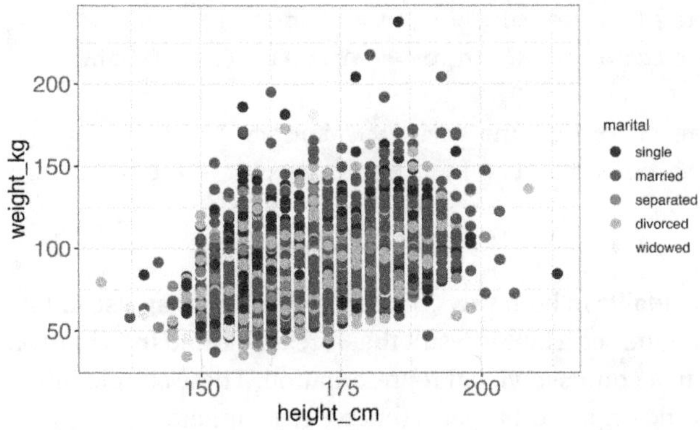

Figure 1.4 Scatterplot with color aesthetic for marital status variable.

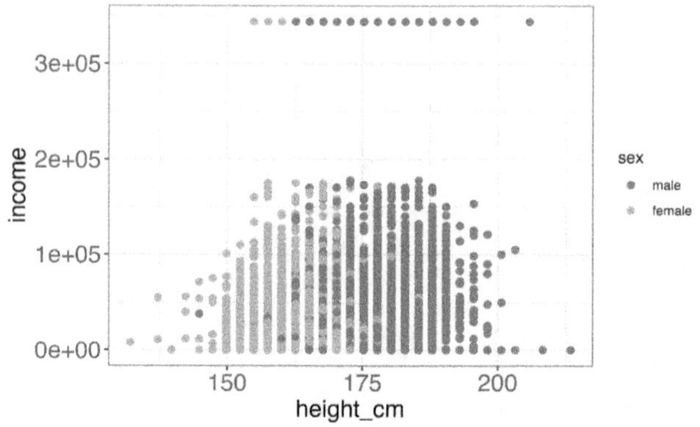

Figure 1.5 Scatterplot with income as dependent variable and color aesthetic for sex variable.

wealthiest, men are largely the majority, two well-known facts of an enduring state of gender inequality.

What if we would like to introduce a fourth variable, for example, the marital status in addition to height, weight, and sex? We have to use another aesthetic in addition to *x*, *y*, and *color*, for example, the *shape* of the markers. We have two possibilities: associate markers' shape to the marital status (`color=sex, shape=marital`) or the sex to the shape (`color=marital, shape=sex`). We try both ways and use package *patchwork* (https://patchwork.data-imaginist.com/) to plot the two graphics side by side (`plot1 + plot2` or `plot1 | plot2`). To have them stacked one over the other, the syntax would be `plot1 / plot2`. Figure 1.6 shows the two alternatives.

```
library(patchwork)

ggplot(data= df, aes(x= height_cm, y= income)) +
  geom_point(aes(color= sex, shape=marital)) -> plot1

ggplot(data= df, aes(x= height_cm, y= income)) +
  geom_point(aes(color= marital, shape=sex)) -> plot2

plot1 / plot2
```

The result is almost unreadable in both ways. This simply shows that just adding more aesthetics does not guarantee a better result that is readable and informative; instead, it easily ends up in a confused visual representation. These simple initial examples have touched some important aspects that we recapitulate:

- The logic of the grammar of graphics.

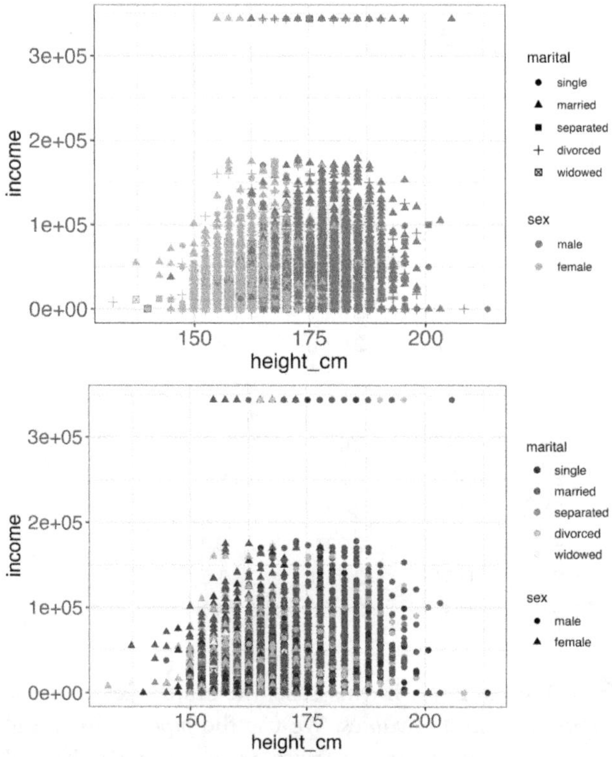

Figure 1.6 (a/b) Scatterplots with four variables.

- The use of aesthetics.
- The indispensable care required to draw a graphic.
- The required caution in interpreting visual results.

Let us now consider another example by using package *WDI* (https://github.com/vincentarelbundock/WDI), containing the World Development Indicators from the *World Bank*. For the sake of precision, the package is not strictly necessary, the same data could be manually collected from the World Bank's *DataBank* (https://data.worldbank.org/).

In particular, we use data about *inflation variations measured on consumer prices*, associated to indicator *FP.CPI.TOTL.ZG* or available from https://data.worldbank.org/indicator/. We use, for instance, US data (different countries could be selected by changing the attribute `iso2c=='US'`).

```
library(WDI)

infl = WDI(indicator='FP.CPI.TOTL.ZG')
```

```
infl= as_tibble(infl)
us_infl= filter(infl, iso2c=='US')

# A tibble: 62 × 5
country iso2c iso3c  year FP.CPI.TOTL.ZG
<chr>    <chr> <chr> <int>          <dbl>
United States      US      USA      2022    8.00
United States      US      USA      2021    4.70
United States      US      USA      2020    1.23
United States      US      USA      2019    1.81
United States      US      USA      2018    2.44
United States      US      USA      2017    2.13
United States      US      USA      2016    1.26
United States      US      USA      2015    0.12
United States      US      USA      2014    1.62
United States      US      USA      2013    1.46
United States      US      USA      2012    2.07
United States      US      USA      2011    3.16
United States      US      USA      2010    1.64
# …
```

The time series goes from 1960 to 2022. In this case, the scatterplot could be produced by associating *years* to *inflation values*. We use the *pipe notation* and add some style options: a specific marker (`shape`) with a custom line width and internal color (`stroke` and `fill`), the marker size (`size`), a certain degree of transparency (`alpha`), custom labels for aesthetics (`labs()`) – either associated to axes, the legend, or as plot title/subtitle – and a graphic theme (`theme()`). Figure 1.7 shows the result.

```
us_infl %>% ggplot(aes(x= year, y= FP.CPI.TOTL.ZG)) +
  geom_point(shape=21, stroke=2, size=5,
             fill="gold", color= "skyblue3", alpha=0.7) +
  labs(x= "Year", y= 'Inflation (%)') +
 theme_light()
```

The options included in this example for customizing the scatterplot cover almost all available possibilities. We can modify the graphic to add more countries, for example, France, Germany, and the United Kingdom.

```
sample_infl= filter(infl, iso2c %in% c('FR','DE','GB','US'))
```

We can draw again the scatterplot, in this case, without the many stylistic options but with *color* as an aesthetic associated to countries and a color palette from *Viridis* (Figure 1.8).

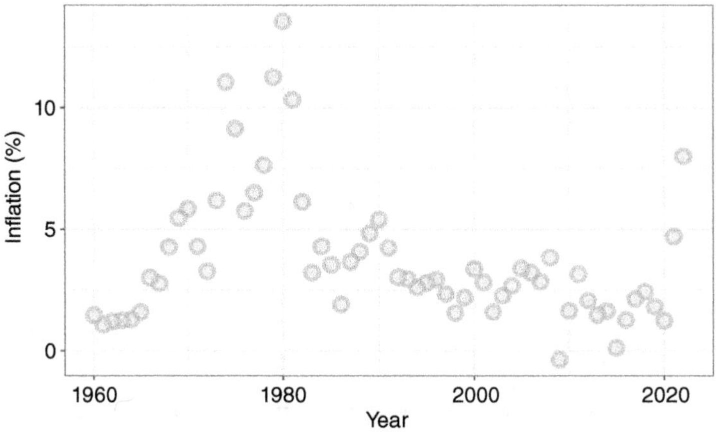

Figure 1.7 United States' inflation values 1960–2022.

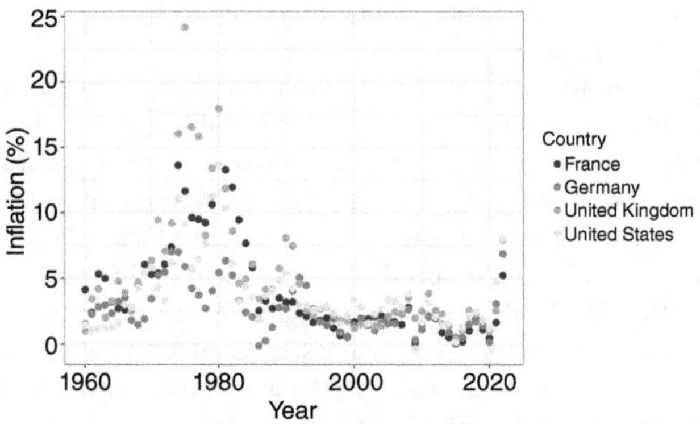

Figure 1.8 Inflation values for a sample of countries.

```
sample_infl %>% ggplot(aes(x= year, y= FP.CPI.TOTL.ZG)) +
  geom_point(aes(color=country), size=2) +
  scale_fill_viridis_d()+
  labs( x= "Year", y= 'Inflation (%)',
        color= "Country" ) +
  theme_light()
```

The result, once again, is not clearly readable, it is difficult to recognize the yearly variations watching dots of same color and even more trying to compare the different countries. This is a typical case of where to prefer a *line plot*, which we will consider in the following section, to a scatterplot, because here it is important to easily recognize groups of points, each one representing a certain entity

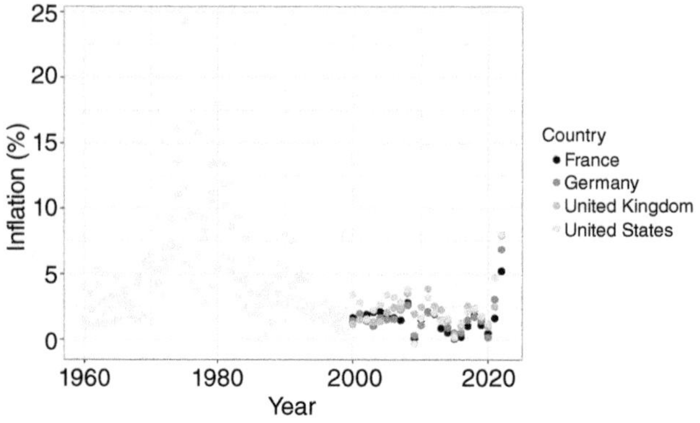

Figure 1.9 Dots colors based on an aesthetic when over a threshold, otherwise as a fixed color.

(a specific country, in our example). Before line plots, to conclude this short introduction to scatterplots, many more examples will be presented in the following chapters, we consider some other cases.

The first one is very common: we want *to color the markers differently based on threshold values*. For example, we want dots over a first threshold in a given color, dots below a second threshold in another color, and those between them in a third color. Or, in a different setting, we want markers colored based on an aesthetic only when they fall over a certain threshold and with a fixed neutral tint when below that threshold; this is because we could be specifically interested in differentiating data points only over the threshold, in order to make an observer focus the attention to them. Same logic could be applied by using shapes rather than colors.

In the following example, we associate the *color* aesthetic to the countries, and we want to show colored markers only for years from 2000 and beyond while using a neutral tint for years before 2000. In this case, we proceed as follows: with function `mutate()` we create a new column *color*, whose values are assigned based on a logical condition, *if* year is *equal or greater* than 2000, then we assign the country name, *otherwise* the value remains undefined.

In the graphic, the aesthetic `color` is associated to the new column *color*. Function `scale_color_manual()` defines the values (using attribute `breaks`) to be associated to colors (using attribute `values`), and, with attribute `na.value`, we assign a fixed color to elements of the column *color* with a missing value (Figure 1.9).

```
color_list= c("black","forestgreen","skyblue3","gold")

sample_infl %>%
  mutate(color = ifelse(year>=2000,
                        as.character(sample_infl$country),
```

```
                          NA_character_)) %>%
ggplot(aes(x= year, y= FP.CPI.TOTL.ZG)) +
geom_point(aes(color=color), size= 2) +
scale_color_manual(breaks = unique(sample_infl$country),
                    values = color_list, na.value= "azure3") +
labs(x= "Year", y= 'Inflation (%)', color= "Country" ) +
theme_light()
```

1.1.2 Repulsive Textual Annotations: Package *ggrepel*

In this example, we define two thresholds for the inflation value and color the points differently. We also add two *horizontal segments* (using function `geom_hline()`) to visually represent the thresholds. Function `scale_color_manual()` allows assigning colors manually to the *color* aesthetic. There exist several variants of *scale* functions, the main ones are `scale_color_*` and `scale_fill_*` (the star symbol indicating that several specific functions are available), respectively, for configuring the aesthetic `color` or the aesthetic `fill`. Moreover, *scale* functions are also important to configure axes values and labels. We will use them in other examples. In addition, we introduce an often very useful package called *ggrepel*, which is the best solution when textual annotations should be added to markers, to show a corresponding value. The problem with textual annotations in scatterplots is that they easily end up overlapping in a clutter of labels only partially readable. Package *ggrepel* automatically separates them or, at least, makes its best effort to produce a comprehensible visualization. It has obvious limits, when markers are too many and too close, there is nothing that even *ggrepel* could do to place all labels in a suitable way, but if markers are a few, which is the correct situation for showing textual labels, the result is usually good. Here we use it to add textual labels only for years with a very high inflation (greater than 5%).

For this example, the logic is the following: with function `cut()`, we can define three ranges of inflation values, i.e. from −2 to 2, from 2 to 5, and from 5 to infinite; variable *val* is defined as a *list* with *key=value* pairs as elements, where keys are the values resulting from function `cut()` and values are color codes; variable *lab* has the different texts to visualize as legend keys.

In the graphic, we have the `color` aesthetic associated to the three values produced by the `cut()` function, and with function `scale_color_manual()` we configure colors corresponding to values of variable *val* and legend names corresponding to variable *lab*. It would be worth making some tests and variations in order to fully clarify the logic of the example. Textual labels are added by loading library *ggrepel* and using function `geom_label_repel()`, which in this case takes a subset of data (variable *highInfl*) and associates values of variable *year* to aesthetic `label`. Figure 1.10 shows the result.

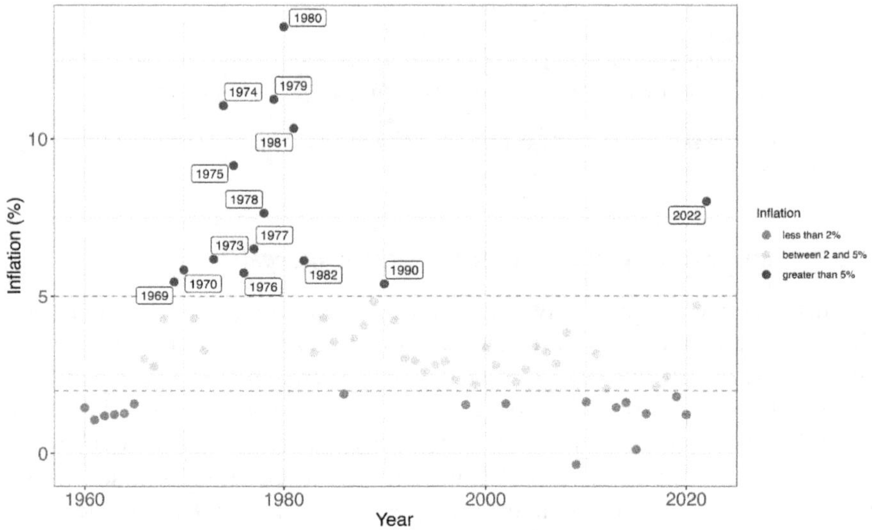

Figure 1.10 Markers colored based on two thresholds and textual labels, US inflation.

```
library(ggrepel)

cut= cut(us_infl$FP.CPI.TOTL.ZG, c(-Inf, 2, 5, Inf))

val= c("(-2,2]" = "forestgreen",
       "(2,5]" = "gold",
       "(5,Inf]" = "darkred")

lab= c("less than 2%", "between 2 and 5%", "greater than 5%")

highInfl= filter(us_infl,FP.CPI.TOTL.ZG>5)

us_infl %>% ggplot(aes(x= year, y= FP.CPI.TOTL.ZG)) +
  geom_point(aes(color= cut), size=3) +
  scale_color_manual(name = "Inflation",
                     values = val,
                     labels = lab) +
  geom_hline(yintercept = 2, linetype = "dashed",
             color = "grey50", linewidth=.5) +
  geom_hline(yintercept = 5, linetype = "dashed",
             color = "grey50", linewidth=.5) +
  geom_label_repel(data=highInfl, aes(label=year))+
  labs( x= "Year", y= 'Inflation (%)' ) +
  theme_light()
```

1.1.3 Scatterplots with High Number of Data Points

With the next example, we show how scatterplots could be employed even with a multitude of data points. In this case, it is not specific values of single data points to provide useful information, if we exclude some exceptional cases, instead, it is the shape of the whole set to inform the reader of a certain phenomenon. For this example, we use datasets with temperature measurements regarding some US cities from Carnegie Mellon University's *Compiled historical daily temperature and precipitation data for selected 210 U.S. cities*. Atlanta, El Paso, Havre (Montana), Milwaukee, New York, and Phoenix have been selected to cover a wide range of climate conditions. Temperatures are measured *daily* by collecting the *minimum* and *maximum temperature*, values are expressed in Fahrenheit degrees (*Note*: readers used to Celsius degrees can convert them using the following formula: *Celsius = (Fahrenheit–32)/1.79999999*).

Time series provided with this set of data, in several cases, cover many decades; for example, years have been selected from 2010 to 2022. Some data-wrangling operations are needed to prepare the data frame. First, because each data series is referred to a single measurement station, there could be more than one for each city, and second, because they are recorded as separate CSV (comma-separated values) datasets. We have chosen data collected from airport measurement stations and, after reading each dataset, a column specifying the city has been added, then separate data frames have been combined to form a single one. The resulting data frame has been transformed into *long form* to have both minimum and maximum temperatures in a single column.

```
c1= vroom('datasets/CarnegieMU/7890488/USW00014839.csv') # Milwaukee
c2= vroom('datasets/CarnegieMU/7890488/USW00023044.csv') # El Paso
c3= vroom('datasets/CarnegieMU/7890488/USW00094728.csv') # New York
c4= vroom('datasets/CarnegieMU/7890488/USW00023183.csv') # Phoenix
c5= vroom('datasets/CarnegieMU/7890488/USW00013874.csv') # Atlanta
c6= vroom('datasets/CarnegieMU/7890488/USW00094012.csv') # Havre, Montana

c1$city= 'Milwaukee'
c2$city= 'El Paso'
c3$city= 'New York'
c4$city= 'Phoenix'
c5$city= 'Atlanta'
c6$city= "Havre (MT)"

cities= bind_rows(c1,c2,c3,c4,c5,c6)

citiesL= pivot_longer(cities, cols = tmax:tmin,
            names_to = "tminmax", values_to = "temp")
```

Years from 2010 to 2022 are selected, then the graphic has been produced. Ticks on axes x and y have been customized according to dates and temperatures; axes and legend values also have been minimally tweaked (functions `scale_x_date()` and `scale_y_continuous()` for axes' ticks, functions `theme()` and `guides()` for axes and legend values). The color palette is set with `scale_color_wsj()` that imitates the typical color scale of *The Wall Street Journal.*

```
filter(citiesL, lubridate::year(Date)>=2010) -> y201022

filter(y201022, tminmax=="tmin") %>%
  ggplot()+
  geom_point(aes(x=Date, y=temp, color=city),
             alpha=0.7, size=0.6, shape=16)+
  scale_color_wsj()+
  scale_x_date(date_breaks = "2 years",
               date_labels = "%Y")+
  scale_y_continuous(breaks = c(-40,-20,0,20,40,60,80,100))+
  labs(x="", y="Temperature (F)",
       color="City", subtitle="Minimum Temperatures 2010-2022")+
  theme_light()+
  theme(axis.text.x = element_text(angle=0, vjust = 0.5)) -> p

p + guides(color= guide_legend(override.aes = list(size=3)))
```

Figure 1.11 shows the result for minimum temperatures. The shape of the multitude of scatterplot markers provides an intuitive information about the seasonal temperature variation, which is qualitatively similar for all cities. The *color* aesthetic, set with city names, offers specific information about cities, although

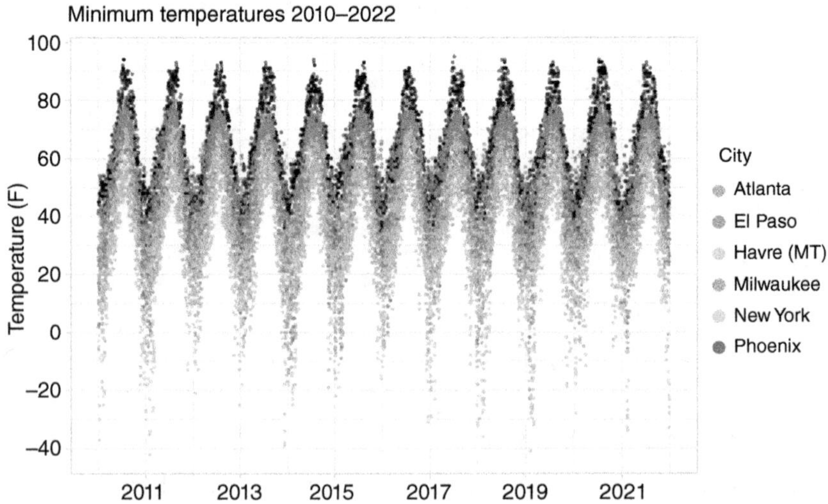

Figure 1.11 Temperature measurement in some US cities, minimum temperatures.

not completely clear, due to markers overlapping. The hottest city, i.e. Phoenix, and the coldest, i.e. Havre, are fairly well recognizable in their most extreme temperatures, but details are muddled for temperatures in the middle range. We will see in a future chapter how to approach a case like this for producing a clearer visualization; for now, it is important to learn that scatterplots are extremely flexible and adaptable to many cases, and creativity could and should be exercised.

1.1.4 Line Plot

The *line plot* is a scatterplot variant that connects with a line the data points *belonging to the same group*, meaning that they share the same value of a certain variable (e.g., they are referred to the same city). The same data points could or could not be visualized with a marker. Let us consider a first example, which will result in an incoherent graphic, but will be useful to understand the main characteristic of line plots, which is the definition of homogeneous groups of data points. We use the previous example with countries and inflation values and add a new layer representing the line plot with function `geom_line()`. Figure 1.12 shows the result, which is problematic.

```
sample_infl %>% ggplot(aes(x= year, y= FP.CPI.TOTL.ZG)) +
  geom_point(aes(color=country), size=2) +
  geom_line(aes()) +
  scale_fill_viridis_d()+
  labs(x= "Year", y= 'Inflation (%)', ccolor= "Country") +
  theme_light()
```

The result is clearly incoherent because the line just connects data points in sequential order, which has no meaning at all. What we would have wanted, instead, was to connect data points belonging to the same country, this way

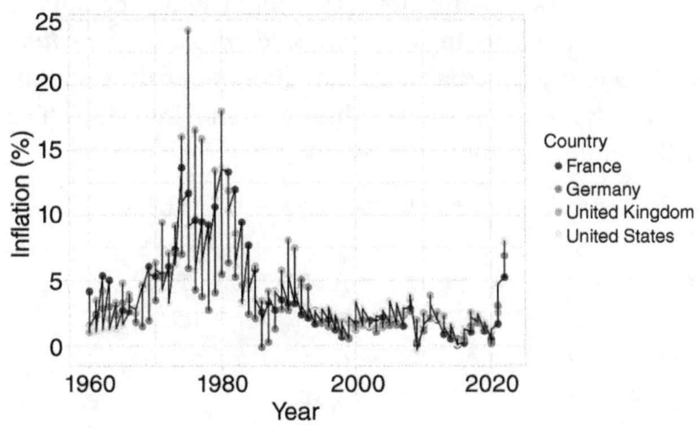

Figure 1.12 A problematic line plot, groups are not respected.

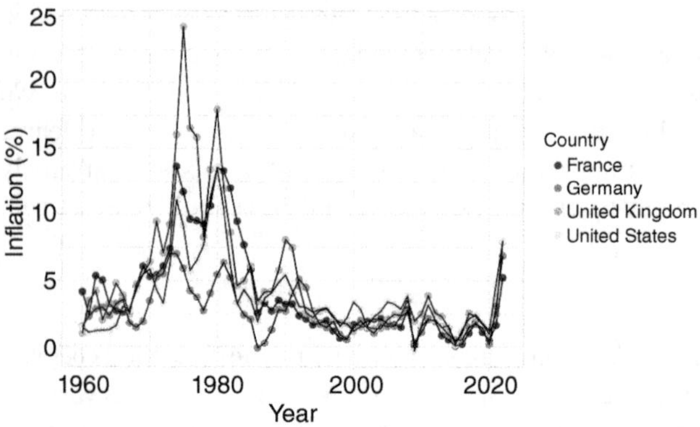

Figure 1.13 Line plot connecting points of same country.

resulting in different lines, one for each country. We should use attribute `group`, which represents a new aesthetic associated to the data frame variable with country names. With attribute `group`, we specify the variable whose unique values define the homogeneous group of points to connect with a line. In the example, we set `group=country`, meaning that points should be logically grouped for same country, and points belonging to the same country should be connected with a line. Figure 1.13 shows the correct line plot.

```
sample_infl %>% ggplot(aes(x= year, y= FP.CPI.TOTL.ZG)) +
  geom_point(aes(color=country), size=2) +
  geom_line(aes(group=country)) +
  scale_fill_viridis_d()+
  labs(x= "Year", y= 'Inflation (%)', color= "Country") +
  theme_light()
```

The readability is still poor, but now the line plot is coherent having one line for each country. We could improve it by removing the scatterplot markers, using *linetype* as an aesthetic in addition to *color* so that lines are different for the different countries, and by tuning other style options such as line color and line width. The result has a better look and is more readable (Figure 1.14).

```
color_list= c("gold","skyblue3","forestgreen","black")

sample_infl %>% ggplot(aes(x= year, y= FP.CPI.TOTL.ZG)) +
  geom_line(aes(color= country, linetype= country),
            linewidth=0.6) +
  scale_color_manual(values = color_list) +
  labs(x= "Year", y= 'Inflation (%)',
       color= "Country", linetype= "Country") +
  theme_light()
```

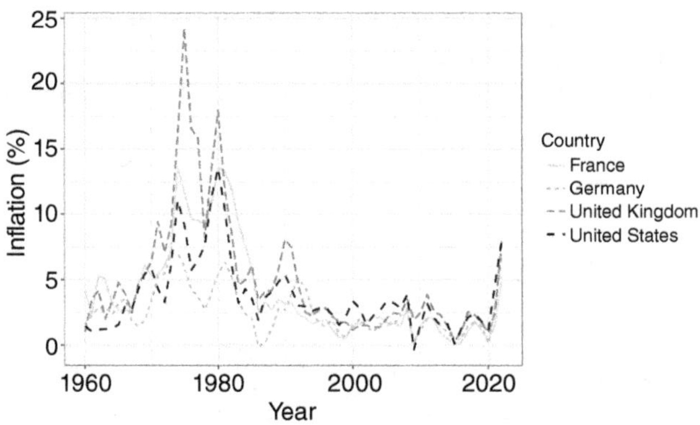

Figure 1.14 Line plot with style options.

> **Tip**
>
> In this last example, the aesthetic `group` has been omitted without influencing the result, because the default behavior for the `geom_line()` function is to use the aesthetic `group` when specified or to use the association defined in another aesthetic, if present. In this case, both the aesthetic `color` and the aesthetic `linetype` are associated to column *countries*, which is correct for setting the groups of lines too. In any case, explicitly specifying the aesthetic `group` would have been also correct.

1.2 Python: Seaborn

With Python's *Seaborn* graphic library, we proceed similarly to what has been done with R's ggplot. Python libraries to import are *NumPy*, *pandas*, *pyplot* module from *matplotlib*, and *Seaborn*. An introductory comment on Seaborn is due. It has been developed as an advanced interface to the pre-existing *matplotlib*, substantially improving several graphical features, which makes it a modern graphical library for data science. It maintains the native approach of the matplotlib library, not based on the grammar of graphics and instead providing for specific functions for each graphic type. It is a simpler approach, convenient for standard graphics with few configurations, but less flexible and adaptable to nonstandard or advanced results. However, it should be noted that also Seaborn is progressively migrating to the grammar of graphics. Starting from version 12.0 of September 2022, a new notation called *Seaborn Objects* has been introduced. It is still in an early stage of development and incomplete, but the direction for its future development is clear and aligned with modern graphical libraries like *ggplot* and *Altair*; some details about the *Seaborn Objects Interface* are present in the *Additional Online Material*.

At any rate, even in the present original form, the Seaborn library is a notable tool and a primary reference for the Python environment.

From the World Bank, we use data about gross domestic product (GDP) growth of several countries.

```
import numpy as np
import pandas as pd
import matplotlib.pyplot as plt
import seaborn as sns

gdp = pd.read_csv('datasets/world_bank/API_NY.GDP.MKTP.
                   KD.ZG_DS2_en_csv_v2_5358346.csv',
                  skiprows=4)
```

	Country Name	Country Code	1960	1961	...	2019	2020	2021
0	Aruba	ABW	NaN	NaN	...	0.635	−18.589	17.172
1	Africa Eastern and Southern	AFE	NaN	0.237	...	2.038	−3.042	4.402
...	...	...	...	...	...	...	...	...
264	Zambia	ZMB	NaN	1.361	...	1.441	−2.785	4.598
265	Zimbabwe	ZWE	NaN	6.316	...	−6.332	−7.816	8.468

A few data-wrangling operations are necessary to prepare the data (i.e., the last useless column is dropped, and the data frame is transformed into long form).

```
gdp=gdp.loc[:, gdp.columns != 'Unnamed: 66']

df=gdp.melt(id_vars=['Country Name','Country Code',
                     'Indicator Name','Indicator Code'],
            var_name= 'Year', value_name= 'GDP')
df.Year=df.Year.astype('int64')
```

	Country Name	Country Code	Year	GDP
0	Aruba	ABW	1960	NaN
1	Africa Eastern and Southern	AFE	1960	NaN
...	...	...	...	...
16489	South Africa	ZAF	2021	4.913097
16490	Zambia	ZMB	2021	4.598734
16491	Zimbabwe	ZWE	2021	8.468017

Figure 1.15 Scatterplot of the United States' GDP time series from the World Bank.

1.2.1 Scatterplot

Function `sns.scatterplot()` produces a scatterplot. Seaborn attributes are intuitive: `hue` corresponds to ggplot `color`, `s` to `size`, `alpha`, `data`, `x` and `y` are the same as ggplot. Legend position should be controlled explicitly and native matplotlib features are needed (e.g., `plt.legend()`, other options exist).

We start with a first simple example by selecting the United States from the data frame in long form, then we add a few stylistic directives and use a light theme (Figure 1.15).

```
us_gdp=df[df['Country Name'] == 'United States']

plt.figure(figsize = (8,5))
plt.rcParams.update({'font.size': 16})
sns.set(style='whitegrid', font_scale=0.9)

g= sns.scatterplot(data=us_gdp, x="Year", y="GDP",
                   color= 'darkmagenta', s=30, )
g.set_title("GDP: United States")
```

Now we consider a group of countries and associate variables to Seaborn function attributes (the term *aesthetics* is not used by Seaborn). We use attribute `hue` for coloring points according to the country (Figure 1.16).

```
sample_gdp=df[(df['Country Name'] == 'United States') |
              (df['Country Name'] == 'France') |
```

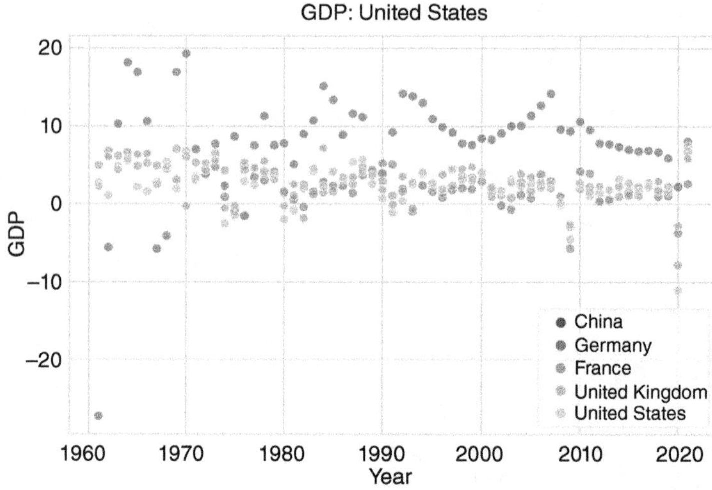

Figure 1.16 Scatterplot of the GDP for a sample of countries.

```
                    (df['Country Name'] == 'Germany') |
                    (df['Country Name'] == 'United Kingdom') |
                    (df['Country Name'] == 'China')]

sns.scatterplot(data=sample_gdp, x="Year", y="GDP",
                s=40, alpha= 0.7, hue='Country Name',
                palette= 'rocket')
plt.legend(loc='lower right')
```

To replicate the example seen with *ggplot* and coloring data points based on a threshold value, Seaborn does not offer many opportunities other than to create two distinct subsets of data points and draw two overlapped scatterplots. In this case, we use point *size* and *transparency* to differentiate data points over or below the threshold. Only one legend is shown, the second would be a duplication (Figure 1.17).

```
subset1= sample_gdp[sample_gdp.Year < 2000]
subset2= sample_gdp[sample_gdp.Year >= 2000]

sns.scatterplot(data=subset2, x="Year", y="GDP",
                s=40, alpha= 1.0, hue='Country Name',
                palette= 'rocket')
sns.scatterplot(data=subset1, x="Year", y="GDP",
                s=20, alpha= 0.5, hue='Country Name',
                palette= 'rocket', legend=False)
plt.legend(loc='lower right')
```

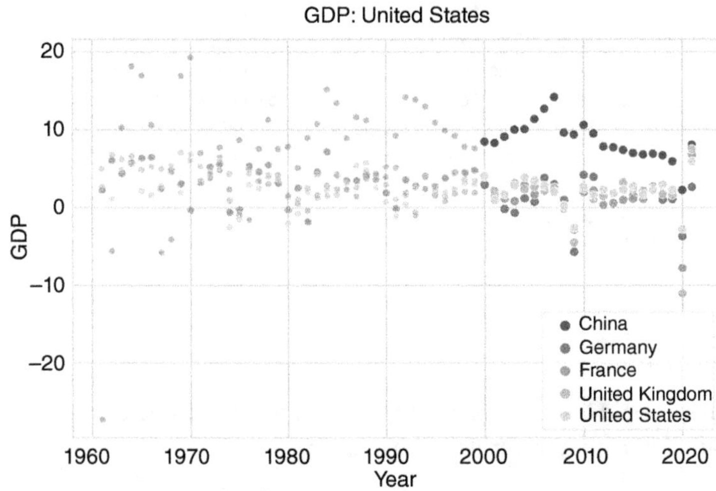

Figure 1.17 Scatterplot with markers styled differently for from year 2000 and beyond.

We could also replicate the example with temperature measurements from some US cities, as collected by Carnegie Mellon University's *Compiled historical daily temperature and precipitation data for selected 210 U.S. cities*. Temperature measurements are recorded *daily* and are referred to as the *minimum* and *maximum temperatures*. The values are expressed in Fahrenheit degrees. The data require some data-wrangling operation to be prepared for visualization. They are the equivalent already seen for R, namely the addition of a new column with the city name, the concatenation of the data frames to form a single one, and the transformation into long form of columns *tmax* and *tmin*. In addition, a few other operations on data types, for selecting only years from 2010 and, in this case, maximum temperatures.

```
# Milwaukee
c1=pd.read_csv('datasets/Carnegie_Mellon_Univ/7890488/USW00014839.csv')
# El Paso
c2=pd.read_csv('datasets/Carnegie_Mellon_Univ/7890488/USW00023044.csv')
# New York
c3=pd.read_csv('datasets/Carnegie_Mellon_Univ/7890488/USW00094728.csv')
# Phoenix
c4=pd.read_csv('datasets/Carnegie_Mellon_Univ/7890488/USW00023183.csv')
# Atlanta
c5=pd.read_csv('datasets/Carnegie_Mellon_Univ/7890488/USW00013874.csv')
# Havre, Montana
c6=pd.read_csv('datasets/Carnegie_Mellon_Univ/7890488/USW00094012.csv')
```

Column *Date* is transformed in *datetime* type and a new column *city* is added with the city name.

```
c1["Date"] = pd.to_datetime(c1["Date"], format="%Y-%m-%d")
c2["Date"] = pd.to_datetime(c2["Date"], format="%Y-%m-%d")
c3["Date"] = pd.to_datetime(c3["Date"], format="%Y-%m-%d")
c4["Date"] = pd.to_datetime(c4["Date"], format="%Y-%m-%d")
c5["Date"] = pd.to_datetime(c5["Date"], format="%Y-%m-%d")
c6["Date"] = pd.to_datetime(c6["Date"], format="%Y-%m-%d")

c1["city"] = "Milwaukee"
c2["city"] = "El Paso"
c3["city"] = "New York"
c4["city"] = "Phoenix"
c5["city"] = "Atlanta"
c6["city"] = "Havre (MN)"
```

The data frames should be concatenated by column to form a single one; then columns *tmax* and *tmin* are transformed into long form.

```
cities= pd.concat([c1,c2,c3,c4,c5,c6], axis=0)

citiesL= cities.melt(id_vars=['Date', 'city'],
value_vars=['tmax','tmin'], var_name="tminmax",
value_name='temp')
```

Now, we could produce the scatterplot. We still select years from 2010 and, this time, maximum temperatures and some style options are added. Figure 1.18 shows the scatterplot.

```
dataT= citiesL[(citiesL.tminmax=="tmax") &\
               (citiesL.Date.dt.year>=2010)]

g= sns.scatterplot(data=dataT, x="Date", y="temp",
  hue="city", s=3, palette="coldwarm",
  hue_order=["Havre (MT)","Milwaukee","New York",
             "Atlanta","El Paso","Phoenix"])

plt.figure(figsize = (8,5), dpi=600)
sns.move_legend(g, "lower left")
plt.title('Maximum Temperatures 2010-2022')
plt.xlabel("")
plt.ylabel('Temperatures (F)')
plt.rcParams.update({'font.size': 16})
```

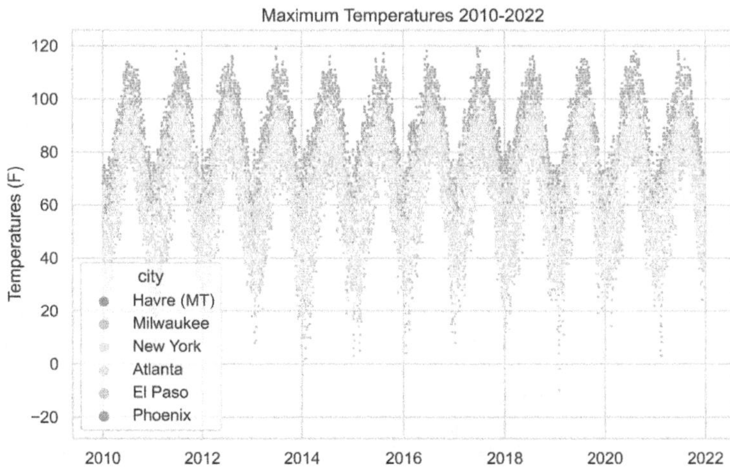

Figure 1.18 Temperature measurement in some US cities, maximum temperatures.

1.2.2 Line Plot

The line plot, as we already know, follows the same logic of the scatterplot, with the additional requirement that groups of points should be correctly managed. Seaborn automatically manages homogeneous data points and just few attributes should be adjusted, with respect to the scatterplot, for example, `linewidth` is needed to change the line width rather than `s` for marker size (Figure 1.19).

```
sns.set(style='white')

sns.lineplot(data=sample_gdp, x="Year", y="GDP",
                        hue='Country Name', linewidth=1,
                        palette= 'viridis')
plt.legend(loc='lower center)
plt.xlabel("")
plt.ylabel('GDP (%)')
```

The line style could be made dependent on variable values by using attribute `style`. In the example, each line style is customized according to country names; other style options in common with the previous graphic have been omitted (Figure 1.20).

```
sns.lineplot(data=sample_gdp, x="Year", y="GDP",
                      hue='Country Name', style='Country Name',
                      linewidth=1, palette= 'viridis')
plt.legend(loc='lower right)
```

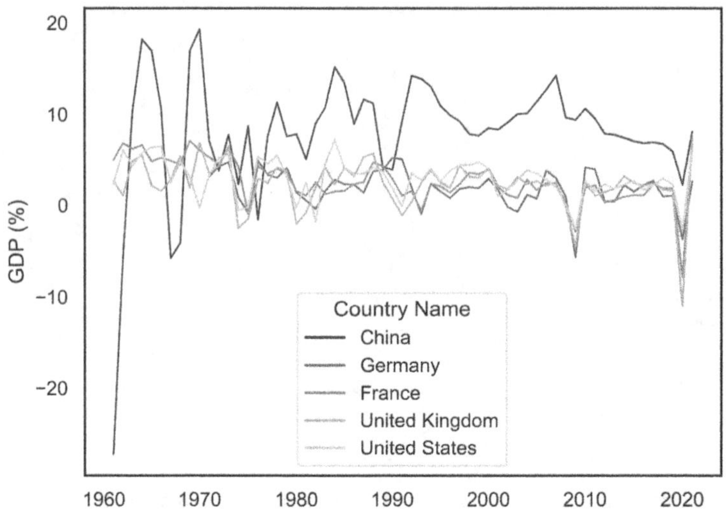

Figure 1.19 Line plot of GDP variations for a sample of countries.

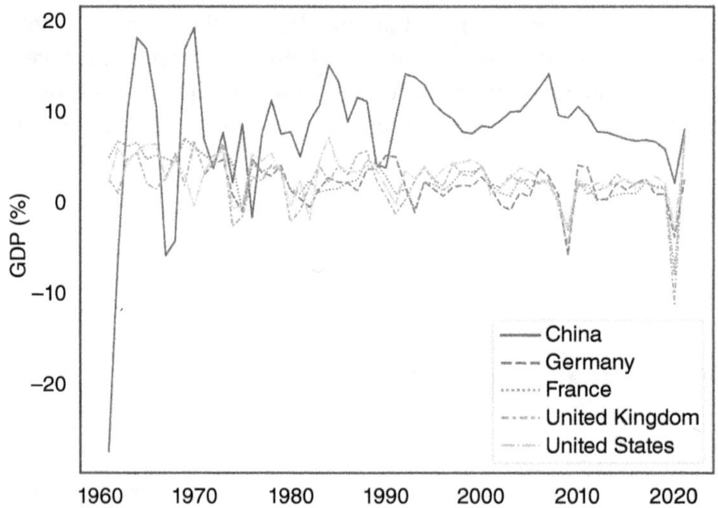

Figure 1.20 Line plot with line style varied according to country.

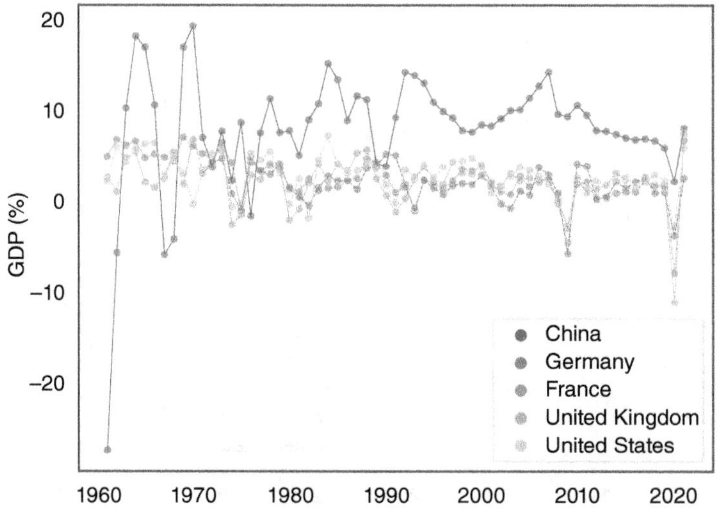

Figure 1.21 Line plot and scatterplot overlapped.

To overlap a scatterplot to the line plot, in order to plot both markers and lines, the two functions could be written in sequence and the graphics are drawn on the same plot. This possibility is not equivalent to the logic of the grammar of graphics with layers of aesthetics, being just distinct plots overlapped on the same plan (Figure 1.21).

```
sns.lineplot(data=sample_gdp, x="Year", y="GDP",
                    hue='Country Name', style='Country Name',
                    linewidth=0.5, palette= 'viridis', legend=False)
sns.scatterplot(data=sample_gdp, x="Year", y="GDP",
                    s=20, alpha= 0.7, hue='Country Name',
                    palette= 'viridis')
```

This just seen is the general technique for Seaborn to overlap different graphics. For specific features, shortcuts often are available. For example, with line plots, in order to show markers, is not necessary to overlap a scatterplot but the handy `markers` attribute set to *True* is sufficient. Shortcuts, however, have often some limitations like in this case where a common style is applied to both markers and lines (see Figure 1.22). If we want different configurations for markers and lines, then the general technique with two plots overlapped is the solution.

```
sns.lineplot(data=sample_gdp, x="Year", y="GDP",
                    hue='Country Name', style='Country Name',
                    linewidth=1, palette= 'viridis', markers=True)
```

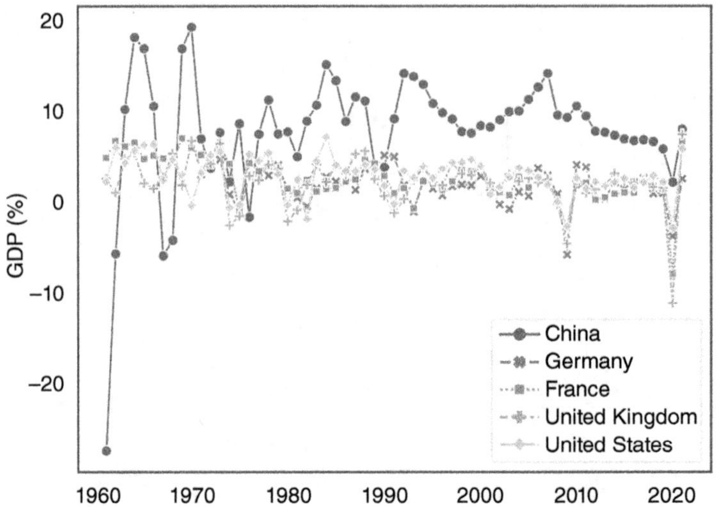

Figure 1.22 Line plot with markers automatically added.

2

Bar Plots

In this section, we introduce the fundamentals of bar plots with ggplot and Seaborn and show their main features. Bar plots, like scatterplots, will be used extensively in following chapters, with more details and variants, so as to appreciate their flexibility.

Dataset

Air Quality Report year 2021 (transl. Report qualità aria 2021), Open Data Municipality of Milan, Italy (https://dati.comune.milano.it/dataset/ds413-rilevazione-qualita-aria-2021).
Copyright: Creative Commons CC BY-4.0.

2.1 R: ggplot

A *bar plot* (or *bar chart*) is the reference type of graphic when categorical variables are handled: each category has a value associated, and a bar is drawn to represent it. Values could depend on another variable, for example, a statistic, or could represent the number of observations that fall in each category. Let us consider a first example using data about *the air quality of the city of Milan, Italy*, which is a heavily polluted city. It is a time series where, for each day of the period, quantities of some pollutants are measured. The variable *pollutant* is categorical, and we want to graphically represent the variations of pollutant levels during the time period. Column names have been translated into English.

Data Visualization in R and Python, First Edition. Marco Cremonini.

Companion website: www.wiley.com/go/Cremonini/DataVisualization1e

```
df=read_csv2("datasets/Milan_municipality/
               qaria_datoariagiornostazione_2021.csv")
df=rename(df, c(station_id=stazione_id, date=data,
                pollutant=inquinante, value=valore))
head(df)
```

```
# A tibble: 6 × 4
  station_id date       pollutant value
       <dbl> <date>      <chr>       <chr>
1          1 2021-12-31 NO2         <NA>
2          2 2021-12-31 C6H6        2
3          2 2021-12-31 NO2         54
4          2 2021-12-31 O3          2
5          2 2021-12-31 PM10        50
6          2 2021-12-31 PM25        32
```

First, a few transformations are needed: column *value* must be converted into numerical type and missing values could be omitted because useless.

```
df$value=as.numeric(df$value)
df%>%filter(!is.na(value)) -> df1
```

With the first bar plot, we want to show, for each pollutant, the total value over the whole period; an aggregation operation is needed.

```
df1%>%group_by(pollutant) %>%
       summarize(total=sum(value)) -> df1_grp
```

```
# A tibble: 7 × 2
  pollutant total
  <chr>      <dbl>
1 C6H6        774.
2 CO_8h       644.
3 NO2       75839
4 O3        34720
5 PM10      26993
6 PM25       9267
7 SO2        1029
```

With this aggregated data frame, the bar plot could be created, adding a few style options, like a color palette. *Color Brewer* (https://r-graph-gallery.com/38-rcolorbrewers-palettes.html) provides a number of predefined palettes for R and it is a common choice, although not much original.

Tip

Many other lists of predefined color palettes are available other than *Color Brewer*: package *ggthemes* has several, and an even larger list is included in *r-color-palettes*. It is worth noting that choosing a color palette is an important choice not to be taken lightly because it could considerably affect the overall quality of a graphic. Colors represent a key aspect of visual communication; several specific publications address the implications of their choice for different audiences and contexts, so choose wisely, always test different alternatives, and do not be afraid of defining your own custom color palette if you think it would be better than the predefined ones.

The ggplot function for bar plots is `geom_bar()` and a key attribute is `stat` (*statistic*). By default, the `stat` attribute has value *count*, meaning that the bar plot requires *a single categorical variable as the independent one (x-axis), and values of the y-axis are calculated as the number of observations falling in each category.* In our case study, it would count the number of measurements for each pollutant. When, instead, *a bar plot with two variables is needed*, one for the categorical values and the second for values associated to each category (in our example, the total quantity of pollutants during the period), the attribute `stat` should be explicitly set to value *identity* (`stat='identity'`). Another important attribute is `position` that controls the visualization of groups of bars, where for each group, bars could be placed beside one to the other (`position='dodged'`) or one on top of the other (`position='stacked'`), which is the default. The next example shows a simple bar plot with two variables, pollutant names on the *x*-axis and their quantities on the *y*-axis, therefore `stat='identity'` is specified. Figure 2.1 shows the result.

```
library(ggthemes)

df1_grp %>% ggplot(aes(x=pollutant, y=total)) +
  geom_bar(aes(fill=pollutant), stat="identity") +
  scale_fill_viridis_d(option = "rocket")+
  theme_clean()
```

Let us see a variant with a *custom palette* and *horizontal orientation of bars* (function `coord_flip()` switches the axes). Bars are also in order for increasing quantity of pollutants by using function `reorder()` for axis *x* (i.e., `x=reorder(pollutant, total)`). Function `reorder()` takes two parameters: the first one is the variable whose elements should be reordered, *pollutant* in our case, and the second is the variable with values to be used for

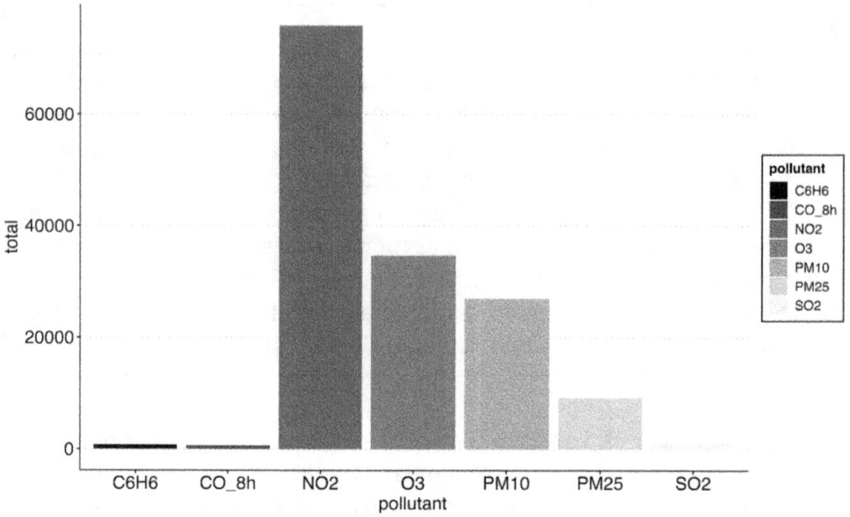

Figure 2.1 Bar plot with two variables.

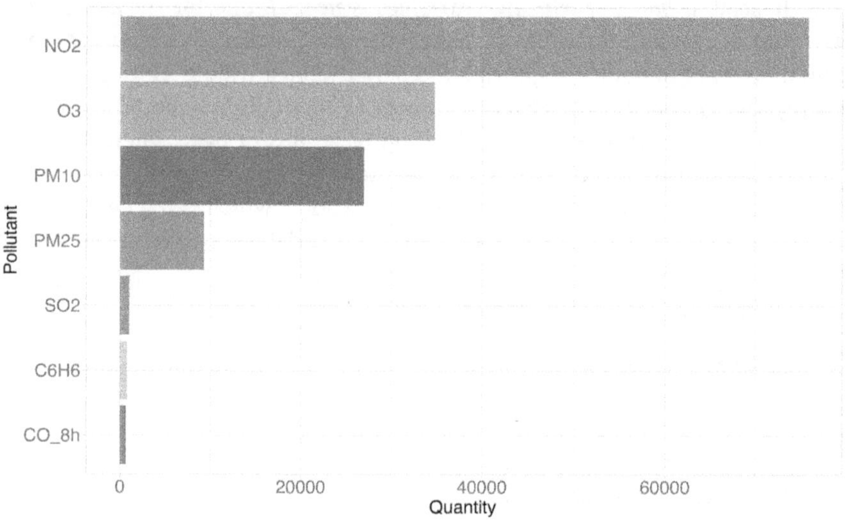

Figure 2.2 Bar plot with custom color palette, horizontal bar orientation, and ordered bars.

defining the order, *total* in our case. We use a custom color palette by specifying colors with their hexadecimal RGB code (RGB is the name of the main color model in use) and axes labels are set with function `labs()`, the legend is omitted (`show.legend=FALSE`) because unnecessary (Figure 2.2).

```
cols=c("C6H6"="#bda50b", "CO_8h"="#a1034a",
"NO2"="#295eb3", "O3"="#94770f", "PM10"="#471870",
"PM25"="#94420f", "SO2"="#356604")

df1_grp %>%
    ggplot(aes(x=reorder(pollutant, total), y=total)) +
    geom_bar(aes(fill=pollutant), stat="identity",
             alpha=0.8, show.legend = FALSE) +
             scale_fill_manual(values = cols)+
    labs(x="Pollutant", y="Quantity")+
    coord_flip()+
    theme_light()
```

2.1.1 Bar Plot and Continuous Variables: Ranges of Values

It often happens that we wish to use values from a continuous variable but still want to produce a bar plot. Being values on a continuous scale, they cannot be used as such (probably there would be just a single data point for each value). The solution is to define *ranges of values* and use those ranges as values of a new categorical variable.

In our example, we may want to divide pollutant quantities into ranges and use a bar plot to count the number of days for each range. The approach is similar to what we have seen in the previous section for coloring scatterplot markers based on thresholds. With pollutants, it should be considered that they have quite different scales, therefore ranges should be defined singularly or for pollutants on similar scales. We consider a single pollutant (i.e., PM10) and use again function `cut()` to define ranges. The new column *range* will record the respective range for each data point.

```
df1_PM10 = filter(df1, pollutant=="PM10")
df1_PM10$value=as.numeric(df1_PM10$value)
```

To define ranges, we consider the minimum and the maximum values, respectively, 10 and 97 for PM10, and define a reasonable number of ranges, for example: <30, 30–40, 40–50, 50–60, 60–70, 70–80, >80.

```
df1_PM10$range <- cut(df1_PM10$value,
                      breaks=c(0, 30, 40, 50, 60, 70, 80, 120),
                      labels=c('<30','30-40','40-50','50-60',
                               '60-70','70-80','>80'))
```

We can produce the bar plot using column *range* and counting the number of observations for each range. This time the `stat='count'` is correct and being the default, it could be omitted (Figure 2.3).

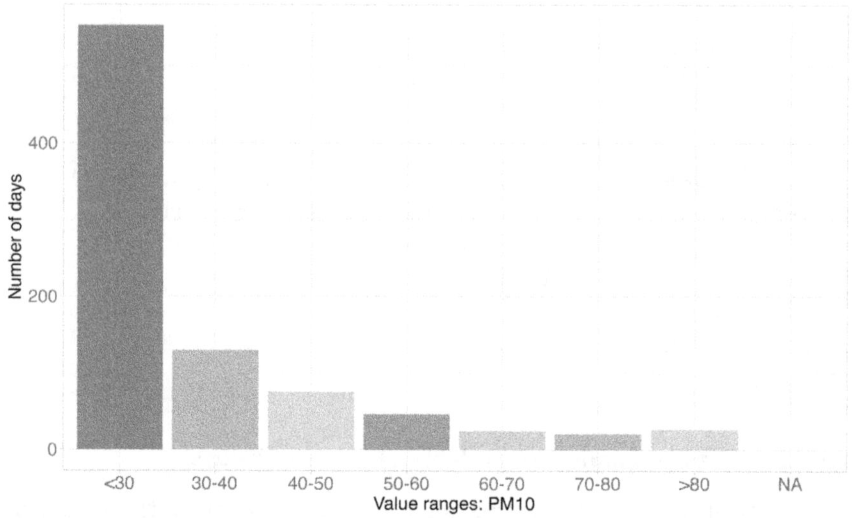

Figure 2.3 Bar plot with ranges of values for PM10 derived from a continuous variable.

```
df1_PM10 %>%
  ggplot(aes(x=range)) +
  geom_bar(aes(fill=range), show.legend = FALSE) +
  scale_fill_tableau(palette = "Miller Stone")+
  labs(x="Value ranges: PM10", y="Number of days")+
  theme_minimal()
```

2.2 Python: Seaborn

We replicate for Seaborn the examples seen with ggplot. First, data should be prepared for plotting.

```
df=pd.read_csv("datasets/Milan_municipality/
                qaria_datoariagiornostazione_2021.csv", sep=";")
df.columns=['station_id', 'date', 'pollutant', 'value']

df["date"]=pd.to_datetime(df["date"], format="%Y-%m-%d")
df=df[~df.isna().any(axis=1)]

df_grp=df.groupby(["pollutant"])[["value"]].sum()
df_grp.reset_index(inplace=True)
```

Now that we have the total quantity for each pollutant, we can start with a simple bar plot using function `sns.barplot()`, to which we add a few options: attribute `order` to order bars, which has a peculiar syntax with the following general template: `order=df.sort_values("variable_y",ascending=`

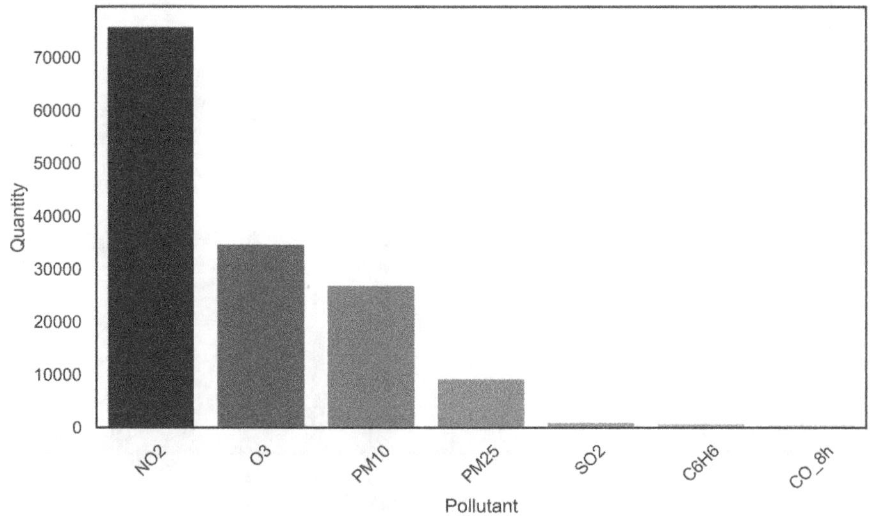

Figure 2.4 Bar plot with ordered bars and x ticks rotated.

`False).variable_x)`, meaning that *variable_x* is the variable whose bars should be ordered, and *variable_y* the variable whose values define the ordering criteria, ascending or descending. As a last option, we rotate the *labels on ticks* of axis *x* by 45° to improve readability and set axes labels (Figure 2.4).

```
sns.barplot(data=df_grp, x="pollutant", y="value",
            order=df_grp.sort_values("value",ascending=
            False).pollutant, palette='mako')

plt.xticks(rotation=45)
plt.xlabel("Pollutant")
plt.ylabel('Quantity')
plt.tight_layout()
```

2.2.1 Bar Plot with Three Variables

We can extend the previous example seen with R to include a third variable, represented by the month. We want to show, for each month, the total quantity of each pollutant. This way we will have groups of bars, one group for each month. We should aggregate the observations for month (method `dt.month` extracts months in numeric form from dates). This time, to differentiate bars based on the pollutant value, we need to associate colors to pollutants with attribute `hue`, and by default in Seaborn, bars in groups are visualized besides one to the other (i.e., dodged). Figure 2.5 shows the result.

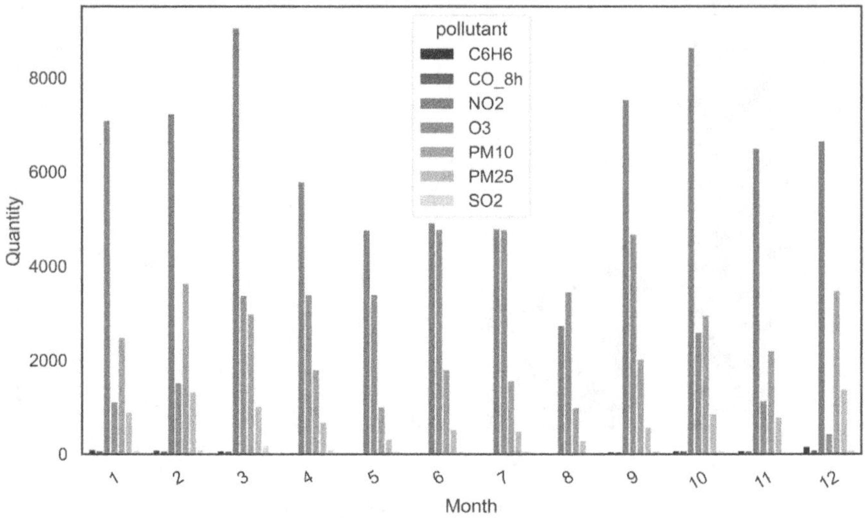

Figure 2.5 Bar plot with three variables and groups of bars.

```
df_grp2= df_py.groupby([df['date'].dt.month, "pollutant"])\
                         [["value"]].sum()
df_grp2.reset_index(inplace=True)
df_grp2= df_grp2.rename(columns={"date":"month"})

sns.barplot(data=df_grp2, x='month', y="value",
            hue="pollutant", palette='mako')

plt.xticks(rotation=30)
plt.xlabel("Month")
plt.ylabel('Quantity')
plt.tight_layout()
```

The bar plot is correct although the style could be improved. For example, we could use *month names* and *move the legend outside the plot*. First, column *month* should be transformed into *datetime* type. Then, we can use method `dt.month_name()` to obtain month names. For the legend, to move it outside the plot, the specific function `sns.move_legend()` has attribute `bbox_to_anchor`, style options in common with the previous graphic have been omitted (Figure 2.6).

Tip

To position a legend outside the plot, to the upper right, the combination `"upper left"` and `bbox_to_anchor=(1, 1)` gives exactly that outcome despite its unintuitive format.

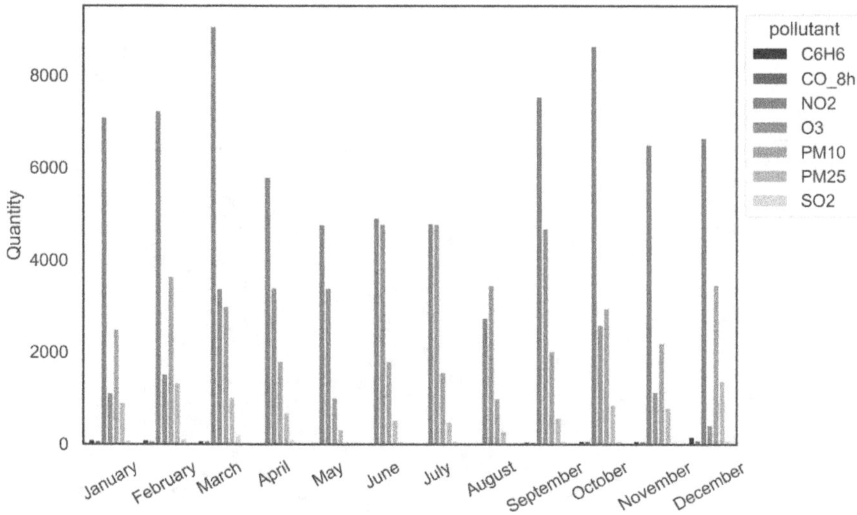

Figure 2.6 Bar plot with month names and the legend moved outside the plot.

```
df_grp2["month"]=pd.to_datetime(df_grp2["month"], format="%m")

g=sns.barplot(df_grp2, x=df_grp2["month"].dt.month_name(),
              y="value", hue="pollutant", palette='mako')

plt.xticks(rotation=30)
plt.xlabel("")
plt.ylabel('Quantity')
sns.move_legend(g, "upper left", bbox_to_anchor=(1, 1))
```

Let us consider a variant by using a color palette (`sns.color_palette()`) and with *stacked bars* rather than dodged, for this attribute `dodge` must be set to *False* (`dodge=False`). Figure 2.7 shows the result, and style options in common with previous plots have been omitted.

```
pal=sns.color_palette("magma")

g=sns.barplot(data=df_grp2,
              x=df_grp2["month"].dt.month_name(), y="value",
              hue="pollutant", dodge=False, palette=pal)
```

2.2.2 Ranges of Values from a Continuous Variable

To create categorical values from a continuous variable, *pandas* offers function `pd.cut()`, very similar to the corresponding R function. In the example, we select a single pollutant (i.e., NO_2) and define a number of value ranges in the new column *range*.

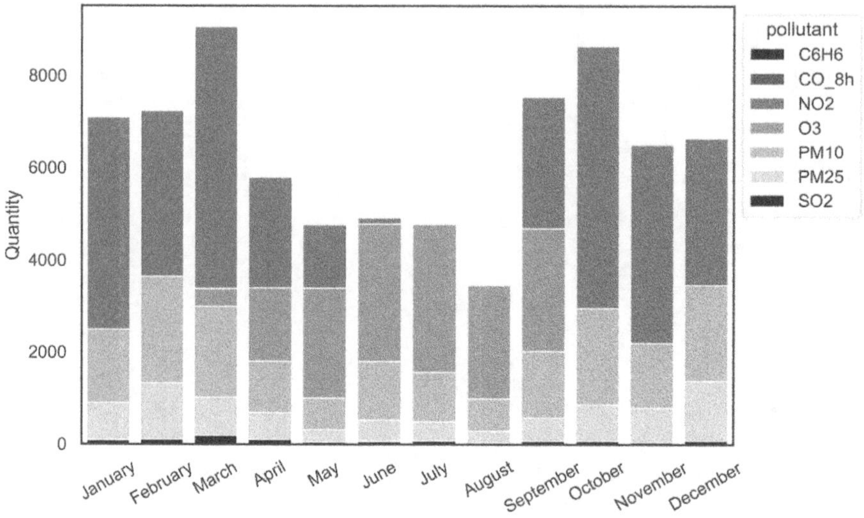

Figure 2.7 Bar plot with stacked bars.

```
df_NO2= df[df.pollutant=="NO2"]

df_NO2[range] = pd.cut(x=df_NO2['value'],
bins=[0, 30, 40, 50, 60, 70, 80, 100, 120, 140, 200],
labels=['<30','30-40','40-50','50-60','60-70','70-80',
        '80-100','100-120','120-140','>140'])
```

	station_id	date	pollutant	value	range
2	2	2021-12-31	NO2	54.0	50–60
8	3	2021-12-31	NO2	51.0	50–60
11	4	2021-12-31	NO2	59.0	50–60
17	6	2021-12-31	NO2	67.0	60–70
20	7	2021-12-31	NO2	54.0	50–60

This time, we want to count the number of observations for each range value, Seaborn distinguishes between two cases: function `sns.barplot()` is for bar plots with *two variables*, while for the case of just *one variable*, it takes function `sns.countplot()`. Figure 2.8 shows the result.

```
plt.figure(figsize = (8,5))
plt.rcParams.update({'font.size': 16})

sns.countplot(data=df_py_NO2, x="range", palette="viridis")
```

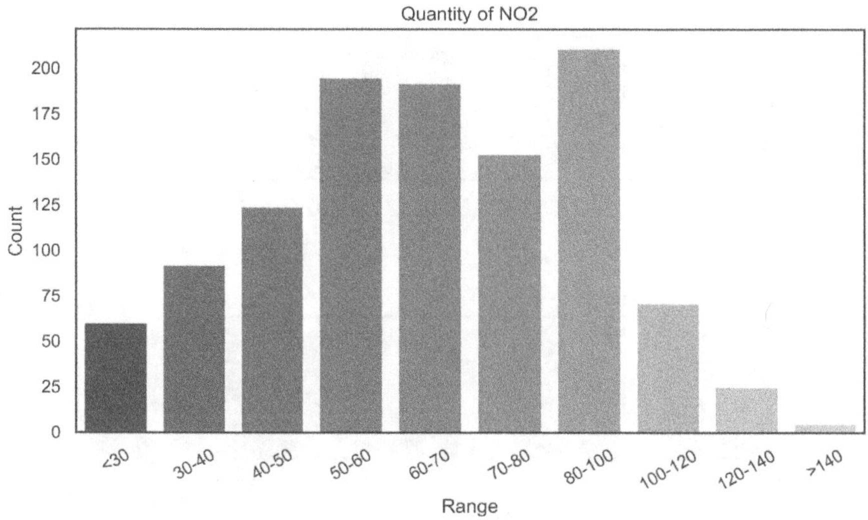

Figure 2.8 Bar plot with ranges of values derived from a continuous variable.

```
plt.xticks(rotation=30)
plt.title("Quantity of NO2")
plt.xlabel("Range")
plt.ylabel('Count')
```

2.2.3 Visualizing Subplots

A useful variant of function `pd.cut()` is function `pd.qcut()`, where the *q* letter stands for *quantile*. With this function, the whole range of variable values is divided into quantiles and the fundamental attribute is `q` that takes two forms:

- `q=<number>` means that the range of values is divided in the specified number of bins, whose limits are automatically set in order to make the number of occurrences for each bin the more balanced as possible (i.e., bin's height will be as alike as possible).
- `q=[list of values]` means that the range of values is divided into the specified quantiles of the distribution (e.g., `q=[0, .2, .4, .6, .8, 1]`).

We can use the `qcut()` function for two examples.

```
df_NO2= df[df.pollutant=="NO2"]
df_NO2['es1'] = pd.qcut(df_NO2['value'], q=4)
df_NO2['es2'] = pd.qcut(x=df_NO2['value'],
                        q=[0, .25, .5, .75, 1])
```

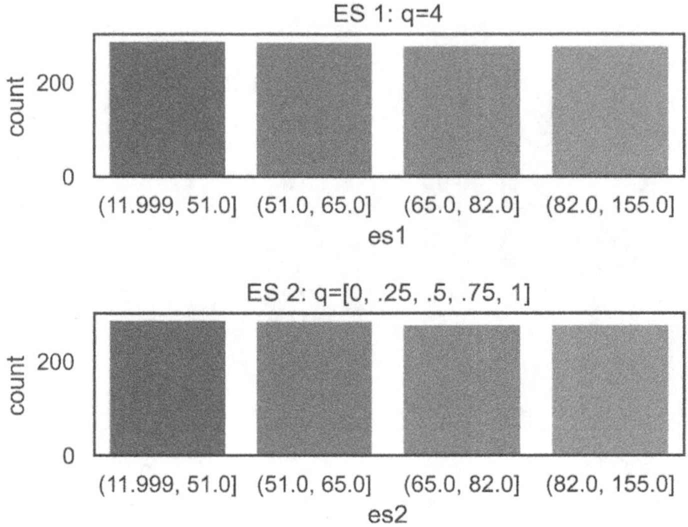

Figure 2.9 Bar plots with quantile representation, subplots, and style options.

In the visualization, we add an important detail to obtain an outcome similar to what we have produced with the R's *patchwork* library that allows drawing multiple plots side-by-side or stacked. In this case, we use matplotlib *subplots*, which lack the intuitive syntax of *patchwork* but provide a wide array of possible visualizations. The function to use is `plt.subplots()`, whose first attribute represents the *number of rows*, the second the *number of columns* (default is 1) of the grid of subplots, `figsize()` specifies the size of the entire plot. Subplots are associated to the standard parameter *ax* (axes), which, in our example, will be an array with two elements, *ax[0]* and *ax[1]*, corresponding to the first and the second subplots. By using *ax[0]* and *ax[1]*, subplots could have specific formatting; in the example, they will have different titles and different axis options (Figure 2.9).

```
df_py_NO2['es1'] = pd.qcut(df_py_NO2['value'], q=4)
df_py_NO2['es2'] = pd.qcut(x=df_py_NO2['value'],
                           q=[0, .25, .5, .75, 1])

f, ax = plt.subplots(2, figsize=(5, 4))
pal=sns.color_palette("viridis")

sns.countplot(data=df_py_NO2, x="es1", palette=pal, ax=ax[0])
sns.countplot(data=df_py_NO2, x="es2", palette=pal, ax=ax[1])

ax[0].set(title="ES 1: q=4")
ax[1].set(title="ES 2: q=[0, .25, .5, .75, 1]")
```

```
ax[0].xaxis.set_tick_params(labelsize=7)
ax[1].xaxis.set_tick_params(labelsize=7)
f.tight_layout()
```

Tip

An R function `qcut()` is included into package *timereg*, it works the same way as the `pd.qcut()`.

3

Facets

Facets represent one of the typical modalities for data visualization. The idea is to have a grid of plots presented as a unique visualization. Graphics presented as facets, however, are not independent and uncorrelated; on the contrary, they are the graphics produced by selecting a specific data frame variable/column, and for each of its unique values, a plot is produced by using common ggplot definition and aesthetics. For example, we may want to visualize the tourist arrivals in some locations on a yearly basis. So, if we have a time series (i.e., the yearly tourist arrivals) but observed in more than one context (e.g., different countries), how would we represent it graphically? There are alternatives. For example, with a line plot, each line representing data of a certain country, or with a stacked bar plot, with each stacked segment corresponding to a country. But we might also prefer to look at the data of the different countries separately rather than condensed into a single plot, for instance for better clarity; in that case, how do we do that? The trivial solution would be to extract subset of rows from the data frame, one subset for each country, and plot them individually. It works, of course, but it is inefficient, and we end up with several distinct plots to manage somehow. Here comes the facet visualization with a clever solution that allows, in a single execution, creating a grid of plots, one for each country with the yearly tourist arrivals. Cases like this are the perfect scenario for facets. It is a smart and convenient solution, but it needs caution because it is easy to end up producing an excessively large grid of plots, which would be computationally intensive and difficult to interpret. In other cases, an ineffective choice of the variable used to produce facets could result in a grid of plots where just a few show informative results, while the others look meaningless. However, when facets are used properly, they usually represent an excellent solution.

Data Visualization in R and Python, First Edition. Marco Cremonini.

Companion website: www.wiley.com/go/Cremonini/DataVisualization1e

Dataset

In this section, we use the dataset *Compiled historical daily temperature and precipitation data for selected 210 U.S. cities*, Yuchuan Lai and David Dzombak, Carnegie Mellon University, and *Air Quality Report year 2021* (transl. Report qualità aria 2021), Open Data Municipality of Milan, already introduced before.

3.1 R: ggplot

3.1.1 Case 1: Temperature

We use the data from Carnegie Mellon University about daily temperature in some US cities in years 2010–2022. To produce a visualization by facets, two formats are available in ggplot: a grid based on distinct values of a single variable (function `facet_wrap()`) or a grid based on the combinations of distinct values from two variables (function `facet_grid()`).

> **Warning**
>
> Each facet is actually a full graphic to be plotted; therefore, a grid of facets could be computationally intensive to produce and/or difficult to read. It is worth estimating in advance the number of facets that would be produced; when facets will be about a dozen, that would already be a significant number of graphics, if their number is in the dozens, that would be probably excessive. Even more care should be taken when function `facet_grid()` is used because combinations of the distinct values of the two variables may grow fast.

In Chapter 1, we saw a scatterplot presenting the daily temperatures for six US cities as a single visualization and commented that, while the overall shape of the scatterplot was informative, it was difficult to clearly recognize data points from all cities. Now, we see how, with a visualization by facets, it is possible to efficiently separate the different cities into individual plots. Variable *city* is used to produce the facets with function `facet_wrap()`. Here we use the same data frame *citiesL* derived in Chapter 1 from reading the datasets and preparing them for visualization. Minimum temperatures are selected, years go from 2010 to 2022. Function `year()` of package *lubridate* extracts the *year* component from a date. Figure 3.1 shows the result with facets.

```
filter(citiesL, lubridate::year(Date)>=2010, tminmax=="tmin") %>%
  ggplot(aes(x=Date, y=temp)) +
  geom_point(aes(color=city),size=0.01, show.legend = FALSE) +
```

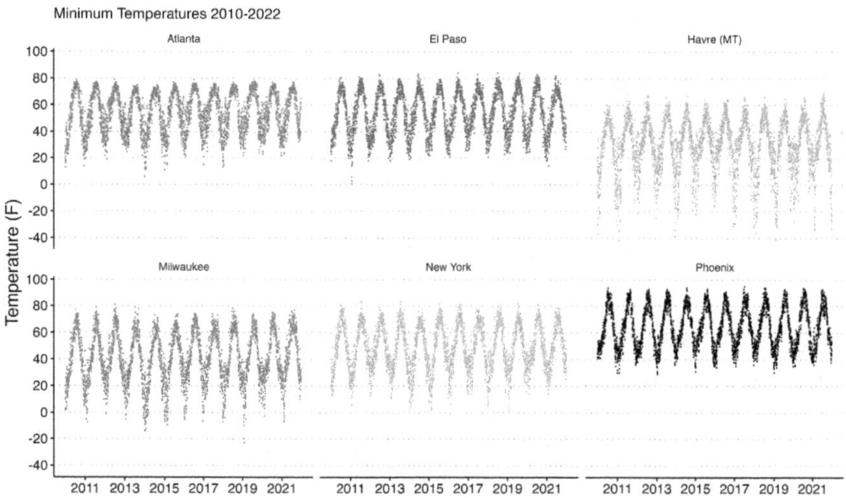

Figure 3.1 Temperature measurement in some US cities, minimum temperatures, visualization by facets.

```
facet_wrap(vars(city), ncol = 3)+
scale_color_wsj()+
scale_x_date(date_breaks = "2 years",
             date_labels = "%Y")+
scale_y_continuous(breaks = c(-40,-20,0,20,40,60,80,100))+
labs(x="", y="Temperature (F)",
     color="City", subtitle="Minimum Temperatures 2010-2022")+
theme_light()
```

3.1.2 Case 2: Air Quality

This time, we reuse the data regarding air quality measurements from the city of Milan. We start by extracting the *month* component from the date with function `month()` of package *lubridate*.

```
df2%>%filter(!is.na(value)) -> df2
df2$value= as.numeric(df2$value)
df2%>%mutate(month= lubridate::month(date)) -> df2
```

```
# A tibble: 4,416 × 5
   station_id date       pollutant value month
        <dbl> <date>     <chr>     <dbl> <dbl>
 1          2 2021-12-31 C6H6          2    12
 2          2 2021-12-31 NO2          54    12
 3          2 2021-12-31 O3            2    12
```

```
 4            2 2021-12-31 PM10          50       12
 5            2 2021-12-31 PM25          32       12
# … with 4,411 more rows
```

We want to show, for each month, the total quantity of every pollutant. First, we need to aggregate and calculate the total quantity for each month and each pollutant.

```
df2%>%group_by(month, pollutant)%>%
      summarize(total=sum(value)) -> df2_grp
```

```
# A tibble: 84 × 3
# Groups:   month [12]
    month pollutant  total
   <dbl> <chr>      <dbl>
 1     1 C6H6         100
 2     1 CO_8h         74
 3     1 NO2         7106
 4     1 O3          1119
 5     1 PM10        2493
 6     1 PM25         910
 7     1 SO2           95.5
# … with 77 more rows
```

Now we can produce bar plots with facets and some style options. We specify month names by replacing month numbers with names. For this, we use function `scale_x_discrete()`. There exist similar functions for the *y*-axis or continuous values (i.e., `scale_y_discrete()`, `scale_x_continue()`, `scale_y_continue()`). In this case, showing the legend would be redundant, we omit it with option `show.legend=FALSE`. Figure 3.2 shows the result.

```
df2_grp %>% ggplot(aes(x=as.factor(month), y=total)) +
  geom_bar(aes(fill=pollutant),stat="identity", show.legend = FALSE) +
  scale_fill_viridis_d(option='cividis')+
  facet_wrap(vars(pollutant), ncol = 3)+
  labs(x="Month", y="Total value ")+
  scale_x_discrete(labels=c("1" = "January", "2" = "February",
                  "3" = "March", "4" = "April", "5"= "May",
                  "6" = "June", "7" = "July", "8" = "August",
                  "9" = "September", "10" = "October",
                  "11" = "November", "12" = "December"))+
  theme_clean()+
  theme(axis.text.x = element_text(angle = 90, hjust = 1),
        axis.text = element_text(size = 12))
```

The result presents inhomogeneous facets, three of them have a scale on axis *y* too different to be represented meaningfully. One possibility to overcome this

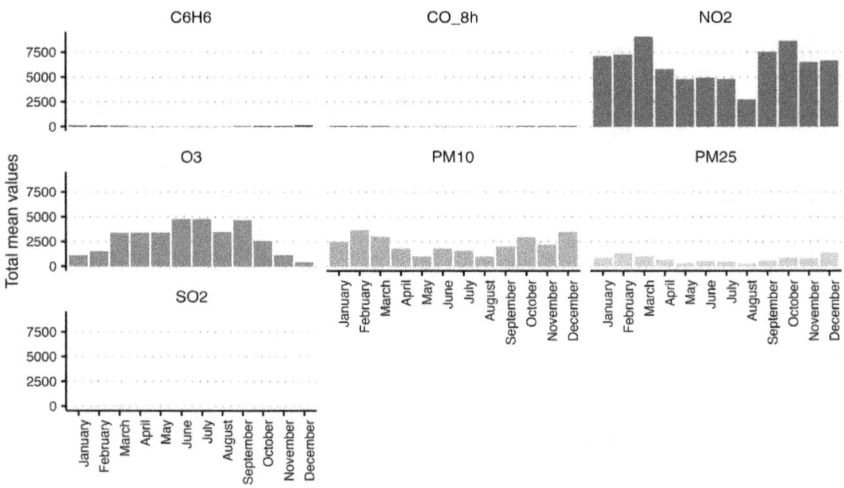

Figure 3.2 Facet visualization with bar plots, some facets not readable due to different scales of pollutant measurements.

problem is to make facet scales on axis *y* independent (or on axis *x*, if that would be the case). This could be done in a simple way by adding attribute `scales` to function `facet_wrap()`, which could have value *free*, *free_x*, or *free_y*, respectively for making both scales independent, only that on the *x*-axis, or on the *y*-axis. In our case, it would be `scales="free_y"`. Figure 3.3 shows how the visualization changes.

```
...
facet_wrap(vars(pollutant), ncol= 3, scales= "free_y")+
...
```

Technically, we have fixed the problem, but caution is nevertheless necessary: the presence of different scales could easily be overlooked by an observer, who as a consequence could be misled into thinking that data in the different facets could be directly compared. That might be the source of severe errors. Depending on how serious this risk is, choosing to plot facets with different scales is worth consideration. Otherwise, a different organization of the plot could be chosen, such as in the following example.

Let us consider a variant by adding a fourth variable, *station_id*, representing the specific monitoring station. We aggregate again to have the totals for each monitoring station, month, and pollutant.

```
df2%>%group_by(station_id, month, pollutant)%>%
      summarize(total=sum(value)) -> df3_grp
```

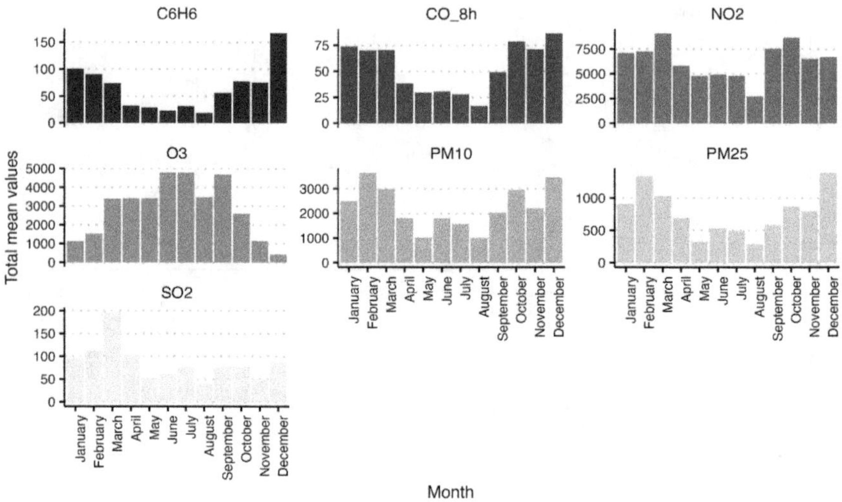

Figure 3.3 Facet visualization with independent scale on *y*-axis.

```
# A tibble: 239 × 4
# Groups:   station_id, month [60]
  station_id month  pollutant total
       <dbl> <dbl> <chr>      <dbl>
 1         2     1 C6H6        25.5
 2         2     1 NO2       1410
 3         2     1 O3         614
 4         2     1 PM10       657
 5         2     1 PM25       508
 6         2     1 SO2         95.5
# … with 233 more rows
```

We can use *month*, *total*, and *pollutant* variables for bar plots, and *station_id* for facets. The style is customized with custom colors. The result shown in Figure 3.4 looks aesthetically pleasant and informative with no risk of ambiguity as for the previous case.

```
df3_grp %>% ggplot(aes(x= as.factor(month), y= total)) +
  geom_bar(aes(fill= pollutant), stat= "identity") +
  scale_fill_viridis_d() +
  facet_wrap(vars(station_id), ncol= 3) +
  labs(x= "Month", y= "Values") +
    scale_x_discrete(labels=c("1" = "January", "2" = "February",
                    "3" = "March", "4" = "April", "5"= "May",
                    "6" = "June", "7" = "July", "8" = "August",
                    "9" = "September", "10" = "October",
```

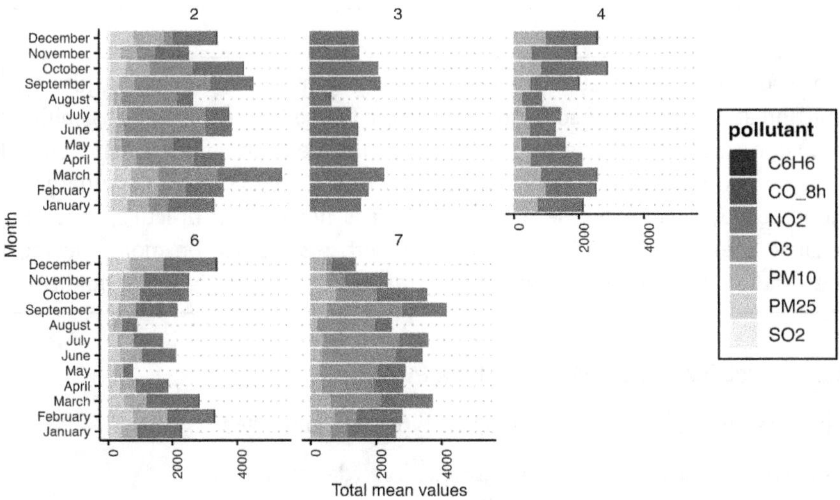

Figure 3.4 Facet visualization with bar plots, facets are all well-readable and balanced.

```
                "11" = "November", "12" = "December"))+
coord_flip() +
theme_clean() +
theme(axis.text.x = element_text(angle = 90, hjust = 1),
      axis.text = element_text(size = 12))
```

3.2 Python: Seaborn

With Seaborn, facets are managed in a peculiar way with two different approaches, a simpler one, but limited in flexibility, and a second a little more complicated but also more general. Let us start with the simple one.

This approach is based on special functions that are *already configured to produce facet visualization*. Each function is suited for a set of graphic types. The main facet-oriented functions are:

- `sns.relplot()` produces facet visualization for *scatterplots* and *line plots*.
- `sns.catplot()` produces facets for the many graphics based on *categorical variables* (e.g., *bar plots, boxplots,* and *categorical scatterplot* variants).
- `sns.displot()` produces facets for *univariate* and *bivariate distributions* (e.g., *histograms* and *kernel density plots*).

To specify the particular type of graphics, all these functions have attribute `kind`, attribute `col` is set to the variable/column used to define the facets.

Tip

These functions could also produce normal graphics without facets, just by omitting attribute `col` specifying the variable to use for facets. This possibility may suggest to always use these functions in place of the more specific ones (e.g., `scatterplot()`, `barplot()`, and `boxplot()`), as (unfortunately) suggested by several online materials. That is not a good practice, though, because these functions have limitations with respect to the more specific ones and are less adaptable, which may result in a poorer graphical quality.

3.2.1 Facet for Scatterplots and Line Plot

With function `relplot()`, two graphic types are supported:

- *scatterplot*, by specifying `kind="scatter"` (default).
- *line plot*, by specifying `kind="line"`.

The usage is simple. We could replicate the previous example with daily temperature from some US cities in years 2010–2022 and use variable *city* for facets. A limitation with respect to specific functions like `scatterplot()` and `lineplot()` is that the plot is not resizable with the usual `plt.figure(figsize = ())` and, in general, many *pyplot*'s methods are not supported, like the one to rotate tick's labels. In the example, we use attribute `kind` set to *scatter* (although, being the default, that would not be necessary), `col` set to *city*, `col_wrap` set to 3 to have a grid with three columns, and `height` set to the single facet's height. In order to rotate tick's labels, we need to adopt a different method with respect to what is seen in previous examples. Figure 3.5 shows the result.

```
g=sns.relplot(data=dataT, x="Date", y="temp", hue="city",
              s=1, palette="magma", kind="scatter",
              col="city", col_wrap=3, height=2.3)
g.tick_params(axis='x', rotation=45)
g.set_axis_labels("",'Temperatures (F)')
```

For a complete overview of the graphical options (e.g., markers, color palette, and proportional sizes), the excellent Seaborn online documentation is the main reference.

3.2.2 Line Plot

For line plots, the only differences with respect to scatterplots are `kind="line"` and `linewidth` to set the line width. The following code is the line plot corresponding to the previous scatterplot.

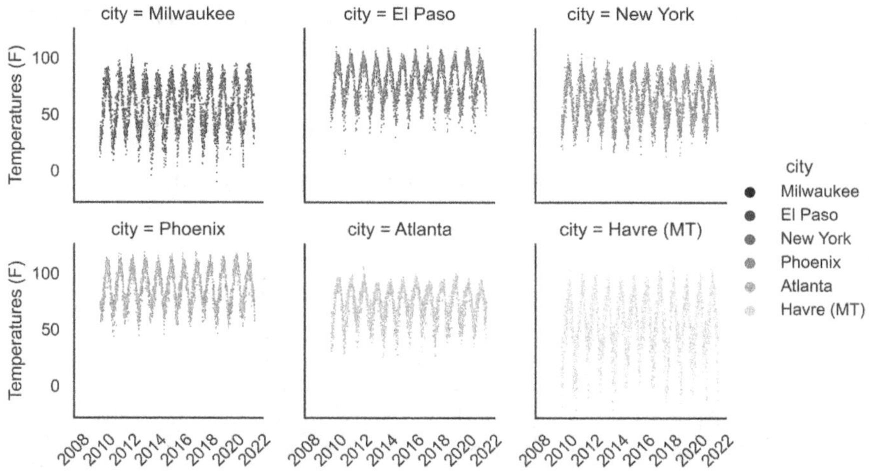

Figure 3.5 Temperature measurement in some US cities, maximum temperatures, facet visualization.

```
g=sns.relplot(data=dataT, x="Date", y="temp", hue="city",
              linewidth=0.3, alpha=0.5, kind="line",
              palette="magma", col="city", col_wrap=3,
              height=2.3)
```

3.2.3 Facet and Graphics for Categorical Variables

With function `catplot()`, we produce facet visualization for graphics of types:

- *strip plot* with `kind="strip"` (default).
- *swarm plot* with `kind="swarm"`.
- *boxplot* with `kind="box"`.
- *violin plot* with `kind="violin"`.
- *boxen plot* with `kind="boxen"`.
- *point plot* with `kind="point"`.
- *bar plot* with `kind="bar"`.
- *count plot* with `kind="count"`.

We will not see examples of all these types of graphics, many of them will be addressed specifically in following sections, and others are just simple variants.

3.2.4 Facet and Bar Plots

To obtain facet visualizations with bar plots, we use `kind=bar`. The result is easy to obtain, but not particularly customizable, unlike the equivalent with ggplot.

We replicate the example seen before with data about the air quality and pollutants in Milan. A few common data-wrangling operations are needed to prepare the data frame.

```
df["data"]= pd.to_datetime(df["date"], format="%Y-%m-%d")
df= df[~df.isna().any(axis=1)]
df_grp1= df.groupby([df['date'].dt.month_name(), "pollutant"])\
                     [["value"]].sum()

df_grp1.reset_index(inplace=True)
df_grp1= df_grp1.rename(columns={"date":"month"})
```

	month	pollutant	value
0	April	C6H6	32.2
1	April	CO_8h	38.3
2	April	NO2	5 798.0
3	April	O3	3 405.0
4	April	PM10	1 806.0
...	...	...	...
79	September	NO2	7 549.0
80	September	O3	4 686.0
81	September	PM10	2 027.0
82	September	PM25	589.0
83	September	SO2	77.0

Let us first use *months* as the facet variable. The result of Figure 3.6 is correct overall, with the exception of the scale on axis *y* that is suitable for certain pollutants only (e.g., bars for C6H6, CO_8h, and SO_2 are always practically invisible).

```
sns.set_theme(style="white",font_scale=0.9)

g=sns.catplot(data=df_grp1, x="pollutant", y="value",
              kind="bar", height=2, col="month",
              col_wrap=3, palette='cubehelix')

g.set_axis_labels("Pollutants",'Quantity')
g.tick_params(axis='x', rotation=45)
```

Let us see a variant that replicates the example seen with ggplot. In this case, we want to have *pollutants* as facets, months on the *x*-axis, and coloring bars for

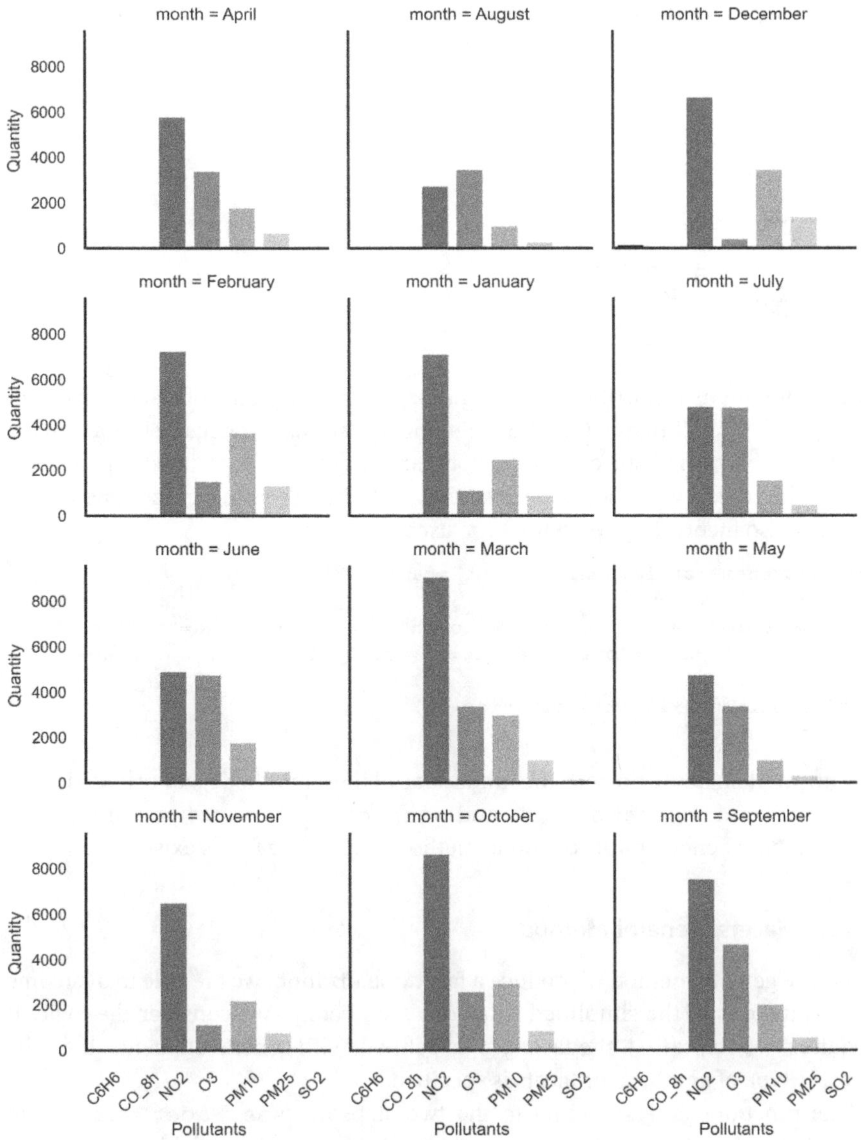

Figure 3.6 Facets and bar plot visualization.

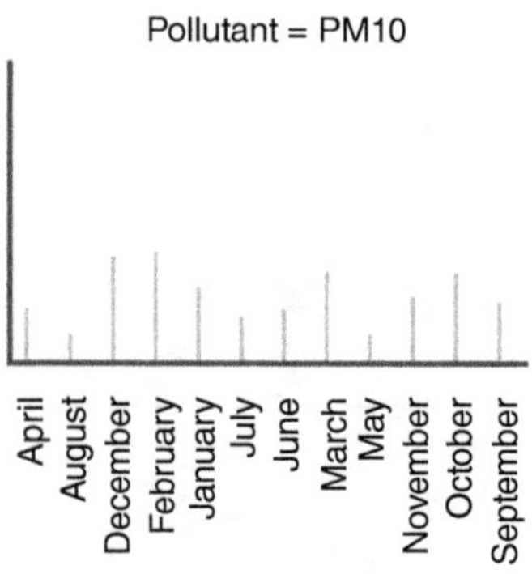

Figure 3.7 Incorrect facet visualization (single facet detail).

each pollutant using attribute hue. Figure 3.7 shows the detail of just one facet for clarity (i.e., for pollutant NO_2), the other ones are similar. The result is not visually correct in this case because Seaborn plots bars as if they were grouped side-by-side, this is the reason why they appear so thin and difficult to recognize. The month order is also incorrect when names are used.

```
sns.set_theme(style="white",font_scale=0.7)

g=sns.catplot(data=df_grp1, x="month", y="value", hue="pollutant",
              kind="bar", height=2, col="pollutant", col_wrap=3)

g.tick_params(axis='x', rotation=90)
g.tight_layout()
```

The problem has to do with the limitations of the simplified facet-oriented functions: relplot(), catplot(), and displot(). To overcome these limitations, a more general but less simple method to visualize facets exists.

3.2.5 Facets: General Method

With the general method to produce a facet visualization, we are able to overcome the limitations of the simplified functions seen before. We consider the logic. It requires two steps: first, the facet grid is defined, with general elements, then the specific type of graphics for facets is specified.

The functions corresponding to the two steps are sns.FacetGrid() and map(). The two functions will be associated by means of a variable representing the graphical object with the following template:

```
g=sns.FacetGrid(general elements)
g.map(specific graphic type and attributes)
```

We can reproduce the previous example to obtain a correct visualization. We also fix the wrong month name order by defining a list with month names correctly

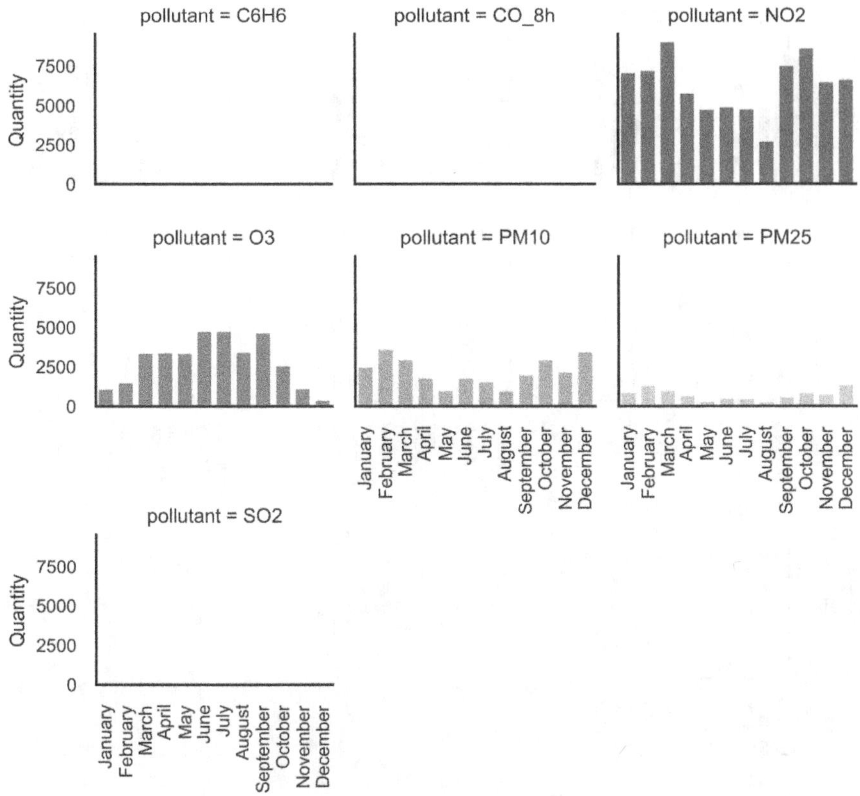

Figure 3.8 Facet visualization with the general method, unbalanced facets.

ordered, with that we configure attribute `order` of function `map()`. Figure 3.8 shows the facet visualization.

```
list=["January", "February", "March", "April", "May",
      "June", "July", "August", "September", "October",
      "November", "December"]

g = sns.FacetGrid(df_grp1, col='pollutant', hue='pollutant',
                  col_wrap=3, height=2, palette='cubehelix')

g.map(sns.barplot, 'month', 'value', order= list)

g.tick_params(axis='x', rotation=90)
g.set_axis_labels("",'Quantity')
g.tight_layout()
```

Technically, the graphic is now correct. Still, the facets are not homogeneous, due to the different scales of the pollutants. We can correct it, similarly to what

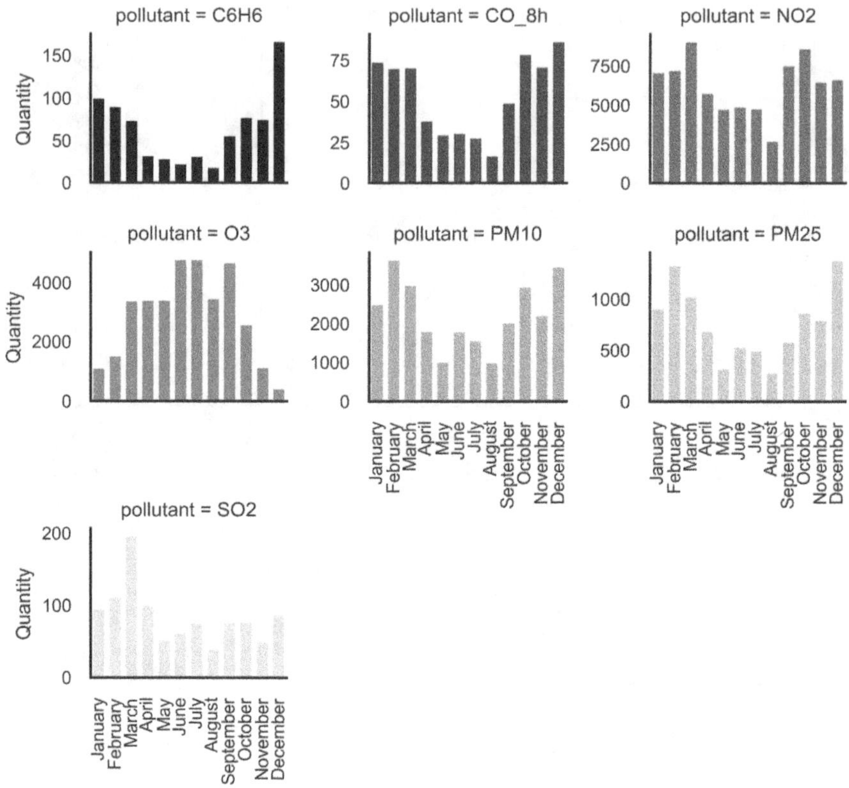

Figure 3.9 Facet visualization with the general method, independent scales.

we did with ggplot, by making scales on the *y*-axis independent. To make that, function `FacetGrid()` has attributes `sharex` and `sharey`, which if *True* use a shared scale for all facets respectively on axis *x* or axis *y*, if *False* otherwise. In our case, we want independent scales on axis *y* (`sharey=False`) and common scales on axis *x* (`sharex=True`). In Figure 3.9 the modified facet visualization is shown.

```
...
g = sns.FacetGrid(df_grp1, col='pollutant', hue='pollutant',
                  col_wrap=3, height=2, sharex=True, sharey=False)
...
```

As observed for the equivalent example in R, a cautionary note is necessary, using different scales in a facet visualization should not be done lightly because observers could easily be misled into thinking that quantities among facets are directly comparable, without noticing that scales are not the same. This misunderstanding might provoke more than a small annoyance.

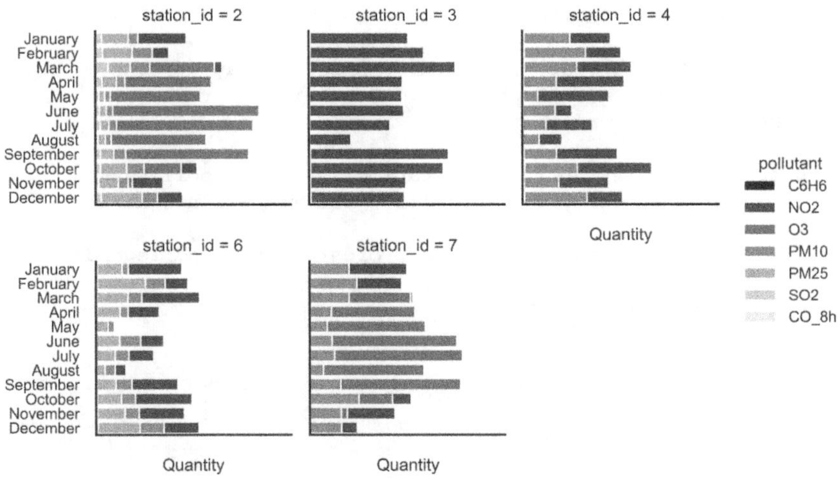

Figure 3.10 Facet visualization with balanced and meaningful bar plots.

Similar to the R section, we show an alternative by employing a fourth variable (*station_id*) for facets, with bars set as *stacked*. Figure 3.10 shows the result.

```
df_grp2= df.groupby(["station_id", df['date'].\
       dt.month_name(), "pollutant"])[["value"]].sum()

df_grp2.reset_index(inplace=True)
df_grp2= df_grp2.rename(columns={"date":"month", "value":"total"})
```

	station_id	month	pollutant	total
0	2	April	C6H6	12.2
1	2	April	NO2	936.0
2	2	April	O3	1 796.0
3	2	April	PM10	457.0
4	2	April	PM25	324.0
...	...	...	...	...
234	7	October	O3	1 267.0
235	7	October	PM10	752.0
236	7	September	NO2	1 367.0
237	7	September	O3	2 317.0
238	7	September	PM10	479.0

```
sns.set_theme(style="white",font_scale=0.7)

list=["January", "February", "March", "April", "May", "June",
      "July", "August", "September", "October", "November",
      "December"]

g2 = sns.FacetGrid(df_grp2, col='station_id', hue='pollutant',
                   palette='cubehelix', col_wrap=3, height=2)

g2.map(sns.barplot, 'total', 'month', order= list).add_legend()

g2.set_axis_labels("Quantity",")
g2.tight_layout()
```

4

Histograms and Kernel Density Plots

A *histogram* is a traditional type of graphics based on a continuous variable. For the values of this variable, it defines a certain number of ranges called *bins* and counts the number of observations for each bin. Visually, it is schematic and typically aesthetically simple, but it may provide useful information about data. For this reason, it is often used as an analysis tool, not just in presentations, in order to study general characteristics of data, such as anomalous distributions. It is important to remember that histograms are most useful when several combinations of *bin width or numerosity* are tested.

Dataset

In this section, we use the dataset *Compiled historical daily temperature and precipitation data for selected 210 U.S. cities*, Yuchuan Lai and David Dzombak, Carnegie Mellon University and *Report qualità aria 2021* (transl. Air Quality Report year 2021), Open Data Municipality of Milan, already introduced before. The following one is new, instead.

Bologna – B&B List, Open Data from Bologna Municipality, Italy (https://opendata.comune.bologna.it/explore/dataset/bologna-rilevazione-airbnb/information/?disjunctive.neighbourhood&disjunctive.room_type),

Copyright: Creative Commons CC BY-4.0.

4.1 R: ggplot

The main ggplot function for histograms is `geom_histogram()` with two main attributes, to be used as alternatives:

- `binwidth` defines the *width of bins*; in this case, the number of bins is derived from the whole range of values divided by the bin's width, and the result is

Data Visualization in R and Python, First Edition. Marco Cremonini.

Companion website: www.wiley.com/go/Cremonini/DataVisualization1e

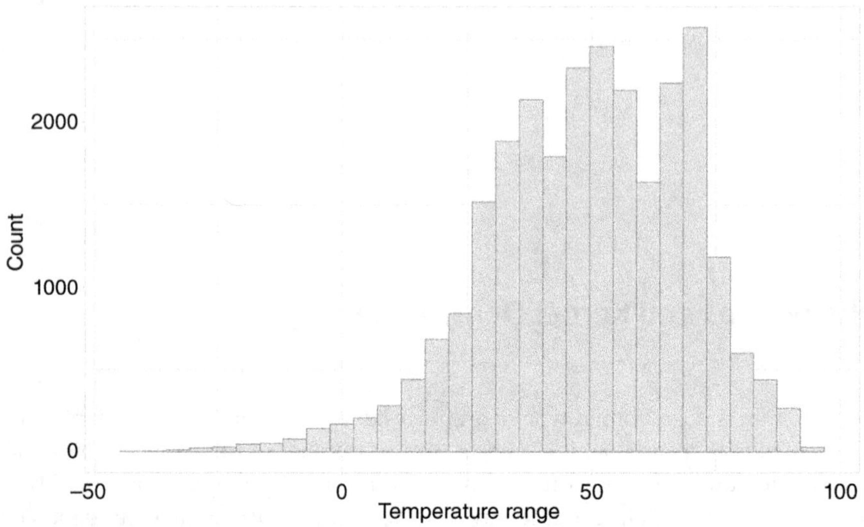

Figure 4.1 Number of bins equals to 30.

usually rounded to the largest integer: *bins=round((max(values)-min(values))/binwidth)*

- `bins` define the number of bins and in this case, it is the bin width to be calculated as *binwidth=round((max(values)-min(values))/bins)*

4.1.1 Univariate Analysis

In short, a univariate analysis means that statistics are analyzed independently, one at time. This is the classical reference case for histograms when the value distribution of a single variable is visually inspected for different bin widths or numbers.

Let us see first an example with daily temperatures of some US cities from years 2010 to 2022. We try with `bins=30`, then with `binwidth=10`. Some style elements are formatted using some of the many options provided by function `theme()`. Figure 4.1 and Figure 4.2 show the histograms for the two cases.

```
# Number of bins: 30

filter(df, tminmax=="tmin", lubridate::year(Date)>=2010)%>%
ggplot() +
  geom_histogram(aes(temp), bins=30,
                 fill="white", color="lightblue", na.rm=TRUE) +
```

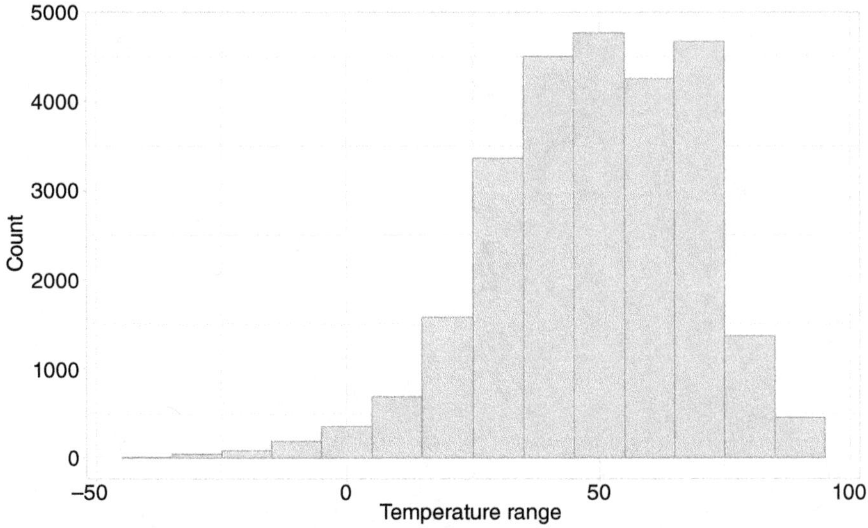

Figure 4.2 Bin width equal to 10.

```
  labs(x="Temperature range", y="Count")+
  theme_clean()+
  theme(panel.grid.major.y = element_blank(),
        legend.position = 'none')+
  theme(axis.text.x =
    element_text(size = 12, hjust = .75))

# Bin width: 5

filter(df, tminmax=="tmin", lubridate::year(Date)>=2010)%>%
ggplot() +
  geom_histogram(aes(temp), binwidth=10,
               fill="white", color="lightblue", na.rm=TRUE) +
  labs(x="Temperature range", y="Count")+
  theme_minimal()+
  theme(panel.grid.major.y = element_blank(),
        legend.position = 'none')+
  theme(axis.text.x =
    element_text(size = 12, vjust = 6, hjust = .75))
```

We could use facets to look at the monthly distribution of temperatures, in function `facet_wrap()`, the notation ~ `Month` is equivalent to `vars(Month)`. Figure 4.3 shows the result.

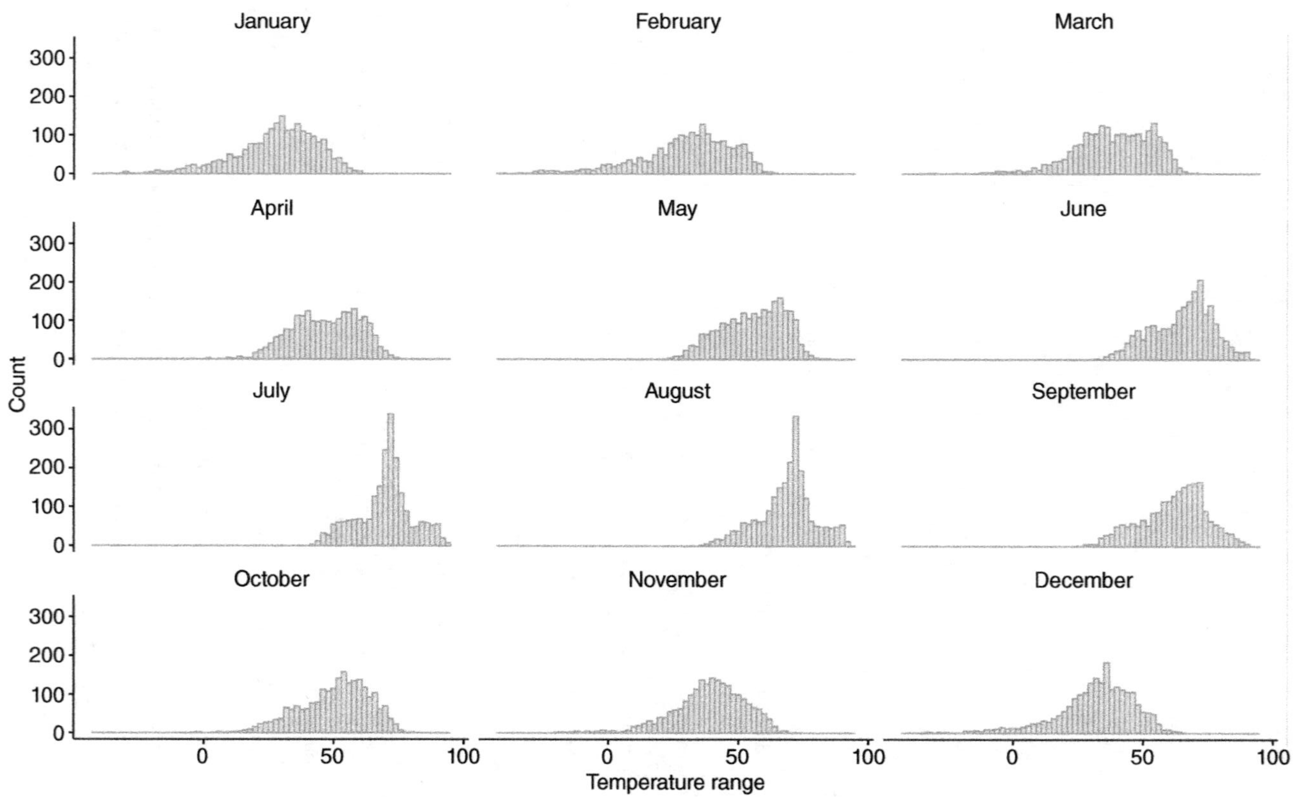

Figure 4.3 Facets visualization with histograms.

Tip

To have month names instead of month numbers as facet's titles, different from the case of axes, a handy `scale_` function is not available. It needs to be a little creative. Here are the steps.
With `mutate()`, a new column *Month* is created with month numbers as values. Then, a second `mutate()` transforms the new column as a factor and associates values (1...12) to levels (*factor level*) ("1"..."12"), and levels to *labels* ("January"..."December"). Function `facet_wrap()` will use labels as titles.

```
mutate(df, Month=month(Date)) %>%
mutate(Month=factor(Month,
            levels = c("1","2","3","4","5","6","7",
                       "8","9","10","11","12"),
            labels = c("January","February","March","April","May",
                       "June","July","August","September","October",
                       "November","December"))) %>%
filter(tminmax=="tmin", lubridate::year(Date)>=2010)%>%
  ggplot() +
  geom_histogram(aes(temp), binwidth=2,
                 fill="lightblue", color="gray50", na.rm=TRUE) +
  facet_wrap(~ Month, ncol = 3)+
  labs(x="Temperature range", y="Count")+
  theme_clean()+
  theme(panel.grid.major.y = element_blank())
```

4.1.2 Bivariate Analysis

In short, bivariate analysis means that two statistics are analyzed together. In this case, graphics have forms less familiar, although aesthetically of greater impact. ggplot utilizes two functions, `geom_bin2d()` and `geom_hex()`, as bivariate extensions of the traditional univariate case. For *kernel density estimate* (*kde*), functions `geom_density2d()` and `geom_density2d_filled()` are available. In this second case, the result will show where, in the bidimensional space of values, points have higher density.

For the example, we use again the datasets of daily temperature of some US cities. In this case, data should be homogeneous, meaning that they could not mix observations collected from contexts having very different characteristics, such as if we were mixing data from Phoenix, one of the hottest US cities with those from Milwaukee, one of the coldest. For this reason, we pick just one city, New York City. Variables are month and temperature.

We start with `geom_bin2d()` and `geom_hex()`; they have simple usage, very similar to the univariate case. Months are obtained with month names through package *lubridate* function `month()` with attribute `label`; other style options have been added, such as `scale_fill_continuous()` to set the color gradient

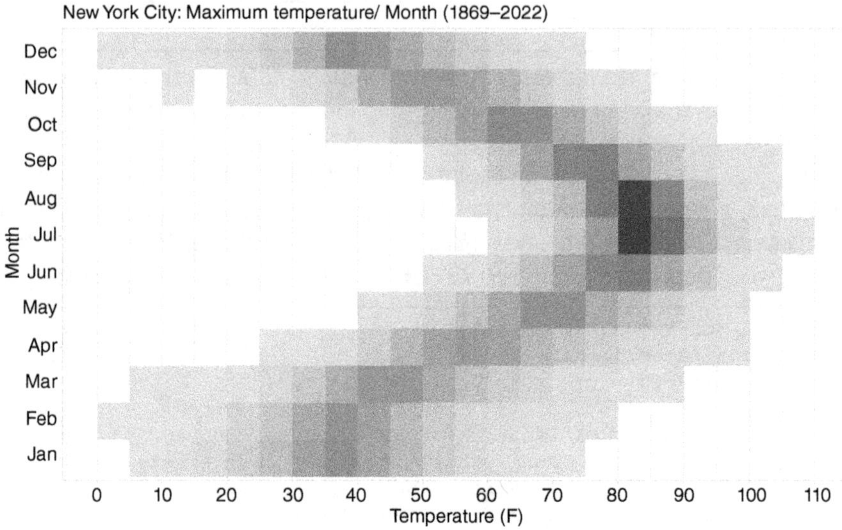

Figure 4.4 Histogram for bivariate analysis with rectangular tiles.

and `scale_x_continuous()` to visualize 10 ticks on the *x*-axis. Finally, with function `theme()`, other formatting options have been adjusted. *Maximum temperatures* have been selected; the bins have a 5 °F range. Figure 4.4 shows the result, which should be *interpreted according to the color scale*, the darker the hue of tiles, the denser the observations; for example, in July and August, temperatures in the range 80–85 °F are the most frequent.

```
filter(df, city=="New York", tminmax=="tmax") %>% ggplot() +
  geom_bin2d(aes(x=temp, y=lubridate::month(Date, label=TRUE)),
             binwidth=5, na.rm=TRUE) +
  scale_fill_continuous(low="lightblue", high="darkred") +
  scale_x_continuous(breaks = waiver(), n.breaks = 10)+
  labs(
    x="Temperature (F)",
    y="Month",
    subtitle="New York City: Maximum temperature/Month (1869-2022)"
  )+
  theme_light() +
  theme(panel.grid.major.y = element_blank(),
        legend.position = 'none',
        axis.text.x = element_text(hjust = .75),
        axis.text = element_text(size = 14),
        axis.title = element_text(size = 14))
```

We try the same but with function `geom_hex()`, which produces a slightly different visual representation with hexagonal tiles instead of rectangular tiles, style options in common with the previous graphic have been omitted; in this case, the

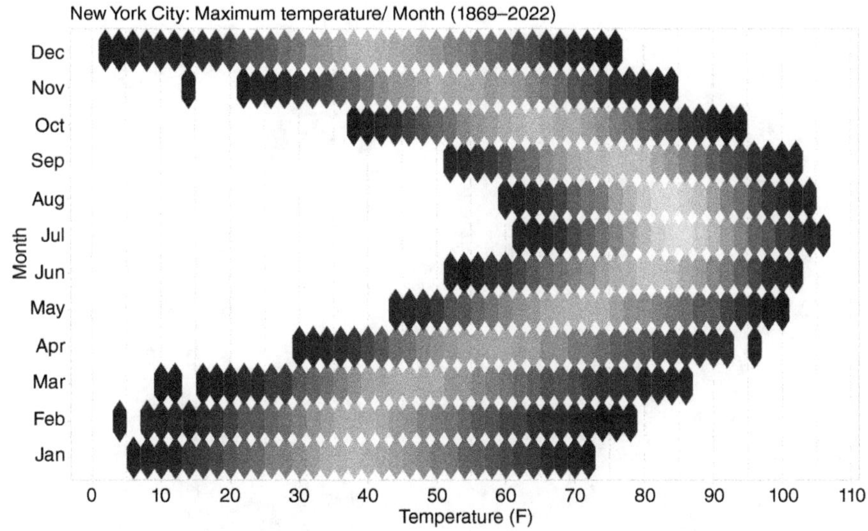

Figure 4.5 Histogram for bivariate analysis with hexagonal tiles.

lighter the hue of tiles, the denser the observations, the bin width is set to 2 for the x-axis (`binwidth=c(2,1)`) (see Figure 4.5).

```
filter(df, city=="New York", tminmax=="tmax") %>% ggplot() +
  geom_hex(aes(x=temp, y=lubridate::month(Date, label=TRUE)),
           binwidth=c(2,1), na.rm=TRUE) +
  scale_fill_continuous(low=low="darkblue", high="gold") +
  ...
```

For these types of graphics, a good choice of colors and style options is important, being the aesthetic impact possibly very effective.

Facet visualization is also possible with bivariate histograms. Here we choose some years (i.e., 1870, 1920, 1970, 2000, 2010, and 2021) and plot the facets for the distribution of maximum temperatures in New York with respect to months. Again, we omit style options in common with previous graphics. Figure 4.6 shows the facet visualization.

```
yearsNY=c("1870","1920","1970","2000","2010","2021")

filter(df, city=="New York", tminmax=="tmax",
       lubridate::year(Date) %in% yearsNY) %>% ggplot() +
  geom_bin2d(aes(x=temp, y=lubridate::month(Date, label=TRUE)),
                 binwidth=5, na.rm=TRUE) +
  facet_wrap(vars(lubridate::year(Date)), ncol= 3)+
  scale_fill_gradient(low="deepskyblue1", high="darkorange") +
...
```

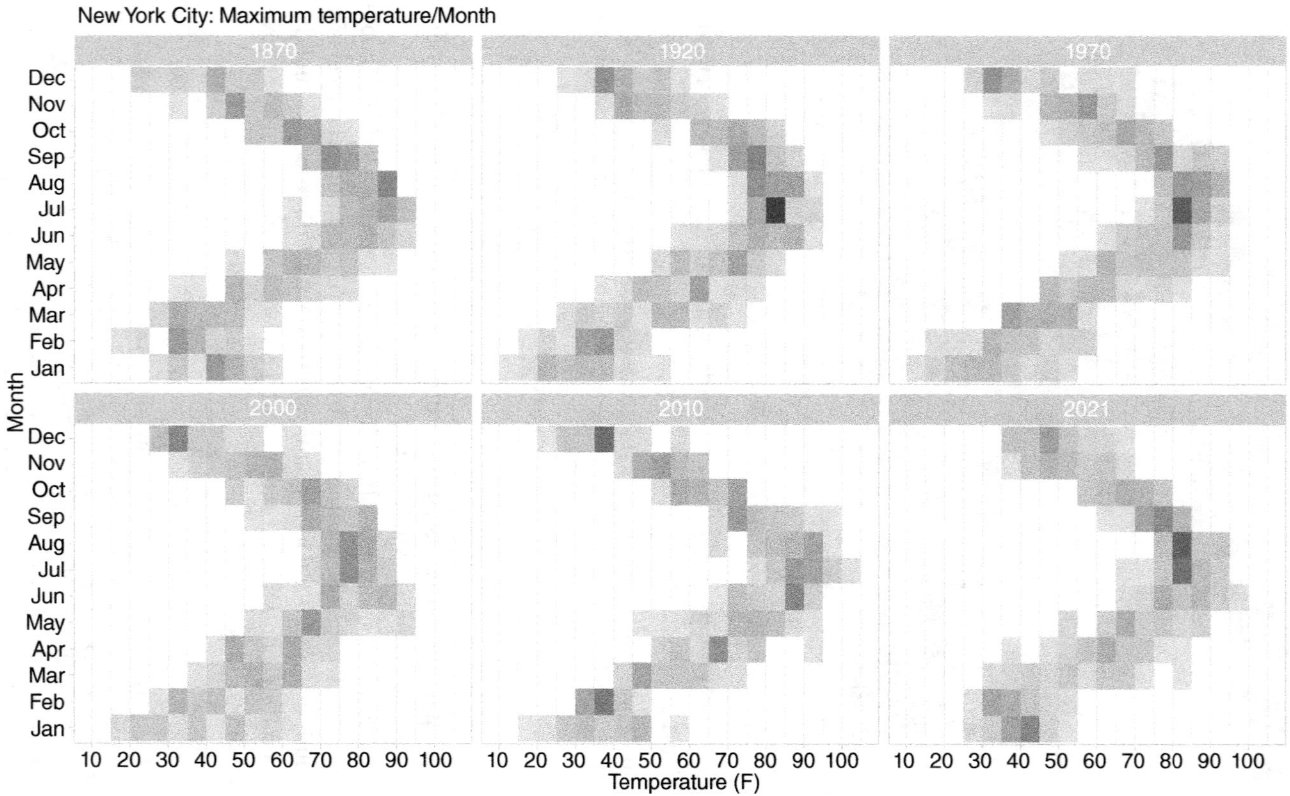

Figure 4.6 Histogram for bivariate analysis with facet visualization.

4.1.3 Kernel Density Plots

We move now to the case of *kernel density plots* using `geom_density2d()` and `geom_density2d_filled()`. Results are qualitatively similar to those obtained with the two previous functions, but some differences are notable, due to the different method of analysis, and a peculiar graphical form. We remain in New York and keep the facet visualization, this time just for years 1940, 1970, 2000, and 2021. For this plot, month names cannot be used as categorical variables for the *y*-axis, numerical continuous values are needed; the number of bins is 20, meaning an approximately 5 °F range of temperature. The plot in Figure 4.7 shows curves representing a certain density level (*isodensity*), the higher the number of curves, the greater the density of data points. For example, we still see that in August, temperatures are densely concentrated around 80 °F; although from 1940 to 2021, a change in temperature distribution is visible.

```
yearsNY=c("1940","1970", "2000","2021")

filter(df, city=="New York", tminmax=="tmax",
       lubridate::year(Date) %in% yearsNY) %>%
  ggplot() +
  geom_density2d(aes(x=temp, y=lubridate::month(Date)),
                 bins=20, na.rm=TRUE) +
  facet_wrap(vars(lubridate::year(Date)), ncol = 2)+
  scale_x_continuous(breaks = waiver(), n.breaks = 10)+
  scale_y_continuous(breaks = waiver(), n.breaks = 12)+
...
```

The result of the second function is qualitatively alike, except that it makes use of a color scale instead of isodensity curves to indicate density levels. We use the same settings as the previous plot, just the function is different. Figure 4.8 shows the result, which is more intuitive than with isodensity curves, although less precise.

```
yearsNY=c("1940","1970", "2000","2021")
filter(df, city=="New York", tminmax=="tmax",
       lubridate::year(Date) %in% yearsNY) %>% ggplot() +
  geom_density2d_filled(aes(x=temp, y=lubridate::month(Date)),
                 bins=20, na.rm=TRUE) +
  facet_wrap(vars(lubridate::year(Date)), ncol = 2)+
  scale_fill_viridis_d(option="plasma")+
  scale_x_continuous(breaks = waiver(), n.breaks = 10)+
  scale_y_continuous(breaks = waiver(), n.breaks = 12)+
...
```

Finally, for curious readers, we also show the results with *minimum temperatures*, still in New York and for the same years of the previous plot (Figure 4.9).

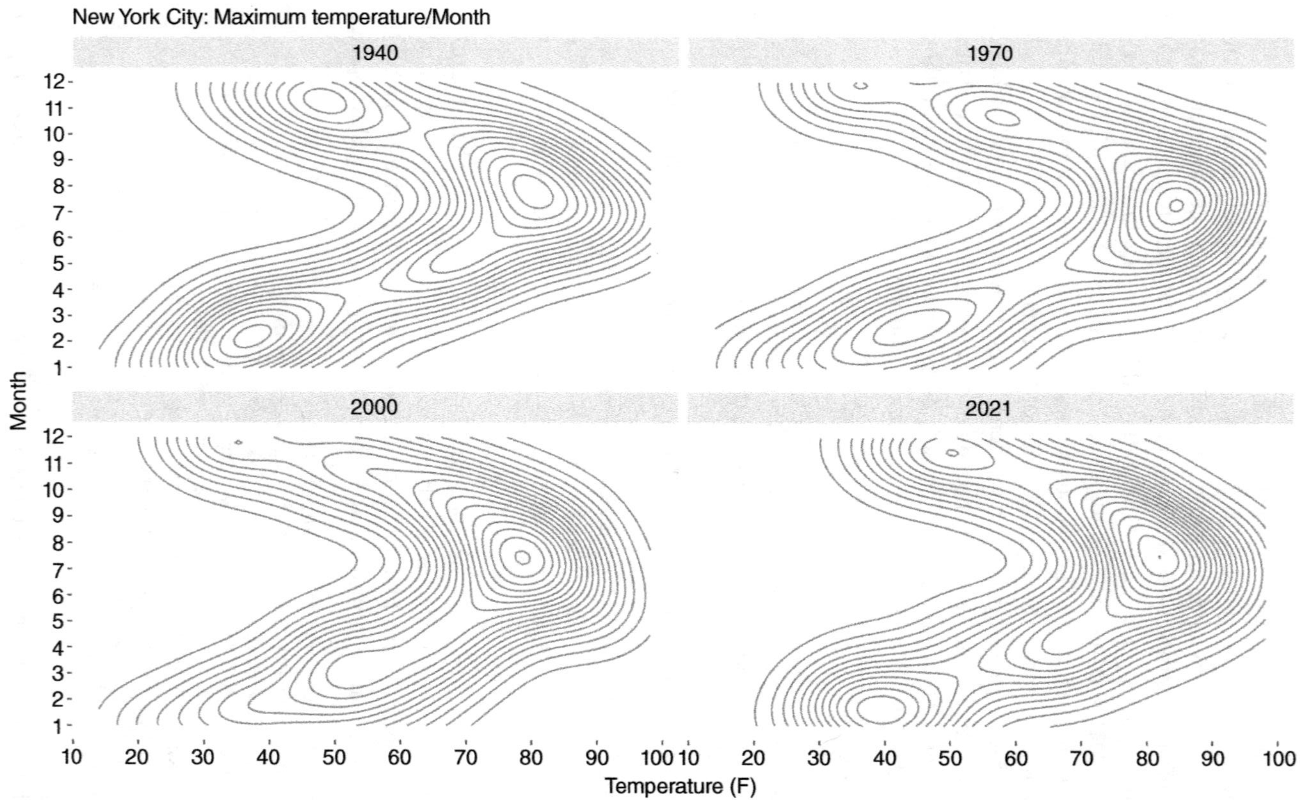

Figure 4.7 Kernel density for bivariate analysis with isodensity curves.

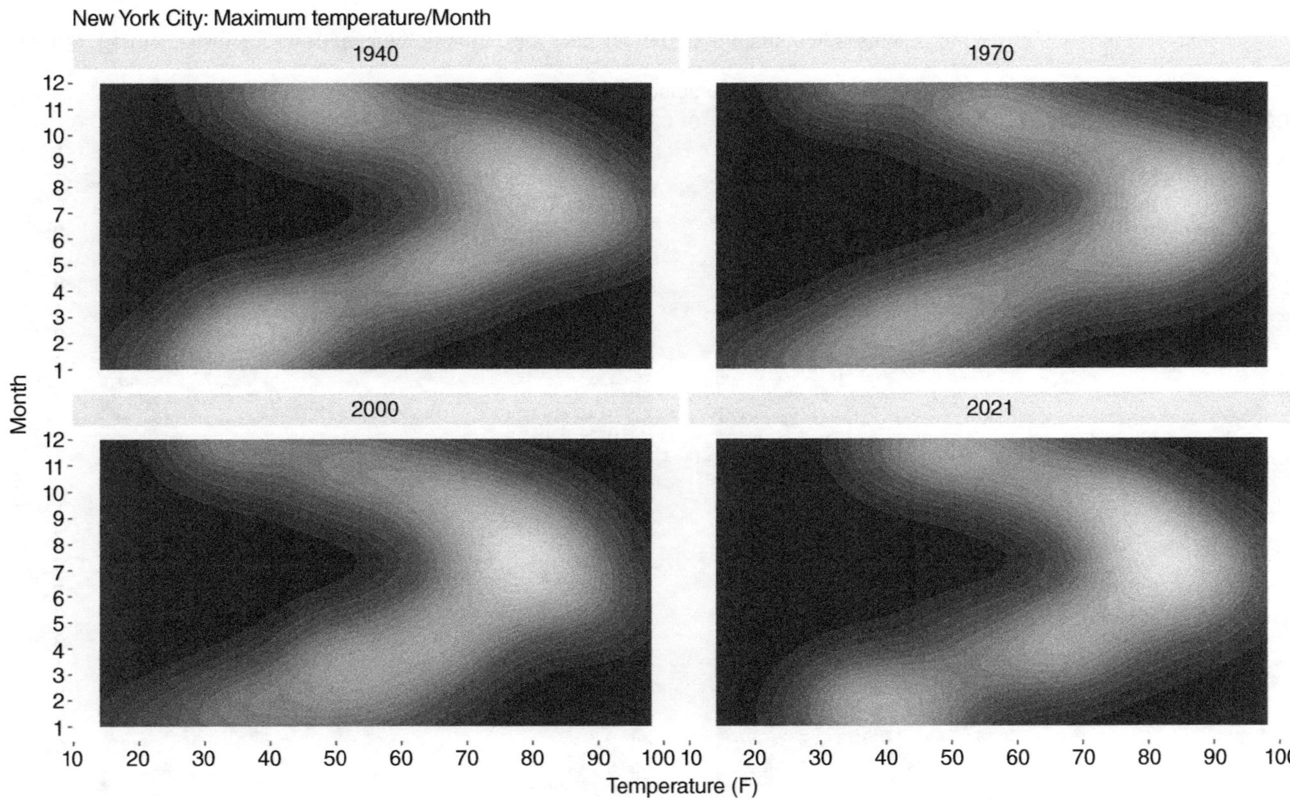

Figure 4.8 Kernel density for bivariate analysis with color gradient, NYC maximum temperatures.

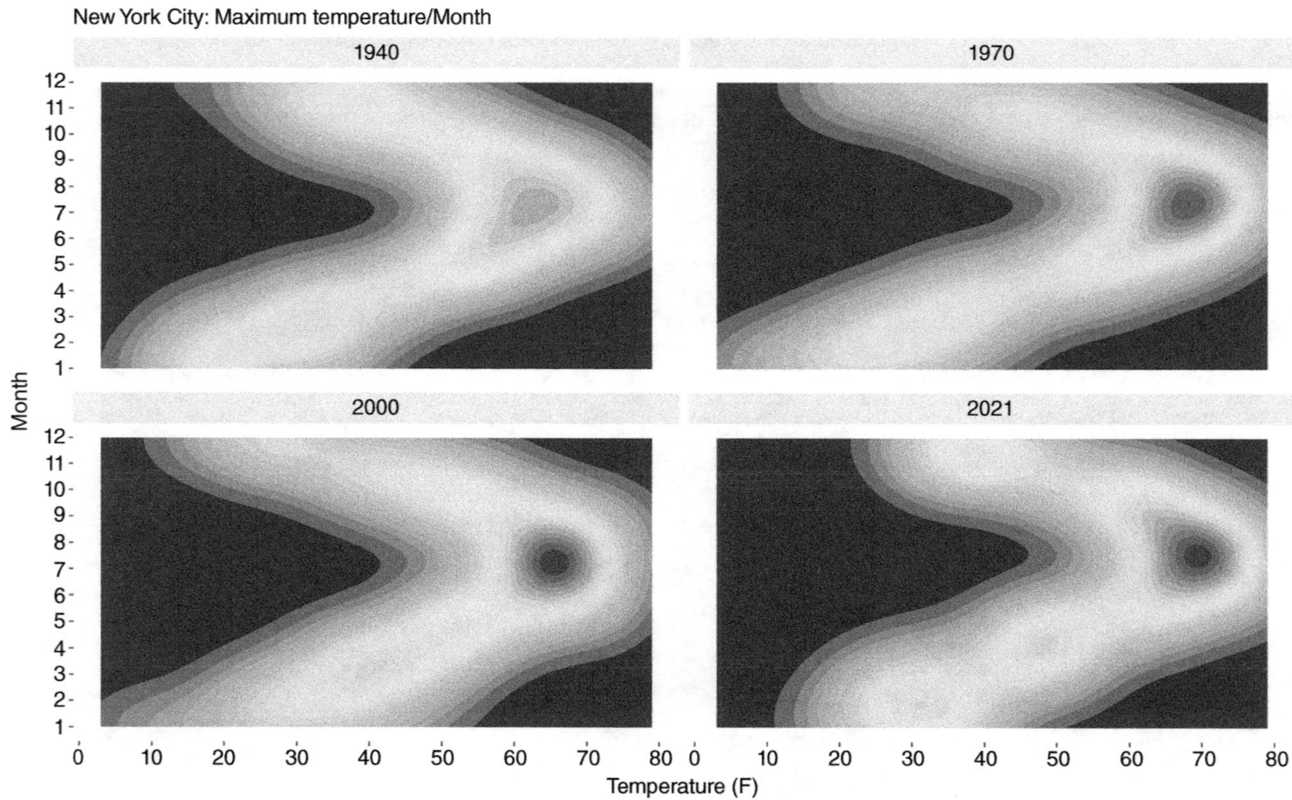

Figure 4.9 Kernel density for bivariate analysis with color gradient, NYC minimum temperatures.

```
yearsNY=c("1940","1970", "2000","2021")
filter(df, city=="New York", tminmax=="tmin",
       lubridate::year(Date) %in% yearsNY) %>% ggplot() +
  geom_density2d_filled(aes(x=temp, y=lubridate::month(Date)),
                        bins=20, na.rm=TRUE) +
  facet_wrap(vars(lubridate::year(Date)), ncol = 2)+
  scale_fill_viridis_d(option="turbo")+
  scale_x_continuous(breaks = waiver(), n.breaks = 10)+
  scale_y_continuous(breaks = waiver(), n.breaks = 12)+
...
```

4.2 Python: Seaborn

Data for this section are from the Open Data of Bologna Municipality, Italy, they contain the list of Bed and Breakfasts (BnB) present in town.

```
df=pd.read_csv("datasets/comune_bologna/bologna-rilevazione-airbnb.csv",
               sep=";")
```

	id	neigh.	price	number_of_ reviews	last_review	reviews_ per_month	avail.
0	209692	Navile	32	22	2021-11-08	0.38	256
1	229114	Navile	80	49	2022-09-12	0.41	125
2	374610	Santo Stefano	48	100	2022-05-05	0.86	29
3	570880	Porto–Saragozza	150	67	2022-07-03	0.54	281
4	684271	Navile	120	4	2018-11-11	0.05	107
...	...	...	...	...	...	...	...

With Seaborn, histograms are produced with function `histplot()`, having the usual two attributes `binwidth` and `bins`, for bin width and number. We start with an example using the *number of reviews* as the continuous variable and we vary bin's width and number.

4.2.1 Univariate Analysis

The bin width is set to 20 (Figure 4.10).

```
g=sns.histplot(data=df, x="number_of_reviews", binwidth=20)

plt.xlabel("Number of Reviews")
plt.ylabel("Number of BnB (count)")
plt.title("binwidth=20")
plt.tight_layout()
```

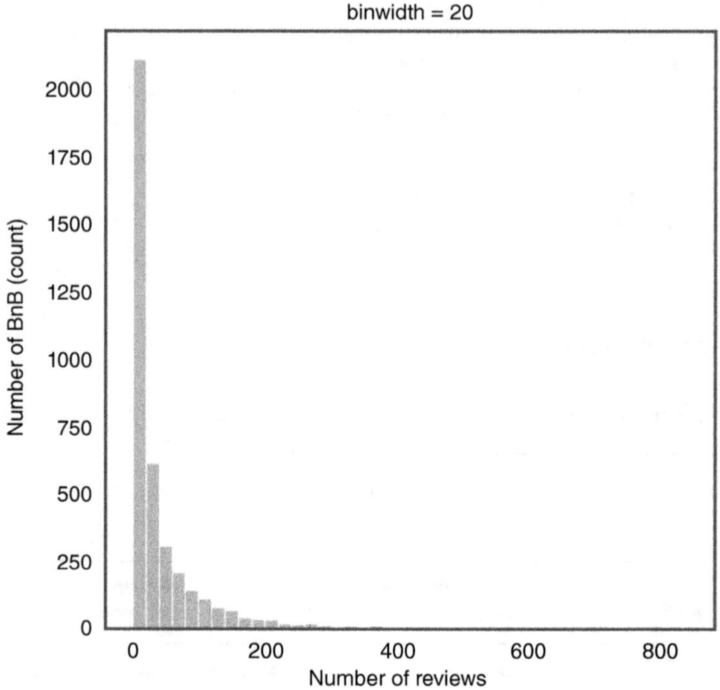

Figure 4.10 Histogram for univariate analysis, bin width equals 20.

To add the kernel density estimate, the attribute is `kde=True` (Figure 4.11).

```
g=sns.histplot(data=df, x="number_of_reviews",
               binwidth=40, fill=False, kde=True)
```

We can try with a third variable for neighborhoods and a stacked layout (attribute `multiple='stack'`); we also omit most expensive BnBs to limit the price range. Unfortunately, the result shown in Figure 4.12 is not clear because bars for BnBs with a high number of reviews are almost invisible. We will improve it later in the chapter.

```
pal=sns.color_palette("cubehelix")

g=sns.histplot(data=df[df.price<750],
              x="number_of_reviews", hue='neighbourhood',
              bins=20, multiple="stack", palette=pal)

plt.xlabel("Number of Reviews")
plt.ylabel("Number of BnB (count)")
plt.title("bins=20")
plt.tight_layout()
```

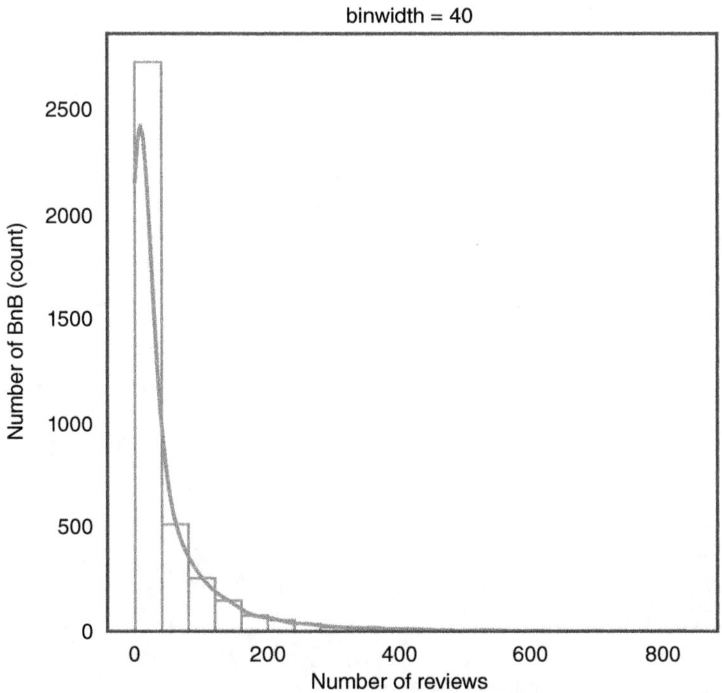

Figure 4.11 Histogram for univariate analysis and kernel density, bin width equals 40.

4.2.2 Bivariate Analysis

We use now function `histplot()` with two variables for a bivariate analysis. We choose the *number of reviews* and *price*. Attribute `discrete` if *True* set `binwidth=1` to the corresponding axis, meaning that each bin corresponds to a single value, which is useful when the variable is categorical. In our first example, we have instead continuous value, then we set `discrete=(False, False)`. Attribute `cbar` controls the visualization of the *color bar*, while `char_kws` represents a method, overly complicated actually, to reduce font size (Figure 4.13).

```
g=sns.histplot(data=df[df.price<750],
               x="number_of_reviews", y='price',
               bins=50, discrete=(False, False),
               cbar=True, cbar_kws=dict(shrink=.75))

plt.xlabel("Number of Reviews")
plt.ylabel("Price")
plt.title("bins=50")
```

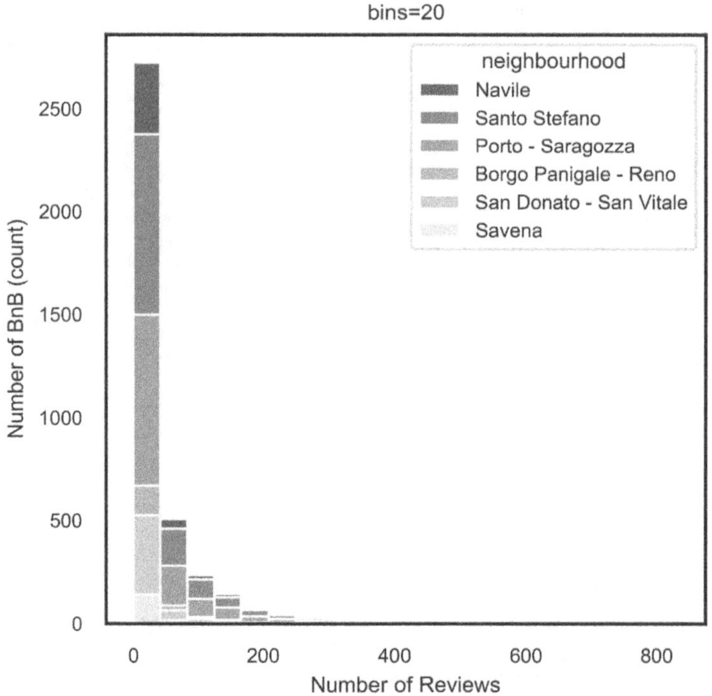

Figure 4.12 Histogram for univariate analysis with stacked bars.

To try with a categorical variable, we could use neighborhoods for the *y* axes, and in this case, we set `discrete=(False,True)`. Figure 4.14 shows the result.

```
g=sns.histplot(data=df[df.price<750],
               x="number_of_reviews", y='neighbourhood',
               bins=30, discrete=(False, True),
               cbar=True, cbar_kws=dict(shrink=.75))
```

As described before, `displot()` function exists for *facet visualization* with univariate and bivariate distributions, whose main graphic types are histograms (`kind="hist"`) and kernel density estimates (`kind='kde'`). Let us consider the case for histograms by using neighborhoods for the facet variable (Figure 4.15).

```
pal=sns.color_palette("crest")

g=sns.displot(data=df[df.price<750],
              x="number_of_reviews",
              y='price', height=2.3,
              kind='hist', col='neighbourhood',
```

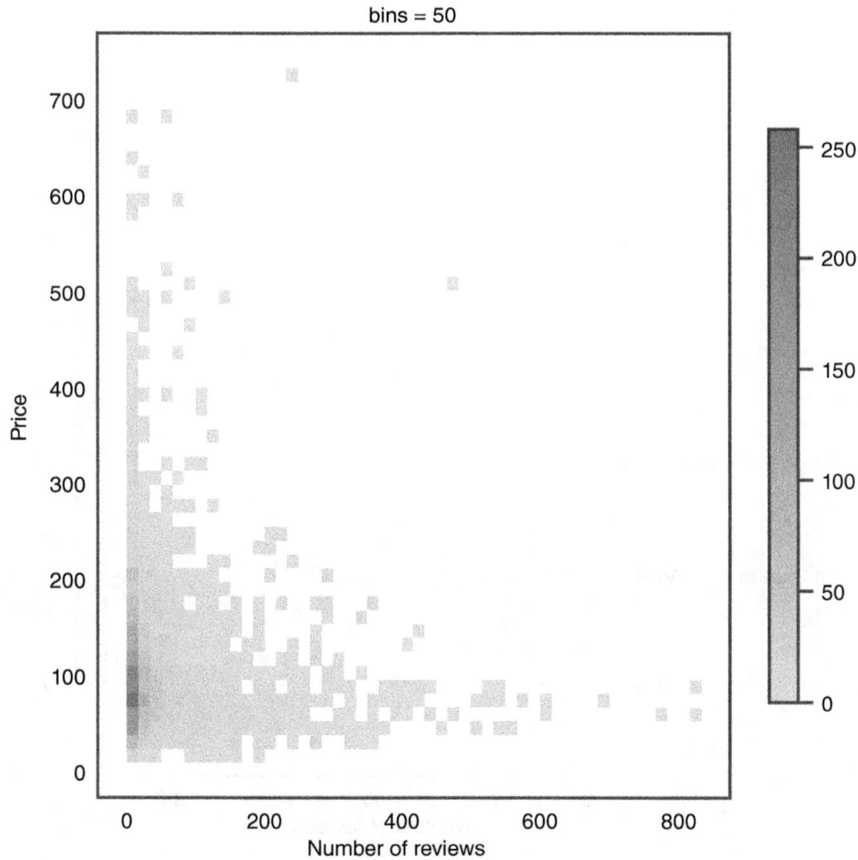

Figure 4.13 Histogram for bivariate analysis and continuous variables.

```
                hue='neighbourhood', col_wrap=3,
                bins=10, discrete=(False, False), palette=pal,
                cbar=True, cbar_kws=dict(shrink=.75),
                legend=False)

g.set_xlabels("Number of Reviews ")
g.set_ylabels("Price")
g.set_titles("Q. {col_name}")
```

4.2.3 Logarithmic Scale

In order to make a visualization clearer when scales vary on several magnitudes, the classical method is to turn to *logarithmic scales*. We can use it for the first

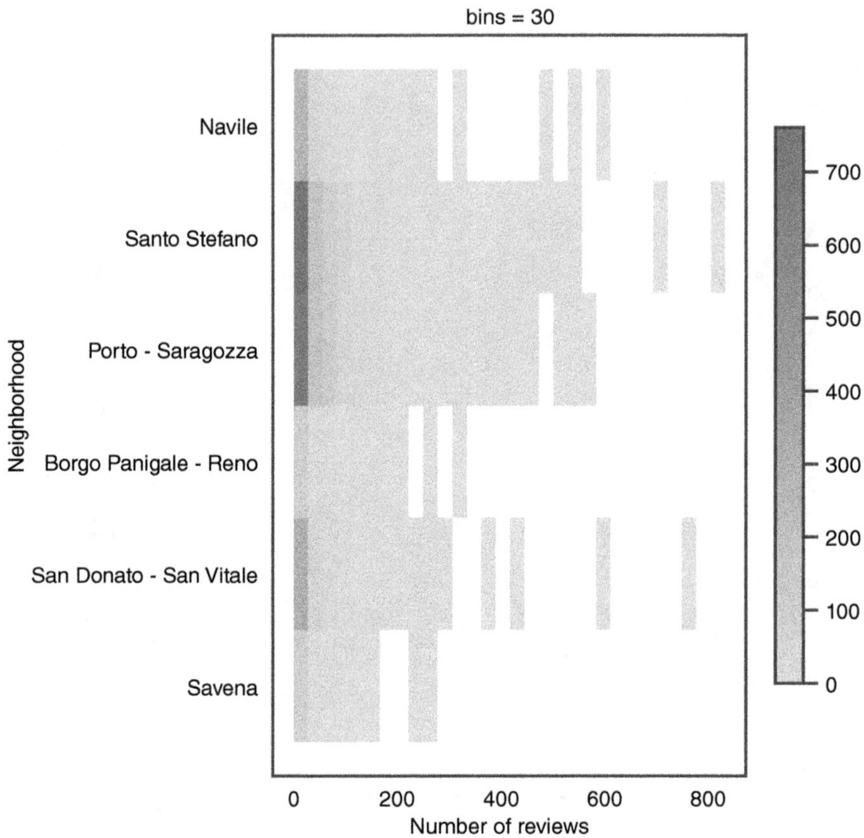

Figure 4.14 Histogram for bivariate analysis with a categorical variable.

example applied to axis *y* with the number of BnBs, which is always greater than zero, so avoiding the problem of *log(0)*, which corresponds to minus infinite (Figure 4.16).

```
g=sns.histplot(data=df, x="number_of_reviews", bins=50)

plt.yscale('log')

plt.xlabel("Number of Reviews ")
plt.ylabel("Number of BnBs (count)")
plt.title("bins=50")
```

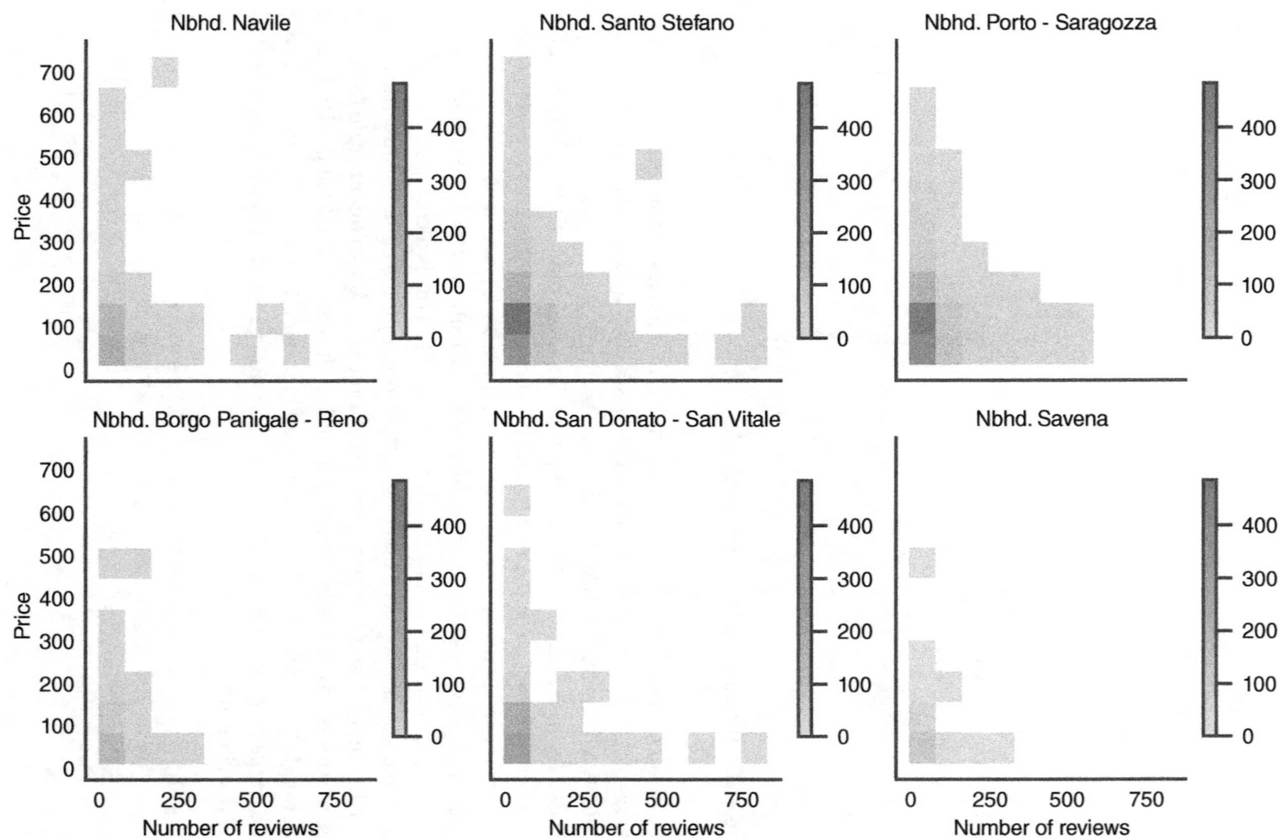

Figure 4.15 Histogram for bivariate analysis and facet visualization.

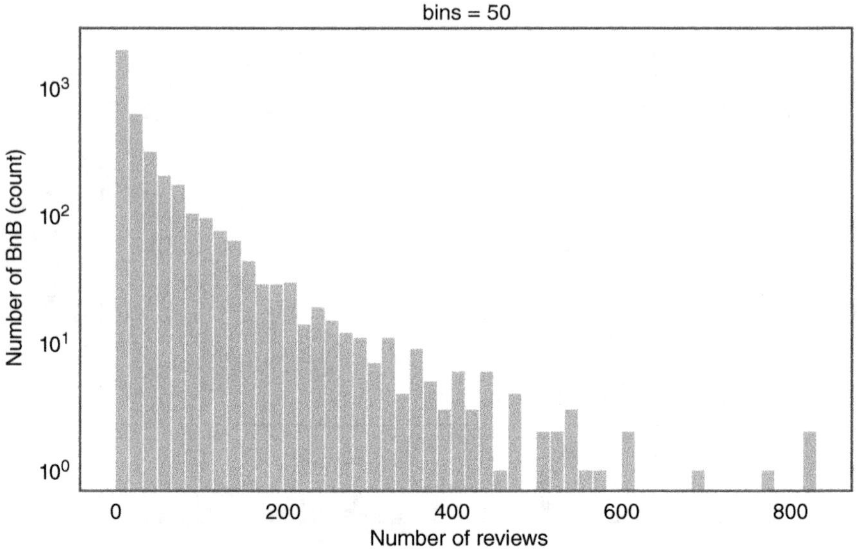

Figure 4.16 Histogram with logarithmic scale.

The result is the classical logarithmic graphic that makes the tail of a distribution more visible; in this case, emphasizing bars associated to BnBs with a high number of reviews, which were almost invisible with a linear scale.

We can try using `bins=100` and apply the logarithmic scale to axis *x*, with the number of reviews, to see the result. The problem is that this time we have many data points corresponding to value zero (i.e., BnBs with no reviews), which would correspond to *log(0)=-inf* and an inevitable visualization error if we would simply set `log_scale=True` in function `histplot()`. This is a common problem of logarithmic scales that has a clever solution in *matplotlib* called *Symmetric log* or *symlog* for short. A symlog turns the logarithmic scale into a linear scale for a tiny range of values around zero, this way avoiding the case of *log(0)* and allowing for a meaningful visualization. The result (see Figure 4.17) shows the presence of a considerable number of BnBs with no reviews and permits visualizing also the tail of the distribution.

```
g=sns.histplot(df, x="number_of_reviews",
               binwidth=2, fill=False)
plt.xscale('symlog')
```

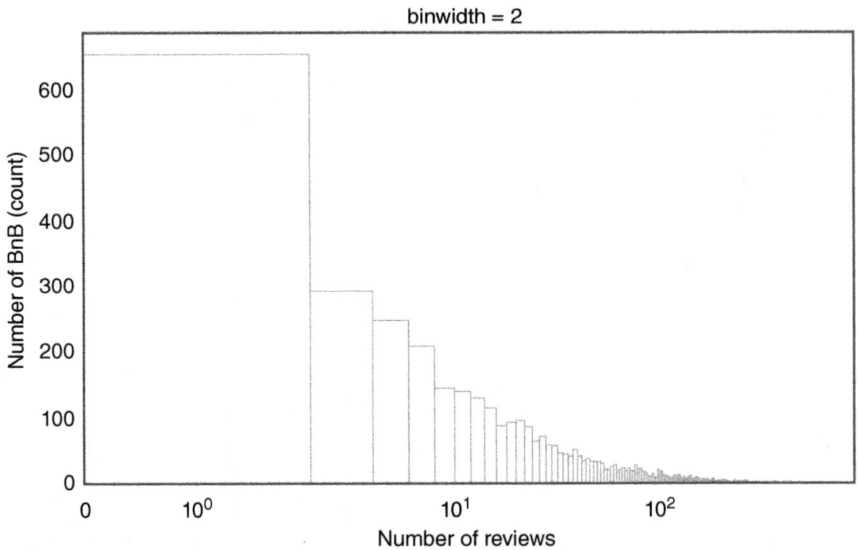

Figure 4.17 Histogram with logarithmic scale and symmetric log.

```
plt.xlim(0,900)
plt.xlabel("Number of Reviews ")
plt.ylabel("Number of BnBs (count)")
plt.title("binwidth=2")
```

We turn now to the previous example with the stacked visualization and improve it to make it more informative. It should be noted how, by changing bin width or number, different details could be observed. Figure 4.18 shows the result for bin width equal to 20, while Figure 4.19 shows the result for bin width equal to 5.

```
g=sns.histplot(data=df[df.price<750],
              x="number_of_reviews", hue='neighbourhood',
              binwidth=20, multiple="stack", palette=pal)

plt.yscale('symlog')
g.legend_.set_title('Neighborhoods')
plt.xlabel("Number of Reviews ")
plt.ylabel("Number of BnBs (count)")
plt.title("binwidth=20")
```

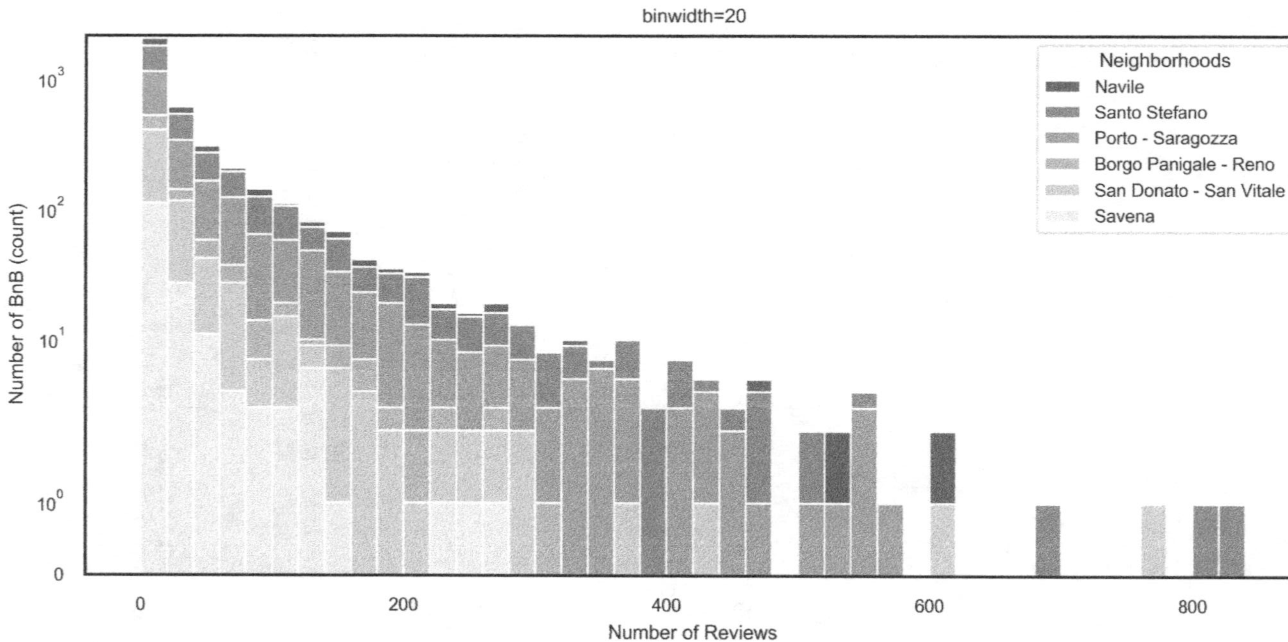

Figure 4.18 Histogram with stacked visualization, logarithmic scale, and symmetric log (bin width equals 20).

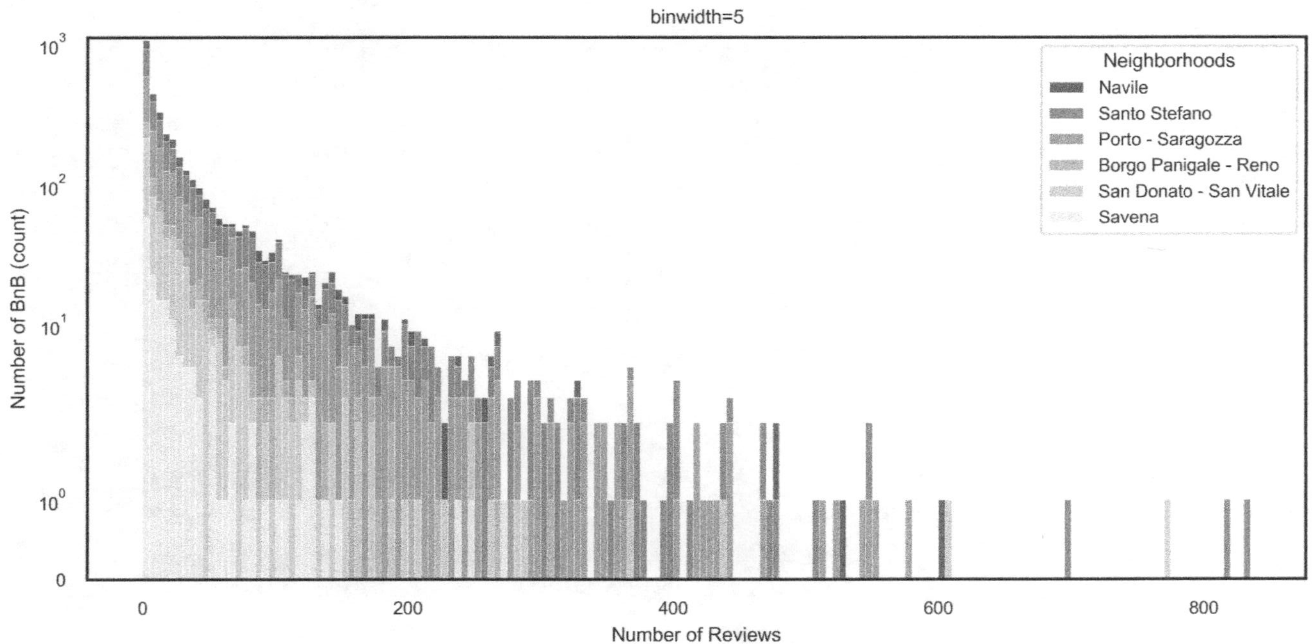

Figure 4.19 Histogram with stacked visualization, logarithmic scale, and symmetric log (bin width equals 5).

5

Diverging Bar Plots and Lollipop Plots

This chapter presents two peculiar types of graphics, *diverging bar plots* and *lollipop plots*, where the second one has an efficient implementation in ggplot but not in Seaborn, which forces to delve into *maplotlib* complications, lacking a specific support. It is of course possible that future versions of Seaborn (v. 12.2 is the one used for this book) will provide a native implementation of lollipop plots.

Dataset

OECD-FAO Agricultural Outlook 2021-2030 by country, Organization for Economic Co-operation and Development (OECD) (https://stats.oecd.org/index.aspx?queryid=107144).

Permitted use: Except where additional restrictions apply as stated above. You can extract from, download, copy, adapt, print, distribute, share, and embed data for any purpose, even for commercial use. You must give appropriate credit to the OECD by using the citation associated with the relevant data, or, if no specific citation is available. You must cite the source information using the following format: OECD (year), (dataset name), (data source) DOI or URL (accessed on (date)). When sharing or licensing work created using the data. You agree to include the same acknowledgment requirement in any sub-licenses that You grant, along with the requirement that any further sub-licensees do the same.

(https://www.oecd.org/termsandconditions/)

5.1 R: ggplot

5.1.1 Diverging Bar Plot

It is not rare to encounter the case of both positive and negative data. When they are associated to a continuous variable, that case is no different than the one

Data Visualization in R and Python, First Edition. Marco Cremonini.

Companion website: www.wiley.com/go/Cremonini/DataVisualization1e

with only positive or only negative data; ggplot just draws the Cartesian plan to show scales with negative and positive values and with graphic functions (e.g., for scatterplots) nothing changes. The same is not completely true for categorical variables when a bar plot has to be produced, this case requires some additional care with respect to the traditional one of all negative or all positive values. For this reason, it is usually identified with the specific adjective of *diverging* bar plot, because the result will show bars in opposite directions for negative and positive values with respect to axis *x* or *y*, depending if the bar plot is visualized vertically or horizontally. Typical examples are associated to variations of a certain quantity that could either increase or decrease along a time period, like countries' gross domestic product (GDP), production of goods, purchases, and population.

For our example, we consider a new dataset from OECD with a time series representing the *production of agricultural goods for a set of countries*. The information we are interested in is the country name, the year of production, and the quantity of a certain commodity. Being interested in visualizing both negative and positive values, we could derive *yearly differences* in production with a simple procedure. For the analysis, we choose a particular product, *wheat*, and calculate yearly differences as the difference between values of two consecutive years.

```
oecd %>%
    filter((Variable=='Production') & (Commodity=="Wheat")) %>%
    select(LOCATION, Country, TIME, Time, Value) -> df
```

There exist several practical ways to calculate differences between consecutive elements of a data frame column, for example, with a *for cycle* that, for each country starts from the second year and compute `df$Value[i] - df$Value[i-1]`. From the data, we know that there are 41 years for each country, so it is easy to move from country to country.

```
df$DIFF=0
num_country= length(unique(oecd$Country))
num_year= length(unique(oecd$TIME))


k=0
for (j in 1:num_country) {
  for (i in 2:num_year) {
       $DIFF[i+k]=df$Value[i+k] - df$Value[i-1+k]
     }
  k=k+41
  }
```

```
  LOCATION Country  TIME   Time  Value    DIFF
  <chr>    <chr>    <dbl> <dbl>  <dbl>   <dbl>
1 AFR      AFRICA    1990  1990 13084.      0
2 AFR      AFRICA    1991  1991 16987.  3903.
3 AFR      AFRICA    1992  1992 11946. -5042.
4 AFR      AFRICA    1993  1993 12954.  1008.
5 AFR      AFRICA    1994  1994 15500.  2547.
6 AFR      AFRICA    1995  1995 13279. -2221.
...
```

An easier solution exists, however, which makes use of R function `lag()` that copies the elements of a column and shifts them down by one line; the result could be then used in a new column (i.e., column *LAG* in the following excerpt of code).

```
df %>% group_by(LOCATION) %>%
   mutate(LAG = lag(Value))
```

```
# Groups:   LOCATION [47]
   LOCATION Country  TIME   Time  Value     LAG
   <chr>    <chr>    <dbl> <dbl>  <dbl>   <dbl>
 1 AFR      AFRICA    1990  1990 13084.     NA
 2 AFR      AFRICA    1991  1991 16987. 13084.
 3 AFR      AFRICA    1992  1992 11946. 16987.
 4 AFR      AFRICA    1993  1993 12954. 11946.
 5 AFR      AFRICA    1994  1994 15500. 12954.
 6 AFR      AFRICA    1995  1995 13279. 15500.
 7 AFR      AFRICA    1996  1996 22135. 13279.
 8 AFR      AFRICA    1997  1997 14837. 22135.
 9 AFR      AFRICA    1998  1998 18437. 14837.
10 AFR      AFRICA    1999  1999 15481. 18437.
# ... with 1,917 more rows
```

With new column *LAG*, we have what we need to easily calculate yearly differences, just by subtracting values of column *LAG* from values of column *Value* and put the result in another new column (i.e., *DIFF*).

```
df %>% group_by(LOCATION) %>%
  mutate(LAG = lag(Value)) %>%
  mutate(DIFF= Value - LAG) -> df2

df2$LAG=NULL
```

```
  LOCATION Country  TIME  Time  Value    DIFF
  <chr>    <chr>   <dbl> <dbl>  <dbl>   <dbl>
1 AFR      AFRICA   1990  1990 13084.      NA
2 AFR      AFRICA   1991  1991 16987.   3903.
3 AFR      AFRICA   1992  1992 11946.  -5042.
4 AFR      AFRICA   1993  1993 12954.   1008.
5 AFR      AFRICA   1994  1994 15500.   2547.
6 AFR      AFRICA   1995  1995 13279.  -2221.
...
```

We just need to remember that, in this particular example, all rows for year 1990, the first of the time series, should be omitted because, for the first row, there is no value for the difference, all the subsequent rows for the year 1990 have meaningless values, being calculated with respect to the last year of the previous country.

```
df2=filter(df2, TIME!=1990)
```

We are ready for visualizing a *diverging bar plot*. A usually good stylistic choice for diverging bar plots is to use a *diverging color palette*, that is a palette that starts from a certain value (e.g., the center of the scale) and uses *two different color gradients* for values above or below that value. For example, one gradient on the blue scale and the other on the red scale, or any other possible variation. With ggplot we can set our custom diverging color palette using function `scale_fill_gradient2()`, which takes three attributes, `mid` for the middle color, `low` and `high` for the colors of the two diverging gradients. For the example, we select data about Argentina (Figure 5.1).

```
df2 %>% filter(LOCATION=="ARG") %>%
  ggplot(aes(x= as.factor(TIME), y=DIFF)) +
  geom_bar(aes(fill = DIFF), stat="identity", show.legend = FALSE) +
  scale_fill_gradient2(low = "darkred",
                       mid = "lightgray",
                       high = "darkblue")+
  labs(
    y= "Wheat production (yearly variations, tons)",
    x="",
    title="Argentina: OECD-FAO Agricultural Outlook 2021-2030"
  )+
  coord_flip()+
  theme_light()+
  theme(axis.text.x = element_text(size = 8),
        axis.text.y = element_text(size = 6))
```

In this case, ordering bars according to the values would not be the most appropriate solution, because maintaining the year order is the most useful information. We can consider a variant, where instead would be useful to order the bars, by considering the whole set of countries and a particular year (i.e., year 2000). We also add the indication of the actual value at the top of each bar by means of function `geom_text()`. Figure 5.2 shows the result.

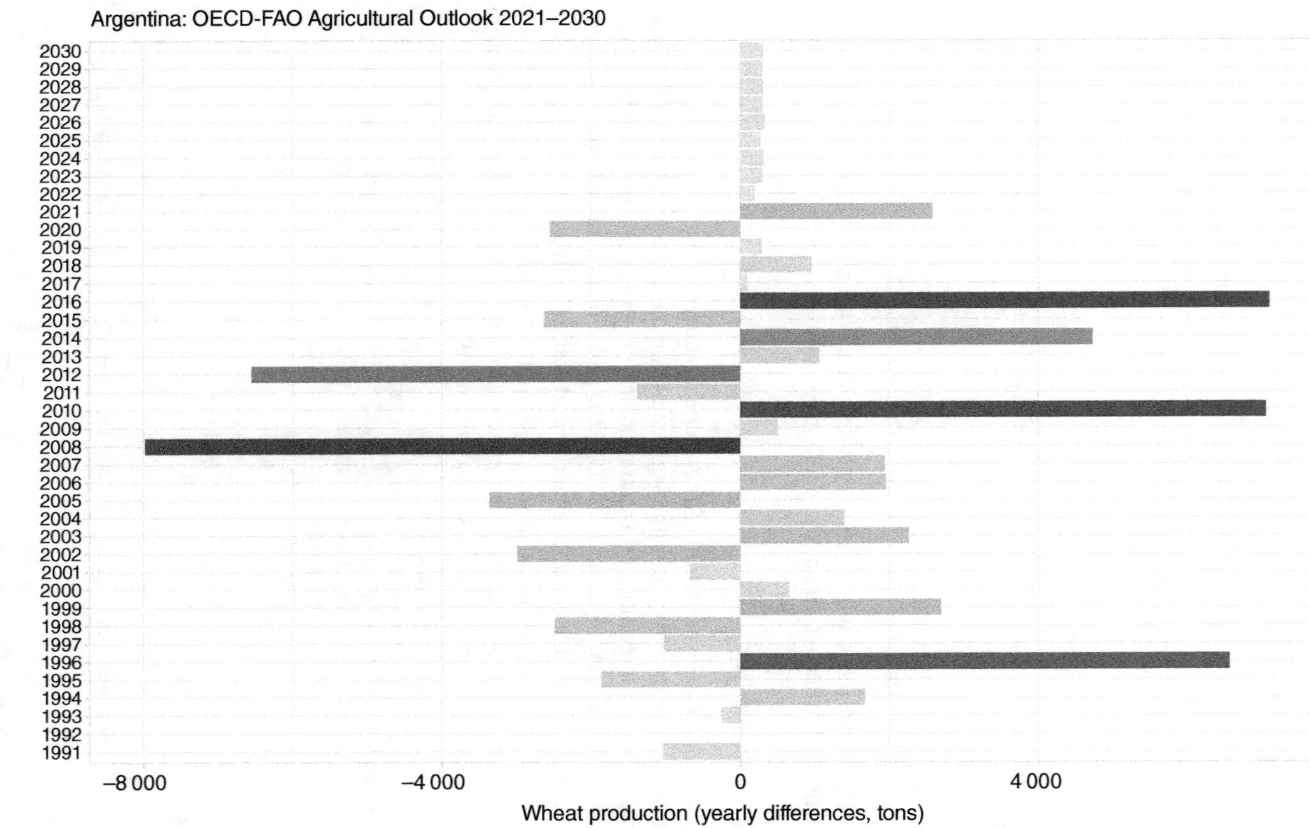

Figure 5.1 Diverging bar plot, yearly wheat production variations for Argentina.

```
df2 %>% filter(TIME==2000) %>%
  ggplot(aes(x= reorder(Country, DIFF), y=DIFF)) +
  geom_bar(aes(fill = DIFF), stat="identity", show.legend = FALSE) +
  scale_fill_gradient2(low = "red",
                       mid = "lightgray",
                       high = "blue")+
  geom_text(aes(label = round(DIFF, 1),
                hjust = ifelse(DIFF < 0, 1.5, -1),
                vjust = 0.5),
            size = 1.5) +
  labs(
    y= "Wheat production (year 2000 variations, tons)",
    x="",
    title="World: OECD-FAO Agricultural Outlook, year 2000"
  )+
  coord_flip()+
  theme_light()+
  theme(axis.text.x = element_text(size = 8),
        axis.text.y = element_text(size = 6))
```

Diverging bar plots, when carefully styled for a good quality appearance, could be particularly effective and aesthetically pleasing.

5.1.2 Lollipop Plot

A *lollipop plot* is a clever *variant of a categorical scatterplot* that simulates a bar plot by substituting bars with points and segments (from here the resemblance with lollipops). It is made by combining a scatterplot (`geom_point()`) to visualize values and segments (`geom_segment()`). Like the previous case of diverging bar plots, when carefully styled, it could be effective and aesthetically good-looking. We consider two layouts with different graphical elements and options, in the second one also aesthetic *size* will be used. The following excerpt of code shows the creation of the lollipop plot and Figure 5.3 shows the result.

```
df2 %>% filter(LOCATION=="ARG") %>%
  ggplot(aes(x= as.factor(TIME), y=DIFF)) +
  geom_point(aes(color=DIFF), size=4, show.legend=FALSE) +
  geom_segment(aes(x=as.factor(TIME), xend=as.factor(TIME),
                   y=0, yend=DIFF, color = DIFF),
               show.legend = FALSE)+
  scale_color_gradient2(low = "darkred",
                        mid = "lightgray",
                        high = "darkblue")+
  labs(
    y= " Wheat production (yearly variations, tons)",
    x="",
    title="Argentina: OECD-FAO Agricultural Outlook 2021-2030"
  )+
  theme_light()+
  theme(axis.text.x = element_text(size = 5),
        axis.text.y = element_text(size=8))+
  theme(axis.text.x = element_text(angle=30, hjust=1))
```

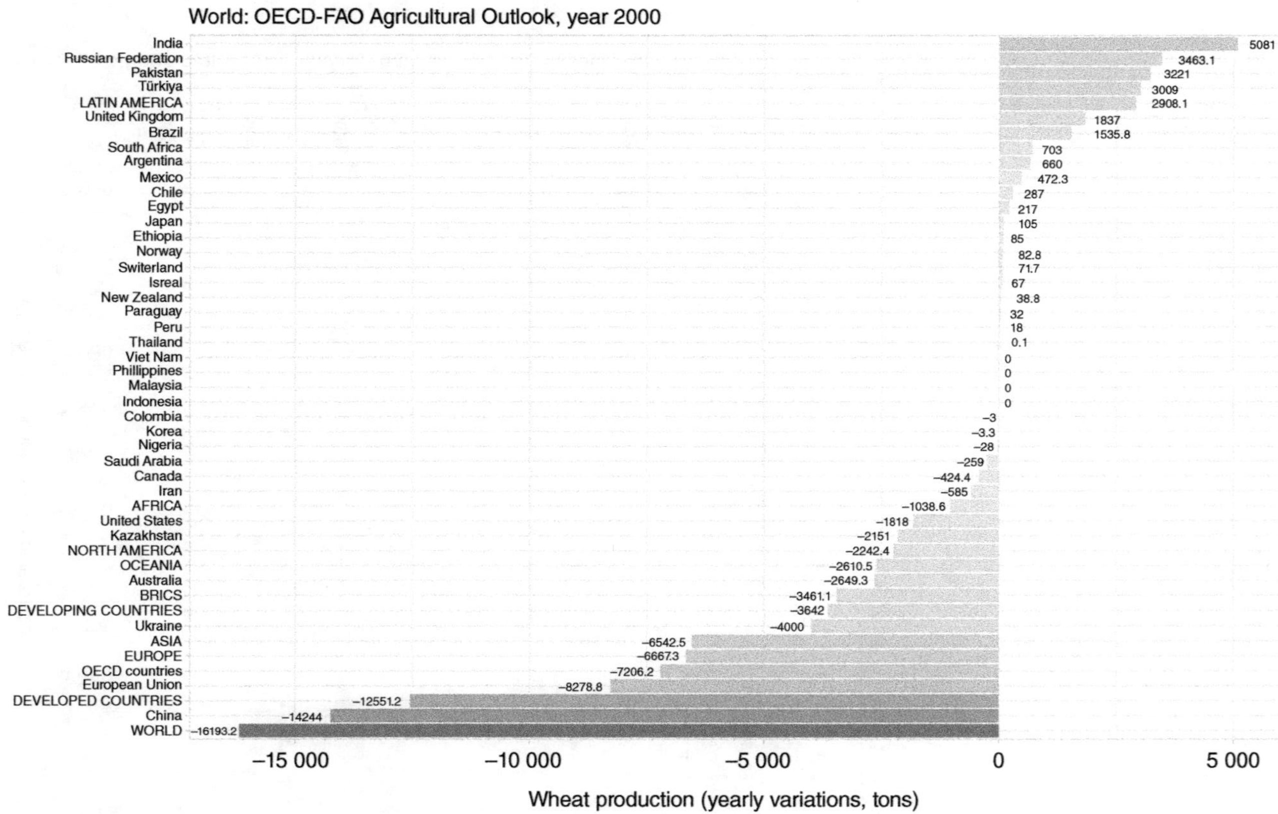

Figure 5.2 Diverging bar plot with ordered bars and annotation, yearly variations in wheat production for year 2000 with respect to year 1999.

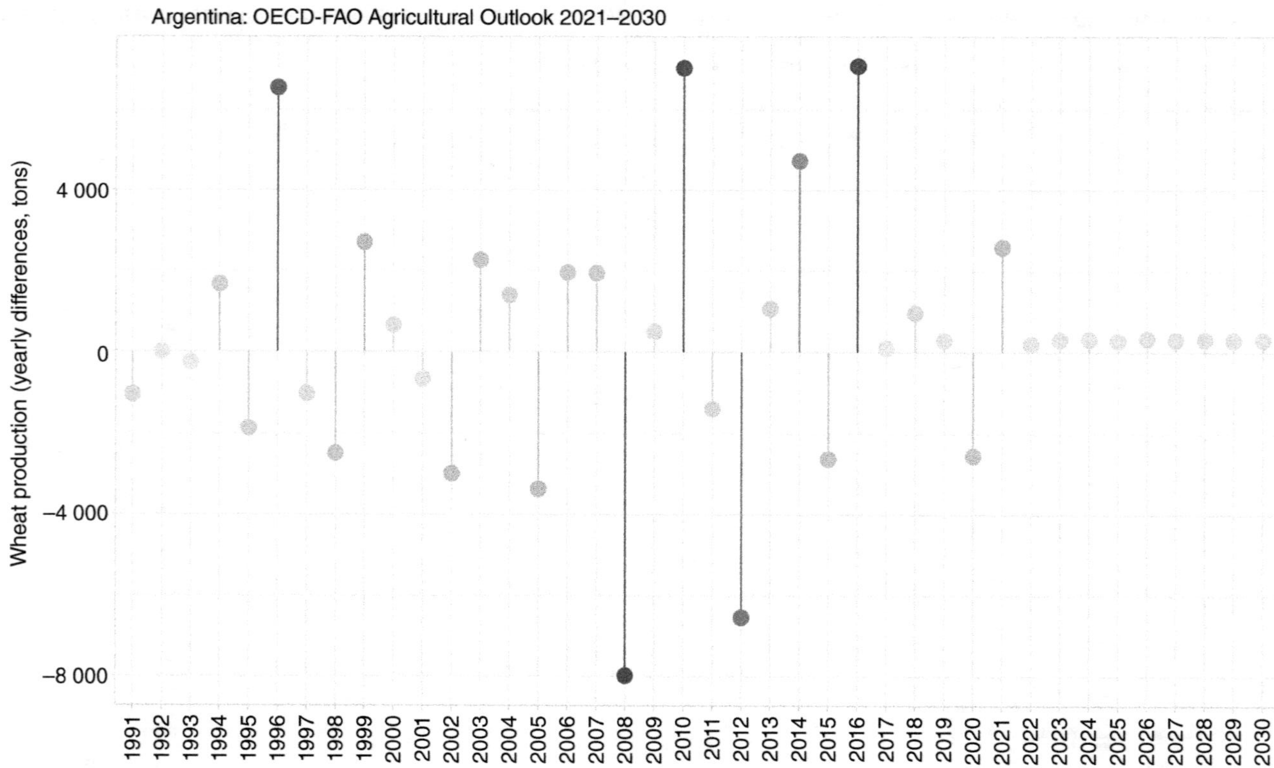

Figure 5.3 Lollipop plot, yearly wheat production variations for Argentina.

With the next example, we reproduce the second diverging bar plot seen before, this time by using a lollipop plot instead of a bar plot (Figure 5.4).

```
df2 %>% filter(TIME==2000) %>%
  ggplot(aes(x= reorder(Country, DIFF), y=DIFF)) +
  geom_point(aes(size=abs(DIFF), color=DIFF), show.legend=FALSE) +
  geom_segment(aes(x=Country, xend=Country, y=0, yend=DIFF-1,
               color=DIFF),
               linewidth=0.4, show.legend = FALSE)+
  scale_color_gradient2(low = "red",
                        mid = "lightgray",
                        high = "blue")+
  geom_text(aes(label = round(DIFF, 1),
                hjust = ifelse(DIFF < 0, 1.5, -1),
                vjust = 0.5),
            size = 1.5) +
  labs(
    y= " Wheat production (year 2000 variations, tons)",
    x="",
    title="World: OECD-FAO Agricultural Outlook, year 2000"
  )+
  coord_flip()+
  theme_minimal()+
  theme(axis.text.x = element_text(size=8),
        axis.text.y = element_text(size=6))
```

5.2 Python: Seaborn

5.2.1 Diverging Bar Plot

We replicate with Python and Seaborn the first diverging bar plot seen with ggplot starting from the necessary data wrangling operations for preparing the data frame.

```
oecd=pd.read_csv("../datasets/OECD/OECD-FAO_Agriculture_20212030.csv")

oecd1=oecd[(oecd.Variable=='Production')&(oecd.Commodity=="Wheat")]\
[['LOCATION', 'Country', 'TIME', 'Value']]
```

	LOCATION	Country	TIME	Value
0	AUS	Australia	1990	15 066.1
1	AUS	Australia	1991	10 557.4
2	AUS	Australia	1992	14 738.7
3	AUS	Australia	1993	16 479.3
4	AUS	Australia	1994	8 961.3
…	…	…	…	…

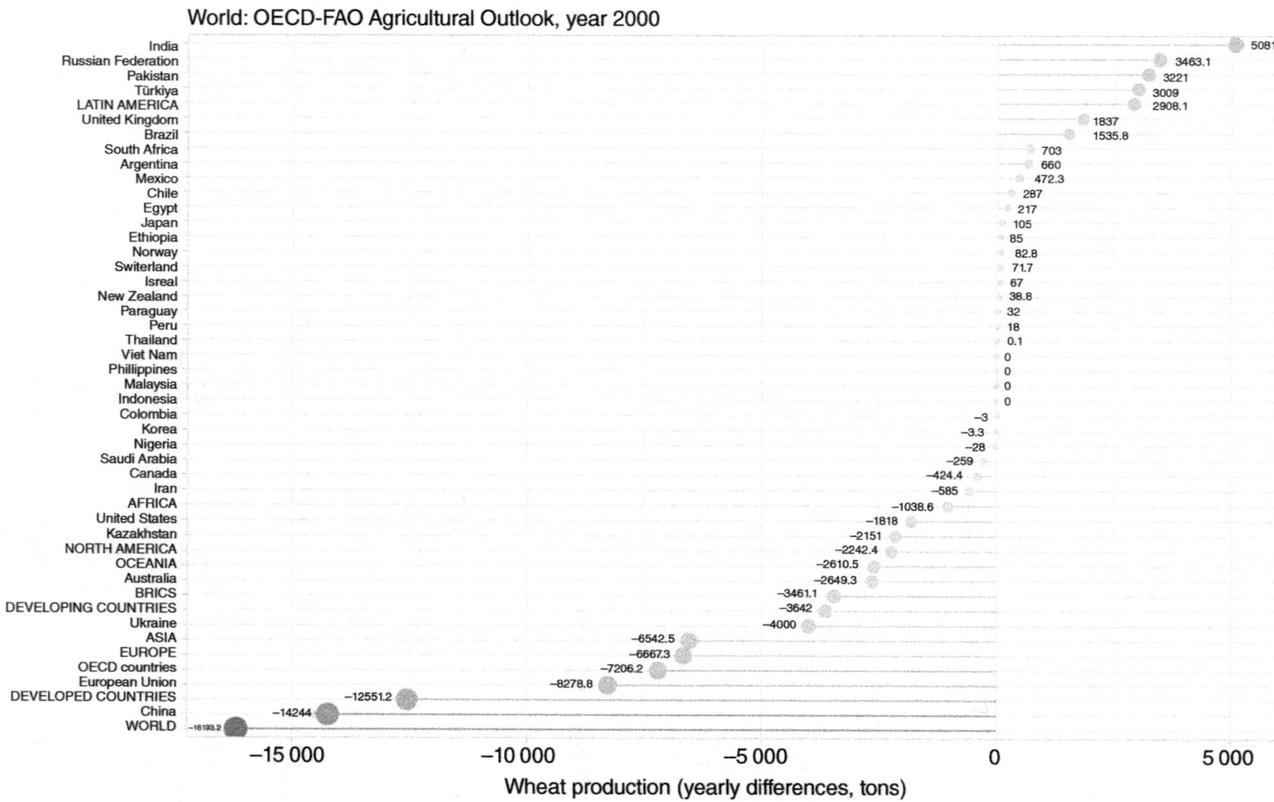

Figure 5.4 Lollipop plot ordered by values and annotation, yearly variations in wheat production for year 2000 with respect to year 1999.

Differences in wheat production from year to year are calculated, first, by creating column *LAG* using Python function `shift()` that copies and shifts column values for the number of specified rows, here just one. Then, the difference could be simply derived by subtracting column *LAG* from column *VALUE*, *DIFF* is the new column.

```
oecd1= oecd1.sort_values(by=['LOCATION','TIME'])

oecd1['LAG']=oecd1.groupby('LOCATION')[['Value']].shift(1)
```

	LOCATION	Country	TIME	Value	LAG
0	AFR	Africa	1990	13 084.2	NaN
1	AFR	Africa	1991	16 987.3	13 084.2
2	AFR	Africa	1992	11 945.7	16 987.3
3	AFR	Africa	1993	12 953.5	11 945.7
4	AFR	Africa	1994	15 500.2	12 953.5
…	…	…	…	…	…

```
oecd1['DIFF']=oecd1.Value-oecd1.LAG
oecd1.drop('LAG', axis=1, inplace=True)
```

	LOCATION	Country	TIME	Value	DIFF
0	AFR	Africa	1990	13 084.2	NaN
1	AFR	Africa	1991	16 987.3	3 903.1
2	AFR	Africa	1992	11 945.7	−5 041.6
3	AFR	Africa	1993	12 953.5	1 007.8
4	AFR	Africa	1994	15 500.2	2 546.7
…	…	…	…	…	…

With these simple operations, the data for all countries are almost ready, we just have to remember that all rows corresponding to year 1990 should be removed because having inconsistent data in production differences. Then, we can select the country for which we want to plot the data, this time it is the United States, and plot.

```
oecd1=oecd1[oecd1.TIME!=1990]

usa=oecd1[oecd1.Country=='United States']
```

To plot the diverging bar plot, we start using the normal Seaborn function `sns.barplot()`, in this example, with years (variable *TIME*) on the *x*-axis and production differences (variable *DIFF*) on the *y*-axis, a few style options are also added. However, this is not sufficient to have a reasonable diverging bar plot because the color scale will not be as we usually want it to be in this case, diverging for positive and negative values. Here comes the tricky part because for that seemingly obvious feature, there is no support from Seaborn and we should turn to *matplotlib* that forces us to manually color each bar.

The logic is as follows: we want to use a diverging palette and a color gradient based on the *height* of each bar, meaning that the higher the bar the darker the hue and different for positive and negative values. This means that first, because of the vertical orientation of bars, we have to collect the *heights* of all bars (`np.array([bar.get_height() for bar in ax.containers[0]])`). Then, we can set the diverging matplotlib's color scale (`mpl.colors.TwoSlopeNorm()`) and for this reason, we had to load the whole *matplotlib* library (`import matplotlib as mpl`), not just the *pyplot* module as usual. Function `TwoSlopeNorm()` is the reference for setting diverging color scales by configuring the *center* of the scale and the two boundaries, with attributes `vcenter`, `vmin`, and `vmax`. After this, we can set the color palette, `bwr` (blue-white-red) in the example, for the color scale (`plt.cm.bwr(divnorm(heights))`). Finally, bars should be individually colored with a *for cycle* that fills each one of them with the color corresponding to the height, positive or negative. It is an overly complicated procedure, indeed, for the result that we want to achieve, which, instead, is quite ordinary. Figure 5.5. shows the result.

```
import matplotlib as mpl

sns.set_theme(style="white", font_scale=0.7)

ax = sns.barplot(usa, x='TIME', y='DIFF',
                 edgecolor='black', linewidth=0.5)

# For all bars, their heights are collected and
# the color scale is configured

heights = np.array([bar.get_height() for bar in ax.containers[0]])
divnorm = mpl.colors.TwoSlopeNorm(vmin=heights.min(),
                                  vcenter=0, vmax=heights.max())

# The color palette (here called bwr) is set for the color scale

div_colors = plt.cm.bwr(divnorm(heights))

# Each bar is individually colored with a for cycle
```

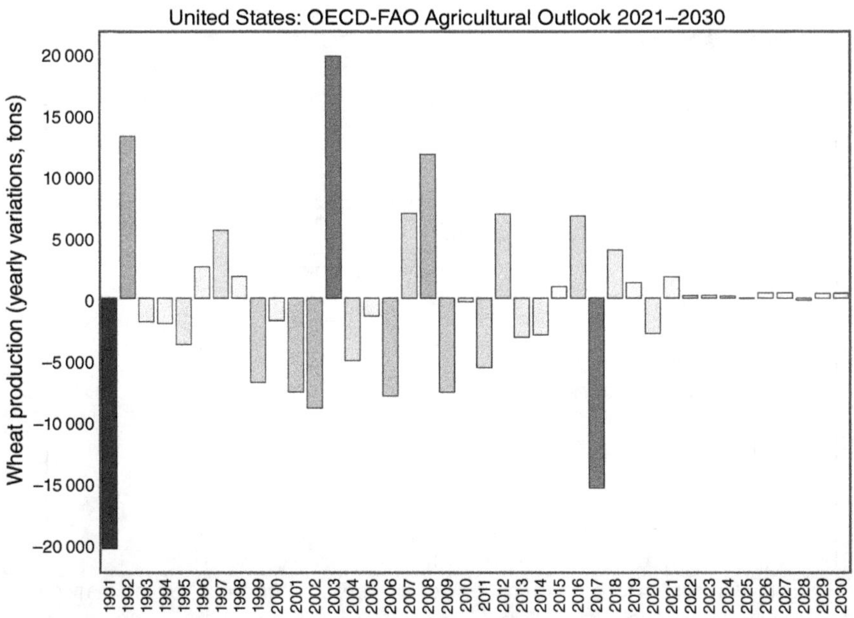

Figure 5.5 Diverging bar plot, yearly wheat production variations for the United States, vertical bar orientation.

```
for bar, color in zip(ax.containers[0], div_colors):
    bar.set_facecolor(color)

# Style options

plt.xticks(rotation=90)
ax.set_ylabel("Wheat production (yearly variations, tons")
ax.set_xlabel("")
plt.title("United States: OECD-FAO Agricultural Outlook 2021-2030")
plt.tight_layout()
```

The plot, however, is likely more readable if bars are horizontal and years on the *y*-axis. That seems trivial, just switching attribute *x* with *y*, or using attribute `direction` of function `sns.barplot()`, should be sufficient. Unfortunately, also this simple variation has hidden subtleties.

Two are the points of attention: first, with horizontal bars, it is no longer bars' *heights* that we should collect, but their *widths*, the code has to be changed accordingly (i.e., `bar.get_height()` becomes `bar.get_width()`); second, if we put years on the *y*-axis, variable *TIME* is numerical and it is not handled as

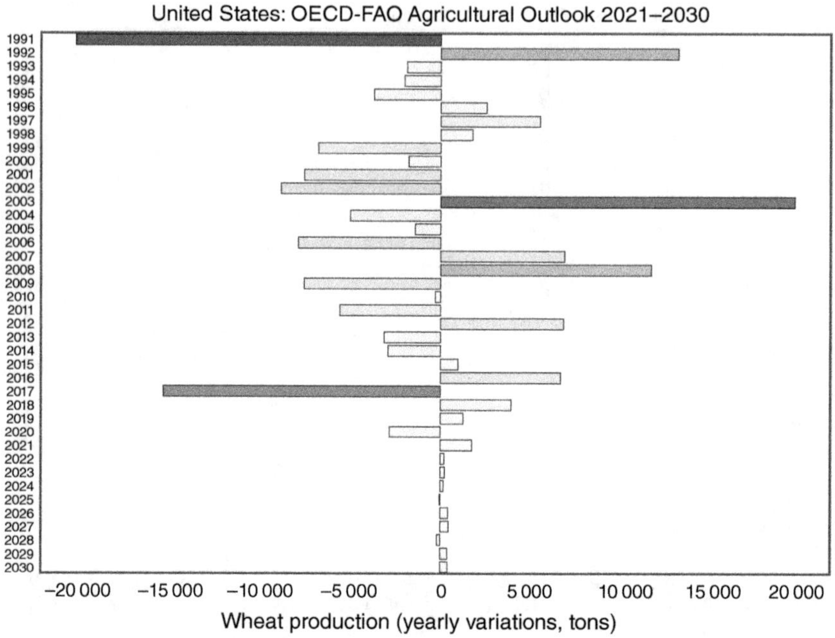

Figure 5.6 Diverging bar plot, yearly wheat production variations for the United States, horizontal bar orientation.

categorical, so the plot becomes a total mess. We have to turn it into *category* data type or create a new one as categorical. In the following example, new column *YEAR* is created as categorical with years as values and categories. Figure 5.6 shows the result.

In conclusion, a little too much trickery to do for producing an ordinary bar plot variation commonly provided by other graphic libraries for data science, a future support for diverging bar plots by Seaborn is awaited.

```
# New column YEAR as categorical with years values as categories
list= usa.TIME.tolist()
usa['YEAR']= pd.Categorical(list, categories=list, ordered=True)

sns.set_theme(style="white", font_scale=0.7)

ax = sns.barplot(data=usa, x='DIFF', y='TIME',
                 edgecolor='black', linewidth=0.5)

widths = np.array( [bar.get_width() for bar in ax.containers[0]])
divnorm = mpl.colors.TwoSlopeNorm(vmin=widths.min(), vcenter=0,
vmax=widths.max())
div_colors = plt.cm.PiYG(divnorm(widths))
```

```
for bar, color in zip(ax.containers[0], div_colors):
    bar.set_facecolor(color)

ax.set_xlabel("Wheat production (yearly variations, tons")
ax.set_ylabel("")
plt.title("United States: OECD-FAO Agricultural Outlook 2021-2030")
plt.tight_layout()
```

6

Boxplots

A *boxplot* is an important type of graphic for categorical variables that has the merit of summarizing several statistics in a compact and intuitive form. Following Figure 6.1 shows the characteristics of a boxplot. Important is to note that the box (i.e., the rectangular area) represents 50% of all data points ($IQR = Q3 - Q1$, with IQR for interquartile range and Q for quartile), or equivalently the range of data points from the 25th to the 75th percentile. For the two segments (called *whiskers*), on top and at the bottom of the box, there is no unique definition, but all of them are substantially equivalent: the interval defined by the two whiskers includes most data points (i.e., at least 95% of them). The only data points not included are *outliers*, usually indicated by single dots.

The term *outlier* needs to be interpreted correctly, though, because if misled, it could provoke serious mistakes in the analysis of results. Data points from observations may fall way far from the median for a number of different reasons. It might be because of some sort of errors (e.g., wrong measurements, mistyped data, or malfunctioning of some instrumentations), which justifies considering them as incoherent data to be omitted that could wrongly affect the statistics and the overall interpretation. But it might also be because of extreme events, meaning exceptionally rare cases that are nevertheless intrinsic to the observed system or phenomenon; in other words, they might be very unusual but not wrong. In that case, considering them as incoherent and omitting them from the analysis could be the source of severe errors. Therefore, outliers of a distribution are initially just data points falling in the tail of the distribution, and that is it. Whether they could safely be omitted, or they should be considered legitimate as all other data points is a matter of knowledge of the observed phenomenon and careful interpretation. This is an important issue to consider because phenomena producing data points far from the median are not rare or necessarily bizarre.

As a graphical tool, a boxplot visualization typically has one categorical variable on the x-axis, when boxplots are drawn vertically, and a continuous variable on the

Data Visualization in R and Python, First Edition. Marco Cremonini.

Companion website: www.wiley.com/go/Cremonini/DataVisualization1e

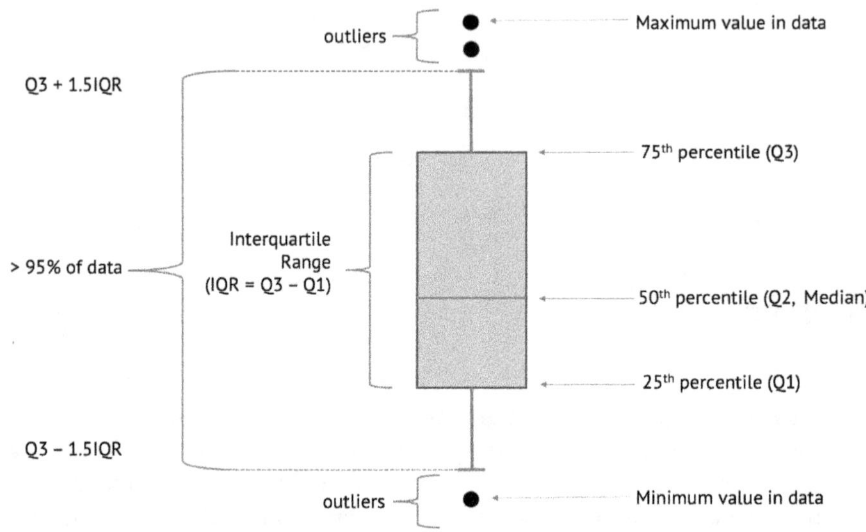

Figure 6.1 Boxplot statistics.

y-axis. Furthermore, being a boxplot aimed at presenting statistics of a distribution, it requires the sample to be statistically significant, so there is no point in producing a boxplot visualization for a few data points. Given these premises, boxplots represent a particularly effective visualization, which, however, requires that readers have sufficient statistical knowledge to correctly interpret them (at least qualitatively), meaning that they are not suitable for all kinds of audiences.

Dataset

In this section, we use the dataset *Report qualità aria 2021* (transl. Air Quality Report year 2021), Municipality of Milan Open Data, already introduced before.

6.1 R: ggplot

For boxplots, similar to what we have done with bar plots, we use *pollutant* as the categorical variable, but this time, rather than aggregating to calculate total quantities, we use all data points to obtain statistics for the boxplot. Let us try with the simplest configuration of function `geom_boxplot()`. Figure 6.2 shows the result.

```
df1 %>% ggplot(aes(x=pollutant, y=value))+
  geom_boxplot(fill="grey80")+
  theme_light()
```

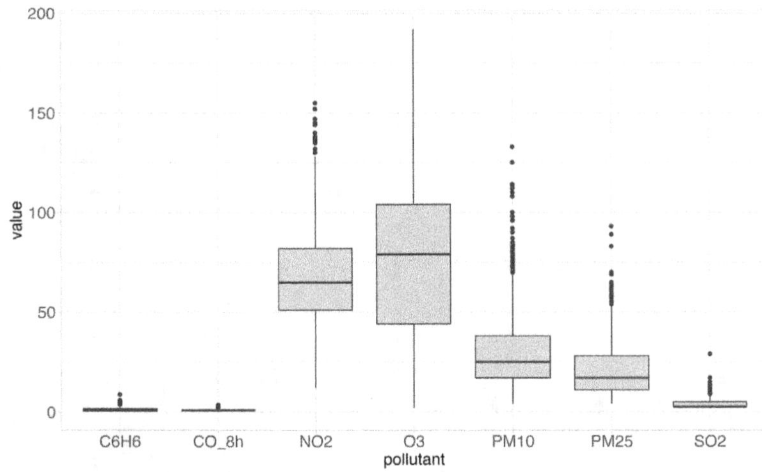

Figure 6.2 Boxplot, air quality in Milan, 2021.

> **Note**
>
> *ggplot* draws whiskers without the horizontal segment at the end, as is typical in most boxplot representations. It is just a stylistic choice; nothing changes in the meaning.

From the example, we note different distributions and statistics for the pollutants but for some of them, boxplots appear shrank at the point of being uninterpretable because of the different scales of values. We had this same problem with bars of the bar plots. Different variations with respect to the median and presence of outliers are also visible, more pronounced for some pollutants. Based on this initial example, we can enrich it with style elements already seen before and add *month* as the third variable. Figure 6.3 shows the result, which, unfortunately, is largely incomprehensible, as it has too many elements put together.

```
months=c("1"="January", "2"="February", "3"="March",
       "4"="April", "5"="May", "6"="June",
       "7"="July", "8"="August", "9"="September",
       "10"="October", "11"="November", "12"="December")

df1 %>% mutate(month=as.factor(month(date))) %>%
  ggplot(aes(x=month, y=value)) +
  geom_boxplot(aes(fill=pollutant)) +
  scale_fill_viridis_d(option='plasma')+
  scale_x_discrete(labels=months) +
```

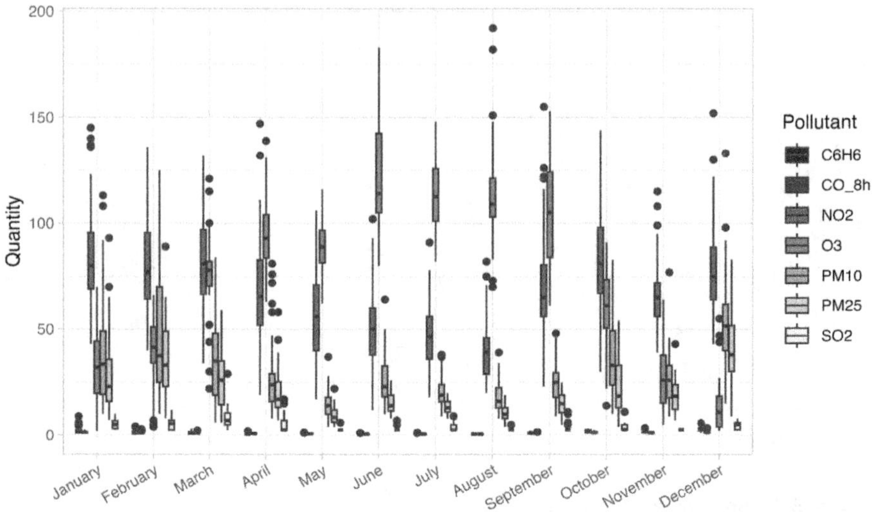

Figure 6.3 Boxplot with three variables, confused result.

```
  labs( x="", y="Value", fill="Pollutant" ) +
  theme_light() +
  theme(axis.text.x = element_text(angle = 30, hjust = 1))
```

To improve the previous plot, we could try with facets, aiming to ease the readability of information. Figure 6.4 shows the result, which is still not satisfactory.

```
months=c("1"="January", "2"="February", "3"="March",
       "4"="April", "5"="May", "6"="June",
       "7"="July", "8"="August", "9"="September",
       "10"="October", "11"="November", "12"="December")

df1 %>% mutate(month=as.factor(month(date))) %>%
  ggplot(aes(x=month, y=value)) +
  geom_boxplot(aes(fill=pollutant)) +
  facet_wrap(vars(pollutant), ncol=4) +
  scale_fill_viridis_d(option='plasma') +
  scale_x_discrete(labels=months)+
  labs( x="", y="Quantity", fill="Pollutant") +
  theme_light() +
  theme(axis.text.x = element_text(angle = 90, hjust = 1))
```

With respect to the previous visualization, this one improved, but still, the problem of the different scales remains, and three facets are almost unreadable. As we

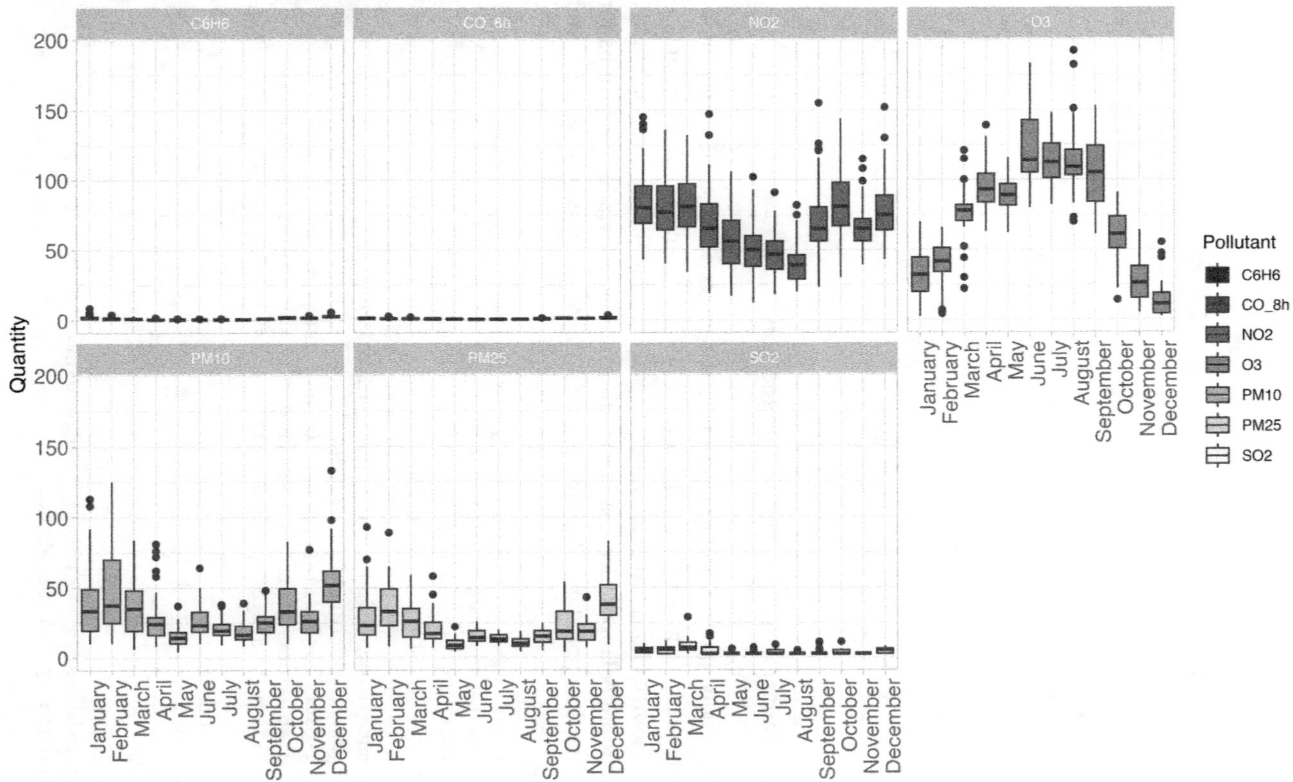

Figure 6.4 Boxplot with three variables, unbalanced facet visualization.

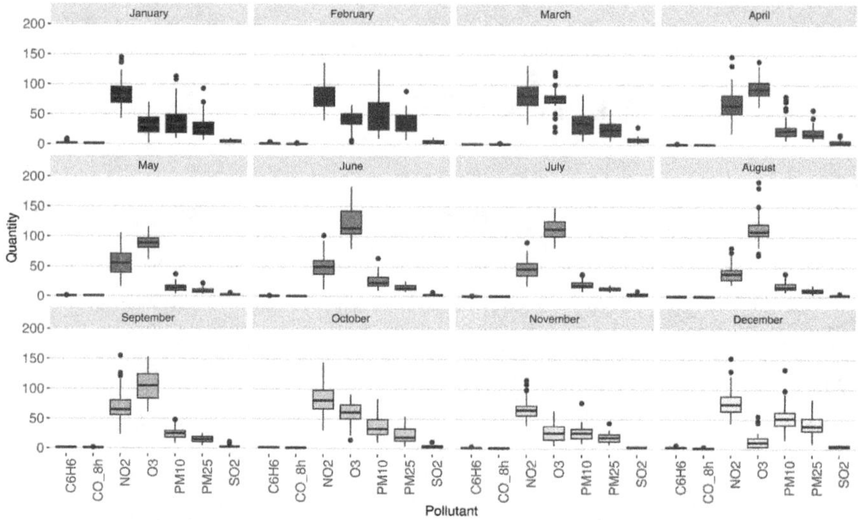

Figure 6.5 Boxplot with three variables, balanced facet visualization.

saw for bar plots, one possibility is to make the facets scale on the *y*-axis independent, but although technically it works, as we have commented before, it also might be a source of misunderstanding for observers. Another option is to modify it to have more balanced facets, and for this example, we could use months for facets rather than pollutants. Figure 6.5 shows the result, now well readable and balanced.

```
months=c("1"="January", "2"="February", "3"="March",
       "4"="April", "5"="May", "6"="June",
       "7"="July", "8"="August", "9"="September",
       "10"="October", "11"="November", "12"="December")

df1 %>% mutate(month=as.factor(month(data))) %>%
  ggplot(aes(x=pollutant, y=value))+
  geom_boxplot(aes(fill=as.factor(month(date))), )+
  facet_wrap(~month, ncol=4, labeller = labeller(month=months))+
  scale_fill_viridis_d(option='plasma', labels=months)+
  labs(
    x="Pollutant",
    y="Quantity",
    fill="Month"
  )+
  theme_hc()+
  theme(axis.text.x = element_text(angle = 90, hjust = 1))+
  theme(legend.position = "none")
```

6.2 Python: Seaborn

The same example presented for ggplot is replicated with Seaborn, with few differences, which makes it particularly easy to create boxplots. For having *month names* correctly ordered, this time, we employ the ordering technique based on an external list that we have seen in a previous chapter for R. The logic in Python is the same, just the technicalities will change. We start by obtaining month names with method `dt.month_name()`, and to add a new feature to the example, we choose names in a different language than the default setting (i.e., English). In this case, we have French month names, so we use attribute `locale='fr_FR'`. and place them in the new column *Month*. Then, we transform the column *Month* with French month names into categorical type with function `pd.Categorical()`, where categories (attribute `categories`) correspond to the ordered list of month names saved into a variable (*month_list*); finally, with attribute `ordered=True`, we specify that the order of the list should be respected. This way, values of column *Month* will be sorted according to the ordered list *month_list*.

Note

A tiny but nevertheless relevant detail should be noted. Month names in Romance languages (e.g., Spanish, French, Italian, and Portuguese) are correctly spelled with lowercase names, and not with the first letter capitalized, such as in English (e.g., in French it is *janvier*, not Janvier, for January). However, the Python *datetime* function `dt.month_name()`, as well as the R's *lubridate* function `month(labels=TRUE, abbr=FALSE)`, defines only capitalized month names. It is incorrect with respect to Romance languages, but it is needed in code otherwise month names are not recognized. This is the reason for capitalized French month names in the following code.

```
month_list=['Janvier','Février','Mars','Avril','Mai',
            'Juin','Juillet','Août','Septembre','Octobre',
            'Novembre','Décembre']

df["Month"]=df['date'].dt.month_name(locale='fr_FR')
df.Month=pd.Categorical(
    df.Month,
    categories = month_list,
    ordered = True)
```

We can now create our first boxplot by means of Seaborn function `sns.boxplot()`. We use three variables (Figure 6.6).

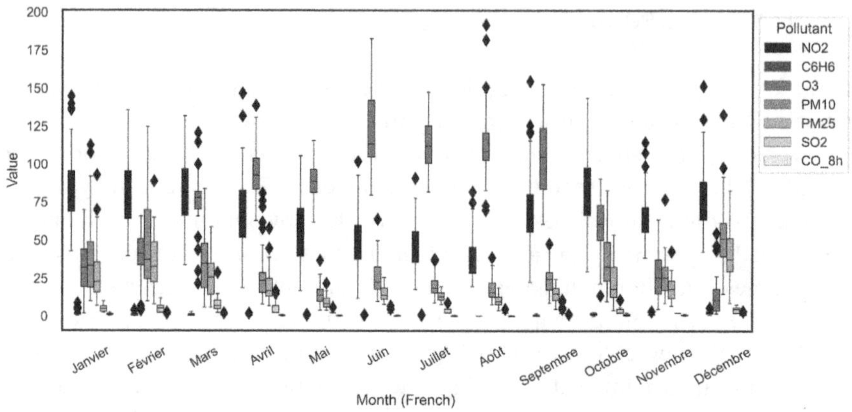

Figure 6.6 Box plot with three variables, the result is confused.

```
g=sns.boxplot(data=df_py, x="Month", y="value",
              hue='pollutant', palette='cubehelix',
              linewidth=0.5)

plt.xticks(rotation=30)
plt.xlabel("Month (French)")
plt.ylabel("Value")
plt.legend(title="Pollutant")
sns.move_legend(g, "upper left", bbox_to_anchor=(1, 1))
```

Similar to the R case, even now the visualization is unclear, with too many graphical elements put together and not well recognizable. Facets would be better and separating months into facets is likely a good choice, as we did before (Figure 6.7).

```
sns.set_theme(style="whitegrid", font_scale=0.8)

g=sns.catplot(data=df_py, x="pollutant", y="value",
              kind="box", height=2, col="Month",
              col_wrap=4, palette='cubehelix',
              linewidth=0.3)

g.set_xticklabels(rotation=90)
g_set_axis_labels("Pollutant","Value")
...
```

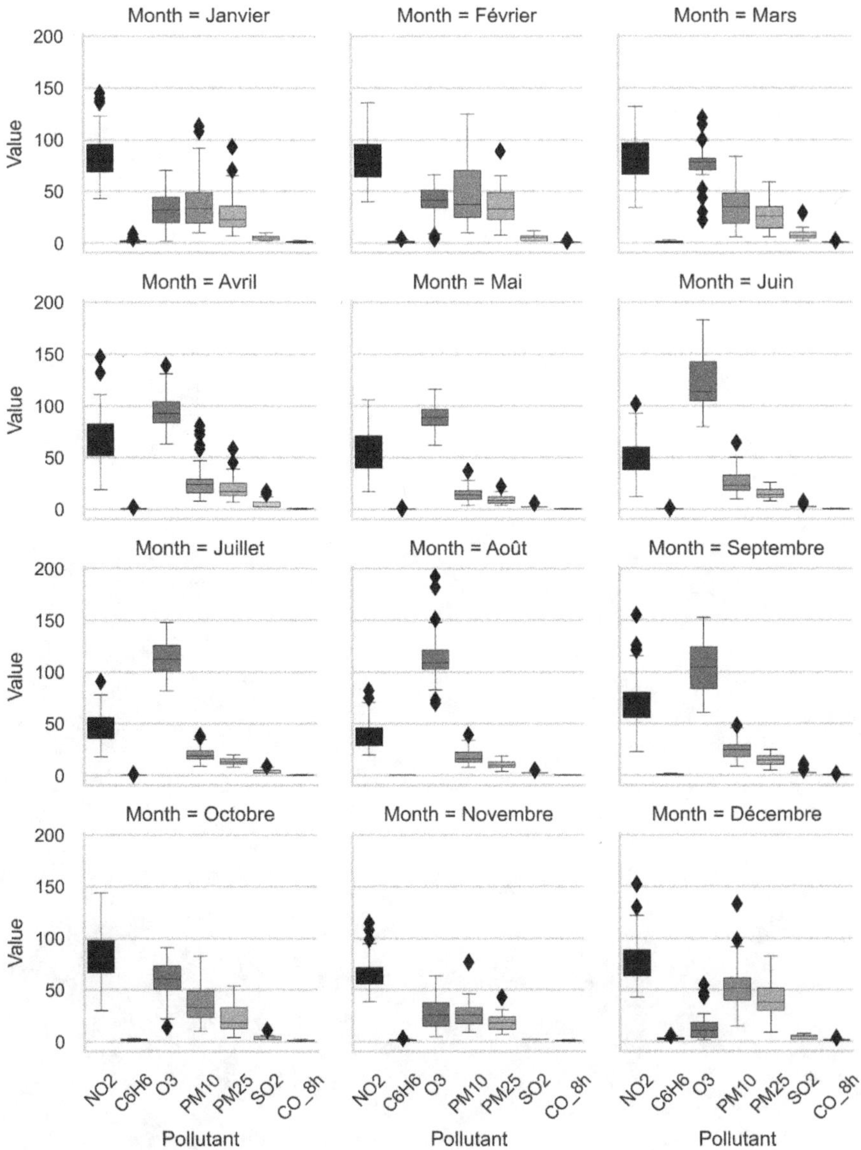

Figure 6.7 Boxplot with three variables, facet visualization.

7

Violin Plots

A *violin plot* is a boxplot variant initially introduced to add the missing information about the actual distribution of data points. Rather than the fixed rectangular boxplot shape, the violin plot adapts its shape to the density of data points for each value of the continuous variable, the shape is larger where data points are more abundant and thinner where they are scarce. This often produces a shape that vaguely reminds a violin, from which the name. The drawback of the violin plot with respect to the boxplot is to be less precise in the representation of descriptive statistics about quantiles of the distribution.

However, another aspect of the violin plot progressively became the most interesting feature of this type of graphics: its suitability to be morphed into new and clever graphical representations by combining it with other types of graphics. It is sometimes surprising to discover the imaginative graphic combinations that make use of the violin plot, mostly because of its elegant and graceful shape. This is the most relevant feature that distinguishes it from the boxplot, while the boxplot is rigorous and severe-looking, possibly intimidating readers not well aware of its statistical meaning, a violin plot in its many variants is pleasant and intuitive, good-looking and curious, although less precise than a boxplot. In conclusion, the violin plot is not just a more graceful but less precise variant of the boxplot. The two types of graphics should actually be considered suitable for different audiences and different visual communication styles.

Dataset

OECD Skills Survey (https://pisadataexplorer.oecd.org/ide/idepisa/report.aspx), OECD 2022 (The Organisation for Economic Co-operation and Development), Pisa Data Explorer (https://www.oecd.org/pisa/data/). The reports produced regard Mathematics, Reading, and Scientific skills for 15-year-old students of

Data Visualization in R and Python, First Edition. Marco Cremonini.

Companion website: www.wiley.com/go/Cremonini/DataVisualization1e

OECD countries. Values are the average results for male and female students for years 2006, 2009, 2012, 2015, 2018, and 2022.

Copyright: You can extract from, download, copy, adapt, print, distribute, share, and embed Data for any purpose, even for commercial use. You must give appropriate credit to the OECD by using the citation associated with the relevant Data [· · ·].

(https://www.oecd.org/termsandconditions/).

Bicycle thefts in Berlin (trans. Fahrraddiebstahl in Berlin) from the Municipality of Berlin, Germany, Berlin Open Data (https://daten.berlin.de/datensaetze/fahrraddiebstahl-berlin). It presents data about bike thefts collected by the German police.

Copyright: Common Criteria Namensnennung 3.0 Deutschland (CC BY 3.0 DE) (https://creativecommons.org/licenses/by/3.0/de/)

7.1 R: ggplot

Let us start with a simple example and elaborate on it. We use first the OECD Skills Survey for Pisa tests, values are referred to the average results and students are divided by gender, male and female. The dataset is in Microsoft Excel format, so it needs package *readxl* to be read and has been slightly modified with respect to the original one (i.e., year values have been copied in all cells, the header simplified, and a new column *Test* added with *MAT* for Mathematics, *READ* for Reading, and *SCI* for Scientific skills).

We start by considering *Mathematics skills*. A few simple data-wrangling operations are needed.

```
library(readxl)

Mat=read_excel("datasets/Eurostat/
             IDEExcelExport-Mar122024-0516PM.xlsx",
              sheet ='Report 1', range='B12:F227', trim_ws=TRUE)
Mat$Female = round(Mat$Female, 0)
Mat$Male = round(Mat$Male, 0)

MatL= pivot_longer(Mat, cols = c(Female, Male),
                   names_to = 'Sex', values_to = 'Avg')
```

In these initial examples of violin plots – which, admittedly, will not look much like violins with this dataset – we aggregate the results referred to the different countries into total results. In following chapters, we will make use again of this dataset with disaggregated data. First, we look at the student distribution, for the different years, with respect to the two subpopulations of male and female students (Figure 7.1).

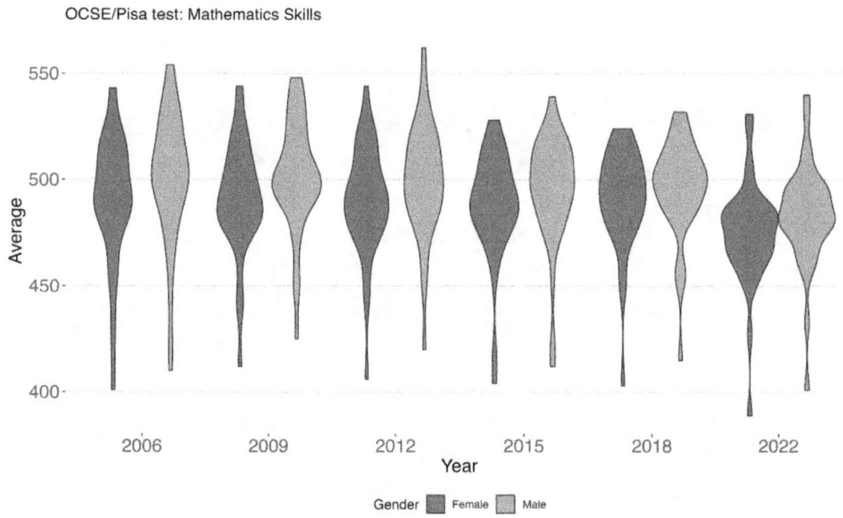

Figure 7.1 Violin plot, OECD/Pisa tests, male and female students, Mathematics skills.

```
library(ggthemes)

ggplot(MatL, aes(x=as.factor(Year) , y=Avg))+
  geom_violin(aes(fill=Sex)) +
  scale_fill_tableau(palette= "Color Blind") +
  labs(
    x="Year", y="Average", fill="Gender",
    title= 'OECD/Pisa test: Mathematics Skills'
  )+
  theme_hc()+
  theme(legend.position = "bottom")+
  theme(axis.text = element_text(size = 16),
        axis.title = element_text(size = 16))
```

The visualization provides intuitive information regarding the distribution of data points. The shape of the violin plot corresponds to the *density of points at each value level.* This is literally how the shape is drawn and it could be seen by comparing the violin plot with a *density plot*, produced by function `geom_density()`. As the following example of Figure 7.2 shows, the violin plot is actually a density plot merged with its mirrored image.

We can produce the density plot by setting test results (column *Avg*) on the *x*-axis, and areas filled with different colors for gender (column *Sex*). The *y*-axis will be automatically associated to the data point density. For better readability,

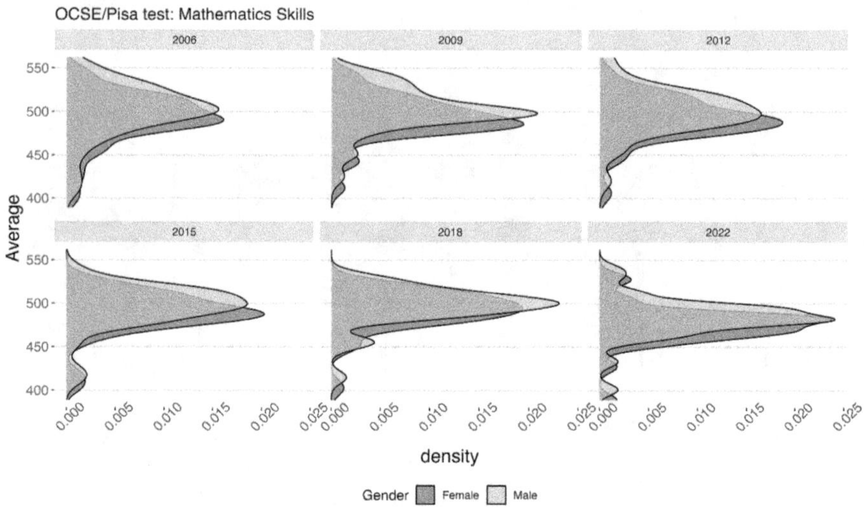

Figure 7.2 Density plot, OECD/Pisa tests, male and female students, Mathematics skills.

facets are configured based on years. Finally, to have an orientation similar to a typical violin plot, we flip the axes (`coord_flip()`).

```
ggplot(MatL, aes(x=Avg, fill=Sex))+
  geom_density(alpha=0.4)+
  coord_flip()+
  facet_wrap(~ as.factor(Year))+
  scale_fill_tableau(palette= "Color Blind") +
  labs(
    x="Average", fill="Gender",
    title= 'OECD/Pisa test: Mathematics Skills'
  )+
  theme_hc()+
  theme(axis.text = element_text(size = 16),
        axis.title = element_text(size = 16))+
  theme(plot.margin = unit(c(0.5,0.5,0.5,0.5),"cm"),
        legend.position = 'bottom',
        axis.text.x = element_text(angle=45))
```

The violin plot and the density plot are scaled differently, but confronting the information they provide, we can immediately recognize that it is the same.

The second important part of the violin plot, in addition to the information about the density of data points, comes from being a variant of the boxplot. The *length of tails* in a violin plot corresponds with the *distance of the farthest outlier in a boxplot*. It could be easily verified by comparing the boxplot of Figure 7.3 with

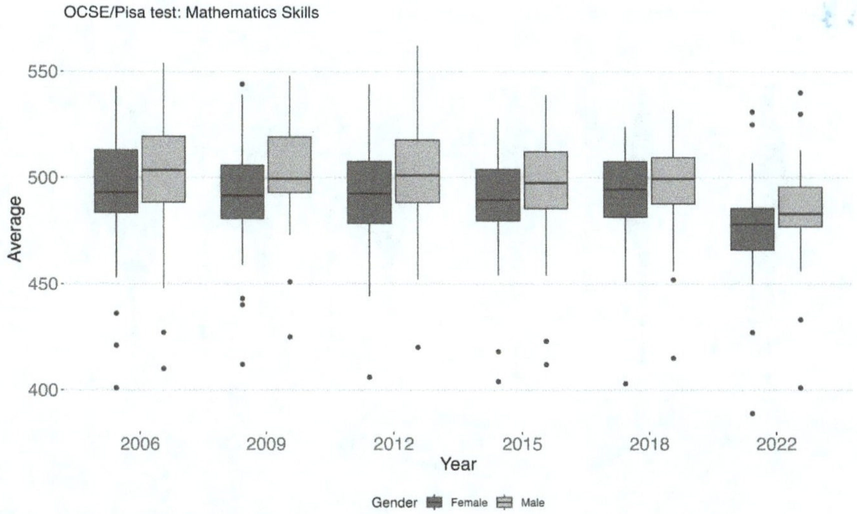

Figure 7.3 Boxplot, OECD/Pisa tests, male and female students, Mathematics skills.

the violin plot of previous Figure 7.1. In the following codes, all instructions that are in common with previous example of Figure 7.1 have been omitted.

```
ggplot(MatL, aes(x=as.factor(Year) , y=Avg))+
  geom_boxplot(aes(fill=Sex)) +
  scale_fill_tableau(...
```

These are the basis for understanding how to use violin plots. But, as said before, violin plots are particularly effective when combined with other graphic types, to produce ingenious representations. Let us see the first two combinations.

7.1.1 Violin Plot and Scatterplot

It is frequent to combine a violin plot with a scatterplot by overlapping one to the other. This way, it is not just the density of data points to be communicated by the violin plot, but data points are also explicitly shown. Clearly, this visualization is better suited for small samples, when visualizing data points conveys information and graphically is well-presented. For large samples, the density is all we need.

Technically, a few adjustments are necessary to produce this type of combined graphics, mostly because what we need is a correct overlapping of the two graphics. In particular, when groups of points are presented (e.g., with aesthetic *color* or *fill*), function `geom_point()` for scatterplots has attribute `group` that instructs ggplot to draw points by respecting the same groups defined in the violin plot, and attribute `position=position_dodge(width=...)` to tell that we

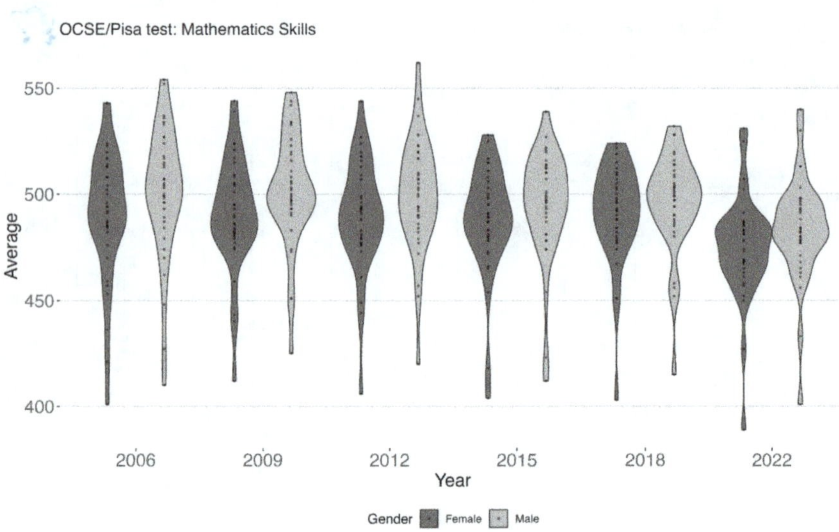

Figure 7.4 Violin plot and scatterplot combined and correctly overlapped and dodged.

want points belonging to different groups presented as dodged, not overlapped. Attribute `width` controls the horizontal alignment. A good value should be found empirically by doing some tests (Figure 7.4).

```
ggplot(MatL, aes(x=as.factor(Year), y=Avg, fill=Sex))+
  geom_violin()+
  geom_point(aes(group=Sex), position=position_dodge
            (width=0.9), alpha=0.5, size=0.5)+
  scale_fill_tableau(...
```

The combined visualization of a violin plot with a scatterplot adds information, but as Figure 7.4 clearly shows, it still presents a recurrent problem: *most scatterplot markers overlap*, which severely reduces the information conveyed by showing data points. This is a general problem of scatterplots that we will consider in a future section. For the moment, we introduce the second common variant of violin plots.

7.1.2 Violin Plot and Boxplot

Since a boxplot is more rigorous in communicating statistical information and a violin plot shows the density of data points and has a more intuitive look, why not combining the two? That is what often happens, aiming at adding up the benefits of both graphic types.

As before, attribute `position=position_dodge()` is key for a correct overlapping and dodging of the two graphics. Additional attributes `alpha`, `size`,

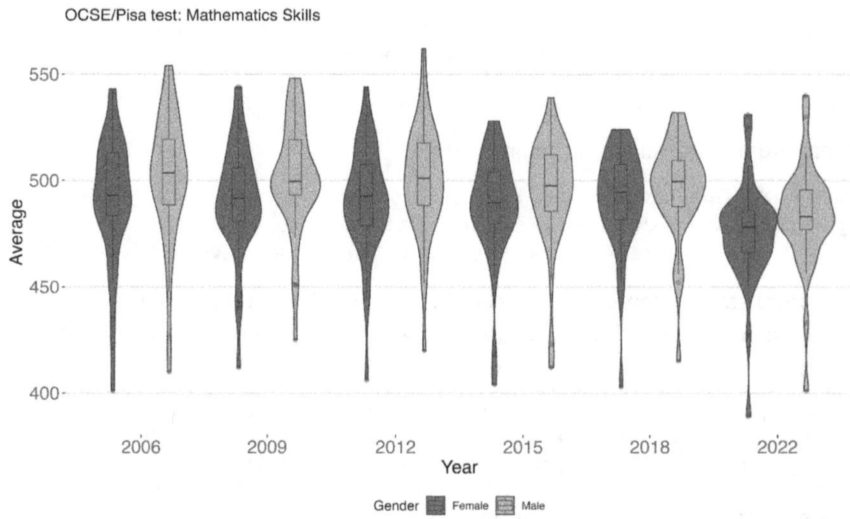

Figure 7.5 Violin plot and boxplot combined and correctly overlapped and dodged.

and `width`, if tuned carefully, allow improving the aesthetic quality of the plot (Figure 7.5).

```
ggplot(MatL, aes(x=as.factor(Year), y=Avg, fill=Sex))+
  geom_violin()+
  geom_boxplot(position=position_dodge(width=0.9),
               alpha=0.4, size=0.3, width= 0.2)+
  scale_fill_tableau(...
```

Finally, we could also read Pisa test results for Reading and Scientific skills, bind rows of the three data frames together, repeat the transformation into long form, and plot the facets by means of variable *Test*. Two details are to note: the first is that for the boxplot, the dots representing outliers are redundant being the violin's tails conveying the same information. These could be omitted with attribute `outlier.shape=NA`; the second is that here we use function `facet_grid()`, not `facet_wrap()`, for the facet visualization; it is only for aesthetic purposes being `facet_grid()` made for facets created with the combination of two variables' values but we have just one, however, using our single variable for rows, we can have facet titles beside each facet instead of on top of them.

```
Rd=read_excel("datasets/Eurostat/IDEExcelExport-Mar122024-0516PM.xlsx",
              sheet = 'Report 2', range = 'B12:F227', trim_ws = TRUE)
Rd$Female = round(Rd$Female, 0)
Rd$Male = round(Rd$Male, 0)
```

```
Sci=read_excel("datasets/Eurostat/IDEExcelExport-Mar122024-0516PM.xlsx",
            sheet = 'Report 3', range = 'B12:F227', trim_ws = TRUE)
Sci$Female = round(Sci$Female, 0)
Sci$Male = round(Sci$Male, 0)
```

Here the transformation into long form.

```
bind_rows(Mat, Rd, Sci) %>%
  pivot_longer(cols= c(Female, Male),
               names_to= 'Sex', values_to= 'Avg') -> pisaMRS
```

The final graphic could be produced (Figure 7.6). We could have added the scatterplot too, but we will show that case later on when we consider how to deal with scatterplot markers that overlap.

```
ggplot(pisaMRS, aes(x=as.factor(Year), y=Avg, fill=Sex))+
  geom_violin(alpha=0.7)+
  geom_boxplot(position=position_dodge(width=0.9),
            alpha=0.9, size=0.3, width= 0.2, outlier.shape = NA)+
  facet_grid(rows = vars(Test))+
  scale_fill_tableau(palette= "Superfishel Stone") +
  labs(
    x="Year", y="Average", fill="Gender",
    title= 'OECD/Pisa test: Mathematics, Reading, and
Scientific Skills'
  )+
theme_hc()+
    theme(axis.text = element_text(size = 14),
        axis.title = element_text(size = 14))+
  theme(legend.position = "bottom")
```

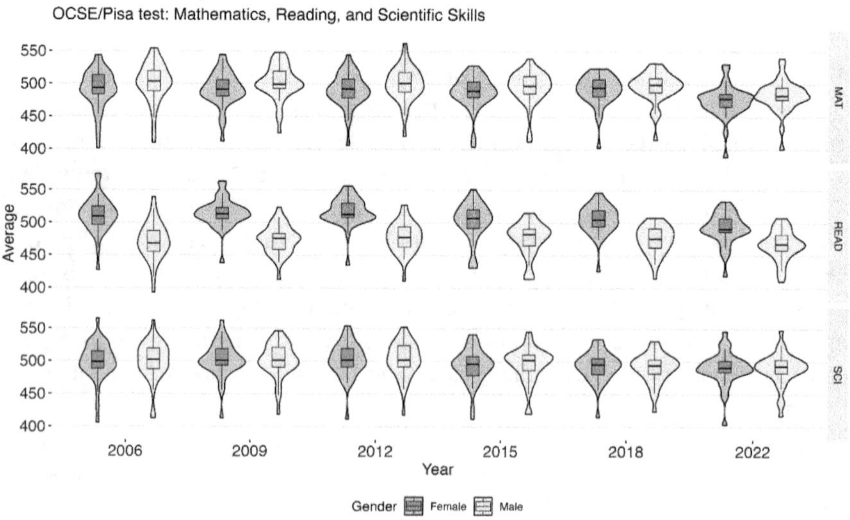

Figure 7.6 OECD/Pisa tests, male and female students, Mathematics, Reading, and Scientific skills.

The result of Figure 7.6 is eye-catching, indeed, and, as a funny note, when I showed it to a person who knows nothing about violin and box plots, her first reaction was "Nice! How cute those little ghostly spinning wheels!" but nevertheless, after that, she got exactly the information conveyed by this compact visualization about young male and female students' skills and the variations along the years. However, it is important to remember that violin plots, and their many combinations, are not just *cute ghostly spinning wheels* but a concentration of statistical information in a very compact form, especially when combined with boxplots.

7.2 Python: Seaborn

With Python, we make use of data about bike thefts in Berlin, Germany.

```
bikes= pd.read_excel("datasets/Berlin_open_data/
                     Fahrraddiebstahl_12_2022_EN.xlsx")
```

The dataset requires some data-wrangling operations to be ready for visualization, in particular, the translation through an online tool from German to English needs a specific care to avoid errors in date formats, errors which might be difficult to spot afterward. In the *Additional Online Material*, all data-wrangling operations, the logic, and the tricky details to take care of are presented, here we use the data frame *bikes* resulting from that preparation.

By checking the range of dates, we figure that dates go from January 1, 2021 to December 9, 2022, therefore we should be aware that for December we have an incomplete time series.

Seaborn function `sns.violinplot()` natively adds the boxplot to the visualization of the violin plot (see Figure 7.7).

```
sns.violinplot(x= bikes["START_DATE"].dt.year,
               y= "DAMAGES", data= bikes,
               palette= "Spectral")
plt.xlabel("")
plt.ylabel("Bike Value")
plt.title("Berlin: bicycle thefts ")
plt.tight_layout()
```

From Figure 7.7, we see that most bikes stolen are in the range of tens to hundreds of euros, while just a few are particularly expensive (thousands of euros). Let us try some variations.

We specify *month* as the variable for the *x*-axis. The result automatically shows the number of observations for each month value on the *y*-axis. Figure 7.8 shows

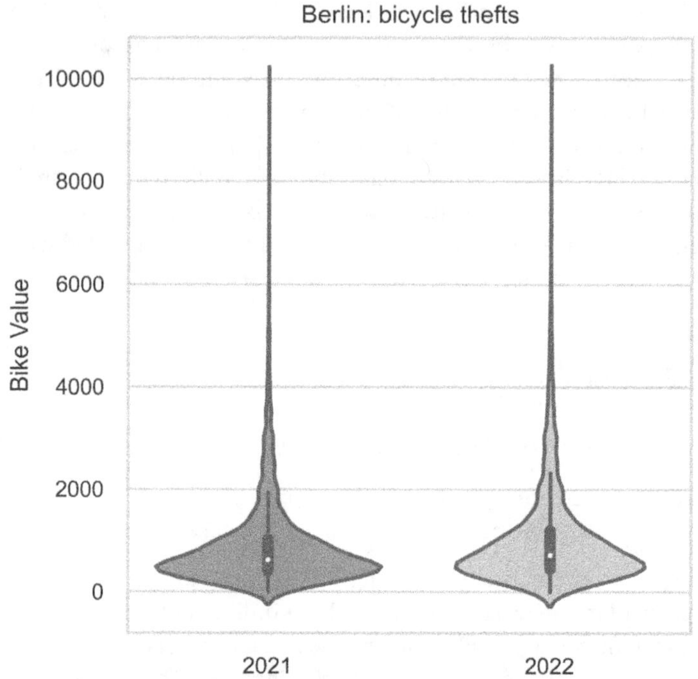

Figure 7.7 Violin plot, bike thefts in Berlin, and bike values.

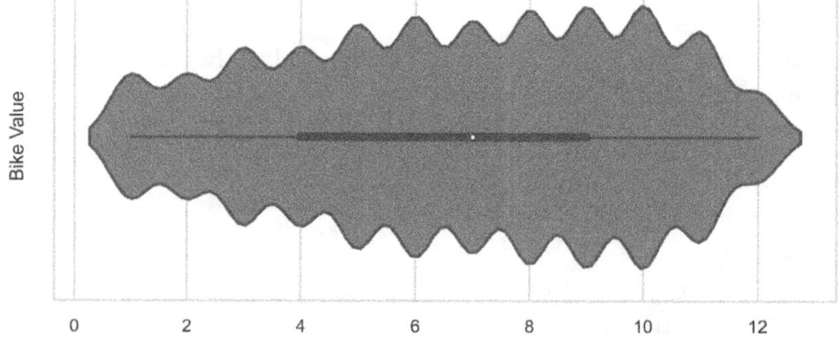

Figure 7.8 Violin plot, bike thefts in Berlin for each month of years 2021 and 2022.

the seasonal variation of bike thefts, the curious shape of the plot seemingly with waves is just the peculiar rendering of the Seaborn function and does not represent data, which are based on a categorical variable (i.e., *months*) in this case. This is an easy way of using the violin plot with Seaborn that sometimes could be useful.

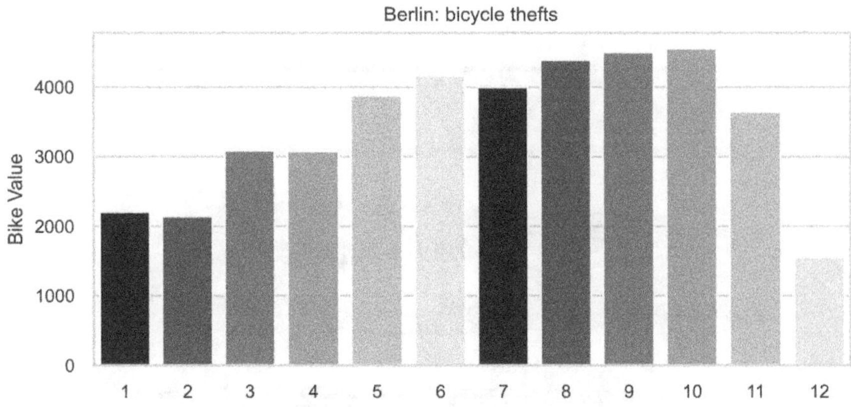

Figure 7.9 Bar plot, bike thefts in Berlin for each month of years 2021 and 2022.

```
sns.violinplot(data=bikes,
               x= bikes["START_DATE"].dt.month)
```

We can verify the same results by calculating the number of thefts for each month and visualizing the bar plot. The shape of the bar plot in Figure 7.9 is equivalent to that of the violin plot of Figure 7.8.

```
bikes2= bikes.groupby(bikes["START_DATE"].dt.month).\
       DAMAGES.count().reset_index()

g= sns.barplot(data= bikes2, x= "START_DATE", y= "DAMAGES",
               palette= 'cubehelix')
```

	START_DATE	DAMAGES
0	1	2 201
1	2	2 140
2	3	3 083
3	4	3 074
4	5	3 877
5	6	4 167
6	7	3 995
7	8	4 387
8	9	4 494
9	10	4 550
10	11	3 642
11	12	1 559

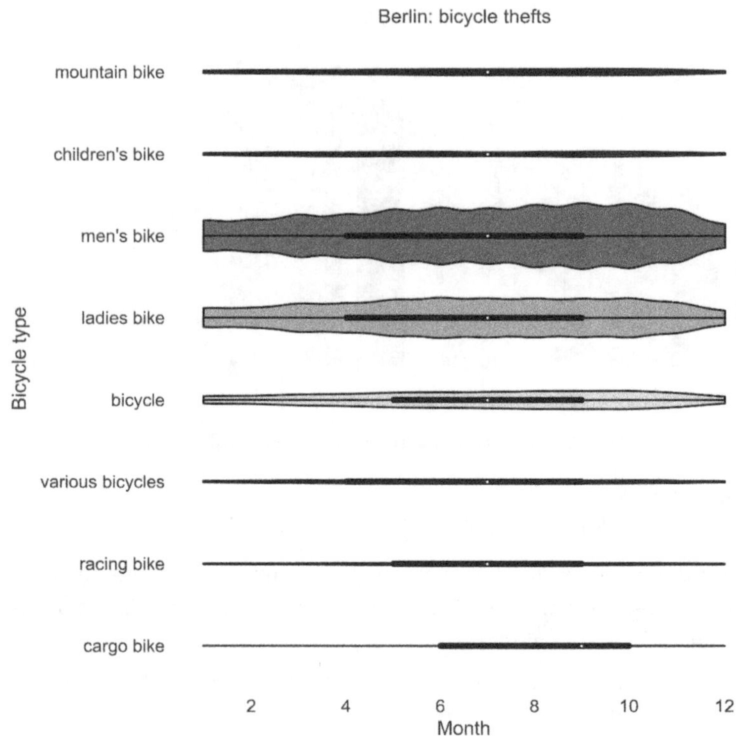

Figure 7.10 Violin plot, bike thefts in Berlin for bike type and month, years 2021 and 2022.

We can now consider *bike types* for axis *y* and use attribute `scale='count'` that scales dimensions with respect to the number of observations. Attribute `cut=0` restricts the shape of the violin plot only to values actually present in data. This may sound bizarre; how could it be that a plot shows inexistent data? Actually, it is what the Seaborn violin plot would do in this case without attribute `cut=0`; violin tails, purely for aesthetic reasons, would be extended beyond the minimum or maximum data point; in this case, we would have seen a tail going in the negative range of the *x*-axis, clearly impossible being *x* the number of thefts. Function `despine()` removes the visualization of Cartesian axes, which might be aesthetically redundant sometimes (Figure 7.10).

```
g= sns.violinplot(data= bici,
                  x= bici["START_DATE"].dt.month,
                  y= "TYPE_OF_BICYCLE",
                  scale= 'count', cut=0,
                  palette= "cubehelix")
sns.despine(left=True, bottom=True)
```

8

Overplotting, Jitter, and Sina Plots

Dataset

In this chapter, we make use again of data from the *OECD Skills Survey*, OECD 2022 (The Organisation for Economic Co-operation and Development), and from *Bicycle thefts in Berlin* (trans. Fahrraddiebstahl in Berlin) from the Municipality of Berlin, Germany, Berlin Open Data, previously introduced.

8.1 Overplotting

Previously, in Figure 7.4, we showed the combination of a violin plot and a scatterplot, and observed that, while the result was correct, scatterplot markers were mostly overlapped, with the actual distribution of data points barely recognizable. Overlapped scatterplot markers are a common problem that goes under the name of *overplotting*.

The easiest way of dealing with overplotting is by adjusting transparency of markers, this way the lighter or darker shade communicates a lesser or higher density. However, transparency alone might be sometimes enough to give a clear information, but insufficient in many cases. Another approach exists and it is called *jittering*. The idea is to introduce a tiny random error in the placement of markers (called *jitter*) in order to plot most of them visibly distinct. The evident drawback of jitter is that the position of markers actually plotted does not correspond any longer to the real data point, and this is acceptable only when the visual effect is more relevant than the exact precision of markers' positions. Also, jittering has limitations, when markers are copious and closely located, the tiny random error introduced might be unable to avoid overplotting. Usually, the degree of such random error is customizable, letting to set more or less jitter, but the stronger the jitter, the less precise the position of markers with respect to real data points.

Data Visualization in R and Python, First Edition. Marco Cremonini.

Companion website: www.wiley.com/go/Cremonini/DataVisualization1e

Hence, there is not a unique solution to deal with overplotting, it should be chosen wisely and tuned case by case.

8.2 R: ggplot

8.2.1 Categorical Scatterplot

Function `geom_jitter()` is equivalent to `geom_point()` but adds a jitter when markers are plotted. Attributes `width` and `height` control the horizontal and vertical extent of the jitter.

> **Note**
>
> With `geom_jitter()`, it is not possible to use at the same time attribute `position` and attributes `width` and `height`. In a previous example with a violin plot and a scatterplot, attribute `position=position_dodge()` was needed to overlap and dodge correctly the two graphics. We will see how to solve this problem.

Let us consider a first example by using `geom_jitter()` with attributes `width=0.2` and `height=0`, without a violin plot. We define a color list and use the same data frame *MatL* of Chapter 7 with data about the Pisa tests for Mathematics skills transformed into long form and grouped for country. For the sake of precision, this type of graphic is often called *categorical scatterplot* or *strip plot*, being defined for a categorical variable. It is only a matter of terminology, nothing substantial changes with respect to generic scatterplots. Figure 8.1 shows the result.

```
colorList= c('#1252b8','#fa866b')

ggplot(MatL, aes(x=as.factor(Year) , y=Avg, color=Sex))+
  geom_jitter(width = 0.2, height = 0, size=3)+
  scale_color_manual(values = colorList) +
    labs(
    x="", y="Test Results", color="Gender:",
    title="OCSE/Pisa test: Mathematics Skills"
  )+
  theme_hc()+
  theme(legend.position = "bottom")+
  theme(plot.margin = unit(c(1,1,1,1),"cm"))+
```

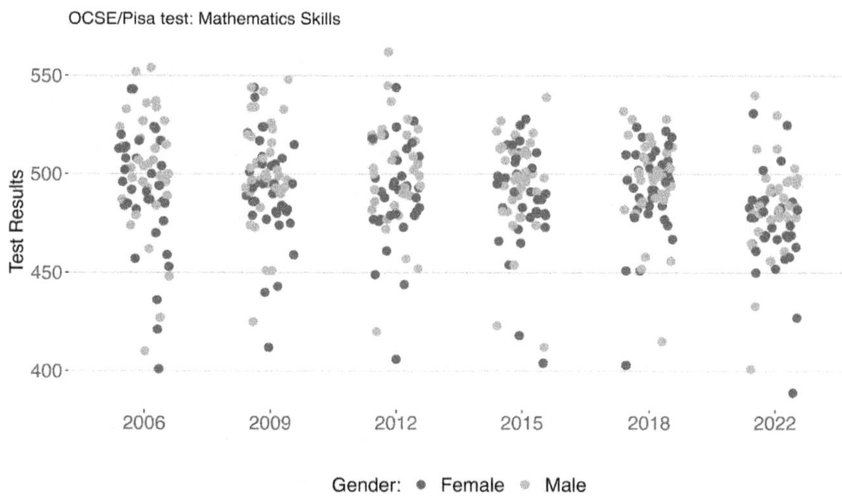

Figure 8.1 Categorical scatterplot with jitter, OECD/Pisa tests results for male and female students, Mathematics skills.

```
theme(axis.text = element_text(size = 16),
      axis.title = element_text(size = 16),
      legend.text = element_text(size = 16),
      legend.title = element_text(size = 16))
```

This way, we have controlled the horizontal jitter effect. In the same way, we could control the vertical jitter. We try two more cases by varying attribute `width`. First, we reduce it to `width=0.1` (Figure 8.2), then increase it to `width=0.3` (Figure 8.3). The different visual effects are evident.

Tip
In genomics, for *genome-wide association studies* (GWAS), it is often employed a graphic type called *Manhattan plot* (a name that may sound a little unfortunate, after September 11, 2001). Several specific R libraries exist to create the many variants of this kind of graphic. However, technically, it still is a categorical scatterplot like the ones just seen, customized with style elements and other graphical components.

8.2.2 Violin Plot and Scatterplot with Jitter

As already observed, function `geom_jitter()` does not allow using at the same time attribute `position` with attributes `width` and `height`, a limitation that

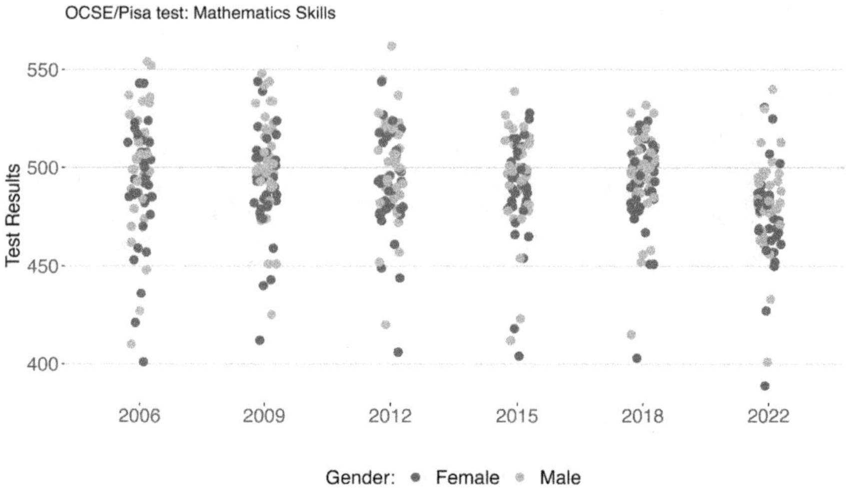

Figure 8.2 Categorical scatterplot with reduced jitter.

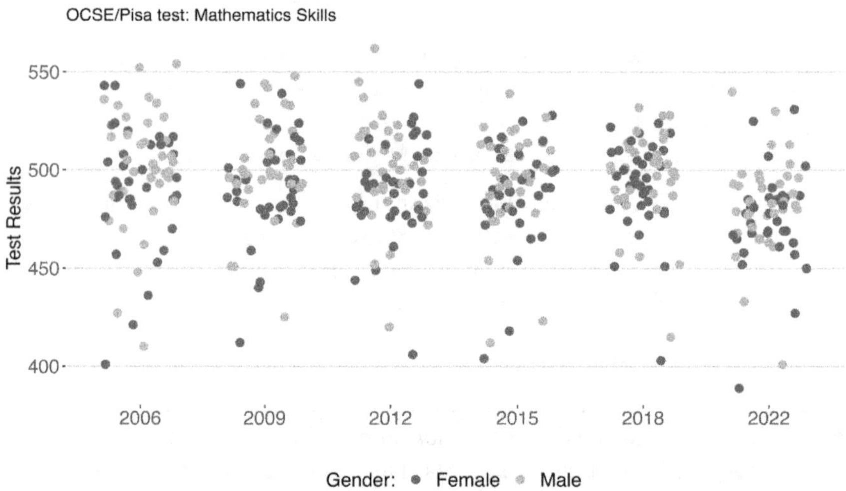

Figure 8.3 Categorical scatterplot with increased jitter.

makes it more difficult to produce a combined graphic between a violin plot and a scatterplot while handling the overplotting with `geom_jitter()`. To this end, a special option has been introduced: `position=position_jitterdodge()`, which has attributes `jitter.width`, `jitter.height`, and the already-known `dodge.width`. We see an example in Figure 8.4, the visual effect improved by reducing the overplotting and making the information about data points clearly visible. Style options in common with previous graphics have been omitted.

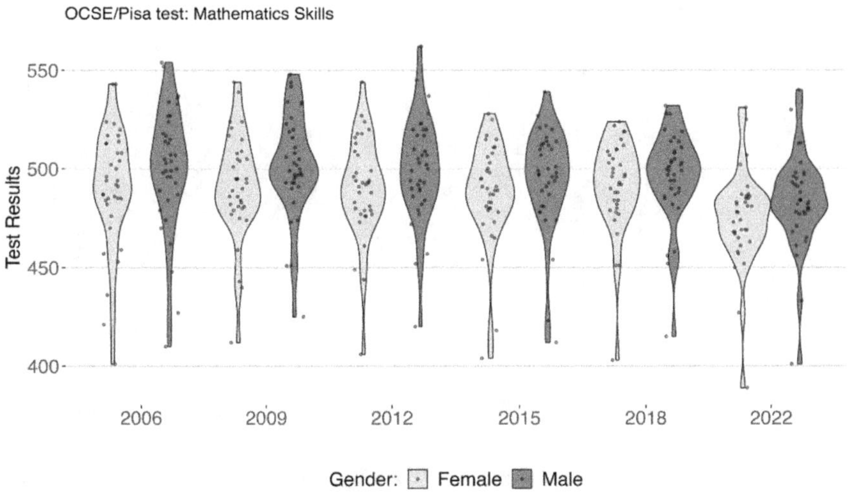

Figure 8.4 Violin plot and scatterplot with jitter, OECD/Pisa tests results for male and female students, Mathematics skills.

```
colorList= c('gold','forestgreen')

ggplot(MatL, aes(x=as.factor(Year), y=Avg, fill=Sex))+
  geom_violin()+
  geom_point(aes(group=Sex),
             position=position_jitterdodge(jitter.width = 0.15,
                                           jitter.height = 0,
                                           dodge.width = 0.9),
             alpha=0.5, size=0.8)+
  scale_fill_manual(values=colorList)+
  labs(...
```

We can do more by combining a violin plot, a scatterplot with jitter, and a boxplot. Attribute `outlier.shape=NA` hides boxplot's outliers, being scatterplot markers already plotted. The graphical result (Figure 8.5) is pleasant and despite the many elements the visual effect is good.

```
colorList= c('gold','forestgreen')

ggplot(pisa, aes(x= as.factor(Year), y= Value, fill=CompLevel)) +
  geom_violin(alpha=0.4) +
  geom_boxplot(position= position_dodge(width=0.9),
             alpha=0.5, size=0.4, width= 0.2,
             outlier.shape= NA) +
  geom_point(aes(group= CompLevel),
       position= position_jitterdodge(jitter.width = 0.15,
                                      jitter.height = 0,
                                      dodge.width = 0.9),
```

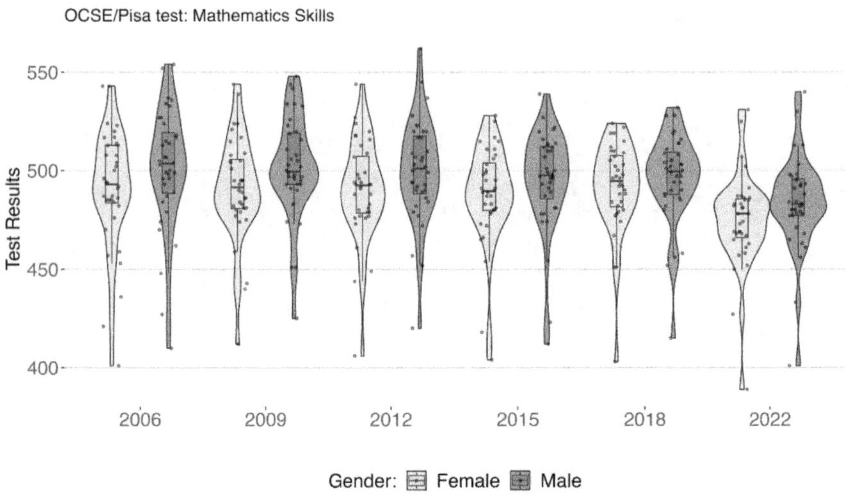

Figure 8.5 Violin plot, boxplot, and scatterplot with jitter, OECD/Pisa tests results for male and female students, Mathematics skills.

```
              alpha=0.5, size=0.7, shape=1) +
  scale_fill_manual(values= colorList)
  ...
```

8.2.3 Sina Plot

We consider now a variant of jittering called *sina plot*. A sina plot is a relatively recent type of graphic, which attracted a good deal of interest because it is not just a simple variant of the basic jittering but it could be considered an alternative visualization to violin plots. For ggplot, it is implemented by function `geom_sina()` of package *ggforce*. The difference with normal jittering is that the points in a sina plot are not displaced randomly but *by complying with the density curve, therefore replicating the shape of a violin plot*. This way, a sina plot provides a solution to overplotting and conveys the same information as a violin plot. We start with the basic example of Figure 8.6, again style options common with previous graphics have been omitted.

```
library(ggforce)
colorList= c('#1252b8','#fa866b')

ggplot(MatL, aes(x=as.factor(Year), y=Avg, color=Sex))+
  geom_sina(size=2)+
  scale_color_manual(values= colorList) +
  labs(...
```

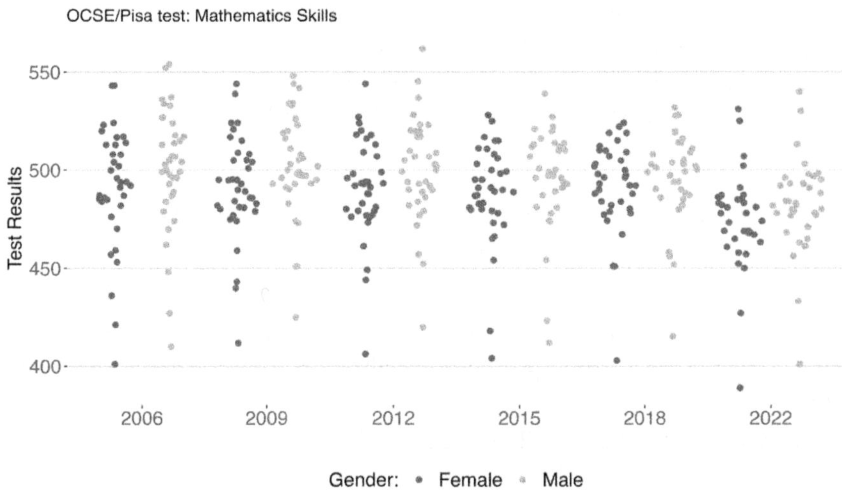

Figure 8.6 Sina plot, OECD/Pisa tests results for male and female students, Mathematics skills.

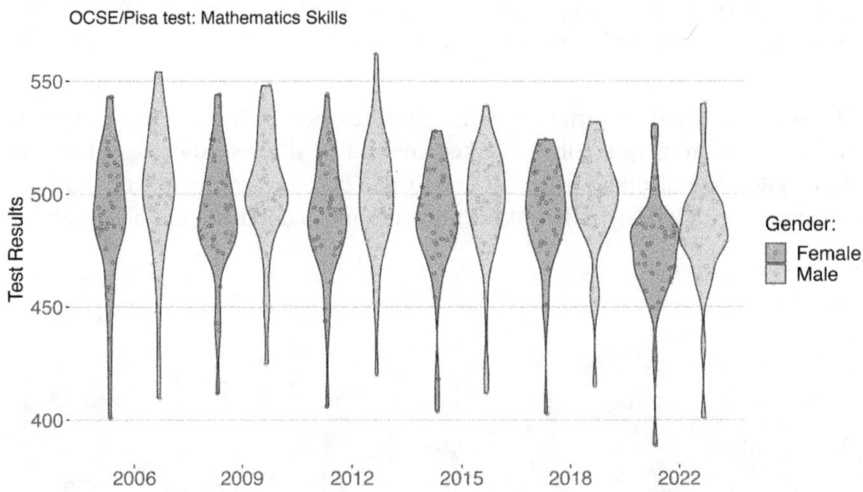

Figure 8.7 Sina plot and violin plot combined, OECD/Pisa tests results for male and female students, Mathematics skills.

A *violin plot and a sina plot could be combined* as well, for a visual effect with better-defined shapes (Figure 8.7), style options common with previous graphics have been omitted.

```
colorList= c('#1252b8','#fa866b')

ggplot(MatL, aes(x=as.factor(Year), y=Avg))+
```

```
  geom_violin(aes(fill=Sex), alpha=0.2)+
  geom_sina(aes(color=Sex), shape=1)+
  scale_color_manual(values = colorList) +
  scale_fill_manual( values = colorList)+
  labs(
    x="", y="Test Results",
    title="OCSE/Pisa test: Mathematics Skills",
    fill="Gender:", color="Gender:") +
    ...
```

Let us try the sina plot with a *boxplot*. The combination could be effective when data points are appropriate to this visualization, even without a violin plot (Figure 8.8).

```
colorList= c('#1252b8','#fa866b')

ggplot(MatL, aes(x=as.factor(Year), y=Avg))+
  geom_boxplot(aes(fill=Sex), alpha=0.7, outlier.shape= NA)+
  geom_sina(aes(color=Sex), shape=1)+
  scale_color_manual(values = colorList) +
  scale_fill_manual(values = colorList) +
   labs(...
```

We see now another variation with attributes `position='identity'` to have separate groups of points stacked instead of dodged and `maxwidth` to control jitter. We also add a logical condition (`color= Avg > 500`) to have some points with a color different from the others. A detail should be noted: the

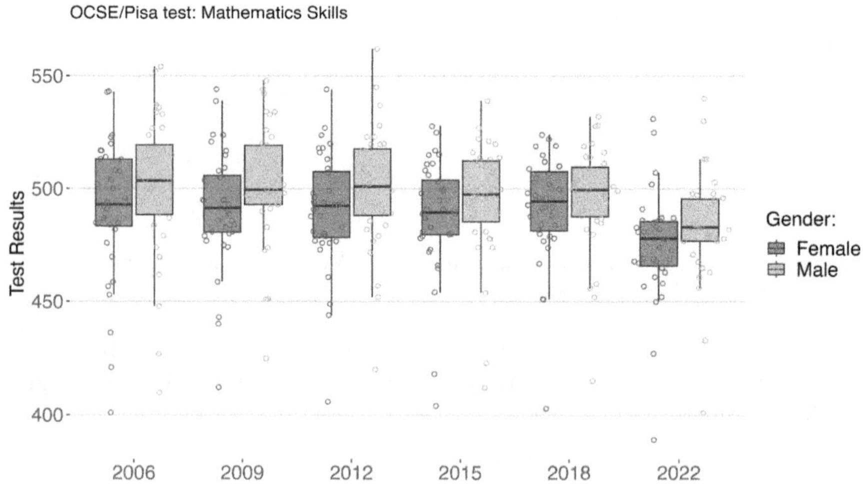

Figure 8.8 Sina plot and boxplot, OECD/Pisa tests results for male and female students, Mathematics skills.

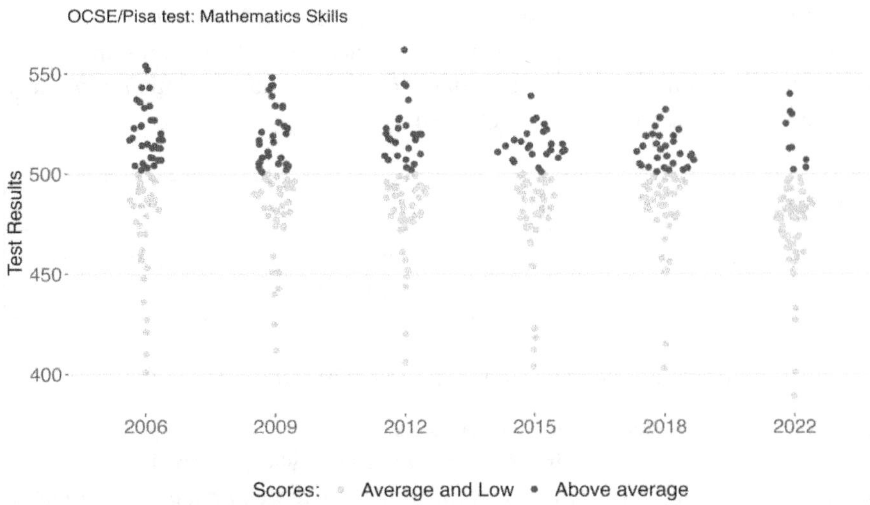

Figure 8.9 Sina plot with stacked groups of data points and color based on logical condition.

logical condition on aesthetic `color` has the consequence that values associated to that aesthetic are *True* and *False*, meaning that in the *legend* the *labels* for the two colors would have been *TRUE* and *FALSE*, barely understandable to a reader. For this reason, we have explicitly reconfigured the legend labels in function `scale_color_manual()`.

Figure 8.9 shows the resulting plot.

```
ggplot(MatL, aes(x= as.factor(Year) , y= Avg)) +
  geom_sina(aes(color= Avg > 500),
            position= "identity",
            maxwidth=0.6, size=2) +
  scale_color_manual(values= c("lightblue","darkred"),
                     labels= c("FALSE"="Average and Low",
                               "TRUE"="Above average")) +
 labs(
    x="", y="Test Results", color="Scores:",
    title="OCSE/Pisa test: Mathematics Skills")+
    ...
```

8.2.4 Beeswarm Plot

A different approach for handling the overplotting problem, especially for categorical data, is provided by the *beeswarm plot*. This is another relatively recent graphic type defined, for ggplot, in a custom package (*ggbeeswarm*) to replicate the corresponding *swarm plot* natively implemented by Seaborn. The features are similar to graphics previously seen in this section. For R, after the installation of package *ggbeeswarm*, the library to load is *ggbeeswarm*.

Warning
Do not mislead the library *ggbeeswarm*, to use for the beeswarm plot, with the similarly named *beeswarm*, installed as a dependency.

Function `geom_beeswarm()` has some peculiar attributes:

- `cex`: controls the distance among markers;
- `dodge.width`: controls distance among markers when grouped;
- `priority`: could have value *ascending* (default), *descending*, *density*, *random*, and *none*, for different layouts of the markers.

Let us consider a basic example. What is shown in Figure 8.10 is the typical *fishbone* deployment of markers in a *beeswarm* plot. The advantage is of providing intuitive information regarding the density of markers for each level of the dependent variable, clearer than in previous graphics. This benefit is, however, paid in terms of precision, the position of markers is no way approximately close to the real data points, much worse than with traditional jittering or sina plot.

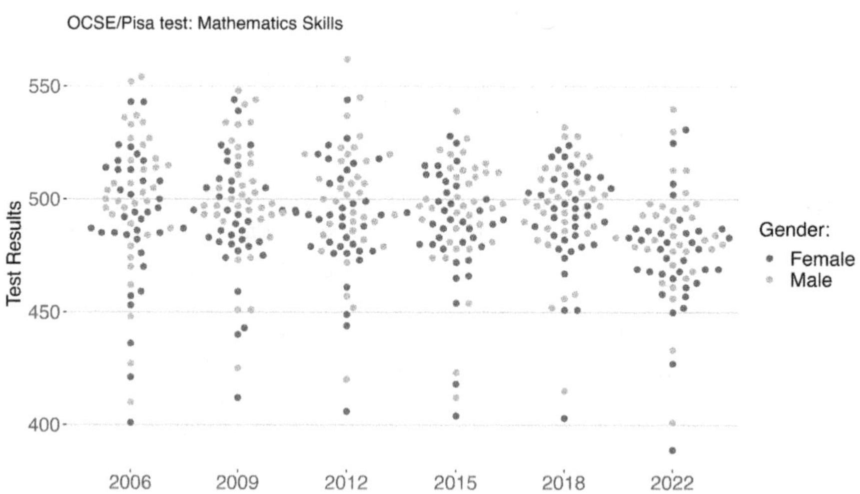

Figure 8.10 Beeswarm plot, OECD/Pisa test results for male and female students, Mathematics skills.

```
library(ggbeeswarm)
colorList= c('#1252b8','#fa866b')

ggplot(pisa, aes(x =as.factor(Year), y= Value,
       color= CompLevel)) +
  geom_beeswarm(size=1, cex=2) +
  scale_color_manual(values= colorList) +
  labs(x="Year", y="Students (%)",
       color="Competence\nLevel") +
  theme_light()+
  theme(plot.margin= unit(c(1,1,1,1),"cm"))
```

8.2.5 Comparison Between Jittering, Sina plot, and Beeswarm plot

In Figure 8.11, the three approaches to overplotting are shown side-by-side together with the representation of overplotting. The differences are easily noted.

Which one to choose? In general, both the sina plot and the beeswarm plot convey an additional information about the distribution of data points with respect to traditional jitter for categorical scatterplots. It could be observed that the sina plot maintains a more realistic representation of the density of the data points, closely resembling a violin plot, while the beeswarm plot prefers a more stylized shape. However, choosing between the sina plot and the beeswarm plot is largely a matter of subjective preference, either aesthetical or of communication style.

8.3 Python: Seaborn

Different from ggplot, Seaborn does not provide a specific control of overplotting, for example, with jittering, for traditional scatterplots. Its approach, instead, is to provide specialized functions for *categorical scatterplots* that natively handle overplotting: *strip plot* (i.e., the traditional categorical scatterplot with jitter) and *swarm plot* (i.e., the same previously called *beeswarm* plot for ggplot). Seaborn functions are, respectively, `stripplot()` and `swarmplot()`.

8.3.1 Strip Plot and Swarm Plot

Strip plots and swarm plots are variants of traditional categorical scatterplots, the first introducing jitter to manage overplotting but weakening the correspondence between the marker's positions and real data points, the second presenting the typical fishbone placement of markers, highlighting their density but almost completely losing the correspondence with real data point positions.

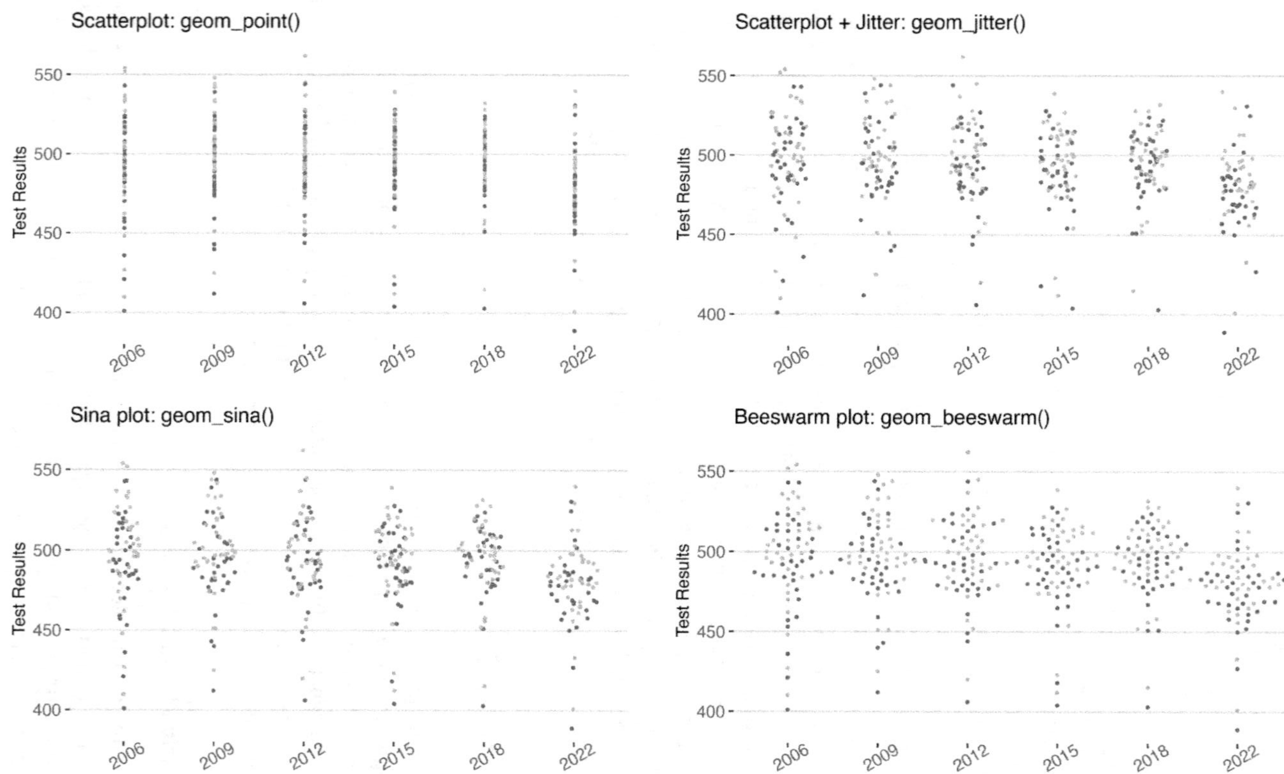

Figure 8.11 Comparing overplotting, jitter, sina plot, and beeswarm plot.

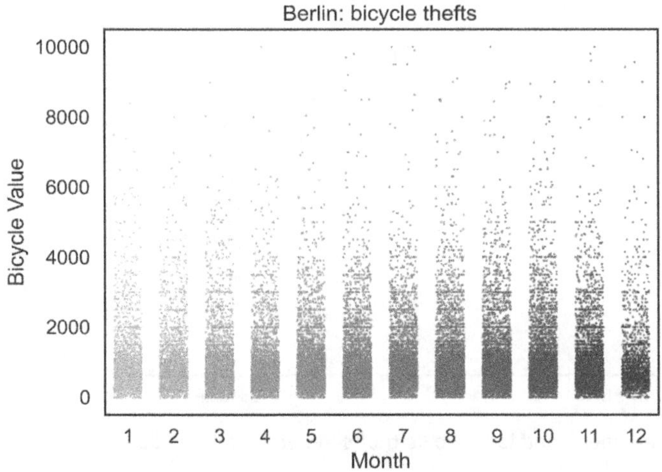

Figure 8.12 Strip plot, bike thefts in Berlin.

We start with a *strip plot*, which lets specifying attributes `jitter`, `size`, and `alpha` to control overplotting. As data, we make use of the dataset about bike thefts in Berlin (see Figure 8.12).

```
g= sns.stripplot(data= bikes,
       x= bici["START_DATE"].dt.month,
       y= "DAMAGES",
       alpha=0.7, size=1.5, jitter=0.3, pal='flare')

plt.xlabel("Month")
plt.ylabel("Bicycle Value ")
plt.title("Berlin: bicycle thefts")
```

With a *swarm plot*, attribute `jitter` is not available. We use a visualization by facets using *month* as the variable. For simplicity, we select just one month, October 2022, and two types of bikes to show the markers grouped (Figure 8.13).

```
bikes_ml=bikes[((bikes["TYPE_OF_BICYCLE"]=="men's bike") | \
                (bikes["TYPE_OF_BICYCLE"]=="ladies bike")) & \
                (bikes["START_DATE"].dt.month==10) & \
                (bikes["START_DATE"].dt.year==2022)]

g=sns.swarmplot(data=bikes_ml,
                x="TYPE_OF_BICYCLE",
                y="START_HOUR",
                size=2.5,
```

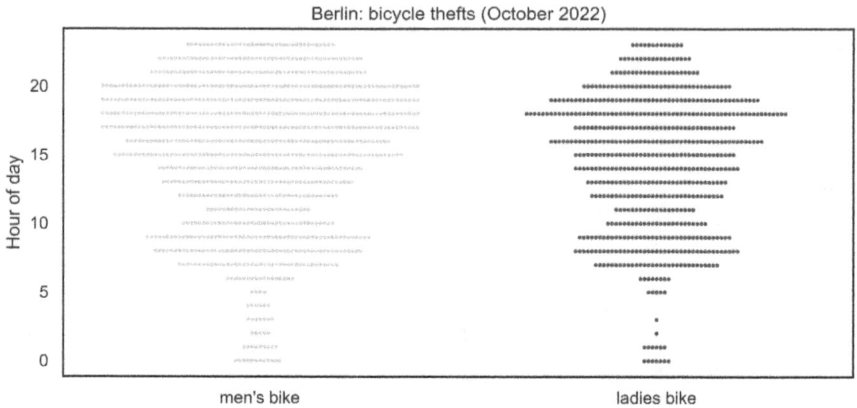

Figure 8.13 Swarm plot, men's and ladies' bike thefts in Berlin, October 2022.

```
                palette={"men's bike": "skyblue", "ladies bike":
                      "darkred"})

plt.xlabel("")
plt.ylabel("Hour of day")
plt.title("Berlin: bicycle thefts (October 2022)")
plt.tight_layout()
```

Graphically, the result is not completely satisfying. It gives an idea of the number of thefts for each hour of day but not much more; in addition, when points reach the maximum width of the virtual column, they are packed together, and details get lost. Generating the swarm plot also takes considerably more time, being computationally intensive, than for the strip plot.

This example shows that choosing between the two types of graphics remains largely an individual choice, but there are some objective elements to consider: *the swarm plot is well-suited for small samples only and with data points not too much concentrated in a small range of values*; for other cases, it is better to use the strip plot.

8.3.2 Sina Plot

Sina plot does not exist as a native graphic type in Seaborn (up to version 12.2, at least), but custom implementations have been proposed and could be considered for use. An excellent one has been realized by Matthew Parker and it is available from his GitHub repository, a Jupyter notebook provides the usage instructions (https://github.com/mparker2/seaborn_sinaplot).

To use custom function `sinaplot()`, it is required to save the two files provided into a local directory called *sinaplot*. The Jupyter notebook or the Python script from which the `sinaplot()` function will be executed should be located in the same *sinaplot* folder. With this, the usual import directive could be executed (`from sinaplot import sinaplot`). The following schema shows the file organization to reproduce.

```
local directory/
|
├── sinaplot /
    |
    ├── init.py
    |
    └── sinaplot.py
├── python script_or_sinaplot.ipynb
|
...
```

Alternatively, a more general solution could be adopted by using Python library *sys* to specify the path to the *sinaplot* directory with the custom function to use.

```
import sys
sys.path.append('path to sinaplot directory')
```

Once the setup is done, usage is simple. Attribute `violin=False` (default *True*) draws only sina plot points without the violin shape, the opposite if set to *True*. For the example, we select just data from January 2021 to 2022, and two types of bikes (Figure 8.14).

```
bikes_ml= bikes[
          ((bikes["TYPE_OF_BICYCLE"]=="men's bike") |
           (bikes["TYPE_OF_BICYCLE"]=="ladies bike")) &
           (bikes["DEED TIME_START_DATE"].dt.month==1)]

g= sinaplot(data= bikes_ml,
    x= bikes_ml["DEED TIME_START_DATE"].dt.year,
    y= "DAMAGES", hue= "TYPE_OF_BICYCLE",
    palette= sns.color_palette(['forestgreen','skyblue']),
    s=2, violin=False)

ax.legend(title="Bike Type ")
ax.set(xlabel=" ", ylabel=" Bicycle Value")
ax.set(title="Berlin: bicycle thefts (January 2021/2022)")
```

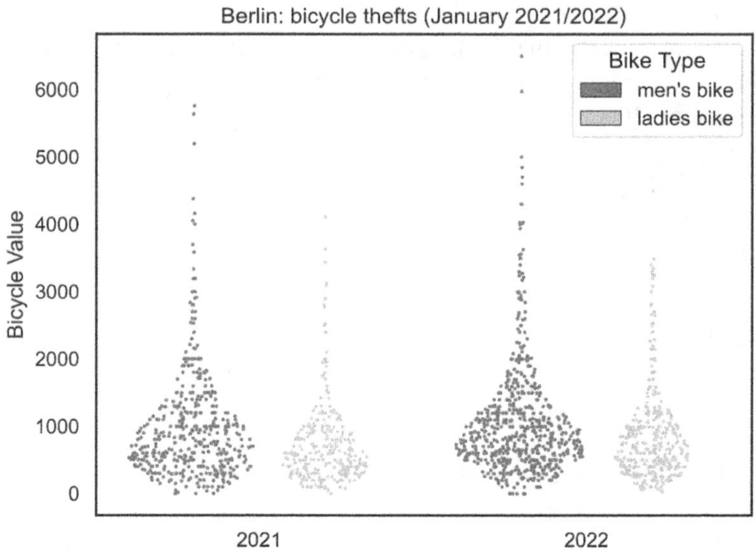

Figure 8.14 Sina plot, men's and ladies' bike thefts in Berlin in January 2021–2022.

9

Half-Violin Plots

The name *half-violin plot* could sound like an oddity, one of those bizarre artifacts that sometimes data scientists and graphic designers create for amusement, but it would be a mistake to consider it that way. Instead, it is a relevant variant of the violin plot that is particularly well-suited to be combined in different fashions to convey a good deal of information in an intuitive and aesthetically pleasant form.

The key premise is that graphics with a symmetric structure (e.g., *boxplots* and *violin plots*) are intrinsically redundant, meaning that the whole information could be provided by just one-half of them. This, on the one side, would allow simplifying the graphic, but aesthetically it would be less agreeable, on the other, it permits replacing one-half of the graphic with something else, like another type of graphic, to increase the informational content of the visualization. Creativity is paramount in this case, as well as good judgment about the effectiveness and interpretability of the visual artifact for data visualization.

We present some cases, others exist, by starting from the basic feature: how to produce just half of a violin plot. In past years, several solutions, both for R and for Python, have been introduced, first as custom functions, then through more stable packages, when the interest in this possibility has gained traction.

Dataset

In this chapter, we make use again of data from the *OECD Skills Survey*, OECD 2022 (The Organisation for Economic Co-operation and Development), and from *Bicycle thefts in Berlin* (transl. Fahrraddiebstahl in Berlin) from the Municipality of Berlin, Germany, Berlin Open Data, previously introduced.

Data Visualization in R and Python, First Edition. Marco Cremonini.

Companion website: www.wiley.com/go/Cremonini/DataVisualization1e

9.1 R: ggplot

9.1.1 Custom Function

Custom function `geom_split_violin()` has been originally proposed on Stack Overflow by user *jan-glx* (https://stackoverflow.com/questions/35717353/split-violin-plot-with-ggplot2) and at the time of writing it does not appear to be available in any package on CRAN (The Comprehensive R Archive Network). The function could be used by manually copying the source code into the same R script or in the same way we previously described for the custom implementation of the sina plot function. The source code is available in the *Additional Online Material – R: half-violin – geom_split_violin.R.* Let us see a basic example, we define a color list and make use of the same data frame *pisa*, created in Chapter 7. Figure 9.1 shows what we expected: just half violins are plotted, clearly resembling density plots (`geom_density()`), with the same information of original violin plots but a more elaborate graphic. It is well-suited when data points are grouped with respect to a variable with just two values (e.g., male/female, North/South, and Republicans/Democrats), so to glue the two halves. Other than that, more creative ways to exploit half-violins become available.

```
colorList= c('#3c77a3','#b1cc29')

ggplot(pisa, aes(x= as.factor(Year) , y= Value,
       fill= Sex)) +
```

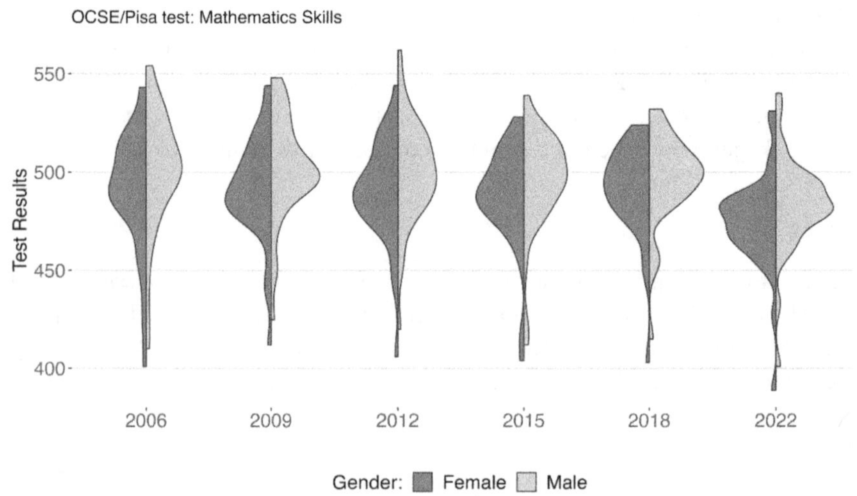

Figure 9.1 Half-violin plot, custom function, OECD/Pisa test results for male and female students, Mathematics skills.

```
  geom_split_violin() +
  scale_color_manual(values= colorList) +
  labs(x=" ", y="Test Results", fill="Gender:",
       title="OCSE/Pisa test: Mathematics Skills"
  )+
  theme_hc()+
  theme(legend.position = "bottom")+
  theme(plot.margin = unit(c(1,1,1,1),"cm"))
```

We can replicate some examples seen with violin plots by using the half-violin graphic type. We choose the most complete, tuning attribute `width` to correctly place the internal boxplot. Once again, the result, shown in Figure 9.2, is aesthetically pleasant and conveys information with a compact and original layout.

```
colorList= c('#3c77a3','#b1cc29')

ggplot(pisa, aes(x= as.factor(Year), y= Value,
               fill= Sex)) +
  geom_split_violin(alpha=0.4) +
  geom_boxplot(position= position_dodge(width=0.2),
             alpha=0.5, size=0.4, width= 0.2,
             outlier.shape= NA) +
  geom_point(aes(group= Sex),
```

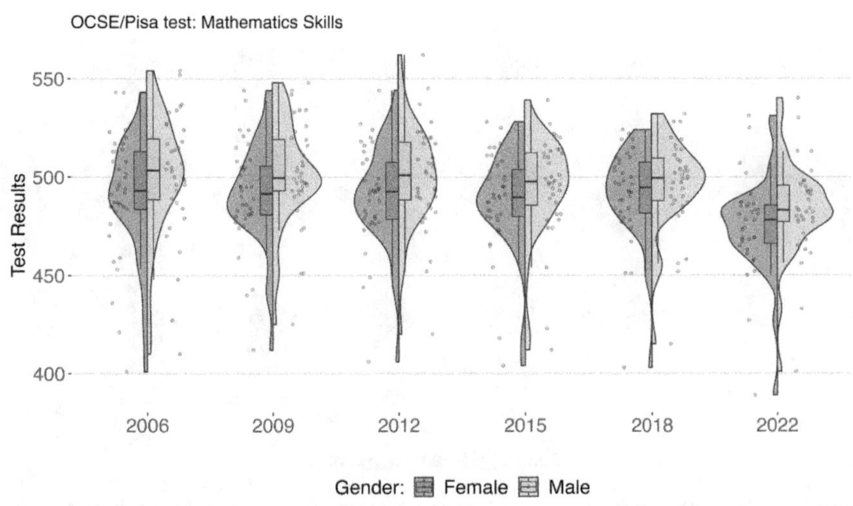

Figure 9.2 Half-violin plot, boxplot, and scatterplot with jitter correctly aligned and dodged, OCSE-PISA tests.

```
        position= position_jitterdodge(jitter.width=0.15,
                                       jitter.height=0,
                                       dodge.width=0.9),
        alpha=0.5, size=0.7, shape=1) +
    scale_fill_manual(values= colorList) +
      labs(x="", y="Test Results", fill="Gender:",
      title="OCSE/Pisa test: Mathematics Skills"
    )+
    theme_hc()+
    theme(legend.position = "bottom")+
    theme(plot.margin = unit(c(1,1,1,1),"cm"))
```

Similar to what we showed in Figure 7.6 of Chapter 7, a facet visualization for Mathematics, Reading, and Scientific skills is an interesting addition to consider the overall picture of Pisa tests and the half-violin plot solution, which is an even more compact form than what we have seen in Figure 7.6. This time, we have also the scatterplot as a graphic layer. In the code, datasets reading operations, binding rows, and long-form transformation are omitted, being identical to those presented in Figure 7.6, the same for style options in common with previous plots. Figure 9.3 shows the result.

```
colorList= c('#3c77a3','#b1cc29')

ggplot(pisaMRS, aes(x=as.factor(Year) , y=Avg, fill=Sex))+
  geom_split_violin(alpha=0.7)+
```

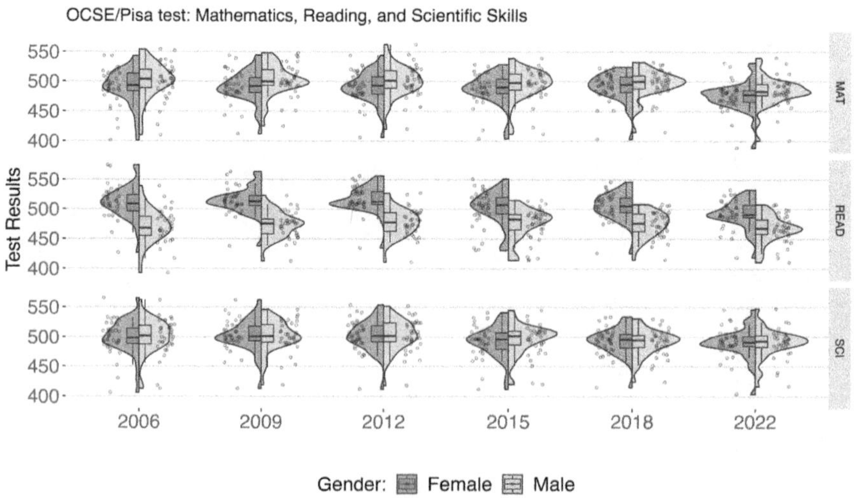

Figure 9.3 OECD/Pisa tests, male and female students, Mathematics, Reading, and Scientific skills.

```
geom_boxplot(position=position_dodge(width=0.2),
           alpha=0.5, size=0.4, width= 0.2, outlier.shape = NA)+
geom_point(aes(group=Sex),
           position=position_jitterdodge(jitter.width = 0.15,
                                         jitter.height = 0,
                                         dodge.width = 0.9),
           alpha=0.5, size=0.7, shape=1)+
  facet_grid(rows = vars(Test))+
scale_fill_manual(values = colorList) +
labs(
  x="", y="Test Results", fill="Gender:",
  title= 'OCSE/Pisa test: Mathematics, Reading, and Scientific Skills'
)+
...
```

9.1.2 Raincloud Plot

A variant of the plot just presented is called *raincloud plot* and combines in a particularly creative fashion a *half-violin plot*, a *boxplot*, and a *dot plot*, the latter another variant of the scatterplot with a stylized layout (`geom_dotplot()`).

Note
The raincloud plot has been presented in the following scientific publication: Allen M, Poggiali D, Whitaker K, Marshall TR, Kievit RA. Raincloud plots: a multi-platform tool for robust data visualization. Wellcome Open Res. 2019 Apr 1;4:63. doi: 10.12688/wellcomeopenres.15191.1. PMID: 31069261; PMCID: PMC6480976.

To implement this example, we need a different function than the previous `geom_split_violin()` because half-violins should have the same orientation (i.e., all left side), a feature not well supported by that custom function. There are alternatives, one available in a package on CRAN is `geom_half_violin()` of package *gghalves*. With attribute `side="l"` (default) only the *left side of the violin* is plotted, similarly `side="r"` draws only the *right side*. Let us see a simple example (Figure 9.4).

```
library(gghalves)
colorList= c('#3c77a3','#b1cc29')

ggplot(MatL, aes(x=as.factor(Year) , y=Avg, fill=Sex))+
  geom_half_violin(side="l")+
  scale_fill_manual(values = colorList) +
  labs(...
```

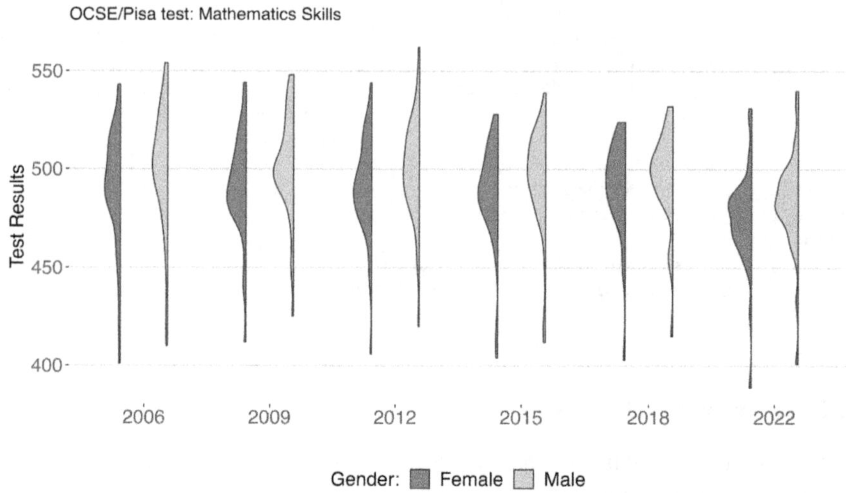

Figure 9.4 Left-side half-violin plots, male and female students, Mathematics skills.

With this as the basis, the *raincloud plot* could be produced. Some care should be taken in order to correctly place the three graphics, the *half-violin plot*, the *boxplot*, and the *dot plot*. In particular, attribute `position=position_nudge()` is needed to overcome the default placement; attribute `stackratio` of `geom_dotplot()` to modify the distance of aligned markers, and attribute `binaxis` defines the axis used to align markers (axis x is the default, we need to specify axis y). The adoption of `facet_grid()` instead of `facet_wrap()` has just an aesthetical reason, that way we have facet titles vertically on the left side rather than on top. In the example, we use a single variable for facets associated to rows of the grid with attribute `rows=vars();` with attribute `switch="y"` facet titles are shown on the right side. As a last detail, by resizing the plot with attribute `width` and `height` of function `ggsave()`, which saves on file the last plot, we improve the excessive vertical closeness of graphics of the original plot, otherwise not easy to tune.

Figure 9.5 shows the result. It is an elaborate combination of three graphics that at first might appear difficult to comprehend, but with some patience and placing one element at time, the logic becomes clear.

```
library(gghalves)
colorList= c('#3c77a3','#b1cc29')

ggplot(pisaMRS, aes(x=as.factor(Year) , y=Avg, fill=Sex))+
  geom_half_violin(side="r", alpha=0.3,
                   position = position_nudge(x = 0.03))+
  geom_boxplot(size=0.4, width= 0.1, outlier.shape = NA,
```

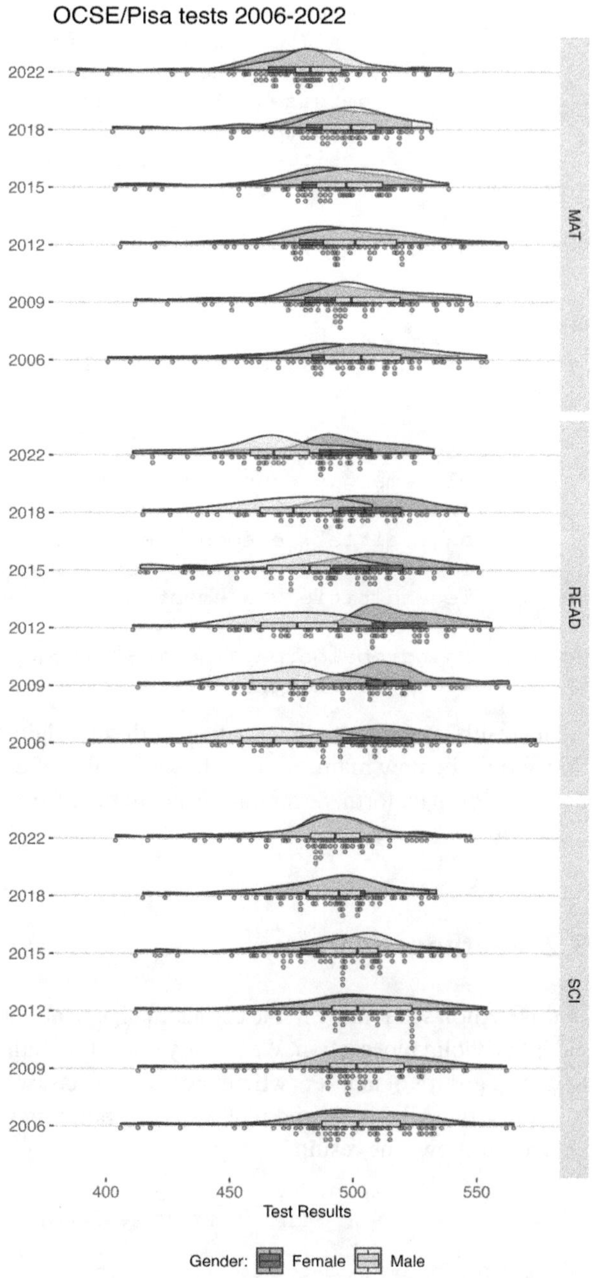

Figure 9.5 Raincloud plot, male and female students, Mathematics, Reading, and Scientific skills.

```
                 position = position_nudge(x = 0.04))+
  scale_fill_manual(values = colorList) +
  geom_dotplot(stackdir="down", binaxis = "y",
                 dotsize=1.6, binwidth = 0.5,
                 stackratio=1.5, width = 0.5,
                 position = position_nudge(x= 0),
                 fill="#345ceb" ,alpha=0.5)+

  facet_grid(rows=vars(Test))+
  coord_flip()+
  labs(
    x="", y="Test Results", fill="Gender:",
    title="OCSE/Pisa tests 2006-2022"
  )+
  theme_hc()+
  theme(legend.position = "bottom")+
  theme(plot.margin = unit(c(1,1,1,1),"cm"))+
  theme(axis.text = element_text(size = 10),
        axis.title = element_text(size = 10),
        legend.text = element_text(size = 10),
        legend.title = element_text(size = 10))

ggsave("raindropPlot.png", dpi=600, bg='transparent',
        width=15, height=30, units="cm")
```

The result is smart and imaginative, with the origin of the name (i.e., raindrop) that should be now manifest. It is, however, also effective in conveying information in a compact form. Several hints about data from the Pisa tests emerge quite evidently.

9.2 Python: Seaborn

In this Python section, we make use again of data about bike thefts in Berlin, as we did in the violin plot section. We already know that half-violin plots are well-suited in case of groups of markers where the variable has two values. For this reason, we select just two bike types and plot the corresponding violin plots for each month. Figure 9.6 shows the result.

```
bikes_ml= bici.query(" TYPE_OF_BICYCLE=='men\\'s bike' | \
                       TYPE_OF_BICYCLE=='ladies bike' ")

g= sns.violinplot(data= bikes_ml,
          x=bikes_ml["START_DATE"].dt.month,
          y= "DAMAGES", hue= "TYPE_OF_BICYCLE",
          palette={"men's bike": '#3c77a3', "ladies bike": '#b1cc29'},
```

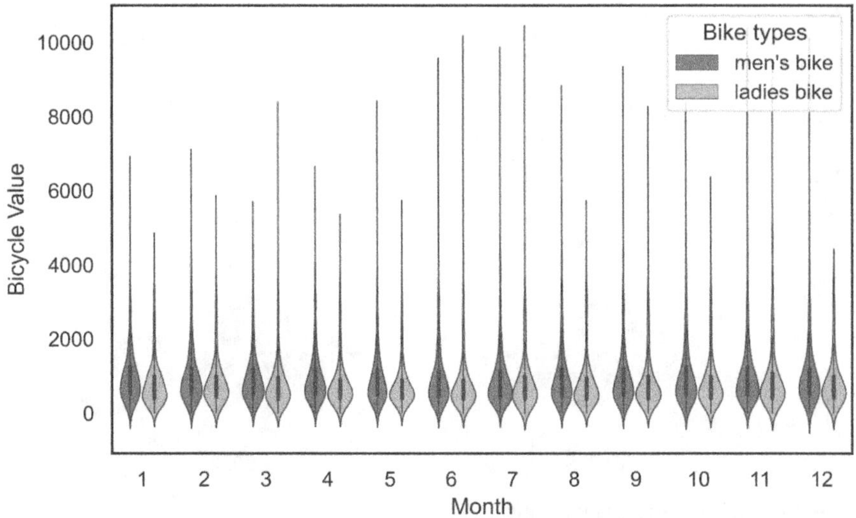

Figure 9.6 Violin plot with groups of two subsets of points, bike thefts in Berlin.

```
         linewidth=0.7)

g.legend_.set_title('Bike types')
plt.xlabel('Month')
plt.ylabel('Bicycle Value')
plt.show()
```

This is an ideal case for a half-violin plot for having a single violin composed of the two halves instead of the two dodged violins. Seaborn supports it natively with attribute `split=True` of function `sns.violinplot()`. To show the result more clearly, we select just one month (i.e., January). With attribute `hue_order`, we could set a specific order of values of the variable used for groups and associated to attribute `hue`. We also add a visual effect with attribute `inner='stick'` that shows the data distribution as lines, while directive `sns.despine(left=True,bottom=True)` removes the external border (see Figure 9.7). By specifying `inner='quart'`, the *quartiles* of the distribution (Q1, median, and Q3) are shown (see Figure 9.8).

```
data= bikes_ml[bikes_ml["START_DATE"].dt.month == 1]

g=sns.violinplot(data= data,
     x= bikes_ml["START_DATE"].dt.year,
     y= "DAMAGES", hue= "TYPE_OF_BICYCLE",
     hue_order= ["men's bike", "ladies bike"],
     palette={"men's bike": '#3c77a3', "ladies bike": '#b1cc29'},
     linewidth=0.1,
     split= True, inner= 'stick')
```

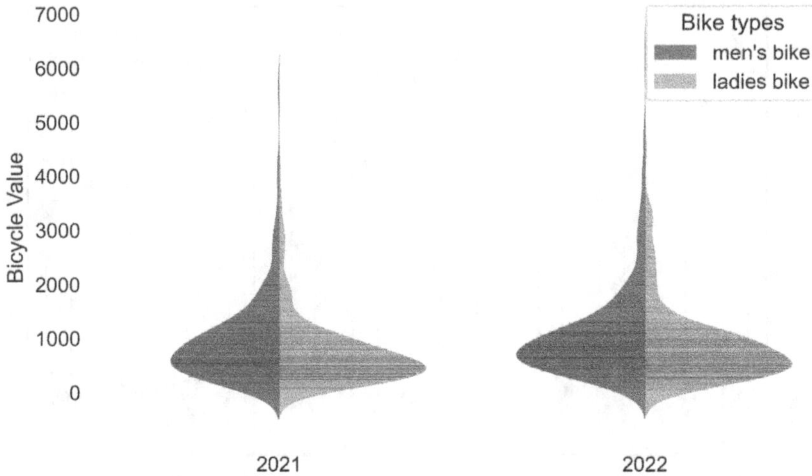

Figure 9.7 Half-violin plots with sticks.

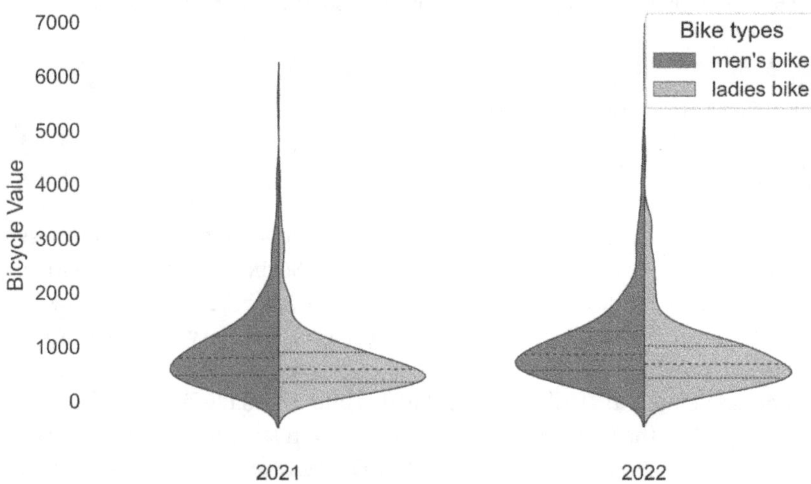

Figure 9.8 Half-violin plots with quartiles.

```
sns.despine(left=True,bottom=True)

g.legend_.set_title('Bike types')
plt.xlabel(")
plt.ylabel('Bicycle Value')
plt.show()
```

10

Ridgeline Plots

10.1 History of the Ridgeline

The *ridgeline plot* is a peculiar type of graphic with a curious history intersecting that of an iconic image, the one presented on the cover of the (once renowned) UK band Joy Division's first album, Unknown Pleasures (1979). The origin of that image has been researched for long by music fans until the definitive explanation was found. It is the white-on-black representation of the 80 pulsations of the first observed pulsar star, named PSR B1919+21 (originally called CP1919 and first observed by Jocelyn Bell Burnell in 1967, at time a Ph.D. student at Cambridge University, UK), vertically aligned one over the other. The original image (Figure 10.1) first appeared in the 1970's Ph.D. thesis of Harold D. Craft, Jr. and in the journal *Scientific American*, which also published that image in 1970, summarized the whole story by interviewing the author, at time a student at Cornell University, now Professor Emeritus at the same university (https://blogs.scientificamerican.com/sa-visual/pop-culture-pulsar-origin-story-of-joy-division-s-unknown-pleasures-album-cover-video/).

The ingenious idea of showing those star pulsations on top of each other to highlight the frequency variations is the same that inspires the *ridgeline plot* where, in place of electromagnetic pulsations, there are *density plots* showing the different value distributions for a set of observations.

The expected visual effect is to compare similar observations collected from different times or contexts, showing them with a visual effect that resembles that of waves flowing. The ridgeline plot is undoubtedly one of the most original and eye-catching types of graphics, but for this reason, it needs to be drawn with special care of all details.

In this section, we show examples only for *ggplot* because it offers a specific library able to produce high-quality ridgeline plots. Unfortunately, this is not the case for Seaborn (at least up to version 12.2), which does not support this type of graphics and no other good custom implementation has been retrieved.

Data Visualization in R and Python, First Edition. Marco Cremonini.

Companion website: www.wiley.com/go/Cremonini/DataVisualization1e

Figure 10.1 "Many consecutive pulses from CP1919," in Harold Dumont Craft, Jr, "Radio observations of the pulse profiles and dispersion measures of twelve pulsars," PhD dissertation, Cornell University, 1970, p. 214, Courtesy of Prof. Harold D. Craft.

With Seaborn, it is possible just to approximately reproduce the graphical layout and visual effect of a ridgeline plot by combining basic elements in an overly complicated and unsatisfactory fashion. We let the possibility to produce good ridgeline plots with Seaborn to future developments.

Dataset

In this chapter, we make use again of data from the *OECD Skills Survey*, OECD 2022 (The Organisation for Economic Co-operation and Development) previously introduced.

10.2 R: ggplot

Package *ggridges*, whose author is Claus O. Wilke, provides the main functions and a sample dataset about temperatures in year 2016 at Lincoln, NE. The specifications with examples are available in the package documentation.

The example of temperatures gathered on an extended time period is well-suited for a ridgeline plot because it represents the same observation taken at different times. The same could have been done by collecting temperatures in the same period (e.g., a month) but from different locations.

In our case study, we want to produce a *ridgeline plot* with data from the *OECD Skills Survey* regarding OECD/Pisa tests, already introduced in Chapter 7, which are the same tests completed by same-age students in different countries. This case has some similarities with that of temperatures but also differences that we should consider:

- They are similar because they are results of the same observation repeated in regional contexts that may differ, climate conditions for temperatures, socioeconomic, political, organizational, and cultural aspects for Pisa tests.
- The main difference with temperatures is that while temperatures are measured on a given scale, Pisa test results do not have an implicit scale for ordering them. Different metrics are possible to use, one should be chosen, and values derived from data.

We present the examples by separating results for Mathematical, Reading, and Scientific skills because a ridgeline plot visualization is effective if data are homogeneous, so to compare them among different contexts. Package *viridis* has color palettes also for discrete variables with numerous values. In our case, we have 35 countries plus the International Average (OECD). Function `geom_density_ridges()` draws the density plots that, when combined, will result in the ridgeline plot. Data frames are the same prepared for visualization in Chapter 7, namely *MatL*, *RdL*, and *SciL*, derived from reading the original datasets and then transformed into long form. Figure 10.2 shows the first resulting plot.

```
library(ggridges)
library(viridis)

MatL%>%
  ggplot(aes(x=Avg, y=Country))+
  geom_density_ridges(aes(fill=Country), scale=2, rel_min_height=0.005) +
  scale_fill_viridis(discrete= TRUE, option= "viridis" )+
  labs(
    x="Test results", y="",
    title="OECD/Pisa test: Mathematics skills"
  )+
  theme_clean() +
  theme(panel.grid.major.y = element_blank(),
        legend.position = 'none')+
  theme(axis.text.x =
    element_text(size = 8, hjust = .75))
```

The first attempt to produce a ridgeline plot is technically correct with density plots that appear sufficiently homogeneous and intuitive. The *viridis* gradient

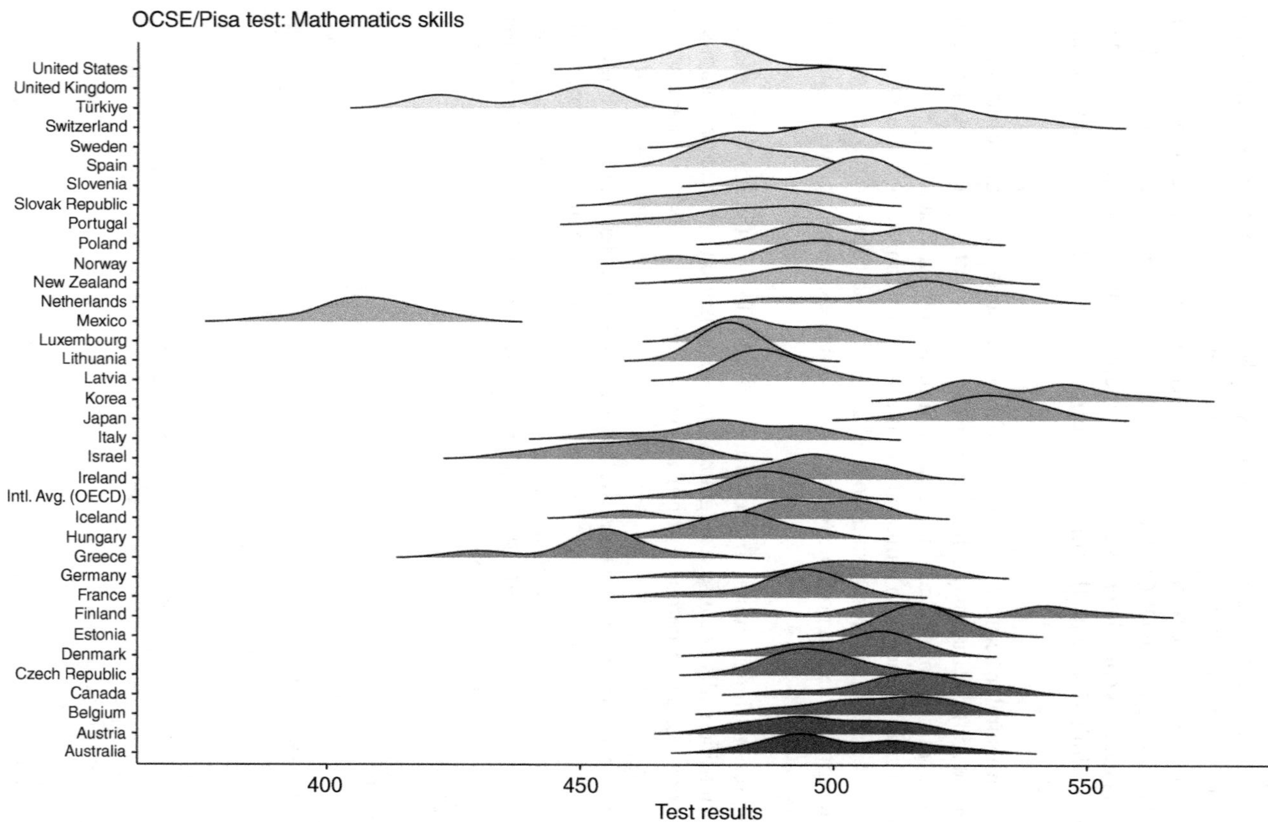

Figure 10.2 Ridgeline plot, OECD-Pisa tests, default alphabetical order based on country names, Mathematics skills.

is pleasant. However, the overall visual effect is somehow confused, grasping the differences among countries requires particular attention and is not immediately clear; it could be improved by ordering the results with respect to a metric based on data, rather than alphabetically by country name. The easiest way is to use a descriptive statistic as a metric; for instance, the arithmetic mean, median, maximum, or minimum value are all possible metrics, and choosing a specific one depends on what information we want to convey.

To realize the solution with a different order of countries, we need a particular technique that allows ordering a data frame with respect to an *external ordered list of items*. The logical steps are as follows:

1. *(a)* First, the list of countries should be ordered based on the metric chosen (e.g., a descriptive statistic) and (*b*) the list of ordered countries should be created.
2. *(a)* Ordered country names of the list should be transformed into categories (R *factor* data type) and (*b*) associated to levels (*factor level*). This way, country names of the data frame will be ordered according to the ordered list.
3. Finally, the data frame is sorted with respect to country names, which will no longer adopt the alphabetical order but the one defined by the external list.

Based on this approach, we could now realize the desired ridgeline plot.

STEP 1a: We choose a specific descriptive statistic as the ordering criteria; in this case, we select the arithmetic mean, and sort the data frame based on mean values.

```
df1_high %>%
   group_by(Country) %>%
   summarize(Mean= mean(Value, na.rm= TRUE)) %>%
   arrange(desc(Mean)) -> df1_sort
```

STEP 1b: Country names (*df1_sort$Country*), sorted based on values of column *Mean*, are transformed into a list of 35 elements.

```
list1 = as.list(df1_sort$Country)
```

STEP 2a: In data frame with Pisa test results (*df1_elev*) country names of column *Country* are transformed into *factor* type.

STEP 2b: With function `fct_relevel()`, each value of column *Country* (now as *factor*) is associated, through its attribute *level*, to the corresponding position of *list1*. For example, Korea is in first position based on mean values of Pisa tests, therefore all rows related to Korea are associated to *factor level 1* and so on for all countries.

STEP 3: Now we can sort the data frame based on the *Country* column, obtaining the ordering based on the factor levels.

```
df1_high %>%
   mutate(Country= factor(Country)) %>%
   mutate(Country = fct_relevel(Country,list1)) %>%
   arrange(Country) -> df_high_factor
```

We can now produce again the ridgeline plot as did before, style directives are omitted for brevity (Figure 10.3).

```
df_high_factor %>%
  ggplot(aes(x= Value, y= Country)) +
  geom_density_ridges(aes(fill= Country),
                      scale= 2, rel_min_height=0.005) +
  scale_fill_viridis(discrete=TRUE, option="viridis") + ...
```

The result is much better than the previous one. Now it is very evident how results of Pisa tests differ for the set of countries. Next, the color gradient is more meaningful this way, highlighting the overall trend.

We can now replicate the same example for *Reading* and *Scientific* skills, just changing the initial data frame, as already did previously for other types of graphics.

For *Reading* skills, there are few changes:

- A different palette from the *Viridis* set (i.e., *plasma*) with the order of color *reverted* with attribute `direction` (i.e., `scale_fill_viridis (discrete=TRUE, option="plasma", direction= -1))`
- Theme *light* a little tweaked to remove major and minor grids for the *x*-axis and the panel's border:

```
theme_light() +
  theme(panel.grid.major.x = element_blank(),
        panel.border = element_blank(),
        panel.grid.minor.x = element_blank(),
        legend.position = 'none')
```

Figure 10.4 shows the result.

Instead, for *Scientific* skills, as a tribute to the first pulsar observed and of Joy Division, we could try to replicate the style of that iconic image (Figure 10.5). In the script, the only differences with what was previously discussed are:

- Data frame is *SciL*, derived from reading the original dataset for Scientific skills and transforming it into long form.
- Colors and line thickness: `geom_density_ridges(fill="black", color="white",size=0.5,scale=1.5, rel_min_height=0.005)`.

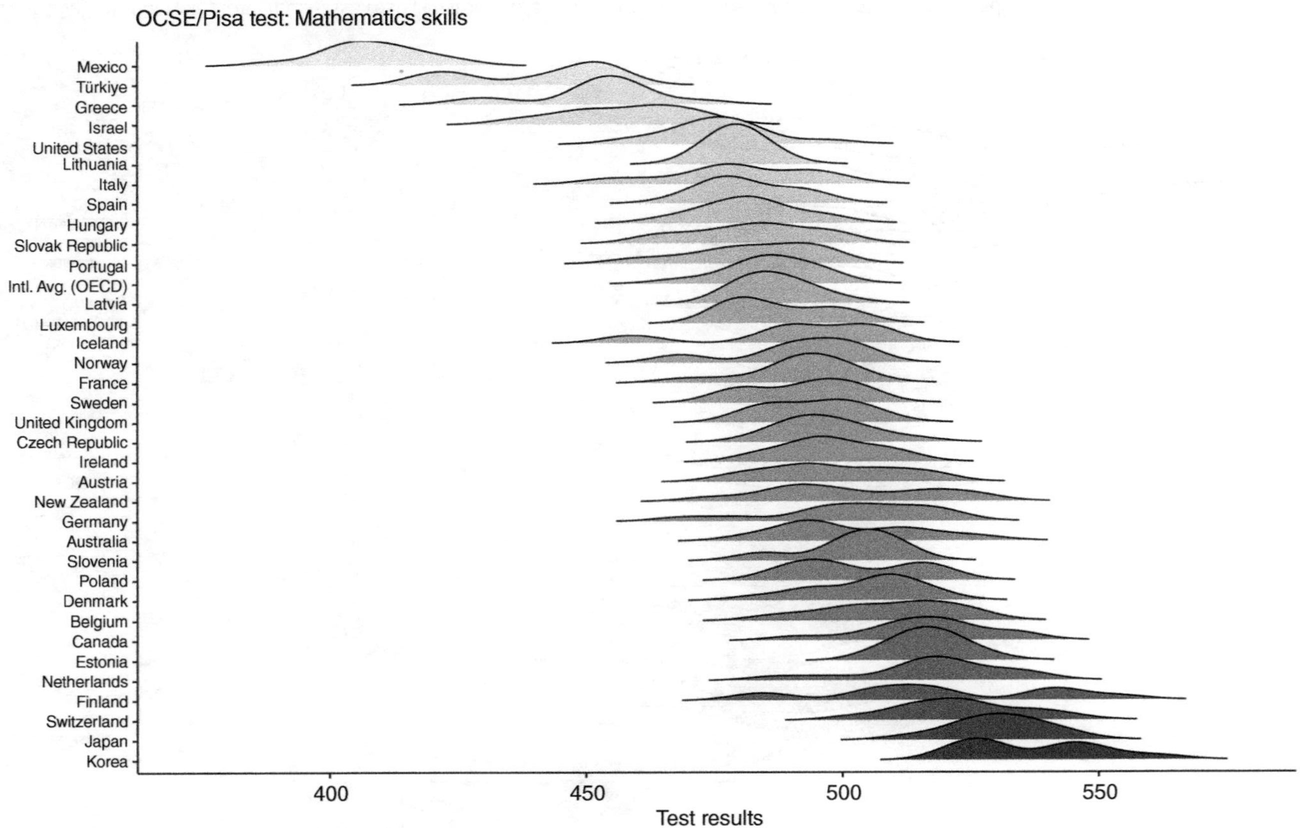

Figure 10.3 Ridgeline plot, OECD-Pisa tests, custom order based on arithmetic mean of test results, Mathematics skills.

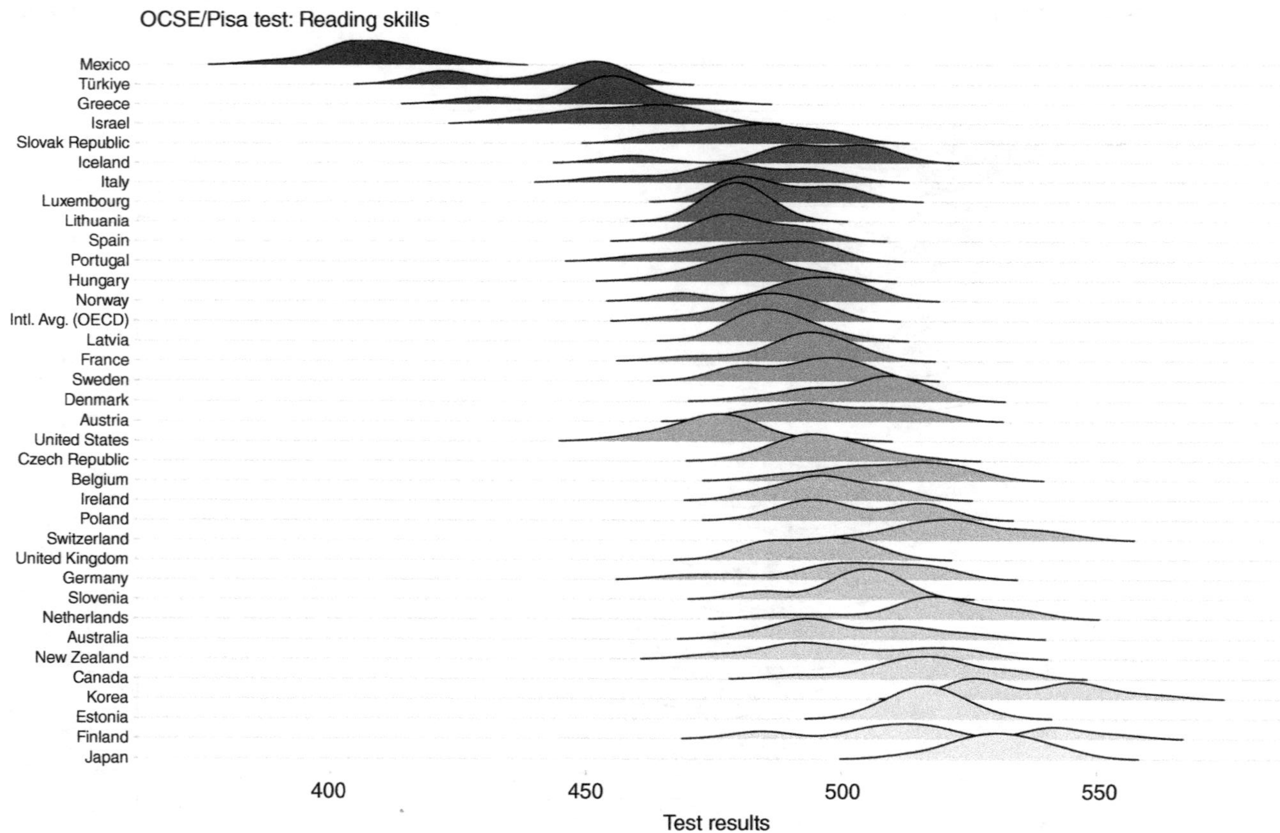

Figure 10.4 Ridgeline plot, OECD-Pisa tests, custom order based on arithmetic mean of test results, Reading skills.

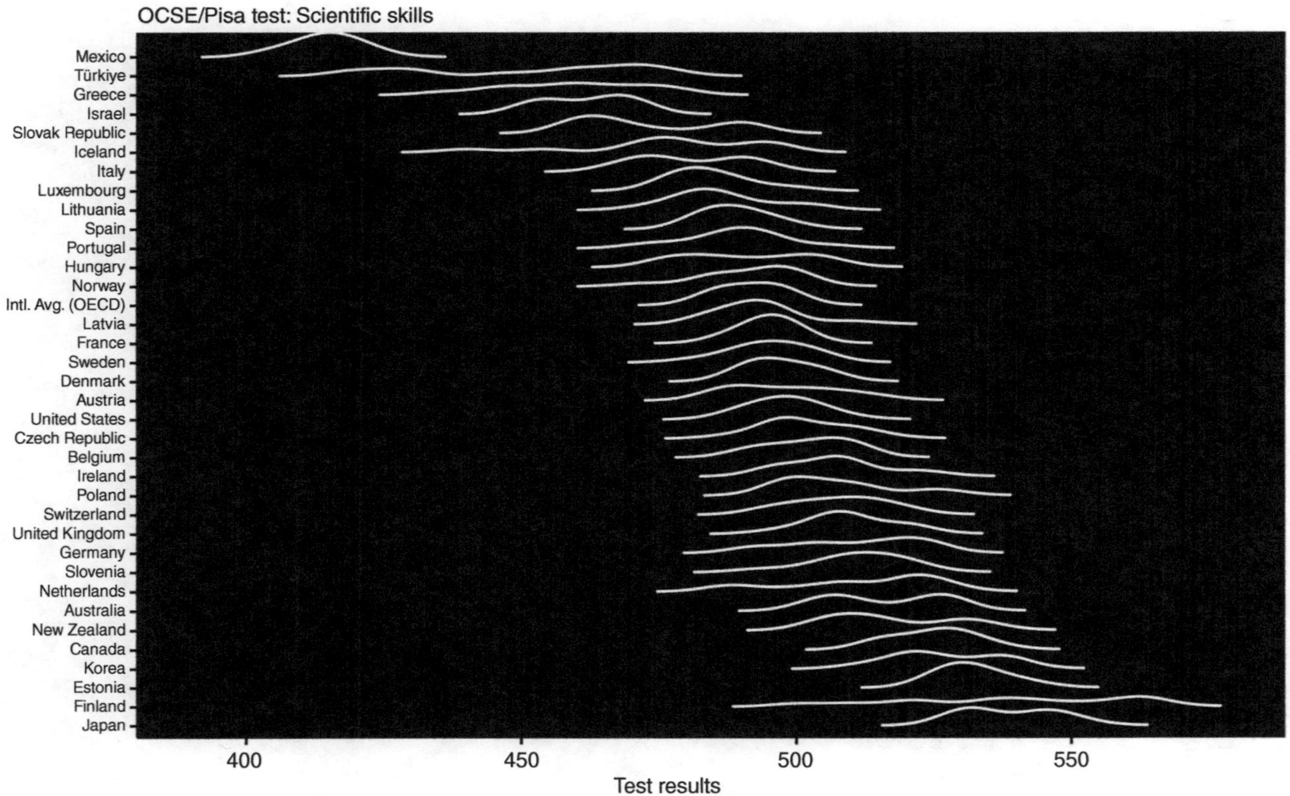

Figure 10.5. Ridgeline plot, OECD-Pisa tests, custom order based on arithmetic mean of test results, Scientific skills, a tribute to pulsar CP1919 and Joy Division.

- The background color: `theme(panel.background=element_rect(fill="black"), axis.text.x=element_text(vjust = 1.5))`.

The excerpt of code shows only the more relevant differences with respect to previous plots.

```
...
  geom_density_ridges(fill="black", color="white", size=0.5,
                      scale = 1.5, rel_min_height = 0.005) +
  labs(...) +
  theme_clean() +
  theme(panel.grid.major.y= element_blank(),
        legend.position= 'none')+
  theme(axis.text.x= element_text(size=8, vjust=6, hjust= .75))+
  theme(panel.background= element_rect(fill= "black"),
        plot.background= element_rect(color='white')
        axis.text.x= element_text(vjust= 1.5))
```

11

Heatmaps

Heatmaps are a type of graphic that is usually easy to produce and could be aesthetically pleasant and effective to convey information in an intuitive way. In practice, what a heatmap shows is a color-based representation of a data frame in rectangular form, with two categorical variables associated to the sides of the heatmap (corresponding to the Cartesian axes), and a third variable, either continuous or categorical, whose values are converted into a color scale. The idea is that, through the color representation, an observer could easily and intuitively grasp the values of the third variable corresponding to the two variables on the axes. The information conveyed by a heatmap is largely qualitative, the color scale usually has quantitative values but, especially with a continuous gradient, the exact value associated to a certain hue is difficult to determine, so what an observer gets is often a broad approximation of the real value. Therefore, with respect to the corresponding data frame, a heatmap is certainly less precise but it gains in simplicity for an observer to get the informational content. In addition to this, heatmaps, being colorful and with their regular structure, are well-adapted to be used in creative ways and combined with different graphical elements.

Dataset

In this chapter, we make use again of data from *Bicycle thefts in Berlin* (transl. Fahrraddiebstahl in Berlin) from the Municipality of Berlin, Germany, Berlin Open Data, previously introduced.

11.1 R: ggplot

We have not yet used the dataset of bike thefts in Berlin with R, so it is worth reminding that, as previously discussed, this case study has some subtleties to

Data Visualization in R and Python, First Edition. Marco Cremonini.

Companion website: www.wiley.com/go/Cremonini/DataVisualization1e

consider when the translated version, from German to English, is used. Problems could arise due to incoherent date formats deriving from intrinsic limitations of automatic translation tools, which suggests caution when dealing with dates. The *Additional Online Material*, in the section dedicated to violin plots (Chapter 7), provides the details of this case and all Python data-wrangling operations to correctly set up the data frame for visualization. The same *Additional Online Material*, in the section dedicated to this chapter on heatmaps, summarizes the same operations for R. Those data-wrangling operations do not present any particular difficulty; however, the subtleties and the logic should be clear in order to fully grasp their meaning.

Here we start with the modified English dataset correctly set up with coherent dates. We read it and adjusted some column names to work more swiftly on them. Then, we aggregate bike values and number of bikes stolen with respect to months and hours of the theft.

```
df= read_csv("datasets/Berlin_open_data/
              Fahrraddiebstahl_12_2022_EN_MOD.csv")

newNames <- c(START_DATE = 'DEED TIME_START_DATE',
              END_DATE = 'DEED TIME_END_DATE',
              START_HOUR = 'TIME_START_HOUR',
              DATE = 'CREATED_AM')
df <- rename(df, all_of(newNames))

bikesR= group_by(df, month(DATE, label=TRUE,
                     abbr=FALSE),
             START_HOUR) %>%
      summarize(TOT_DMG= sum(DAMAGES), NUM= n()) %>%
      rename(MONTH = 1)

# A tibble: 288 × 4
# Groups:   MONTH [12]
   MONTH        START_HOUR TOT_DMG   NUM
   <ord>             <dbl>   <dbl> <int>
 1 January               0   28696    29
 2 January               1    7746    13
 3 January               2    8255    11
 4 January               3    8328    11
 5 January               4    6073     6
# … with 283 more rows
```

Let us check the data type of column *MONTH*, it is of *factor* type with values correctly ordered (we have assumed to have already sorted it based on the external ordered list with month names, as seen in previous chapters).

```
class(bikesR$MONTH)
[1] "ordered" "factor"
```

ggplot offers a basic support for heatmaps with functions `geom_tile()` and `geom_rect()`, very similar, and `geom_raster()`, more efficient in some specific cases (i.e. same-size tiles). Different from Seaborn, as we will see, which requires the data frame in rectangular form (i.e. wide form), *ggplot* functions work on data frames in *long form*, namely they require three columns respectively for data corresponding to the *x*-axis, the *y*-axis, and the color scale. Knowing this, we could create our first heatmap, with the caveat that looking at the result we should remember that the dataset has incomplete values for December, which is certainly underestimated (Figure 11.1).

```
bikesR %>% ggplot(aes(x=START_HOUR, y=MONTH)) +
  geom_tile(aes(fill=NUM))+
  scale_x_continuous(breaks= c(0,2,4,6,8,10,12,14,16,18,20,22))+
  labs(x= "Hour of day", y= "", fill="Bikes\nstolen") +
  theme_clean()+
  theme(axis.text = element_text(size= 14),
        axis.title = element_text(size= 14))
```

We can produce a second heatmap improving the visual presentation and with some better-crafted elements, such as reversing the ordering of values on the *y*-axis

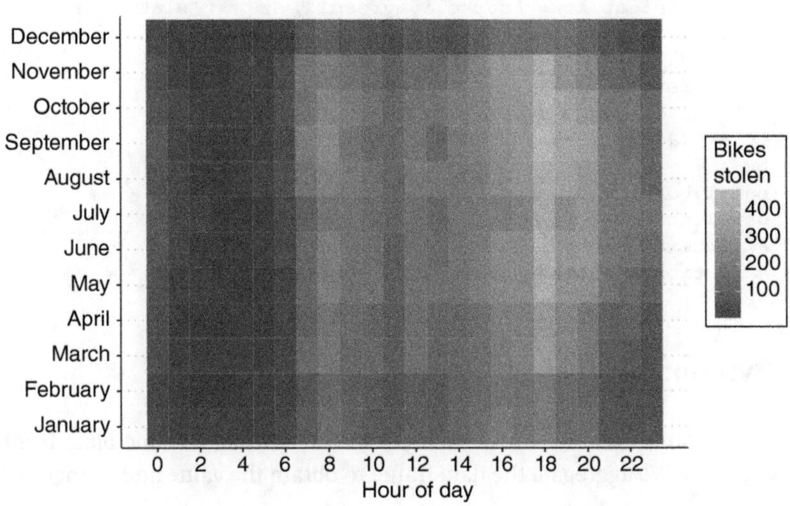

Figure 11.1 Heatmap, bike thefts in Berlin for months and hours of day.

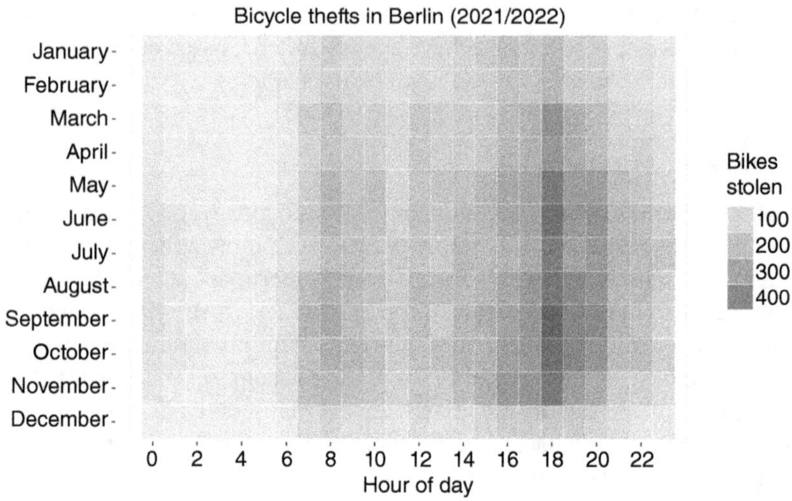

Figure 11.2 Heatmap, bike thefts in Berlin for months and hours and style elements.

through directive `scale_y_discrete(limits=rev)` and some other tweaks (Figure 11.2).

```
min_lim= min(bikesR$NUM)
max_lim= max(bikesR$NUM)

bikesR %>% ggplot(aes(x=START_HOUR, y=MONTH)) +
  geom_tile(aes(fill= NUM), color= "white") +
  scale_fill_gradient(low= "darkolivegreen1", high= "slateblue4",
          limits= c(min_lim, max_lim),
          guide= guide_legend(title="Bikes\nstolen")) +
  scale_y_discrete(limits= rev) +
  labs(x= "Hour of day", y= "",
       title= "Bicycle thefts in Berlin (2021/2022)") +
  theme_bw() +
  theme(panel.border= element_blank(),
        panel.grid.major= element_blank(),
        axis.text= element_text(size=12),
        axis.title= element_text(face='bold'))
```

11.2 Python: Seaborn

We still use the same dataset of bike thefts in Berlin with data frame *bikes* from previous chapters. We aggregate the data frame to obtain the value and number of bikes stolen for each month and hour of day. First, we rename some columns for simplicity.

```
bikes.columns= ['DATE','START_DATE','START_HOUR',
                'END_DATE','END_HOUR','LOR','DAMAGES',
                'EXPERIMENT','TYPE_OF_BICYCLE',
                'OFFENSE', 'DETECTION']


bikes2= bikes.groupby([bikes['DATE'].dt.month_name(),
                       'START_HOUR'])\
       ['DAMAGES'].agg(TOT_DMG= 'sum', NUM= 'count').\
       reset_index()
```

Now we want to correctly sort the new data frame *bikes2* with respect to month names. We need to employ the known technique based on an external list. Here we show a tiny variant, deriving the month list instead of manually writing it.

```
monthList= pd.date_range(
                start='2022-01-01',
                end='2022-12-01', freq='MS')
monthName=
    monthList.map(lambda x: x.month_name()).to_list()


bikes2.DATE= pd.Categorical(bikes2.DATE,
    categories= monthName, ordered= True)


bikes2.sort_values('DATE', inplace= True)
```

To generate a heatmap, Seaborn requires having the data frame in *rectangular form* with an *index* composed of a *single level*, meaning we need data in the wide format. The resulting heatmap will have, on the *y*-axis, the values of the index, and as values corresponding to the *x*-axis, the column names. Tiles of the heatmap will be colored according to values of elements of the rectangular data frame. If the explanation sounds not easy to understand, there is a better way to say it: look at the data frame in rectangular form, the Seaborn heatmap is exactly its translation into a colorful rectangular graphic.

For the example, we transform data frame *bikes2* into wide form by using column *START_HOUR* for new column names and the number of bikes stolen for values.

```
bikes_wide= pd.pivot_table(bikes2, values= 'NUM',
              index= 'DATE', columns= 'START_HOUR')
```

START_HOUR DATE	0	1	2	3	...	21	22	23
January	29	13	11	11	...	69	65	53
February	28	10	3	5	...	76	64	49
March	50	18	15	10	...	108	95	58
April	47	21	14	9	...	118	124	75
May	58	23	29	14	...	189	157	105
June	79	51	24	13	...	211	195	146
July	88	47	37	15	...	218	206	173
August	72	51	19	19	...	212	215	131
September	88	42	29	18	...	222	184	123
October	67	51	19	18	...	204	202	130
November	54	25	15	14	...	136	127	79
December	23	14	9	4	...	72	46	31

Now that we have the data frame in rectangular form, the Seaborn heatmap is very easy to produce with function `sns.heatmap()`, we just need to select a color palette, as we wish; a few style options have been applied (Figure 11.3)

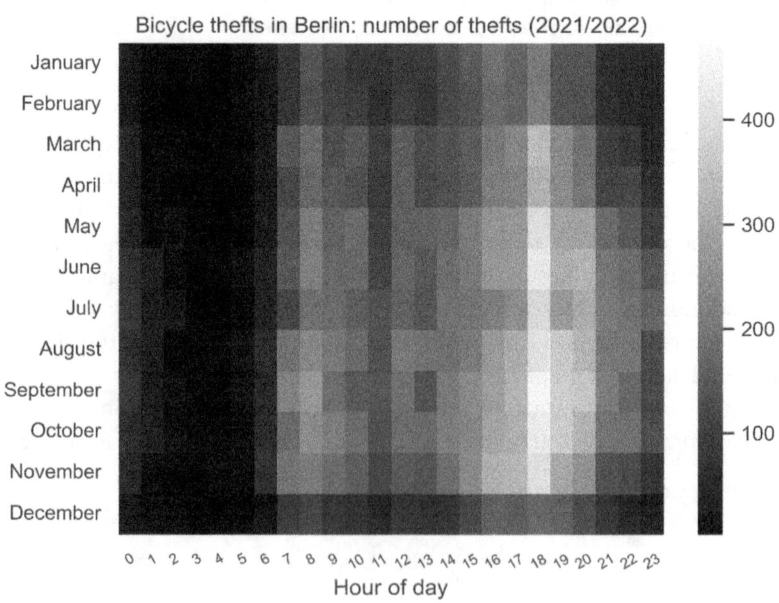

Figure 11.3 Heatmap, number of bike thefts in Berlin for months and hours.

```
sns.set_theme(style="white")

g= sns.heatmap(bici_wide, cmap="mako", ax=ax)

g.xaxis.set_tick_params(labelsize=8, rotation=30)
plt.xlabel("Hour of day")
plt.ylabel("")
plt.title("Bicycle thefts in Berlin: number of thefts (2021/2022)")
plt.tight_layout()
```

We can repeat it, this time by using bikes value for the wide form transformation (Figure 11.4).

```
bikes_wide2= pd.pivot_table(bikes2, values= 'TOT_DMG',
                            index= 'DATE',
                            columns= 'START_HOUR')

sns.set_theme(style="white")

g= sns.heatmap(bici_wide, cmap="cubehelix")

g.xaxis.set_tick_params(labelsize=8, rotation=30)
plt.xlabel("Hour of day")
plt.ylabel("")
plt.title("Bicycle thefts in Berlin: bikes value (2021/2022)")
plt.tight_layout()
```

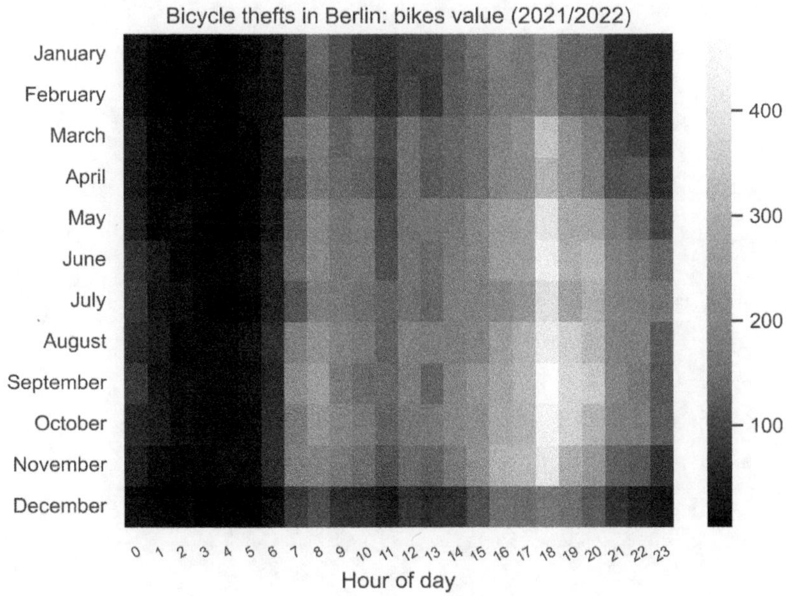

Figure 11.4 Heatmap, value of stolen bikes in Berlin for months and hours.

12

Marginals and Plots Alignment

So-called *marginals* are a family of graphics made by the combination of different plots with a main one presented in the central position and one or two others associated to the *x* and *y* axes. For example, we may have a scatterplot as the main graphic and histograms, density plots, or boxplots associated to the axes. Several other variants are possible.

Dataset

In this chapter, we make use again of data from *Bicycle thefts in Berlin* (transl. Fahrraddiebstahl in Berlin) from the Municipality of Berlin, Germany, Berlin Open Data, previously introduced.

12.1 R: ggplot

Dataset read and change of column names are the same as already shown before, here omitted. We aggregate values for year, month, and bike type, calculating bike values, and number of stolen bikes.

```
bikesR= group_by(df,
                 year(DATE),
                 month(DATE, label=TRUE, abbr=FALSE),
                 TYPE_OF_BICYCLE) %>%
        summarize(TOT_DMG= sum(DAMAGES), NUM =n()) %>%
        rename(YEAR = 1, MONTH_CREATED = 2)
```

12.1.1 Marginal

Features to produce *marginal* graphics are offered by package *ggExtra* with function `ggMarginal()`.

Data Visualization in R and Python, First Edition. Marco Cremonini.

Companion website: www.wiley.com/go/Cremonini/DataVisualization1e

We create a first simple example by defining a scatterplot with some style elements and assigning it to variable *p*. For convenience, we omit the two bike types with the lowest number of thefts and plot the number of thefts with respect to the average value of stolen bikes for bike type. We add also *shape* as an aesthetic to observe the effect on black and white support, as is the paper edition of the book. Function `scale_color_brewer()` permits to select a color palette among those defined by *Color Brewer*.

```
library(ggExtra)
library(ggthemes)

filter(bikesR, TYPE_OF_BICYCLE!="children's bike",
                TYPE_OF_BICYCLE!='mountain bike') %>%
  ggplot(aes(x= NUM , y= TOT_DMG/NUM)) +
  geom_point(aes(color=TYPE_OF_BICYCLE, shape=TYPE_OF_BICYCLE),
             alpha=0.8, size=3)+
  scale_color_brewer(palette = 'Paired')+
  labs(
    x="Number of stolen bikes x month",
    y="Average bike value",
    color="Bike type", shape="Bike type"
  ) +
  theme_hc() + theme(legend.position = "left") -> p
```

Following this, we specify the graphic type to add as *marginal*. We chose a *histogram* with 20 bins. The first attribute is variable *p1* with the scatterplot just defined. As it could be seen from Figure 12.1, histograms on the axes show the distribution of corresponding axis *x* and axis *y* values, shapes, when not too cluttered, help to distinguish categories when colors are not clearly discernible.

```
ggMarginal(p,
  type= "histogram",
  fill= "lightblue",
  xparams= list(bins=20))
```

12.1.2 Plots Alignment

In order to see the marginal variants with *boxplots* and *density plots*, we introduce a new possibility to define the layout of the result that would permit to align different plots in different ways. Several solutions exist for that feature, with different degrees of difficulty. Previously, we already saw an example by using packet *patchwork*, which is the easiest, but unfortunately does not support graphical objects produced with *ggMarginal* and cannot be fine-tuned. We present one of the most flexible solutions for plot alignment provided by package *gridExtra*.

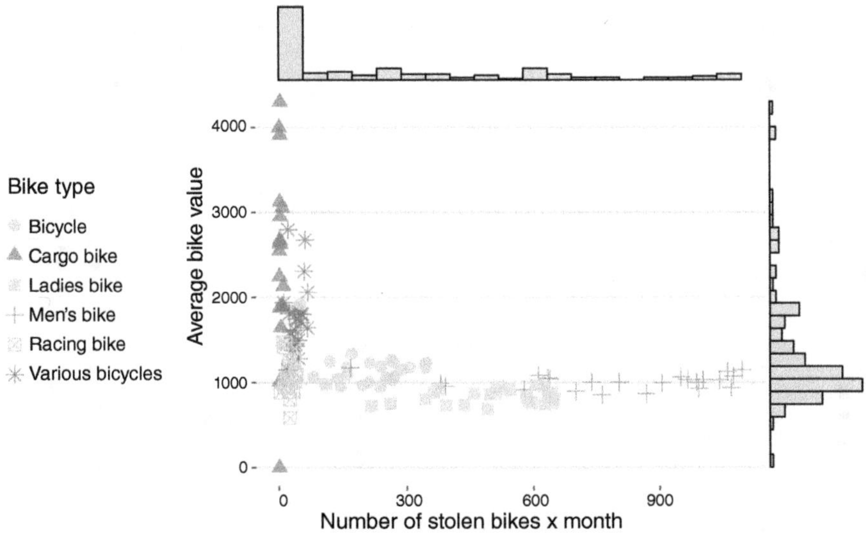

Figure 12.1 Marginal with scatterplot and histograms, bike thefts in Berlin (2021–2022).

With *gridExtra*, it is possible to create complex layouts with different graphical objects and images. Here, we use it in a simple way, just to vertically align three plots: the one created in *p1* and two variants. The main function is `grid.arrange()`, which lets specify the number of rows (attribute `nrow`) and columns (attribute `ncol`) of the grid. The creation of ggplot object *p* is identical to the previous example and is omitted. Figure 12.2 shows the result.

```
library(gridExtra)

... -> p


p1 <- ggMarginal(p, type= "histogram",
                 fill= "lightblue",
                 xparams= list(bins=20))
p2 <- ggMarginal(p, type= "boxplot",)
p3 <- ggMarginal(p, type= "density")

grid.arrange(p1, p2, p3, ncol=1)
```

More elaborate alignments and the tuning of fine details, such as to have a single legend, might require solutions that could be surprisingly overly complicated.

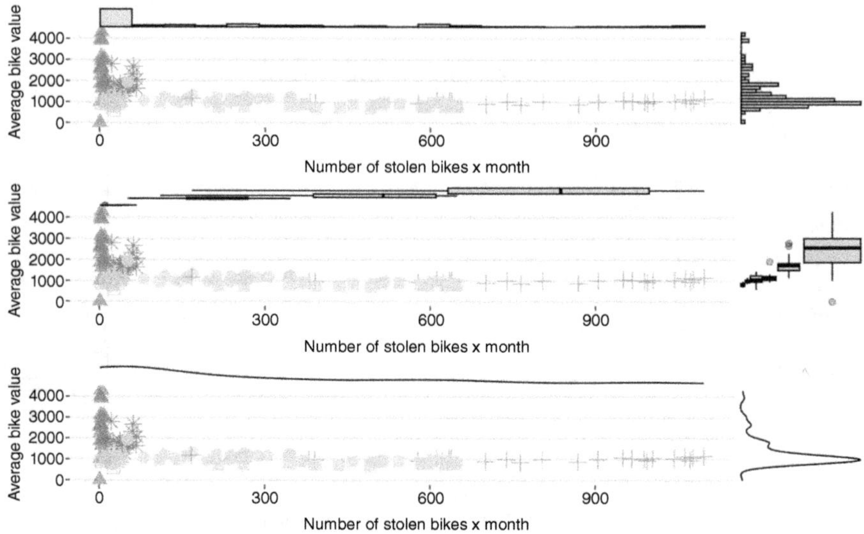

Figure 12.2 Plots aligned in a vertical grid, marginals, bike thefts in Berlin (2021–2022).

12.1.3 Rug Plot

A *rug plot* is a kind of density plot that, instead of density curves, shows small segments, whose density represents the density of data points. It is not a particularly relevant type of graphics, but its visual effect could be agreeable in some cases.

To create a rug plot, there exists function `geom_rug()`. Usage is simple and rug plots could be added as marginals as we have seen in previous examples. In the following example, we add some style options: we move the rug plot right-top (attribute `sides`) and external with respect to the axes (attribute `outside`). Function `coord_cartesian()` with attribute `clip='off'` adds a stylistic variant by hiding the Cartesian axes. Like for the previous example, the creation of ggplot object *p* is omitted, being the same as described in Figure 12.1. The result is shown in Figure 12.3.

```
... -> p

p + geom_rug(length = unit(0.1, "npc"), sides="rt",
             linewidth= 0.1, alpha= 1/2, outside= TRUE)+
  coord_cartesian(clip = "off") +
  theme(plot.margin = margin(1, 1, 1, 1, "cm"))
```

We change graphic type and present another variant, a little more imaginative. We use hours of day as the variable for the *y*-axis, hence a categorical variable, the number of stolen bikes for axis *x*, and bike types for *color* aesthetic, meaning

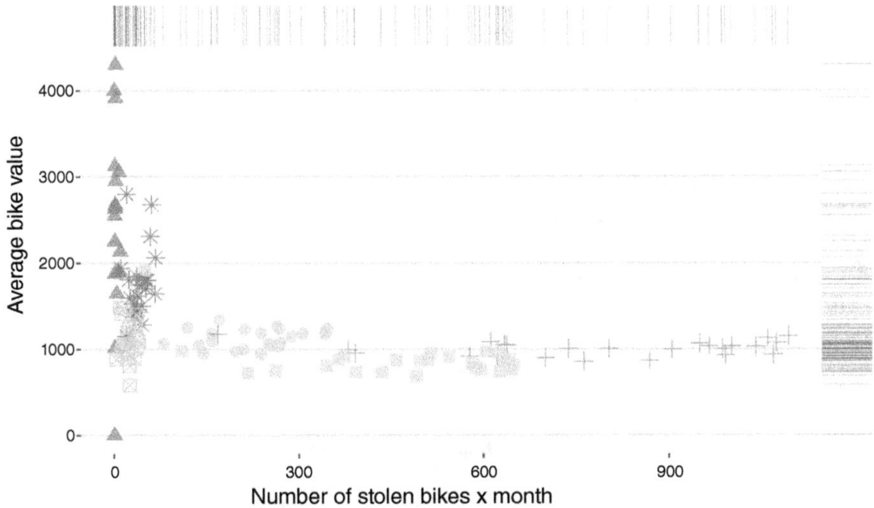

Figure 12.3 Marginal with scatterplot and rug plots, bike thefts in Berlin (2021–2022).

that we will have a categorical scatterplot horizontally oriented. With function `pretty_breaks()` of package *scales*, part of *tidyverse*, we could adapt ticks of the *x*-axis (e.g. ticks every 10 units). In this case, the same would not be correct for the *y*-axis too, because there we have hours, which should be exactly 24 for the day. The `pretty_breaks()` function, instead, tries to adjust ticks and we would end up with days of more or less than 24 hours. We add the rug plot as marginal for the *x*-axis placed on top, move the legend to the bottom, and define a color palette (Figure 12.4).

```
bike_types= c("ladies bike","men's bike","mountain bike")

filter(df_viz, TYPE_OF_BICYCLE %in% bike_types) %>%
  ggplot(aes(x= NUM , y= START_HOUR)) +
  geom_point(aes(color=TYPE_OF_BICYCLE), alpha=0.5, size=2.5)+
  scale_color_viridis_d()+
  scale_y_continuous(breaks = c(0,1,2,3,4,5,6,7,8,9,10,11,12,13,
                                14,15,16,17,18,19,20,21,22,23))+
  scale_x_continuous(breaks = scales::pretty_breaks(n = 10))+
  labs(
    x="Number of stolen bikes", y="Hour of day", color="Bike type"
  ) +
  geom_rug(aes(color=TYPE_OF_BICYCLE),
           length = unit(0.1, "npc"),
           outside = TRUE, sides = "t") +
  coord_cartesian(clip = "off") +
  theme_hc() + theme(legend.position = "bottom") +
  theme(plot.margin = margin(1, 1, 1, 1, "cm"),
        axis.text = element_text(size=8))
```

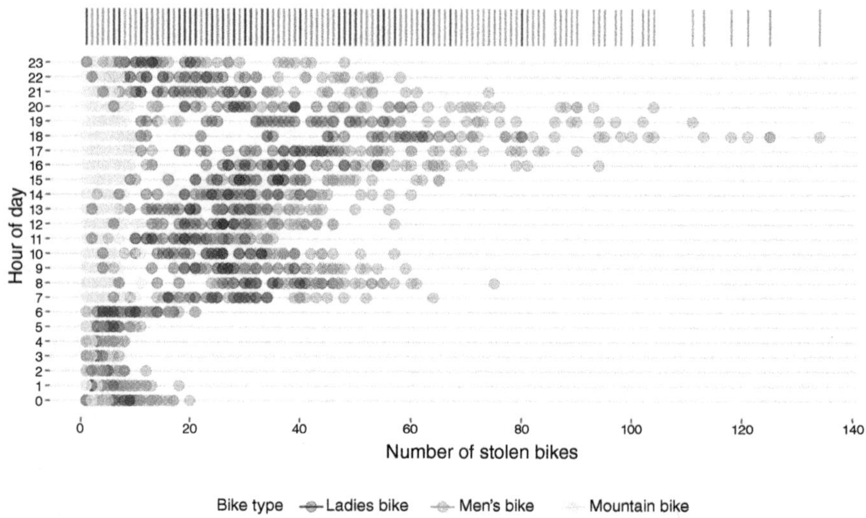

Figure 12.4 Marginal with categorical scatterplot and rug plot, number of stolen bikes in Berlin for hours and types of bikes (2021–2022).

12.2 Python: Seaborn

12.2.1 Subplots

With Python, we start from plot alignment, which requires the definition of *subplots*. The technique is derived from *matplotlib*, not native to Seaborn. Again, we omit the dataset read and column renaming. We aggregate for month and bike type.

```
bikes2= bikes.groupby([bikes['DATE'].dt.month_name(),
                        'TYPE_OF_BICYCLE'])['DAMAGES'].\
        agg(TOT_DMG= 'sum', NUM= 'count').\
        reset_index()
```

We create two *subplots*, respectively, with a *scatterplot* and a *boxplot*, and add few style elements. To do this, we need to define the number of subplots (`plt.subplots(1, 2,...)`) and possibly their relative proportion; in this case, the first will have a length three times the second (`gridspec_kw=dict (width_ratios=[3,1])`). Variable *ax* is a vector whose elements *ax[0]* and *ax[1]* correspond to the first and the second subplot.

```
sns.set_theme(style="white")


f, ax = plt.subplots(1, 2, figsize=(7, 4),
            gridspec_kw= dict(width_ratios= [3,1]))
```

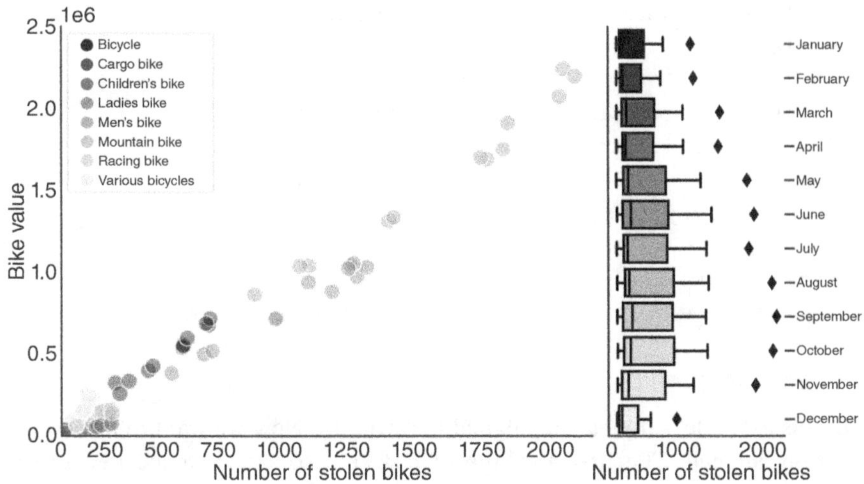

Figure 12.5 Subplots, a scatter plot and a boxplot horizontally aligned, stolen bikes in Berlin (2021/2022).

Now we can draw the two graphics corresponding to the subplots, respectively, a scatterplot for the first one and a boxplot for the second.

The two subplots associated to *ax[0]* and *ax[1]* could be configured separately in their elements, such as the limits of the scales and the visualization of the legend (Figure 12.5).

```
sns.scatterplot(data= bikes2, y= "TOT_DMG",
                x= "NUM", hue= "TYPE_OF_BICYCLE",
                s=80, alpha=.6, legend=True,
                palette="cubehelix", ax= ax[0])

sns.boxplot(data= bici2, y= "CREATED_AM", x= 'NUM',
            palette="cubehelix", ax= ax[1])

# Style elements

ax[0].set(
    xlim=(0, 2200), ylim=(0, 2.5e+06),
    xlabel='Number of bikes (month)',
    ylabel='Value (month)',
)
ax[0].legend()

ax[1].set(
```

```
    xlabel=' Number of bikes (month)',
    ylabel="
)
ax[1].yaxis.set_label_position("right")
ax[1].yaxis.tick_right()

# Despine subplots

for ax in ax.flat:
  sns.despine(bottom=False, left=False, ax=ax)

f.tight_layout()
```

In this example, subplots are aligned horizontally. Now we want to have them vertically aligned. The first attribute of `plt.subplot()` is associated to the *rows* of the subplot grid, so we set it to 2. The second attribute is associated to the *columns* of the subplot grid, 1 is the default and could be omitted. This time we should specify the relative proportion between subplot heights, which in this case will be that the second one should be three times the height of the second (`height_ratios=[1,3]`). The remaining part is the same as the previous example with *ax[0]* and *ax[1]* associated to the first and second subplots (the same code is omitted). Figure 12.6 shows the result.

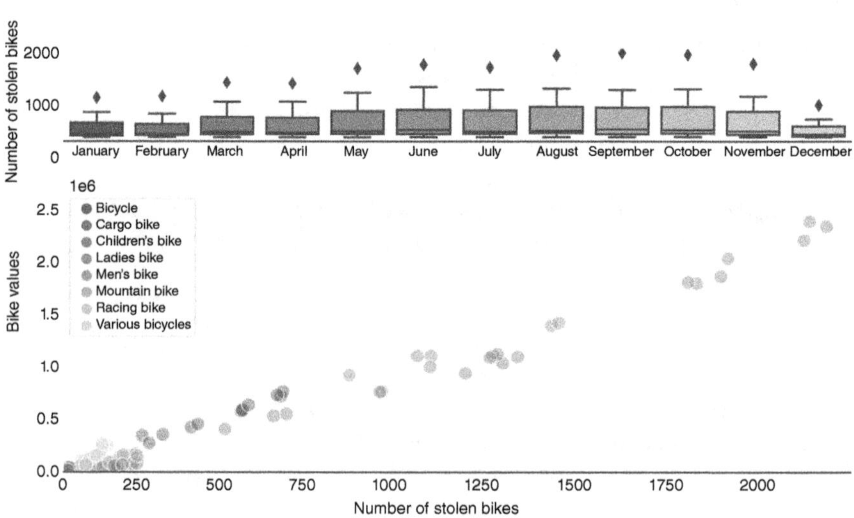

Figure 12.6 Subplots, a scatter plot and a boxplot vertically aligned, stolen bikes in Berlin (2021–2022).

```
sns.set_theme(style="white")

f, ax = plt.subplots(2, figsize=(8, 4),
          gridspec_kw= dict(height_ratios= [1,3]))
...
# Despine subplots

for ax in ax.flat:
  sns.despine(bottom=False, left=True, top=True, right=True, ax=ax)
```

12.2.2 Marginals: Joint Plot

We consider marginals in Seaborn by still using data frame *bikes2*. Different from ggplot, Seaborn natively implements marginals in two forms, respectively, called *Joint plot* and *Joint grid*. We start with the first one and show a simple example. The Seaborn function to use is `sns.jointplot()`. It works in a simplified way, the marginal type of graphic is automatically selected according to a simple rule: if the main graphic does not use attribute `hue`, then *histograms* are placed on axes as marginals, otherwise, if the main graphics does use the `hue` attribute, then *density plots* are placed on the axes.

We produce the joint plot with some style elements. Since we will use the `hue` attribute, we expect to see density plots as marginals. The legend is placed with a *matplotlib* directive (Figure 12.7).

```
sns.set_theme(style="ticks")

g= sns.jointplot(data= bici2, y= "TOT_DMG", x= "NUM",
          hue= "TYPE_OF_BICYCLE",
          ratio=3, alpha=0.7, palette='inferno',
          s=100, kind= "scatter")

# limits of axes values
g.ax_marg_x.set_xlim(0, 2200)
g.ax_marg_y.set_ylim(0,2.5e+06)

g.ax_joint.legend_._visible= False
g.fig.legend(bbox_to_anchor= (1.0, 1.0), loc=1)
plt.ylabel("Bike values")
plt.xlabel("Number of stolen bikes")
```

12.2.3 Marginals: Joint Grid

The *Joint grid* is the extended version of the Joint plot, which specifies explicitly the configuration. The logic is similar to what we have seen for facets, whose

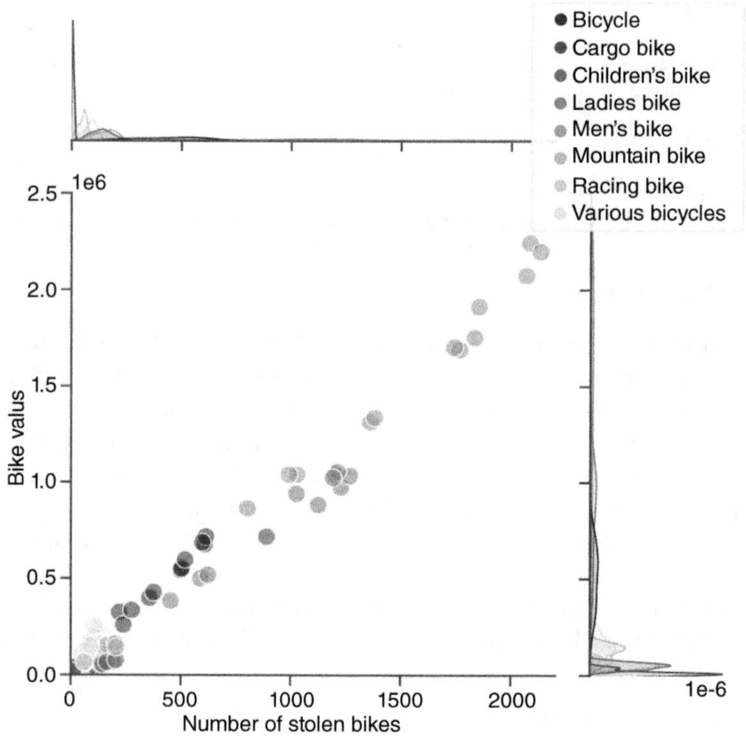

Figure 12.7 Joint plot with density plots as marginals, stolen bikes in Berlin (2021–2022).

general approach combines functions `FacetGrid()` with `map()`, the first to define general attributes and the facet grid, the second to associate to facets a specific graphic type.

For *Joint grid* graphics, it exists a similar approach that combines three functions:

- `JointGrid()` defines the grid for the main plot and the two marginals, and possibly additional graphical elements associated to variables.
- `plot_joint()` defines the type for the main plot and optional elements.
- `plot_marginals()` defines the type for marginals and optional elements.

This way a fine-grained control of the graphic is granted. We use the joint grid with a rug plot as marginals with function `sns.rugplot()`. Attribute `ratio` controls the size proportion between the main plot and marginals. Figure 12.8 shows the result.

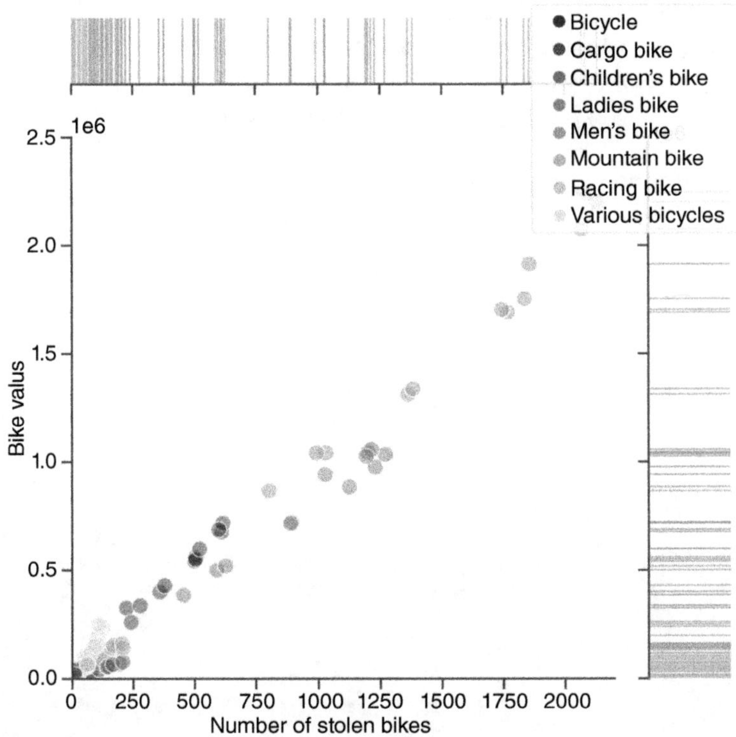

Figure 12.8 Joint grid with scatterplot and rug plots as marginals, stolen bikes in Berlin (2021–2022).

```
g= sns.JointGrid(data= bikes2,
                 y= "TOT_DMG", x= "NUM",
                 hue= "TYPE_OF_BICYCLE",
                 space=0, ratio=5)

# Main graphic
g.plot_joint(sns.scatterplot, s=80, alpha=.6,
             legend=True, palette= 'inferno')

# Marginals
g.plot_marginals(sns.rugplot, height=1,
                 color="teal", alpha=.8)

# Optional element for axes
```

```
g.ax_marg_x.set_xlim(0, 2200)
g.ax_marg_y.set_ylim(0, 2.5e+06)
g.set_axis_labels(xlabel='Number of stolen bikes',
                  ylabel='Bike values', fontsize=12)

g.ax_joint.legend_._visible= False
g.fig.legend(bbox_to_anchor=(1.0, 1.0), loc=1)
```

13

Correlation Graphics and Cluster Maps

C*orrelation graphics* are a family of graphics aimed at showing the possible statistical correlation between variables. With respect to case studies discussed in previous sections, for instance, we may want to know which is the correlation between the hour of day or the month with bike thefts in Berlin. From the statistical *correlation index* is then possible to analyze the possible cause–effect relationship between two variables. For example, is it true that thefts happen more frequently in certain hours of the day or in certain months? Intuitively we might be tempted to answer positively, but intuition often fails us when correlation is inquired and it is not rare to end up misleading pure chance with causality or imagining a direct correlation between two events when instead they are correlated with a third one (e.g., seasonal phenomena), somehow hidden or ignored.

Data science and statistics have a long history of mistakes of this sort, seeing correlation where there is none because finding causes for an effect is a desire deeply buried into the human nature or, sometimes, just the most convenient answer. For this reason, when analyzing data, one should be conscious of this always looming risk and proceed with extreme caution before stating the presence of causality. Data visualization, as a language for communicating knowledge from data, could also easily mislead an observer, either inadvertently or due to voluntary manipulations, into the belief that a certain graphic demonstrates causation. It is almost never the truth, a graphic is not meant to demonstrate causation, it just reflects how data appear, not the reason why they appear that way. Finding meaning into data, like establishing causality between events, is only the result of a correct and insightful analysis, not of just a table with numerical values or a plot representing them. This is one of the most important lessons to keep in mind.

In the *Additional Online Material*, section *Correlation indexes, correlation analysis, and normality test*, a summary of the basic knowledge for correlation analysis is presented. That section is not intended to replace basic statistical training, widely available in print or online sources, just a short reminder of the importance of those competencies. Many readers of this book would certainly have them.

Data Visualization in R and Python, First Edition. Marco Cremonini.

Companion website: www.wiley.com/go/Cremonini/DataVisualization1e

Dataset

In this chapter, we make use again of data from *Bicycle thefts in Berlin* (trans. Fahrraddiebstahl in Berlin) from the Municipality of Berlin, Germany, Berlin Open Data, previously introduced.

13.1 R: ggplot

13.1.1 Cluster Map

We start with a graphic type that goes often under the name of *cluster map* and represents an extension of traditional heatmaps, enhancing them with graphical elements derived from *clusterization* methods, which are statistical methods aimed at grouping observations based on *similarity* or *correlation metrics.* The goal is to recognize which observations are more similar, with respect to a statistical criterion, and divide the sample into clusters of observations that are more alike with each other than with respect to all others. The information provided is that observations in the same cluster have something in common, which depends on the specific clusterization metric employed, more than what they have in common with respect to observations not belonging to the cluster.

Ggplot (up to version ggplot2 3.4.1, at least) does not natively support cluster maps, like instead, Seaborn does. Standard functionalities for R cluster maps are available in package *stats* through function `stats::heatmap()`. In addition to these base features, other custom solutions have been presented but, up to now, none seems to have reached a sufficient maturity level to be considered a reference solution. We will show examples with `stats::heatmap()`, which as data requires a *matrix with numerical values only.* A matrix is a tabular data representation, but it is not the same as a data frame, being a bare table of values of same type with row and column names, nothing more. Function `stats::heatmap()` creates a cluster map by using row and column names for axes x and y, and matrix values for the color scale of tiles.

We use again data frame *bikes* and, this time, we need to bring them into *wide* form. We choose column *START_HOUR* as values. We also add prefix *h* to hours to avoid backticks in column names.

```
bikes_wide= pivot_wider(bikes, id_cols=MONTH_CREATED,
                              names_from =START_HOUR,
                              names_prefix='h',
                              values_from= NUM)
```

```
   MONTH           h0  h1  h2  h3  h4  h5  h6  ...
 1 January         29  13  11  11   6  16  35  ...
```

```
 2 February        28  10   3   5   8  22     34  ...
 3 March           50  18  15  10  11  18     38  ...
 4 April           47  21  14   9  10  15     39  ...
 5 May             58  23  29  14   8  16     42  ...
 6 June            79  51  24  13  16  32     61  ...
 7 July            88  47  37  15  12  23     57  ...
 8 August          72  51  19  19  24  37     75  ...
 9 September       88  42  29  18  21  34     62  ...
10 October         67  51  29  19  18  27     73  ...
11 November        54  25  15  14  23  23     71  ...
12 December        23  14   9   4   8   8     20  ...
```

Now the data frame is in *rectangular* form and has no missing values, this is the basis. Still, it is not sufficient, a matrix should have only values of same type, row and column names, and function `stats::heatmap()` requires numerical values only. Data frame *bikes_wide*, instead, has the alphanumeric column *MONTH* and has no row names. It should be further manipulated by transforming column *MONTH* into row names, then it could be converted into a matrix.

```
bikes_matrix  <- bikes_wide %>%
     remove_rownames() %>%
     column_to_rownames(var= 'MONTH')

bikes_matrix= as.matrix(bikes_matrix)
```

```
         h0 h1 h2 h3 h4 h5 h6  h7  h8  h9 h10 h11 h12 h13 h14 ...
January  29 13 11 11  6 16 35  89 144 110  87  82  97  95 124 ...
February 28 10  3  5  8 22 34  89 136 114 102  79 107  88 127 ...
March    50 18 15 10 11 18 38 152 193 137 152 109 168 135 146 ...
April    47 21 14  9 10 15 39 124 184 154 139 102 170 129 139 ...
May      58 23 29 14  8 16 42 146 232 176 192 112 173 174 183 ...
June     79 51 24 13 16 32 61 156 235 186 187 120 180 159 199 ...
...
```

Matrix *bikes_matrix* is correctly organized and could now be used with function `stats::heatmap()`, which is not a ggplot function, therefore it should be called prefixing `stats::` or explicitly loading the *stats* library. Attribute `scale` selects if values will be scaled (i.e., standardized) *by row* or *by column*, meaning that to each value the minimum row or column value is subtracted, and the result divided by the maximum row or column value.

Standardization with respect to a dimension (rows or columns) permits to show *relative variations of values with regard to the non-standardized dimension*. For example, if bike thefts are standardized (i.e., scaled) with respect to months, hence by row, we highlight relative variations of thefts among hours of day, independently from the seasonal variability of months. Vice versa, if bike thefts are scaled

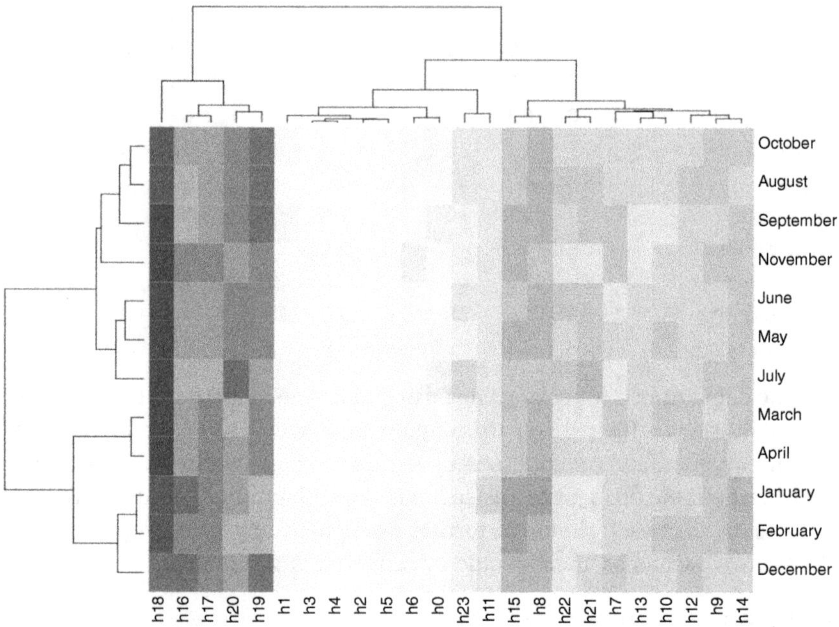

Figure 13.1 Cluster map, bike thefts in Berlin (2021–2022), values scaled by rows.

with respect to hours of day, hence by column, it is the relative variation of thefts among months to be highlighted, independently from the variability among hours of day.

Attribute `margins` control the visualization of values on the axes. In the following example, we *scale by row* (`scale='row'`), hence the color gradient is communicating relative variation among hours of the day (Figure 13.1).

```
stats::heatmap(bikes_matrix,
                    scale= 'row', margins= c(2,0))
```

The result is not just a simple heatmap as seen before but has statistical information about clusters of observations. The color scale communicates variations in the number of thefts (dark is the highest, light is the lowest), but it is the graphical element on the axes to inform us about clusters and how *columns*, in this case, since we have scaled by row, have been reordered. Hours have been reordered by respecting their similarity in terms of thefts along the whole year, for example, from 16:00 to 19:00 (i.e., columns *h16-h19*) they are similar, same between 00:00 and 06:00 (i.e., columns *h0-h6*), and the graphic on top of the cluster map shows the details. That type of graphics is called *dendrogram* and shows clusters at different levels, with lower levels representing the more similar clusters. So, for instance, looking at the lowest level of the dendrogram on top side, hours 19:00 and 20:00 are very similar, so are 16:00 and 17:00; moving to the upper level, we see that the two clusters 19:00 and 20:00 and 16:00 and 17:00 form a cluster together, meaning they are similar but somehow less similar than the clusters considered individually, moving up again we discover that the combination of clusters 19:00 and 20:00/16:00 and 17:00 is similar to 18:00 but yet somehow less so than the two separated. This is how a dendrogram is read, bottom-up.

The dendrogram on the left side shows clusters of rows (i.e., months) with the same logic explained for columns. In this case, we could have hints about similarity among months, but the color scale does not represent them. Let us try now to *scale by column* (Figure 13.2).

```
colors <- colorRampPalette(cividis(9,
                            direction = -1))(25)

stats::heatmap(test, scale = "col",
               margins = c(2,0), col=colors)
```

The color scale now shows relative variations of bike thefts among months (dark is the highest, light is the lowest), with dendrograms having the same meaning as

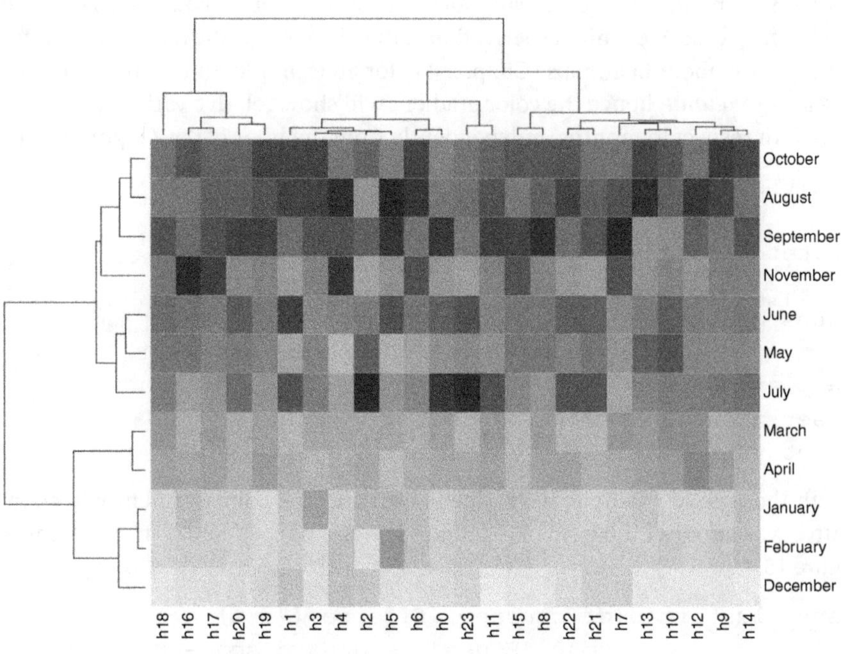

Figure 13.2 Cluster map, bike thefts in Berlin (2021–2022), values scaled by columns.

described in the previous example. In this case, scaling by hours (i.e. columns), differences among months look less marked than among hours of day shown in Figure 13.1, however, winter months have visibly less thefts, then they rise in spring, and in summer and autumn they do not exhibit large variability. Not truly surprising as a conclusion, but so is statistics that often is necessary to state what is common sense but in a methodologically sound way.

13.2 Python: Seaborn

13.2.1 Cluster Map

Cluster maps in Seaborn are natively supported as an extension of heatmaps through function `sns.clustermap()`. The usage requires package *scipy*. Let us consider the two base cases. Attribute `standard_scale` controls *standardization* (i.e., *scaling*), which could be produced *by row* (`standard_scale=0`) or *by column* (`standard_scale=1`). As already discussed in the previous section, standardization with respect to one dimension allows showing relative variation of values for the other dimension. The data frame used for function `sns.clustermap()` has the same requirement of data frames for Seaborn heatmaps, it should be in *rectangular form*, but should not be a matrix, as we have seen for the R case. We omit the derivation of that data frame; the reader could refer to the section about heatmaps (Chapter 11) for an example. In the first example, we scale by *column*, hence the color gradient will show relative variations of bike thefts with respect to months, independently from the hour of day (Figure 13.3).

```
import scipy

sns.set_theme(color_codes=True)

g= sns.clustermap(df_cluster, figsize= (7, 5),
                  cmap="Blues", standard_scale= 1)
ax= g.ax_heatmap
ax.set_xlabel("Hour")
ax.set_ylabel("")
```

With the second example, we scale by *row*, thus the color gradient will show relative variation of bike thefts among hours, independently from months (Figure 13.4).

```
g=sns.clustermap(df_cluster, figsize=(7, 5),
                 cmap="Blues", standard_scale=0)
ax = g.ax_heatmap
```

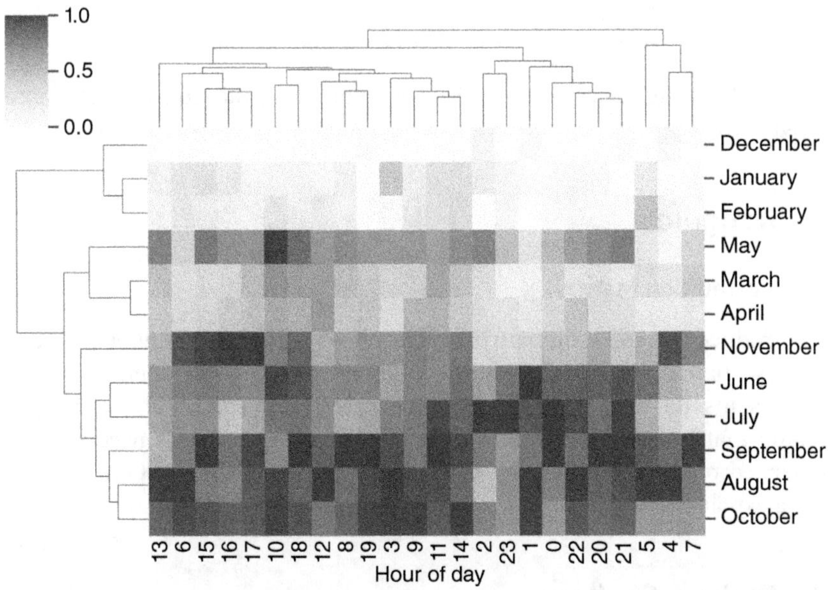

Figure 13.3 Cluster map, stolen bikes in Berlin (2021–2022), scaled by columns.

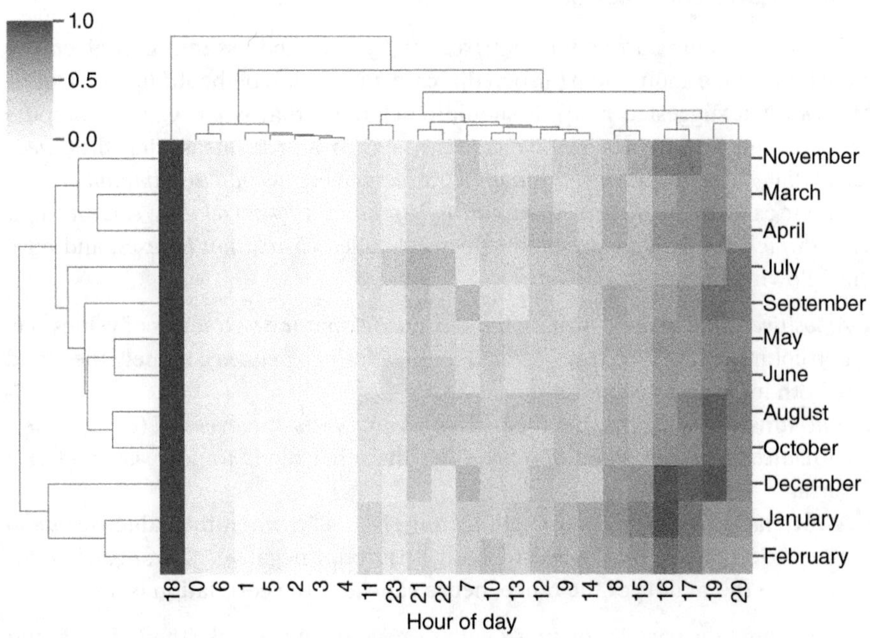

Figure 13.4 Cluster map, stolen bikes in Berlin (2021–2022), scaled by rows.

```
ax.set_xlabel("Hour")
ax.set_ylabel("")
```

Except for few differences, results of Seaborn cluster map are equivalent to those produced with R.

13.3 R: ggplot

13.3.1 Correlation Matrix

How to produce a correlation matrix in R is presented in the *Additional Online Material*, section *Correlation indexes, correlation analysis, and normality test*, which presents the basic information to correctly interpret the meaning of correlation matrixes and correlation indexes, a knowledge that is necessary for any linear correlation analysis. We forward the reader to that section, without repeating explanations here.

13.4 Python: Seaborn

13.4.1 Correlation Matrix

Before introducing correlation matrixes for Python, and assuming as given the basic knowledge about them (also in this case, the section of the *Additional Online Material* is a suggested read), it should be clarified that what we will compute are so-called *Pearson correlation matrixes*, which aim at measuring the *linear correlation degree between continuous variables having normal distribution.*

In our case study, *a correlation matrix is produced by correlating columns of a data frame.* The single computed values are called *correlation indexes*, and have the following meaning:

- *A positive value* of the correlation index means that the two series of values (i.e. two columns) are *directly correlated* (or *positively correlated*), namely they tend to both increase or decrease.
- *A negative value* means that the two series are *inversely correlated* (or *negatively correlated*), namely when one increases the other tends to decrease, and vice versa.
- A correlation index is *a value in the range [−1, +1]*, when the value is *close to +1 or −1*, it means that the correlation, positive or negative, is *strong*, while for values in the middle of the range, hence *close to 0*, the correlation is *weak*.

To compute the correlation index with respect to hours of bike thefts, we should have the data frame in rectangular form with hours as columns and all columns defined as numeric. The row index produced by the wide form transformation should be dropped and the column index should have no name. We use data frame *bikes_wide* from the heatmap section of Chapter 11.

```
# The row index is dropped
bikes_corr= bikes_wide.reset_index(drop=True)

# The column index with no name
bikes_corr.rename_axis(None, axis=1, inplace=True)
```

	0	1	2	3	4	5	6		17	18	19	20	21	22	23
0	29	13	11	11	6	16	35	...	168	207	139	142	69	65	53
1	28	10	3	5	8	22	34	...	168	217	140	135	76	64	49
2	50	18	15	10	11	18	38	...	240	357	250	203	108	95	58
3	47	21	14	9	10	15	39	...	230	329	252	205	118	124	75
4	58	23	29	14	8	16	42	...	277	425	303	304	189	157	105
5	79	51	24	13	16	32	61	...	281	448	317	341	211	195	146
6	88	47	37	15	12	23	57	...	250	411	278	324	218	206	173
7	72	51	19	19	24	37	75	...	317	429	371	339	212	215	131
8	88	42	29	18	21	34	62	...	327	473	383	371	222	184	123
9	67	51	29	19	18	27	73	...	319	452	379	334	204	202	130
10	54	25	15	14	23	23	71	...	335	427	306	263	136	127	79
11	23	14	9	4	8	8	20	...	144	163	150	119	72	46	31

With the data frame correctly configured, we can create the correlation matrix. Correlation is among columns, therefore for N columns, the result will be a matrix N × N; here we have 24 hours, and it results in a 24 × 24 correlation matrix. The function is the standard `corr()`.

```
corrHour= bikes_corr.corr()
```

	0	1	2		21	22	23
0	1.000000	0.889854	0.874354	...	0.957273	0.935459	0.938598
1	0.889854	1.000000	0.761488	...	0.919318	0.948467	0.923206
2	0.874354	0.761488	1.000000	...	0.888029	0.841235	0.884983
...	...	...	...	...	...	...	...
21	0.957273	0.919318	0.888029	...	1.000000	0.976417	0.947220
22	0.935459	0.948467	0.841235	...	0.976417	1.000000	0.957711
23	0.938598	0.923206	0.884983	...	0.947220	0.957711	1.000000

The typical feature of a correlation matrix is to always have the *main diagonal with all values equal to +1* (being a series perfectly correlated with itself) and to be *specular* with respect to the diagonal (being the correlation between *series1* and *series2* the same that between *series2* and *series1*).

13.4.2 Diagonal Correlation Heatmap

With correlation matrixes, we need an appropriate visualization and Seaborn comes to help with *diagonal correlation heatmaps*, a smart adaptation of heatmaps that produces a *triangular heatmap*, because only half of a correlation matrix is necessary, the other half being just its specular image. The following code shows how to produce the diagonal correlation matrix with Seaborn function `sns.heatmap()`. Inline comments guide the comprehension. Figure 13.5 shows the result.

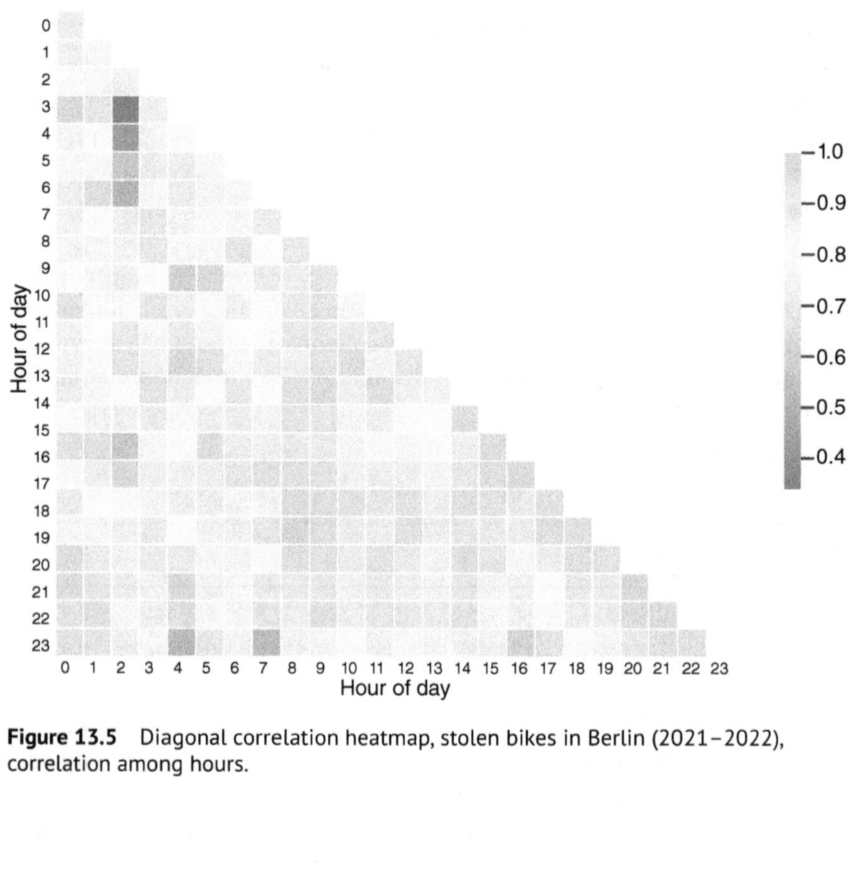

Figure 13.5 Diagonal correlation heatmap, stolen bikes in Berlin (2021–2022), correlation among hours.

```
sns.set(style="white", font_scale=0.7)

# Mask to omit the upper triangular half of the
# correlation matrix (values above the main diagonal)

mask= np.triu(np.ones_like(corrHour, dtype=bool))

# Divergent color palette

cmap= sns.diverging_palette(200, 20, as_cmap=True)

# Diagonal correlation heatmap, configured by setting the central
# value of the gradient with the approximate value of the
# mean of correlation indexes (0.7), manually calculated

g= sns.heatmap(corrHour, mask=mask, cmap=cmap, vmax=1.0,
            center=0.7, square=True, linewidths=.5,
            cbar_kws={"shrink": .5})

g.yaxis.set_tick_params(labelsize=8, rotation='auto')
g.set(xlabel='Hour of day', ylabel='Hour of day')
```

We repeat it by correlating *months*, rather than hours. Months are the rows of the data frame *bikes_corr* previously produced, we need them as columns, so we compute the *transpose*. Then we proceed in the same way just seen.

```
bikes_corrT= bikes_corr.T
corrMonth= bikes_corrT.corr()
```

	0	**1**	**2**		**9**	**10**	**11**
0	1.000000	0.992954	0.949250	...	0.944543	0.973583	0.965773
1	0.992954	1.000000	0.967423	...	0.954703	0.978279	0.964437
2	0.949250	0.967423	1.000000	...	0.971824	0.976873	0.964857
...	...	...	...	...	...	...	...
9	0.944543	0.954703	0.971824	...	1.000000	0.970778	0.964352
10	0.973583	0.978279	0.976873	...	0.970778	1.000000	0.984198
11	0.965773	0.964437	0.964857	...	0.964352	0.984198	1.000000

Now the correlation matrix is 12×12 and we can produce the diagonal correlation heatmap. Figure 13.6 shows the result, which still to improve a little, months are shown from 0 to 11 and the ordering on the y-axis would be better if reversed, just small tweaks.

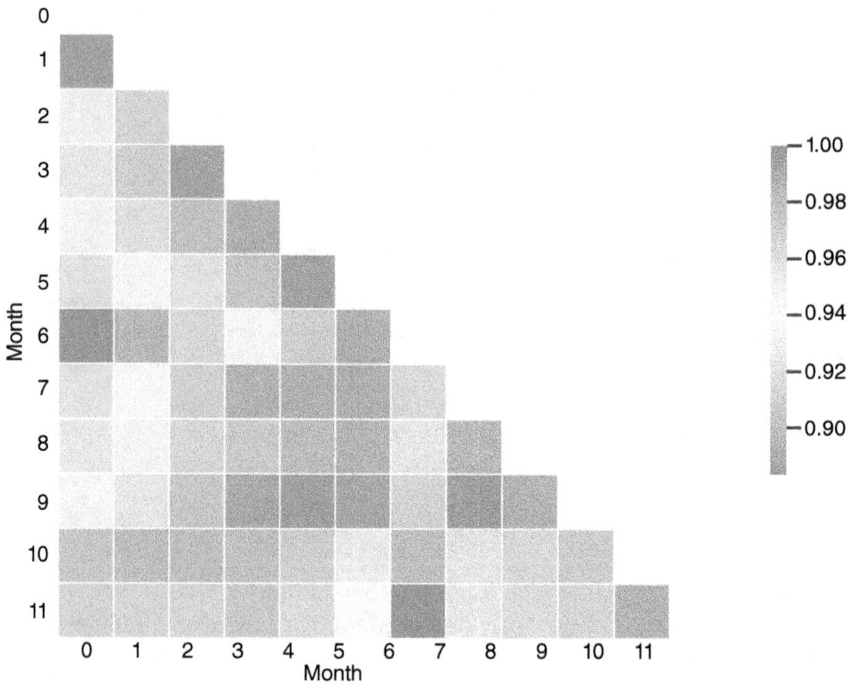

Figure 13.6 Diagonal correlation heatmap, stolen bikes in Berlin, correlation among months.

```
mask= np.triu(np.ones_like(corrT, dtype=bool))

cmap= sns.diverging_palette(200, 20, as_cmap=True)

sns.heatmap(corrMonth, mask=mask, cmap=cmap, vmax=1.0,
            center=0.94, square=True, linewidths=.5,
            cbar_kws={"shrink": .5})
```

13.4.3 Scatterplot Heatmap

Seaborn offers another interesting visualization for correlation matrixes, again as a smart variant of a traditional graphic. The idea is to use *a scatterplot as a heatmap* to represent a correlation matrix and it takes the name of *scatterplot heatmap*.

For the example, we use function `relplot()`, the general function for facet-ready plots supporting scatterplots. The logic we want to realize is to mimic a heatmap, so it should look rectangular (not triangular like the diagonal correlation heatmap) with scatterplot markers as heatmap tiles.

This graphic should be carefully crafted, being a peculiar adaptation of one type of graphic to simulate another one, in order to obtain an eye-catching and particularly pleasant visual effect. Let us delve into the details. Being a scatterplot, the reference format is the *long* form, not the wide one as for heatmaps, so we need to transform the previous correlation matrix into long form. We use data frame *corrHour*, with correlations among hours of day.

```
corrHour_Long= corrHour.stack().\
               reset_index(name= "correlation")
```

	level_0	level_1	correlation
0	0	0	1.000000
1	0	1	0.571533
2	0	2	0.512906
3	0	3	0.446323
4	0	4	0.279243
...	...	...	...
571	23	19	0.555608
572	23	20	0.682778
573	23	21	0.731613
574	23	22	0.811389
575	23	23	1.000000

Combinations of values from columns *level_0* and *level_1* correspond to all elements of the correlation matrix, while column *correlation* has correlation indexes. With the data frame in this form, we could imitate the heatmap. Directive `g.ax.invert_yaxis()` lets inverting the ordering on axis *y*, so to have the usual scales of Cartesian axes both increasing from the origin. Construct `for_artist in g.legend.legendHandles`, at the end of the script, is a little tweak that permits having markers in the legend with a colored border, like in the graphic. The script presents some inline comments to guide the comprehension. Figure 13.7 shows the result.

```
sns.set(style="white")

# Custom diverging color palette
ccolor=sns.diverging_palette(20, 220, l=55, s=90, center="light",
                             n=4, as_cmap=True)
```

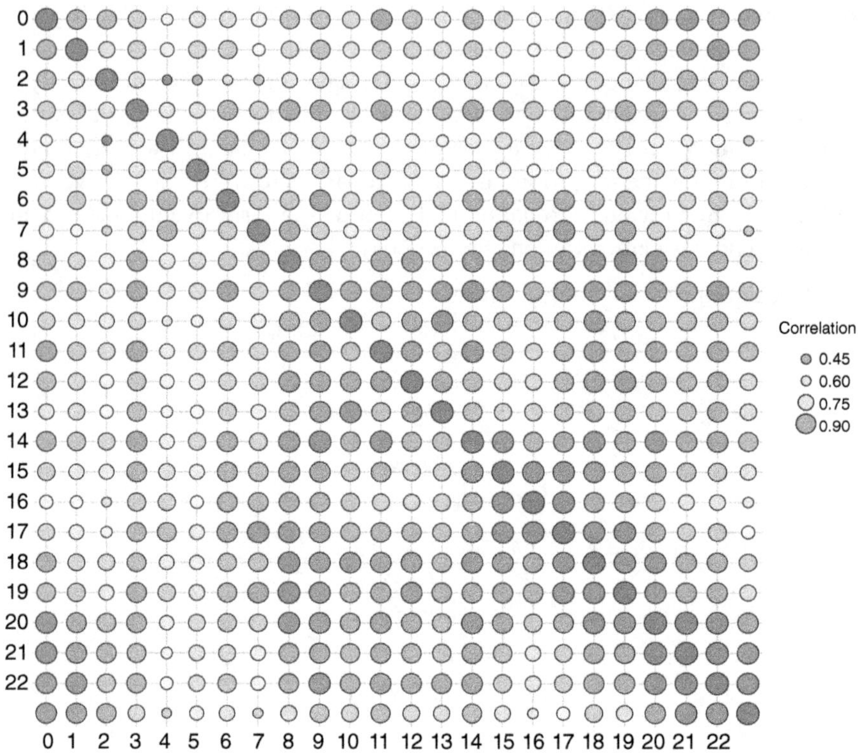

Figure 13.7 Scatterplot heatmap, stolen bikes in Berlin (2021–2022), correlation between hours (it is suggested to look at the colored version of this figure from the Additional Online Material for an optimal view of the many hues).

```
# Draw scatterplot markers by changing their size
# edgecolor is the marker's border
g = sns.relplot(
    data=corr_Long,
    x="level_0", y="level_1", hue="correlation", size="correlation",
    palette=ccolor, edgecolor="0.1",
    height=8, sizes=(50, 250), size_norm=(.50, 1.0),
)

# Invert y axis
g.ax.invert_yaxis()

# Style options
g.set(xlabel="", ylabel="", aspect="equal")
g.despine(left=True, bottom=True)
```

```
g.ax.xaxis.set_ticks(np.arange(0, 23, 1))
g.ax.yaxis.set_ticks(np.arange(0, 23, 1))
g.ax.margins(.02)

# Set border in legend keys like in scatterplot markers
for artist in g.legend.legendHandles:
    artist.set_edgecolor(".1")
g.tight_layout()
```

Part II

Interactive Graphics with Altair

With *Altair*, a Python-based graphical library, we enter into the realm of *interactive graphics* with graphics that take the form of HTML or JSON objects (other formats are available). We will still see some static graphics, similar to those presented in Part 1 of the book, because we need them as building blocks for interactive ones, however, the main interest now is not specifically on them but on the logic and mechanisms supporting the interactivity of those visual objects with actions performed by the observer. Hence, graphics become responsive to user's choices, they dynamically adapt through user's inputs, which may take different forms like mouse clicks and hovering, or gestures on the touchpad/touchscreen.

This novelty is not a small improvement over static graphics; instead, it is a true change of perspective. While static graphics still have roots in traditional schemas and diagrams, for some, those roots may look distant. Interactive graphics, being reactive and dynamic, cater to the web and offer a completely different user experience. It is no longer just a visual language for communicating information to passive observers, but an interactive association between visual objects and active observers involving actions and responses that should be imagined, designed, and developed since the beginning of a data visualization project. Interactivity is not just an add-on to static objects; it is the nature of these dynamic visual objects. Another important difference is that with interactive graphics, the connection with a print representation no longer exists, or it is extremely weak. On paper, we could only reproduce some screenshots of an interactive graphic, a poor approximation of the real experience. This difference, again, should not be minimized, they truly are artifacts for digital consumption, not for paper. Hence, by considering Altair is not just an exercise in learning another fancy graphical tool, but it is

Data Visualization in R and Python, First Edition. Marco Cremonini.

Companion website: www.wiley.com/go/Cremonini/DataVisualization1e

the means to enter a new dimension of data visualization, with a different context, relation with observers, and mode of thinking about visual objects.

More specifically, Altair is an evolved front end of *Vega-Lite* (https://vega.github.io/vega-lite/), a well-known library for interactive graphics with a syntax based on the grammar of graphics and JSON format. Being a front end, Altair masks the specifics of Vega-Lite with its own syntax, which is intuitive and should look familiar to the readers of this book. Sometimes it happens that some typical features of Vega-Lite become visible, but they are limited cases. In general, the graphical quality of Altair is excellent, and it adopts a clear and clean logic for producing the graphics and the associated interactive actions, a remarkable legacy from Vega-Lite.

14

Altair Interactive Plots

Dataset

Tourist/visitor arrivals and tourism expenditure, Open Data United Nations (http://data.un.org/). Tourist arrivals and expenditure for different countries and years.

Copyright: "All data and metadata provided on UNdata's website are available free of charge and may be copied freely, duplicated, and further distributed provided that UNdata is cited as the reference." (Terms and Conditions of use, http://data.un.org/Host.aspx?Content=UNdataUse).

Standard country or area codes for statistical use (M49) from the Statistics Division of the United Nations. Official denominations, codes, and information of countries (https://unstats.un.org/unsd/methodology/m49/overview/).

Copyright: Public domain

Crime at Sea: A Global Database of Maritime Pirate Attacks (1993–2020). Data regarding pirate attacks on sea between January 1993 and December 2020.

Source: Benden, P., Feng, A., Howell, C., & Dalla Riva, G. V. (2021). «Crime at Sea: A Global Database of Maritime Pirate Attacks (1993–2020)». *Journal of Open Humanities Data*, 7, 19. DOI: http://doi.org/10.5334/johd.39

Copyright: Creative Commons Attribution-ShareAlike 4.0 International License (CC BY-SA 4.0). (https://openhumanitiesdata.metajnl.com/article/10.5334/johd.39/, https://creativecommons.org/licenses/by-sa/4.0/)

Goods loaded worldwide from the United Nations Conference on Trade and Development (UNCTAD STAT). Data on products shipped on sea (billions of tons) (Handbook of Statistics 2022) (https://unctadstat.unctad.org/EN/Index.html).

Copyright: Creative Commons Attribution 3.0 IGO (CC BY 3.0 IGO) (https://unctadstat.unctad.org/UnctadStatMetadata/Documentation/UNCTAD_CreativeCommonsLicense3.0_IGO_EN.pdf, https://creativecommons.org/licenses/by/3.0/igo/)

Data Visualization in R and Python, First Edition. Marco Cremonini.

Companion website: www.wiley.com/go/Cremonini/DataVisualization1e

2007 – 2022 Point-in-Time Estimates by State, from the US Department of Housing and Urban Development. Data regarding the number of homeless persons at national and state level, from year 2007 and 2022 (https://www.hudexchange.info/resource/3031/pit-and-hic-data-since-2007/).

Copyright: CC0 1.0 Universal (CC0 1.0) Public Domain Dedication. (https://www.hudexchange.info/about/, https://creativecommons.org/publicdomain/zero/1.0/)

14.1 Scatterplots

We start from the fundamental graph type for continuous variables, the *scatterplot*, and its important variant the *line plot*, which Altair obviously supports, as well as many other graphic types that a modern data visualization library is expected to offer.

An important technical aspect of Altair to know immediately is that there is a *standard limitation* on the amount of local data that could be used. The default threshold limits *datasets to 5000 at most*. The threshold is configurable and could be changed, but it is important to understand the reason for such a limitation, apparently incomprehensible if one comes from experiencing with static graphic libraries like ggplot and Seaborn. 5000 rows for a dataset means a small dataset, open data could easily have tens of thousands of rows, and datasets in the order of millions of rows are not unusual at all. So why is there that low threshold in Altair?

The reason is in the interactive nature of the Altair graphics. A static graphic is just an image, there is no data in there. But an interactive data is a dynamic object that should reconfigure itself when the observer interacts with it, and to do that it has to have the data. So, if the data are local, it means they are stored *inside* the Altair object, which also means that the more the data, the larger the size of the Altair object, HTML or JSON, and the more difficult is to store, access, or transmit it. We will see an example later in the chapter. This is why it is convenient to put a threshold on local data, which could be changed if you wish, but being aware of the possible consequences. There is an alternative, of course, larger datasets should be *remotely accessed by an Altair object*, rather than storing all data as local data. This is the suggested solution: put the data on an online accessible location and configure the URL. It could be GitHub, an online repository, or something else of your own and you can use even the largest datasets with Altair. In the examples, we use the simplest solution of reading data locally, the official Altair documentation provides information for changing the default threshold and for configuring a remote access to data.

14.1.1 Static Graphics

We make use of dataset *Tourist/visitor arrivals and tourism expenditure* from the United Nations (UN). Colum *Value* adopts comma as thousand separators, therefore, to read it correctly, attribute `thousands` has to be specified because the default is to have no separator and values would be interpreted as alphanumeric.

```
import numpy as np
import pandas as pd
import altair as alt

df= pd.read_csv("datasets/
   UN/SYB65_176_202209_Tourist-Visitors Arrival and Expenditure.csv",
   thousands=',')
```

	Region/ Country/ Area	Country	Year	Series	Tourism arrivals series type	Value
0	4	Afghanistan	2010	Tourism expenditure	NaN	147
1	4	Afghanistan	2018	Tourism expenditure	NaN	50
2	4	Afghanistan	2019	Tourism expenditure	NaN	85
3	4	Afghanistan	2020	Tourism expenditure	NaN	75
4	8	Albania	2010	Tourist/visitor arrivals	TF	2191
...	...	...	...	...	...	...

The data frame should be prepared for visualization as a scatterplot. Rows mix two series, one for expenditures and the other for number of arrivals, we separate them by transforming in wide form column *Series* to have a column as monetary values (millions of dollars) and the other as number of tourists (thousands). Then, we add a new column *Per_capita_Exp(x1000)* with the per capita expenditure for tourists (thousands of dollars), which is a relative information that could be used to compare the different countries, where absolute values would not have permitted doing that.

```
df1= df.pivot(index= ['Country','Year'], columns= 'Series',
              values= 'Value').reset_index()

df1.columns= ['Country','Year','Expenditure','Arrivals']
df1["Per_capita_Exp(x1000)"]= (df1.Expenditure/df1.Arrivals).round(3)
```

	Country	Year	Expenditure	Arrivals	Per_capita_Exp (x1000)
0	Afghanistan	2010	147.0	NaN	NaN
1	Afghanistan	2018	50.0	NaN	NaN
2	Afghanistan	2019	85.0	NaN	NaN
3	Afghanistan	2020	75.0	NaN	NaN
4	Albania	1995	70.0	NaN	NaN
...	...	...	...	...	...
1229	Zimbabwe	2005	99.0	1559.0	0.064
1230	Zimbabwe	2010	135.0	2239.0	0.060
1231	Zimbabwe	2018	191.0	2580.0	0.074
1232	Zimbabwe	2019	285.0	2294.0	0.124
1233	Zimbabwe	2020	66.0	639.0	0.103

First, we omit rows with missing values in expenditures or arrivals, which are of no interest for the graphic. Easier would have been to omit those with missing values in the per capita expenditure column, but a little reminder about the composition of logical conditions could be useful.

```
df2= df1[ ~((df1.Expenditure.isna()) | (df1.Arrivals.isna())) ]
```

Now, we create the scatterplot and add some style options for the axes, the legend, the color palette, the theme, etc. Variables in Altair could be annotated with their type, either in the extended form by using attribute `type` or in the compact form with a capital letter indicating the type, *Q* for *quantitative*, meaning numerical variables, *O* for *ordinal*, meaning categorical variables and others that we will see. It is not always needed to specify the data type, here we use it for completeness. From the following example, a reader could try to selectively remove the data type specification in order to learn where it was not necessary and where, instead, it would change the result when not specified.

Let us consider one element at time starting with the general definition of an Altair graphic with function `alt.Chart()`. The data frame is the first attribute, *df2* in our case. To draw a parallel with ggplot, this operation is the equivalent of the `ggplot()` function.

Now, we should define the specific type of graphic we wish to produce. In this case, it is a scatterplot, so we use function `mark_circle()`, applied to the Altair chart object previously created, then we could specify the characteristics of the markers, such as their size (attribute `size`) or transparency (attribute `opacity`).

The specification of graphical elements, such as the marker characteristics, could be done in different ways. It could be *local* to the specific function (e.g., `mark_circle()`), in this case, is applied only to the markers produced by that function, it could be *global*, meaning valid for all graphical elements, when applied to the chart object (e.g., `p1.configure_mark(opacity=0.5, size=80)`), or could be in the *encoding*, which we will introduce soon (e.g., `opacity=alt.value(0.5), size= alt.value(80)`). Here, we specify size and opacity locally.

```
p1 = alt.Chart(df2)
p1.mark_circle(size=80, opacity=0.7)
```

The two instructions could have been concatenated as well.

```
alt.Chart(df2).mark_circle(size=80, opacity=0.7)
```

We consider now, the *encoding*, defined with function `encode()`, which represents the general way to define properties for graphical elements such as the variables for the Cartesian axes, color, size, etc. (in other terms, properties of the aesthetics of the grammar of graphics). In the encoding, we specify the variables for axes *x* and *y* with their attributes (`x` and `y`) and data type (functions `X()` and `Y()`), titles (in function `Axes()` with attributes `axis` and `title`), and padding (in function `Scale()` with attributes `scale` and `padding`). For the data types, we show both the compact form (e.g., '`Arrivals:Q`') and the extended form (e.g., `'Expenditure', type='quantitative'`).

```
alt.Chart(df2).mark_circle(size=80, opacity=0.7).encode(

# For axes x and y we define a title, for axis y the padding,
# meaning the distance of markers from the axis

    x= alt.X('Arrivals:Q',
             axis= alt.Axis(title='Arrivals (thousands)')),

    y= alt.Y('Expenditure',
            type= 'quantitative',
            axis= alt.Axis(title='Expenditure (millions $)'),
            scale= alt.Scale(padding=1)),
```

Finally, we add a third variable (*Year*) associated to the *color* aesthetic (attribute `color` and function `Color()`); to specify a color palette we use again function `Scale()`; the legend is placed on top of the graphic with attribute `legend` and function `Legend()`. With knowledge of ggplot acquired in Part 1 of this book, the Altair syntax should look familiar. Figure 14.1 shows the Altair scatterplot for this example.

```
    color= alt.Color('Year:O',
             scale= alt.Scale(scheme='viridis'),
             legend= alt.Legend(title="Years", orient="top")))
```

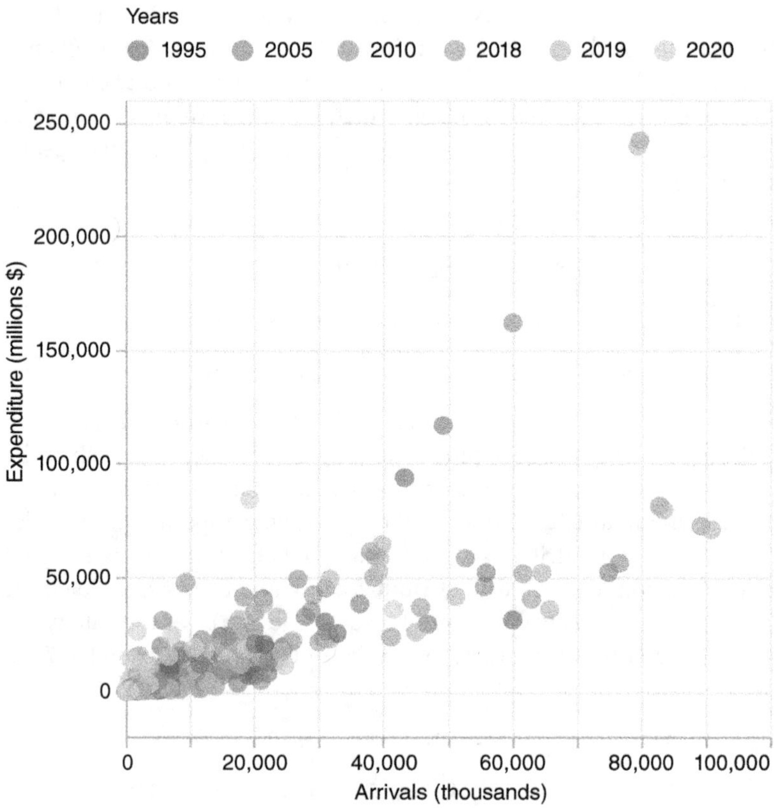

Figure 14.1 Altair, scatterplot with color aesthetic and style options.

In general, Altair produces graphics of excellent quality that can be exported into different formats: PNG/JPG, SVG, HTML, and JSON.

14.1.1.1 JSON Format: Data Organization

Let us delve into some details by saving the previous plot as a JSON file and looking at its content. The following excerpt of code is the beginning of the JSON data structure. JSON follows the Python *dictionary* specifications, keys *mark* and *type* with value *circle* could be seen, corresponding to Altair function `mark_circle()`, followed by local attributes *opacity* and *size*, then *encoding* and so on. It is the JSON equivalent of the Altair script.

```
"mark": {
  "type": "circle",
  "opacity": 0.7,
  "size": 80
```

```
},
"encoding": {
  "color": {
    "field": "Year",
    "legend": {
      "orient": "top",
      "title": "Years"
    },
```

But, if we move down in the JSON structure, we find something else.

```
"datasets": {
  "data-afce4904be12f430c4cee42cfa3e79c6": [
    {
      "Country": "Albania",
      "Year": 2010,
      "Expenditure": 1778,
      "Arrivals": 2191,
      "Per_capita_Exp(x1000)": 0.812
    },
    {
      "Country": "Albania",
      "Year": 2018,
      "Expenditure": 2306,
      "Arrivals": 5340,
      "Per_capita_Exp(x1000)": 0.432
    },
    ...
```

This is the full data frame used for plotting the graphic, which, as said before, when accessed locally, is stored *within* the Altair object. And the same happens if we produce an interactive graphic in HTML format, inside it has the full data frame, if read locally. This should convince everyone that having a limitation on the size of data to be accessed locally is a wise choice, configurable at will, but being aware of the possible consequences.

14.1.1.2 Plot Alignment and Variable Types

We consider how the result may change by specifying different data types for a variable. We use variable *Year*, associated to the *color* aesthetic, and add some new features: how to align more Altair graphics and how to specify their width and height. In particular, we will see:

- *Horizontal alignment* by using function `alt.hconcat()` and for *vertical alignment* function `alt.vconcat()`.

- *Width* and *height* specification with method and attributes `properties (width= , height= )`.
- The definition of a base graphic and the following instantiation into different plots.

We start by assigning the Altair graphic to object *base*, without fully specifying the graphics but just the common characteristics of graphics that will be instantiated from it.

```
base= alt.Chart(df2).mark_circle(size=80, opacity=0.7).encode(
    x= alt.X('Arrivals:Q',
            axis= alt.Axis(title='Arrivals (thousands)')),
    y= alt.Y('Expenditure',
            type='quantitative',
            axis= alt.Axis(title='Expenditure (millions $)'))

# Setting width and height

).properties(
    width=150,
    height=150
)
```

At this point, the graphic is represented by object *base* and not visualized yet. Now, we use *base* to define three different graphics, each one with a different feature, which, in this case, will be a different data type for variable *Year* associated to markers color (i.e., *quantitative* (Q), *ordinal* (O), *nominal* (N), corresponding to numerical, categorical, and alphanumerical). Finally, we will visualize the three graphics horizontally aligned in Figure 14.2.

```
# Horizontal alignment

alt.hconcat(
   base.encode(color='Year:Q').properties(title='quantitative'),
   base.encode(color='Year:O').properties(title='ordinal'),
   base.encode(color='Year:N').properties(title='nominal')
)
```

As it is evident from the results, by changing the data type associated to the *color* aesthetic, the color palette automatically changes to adapt to the specific data type. It is a continuous palette when data are numerical, a discrete palette with sequential gradient when categorical, and a discrete palette when alphanumerical.

14.1.2 Facets

We introduce *facets*. For a visualization by facets, as we already know, we should specify a variable whose unique values will be associated to facets. In our example, we use *Year*. We also change graphical function from `mark_circle()`

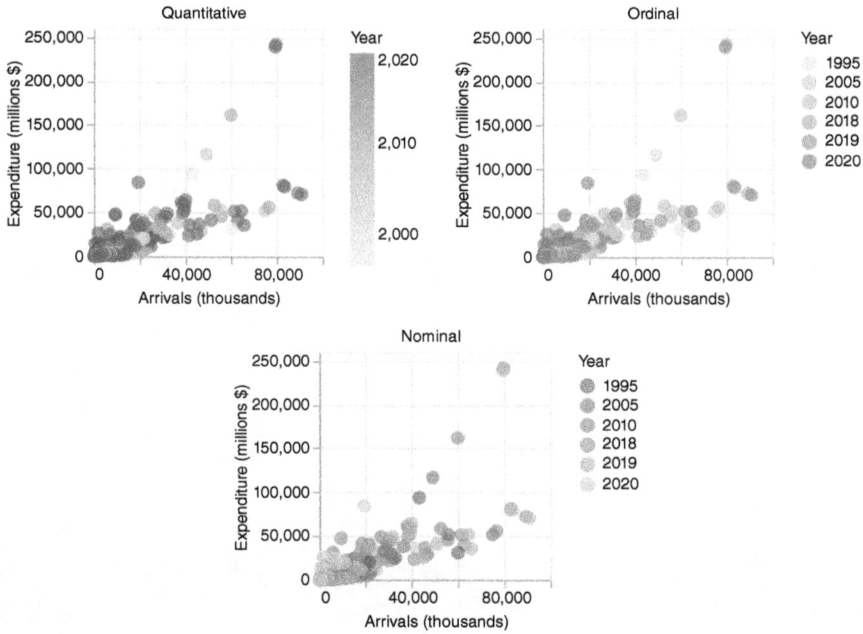

Figure 14.2 Altair, horizontal alignments of plots and differences from assigning different data types to variable Year.

to `mark_point()`, it is still a scatterplot but the marker's shape changes, from dots to rings. With method `facet` we specify variable *Year* and the grid of facets, in this case with three columns, using attribute `columns` (to specify the number of rows, there is attribute `rows`). Figure 14.3 shows the result.

```
alt.Chart(df2
).mark_point(
    size=40,
    opacity=0.5
).encode(
    x= 'Arrivals:Q',
    y= 'Expenditure:Q'
).properties(
    width=150,
    height=150
).facet(
    facet= 'Year:O',
    columns=3 )
```

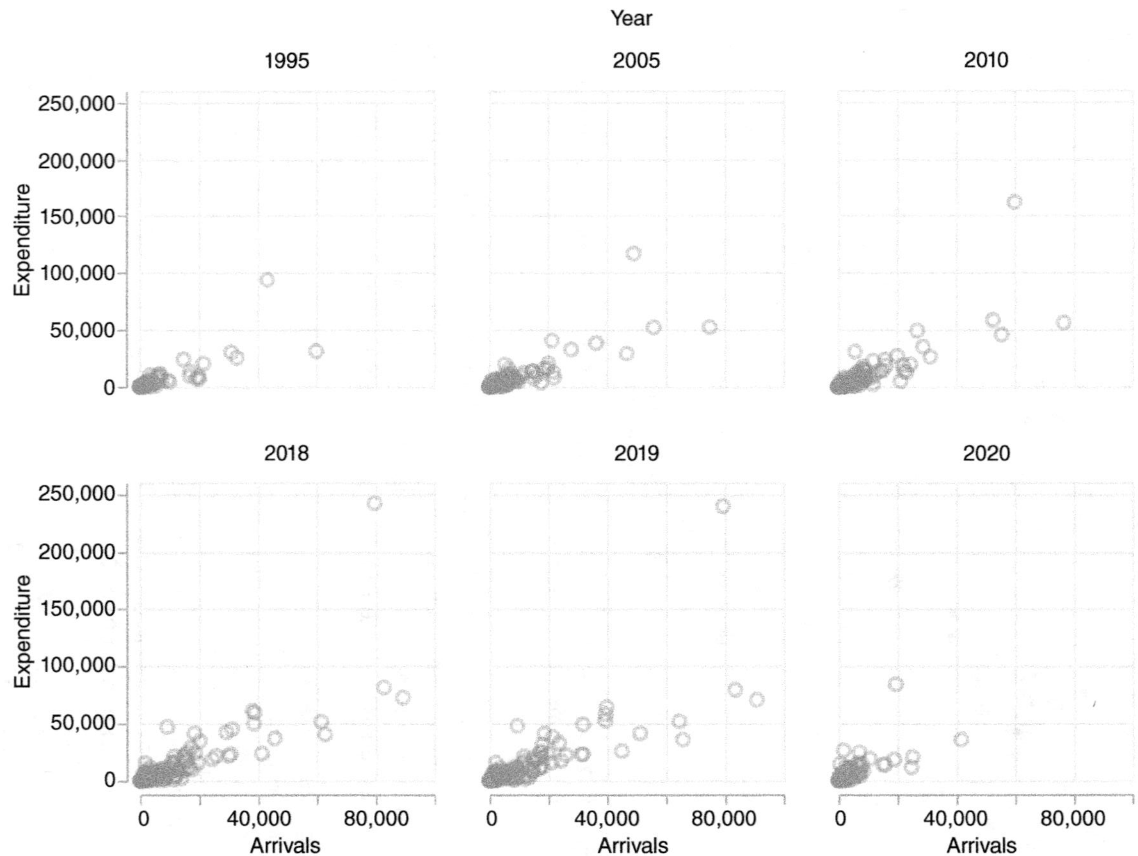

Figure 14.3 Altair, facet visualization.

14.1.3 Interactive Graphics

We have seen a few examples of static graphics with basic elements and options. Others will be presented in the following examples, now it is time to move to the real deal of the Altair library: interactive graphics.

14.1.3.1 Dynamic Tooltips

We return to the first example and add to it the first interactive element: the *dynamic tooltip*, which is a box with a content that pops up when the mouse pointer hovers on a marker or other elements associated to dynamic tooltips (usually there is a difference between *tooltip* and *popup*, the former appears when the mouse hovers on the graphical element, the latter requires the user to click on the element, therefore, these Altair objects are correctly named tooltips).

Information shown in the tooltip is configurable based on data frame variables. In the example, for each marker, we want to show the country name and the per capita tourist expenditure. Tooltips are another aesthetic of Altair graphics, so their configuration is easily done in the *encoding* with attribute `tooltip` associated to the list of variables whose values will be shown in the tooltip. Figure 14.4a and Figure 14.4b shows two screenshots with different tooltips.

```
alt.Chart(df2).mark_point(size=80, opacity=0.7).encode(
     x= alt.X('Arrivals',
              axis= alt.Axis(title='Arrivals (thousands)')),
     y= alt.Y('Expenditure',
              axis= alt.Axis(title='Expenditure (millions $)')),
    color= alt.Color('Year:O', scale= alt.Scale(scheme='viridis')),

# Tooltip specification

    tooltip= ['Country:N','Per_capita_Exp(x1000)']
)
```

This is the first example of an interactive graphic, whose presentation on paper or in static formats cannot be complete; only a few screenshots can be shown. In all cases, screenshots presented in this book have been selected to be informative for the reader to grasp the real functionality. However, for a better and more complete experience with interactive graphics, all interactive graphics are available in the HTML version in the *Additional Online Material*. To visualize these, you need a JavaScript front end, such as notebook environments like Jupyter Lab or Zeppelin with an active web connection (https://altair-viz.github.io/user_guide/display_frontends.html) or they can be imported into web dashboards (more on this in Part 3 of the book).

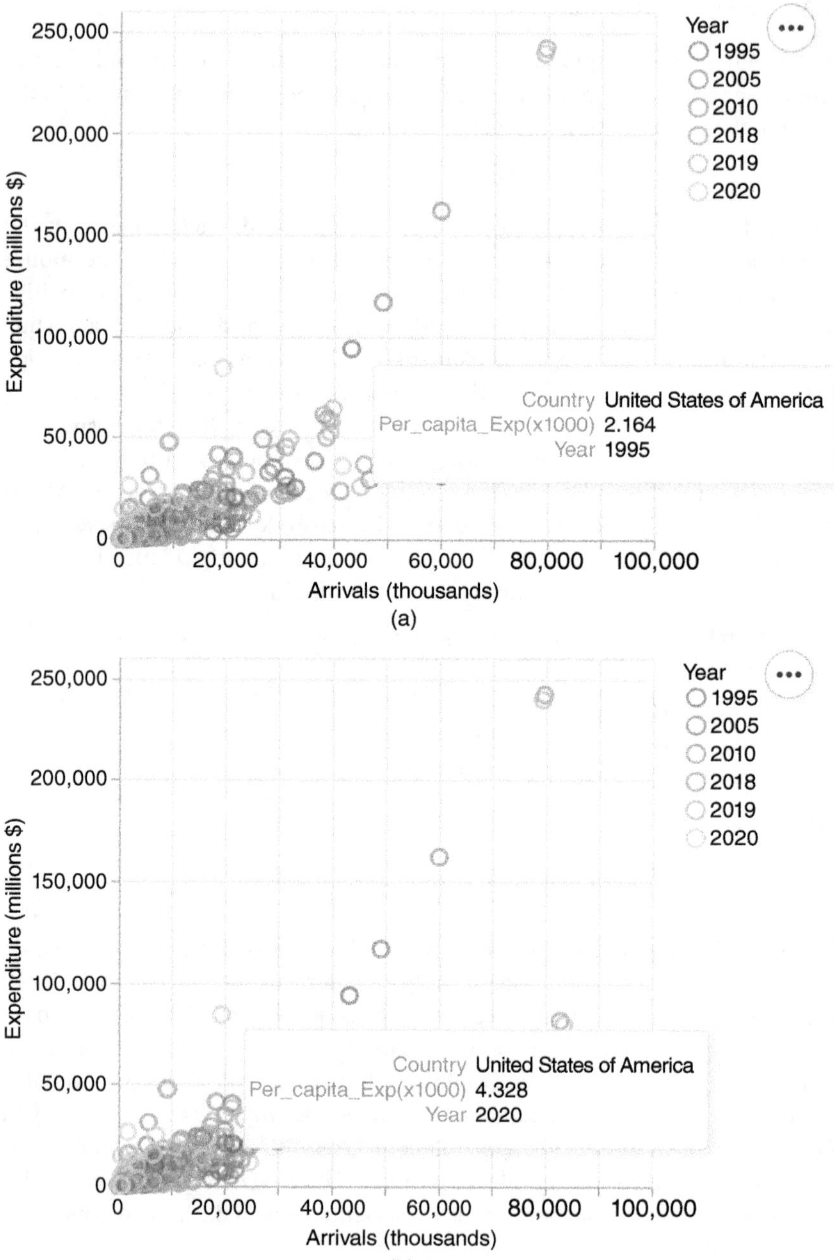

Figure 14.4 (a) Dynamic tooltip (example 1). (b) Dynamic tooltip (example 2).

14.1.3.2 Interactive Legend

We add the *interactive legend*, where *every key of the legend is an active element, whose selection modifies the graphic visualization*. In the following example, a user needs to click on a legend key (i.e. a year) and only scatterplot markers corresponding to that year will be visualized. To start, the operation of selecting values of variable *Year* from the legend should be defined. In practice, those legend elements will be turned into *radio buttons*, the typical widget of graphical interfaces that shows a list of choices with a button associated where only one of those buttons could be selected. In our case, the selection of a single key on the legend should correspond to a selection of all markers related to that key. For instance, if we select year 2010 on the legend, all markers referring to year 2010 should be selected. For this reason, we need a method able to select multiple elements on the graphic, it is provided by function `alt.selection_point()` (see the following *Note*), which implements a selection operation of data points with attribute `fields` and should be connected to the legend through attribute `bind='legend'`.

```
selection= alt.selection_point(fields=['Year'], bind='legend')
```

> **Note**
>
> For the examples, we use the new methods from Altair 4, which has deprecated some previous methods. Specifically, `alt.selection_multi()` and `alt.selection_single()` have been superseded by `alt.selection_point()`; `alt.selection(type='interval')` is to be replaced by `alt.selection_interval()`; and `add_selection()` by `add_params()`.
>
> The older versions still work, but being deprecated, they will stop being supported in future releases of Altair. However, since many examples of Altair scripts that could be found are based on the older functions, it is worth knowing that they could be easily adapted to the new syntax.

We have defined the selection criteria and associated it to the legend. Now, we need to specify the graphic and the dynamic actions that will modify it according to the selection on the legend. The *action* represents what should be done after a selection is performed, for example, if we select year 2012 on the legend, what should happen on the graphic? In our case, we want that all markers relative to year 2012 stay visible as originally were, and all other markers become invisible or shaded somehow. Then, for markers of the selected year, we are not going to do anything; they are fine as they are. We need to modify the others. The easiest way is to twist the *transparency*, making them more faded or completely transparent, or to manage colors, for example changing the hue into a neutral, inconspicuous tone like pale gray or the like. Here, we twist the transparency with attribute `opacity`. For markers of the selected year, we keep the full colors, for markers of other years, we set a high level of transparency. Technically, it is a condition logically equivalent to an *if-else* construct, it has two possibilities, the first if the condition is true, and the second if it is false. The Altair function is `alt.condition()`, the logical condition is implemented by the selection criteria (variable *selection*), meaning that if the year is selected on the legend, the two possibilities for true and false are the different levels of transparency (i.e. `alt.value(0.9), alt.value(0.1)`).

```
opacity= alt.condition(selection, alt.value(0.9), alt.value(0.1))
```

This way, the aesthetic *opacity* in the encoding varies according to the selection on the legend.

The second necessary step is to specify that an interactive selection (represented by variable *selection*) is associated to the graphic, this is needed for every selection operation. Method `add_params(selection)` should be used. Here is the full script.

```
selection= alt.selection_point(fields=['Year'], bind='legend')

chart= alt.Chart(df2).mark_circle(size=80, opacity=0.7).encode(
    x= alt.X('Arrivals',
             axis= alt.Axis(title='Arrivals (thousands)')),
     y= alt.Y('Expenditure',
             axis= alt.Axis(title='Expenditure (millions $)')),
    color= alt.Color('Year:O',
                     scale= alt.Scale(scheme='viridis')),
    tooltip= ['Country:N','Per_capita_Exp(x1000)'],

    opacity= alt.condition(selection, alt.value(0.9),
                                      alt.value(0.1))
).add_params(
    selection
)
chart.show()
```

The two screenshots, Figure 14.5a and Figure 14.5b show how the transparency of different markers changes by changing the legend selection.

14.1.3.3 Dynamic Zoom

The *dynamic zoom* is another interactive element that lets zooming in and out on the graphic and moving it with the mouse. It is the same common functionality we are used to with online maps through the mouse or gestures on the touchpad, scrolling activates the zoom, while clicking and moving shifts the graphic. With an Altair graphic, it could be particularly useful to inspect details that at standard zoom level are difficult to evaluate, such as when markers are very close or appear overplotted. By zooming in or out, the *scales* are dynamically recalculated, so, for

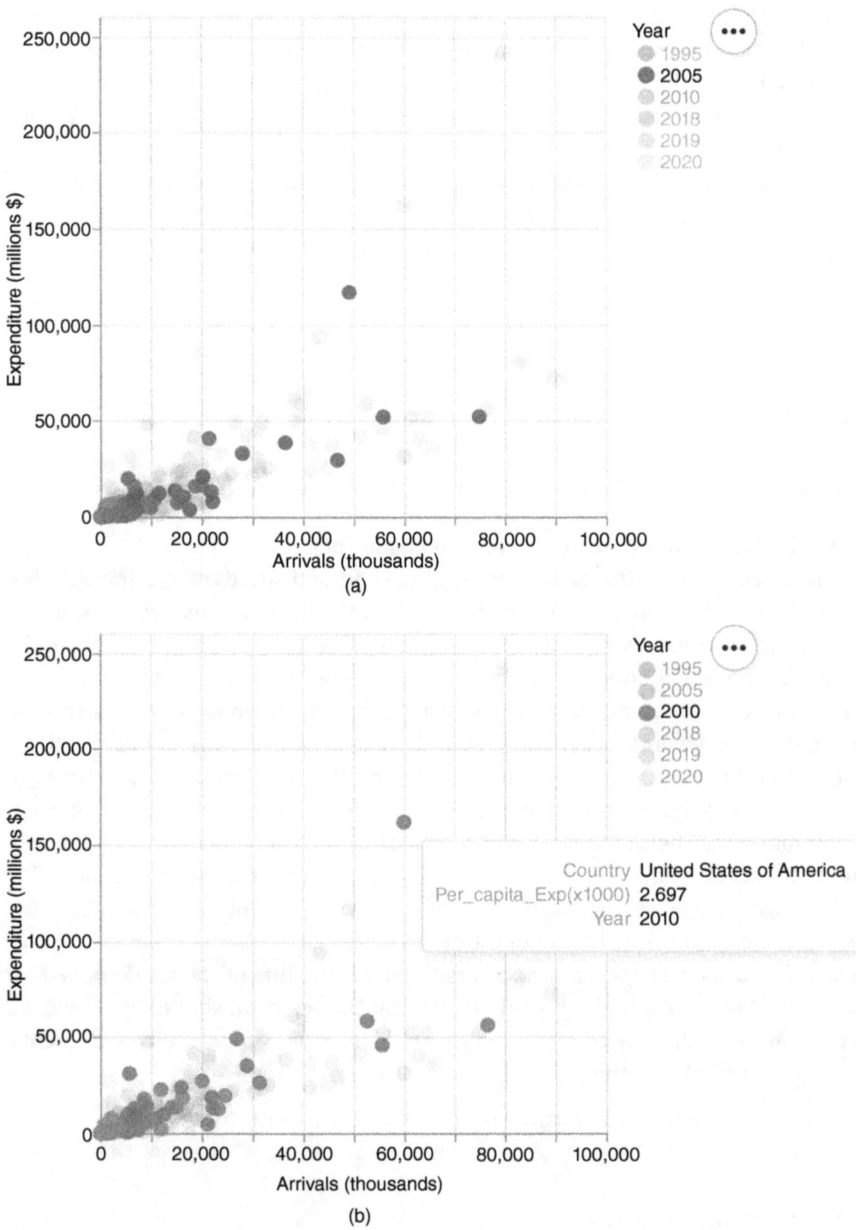

Figure 14.5 (a) Dynamic legend, year 2005. (b) Dynamic legend, year 2010.

example, if the standard scale has thousands as units, by zooming in it is possible to look at details at scale of hundreds or tens. In the example, screenshots of Figure 14.6a and Figure 14.6b show the two cases, the first has been zoomed in to scales of tens of thousands for the arrivals, while in the second the scale is zoomed out up to millions of tourist arrivals and the plot moved.

To add the dynamic zoom is very easy, it is done by simply specifying the method `interactive()` with no attribute.

```
selection= alt.selection_point(fields=['Year'], bind='legend')

alt.Chart(df2).mark_point(...
).add_params(
   selection

# Dynamic zoom
).interactive()
```

In the same way, the dynamic zoom is compatible with a visualization by facets.

14.1.3.4 Mouse Hovering and Contextual Change of Color

We have seen that with mouse hovering we can activate dynamic tooltips, but we could do even more, for example, we could activate a *contextual change of color of the markers*. Specifically, we want to highlight the marker over which the mouse is positioned and, contextually, shade the others. We could also combine this action with dynamic tooltips. The logic is similar to what we have seen with the interactive legend, a certain action, here mouse hovering, should activate a selection, in this case of a single marker, and the selection should be used in the encoding to dynamically change an aesthetic of the graphic, again the color of the markers. The difference with the case of the interactive legend is that in function `selection_point()` the selection is associated to mouse hovering with attribute `on='mouseover'`. In the scatterplot definition, we still have the aesthetic *color* associated to a condition (`color=alt.condition()`), in this case, it is not the transparency to be modified but the hue of the markers, red for the selected marker, gray for the others. Finally, the selection should be associated to the graphic with method `add_params()`. The script shows the new elements, and Figure 14.7 shows the result.

```
hover= alt.selection_point(on='mouseover',
                           nearest=True, empty=False)

alt.Chart(df2).mark_point(...

     color= alt.condition(hover, alt.value('red'),
                          alt.value('gray'))
).add_params( selection
).interactive()
```

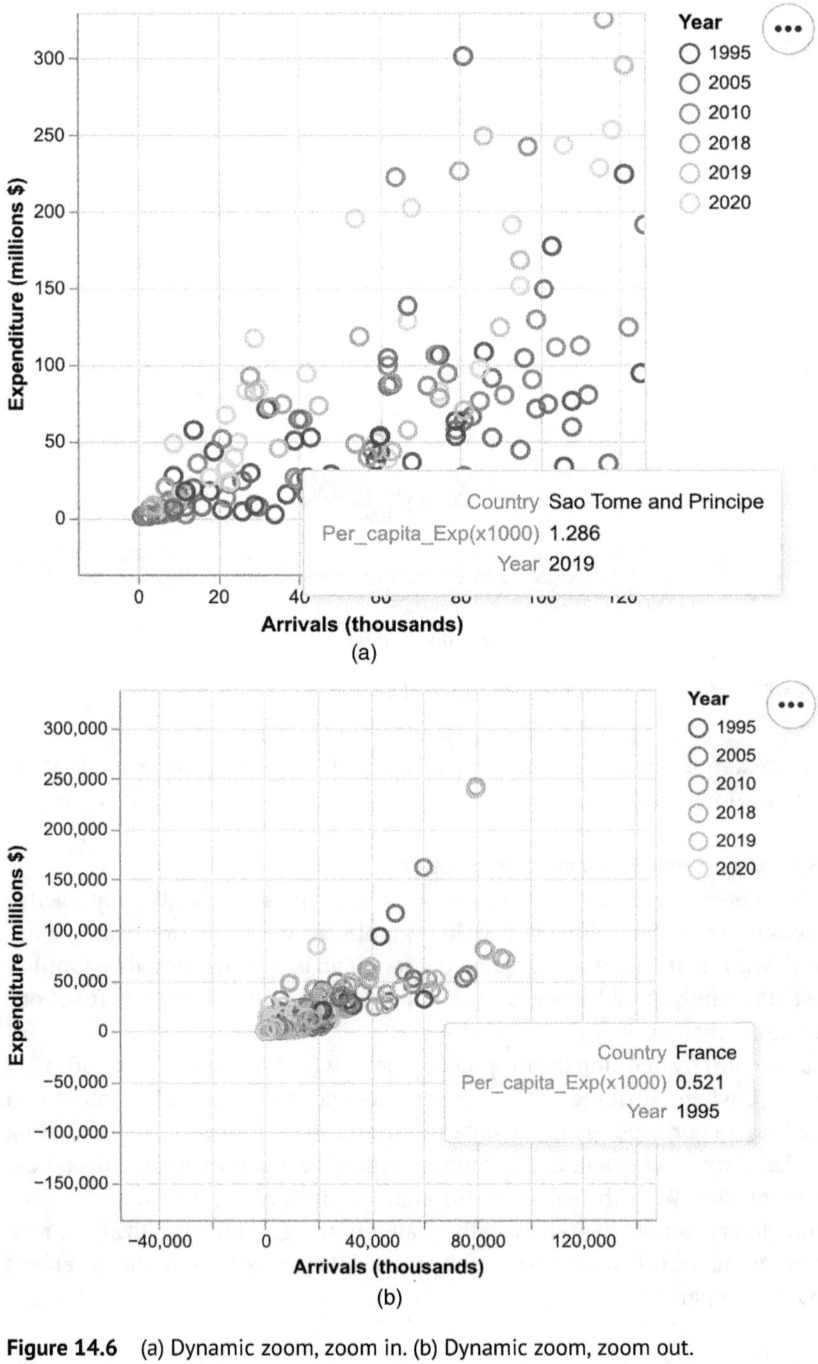

Figure 14.6 (a) Dynamic zoom, zoom in. (b) Dynamic zoom, zoom out.

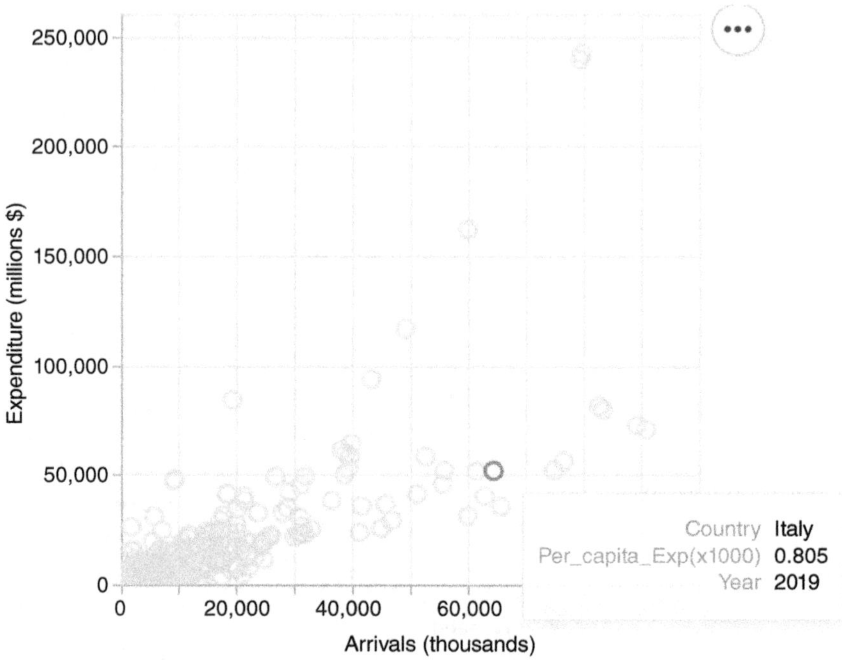

Figure 14.7 Mouse hover, contextual change of color.

For this example, in the tooltip, the year is also present. The same could be done for visualization by facets.

14.1.3.5 Drop-Down Menu and Radio Buttons

Drop-down menus and *radio buttons* are other two typical elements of interactive interfaces that could be added to an Altair graphic as well. The first example has a drop-down menu with a list of years to select. The logic now should be familiar because it is similar to what we have seen previously, only the specific functions and methods change.

Here, we start by defining the drop-down menu with function `alt.binding_select()`, where attribute `options` specifies the list of selectable values and attribute `name` corresponds to the data frame column name with corresponding values (i.e. *Years*). As usual, this definition should be assigned to an object, here *input_dropdown*. With the selection through the drop-down menu, we proceed as in previous example by dynamically changing the graphic visualization, now both modifying the transparency and the color aesthetics, so to combine the effects already seen separately.

```
input_dropdown= alt.binding_select(options=[1995,2005,2010,
                                            2018,2019,2020],
                                   name='Year')
```

For the selection, it uses attribute `fields` to specify the data frame column with data points to select, it corresponds to the same column used for the definition of the drop-down menu (i.e. *Year*), and it is connected to the variable representing the drop-down menu with attribute `bind`.

```
selection= alt.selection_point(fields=['Year'],
                               bind= input_dropdown)
```

The actions in the encoding part are similar to those already discussed before. In the following, the full script is presented, and Figure 14.8 shows the result.

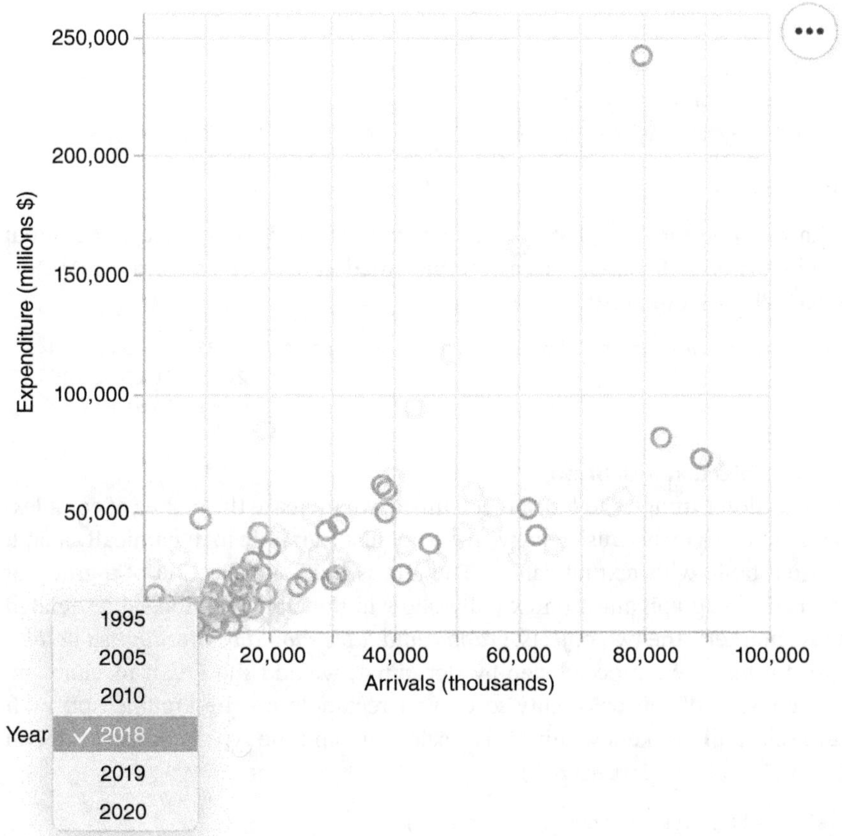

Figure 14.8 Drop-down menu.

```
# Drop-down menu definition
input_dropdown= alt.binding_select(options=[1995,2005,2010,
                                            2018,2019,2020],
                                            name='Year')
# Selection
selection= alt.selection_point(fields=['Year'],
                                bind= input_dropdown)

# Actions
change_color= alt.condition(selection,
                     alt.Color('Year:N', legend=None),
                     alt.value('lightgray'))

change_opacity= alt.condition(selection,
                     alt.value(1.0), alt.value(0.3))

# Graphic
alt.Chart(df2).mark_point(...
    color= change_color,
    opacity= change_opacity

).add_params( selection )
```

With radio buttons we proceed the same way, the only difference is the initial definition, now of radio buttons with function `alt.binding_radio()`. Figure 14.9 shows the result.

```
input_dropdown= alt.binding_radio(options=[1995,2005,2010,
                                           2018,2019,2020],
                                           name='Year')
```

14.1.3.6 Selection with Brush

With selection through the *brush* mechanism, we increase the degree of complexity and interactivity because now we have not just a graphic to dynamically adapt, but also a table with textual values. The aim is to allow selection of a group of markers on the graph and, contextually, show in the table only the values related to those markers, the two objects, *graphic and table should be coordinated in their reconfigurations.* We proceed step-by-step. First, we add the brush mechanism, which consists of the possibility to draw a rectangle on the graphic and with that to select all markers within. It is a selection, and the type is now an interval (`alt.selection_interval`).

```
brush= alt.selection_interval()
```

Then, we define the graphic, still a scatterplot (`mark_circle()`) and add to it the selection with brush (`add_params()`). This just gives us the brush

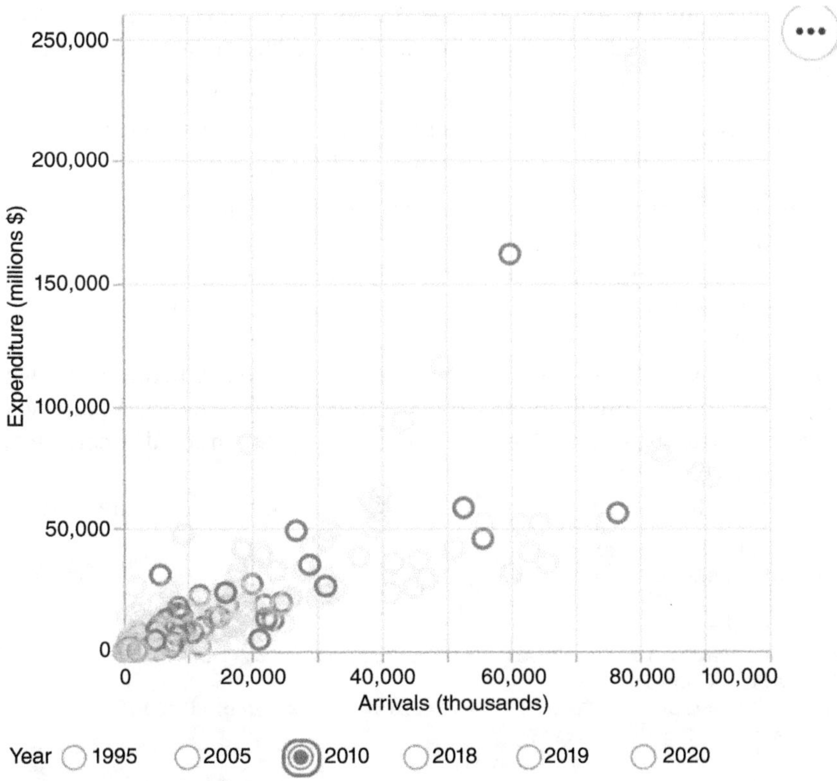

Figure 14.9 Radio buttons.

mechanism on the graphic. We need now to synchronize the table with that selection, meaning that the selection of data points operated with the brush should correspond to a selection of rows on the data frame to visualize in the table. We delve into the details step-by-step.

STEP 1. Variable *ranked_text* represents a table (`mark_text()`) *composed by a single column*:

- Rows (axis *y*) are associated to row numbers (*'row_number:O'*) but not visualized (*axis=None*).
- Row numbers are dynamically modified (`transform_window`).
- Table values correspond to the data points selected with the brush on the graphic (`transform_filter`).
- The number of visualized rows is limited for visualization purposes (less than 15 in the example) with method `transform_filter` and function `datum.rank()`.

STEP 2. This represents the encoding of table *ranked_text* and it should be repeated as many times as the table columns to visualize (remember that each table has just one column):

- Country, arrival, and expenditures are the three columns we want to show.
- For each one of them, its width (attribute `witdh`) is specified.

At this point, technically, we have three tables of one column each associated to different data frame columns.

STEP 3. We specify the horizontal alignment of the three tables of one column, so as to resemble a single table with three columns (function `hconcat()`) and save in variable *data*.

STEP 4. Finally, we have object *plot* for the graphic and *data* with the table, what is still missing is their visualization. We want them side-by-side, so again function `hconcat()`. With `resolve_legend()` the legend position could be corrected, but this is just a tiny detail.

Here is the full script and two screenshots in Figure 14.10a and Figure 14.10b.

```
# Selection with brush
brush= alt.selection_interval(type='interval')

# Scatterplot
plot= alt.Chart(df2).mark_circle(size=80, opacity=0.7).encode(
    x= alt.X('Arrivals:Q',
            axis= alt.Axis(title='Arrivals (thousands)')),
    y= alt.Y('Expenditure',
            type= 'quantitative',
            axis= alt.Axis(title='Expenditure (millions $)')),

    color= alt.Color('Year:O',
                    scale= alt.Scale(scheme='viridis'),
                    legend= alt.Legend(title="Years",
                                    orient="top"))

).properties( width=300, height=300
).add_params( brush )

# Table definition
ranked_text= alt.Chart(df2).mark_text().encode(
    y= alt.Y('row_number:O',axis=None)
).transform_window(
    row_number= 'row_number()'
).transform_filter(
    brush
).transform_window(
    rank= 'rank(row_number)'
).transform_filter(
    alt.datum.rank < 15
)
```

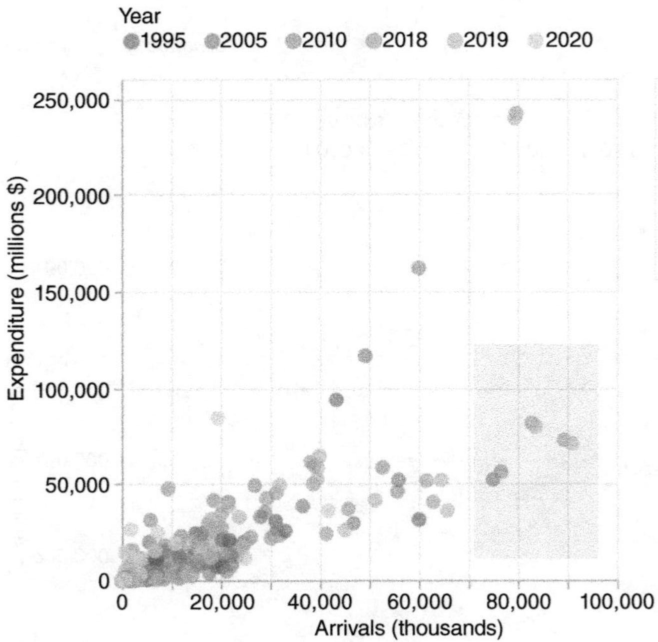

Country	Arrivals	Expenditure
France	74988	52126
France	76647	56178
France	89322	72518
France	90914	70776
Spain	82808	81420
Spain	83509	79611

(a)

Figure 14.10 (a) Selection with brush and synchronized table (example 1). (b) Selection with brush and synchronized table (example 2).

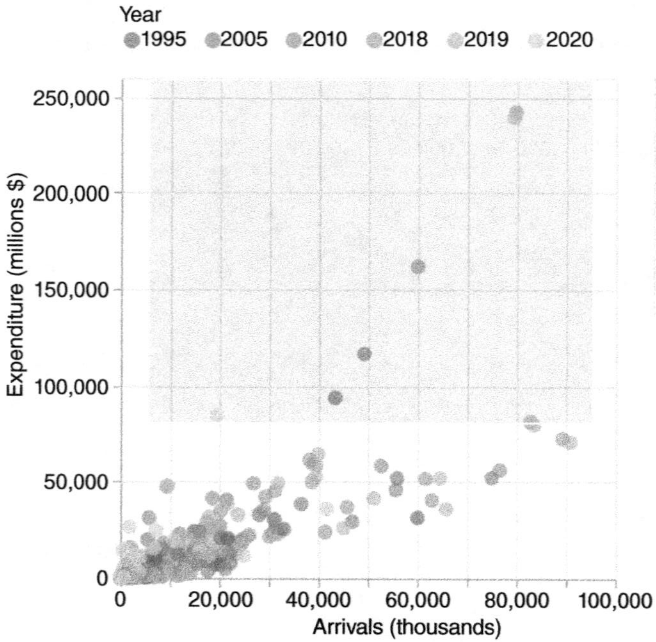

Country	Arrivals	Expenditure
Spain	82808	81420
United States of America	43318	93743
United States of America	49206	116682
United States of America	60010	161821
United States of America	79746	241984
United States of America	79442	239447
United States of America	19457	84205

(b)

Figure 14.10 (*Continued*)

```
# Encoding of columns
country= ranked_text.encode(text= 'Country:N'
).properties(width=150, title='Country')

arrivals= ranked_text.encode(text= 'Arrivals:N'
).properties(width=100, title='Arrivals')

expenditure= ranked_text.encode(text= 'Expenditure:N'
).properties(width=100, title='Expenditure')

# Table visualization
data= alt.hconcat(country, arrivals, expenditure)

# Graphic and table visualization
alt.hconcat(plot, data
).resolve_legend( color="independent" )
```

This type of interactive graphics is flexible and permits to produce interesting visualization for every group of data points. For example, with brush, we can select countries with a number of arrivals greater than a certain threshold or with per capita expenditure less than another threshold and so forth and look at the corresponding tabular values. Basically, it is a way to execute logical conditions through gestures on the graphics. With different visualizations of the scatterplot is also possible to implement other selection criteria.

There are limitations to consider, though. We could possibly want to add the dynamic zoom, for example, in order to select through the brush at different scales. It is a possibility that could be added to the script, but a problem would arise. It is likely that the zoom mechanism will not function correctly because *the same gesture* with the mouse or on the touchpad would likely be associated to different actions: zooming in and out and defining the brush area. In that case, one of the two should be remapped to a different gesture on the computer. A second limitation is the table size because it is not dynamically adjusted to fit the actual length of the shown text, but it is a static parameter in the script specification or set by default. Therefore, a text larger than the preset column width will overflow the table, with a loss of visualization quality. This aspect should be dealt manually, either by configuring the column width larger than the largest textual value or shortening too long textual values or both. An alternative is to visualize the graphic and the table vertically aligned with function `vconcat()`, which does not solve the problem by itself, but would give more space to enlarge the table. In any case, tests are needed to find the right trade-off.

Another useful case study for the brush mechanism is to allow observing *the same selection of data points in two different graphics by synchronizing their reconfiguration*. It is an interesting possibility supported by Altair. The following example shows this case. We have a base graphic (object *plot*) without the association of a variable to axis *y* and two conditions: one applied to aesthetic *color* and the other to *transparency*, both dependent on brush selection. The logic is similar to what we have previously seen, for selected markers the color and transparency will remain unchanged, for the others they will change. This for the *base* graphic. The next step is to instantiate two specific graphics, from the base one (*plot1* and *plot2*), each with *a different variable associated to axis y*. So, they are different graphics. Finally, they should be synchronized to have that a brush selection on one will produce a reconfiguration also of the other *for the same data points*. The full script is presented, and screenshots are shown in Figure 14.11a and Figure 14.11b.

```
# Brush definition
brush= alt.selection_interval()

# Base graphic, axis y is missing
plot= alt.Chart(df2).mark_circle(size=80).encode(
        x= alt.X('Arrivals:Q',
            axis= alt.Axis(title='Arrivals (thousands)')),

# Conditions on color and transparency
    color= alt.condition(brush, 'Year:O', alt.value('lightblue'),
                    scale= alt.Scale(scheme='magma'),
                    legend= alt.Legend(title="Years",
                    orient="top")),
    opacity= alt.condition(brush, alt.value(1.0), alt.value(0.3))

).properties(width=300,height=300
).add_params(brush)

# Graphics: plot1 has axis y associated to Expenditure
# plot2 has axis y associated to Per_capita_Exp(x1000)
plot1= plot.encode(
         y= alt.Y('Expenditure:Q',
            axis= alt.Axis(title='Expenditure (millions $)')),)

plot2= plot.encode(
         y=alt.Y('Per_capita_Exp(x1000)',
           axis= alt.Axis(title='Per_capita Expenditure (thousands)')),)

alt.hconcat(plot1, plot2)
```

14.1.3.7 Graphics as Legends

A curious possibility offered by Altair is to *replace a legend with an interactive graphic*. We have already seen interactive legends, but the limitation is that they work as radio buttons, so just one value could be selected. If we want the possibility of a *multiple selection*, this ingenious workaround comes to help. The logic is similar to what we have just seen, two graphics are synchronized so that the selection on one automatically reconfigures also the second. Let us start by

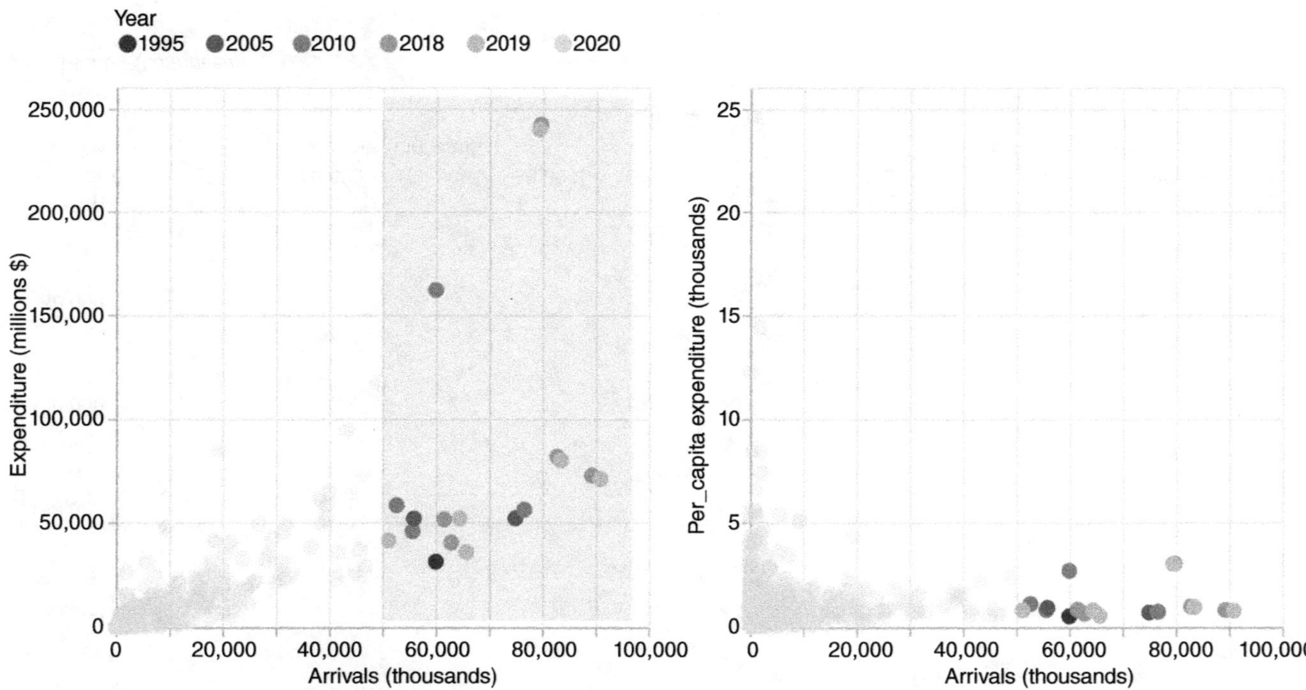

(a)

Figure 14.11 (a) (Left plot) brush selection; (right plot) synchronized plot, same data points colored. (b) (Left plot) synchronized plot, same data points colored; (right plot) brush selection.

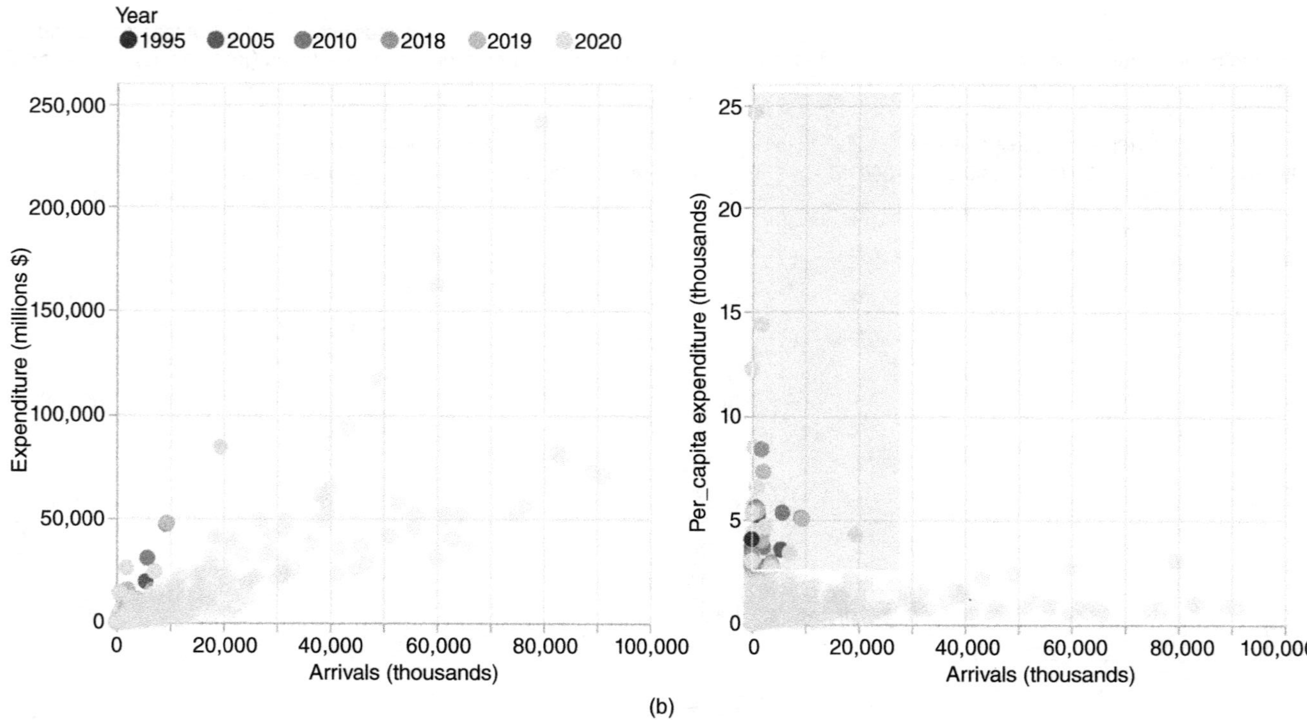

Figure 14.11 (*Continued*)

defining a multiple selection with `selection_point()` over values of data frame column *Year*, followed by the usual condition to change markers color based on the selection. We have already seen this.

```
selection= alt.selection_point(fields=['Year'])

change_color= alt.condition(selection,
               alt.Color('Year:O', legend=None,
                         scale= alt.Scale(scheme='plasma')),
               alt.value('lightgray'))
```

Now we need to define the main graphic and a second one acting and looking like a legend. The main graphic is still our scatterplot with aesthetic *color* associated to the selection. Instead, the graphic mimicking a legend could be defined having a *rectangular shape* with `mark_rect()` and only axis *y*, with no *x* (technically it is a heatmap with a single column). Axis *y* will be associated to column *Year* and to the condition for changing colors. To this graphic is also associated the selection, to reconfigure its colors too. The result is very similar to an actual legend and allows for multiple selections (usually using the uppercase key). This way, we may select all combinations of years. The full script is presented, and screenshots are shown in Figure 14.12a and Figure 14.12b.

```
# Main graphic
plot= alt.Chart(df2).mark_point(size=80, opacity=0.7).encode(
        x= alt.X('Arrivals',
             axis= alt.Axis(title='Arrivals (thousands)')),
        y= alt.Y('Expenditure',
             axis= alt.Axis(title='Expenditure (millions $)')),
        color= change_color,
        tooltip= ['Country:N','Per_capita_Exp(x1000)']
)

# Second graphic as a legend, only axis y is defined
legend= alt.Chart(df2).mark_rect().encode(
            y= alt.Y('Year:O', axis= alt.Axis(orient='right')),
            color= change_color
).add_params(
    selection )

# Visualization
plot | legend
```

To be noted how the two plots have been horizontally aligned. The notation `plot1 | plot2` corresponds to `hconcat(plot1,plot2)`, whereas `plot1 & plot2` corresponds to `vconcat(plot1,plot2)` for vertical alignment.

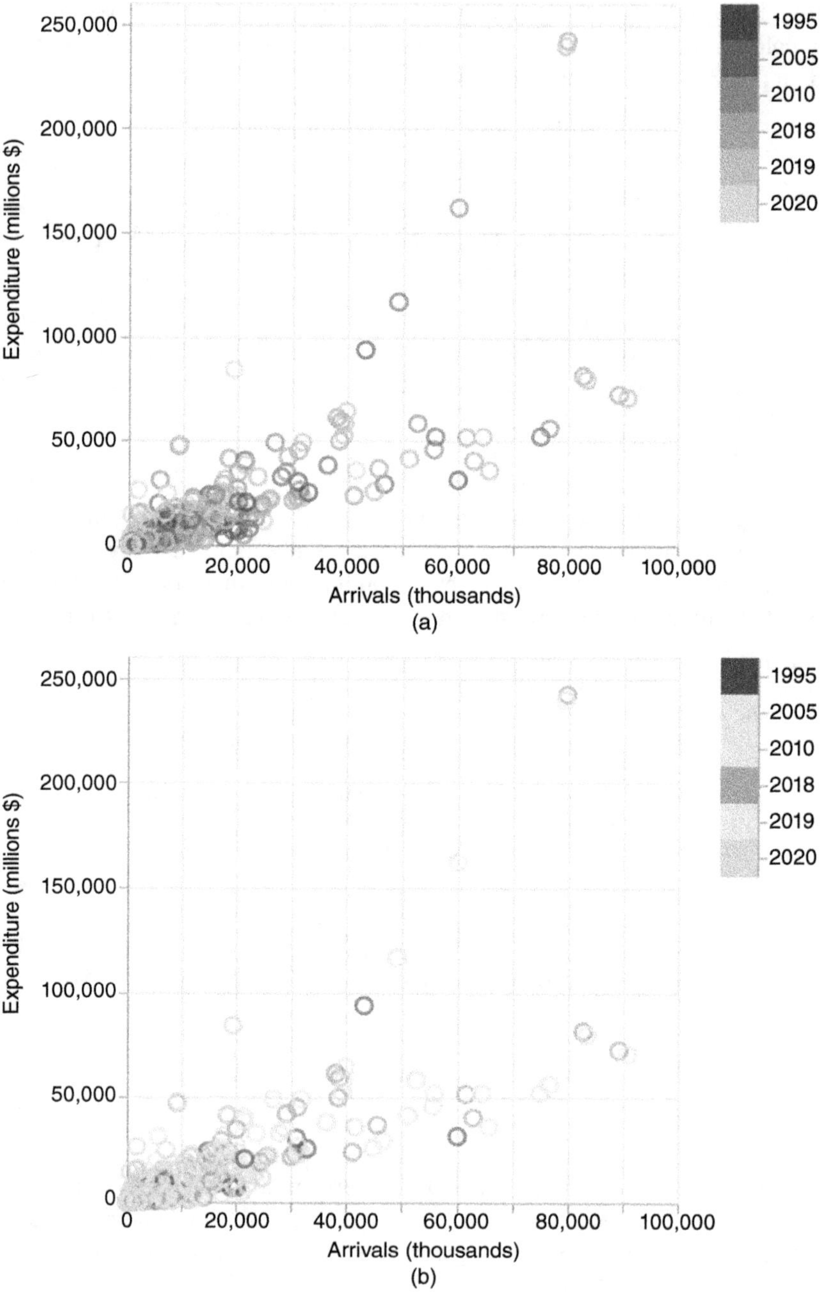

Figure 14.12 (a) Plot as interactive legend, all years selected. (b) Plot as interactive legend, only years 1995, 2010 and 2020 selected and the scatterplot reconfigured.

14.2 Line Plots

14.2.1 Static Graphics

We see now line plots in Altair and the peculiar interactive actions that could be introduced.

First, we use dataset *UNSD – Methodology* from the United Nations that contains official denominations, codes, and geographical information.

```
country= pd.read_csv("datasets/UN/UNSD — Methodology.csv", sep=';')
```

	Global Code	Region Name	Sub-region Name	Country or Area	M49 Code	ISO-alpha2 Code	ISO-alpha3 Code
0	1	Africa	Northern Africa	Algeria	12	DZ	DZA
1	1	Africa	Northern Africa	Egypt	818	EG	EGY
2	1	Africa	Northern Africa	Libya	434	LY	LBY
3	1	Africa	Northern Africa	Morocco	504	MA	MAR
4	1	Africa	Northern Africa	Sudan	729	SD	SDN
...	...	...	...	...	...	...	...

The data frame should be prepared for visualization. Data-wrangling operations are presented in the *Additional Online Material – Altair – Line plot: transformations*. We want to show line plots regarding continents (column *Region*) with respect to the mean per capita expenditure for tourist. We aggregate to obtain the means and visualize.

```
df2_ext= df1_ext.groupby(['Region Name', 'Year'])\
[['Expenditure','Arrivals','Per_capita_Exp(x1000)']].mean().\
      round(3).reset_index()
```

	Region Name	Year	Expenditure	Arrivals	Per_capita_Exp (x1000)
0	Africa	1995	332.054	504.133	0.816
1	Africa	2005	713.625	951.638	0.760
2	Africa	2010	1051.854	1339.542	0.792
3	Africa	2018	1318.022	1857.538	0.961
4	Africa	2019	1371.114	2047.057	0.909
...	...	...	...	...	...

The line plot is similar to the scatterplot, only the function to be called changes, it is `mark_line()`.

```
alt.Chart(df2_ext).mark_line().encode(
    x= alt.X('Year:O',
         axis= alt.Axis(title='Year')),
    y= alt.Y('Per_capita_Exp(x1000):Q',
         axis= alt.Axis(title='Mean Per_capita Expenditure
                                 (thousands)')),
    color= alt.Color('Region Name:N',
             scale= alt.Scale(scheme='magma'),
             legend= alt.Legend(title="Regions", orient="bottom"))
).properties(width=300,height=300)
```

Previously, we have used standard *pandas* functions to aggregate values and obtain the means, but the same could have been done *directly in the Altair graphic* with attribute `aggregate='mean'`. Here the script using the original *df1_ext* data frame and aggregation in the Altair graphic.

```
alt.Chart(df1_ext).mark_line().encode(...

    y= alt.Y(field='Per_capita_Exp(x1000)',
           aggregate='mean',
           type='quantitative',
           axis=alt.Axis(title='Mean Per_capita Expenditure
                                (thousands $)')),
    ...
```

If we wish to show both the mean per capita expenditure and the total expenditure (`aggregate='sum'`), the possibility to define them directly into Altair would be handy. The following script presents them both together with the total of arrivals. Figure 14.13 shows the plots aligned.

```
plot1= alt.Chart(df1_ext).mark_line().encode(
    x= alt.X('Year:O', axis= alt.Axis(title='Year')),
    y= alt.Y(field='Per_capita_Exp(x1000)', aggregate='mean',
         type='quantitative',
         axis= alt.Axis(title='Mean Per_capita Expenditure
                                 (thousands $)')),
    color= alt.Color('Region Name:N',
             scale= alt.Scale(scheme='magma'),
             legend= alt.Legend(title="Regions", orient="bottom"))
).properties(width=200, height=250)

plot2 = alt.Chart(df1_ext).mark_line().encode(
    x= alt.X('Year:O', axis=alt.Axis(title='Year')),
    y= alt.Y(field='Expenditure', aggregate='sum',
           type='quantitative',
           axis= alt.Axis(title='Total Expenditure (millions $)')),
    color= alt.Color('Region Name:N',
      scale= alt.Scale(scheme='magma'))
).properties(width=200, height=250)
```

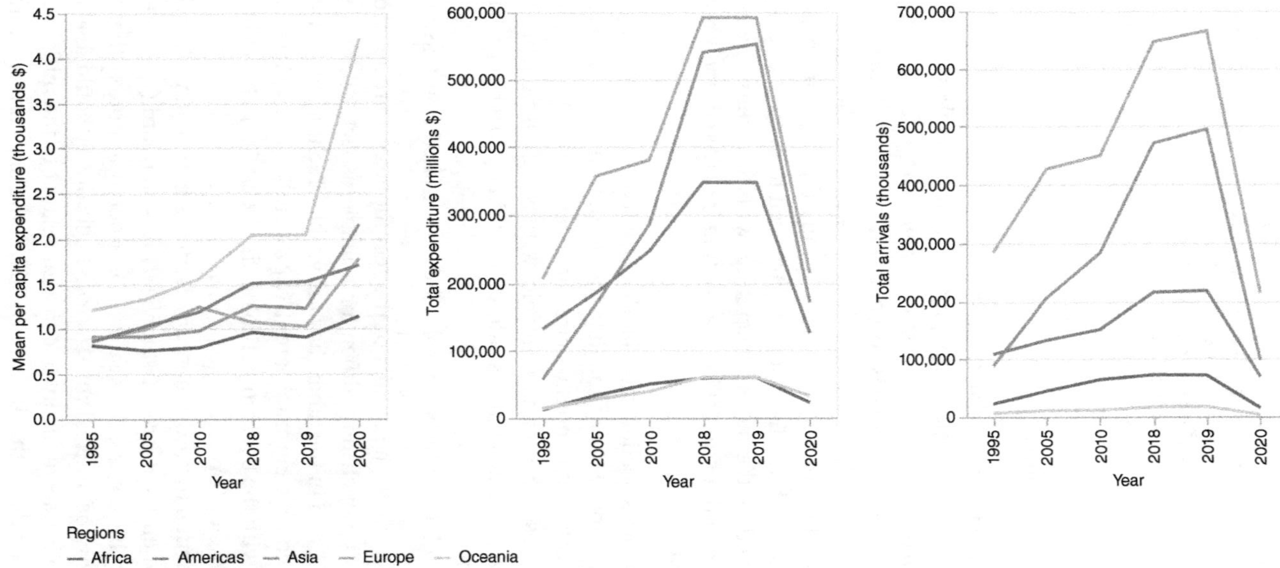

Figure 14.13 Line plots, mean per capita, total expenditure, and total arrivals.

```
plot3= alt.Chart(df1_ext).mark_line().encode(
    x= alt.X('Year:O', axis= alt.Axis(title='Year')),
    y= alt.Y(field='Arrivals', aggregate='sum', type='quantitative',
         axis= alt.Axis(title='Total Arrivals (thousands)')),
    color= alt.Color('Region Name:N',
      scale =alt.Scale(scheme='magma'))
).properties(width=200, height=250)

plot1 | plot2 | plot3
```

14.2.2 Interactive Graphics

14.2.2.1 Highlighted Lines with Mouse Hover

In the first example of interactive line plot, we add a simple visual effect: *lines are highlighted when the mouse hovers on them*. The effect is simple but to realize it, there are some subtleties to consider. The first is that the action is not actually triggered by the lines, but by markers, with the same mechanism of scatterplot examples already seen. This means that a scatterplot should be introduced, together with the line plot, we just need to make it not visible to the observer but detected by the mouse. Therefore, with functions `mark_point` or `mark_circle`, we add a scatterplot that should be layered upon the line plot. Here are the logical steps:

1. First, we define the selection criteria, the variable is called *highlight* and it is associated to the mouse hover and data frame column *Region Name*.
2. Line plot and scatterplot should share the same axes definitions to be overlapped, for this reason we define a *base* plot with common elements that will be instantiated into a line plot and a scatterplot, similarly to what we have already done in previous examples.
3. Finally, the line plot and the scatterplot are instantiated from the *base* plot.

In order to better show the details of the technique, we create two graphics, *points1* and *points0*, which only differ for a single aspect: one has scatterplot markers not visible, and in the other they are visible. Technically, in the first one, the scatterplot is completely transparent (`opacity=alt.value(0.0)`) and markers are filled with the background color (*fill='white'*), in the second, instead, there is no transparency (`opacity=alt.value(1.0)`).

We also add an action to lines, whose *size* is an aesthetic and varies with respect to the selection: when *not selected* (*~highlight*) it is standard (`alt.value(1)`), when *selected* it is thicker (`alt.value(3)`). A detail to note is that the logical condition checks if the line is *not selected*. Logically, it could have been the opposite, but there is a technicality to consider related to the initial value: when no selection has been done, the first value is used, the one corresponding to *True*. By checking if a line is not selected, the initial value is the standard thickness of size 1. The reader could try to invert the condition (i.e. `(highlight, alt.value(3), alt.value(1))`) and, initially, she/he would see all lines with thickness of size 3.

The overlapping of the two graphics is done with the plus symbol + (e.g. `lines + points1`). Therefore, with `lines + points1`, Altair first draws the lines, then it overlays points to them. This is the reason to specify the size in the line plot because it is created first. The opposite would be necessary if we reverse the order (i.e. `points1 + lines`). The same we do for the second graphic with `lines + points0`, finally the two plots are aligned horizontally. The full script follows, and Figure 14.14 shows the result.

```
# Selection associated to mouse hover

highlight= alt.selection_interval(on='mouseover',
             fields=['Region Name'], nearest=True)

# Base plot, the specific graphic is not set

base= alt.Chart(df2_ext).encode(
    x= alt.X('Year:O', axis= alt.Axis(title='Year')),
    y= alt.Y('Per_capita_Exp(x1000):Q',
         axis= alt.Axis(title='Mean Per_capita Expenditure
                          (thousands)')),
    color= alt.Color('Region Name:N',
             scale= alt.Scale(scheme='magma'),
             legend= alt.Legend(title="Regions",
                              orient="right")))

# First scatterplot with visible points

points1= base.mark_point(fill='white').encode(
           opacity= alt.value(1)
).add_params( highlight )

# Second scatterplot with invisible points

points0= base.mark_point().encode(
           opacity= alt.value(0)
).add_params( highlight )

# Line plot
lines= base.mark_line().encode(
    size= alt.condition(~highlight, alt.value(1), alt.value(3))
).properties( width=300,height=300 )

# Plots overlapping and alignment

(lines + points1) | (lines + points0)
```

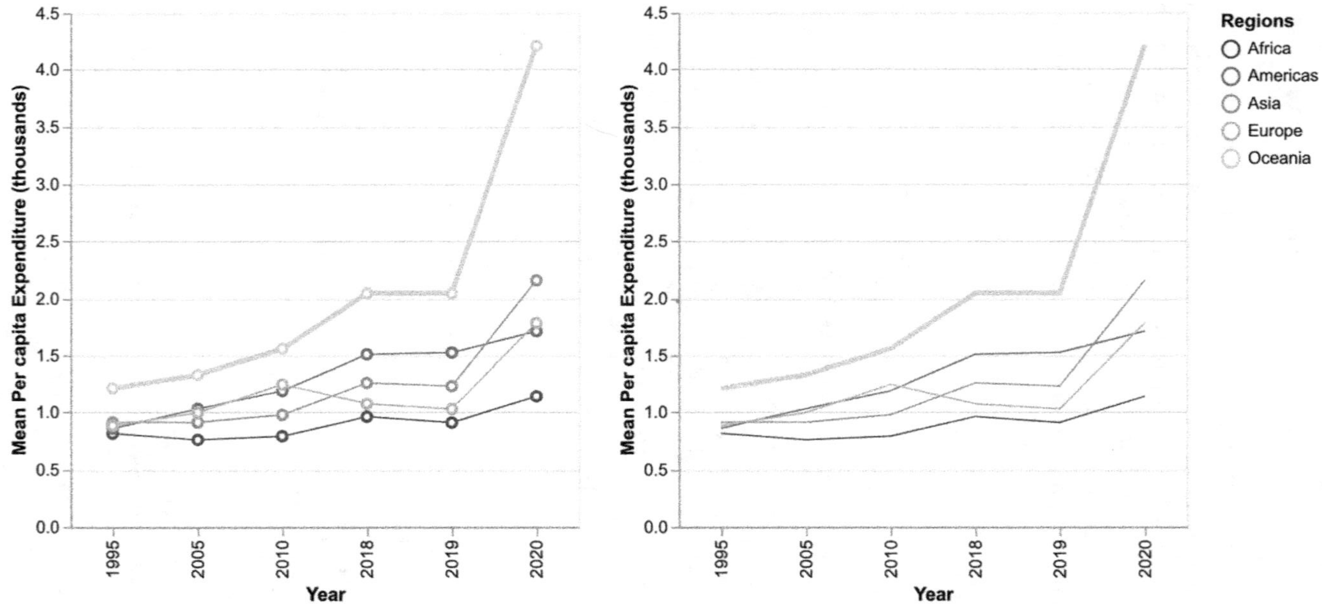

Figure 14.14 Line plots with mouse hover, Oceania's line is highlighted (the mouse over is not visible in screenshots).

14.2.2.2 Aligned Tooltips

We want to *add dynamic tooltips to line plots*. With scatterplots it was very easy, but line plots present a new difficulty because the effect we want to obtain is not that simple. We do not want to show the tooltip for just a single line, which actually will only be a point on the overlapped scatterplot, which would be the same as simply showing the scatterplot. What we want is to show all tooltips for all points corresponding to a certain coordinate on the *x*-axis. For example, when the mouse hovers over a point in Figure 14.14, let us say the one corresponding to year 2019 for Americas, we want to show all tooltips related to year 2019 for all regions, not just Americas. That is more complicated and needs an ingenious solution.

As did before, we start by defining the selection criteria. The new idea is to select a single marker of the scatterplot, that will be not visible to the observer (the scatterplot is fully transparent), associated to the coordinate on the *x*-axis, therefore related to a specific value of *Year*. This is the basis to show all the other tooltips for that coordinate. Then, we define the line plot as a static graphic.

```
# Selection criteria

selection= alt.selection_point(nearest=True,
                         on='mouseover',
                         fields=['Year'], empty=False)

# Line plot

line= alt.Chart(df2_ext).mark_line().encode(
    x= alt.X('Year:O', axis =alt.Axis(title='Year')),
    y= alt.Y('Per_capita_Exp(x1000):Q',
    axis= alt.Axis(title='Mean Per_capita Expenditure
                         (thousands)')),
    color= alt.Color('Region Name:N',
             scale= alt.Scale(scheme='magma'),
             legend= alt.Legend(title="Regions",
             orient="right")))
```

Now comes the ingenious solution. The *first scatterplot* should be associated only to the *x*-axis, with no *y*-axis defined, which would be a series of points aligned horizontally on the *x*-axis (and invisible). To these points, we associate the selection. In order to see the mechanism more clearly, it is possible to temporarily make them visible by changing the transparency from 0 to 1.

```
points0= alt.Chart(df2_ext).mark_point().encode(
           x='Year:O',
           opacity= alt.value(0),
).add_params( selection )
```

The *second scatterplot* has markers visualized for a better graphical effect. We can add it by using the line plot definition with `line.mark_point()` and associate to it a condition changing the transparency: when the mouse hovers on the *x* coordinate (i.e. a certain year) there is no transparency and markers on the line become visible, otherwise the transparency is full and markers are hidden.

```
points1= line.mark_point().encode(
            opacity= alt.condition(selection,
                     alt.value(1), alt.value(0)))
```

We also want *textual values* to be shown representing the values of corresponding markers when they become visible. Again, when the mouse hovers on one marker, we want to show all values of points with same *x* coordinate. It is the same mechanism used to show markers of the second scatterplot, so, again, the line plot definition is used, now as `line.mark_text()`. Attributes `align`, dx, and dy, adjust the text position with respect to the scatterplot points.

```
text= line.mark_text(align='right', dx=-5, dy=-7).encode(
        text= alt.condition(selection,
                'Per_capita_Exp(x1000):Q', alt.value(' ')))
```

The last graphical element we want to introduce to improve the readability is a *vertical line* (function `mark_rule()`) corresponding to the *x* coordinate for which points and textual values are visualized. This time, it does not depend on the line plot but just on the *x* coordinate and the mouse hover. Function `transform_filter()` is used with the selection to visualize this vertical line when the selection is true.

```
rules= alt.Chart(df2_ext).mark_rule(color='gray').encode(
          x='Year:O'
).transform_filter( selection )
```

We have all elements, this time the graphic has a degree of complexity clearly higher than the previous cases because we should combine a line plot (object *line*), a scatterplot with invisible points to activate the selection (object *points0*), a second scatterplot with visible points and dynamic actions (object *points1*), textual elements with a dynamic action (object *text*), and a vertical line with a dynamic action (object *rules*). In order to combine them all in a single graphic, we need to explicitly use layers, directly inherited from the grammar of graphics, with function `alt.layer()`.

```
alt.layer(
    line, points0, points1, rules, text
).properties( width=300, height=500 )
```

The visual effect of this solution could vary from case to case. In particular, visualizing the textual values is effective when the result is sufficiently separated to be clearly read. On the contrary, if lines of the line plot are too close to one another, the textual labels will overlap, resulting in practically unreadable and the overall effect will appear confused. Figure 14.15a and Figure 14.15b show two screenshots for x coordinates that let textual labels to be read sufficiently well; that would not be the case for years where lines are very close to each other.

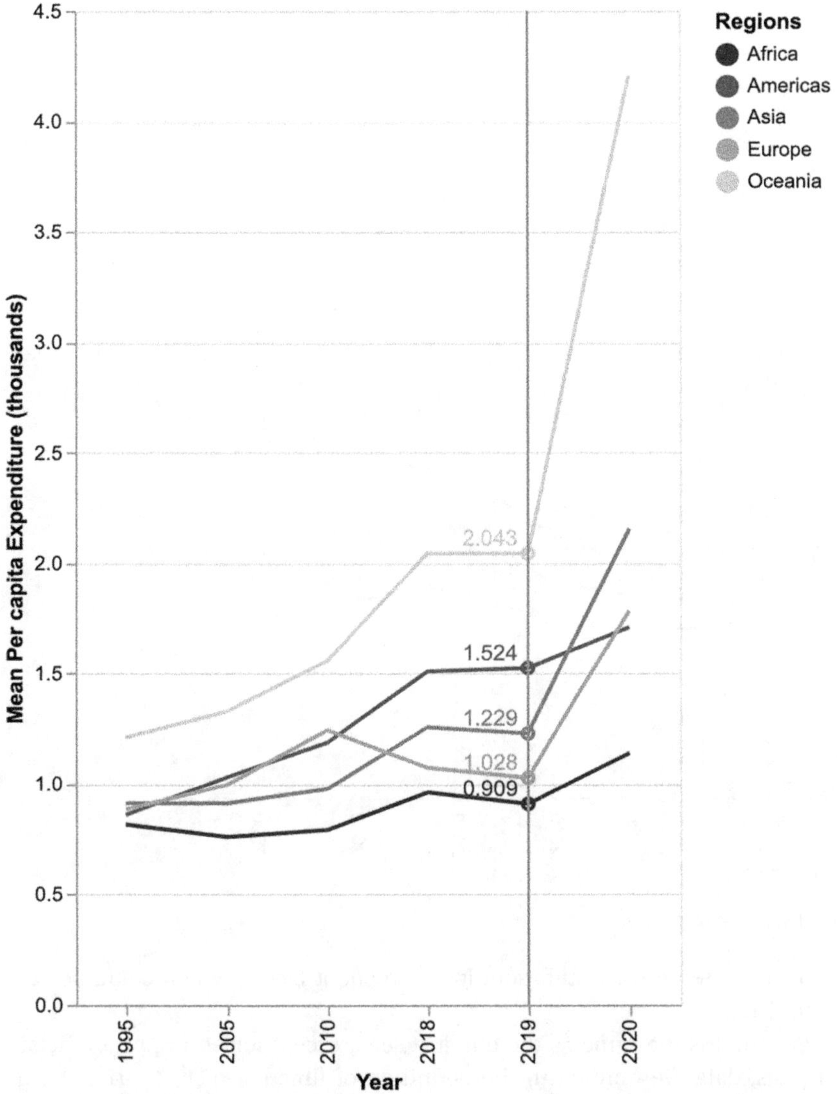

Figure 14.15 (a) Line plot with mouse hover and coordinated visualization of all values and the vertical segment for the corresponding year (example with year 2019). (b) Same for year 2018.

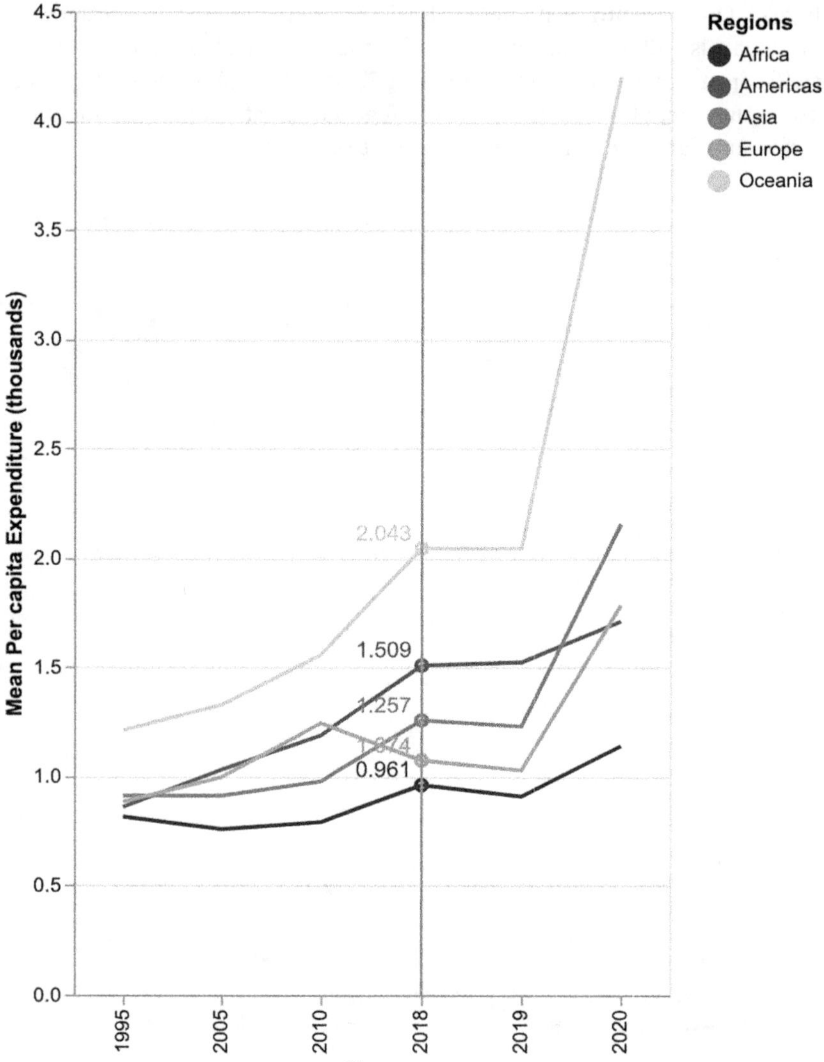

Figure 14.15 *(Continued)*

A possible alternative to this solution is to adopt facets, which could be kept synchronized.

The solution is the same as the one just seen, except for an important detail: in all plots, data are omitted in the definition of function `alt.Chart()` (e.g., `line=alt.Chart().mark_line().encode(...)`). Instead, they are defined globally in facet specification, which will be concatenated with layers definition, as in the following excerpt of code. That way, we will have each region in a facet, and for all of them the dynamic mechanisms will be replicated and synchronized, as shown in Figure 14.16.

```
alt.layer(line, points0, points1, rules, text).facet(
   column='Region Name', data=df2_ext)
```

14.3 Bar Plots

14.3.1 Static Graphics

After scatterplots and line plots, we consider *bar plots*, the typical graphic type for categorical variables. As before, we start from the static definition followed by interactive components. We will see some of the main aspects, for the full list, we forward the reader to the Altair official documentation. As data, we will use dataset *Crime at Sea: A Global Database of Maritime Pirate Attacks (1993–2020)*.

```
df= pd.read_csv("datasets/Pirate_Attacks/pirate_attacks.csv")
```

date	longitude	latitude	location_description	eez_ country	vessel_name
1993-01-02	116.9667	19.700000	Hong Kong – Luzon – Hainan	TWN	Mv Cosmic Leader
1993-01-04	116.0000	22.350000	Hong Kong – Luzon – Hainan	CHN	Mv Tricolor Star III
1993-01-06	115.2500	19.670000	Hong Kong – Luzon – Hainan	TWN	Mv Arktis Star
1993-01-08	124.5833	29.900000	East China Sea	CHN	Ussurijsk
1993-01-12	120.2667	18.133333	Hong Kong – Luzon – Hainan	PHL	Mv Chennai Nermai

The data frame needs some transformations to be ready for visualization. We aggregate data based on the number of attacks for year and month and execute a few other simple data-wrangling operations.

```
df['date']= pd.to_datetime(df['date'], format='%Y-%m-%d')
df['Year']= df['date'].dt.year
df['Month']= df['date'].dt.month

df1= df.groupby(['Year',"Month"])[['date']].\
count().reset_index().\
rename(columns= {"date": "Attacks"})
```

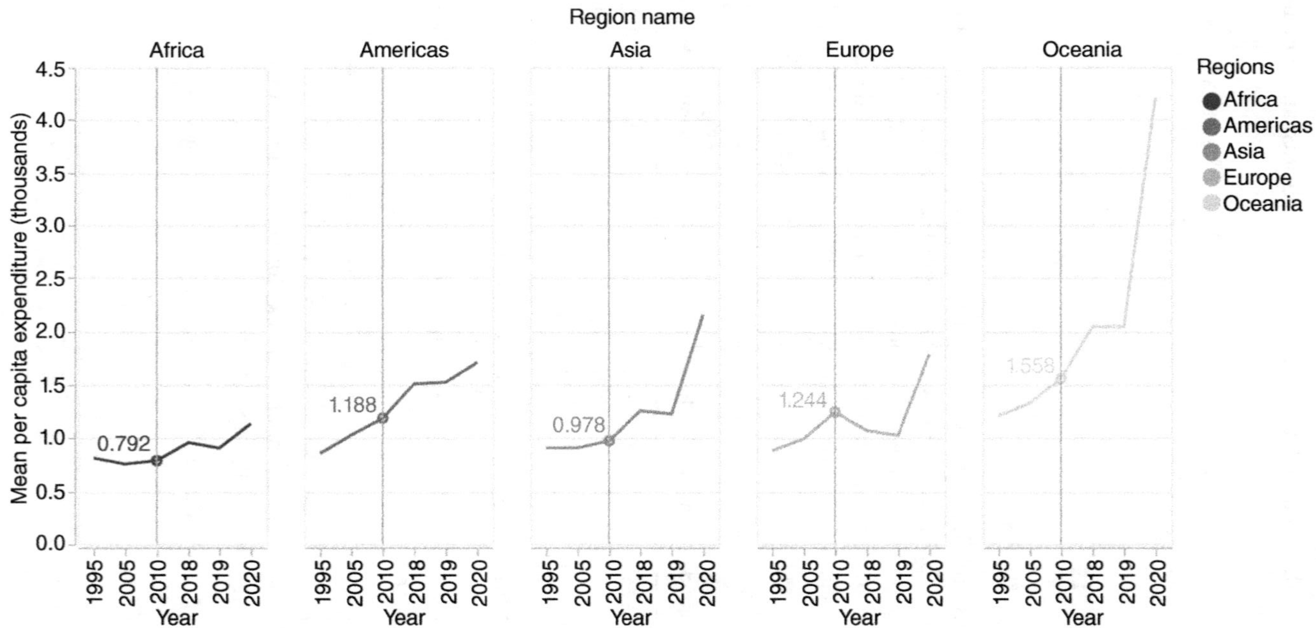

Figure 14.16 Line plot with mouse hover and coordinated visualization in all facets for the corresponding year (example with year 2010).

	Year	Month	Attacks
0	1993	1	11
1	1993	2	13
2	1993	3	10
3	1993	4	13
4	1993	5	9
...	...	...	...
331	2020	8	8
332	2020	9	8
333	2020	10	18
334	2020	11	24
335	2020	12	16

The Altair function for bar plots is `mark_bar()`. The following example presents the number of pirate attacks during the years together with the arithmetic mean, shown with a horizontal line (function `mark.rule()`) (see Figure 14.17).

```
df2= df1.groupby('Year')[['Attacks']].sum().reset_index()

plot= alt.Chart(df2).mark_bar(fill='lightblue').encode(
    x='Year:O',
    y= alt.Y('Attacks:Q',
```

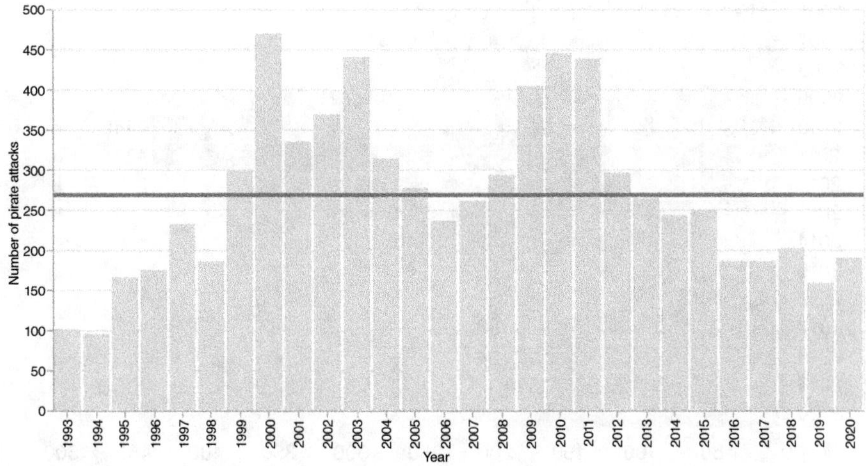

Figure 14.17 (Left): Bar plot with segment for the arithmetic mean.

```
        axis= alt.Axis(title='Number of Pirate Attacks')))

stat= alt.Chart(df2).mark_rule(color='red', size=3).encode(
    y= 'mean(Attacks):Q')

(plot + stat).properties(width=600)
```

As a second basic example, we use the original data frame *df1* and native Altair aggregation features (`aggregate='sum'`), then we plot it horizontally by exchanging the axes definition and add the information about the actual value at the end of each bar using function `mark_text()`, associated to bar definition. Attribute `text` has the sum of monthly attacks as value. Figure 14.18 shows the result.

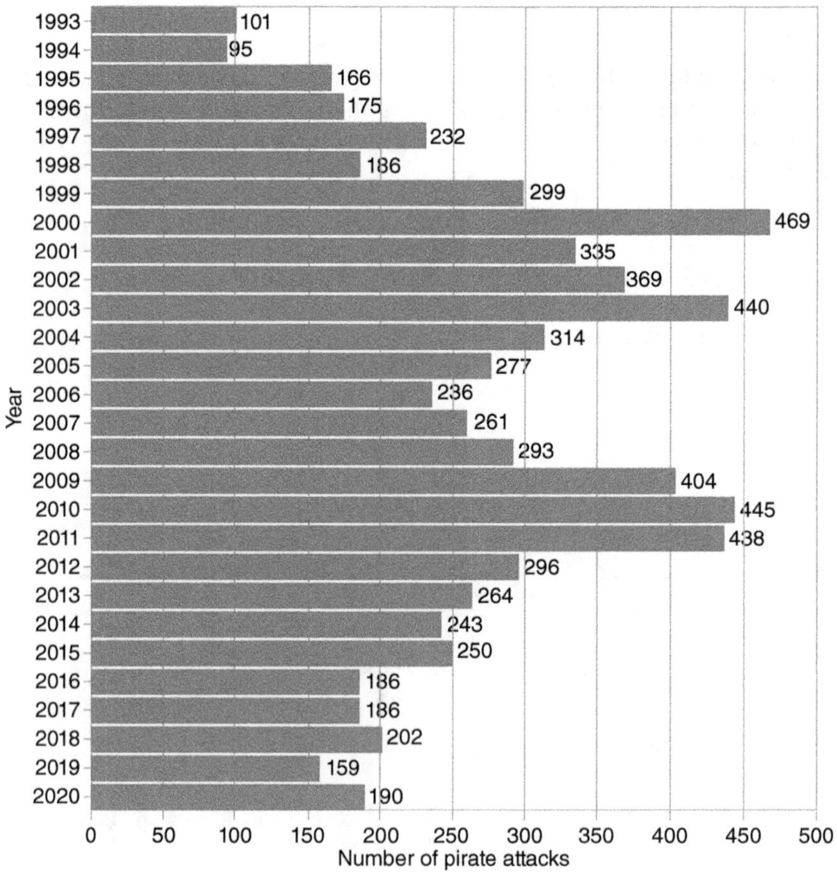

Figure 14.18 (Right): Bar plot with horizontal orientation and annotations.

```
bars= alt.Chart(df1).mark_bar(fill='teal').encode(
    y= 'Year:O',
    x= alt.X(field='Attacks',
         aggregate='sum', type='quantitative',
         axis= alt.Axis(title='Number of Pirate Attacks')),)

text= bars.mark_text( align='left', baseline='middle', dx=3
).encode( text='sum(Attacks)')

(bars + text).properties(height=450)
```

14.3.1.1 Diverging Bar Plot

Diverging bar plots are an important variant of traditional bar plots, with both positive and negative values that lead to the typical configuration of bars oriented in opposite directions. To present this case, we need to build a data frame with positive and negative values; in our case, it could be done by calculating differences in pirate attacks over consecutive years. Python function `shift(1)` permits to copy the values of a column and shift them down one element. This way, with the exception of the first element, we will have, in two columns, the value of pirate attacks for a certain month and year and beside the value of the previous month (column *lag*), which makes it very convenient to calculate the difference for consecutive months in another new column (*diff* in the example).

```
df1['lag']  = df1['Attacks'].shift(1)
df1['diff']= df1['lag']-df1['Attacks']

df1= df1.assign(Date = df1.Year.astype(str) + '-' +
                       df1.Month.astype(str))
df1['Date']= pd.to_datetime(df1.Date,format='%Y-%m')
```

	Year	Month	Attacks	lag	diff	Date
0	1993	1	11	NaN	NaN	1993-01-01
1	1993	2	13	11.0	−2.0	1993-02-01
2	1993	3	10	13.0	3.0	1993-03-01
3	1993	4	13	10.0	−3.0	1993-04-01
4	1993	5	9	13.0	4.0	1993-05-01
...	...	...	...	...	...	...
331	2020	8	8	9.0	1.0	2020-08-01
332	2020	9	8	8.0	0.0	2020-09-01
333	2020	10	18	8.0	−10.0	2020-10-01
334	2020	11	24	18.0	−6.0	2020-11-01
335	2020	12	16	24.0	8.0	2020-12-01

This way, we have obtained a column with positive and negative monthly variations. We could do the same for yearly variations, so as to have two time series to visualize as diverging bar plots. We use different colors for positive and negative values, in addition to the different orientations, which will be applied by means of a logical condition, similar in logic to those already seen in previous examples. Here there is a difference due to the fact that, logically, we should check whether the value of column *diff* is greater than zero, but technically this condition requires the `alt.datum` method to be executed (`alt.datum.diff >= 0`). The complete script follows, and Figure 14.19 shows the diverging bar plot for both time series.

```
# Data aggregation
temp= df1.groupby('Year')[['diff']].sum().reset_index()

# Diverging bar plot for monthly variations

plot1= alt.Chart(df1).mark_bar().encode(
         x= alt.X('Date:T', axis= alt.Axis(title=None)),
         y= alt.Y('diff:Q',
              axis= alt.Axis(title='Difference in Number of
                                   Pirate Attacks')),
         color= alt.condition(alt.datum.diff >= 0,
                    alt.value("black"), alt.value("orange"))
).properties(height=200,width=800, title='Monthly variations')

# Diverging bar plot for yearly variations

plot2= alt.Chart(temp).mark_bar().encode(
         x= alt.X('Year:O', axis= alt.Axis(title=None,
              labels=False, ticks=True)),
         y= alt.Y('diff:Q',
              axis= alt.Axis(title='Difference in Number of
                                  Pirate Attacks')),
         color= alt.condition( alt.datum.diff >= 0,
                   alt.value("black"), alt.value("orange"))
).properties(height=200,width=800, title='Yearly variations')

# Vertical alignment
plot2 & plot1
```

14.3.1.2 Plots with Double Scale

A different variant, although not truly specific to bar plots, is the case of two different plots overlapping, *each one with its own scale.* For the second graphic, we use dataset *Goods loaded worldwide*, related to global maritime shipping, which we want to confront with data about pirate attacks, in the not unreasonable hypothesis that the two phenomena could be somehow correlated (remember, a visualization does not demonstrate causation, at most, it could provide an initial hint for a more

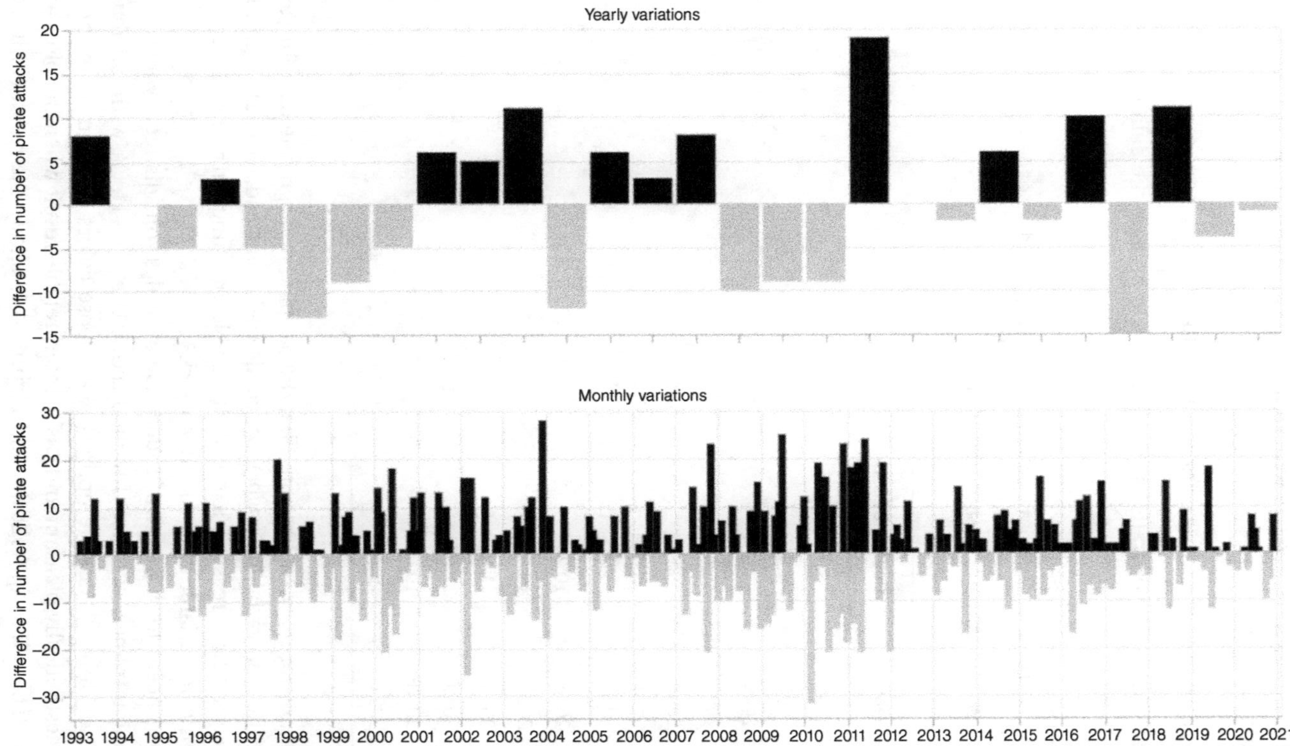

Figure 14.19 Diverging bar plots, pirate attacks, yearly and monthly variations.

accurate analysis unless we have other contextual information). For goods loaded, we use a line plot and an *area plot* with some style options for improving the visual quality and readability.

```
trade= pd.read_csv("datasets/UN/HBS2022_5.1Fig1.csv")
```

Some data-wrangling operations are necessary to prepare the data frame, they are simple.

```
trade= trade.iloc[0:26,:]
trade['Goods loaded']= pd.to_numeric(trade['Goods loaded']).round(3)
trade['Category']= pd.to_numeric(trade['Category'])
trade.columns= ['Year','Goods_loaded']
```

	Year	Goods_loaded
0	1996	4.758
1	1997	4.953
2	1998	5.631
3	1999	5.683
4	2000	5.984
5	2001	6.020
...	...	...
20	2016	10.247
21	2017	10.714
22	2018	11.019
23	2019	11.071
24	2020	10.645
25	2021	10.985

We are ready for the visualization. First the bar plot, we aggregate data for year and define the plot (variable *barplot*). For goods loaded, instead, we use two graphics for purely aesthetic reasons: a line plot (variable *line*, function `mark_line()`) and an *area plot* (variable *area*, function `mark_area()`).

Now, we need to have two independent scales on distinct *y*-axes for the two data frames, we use function `resolve_scale()` with attribute `y='independent'`. As style options, we choose colors and transparency to obtain an aesthetically pleasant and easily interpretable result when the plots are overlapped. The full script follows, and Figure 14.20 shows the result (hint: the hypothetical correlation between the two phenomena seems unsupported).

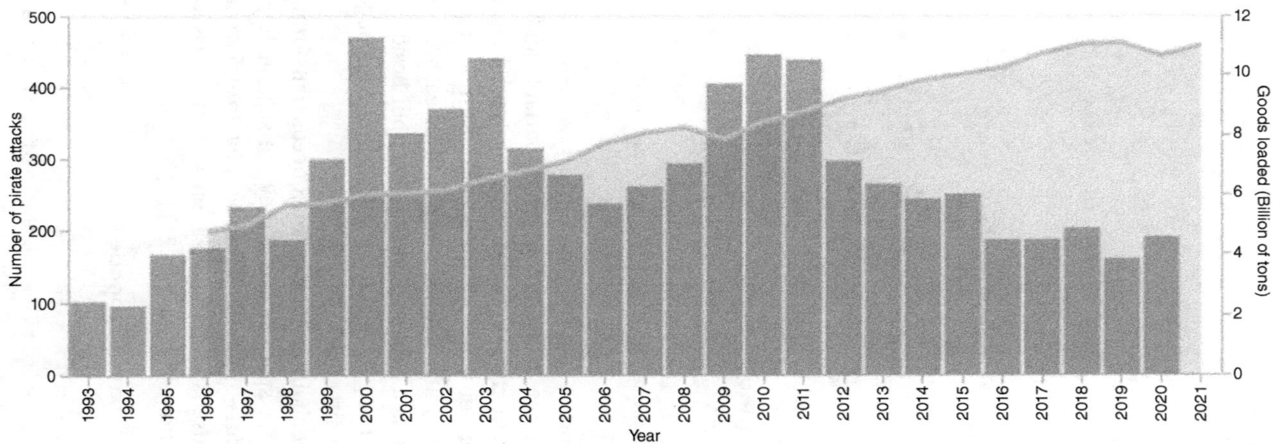

Figure 14.20 Plot with two distinct *y*-axes and corresponding scales.

```
# Aggregation
df2= df1.groupby('Year')[['Attacks']].sum().reset_index()

# Bar plot (pirate attacks)

barplot= alt.Chart(df2).mark_bar(color='gray').encode(
    x= 'Year:O',
    y= alt.Y('Attacks:Q',
         axis= alt.Axis(title='Number of pirate attacks')))

# Line plot (goods loaded)

line= alt.Chart(trade).mark_line(color='orange', size=3).encode(
    x= 'Year:O',
    y= alt.Y('Goods_loaded:Q',
         axis=alt.Axis(title='Goods loaded (Billions of tons)')))

# Area plot (goods loaded), based on the line plot definition

area= line.mark_area(color='teal', opacity=0.3)

# Line plot and area plot combined
arealine = (line + area)

# Full composition with independent scales
(barplot + arealine).resolve_scale(y='independent')
```

14.3.1.3 Stacked Bar Plots

With bar plots, it is possible to use a categorical variable and color differently data belonging to different categories. Two are the typical layouts: *stacked bar plots* (colored bars are on top one with the other to form a single composite bar for each categorical value) and *dodged bar plots* (for each categorical value of the Cartesian axis, there is a group of colored bars put beside). Altair supports the stacked layout but, strangely, lacks the support for the dodged one. For this reason, we show only the first case.

We still use the dataset about pirate attacks. It needs transformations to be prepared for visualization; for space reasons, they are separately presented in the *Additional Online Material – Altair – Stacked bar plot: transformations*. The result is data frame *df6*, that is used in the visualization. Colors are associated to country names (variable *country name*) (Figure 14.21).

```
alt.Chart(df6).mark_bar().encode(
    x='Year:O',
    y=alt.Y('Attacks:Q',
        axis= alt.Axis(title='Number of pirate attacks')),

    color= alt.Color('country_name:N',
```

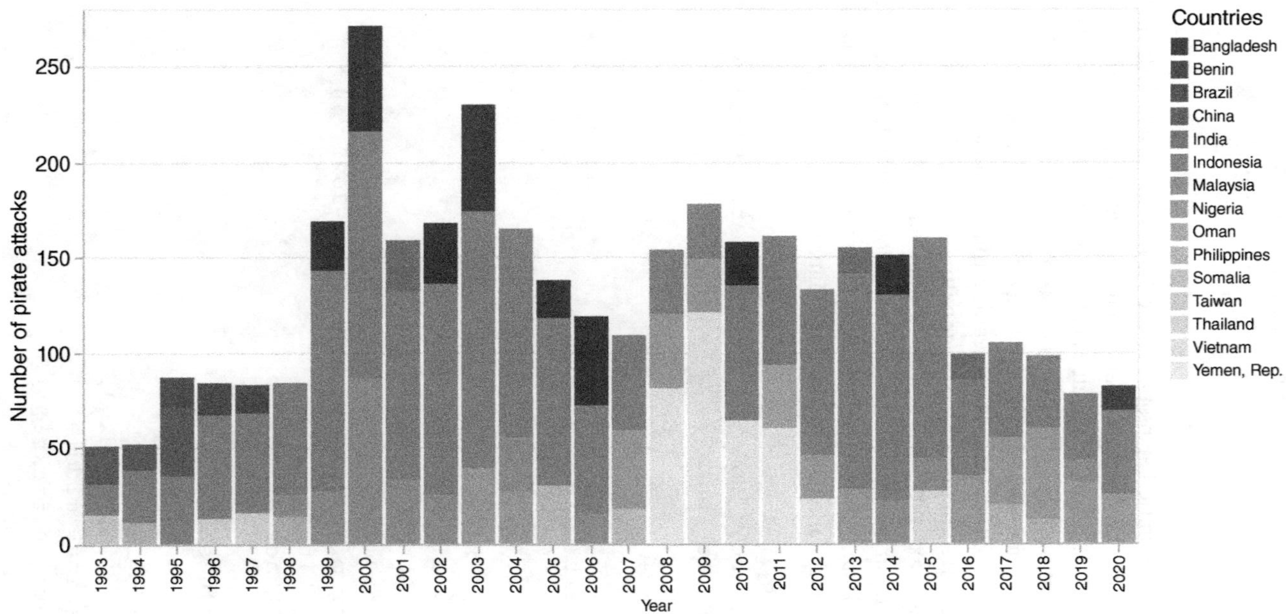

Figure 14.21 Stacked bar plot, pirate attacks, and countries where they took place.

```
                scale=alt.Scale(scheme='plasma'),
                legend=alt.Legend(title="Countries",
                                  orient="right")))
```

14.3.1.4 Sorted Bars

As a final feature for static bar plots, we see how to sort bars with respect to a quantitative variable. The dataset is still that of pirate attacks. We need a logical condition to select a subset of values (function `transform_filter`), this time based on the number of attacks (`alt.datum.Attacks > 50`). We want the bars, each one referred to a country, sorted for number of attacks. Attribute `sort=-x` will be specified for axis *y*, meaning that countries (i.e., values of the *y*-axis) should be sorted in *decreasing order* with respect to the number of attacks (i.e., values of the *x*-axis). We also add the textual value of the number of attacks at the end of each bar, as we have seen in a previous example by using function `mark_text()`. Data frame *df5* is the result of some common transformations presented in the *Additional Online Material* (Figure 14.22).

```
# Aggregation
data= df5.groupby('country_name')[['Attacks']].\
agg('sum').reset_index()

# Bar plot

plot= alt.Chart(data).mark_bar(
).encode(
   y= alt.Y('country_name:N',
        sort='-x',
        axis= alt.Axis(title='')),
   x= alt.X('Attacks:Q',
        axis= alt.Axis(title=
      'Number of pirate attacks (1993-2020)'))
).transform_filter(
     'datum.Attacks > 50')

# Textual values

text= plot.mark_text(
        align='left', dx=3,
        baseline='middle'
).encode( text='Attacks:Q')

plot + text
```

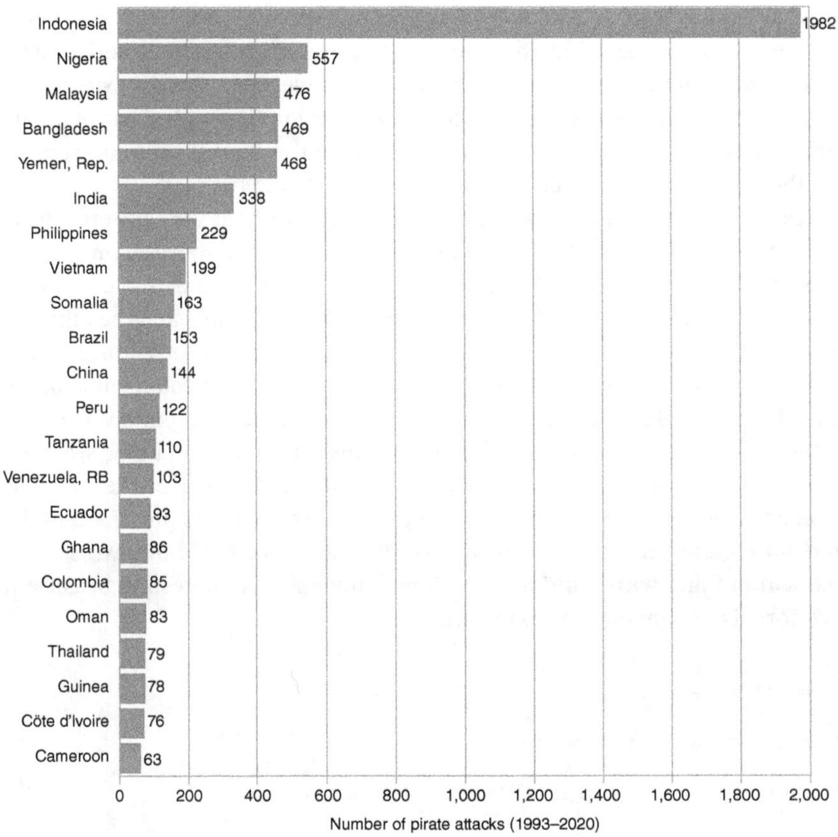

Figure 14.22 Bar plot with sorted bars and annotations.

14.3.2 Interactive Graphics

14.3.2.1 Synchronized Bar Plots

We move to interactive features of bar plots starting with a case where interactivity may offer a possibility otherwise not easy to obtain. We use the two last static bar plots just seen: the *stacked bar plot*, which could present many details in a compact form but tends to become increasingly difficult to read when the number of elements increases, and the *bar plot with sorted bars*, which, on the contrary, is easy to read but may lack details if the number of bars has been limited, for example. We could make them *mutually interactive and synchronized* so that by selecting one or more elements on one of the two bar plots, we can automatically see the corresponding elements in the other one. That might be particularly useful, for example, we can select some countries in the sorted bar plot, which is an easy action being the names of countries explicitly listed and see where those countries are placed in the stacked bar plot, where it could be less easy to recognize a country by looking at the color scale legend. The opposite is also possible, we want to know which is a certain country in the stacked bar plot, and again the color palette legend could be difficult to interpret if hues are similar, while the information could be easily visible in the sorted bar plot.

To realize this feature, we proceed in a way similar to what we have previously seen with scatterplots. We start by defining a multiple selection based on country names with function `alt.selection_point()`. Then, we define conditions for changing colors to bars so that those selected have full colors and the others, a neutral tint. The conditions will be different for the two bar plots (*change_color1* and *change_color2*): in the sorted bar plot, bars have a uniform color, while in the stacked bar plot, color is an aesthetic referred to country names. Finally, we want the interactivity to be *bidirectional*, meaning that the initial manual selection could be done in both plots. Data frame *df5* is the same used in the previous section and has been derived through common transformations presented in the *Additional Online Material*. Figure 14.23a and Figure 14.23b show two screenshots, without and with multiple selections. The result is interesting because it allows for all combinations of countries.

```
data= df5.groupby('country_name')[['Attacks']].\
agg('sum').reset_index()

# Multiple selection based on country names

selection= alt.selection_point(fields=['country_name'])

# Conditions for changing color of bars

change_color1= alt.condition(selection,
                   alt.value('teal'), alt.value('lightgray'))

change_color2= alt.condition(selection,
                   alt.Color('country_name:N'),
                   alt.value('lightgray'))

# Sorted bar plot, it shows the 40 countries with more pirate attacks

bar_ordered= alt.Chart(data).mark_bar().encode(
    y= alt.Y('country_name:N', sort='-x',
         axis= alt.Axis(title='')),
    x= alt.X('Attacks:Q',
         axis= alt.Axis(title='Number of pirate attacks (1993-2020)')),
    color= change_color1,
).transform_filter('datum.Attacks > 40'
).add_params( selection )

# Stacked bar plot, all countries with more than 10 attacks
```

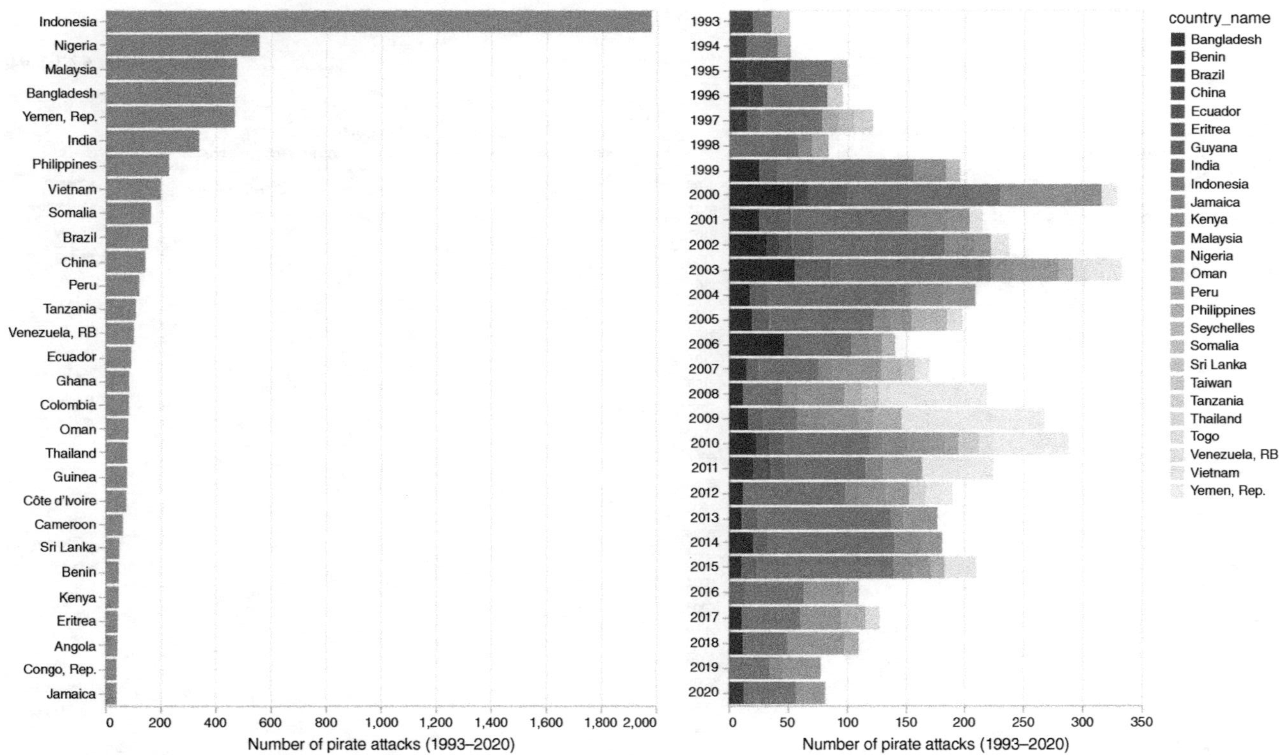

(a)

Figure 14.23 (a) Synchronized bar plots, default visualization, without selection. (b) Synchronized bar plots with multiple selections of countries.

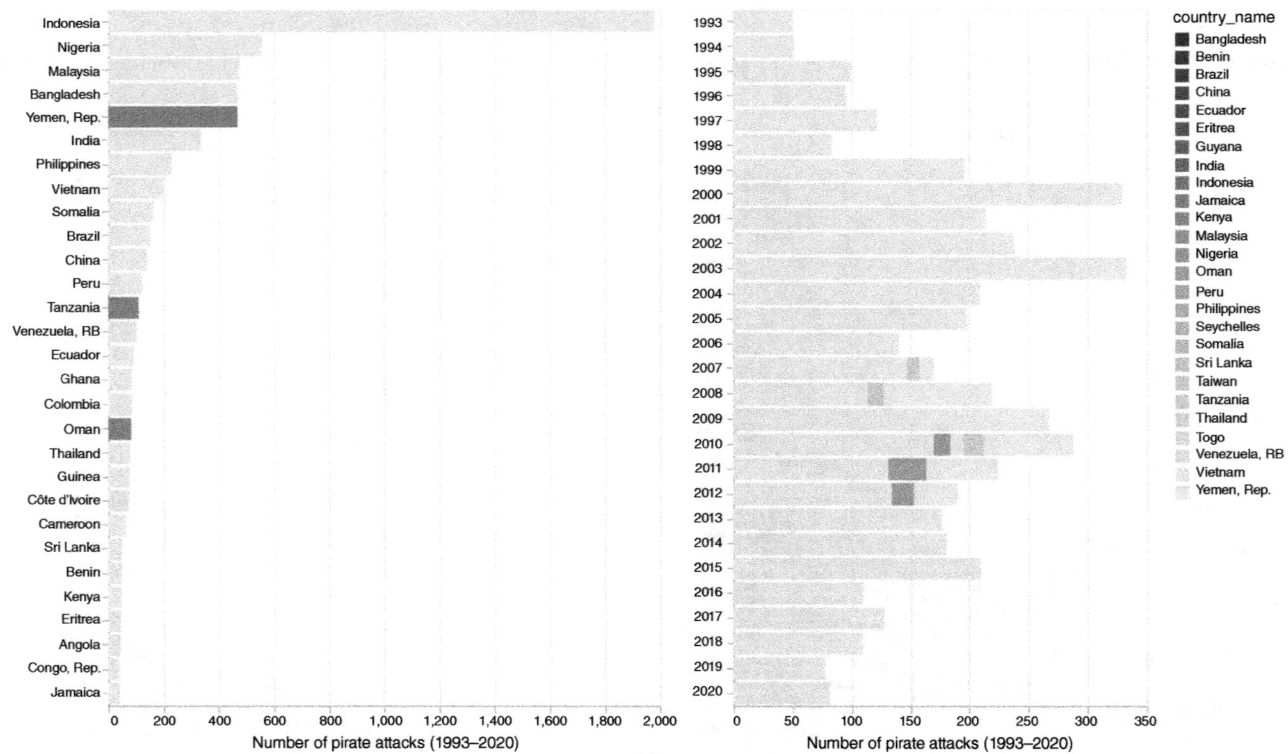

(b)

Figure 14.23 (*Continued*)

```
bar_stacked= alt.Chart(df5).mark_bar().encode(
    y= alt.Y('Year:O',
         axis= alt.Axis(title=None)),
    x= alt.X('Attacks:Q',
         axis= alt.Axis(title='Number of pirate attacks (1993-2020)')),
    color= change_color2,
).transform_filter('datum.Attacks > 10'
).add_params( selection)

bar_ordered | bar_stacked
```

14.3.2.2 Bar Plot with Slider

We introduce the dataset regarding *homeless persons in the United States – 2007 – 2022 – Point-in-Time Estimates by State*, from the US Department of Housing and Urban Development, and select the total amount for each year of the survey. As usual, some common data-wrangling operations are needed to prepare the data frame (i.e., *df_hl1*) for visualization. They are presented in the *Additional Online Material – Altair – Bar plot with slider 1: transformations.*

Let us consider a first simple example of *bar plot with slider*. A *slider* is a graphical element that allows selecting a range of values, quite often without exact precision if the minimum step is not small, but it is anyway a popular and handy widget for interactively selecting and changing ranges. We need to define the slider object as associated to a range with function `alt.binding.range()`, by setting the minimum and maximum values of the scale and the step of the slider (i.e. the minimum increment associated to a movement of the slider). After that, we define a base plot (object *base*) to be used to instantiate the final bar plots. It will be just an Altair *Chart* associated to data and the slider selection regarding a range of years. Next, the definition of the color scale is added.

```
# Slider definition and selection criteria

slider= alt.binding_range(min=2015, max=2022, step=1)

select_year= alt.selection_point(name='Year', fields=['Year'],
                              bind= slider, init={'Year': 2022})

# Base plot with data, selection

base= alt.Chart(df_hl1).add_params(
    select_year
).transform_filter(
    select_year
).properties(
    width=250
)

# Color scale
```

```
color_scale = alt.Scale(domain=['Overall Homeless','Male',
                        'Female','Transgender','Not_S_M_F'],
                        range=['gray','gold', 'darkgreen',
                               'blue','magenta'])
```

With these elements, we can define the four final plots that will respond to the interactive selection operated through the slider. For all, category *Overall Homeless* is omitted from data (`alt.datum.Category != 'Overall Homeless'`), because being the total of all values, in the visualization it will be too large with respect to the scale of individual categories, producing a bad visual effect. Individual plots are derived from the *base* plot: plots *left* and *right* are bar plots (function `mark_bar()`), while *middle1* and *middle2* are textual tables (function `mark_text()`). Bars in the *left* plot are sorted with function `alt.SortOrder()`. With the slider, a range of years is selected and both bar plots and tables are automatically updated. Finally, the four plots are aligned together. Figure 14.24 shows the result with a certain range of years selected.

```
# Bar plots left and right

left= base.transform_filter(
    alt.datum.Category != 'Overall Homeless'
).encode(
    y= alt.Y('Category:N', axis=None),
    x= alt.X('Value:Q', title='Population',
         sort=alt.SortOrder('descending')),
    color= alt.Color('Category:N', scale=color_scale,
                     legend=None)
).mark_bar().properties(height=150,title='Gender')

right= base.transform_filter(
    alt.datum.Category == 'Overall Homeless'
).encode(
    y= alt.Y('Category:N', axis=None),
```

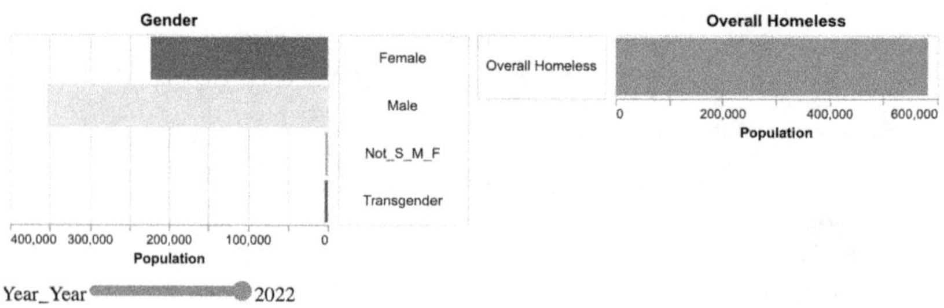

Figure 14.24 Bar plots and tables synchronized with slider, homeless in the United States, year 2022.

```
    x= alt.X('Value:Q', title='Population'),
    color= alt.Color('Category:N', scale=color_scale, legend=None)
).mark_bar().properties(height=50, title='Overall Homeless')

# Textual tables middle1 and middle2

middle1= base.transform_filter(
    alt.datum.Category != 'Overall Homeless'
).encode(
    y= alt.Y('Category:N', axis=None),
    text= alt.Text('Category:N'),
).mark_text().properties(height=150,width=100)

middle2= base.transform_filter(
    alt.datum.Category == 'Overall Homeless'
).encode(
    y= alt.Y('Category:N', axis=None),
    text= alt.Text('Category:N'),
).mark_text().properties(height=50,width=100)

alt.concat(left, middle1, middle2, right, spacing=5)
```

This is a very basic example; we elaborate it some more to show further details and improve the aesthetic quality. We still use the same mechanisms, but now we consider the US States separately and ethnic categories used in population statistics. Again, the data frame (i.e., *df_hl2*) requires some common transformations, shown in the *Additional Online Material – Bar plot with slider 2: transformations*. In our case, we want to show statistics related to Whites compared to those about Blacks and Hispanics/Latinos. We orient the plots vertically, similar to diverging bar plots, to have a compact visualization. We also take care of some style elements like the transparent border for the middle plot with state codes. There is a tiny detail to consider: possessions of American Samoa (AS) and Northern Mariana Islands (MP) have no values, so we omit them. Figure 14.25a and Figure 14.25b show two screenshots for years 2022 and 2021.

```
df_hl2= df_hl2[(df_hl2.State!="AS") & (df_hl2.State!="MP") &
               (df_hl2.State!="Total")]

# Slider, selection, and color scale

slider= alt.binding_range(min=2015, max=2022, step=1)

select_year= alt.selection_point(name='Year', fields=['Year'],
                                 bind=slider, init={'Year': 2022})

color_scale= alt.Scale(domain=['White','Black', 'Lat/Hisp'],
                       range=['darkred','#2f89de','gold'])
```

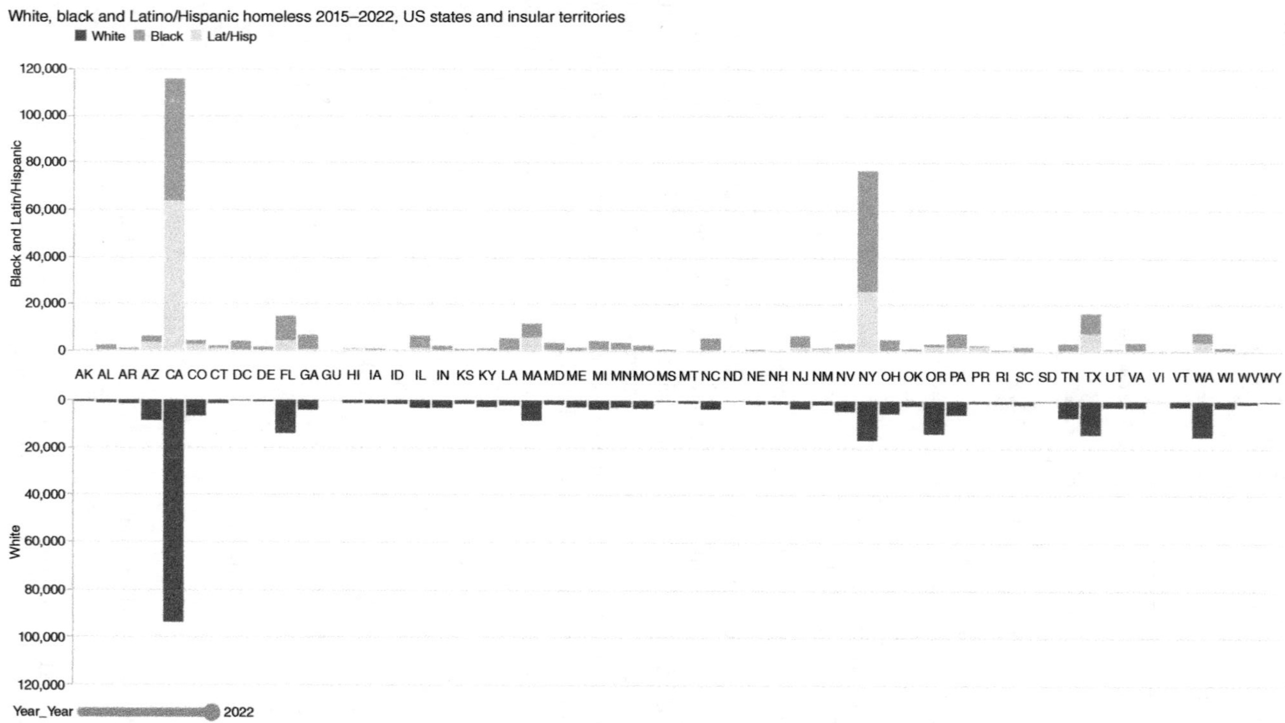

(a)

Figure 14.25 (a) Bar plots and slider, homeless in the US States (year 2022). (b) Bar plots and slider, homeless in the US States (year 2021).

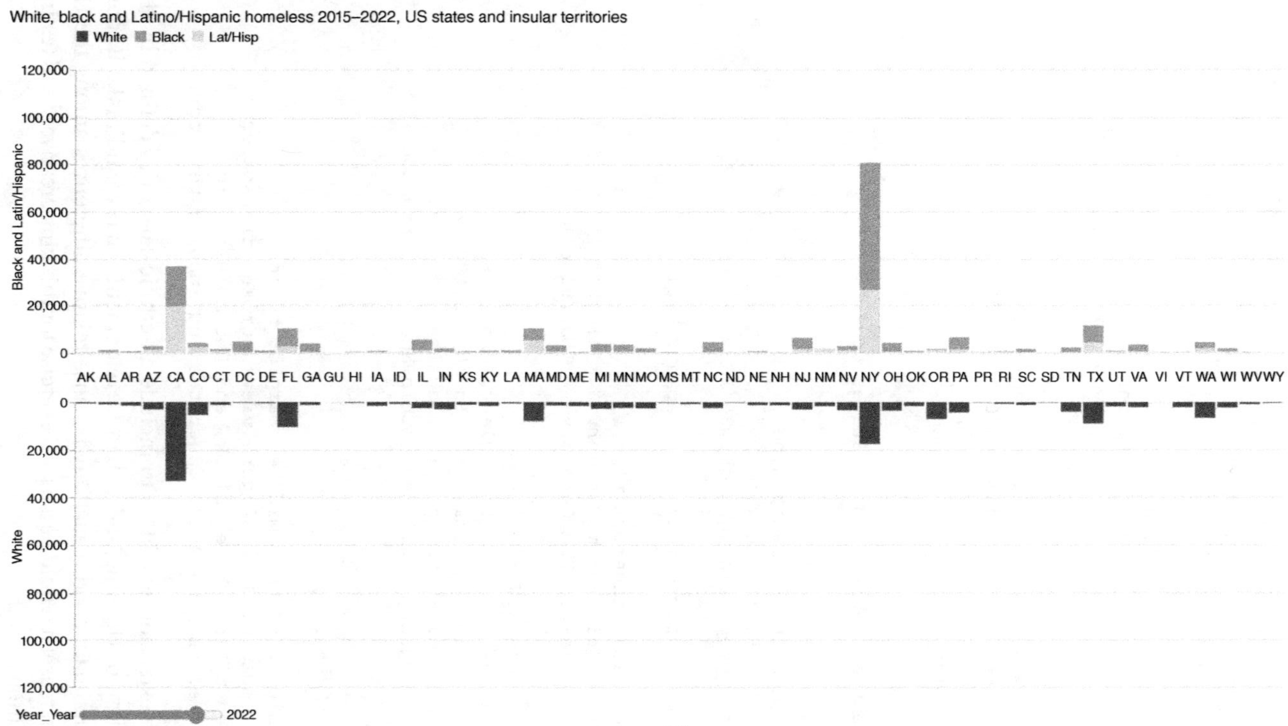

(b)

Figure 14.25 (*Continued*)

```
# Base plot

base= alt.Chart(df_hl2).add_params( select_year
).transform_filter( select_year
).properties( height=250 )

# Upper bar plot for Whites
barplot_bottom= base.transform_filter(
                    alt.datum.Category == 'White').encode(
    x= alt.X('State:N', axis=None),
    y= alt.Y('Value:Q', title='White',
         sort= alt.SortOrder('descending'),
         scale= alt.Scale(domain=(0, 120000))),
    color= alt.Color('Category:N',
    scale= color_scale, legend=None)
).mark_bar()

# Middle textual table with US States codes

middle= base.encode(
    x= alt.X('State:N', axis=None),
    text= alt.Text('State:N'),
).mark_text().properties( height=20 )

# Lower bar plot for Blacks and Hispanic/Latinos

barplot_top= base.transform_filter(
               (alt.datum.Category == 'Black') |
               (alt.datum.Category == 'Lat/Hisp')
).encode(
    x= alt.X('State:N', axis=None),
    y= alt.Y('Value:Q', title='Black & Latin/Hispanic',
           scale= alt.Scale(domain=(0, 120000))),
    color= alt.Color('Category:N', scale=color_scale,
           legend= alt.Legend(title=None, orient="top"))
).mark_bar()

# Plot alignment

alt.vconcat(barplot_top, middle, barplot_bottom ,
            spacing=5).configure_view( stroke='transparent'
).properties(title='White, Black, and Latino/Hispanic
        Homeless 2015-2022, US states and insular territories')
```

A possible extension would be to include all ethnic categories defined by the US Department of Housing and Urban Development. That would make it more difficult to maintain good readability because relative differences among the US States will increase; it would be a useful exercise for thinking creatively and testing possible solutions.

14.4 Bubble Plots

14.4.1 Interactive Graphics

14.4.1.1 Bubble Plot with Slider

A type of graphic that could be effective and pleasant, supported by all modern graphical libraries like ggplot and Seaborn, is the *bubble plot*, which could be adopted either for categorical or continuous variables. It is a scatterplot variant that makes use of marker *size* as an aesthetic, so that the higher the value of the associated variable, the greater the *area* of the circle. In the following example, we will see it for Altair in an interactive plot with slider, again associated to years and with data about homeless population in the US States. A detail to note is that the scale on the *y*-axis has been configured *not to be rescaled*, so that different years could be compared based on the same quantitative scale. In code, we set the scale with `alt.Scale(domain=(100, 20000, 120000)`, where 100 and 120000 are the minimum and maximum values and 20000 is the increment for visualizing markers with different areas. Bubble size is defined as an aesthetic depending on column *Value* (`size= alt.Size('Value:Q' ...)`). Data frame *df_hl2* is the same as the previous example and derived from the dataset in the *Additional Online Material*. Figure 14.26a and Figure 14.26b show two screenshots for years 2022 and 2021. The result, if data allow for producing different bubbles, could be eye-catching and easy to interpret, although values are never precise, but if an approximate evaluation is sufficient, the bubble plot is a choice to consider.

```
# Slider definition and selection criteria

= alt.binding_range(min=2015, max=2022, step=1)

select_year= alt.selection_point(name='Year',
                fields=['Year'], bind=slider, init={'Year': 2015})

# Base plot

base= alt.Chart(df_hl2).add_params( select_year
).transform_filter( select_year ).properties( height=300 )


# Bubble plot

plot= base.mark_circle().encode(
    y= alt.Y('Category:N',title=None),
    x= alt.X('State:N',title=None),
    size= alt.Size('Value:Q',
            scale= alt.Scale(domain=(100, 20000, 120000)),
    legend= alt.Legend(title='Population', orient="top")),
```

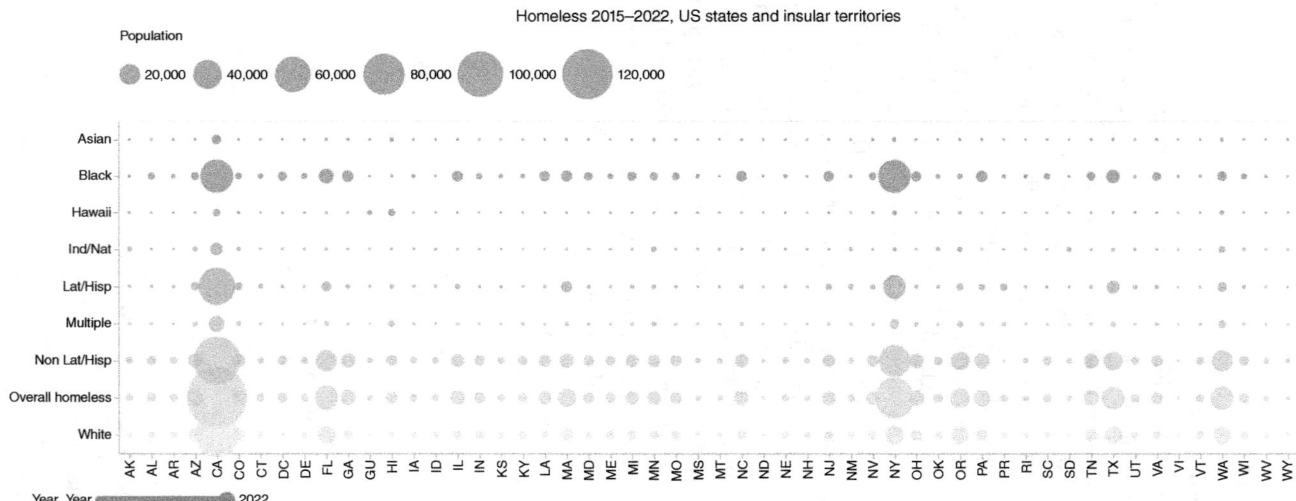

(a)

Figure 14.26 (a) Bubble plot and slider, homeless in the US States (year 2022). (b) Bubble plot and slider, homeless in the US States (year 2021).

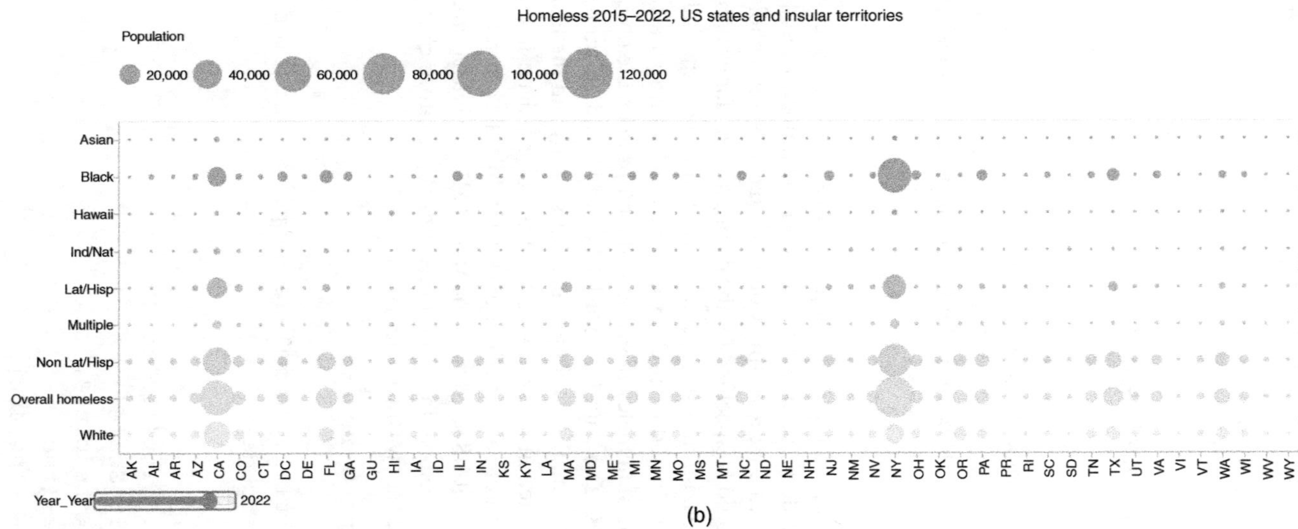

(b)

Figure 14.26 (*Continued*)

```
    color= alt.Color('Category:N',
            scale=alt.Scale(scheme="darkblue"), legend=None))

plot.properties(title='Homeless 2015-2022,
                       US states and insular territories')
```

14.5 Heatmaps and Histograms

14.5.1 Interactive Graphics

We conclude this Part 2 dedicated to Altair and interactive graphics by adding a few more details with two popular types of graphics. As data, we still use those about homelessness in the US States from the US Department of Housing and Urban Development.

14.5.1.1 Heatmaps

An Altair heatmap is produced following the same logic we have described for ggplot: variables should be in *long*-form and corresponding to *x* and *y* Cartesian axes, with the color scale representing values. As usual, several choices could be made and options could be specified for the color gradient, for example by setting the minimum and maximum values, and the central value, especially important for *divergent palettes*. In the example, we want to visualize as a heatmap the percentual variations of homelessness and add *tooltips* to let the observer inspect actual values of tiles. The data frame used before should be transformed into long-form (the transformation is simple and not shown) and the heatmap could be produced with function `mark_rect()`. The color palette is divergent and configured with minimum and maximum values, while the central value is set to 0. Again, we should omit US possessions of AS and MP, module *datum* is imported for specifying the corresponding conditions into the `transform_filter()` function. Figure 14.27 shows the result.

```
from altair import datum

alt.Chart(df1, title="Homeless people (variation (%)"
).mark_rect().encode(
    y='State:N',
    x='Time:N',
    color= alt.Color('Value:Q',
      scale= alt.Scale(
        scheme="redblue",
        reverse=True,
        domain=[-100,400],
        domainMid=0, clamp=True),
```

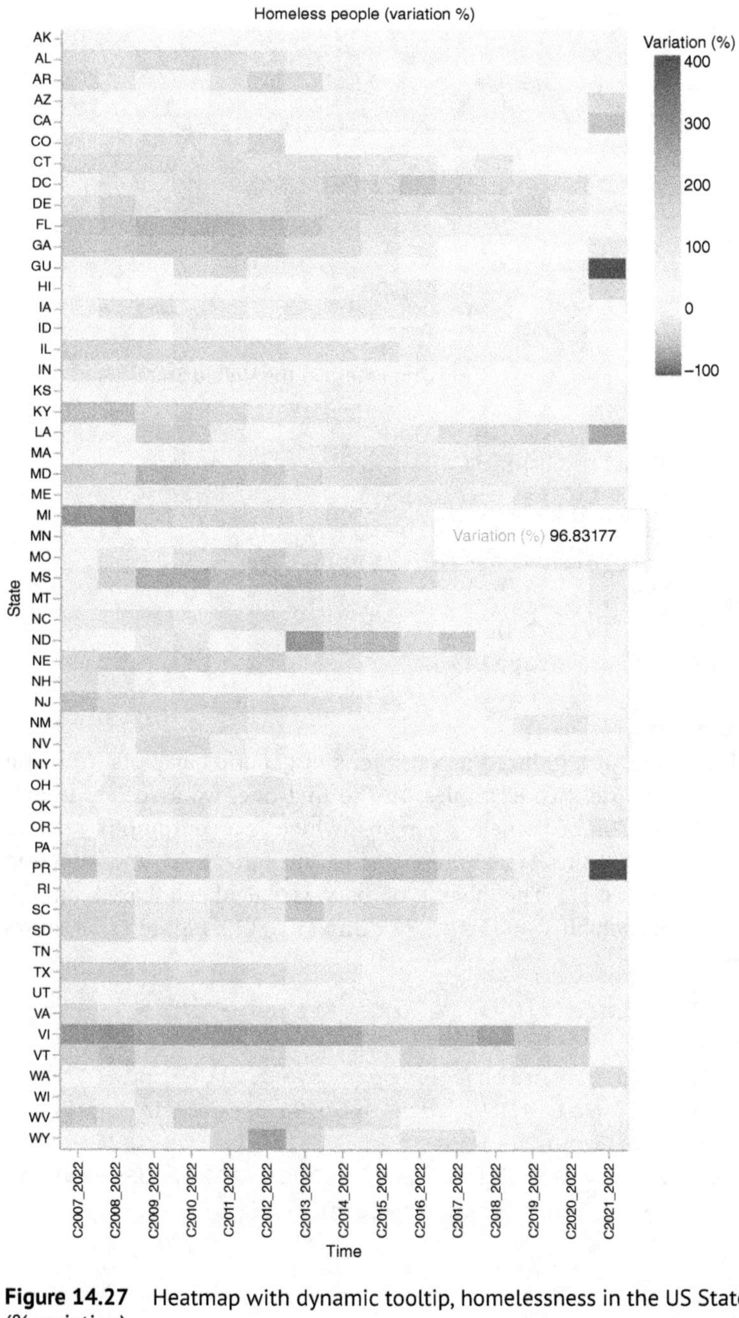

Figure 14.27 Heatmap with dynamic tooltip, homelessness in the US States (% variation).

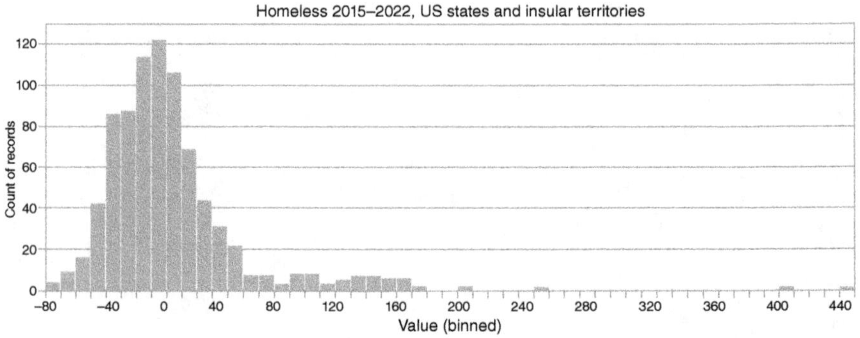

Figure 14.28 Univariate histogram, 100 bins, homeless in the United States (% variation).

```
        legend= alt.Legend(
          title=" Variation (%)")),
    tooltip= [alt.Tooltip('Value:Q',
              title='Variation (%)')]
).transform_filter(
    (datum.State != 'MP') &
    (datum.State != 'Total'))
```

14.5.1.2 Histograms

Univariate histograms are produced as variations of generic bar plots (function `mark_bar()`). Let us see two examples. In the first one, we associate to axis x the percentual variation of homeless persons, which is a continuous variable that is binned into 100 bins (maximum) using attribute `bin` and function `alt.Bin(maxbins=100)`. The height of bars is calculated based on the number of values for each bin (`y=alt.Y('count():Q')`). Figure 14.28 shows the histogram.

```
df_h= df1[(df1.State!='MP') & (df1.State!='AS')]

base= alt.Chart(df_h).mark_bar(opacity=0.8).encode(
        x= alt.X('Value:Q', bin= alt.Bin(maxbins=100)),
        y= alt.Y('count():Q'),
).properties(title='Homeless people 2015-2022, US states
                     and insular territories')
```

As a second example, we produce a *bivariate histogram*, which is a variation of the heatmap (function `mark_rect()`). On the *x*-axis, we still have the percentual variation of homeless persons, now made categorical by binning it into 20 bins. The second variable for *y*-axis is *Time*, which is already expressed as categorical time periods. The color gradient is associated to the number of data points for each tile. We also improve the visualization by overlapping a *scatterplot*, to visualize the actual density of data points. The visual effect, when carefully styled, could be effective and pleasant (Figure 14.29). Last, we make a little variation by showing *ticks* (function `mark_tick()`) instead of points, which technically means to replace the scatterplot with a rug plot (Figure 14.30).

```
# Base plot as a heatmap variation

base= alt.Chart(df_h).mark_rect().encode(
    x= alt.X('Value:Q', bin=alt.Bin(maxbins=20)),
    y= alt.Y('Time:N'),
    color= alt.Color('count()',
        scale= alt.Scale(scheme='purpleblue'),
        legend= alt.Legend(title=Number of points)))

# Overlapped scatterplot

scatter1= alt.Chart(df_h).mark_circle(size=5,color='black'
).encode(
    x= alt.X('Value:Q',title='Values (binned)'),
    y= alt.Y('Time:N',title=None))

# Overlapped rug plot

scatter2 = alt.Chart(df_h).mark_tick(size=15,color='brown'
).encode(
    x= alt.X('Value:Q',title='Values (binned)'),
    y= alt.Y('Time:N',title=None))

plot1= base + scatter1
plot2= base + scatter2

hconcat(plot1, plot2).properties(
    title='Homeless people 2015-2022,
           US states and insular territories')
```

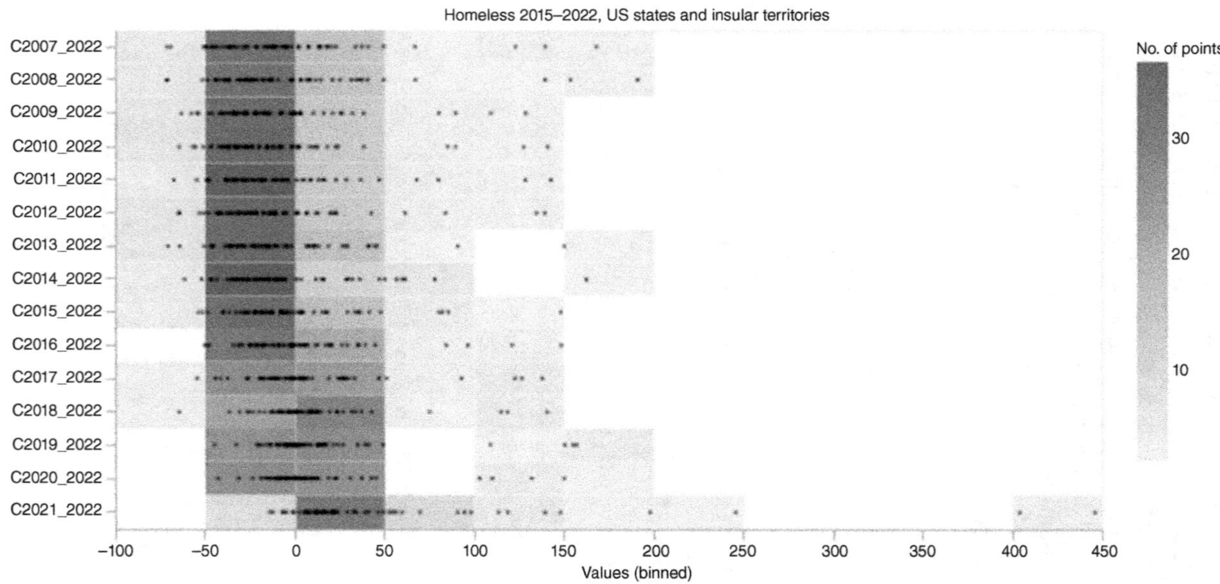

Figure 14.29 Bivariate histogram, 20 bins, and scatterplot, homeless in the United States (% variation).

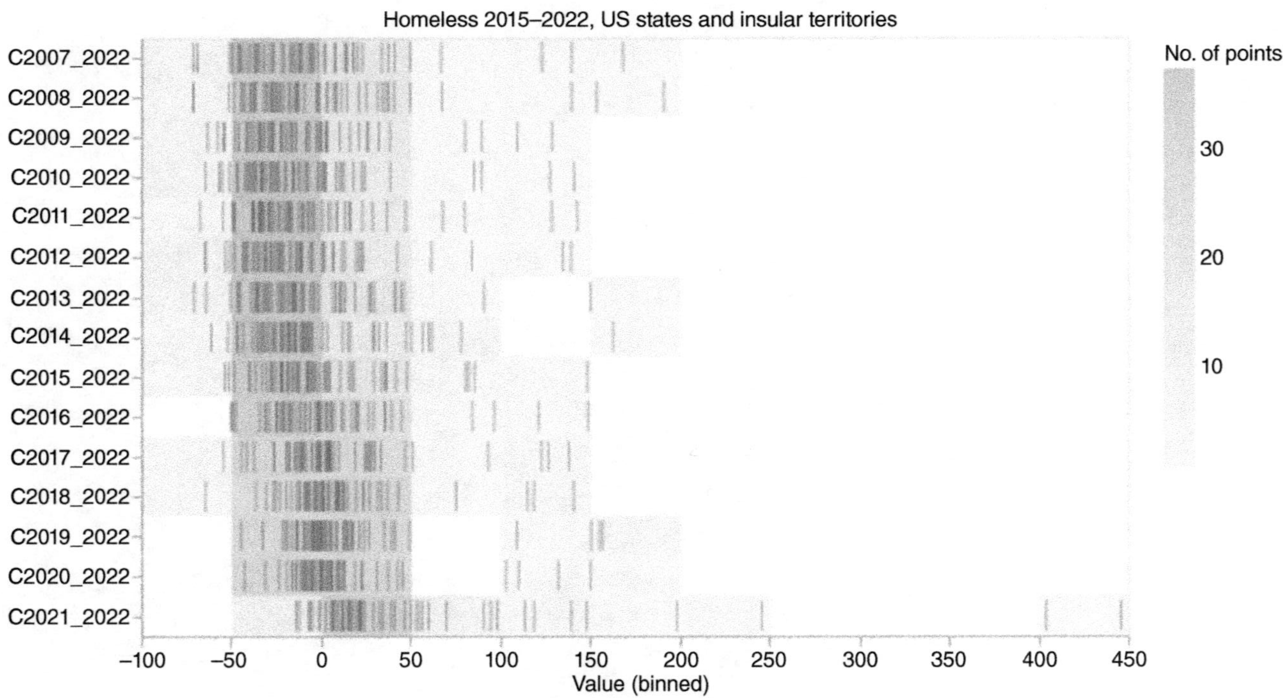

Figure 14.30 Bivariate histogram, 20 bins, and rug plot, homeless in the United States (% variation).

Part III

Web Dashboards

A *web dashboard* represents the conclusion of a journey into data visualization projects being the final step of a pipeline started with static graphics and moved to interactive ones, which are clearly already web oriented.

Dashboards are actually true web applications, composed by several elements and functionalities, integrating different technologies and methodologies, whose complexity could easily grow fast. In short, web dashboards combine data science visualization with web applications in a coherent and usable way. That is great when effective, but it requires different skills, the necessary amount of practice, and a lot of attention to detail. However, with patience and method, everybody could learn to design and build good web dashboards, provided that the fundamental skills have been acquired. It may take some time, but it is feasible, be confident about this.

From data science, dashboards inherit data import, wrangling, and visualization to feed them with data-oriented informative content. From web applications, instead, dashboards make use of web technologies, remote connections and provision of pages, and web standards for interoperability and content layout. Dashboards should also be deployed into a production environment, be it on the open web or in corporate intranets, for the content provision to many simultaneous user accesses. This brings typical problems of scalability and reliability of web applications that web dashboards have to deal with. In this book, we will not tackle deployment problems, scalability, and reliability of web accesses, as well as with security, these are issues commonly discussed in technical documentation for specific solutions or mainly dedicated to web applications. We focus on the visualization aspects, but it is however important to know that when a dashboard is deployed in a production environment, those operational aspects are paramount.

Data Visualization in R and Python, First Edition. Marco Cremonini.

Companion website: www.wiley.com/go/Cremonini/DataVisualization1e

For what concerns us, the most important aspect to learn is the concept of *reactive logic* that represents the basis for understanding the functioning principle of all dashboards, regardless of the specific technology or tool. The concept of reactive logic is the theoretical ground for learning to programmatically define *reactive events*, the core components of dashboards, namely the implementation of the logic that allows for intercepting client-side user interactions with the graphical interface and *reacting* to them server-side through the functionalities that have been defined, by adapting the visual content, modifying the data, and, this the most important aspect, maintaining the overall consistency of the information presented. This has to be granted for all users possibly interacting, simultaneously or not, with the dashboard, each one of them has to always see a coherent information, resulting from her/his own actions.

Dashboards are technologically advanced digital artifacts and to build them there exist several commercial solutions and some excellent open-source ones. We are interested in the latter, specifically for R and Python environments: *Shiny* for R and *Plotly/Dash* for Python (this last one, specific for Python data science projects, where the *Apache* family of tools is Python-compatible and more suited for enterprise projects managing large data streams). Shiny and Plotly/Dash are both advanced tools with several common aspects, although realized differently. The first is that both allow for a fine-grained level of control of the dashboard, with low-level implementations exposing the basic mechanisms to the developers with no use of GUIs (Graphical User Interfaces) or high-level predefined constructs. This, as usual, makes the learning curve steeper at the beginning, but it provides clear and necessary understanding of the logic and mechanisms, and, with practice, permits to develop custom solutions of high quality and creativity, a combination that commercial solutions sometimes do not consent. Shiny and Plotly/Dash are also tools with a wide user base, they are commonly used by many professionals and organizations, so they are not just good platforms for learning, but professional, enterprise-level tools. Remember, never believe those telling you that low-level tools are outdated and that GUI-based ones are the modern choice. It is patently not true, possibly told by someone who really does not have a clue about what a low-level, open-source tool is capable of, often better than GUI-based, commercial ones. There is ample room for both kind of tools on the market and in organizations, important is to know what kind of solutions each one is offering.

Both Shiny and Plotly/Dash are rich in functionalities and are highly configurable, in this book we could only see the main features, those necessary to learn the reactive logic and how to configure the layout. In addition, all examples that will be presented could have been realized in several alternative ways, equally effective and possibly better. The goal is not to show the best way to produce a certain case study but to demonstrate the possibilities and inspire other applications. We will proceed incrementally, step-by-step, always starting

Figure 1 Design for Tandem Cart, 1850–74, Gift of William Brewster, 1923, The Met, New York, NY. Source: The Metropolitan Museum of Art / Public Domain.

with a simple, rudimental dashboard and enriching it with new elements, either interactive, aesthetical, or of the layout. Another goal is to foster creativity, that dashboards make possible to exercise. It is with a certain degree of disappointment that many real dashboards look too similar one to the other, all seemingly derived from the same few templates. For some applications that is perfectly fine, there is no need of creativity, just efficient functionalities presented rationally. But that is not always the case, there are plenty of occasions where creativity would make a remarkable difference, and it should be exercised, it does not come for granted or just as a gift of nature. Last, it should be conceded that dashboards have made a long journey from their inception to our days (Part 3, Figure 1).

Dataset

Low achieving 15-year-olds in reading, mathematics, or science by sex from Eurostat (source OECD) (https://ec.europa.eu/eurostat/databrowser/view/EDUC_OUTC_PISA__custom_3152295/). It contains results from OECD/PISA tests from 15-year-old students on mathematics, science, and reading skills.

Copyright: Creative Commons Attribution 4.0 International (CC BY 4.0) (http://creativecommons.org/licenses/by/4.0/, https://commission.europa.eu/legal-notice_en#copyright-notice).

15

Shiny Dashboards

15.1 General Organization

A Shiny dashboard has generally a schema composed of three fundamental elements: the graphical user interface definition (*User Interface*), the definition of actions, either reactive or nonreactive, to execute on data and variables (*Server Logic*), and the execution of the application (*Run App*). In our examples, we will follow this schema, incrementally adding elements to the dashboard, with the user interface and the server logic always kept clearly distinct. From the following schema, some key Shiny functions are shown for the user interface: `fluidPage()` for the definition of the dynamic layout, composed of rows (function `fluidRow()`), each one possibly separated in columns (function `column()`).

```
##### USER INTERFACE #####
ui <- fluidPage(
  titlePanel( ),
  fluidRow(
    column(  )
    ),
  ...
  )

##### SERVER LOGIC #####
server <- function(input, output, session) {
  ...
  }

##### RUN APP #####
shinyApp(ui, server)
```

Data Visualization in R and Python, First Edition. Marco Cremonini.

Companion website: www.wiley.com/go/Cremonini/DataVisualization1e

The definition of the user interface is tightly related to characteristics and limitations of a web application and to the current HTML standard. From this comes the fact of considering the web page as a *virtual grid* composed by rows and columns to be used for placing graphical elements of the dashboard. The maximum number of virtual columns is 12, of same size, while rows are unlimited in number and have variable height. This difference between rows and columns is largely motivated by an intrinsic difference between horizontal and vertical scrolling. Vertical scrolling of a web page is typically an intuitive and well-established gesture and does not pose usability problems (relatively speaking, of course, an excessively long page is not user-friendly); on the contrary horizontal scrolling is perceived as annoying and information falling out of the page width might go unnoticed, so it makes sense to limit it. Basic graphical elements of a dashboard layout, such as the drop-down menu, the checkbox and radio button, or the slider are *input elements*, meaning they are used to collect user choices and reconfigure the visualization or perform some actions on data. *Output elements*, instead, are typically those used to produce information, for instance in graphics or data tables. Other output elements are those that modify something through actions, for example, a user selection could be modified as a result of an output element. Furthermore, a dashboard could have a single page or several pages through the definition of *tabs* (in this case it is a *multi-page dashboard*). Moving to advanced web layouts, other elements and solutions could be added, as is customary in modern web applications. In the user interface, we often want to specify titles, a header, a sidebar, and possibly a navbar, in addition to the definition of the virtual grid and all input and output elements that should be visualized. The typical programmatic construct that we will use in the user interface definition is as follows:

```
fluidRow(
    column(  )
    ),
```

With this construct, we specify a row in the virtual grid of variable size (`fluidRow()`) and within that row a column (`column()`). The column could be configured with a certain width as the number of columns of the virtual grid, so, for example, `column(6, ...)` specifies a width equal to 6 virtual columns, or 50% of the page width, being 12 the virtual columns; `column(3, ...)` corresponds to 25% of the page width, and so on. This also means that, on a single row, more columns could be defined, possibly each one with a relative size, corresponding to graphical elements aligned *horizontally*. Instead, several rows are visualized *vertically* aligned.

We can now start with a first simple example, just focusing on the user interface with no server-side actions. First, we import R libraries *tidyverse* and *shiny* and read the dataset with Pisa test results for low-achieving students from Eurostat. It is in compressed form but both functions `read_csv()` and `vroom()` (in this case package *vroom* is necessary) are able to read it directly and extract the CSV dataset. For ease of comprehension, we replace string *EF461*, indicating mathematics tests, with *MAT* and obtain the list of countries and tests (i.e., reading comprehension and scientific knowledge are the other two tests, respectively indicated with READ and SCI in the following).

```
library(tidyverse)
library(shiny)

pisa= read_csv("datasets/Eurostat/
        educ_outc_pisa__custom_4942428_linear.csv.gz")

pisa$field= str_replace_all(pisa$field, 'EF461','MAT')

choice_test= unique(pisa$field)
choice_geo= unique(pisa$geo)
```

As we have seen, the user interface is created with function `fluidPage()`. As input elements, we choose two drop-down menus (function `selectInput()`), respectively to select a test and a country from the lists; we place them aligned vertically in two rows. As output elements, we want two textual tables (function `tableOutput()`), this time horizontally aligned, to visualize the data corresponding to the choices activated with the drop-down menus. These are the specifics of our first Shiny user interface. To recap, we will have two rows, two drop-down menus, and two textual tables. Each element should be specified in a column (function `column()`). We also add a title with function `titlePanel()`.

More specifically, all input and output elements would be associated to an *identifier*, which will become necessary in the server logic to associate actions to elements. Our identifiers will be called *test* and *country* for drop-down menus, *table1* and *table2* for tables. Attribute `choice` of function `selectInput()` is used to refer to the list of items to visualize, respectively the variable with the list of tests (*choice_test*) and the variable with the list of countries (*choice_geo*) defined in the previous excerpt of code.

```
####### USER INTERFACE ########
ui <- fluidPage(

# Title
    titlePanel("PISA test: Low achieving 15-year-olds in
                reading, mathematics or science by sex"),

# Drop-down menus, vertically aligned
```

```
    fluidRow(
      column(6,
        selectInput("test", "TEST", choices= choice_test)
      )
    ),

    fluidRow(
      column(6,
        selectInput("country", "COUNTRY", choices= choice_geo)
      )
    ),

# Textual tables, horizontally aligned
    fluidRow(
      column(4, tableOutput("table1")),
      column(4, tableOutput("table2")),
    )
)

######## SERVER LOGIC #########
server <- function(input, output, session) { }

######## RUN APP #########
shinyApp(ui, server)
```

From RStudio, we can execute *RunApp* and, if we do not make any error, the result will be that a local *http service* is started and a message like *Listening on http://127.0.0.1* will appear on the console, informing us that our new Shiny dashboard is listening on the localhost network port and ready to receive inputs through the user interface. RStudio permits to visualize the *rendering* of the dashboard in the *Viewer* panel (a choice suggested only for very early tests) or to open a new window/tab in the predefined web browser (the preferred choice).

The dashboard produced at this point is obviously rudimentary, however, it is a start and we have already placed some elements on the page, while data are read from the dataset. The two tables are still missing, we have just defined them as output elements, but not produced as yet. For this, we need a *server logic to define actions to be executed as a response to changes in input elements and for producing some outputs*. Let us consider the logic first.

What we want to achieve is that, whenever a Pisa test or a country is selected through one of the drop-down menus, the two tables should be reconfigured with the corresponding data. This simple task hides a detail that is of paramount importance for all reactive actions: *only when an input element changes, actions should be triggered, and output elements updated*. This means that for every update to output elements, data should be read again, which is a computationally intensive and network-based (in a production environment) operation that should be done only when necessary because it may have a significant latency and require data-wrangling operations, all tasks that introduce delays and affect usability. Therefore, the key aspect in managing reactive actions is *to produce an output if and only if an input element has been modified*. In our case, tables rendering should not be recalculated when input elements have not been modified, but restored from a *local cache memory*, which is a copy of the previous state of the dashboard that is simply rendered again with no access to data, network, and so on. This is one of the main reasons for paying great attention and care when reactive actions are defined because correctly managing them is fundamental for a dashboard, and the more a dashboard is complex, the more important is to configure reactive actions correctly.

Let us consider the two tables. Input elements are the drop-down menus, which, when modified, will communicate the new values to use for reconfiguring the tables. Shiny defines such elements as *reactive objects*, meaning that they could trigger reactive actions in the server logic, so they have to be monitored for any change. Function `reactive()` (and the similar `eventReactive()`) is the main one for the definition of a reactive action in the server logic. In our case, the reactive action has to be executed if and only if the corresponding reactive object changes, meaning a new selection is done through the drop-down menus. We start with the first drop-down menu, that of Pisa tests. We have defined it with `selectInput("test", "TEST", choices=choice_test)`, where the first attribute is the identifier (attribute `inputId`), the second is the title to be visualized, and the third the list of values, here stored in variable *choice_test*.

The *inputId* (i.e. *test*) uniquely identifies an input element in the server logic, equally for *outputId* identifying an output element. In the server logic, we will refer to them with the *dollar symbol* $ prefixed by *input*, for an input element, or *output* for an output element (in this case the drop-down menu will be referred as `input$test`). Similarly, the drop-down menu for countries (with identifier *country*) will be referred as `input$country`. With this, we can write in the server logic the data selection operations based on inputs from drop-down menus.

```
pisa %>% filter(field == input$test)
pisa %>% filter(field == input$country)
```

These are just the filtering operations; we still have to define them as reactive actions. For this we need to enclose each one of them into function `reactive()`.

```
selected1 <- reactive(pisa %>% filter(field == input$test))
selected2 <- reactive(pisa %>% filter(field == input$country))
```

This is the fundamental step because in this way we are correctly managing reactive objects and reactive actions for this case.

Now we should produce the two tables. The basic function is `renderTable()`, whose content will be the data to be visualized as a table. In our example, we execute two different actions for the two tables. In the first one, we show, for each country and gender, the arithmetic means on all years for students with low skills. It is a common aggregation operation to be executed on variable *selected1()*. In the second table, we show all values, not aggregated, and we use variable *selected2()* as data.

Let us make a pause. You may have noticed something strange: why are variables with data stated with parenthesis (i.e. *selected1()* and *selected2()*)? Functions have parenthesis, not variables, so why is that? Here lies a fundamental difference between a dashboard and a normal R script. In a normal R script, variables are just R objects, but in a Shiny dashboard, there are variables that are common R objects, but there are also variables that are something different, they are *reactive objects*. Here, *selected1()* and *selected2()* are reactive objects because they depend on input elements and the associated reactive actions. Specifically, they are defined as type *reactiveExpr*, meaning that they technically are functions, therefore they should be written with parenthesis. From this example comes an important rule for Shiny dashboards: *all reactive objects are functions, not simple R objects.*

A last aspect remains to be specified: in which graphical objects of the user interface should the two reactive objects *selected1()* and *selected2()* be visualized? Values of *selected1()* and *selected2()* are in tabular form, so they should be the corresponding graphical objects of the user interface. There, we had defined `tableOutput("table1")` and `tableOutput("table2")`, with *table1* and *table2* as *outputId* identifiers. Similar to the case of input elements, for output elements the syntax to use will be like `output$...`, therefore, the result of the first `renderTable()` function will be assigned to `output$table1`, the second to `output$table2`. The complete code for the server logic part follows.

```
server <- function(input, output, session) {

# Reactive objects selected1 and selected2 associated to
# reactive actions for data selection

   selected1 <- reactive(pisa %>% filter(field == input$test))
   selected2 <- reactive(pisa %>% filter(geo == input$country))

# Tables rendering

# First table
   output$table1 <- renderTable(
      selected1() %>%
        group_by(geo, sex) %>%
        summarize(Mean= mean(OBS_VALUE, na.rm=TRUE))
   )
```

```
# Second table
   output$table2 <- renderTable(
     selected2() %>% select(4,5,7,8,9)
   )
}
```

Putting together the user interface and the server logic parts, we can run the complete Shiny dashboard of our first example. It is still the bare minimum for a dashboard, but nevertheless it is a fully functioning and complete dashboard with all fundamental parts. From this one, we will move on adding elements and complicating the interface and the logic. Figure 15.1a and Figure 15.1b show two screenshots with different selections from drop-down menus and corresponding tables.

The following step is to add a graphic that should be dynamically redesigned when input elements change. The logic is similar to what discussed for tables, it changes how to obtain the result. A graphic is again an output element that should be placed in a certain row and column of the user interface with a specified size. We put it on the same row of tables with function `plotOutput()` having *pisa_MF* as the *outputId*. This is all the user interface needs to know. Now we turn to the server logic. Again, the key is to correctly manage reactive events. For the example, we want to produce a simple *line plot* by using the same data used for the corresponding table, which, for now, allows us not to define another reactive event and object. The syntax for plots is similar to that for tables, function `renderPlot()` is needed and within that function, the graphical object should be included. In our case, the graphic is produced with *ggplot*, therefore we can either directly write ggplot operations inside the `renderPlot()` function or write them separately with a custom function and use that function within the `renderPlot()`. This time, we write ggplot operations directly. Other tweaks are represented by the default values for the drop-down menus with attribute `selected` and to have kept just one table in the user interface in order to have a compact visualization of a table and the corresponding plot.

```
###### USER INTERFACE
ui <- fluidPage(

  titlePanel("PISA test: Low achieving 15-year-olds"),

  fluidRow(
    column(6, selectInput("test", "Test",
           choices = choice_test, selected='READ')
    )
  ),

  fluidRow(
```

PISA test: Low achieving 15-year-olds in reading, mathematics or science by sex

TEST

MAT ▾

COUNTRY

AL ▾

geo	sex	Mean
AL	F	54.60
AL	M	57.40
AL	T	56.02
AT	F	21.80
AT	M	18.42
AT	T	20.10
BE	F	19.28
BE	M	17.95

field	sex	geo	TIME_PERIOD	OBS_VALUE
MAT	F	AL	2009.00	66.30
MAT	F	AL	2012.00	60.30
MAT	F	AL	2015.00	51.20
MAT	F	AL	2018.00	40.60
MAT	M	AL	2009.00	69.10
MAT	M	AL	2012.00	61.00
MAT	M	AL	2015.00	55.40
MAT	M	AL	2018.00	44.10

(a)

PISA test: Low achieving 15-year-olds in reading, mathematics or science by sex

TEST

READ ▾

COUNTRY

IT ▾

geo	sex	Mean
AL	F	46.60
AL	M	65.96
AL	T	56.38
AT	F	15.58
AT	M	26.70
AT	T	21.18
BE	F	14.41
BE	M	22.67

field	sex	geo	TIME_PERIOD	OBS_VALUE
MAT	F	IT	2003.00	34.00
MAT	F	IT	2006.00	35.70
MAT	F	IT	2009.00	26.40
MAT	F	IT	2012.00	26.70
MAT	F	IT	2015.00	25.80
MAT	F	IT	2018.00	25.10
MAT	M	IT	2003.00	29.70
MAT	M	IT	2006.00	30.20

(b)

Figure 15.1 (a) Shiny, test MAT, and country AL (Albania) selected. (b) Shiny, test READ, and country IT (Italy) selected.

```
    column(6, selectInput("country", "Country",
           choices = choice_geo, selected="IT")
    )
  ),

  fluidRow(
    column(4, tableOutput("table1")),
    column(4, plotOutput("pisa_MF"))
    )
  )

###### SERVER LOGIC
server <- function(input, output, session) {

   selected1 <- reactive(pisa %>%
                   filter( (geo == input$country) &
                           (field==input$test) &
                           (sex!="T") &
                           (!is.na(OBS_VALUE))
                         )
                      )

   output$table1 <- renderTable(
                  selected1() %>% select(4,5,7,8,9)
                    )

   output$pisa_MF <- renderPlot({

     selected1() %>% ggplot()+
       geom_line(aes(x=as.factor(TIME_PERIOD), y=OBS_VALUE,
                    color=sex, group=sex), linewidth=1)+
       labs(x="" , y="Low achieving 15-year-olds (%)",
            color="Gender" )+
       theme_bw()+
       theme(
         axis.text = element_text(size = rel(1.3)),
         axis.title = element_text(size = rel(1.5)),
         legend.title= element_text(size = rel(1.5)),
         legend.text= element_text(size = rel(1.3))
       )
   })
}

##### RUN APP
shinyApp(ui, server)
```

Figure 15.2a and Figure 15.2b show two screenshots for different selections with the corresponding table and plot.

15.2 Second Version: Graphics and Style Options

At this point, we know how to place elements in the user interface and to define actions in the server logic. We can extend the first example by adding a second graphic and taking better care of the style. Specifically, we want to include the following elements:

- As a second plot, we reuse the *ridgeline plot* presented in Part 1, which also uses OECD/Pisa data, in that case, divided by skills and gender.
- The style of the first graphic will be improved by introducing a scatterplot and specifying some style options.
- Graphical themes could be applied, for example by using package *shinythemes*; we try with both light and dark themes. Themes employed are among those freely available through *Bootswatch* (https://bootswatch.com/), a common choice in web dashboards and applications.

In the *user interface*, in order to configure a theme from package *shinythemes*, it suffices to refer to it inside the *FluidPage* function, such as:

```
fluidPage(theme= shinytheme("cosmo"), ...
```

It also exists a special selector that automatically adds a drop-down menu with the list of available themes and allows for changing the theme dynamically when the dashboard is operating. It is a convenient feature to make tests on a dashboard without stopping it, changing the code, and restarting. To have this special selector, the following instruction should be added:

```
shinythemes::themeSelector(),
```

As a last modification to the user interface, we want to show a second plot, so we have to define it. We want it beside the first plot, then on the same row as a new column (`column(4, plotOutput("pisa_ridges"))`).

More relevant are changes to make to the *server logic*. Let us start with creating the second plot, then we will deal with style options. The ridgeline plot, different from the first line plot, does not depend on country selection because it shows all countries. We have to change the data selection, meaning to create a new reactive action and reactive object. We also omit missing values and total values in order to keep only data for male and female students.

PISA test: Low achieving 15-year-olds

Test

READ

Country

KR

field	sex	geo	TIME_PERIOD	OBS_VALUE
READ	F	KR	2000	3.70
READ	F	KR	2003	4.40
READ	F	KR	2006	3.30
READ	F	KR	2009	2.40
READ	F	KR	2012	4.50
READ	F	KR	2015	7.60
READ	F	KR	2018	11.20
READ	M	KR	2000	7.30
READ	M	KR	2003	8.40
READ	M	KR	2006	8.20
READ	M	KR	2009	8.80
READ	M	KR	2012	10.40
READ	M	KR	2015	19.20
READ	M	KR	2018	18.70

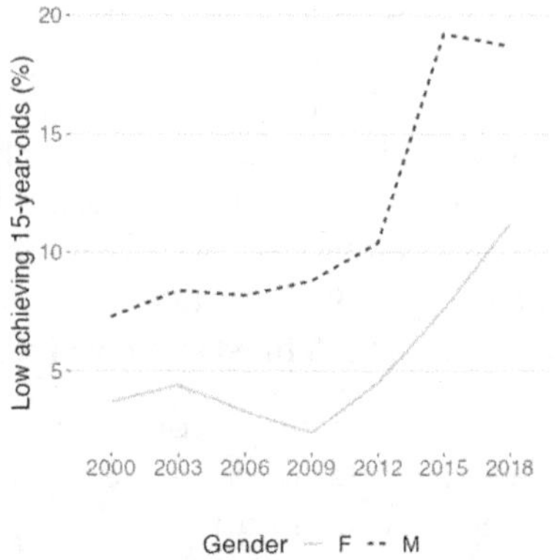

(a)

PISA test: Low achieving 15-year-olds

Test

MAT

Country

KR

field	sex	geo	TIME_PERIOD	OBS_VALUE
MAT	F	KR	2003	11.00
MAT	F	KR	2006	8.70
MAT	F	KR	2009	7.00
MAT	F	KR	2012	9.10
MAT	F	KR	2015	13.00
MAT	F	KR	2018	14.40
MAT	M	KR	2003	8.50
MAT	M	KR	2006	9.10
MAT	M	KR	2009	9.10
MAT	M	KR	2012	9.20
MAT	M	KR	2015	17.80
MAT	M	KR	2018	15.60

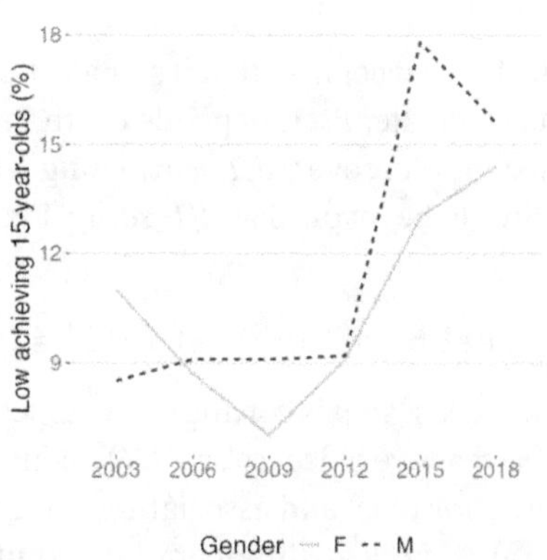

(b)

Figure 15.2 (a) Table and plot, test READ and country KR (Korea) selected. (b) Table and plot, test MAT and country KR selected.

```
selected2 <- reactive(pisa %>%
                    filter( (field == input$test) &
                    (sex != "T") & (!is.na(OBS_VALUE)))
                )
```

The other relevant feature of the ridgeline plot is to show values of the categorical variable sorted by a certain metric. In Part 1, we sorted it based on the arithmetic mean of test results for each country, through an external ordered list. To do the same in the dashboard, we have to reproduce the solution and the difference, once again, is made by reactive events. The ordered list should be recalculated when the selection of test changes (e.g. from MAT to READ), which makes the sorting of countries another reactive event. In the following excerpt of code, we group for country and aggregate to obtain the test arithmetic mean, then we sort the result. It has to be defined as a reactive event.

```
df1_sort= reactive(selected2() %>% group_by(geo) %>%
    summarize(Mean= mean(OBS_VALUE, na.rm=TRUE)) %>%
    arrange(desc(Mean))
    )
```

The following step is to transform into type *list* the column with country names. The original version, with names adapted to the current example, would be like `list1= as.list(df1_sort$geo)`. However, if we try with this solution, an error is raised by the Shiny interpreter:

```
Error in '.getReactiveEnvironment()$currentContext()':
! Operation not allowed without an active reactive context.
You tried to do something that can only be done from inside a reac-
tive consumer.
```

Reading it, we recognize that it signals the necessity of a reactive context because the object to create, *list1*, depends on the reactive object *df1_sort*, created in the previous step. Moreover, *df1_sort*, being a reactive object, is actually a function that requires to be invoked as *df1_sort()*. Fixing the mistakes, we obtain the correct form:

```
list1= reactive(as.list(df1_sort()$geo))
```

Finally, the last step is sorting with respect to the external list, which consists of using data (reactive object *selected2()*), converting the column with country names (*geo*) into *factor* type, and associating categories (*level*) to the sorted list *list1*. As it should be already clear, this operation requires a reactive context, being dependent on the two reactive objects *selected2()* and *list1()*.

```
df_elev_factor= reactive(
                    selected2() %>%
```

```
        mutate(geo= factor(geo)) %>%
        mutate(geo= fct_relevel(geo, list1() )) %>%
        arrange(geo)
      )
```

Now that we have correctly managed reactive events, we can turn our attention to graphical aspects. The ridgeline plot could be easily adapted from what we have seen in Part 1. Equally, overlapping a scatterplot to the line plot is just a simple modification to the ggplot script. What is new in this example are Shiny themes and how to use them. An important detail is that Shiny does not automatically adapt the aesthetic features of a graphic to those of a theme, for instance, the background, the legend, axes fonts, and title fonts are kept as in the original graphic instead of being made the same of the theme. Such details might be unimportant with light themes but become relevant when dark themes are used because they are evidently misaligned and create an impression of poor quality, when not truly a mistake such as with black fonts over a black background. These details must be considered and fixed. In the following excerpt, style options are presented in order to comply with a dark theme too. They make use of ggplot function `theme()`, which allows for a fine-grained control of style options.

```
theme(
  panel.background= element_rect(fill='transparent'),
  plot.background= element_rect(fill='transparent', color=NA),
  panel.grid.major= element_line(color ='lightgray'),
  panel.grid.minor= element_line(color ='lightgray'),
  legend.background= element_rect(fill='lightgray'),
  legend.box.background= element_rect(fill='transparent'),
  axis.text= element_text(size = rel(1.3),color ='gray50'),
  axis.title= element_text(size = rel(1.3),color ='gray50')
)
```

To these options, another one should be added, which is needed in the `renderPlot()` function to define the graphic background as *transparent*:

```
renderPlot({
   ...
}, bg="transparent")
```

The complete code for this version is available in the *Additional Online Material – PISA Test Dashboard, Second Version.* Figure 15.3a and Figure 15.3b show two screenshots of the result, one with a light theme, the other with a dark theme. To note, on top-right, there is the *theme selector* widget.

With these configurations, the aesthetic quality of our dashboard, rudimentary in the first version, has definitely improved. It is still a simple dashboard with minimal functionalities, but we were able to add fast a number of noticeable enhancements.

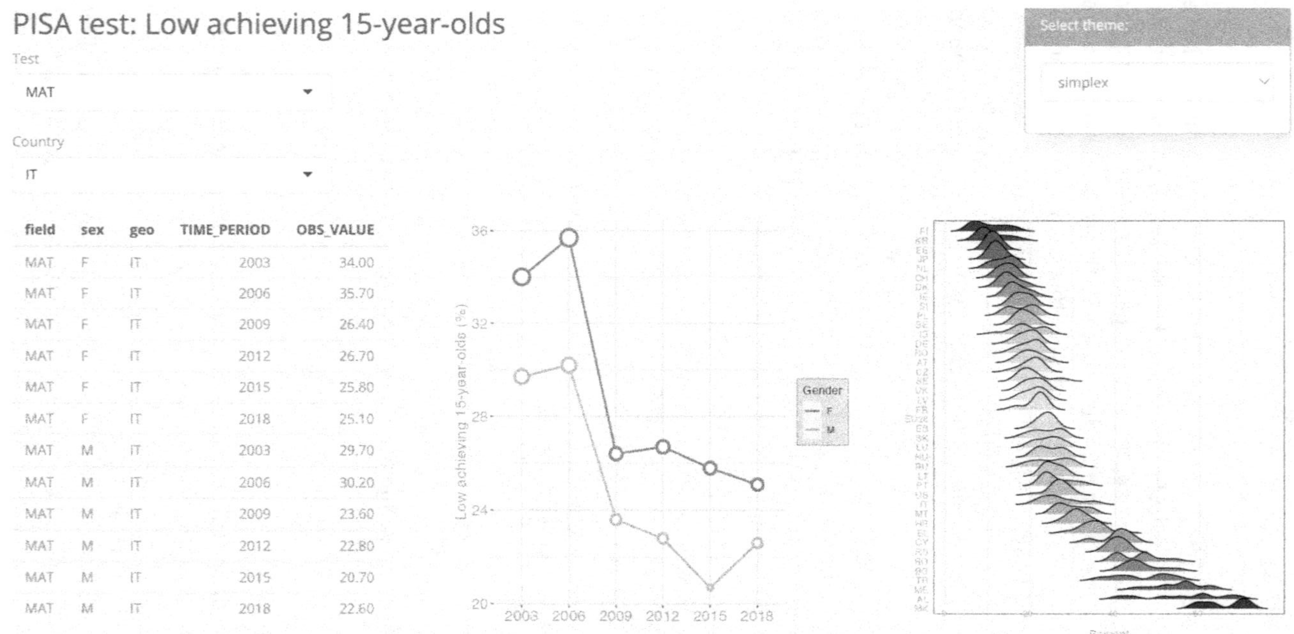

(a)

Figure 15.3 (a) A table, two plots, and light theme. (b) A table, two plots, and dark theme with style options.

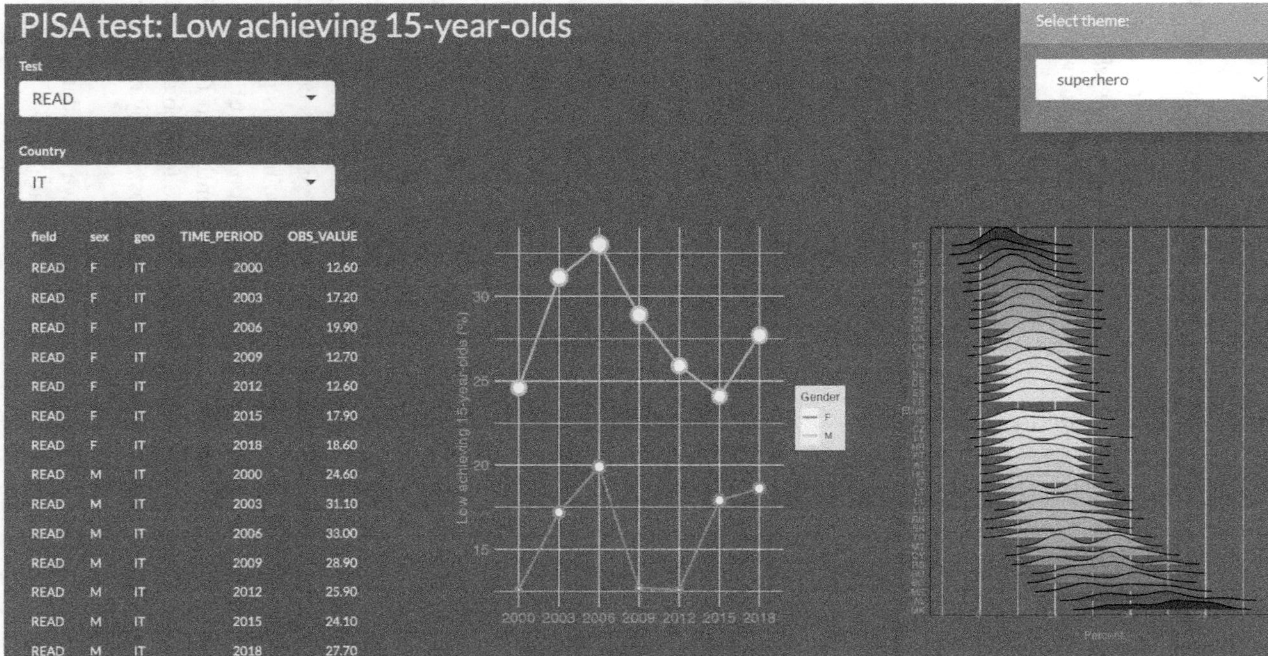

(b)

Figure 15.3 *(Continued)*

15.3 Third Version: Tabs, Widgets, and Advanced Themes

We keep improving our dashboard by introducing other elements frequently used:

- *tabs* (function `tabsetPanel()`) to configure a *multi-page layout*.
- A *widget* (a preconfigured graphical element) to have a *multiple selection box* (function `multiInput()`). In order to use widgets, package *shinyWidgets* is required.
- An advanced table rendering (function `renderDataTable()`) from package *DT* (DT is the actual package name and stands for Data Table), which supports *JavaScript* functionalities for sorting columns, selection, and others.
- An alternative theme package called *bslib*.
- A package called *thematic* that supports a unified management of graphical themes for R and Shiny.

In particular, *bslib* (https://rstudio.github.io/bslib/index.html) is useful to integrate *Bootstrap* (https://getbootstrap.com/) into the dashboard, a widely adopted toolkit for website configuration, which supports CSS style sheets, JavaScript functionalities, and other features. A detailed presentation of *Bootstrap* is out of the scope of this book, but it would be useful to read its documentation to learn the many ways it permits to customize a dashboard with tools typical of web frontends. With *bslib* it is possible to also use free themes from *Bootswatch* (https://bootswatch.com/), the same available with *shinythemes*, and customize them with a simple GUI. Instead, *thematic* (https://rstudio.github.io/thematic/) supports a centralized management of ggplot and Shiny graphical themes, with also a functionality called *automatic styling* to solve a problem that we already know about, namely the fact that ggplot graphics are not integrated with a Shiny dashboard's CSS style sheet, leaving several elements with their original colors. Previously, we solved it by manually configuring style options through the `theme()` ggplot function, the Thematic's *automatic styling* is configured to automatically adjust such options. In general, it is effective but it is possible that some details slip away and still require a manual intervention with `theme()`. The combination between *bslib* and *thematic* supports efficiently also *Google Fonts* (https://fonts.google.com/), another widely adopted choice for web applications. Finally, for *Shiny Widgets*, a gallery is available at: https://shiny.rstudio.com/gallery/widget-gallery.html.

Let us delve into the technical details. The first element we consider is thematic automatic styling, which is defined outside the user interface.

```
thematic_shiny(font='auto')
```

With this, thematic functionalities are activated, and graphics are adapted to the selected theme. Specific fonts or font families, for instance from *Google Fonts*, could be indicated, or the choice is left to the tool with `font='auto'`.

In the *user interface*, the theme definition is set with *bslib* function `bs_theme()`. We do not specify a certain theme because we want to use the selector. On the contrary, a theme could be indicated, attributes are the Bootswatch version (attribute `version`, the current one at the time of writing is 5) and the theme's name (attribute `bootswatch`).

```
theme = bslib::bs_theme(),
```

Next, in the user interface, we want to include the *widget for the multiple selection*. It exists the simple version with standard Shiny element `selectInput()` already seen in the previous versions of the example, which supports attribute `multiple=TRUE`, which makes it possible to select more values from the drop-down menu. However, with widget `multiInput()` a richer layout is provided. The first attributes are the same of function `selectInput()`, specific are instead attribute `selected`, configured with elements selected by default, and attribute `options` as a list with the activation of the search functionality and the labels for selected and nonselected values.

```
multiInput(
    inputId= "country", label= "Countries :",
    choices= unique(pisa$COUNTRY),
    selected= "United States of America",
    width= '100%',
    options= list(
                enable_search= FALSE,
                non_selected_header= "List:",
                selected_header= "Selected:"
                )
          )
```

To transform our single-page dashboard into a multi-page one, tabs should be introduced following the schema shown here:

```
tabsetPanel(
      id= ,
      tabPanel(
          id="IdTab1",
          fluidRow(...)
          ),

      tabPanel(
          id="IdTab2",
```

```
            fluidRow(...)
            ),
        ...
        )
```

The general container is configured with function `tabsetPanel()` that includes an element `tabPanel()` for each tab. Each element `tabPanel()`, in turn, defines its own page layout with the usual sequence of rows through `fluidRow()`, each one subdivided into columns with `column()` as we have seen for the single-page case.

Another useful improvement to introduce is of programmatic nature. In the previous versions, we have produced the ggplot graphic by including the ggplot script into function `renderPlot()`. That would be a fair choice only for simple and short ggplot scripts, but it becomes a bad practice when the ggplot script is somehow more elaborate than the basic level. It is a bad practice because it easily generates confusion in the code, mixing ggplot logic with Shiny logic. Much better would be to keep different things separate, the ggplot script out of the Shiny dashboard configuration and in `renderPlot()` just use a standard construct with the ggplot object. That is possible by defining as a custom function the ggplot script, such as `plot_tabs <- function(data) {...}`. The definition of this custom function contains the normal ggplot script, and once invoked, the result will be the ggplot object representing the plot. To recap, the *good practice* is:

- define a *custom function*, outside the dashboard, with the ggplot script to produce a certain graphic.
- inside function `renderPlot()` of the *server logic*, invoke the custom function with its parameters.

For beginners, this good practice might look like an additional level of complexity, but actually it is the opposite, with a little effort the code is much more readable, clear, and manageable. It is a little effort well spent. In the following, the excerpt with the definition of custom function *plot_tabs*, having the schema:

```
function_name <- function(parameters) {ggplot script}
```

Just remember that this function definition should be placed outside the user interface and the server logic, and before it is invoked; at the very beginning, before everything else, is usually a good choice.

```
plot_tabs <- function(data) {

  data %>% ggplot() +
    geom_line(aes(x=YEAR ,y='VALUE (%)',
                  color=COUNTRY, linetype=COUNTRY, group=COUNTRY),
              linewidth=0.7) +
```

```
    geom_point(aes(x=YEAR, y='VALUE (%)',
                   color=COUNTRY),
               size=2, shape=21, fill="white") +
    facet_wrap(vars(GEN), ncol=1) +
    labs(x="" , y="Low achieving 15-year-olds (%)",
         color="Country", linetype='Country') +
    scale_color_viridis_d() +
    theme_minimal() +
    theme(1)
    )
}
```

For the *server logic*, we could activate the panel *Theme customizer* with function `bs_themer()` to insert the theme selector and make tests by changing the dashboard's theme.

15.4 Observe and Reactive

In managing reactive events and objects, we could meet a situation different from the ones seen before, which were all cases of events that triggered a recalculation of a new result, for instance, a new selection of rows from a data frame, after an input element was changed. Such cases where a result is updated are typical of function `reactive()`, as we did before. However, actions associated to *tabs* are of different nature. They clearly are reactive contexts because by changing input elements (e.g. tests or country selection), table data and plots included in all tab pages should change, but they are not simply a recalculation and an update of output elements, reactive events associated to tabs are *object rendering actions*. Shiny documentation explains this scenario: " Use `observeEvent` whenever you want to *perform an action* in response to an event. (Note that "recalculate a value" does not generally count as performing an action-see `eventReactive` for that.) The first argument is the event you want to respond to, and the second argument is a function that should be called whenever the event occurs." (Source: https://shiny.posit.co/r/reference/shiny/0.11/observeevent)

In our case, changing tab is exactly that type of event, which, as a consequence, would require function `observeEvent()`. The general scheme is as follows:

```
observeEvent(input$tabs, {
... actions for all tab pages
}
```

Alternatively, a logical condition of type *if-else-if* could be used to specify the execution of different actions based on the selected tab (Note: it requires to specify the tab identifier.)

```
observeEvent(input$tabs, {
  if(input$tabs == "tab1"){
  ... tab1 actions
  } else if(input$tabs == "tab2"){
  ... tab2 actions
  } else {
  ... tab3 actions
  }
}
```

In the dashboard that we are producing, the tab management will follow the logic described as under:

```
observeEvent(input$tabs, {

    if(input$tabs == "MAT") {
    # tab MAT
      ...
      plot and table rendering
      ...}
    } else if (input$tabs == "READ") {
    # tab READ
      ...}
      plot and table rendering
      ...
    } else {
    # tab SCI
      ...
      plot and table rendering
      ... }
  })
```

Use cases for function `observeEvent()` and of similar `observe()` are many and include scenarios where reactive contexts are not simply those of an input element that changes, but, for example, several events combined that should take place for a reactive action to be executed, or an event that is associated to a button and should change several objects or widgets at the same time.

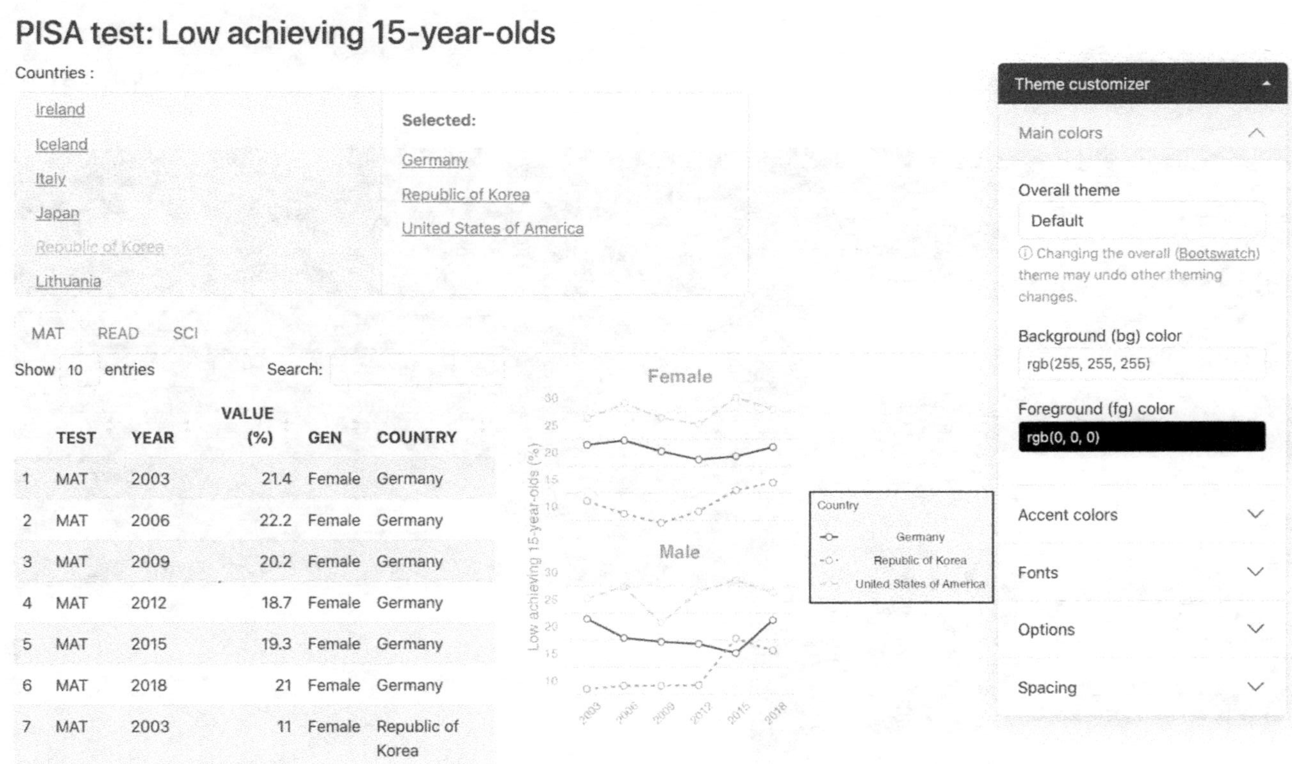

(a)

Figure 15.4 (a) Tab MAT, default theme. (b) Tab READ, dark theme. (c) Google fonts.

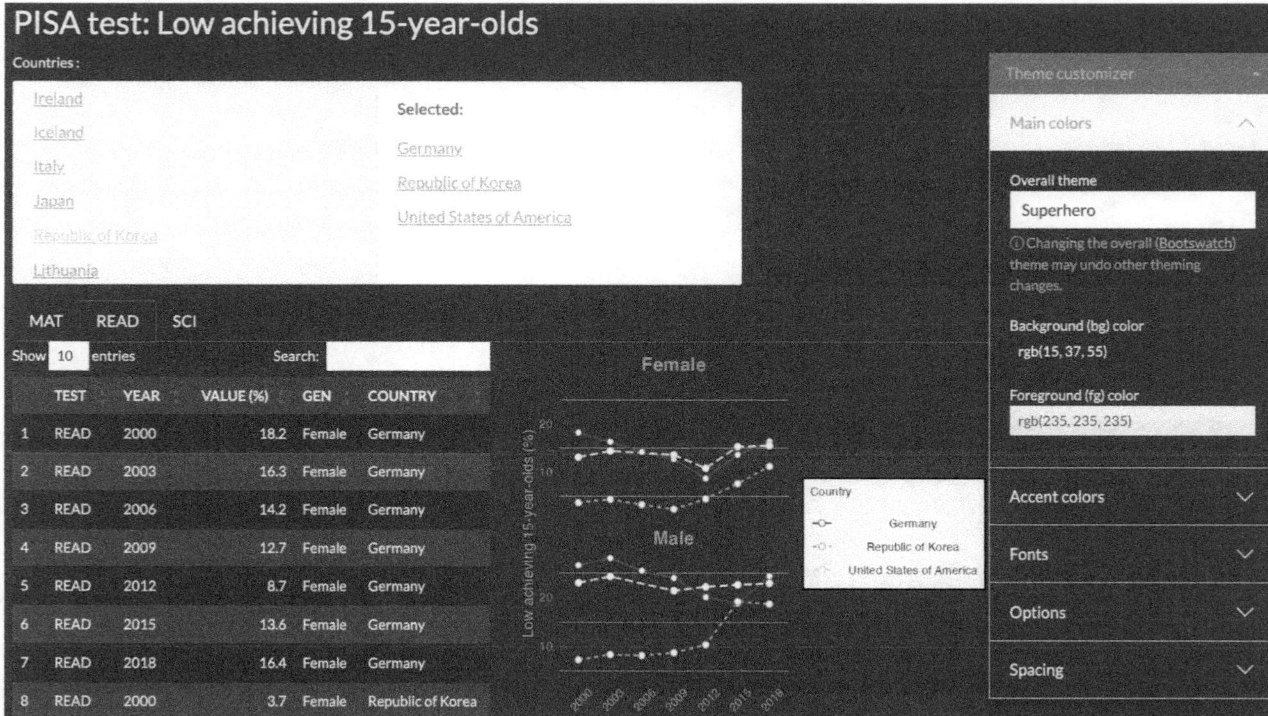

(b)

Figure 15.4 (*Continued*)

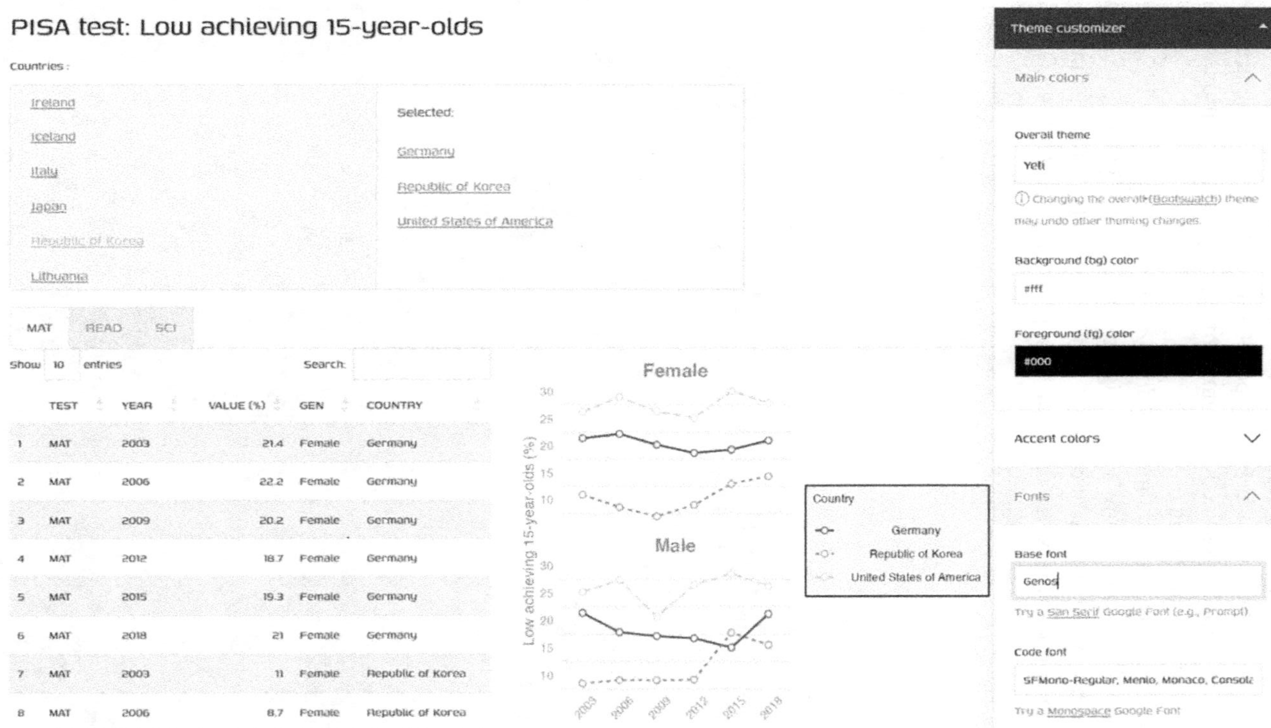

(c)

Figure 15.4 (*Continued*)

We also keep all style configurations specified through ggplot function `theme()` because Thematic is unable to uniformly reconfigure all graphical elements – for example, facets titles and axes labels. It is possible to test which configurations thematic is able to manage by selectively commenting single configurations of the `theme()` function and checking the result.

The complete code is available in the *Additional Online Material – PISA Test Dashboard, Third Version*. Figure 15.4a, Figure 15.4b, and Figure 15.4c show screenshots of the dashboard with different themes, the *default* theme, and the *Superhero* theme, respectively, for different tabs, plus an example using Google Fonts (i.e. *Genos*).

16

Advanced Shiny Dashboards

Dataset

The Himalayan Database Version 2, The Himalayan Database a Nonprofit Organization, Ann Arbor, Michigan, US (https://www.himalayandatabase.com/index.html). It contains information on all expeditions to Himalayan peaks, from 1905 to the Spring of 2022. For the examples, we have selected data regarding expeditions to Mount Everest.

Copyright: Released to the general public at no charge. (https://www.himalayandatabase.com/downloads.html)

16.1 First Version: Sidebar, Widgets, Customized Themes, and Reactive/Observe

With this second Shiny dashboard, we increase the complexity level by adding other graphical elements, reactive events, a more elaborate layout, and finally by integrating interactive Altair plots. The first element we will consider is very typical of dashboards and it can be seen in almost all instances: the *sidebar*, the left-side panel where widgets, options, and selectors are usually placed. We will add some new widgets to the sidebar, but in particular we will discuss a special case: a widget whose aim is not just to let the user make a choice among some alternatives but to modify the actions of other widgets.

Data and the dashboard organization will require more elaborate actions and the usage of both `reactive()` and `observe()` functions for managing the different types of reactive events, those aimed at recalculating values (i.e., *reactive*) and those triggered to execute other actions different from recalculating values (i.e., *observe*). This case will also require a particular care of graphical details, such as to modify textual values in order to make them compatible with the visualization on the dashboard and exploit CSS style sheet functionalities for the graphical

Data Visualization in R and Python, First Edition. Marco Cremonini.

Companion website: www.wiley.com/go/Cremonini/DataVisualization1e

theme. This level of attention to detail and their management is a necessary effort when working on dashboards; it does not suffice to produce a dashboard that works correctly and is passably clear to interact with, instead a dashboard should be graphically well-organized, carefully crafted, and aesthetically pleasant. The appearance is not less important than functionalities in a dashboard, it is part of its quality and effectiveness. For this second dashboard, we will spend more effort for its aesthetic to demonstrate that such aspects should not be overlooked.

Furthermore, when the complexity of the artifact grows, it becomes very important to pay attention to the *organization of code* (not to say its quality). The dashboard's code should be written orderly and clearly; different modules and functionalities should be accompanied by comments and explanations, especially when a nonintuitive solution has been applied; the code should be correctly indented even when not mandatory by the language, and different functionalities should be placed in separate modules, rather than writing a flat long sequence of instructions. These are all basic simple rules for good programming that have their motivation both in the possible reuse of code and, most important for us, in debugging the dashboard and fix errors. What should be clear is that it is the ultimate goal to produce a correctly functioning error-free dashboard, but this does not imply that no errors should be made in all steps of the development. Errors are inevitable during development, so is the necessity to debug the code, and thoroughly test all intermediate artifacts and the final product. A well-ordered code is important, also by considering that debugging a dashboard is more complicated than debugging a traditional R or Python script, because of the reactive events, whose logic could be complex and may hide subtle errors not easy to detect.

Let us introduce the new elements for this second Shiny dashboard.

Customized bslib theme. Preconfigured Bootswatch themes (or of *shinythemes*) are useful and well-done but generic and unoriginal. In a dashboard project, it is often appreciated a certain degree of customization, not only operational but also aesthetical, instead of just applying an ordinary graphical theme. For this, a graphic project and manual customizations are required. In our case, we will present some examples by manually customizing some elements of the layout by means of *bslib*, which supports configurations of the HTML page and CSS style sheets. We will also make use of *Google Fonts* and personalized colors chosen with a *Color Picker* (we suggest trying to modify the choices of the example and test different outcomes).

Sidebar. The first new dashboard element of the user interface is the *sidebar*, which could be defined according to the following schema with functions `sidebarLayout()` and `sidebarPanel()`, with parameter `width` to set the sidebar width:

```
sidebarLayout(
    sidebarPanel(
```

```
        ...
        widgets, text, graphical elements
    )
, width = ...)
```

Widgets. We introduce new widgets, in addition to those already presented in the first dashboard, namely the drop-down menu (function `selectInput()`) and the multiple selection box (function `multiInput()`). The new ones are:

- *slider* for the selection of a range of values (function `sliderInput()`).
- *single or multiple checkbox* (functions `checkboxInput()` and `checkbox-GroupInput()`).
- *button* (function `actionButton()`).

All these widgets are configured in a similar way of the ones already seen, with first attribute `id` as the identifier, needed in the server logic to handle input or output from/to that widget, then a title or text to visualize, and some specific attributes like minimum and maximum values for the slider, a list of choices for the checkboxes and so on. The same applies to other widgets not presented in this book.

Main panel. The new user interface element *main panel* (function `main-Panel()`) defines the page space except the sidebar (and other similar elements like the *navbar*, the panel on top of the page typically used for navigating into the dashboard or menus, we will not use it). In the main panel, we define the usual layout of the user interface with rows (`fluidRow()`) and columns (`column()`).

Custom functions. This is not a real novelty; we have already made use of one of them for creating the ggplot graphic in the first dashboard. This time we will have more graphics to include, so the convenience of separating the code for producing them from the server logic is even greater.

16.1.1 Button Widget: Observe Context

The *button* widget allows us discussing an interesting case of an *observe* context (functions `observeEvent()` or `observe()`), because the reactive action to perform is not a recalculation of some values. What we wish to achieve is different.

From the data frame, we want to show with a checkbox all expedition results (i.e., unique values of data frame column *Result*), such as "Success," "Bad Weather," and "Accident." The checkbox permits a multiple choice, and its identifier is *result*. By changing the selection, the visualization on the dashboard is updated. There is an additional feature, though. With a *button* widget (identifier *selectall*), we want to add the possibility to automatically *select all checks*, which is useful instead of manually select each one of them. The logic of the action associated to the button should be as follows:

- *if* button *selectall is not selected*, then data frame rows are filtered based on the checkbox choice of expedition results and visualized in the dashboard tables and graphics.
- *otherwise*, *if* button *selectall is selected*, then all checks in the checkbox are marked as selected and all expeditions are used for visualization.

This is a situation in which an input element (button *selectall*) is used for modifying a logical condition on data and the state of another input element. It is clearly a reactive context because input data should be read again if and only if the input element is modified, but it is also not a simple recalculation. Therefore, it needs function `observeEvent()` or `observe()`.

A question may arise: what if we use by mistake `reactive()` rather than `observe()`? Such error is certainly easy to do, and it does not produce a blocking condition when the dashboard is run. Everything will seem to work smoothly, but trying to click on the button, nothing will happen, and the reason is that function `reactive()` does not support that kind of event, it just does nothing. Testing the dashboard would easily reveal that something is off.

Some other details need a closer look. The first one is that the function used to modify the values of the checkbox (i.e., `updateCheckboxGroupInput()`) requires as first attribute the *session identifier* that the Shiny server is handling. It is the same parameter that appears in `server <- function(input, output, session)`. Session management has mostly to do with the management of concurrent accesses from multiple users, which is customary for a web application. In that case, every user should see the results of her/his own interaction with the application, something similar to what happens on an e-commerce site, each customer must only see her/his cart, not those of others, even when purchasing items at the same moment. This is the meaning of sessions, to keep users separate. These details are important in the deployment phase in a production environment, we do not delve into them and forward the interested readers to the official Shiny documentation. However, the reason for that attribute in function `updateCheckboxGroupInput()` is similar, if several users are accessing the dashboard and one of them clicks on the *selectall* button, that action should select all results just for her/him, not for all connected users.

16.1.2 Button Widget: Mode of Operation

A second important detail related to the *button* widget is its mode of operation. It could be easily mistaken to be similar to a checkbox that has only two states for each check, selected or not selected, 1 and 0 in numerical values. On the contrary, a button is basically a *counter*, every time the button is clicked, there is a value associated that is incremented by one, representing the number of times the button has been clicked. This behavior is easily observable; it suffices to add an instruction in the server logic to write on the RStudio console the button's value. To do that, we can just use standard `print()` and `cat()` R functions, the syntax between them is a little different but they are basically equivalent, choose the one you like more. So, for example, we may add in the server logic the following instruction: `cat("ALL RESULTS: ", input$selectall, "\n")` and expect to see the value of button *selectall* written on the console. Unfortunately, we would receive an error message:

```
Error in input$selectall :
Can't access reactive value 'selectall' outside of
reactive consumer.
Do you need to wrap inside reactive() or observe()?
```

We already know that error message, it is about the reactive context that we forget to define. But why should we have to deal with a reactive context just for printing values of a button? The answer is always the same, we are using the state of the input element `input$selectall` that is interactive, hence monitored as a reactive event, therefore the need to define a reactive context. Having understood this, however, should we use `reactive()` or `observe()`? Are we recalculating a value? No, then it is `observe()`. We add the equivalent instruction for printing values of the checkbox.

```
observe(cat("ALL RESULTS: ", input$selectall, "\n"))
observe(cat("RESULTS: ", input$result, "\n"))
```

Now, we can try clicking several times on the button and look at the console to check the outcome:

```
ALL RESULTS:  0
RESULTS:  Success Success (Claimed)

ALL RESULTS:  1
RESULTS:  Accident Attempt Rumored Bad Conditions Bad
Weather Did not Climb Illness, AMS Lack of Supplies Lack
of Time Not to Reach BC Other Route Difficulty Success
Success (Claimed)
Success (Subpeak, ForeSmt) Unknown

ALL RESULTS:  2
RESULTS:
```

```
ALL RESULTS:  3
RESULTS:  Accident Attempt Rumored Bad Conditions Bad
Weather Did not Climb Illness, AMS Lack of Supplies Lack
of Time Not to Reach BC Other Route Difficulty Success
Success (Claimed)
Success (Subpeak, ForeSmt) Unknown

ALL RESULTS:  4
RESULTS:
...
```

We have the confirmation of what was said before. When the dashboard is executed the first time, button *selectall* has value 0 (*ALL RESULTS: 0*) and the checkbox has the default values *Success* and *Success (Claimed)*. When the button is first clicked, *selectall* has value 1 (*ALL RESULTS: 1*) and the checkbox has all checks selected. If it is clicked the second time, *selectall* has value 2 and all checks are deselected. Clicking the third time, *selectall* has value 3 and the checkbox has again all checks selected. The fourth time, *selectall* has value 4 and no check selected, and so on. The mode of operation is clear, for *selectall* = 0 nothing has been done except setting the default values, if any; for *selectall* = (1, 3, 5, 7, …) all checks of the checkbox are selected; for *selectall* = (2, 4, 6, 8, …) no check is selected. The programmatic logic is:

- For *odd values* of *selectall*, data frame rows should be filtered with a logical condition representing the manually selected checks on the checkbox.
- For *even values* of *selectall*, data frame rows should not be filtered based on any logical condition because all checks are selected.
- For *zero*, the default values are used to filter data frame rows.

The following question is: How do we recognize even values from odd values in R? There certainly are custom functions that do that but looking for them is unnecessary and a waste of time because there is a simple and basic method: *divide the value by 2 and look at the rest, if it is 0 then the value is even, if it is 1 then the value is odd.* In addition, R offers a handy notation to obtain the rest of a division, the *double percent symbol* `%%`. Hence, the condition `input$selectall%%2 == 0` is *True* for even values of *selectall*, and *False* for odd values.

Another detail that will be found in the code is the strange instruction `freezeReactiveValue(input, "result")`. What is that? It is not strictly needed, if omitted the dashboard functioning is still correct, but it adds a useful functionality to avoid the so-called *flickering*, which is the annoying condition when the dashboard is updating the visualization because some input element was changed and, during the reconfiguration, for a short time, it could show incoherent results. That is flickering, when a temporary inconsistent state becomes visible. Function `freezeReactiveValue()` freezes the graphical update of a reactive element, in our case *result*, until a coherent state of all reactive elements have been reached. The code for the button widget follows.

```
observeEvent(input$selectall, {

# selectall equals to 0
  if(input$selectall == 0) return(NULL)

# Even values of selactall
  else if (input$selectall%%2 == 0)
  {
    freezeReactiveValue(input, "result")
    updateCheckboxGroupInput(session,"result","Result",
                             choices= sort(unique(him$Result)),
                             inline=TRUE)
  }
  else

# Odd values of selectall
  {
    freezeReactiveValue(input, "result")
    updateCheckboxGroupInput(session,"result","Result",
                             choices= sort(unique(him$Result)),
                             selected= sort(unique(him$Result)),
                             inline=TRUE)

    }
})
```

16.1.3 HTML Data Table

The last detail that we should analyze regards table formatting, which may hide a tiny subtle difficulty. Let us see the excerpt of code, simplified for ease of comprehension:

```
output$exped <- DT::renderDT(DT::datatable(data= table_data(),
                     options= list(
                      ...
                      )) %>% DT::formatStyle(
                               columns= colnames(.$x$data),
                               fontSize= '70%',
                               textAlign= "center"))
```

This piece of code executes the rendering of the data table (function `DT::renderDT()`) as output element of the user interface. That function requires data to render being in HTML format, and this is the task of function `DT::datatable()` that takes tabular textual data (a matrix or a data frame) and transforms them into an HTML table. The data frame is provided by the reactive object `table_data()`, which we have created with a `filter()` instruction and the original data frame. The resulting HTML table should be formatted with function `DT::formatStyle()`, reducing font size and centering the text, for example. Here comes the subtle problem. Function `formatStyle()`, has first attribute `table` that requires an HTML table, the one created with `datatable()` and passed with the pipe; with attribute `columns` the names of columns to be formatted are specified. We want to format *all columns*; how can we specify that? The trivial solution is to explicitly list them all, it works but it is not a general solution. We want to specify it so that all columns are automatically formatted, it does not sound difficult but instead, it is not as easy as it looks like. To understand the problem clearly, a toy example would help.

First, what we need is to obtain all column names from the table created with `datatable()`. As a toy example, we can try using just `datatable()` with data frame *him*, the original one produced by reading the dataset, and the common R function `colnames()`. Then, we test two simple operations: first we format a single column (i.e., *Year*) just coloring red its values; second we try the same with all columns, by using `colnames()` to obtain the list of names, expecting to see all columns values colored red.

```
> colnames(him)
 [1] "Year" "Season" "Host" "Nationalities" "Leader (s)" "Route(s)"
 [7] "Result" "Smtrs" "Dead" "Exped ID" "Nation"

# Tests:
# 1) Just column Year is formatted by coloring red its values
> datatable(data= him) %>% formatStyle(columns="Year",
                                       color='red')
# 2) Same but for all columns by using colnames(.)
> datatable(data= him) %>% formatStyle(columns=colnames(.),
                                       color='red')
```

The result is that, with the first test, we correctly obtain values of column *Year* colored red. But with the second, by using the normal dot notation from *magrittr* to specify where to place data passed through a pipe, no value is colored red. The formatting has not been applied to any column. Something is wrong. The problem, as said, is subtle, and it has to do with the fact that the table produced by `datatable()` is not a normal R data frame, so the traditional dot notation with pipe does not work. A particular syntax is needed: `.$x$data`, which means that from data passed by pipe (the dot notation), which is an HTML table, data used by `datatable()` are considered (`$data`), and of them all columns (`$x`). It is certainly not crystal clear as a syntax, but it is correct, and by using it we have all values colored red in our toy example.

```
datatable(data=him) %>% formatStyle(columns=colnames(.$x$data),
                                    color= 'red')
```

The dashboard code reflects exactly what we have discussed with the toy example, it just applies different formatting operations. The complete code for this first version of the second Shiny dashboard is available in the *Additional Online Material – Himalayan Database Dashboard, First version*. Figure 16.1a, Figure 16.1b, and Figure 16.1c show some screenshots of the dashboard with the default configuration and a custom range of years, button *Select All* clicked, and a few nationalities selected. The possibilities are clearly many more.

16.2 Second Version: Tabs, *Shinydashboard*, and Web Scraping

The first version is already an acceptable dashboard, still simple but neat, and most of all it is still largely customizable by configuring the many style options of the layout. We focus on a different aspect, though. The visualization is dense and trying not to make the page excessively long, a first improvement would be to make it a multi-page dashboard by introducing *tabs*. It is not difficult, as we have seen with the first dashboard of the previous chapter, the overall page organization remains the same, with the addition of a main element `tabsetPanel()` and elements `tabPanel()`, one for each tab with its own page layout. We will not go through it again with a detailed explanation, there is no difference with respect to the previous chapter, just adaptations.

16.2.1 Shiny Dashboard

We consider, instead, a new package called *shinydashboard* that helps in the configuration of a Shiny dashboard. It could be useful and it is reliable, but it is often observed that it produces dashboards that look too similar and conventional like a template endlessly reused. It is true, but that is mostly due to a certain laziness in sticking with default configurations, because there is actually no hard constraint for personalizing a dashboard produced with the help of this package. The same criticism, as we have observed before, holds for all tools and solutions that make use of predefined templates and themes, for example it applies to Bootswatch themes as well, which are many but still tend to a certain degree of stylistic homologation. The same is also true for many predefined color palettes and for most commercial products for dashboard development, which often limit the customization options. The truth is that choosing among preset configurations is easy and quick, and almost always, among predefined alternatives, a few are clearly better than the others, so the choice falls preferably on those few. The definition of a personalized style and layout, not conformist, not homologated with common templates, is more difficult than it may seem; it

(a)

Figure 16.1 (a) Layout with default configuration with years range 2000–2021. (b) Select All button clicked. (c) Only Italy, USA, and UK chosen.

(b)

Figure 16.1 (*Continued*)

(c)

Figure 16.1 (*Continued*)

takes a considerable amount of time and effort, many attempts and adjustments, and it also requires great care of the details. It is not by chance that professionals skilled in that area are often in great demand.

For our examples, we will use *shinydashboard* and apply some personalization, in order to give a glimpse of the many possibilities. The library offers several specific functions for typical components of a user interface, another reason to clearly organize it in separate modules: functions `dashboardHeader()`, `dashboardSidebar()`, `dashboardBody()`, and `dashboardPage()` are specific for the corresponding components, header, sidebar, body, and page. The reference schema for the organization is as follows:

```
dashboardPage(
  dashboardHeader(),
  dashboardSidebar(),
  dashboardBody()
)
```

An even better organization makes use of variables to handle the different parts of a dashboard. Let us see how by starting with the user interface. Instead of defining all user interface components as values of a single `ui` object, as we did until now, we could assign

the different components of the user interface to specific variables, and organize the dashboard with those specific variables, rather than with the general `ui` one. An example could be to use the following definitions:

- *header* (`header <- dashboardHeader()`): we use it to define all features of the dashboard's header.
- *sidebar* (`sidebar <- dashboardSidebar()`): for all features of the sidebar, such as the element `sidebarMenu()` and widgets.
- *body* (`body <- dashboardBody()`): for all features referred to the main page, graphical objects, tables, and for multi-page dashboards the `tabsetPanel()` and specific tab layouts.

Finally, since to run a Shiny app we need to invoke `shinyApp(ui,server)`, all specific variables should be combined with `dashboardPage()` into the standard general `ui` variable.

```
ui= dashboardPage(header, sidebar, body, skin = "blue")

shinyApp(ui, server)
```

For stylistic personalization, some predefined *skins* exist, "*blue*" is the standard one, and others are "*black*," "*purple*," "*green*," "*red*," and "*yellow*." However, variations among these skins are limited to the header panel color and a little more.

That produces the most manifest homologation effect, other than the layout organization; dashboards produced this way are essentially all alike, most of them with the blue header, but a little to nothing changes by choosing a different skin. For true personalization, it is required, at least, to work on the CSS style sheet, the same way it is done with a traditional website or application. It is possible either to connect to the dashboard a custom CSS style sheet or to work with inline definitions (e.g., `tags$head(tags$style(HTML('...'))`), which is the Shiny syntax that translates CSS declarations. In the following excerpt, we change the background and font color. Technical details are available in the official documentation of package *shinydashboard* (http://rstudio.github.io/shinydashboard/appearance.html) with additional functionalities here not presented.

```
tags$head(tags$style(HTML('
            .skin_blue, .sidebar-menu, #season a {
               color: #e6e5e3;
               background-color: #2b447a;
            }
            .skin_blue, .shiny-options-group span {
                color: #e6e5e3;
            }
            .skin_blue, .control-label {
                color: #e6e5e3;
            }
            .skin_blue, .checkbox span {
                color: #e6e5e3;
            }'
))),
```

16.2.2 Web Scraping of HTML Tables

We move now to consider the second main novelty of this dashboard version, the *web scraping of HTML tables*. With this, we wish to enrich the dashboard with tabular information freely available from websites, without necessarily downloading it, and transform into a local CSV dataset for traditional data import. This is where web scraping techniques and tools are useful for retrieving information directly from the web source. Alternatively, we might use APIs (*Application Programming Interfaces*), namely specific functions made available by the owner of the online source to let remote users access information. If available, APIs are the best choice to access online information, but if not available, web scraping may help. With web scraping techniques, data are collected straight from the HTML source by selecting the elements to collect.

It is, however, necessary to know that web scraping is subject to an ever-ending debate regarding its legitimacy as a way to collect information from public sources. Information on public websites is freely accessible, which technically means that a user downloads it locally to read it, however, information on public sources is still a proprietary information and it is questionable if a programmatic collection through automatic tools is or is not acceptable. There are legitimate concerns regarding the possible performance degradation if a web server is heavily loaded with collections of large bunches of data, possibly systematically repeated. There are also legitimate doubts regarding the fundamental difference between users individually accessing online information, the reason why a website is online, and the programmatic collection of information by automatic means, which is not the purpose of the website. In short, web scraping is not in general forbidden or a sneaky action possibly unlawful and it is normally made available by standard libraries and tools (e.g., R and Python data science libraries), but it is possible that the online source owner decides to block that kind of activity and even to blacklist the source IP address if they detect a systematic web scraping activity. For example, do not try to web scrape Amazon, they will not tolerate such attempts.

At any rate, for our purposes and examples, we are not interested in systematically web scraping a large amount of data or proprietary data for which the owner forbids web scraping attempts, but we limit our attention to the most innocuous and simple of online data: *HTML tables from static pages*. That is easy to do and problem-free, dynamic content generated by JavaScript is more difficult to retrieve, you can try it without fear of triggering angry reactions.

We wish to retrieve data from two HTML tables, one present in the Wikipedia page “List of people who died climbing Mount Everest” (https://en.wikipedia.org/wiki/List_of_people_who_died_climbing_Mount_Everest), regarding mortal accidents that happened during expeditions; the other from *The Himalayan Database*, by selecting the *Peak Ascents Report* with Mount Everest code (*Peak ID: EVER*) (https://www.himalayandatabase.com/scripts/peaksmtr.php), which provides the full list of Everest expeditions members (at the time of writing, 11 341 members).

Let us consider the basic logic for retrieving those data by means of R functionalities and inserting them into the Shiny dashboard. First, we need package *rvest*, included into *tidyverse*. The general idea is that we read the HTML page corresponding to a certain URL, then from the page source, we retrieve the table we are interested in and transform it into a data frame. Let us consider the corresponding code for the Wikipedia table:

```
library(rvest)

# Read the HTML page
```

```
url <- ("https://en.wikipedia.org/wiki/
              List_of_people_who_died_climbing_Mount_Everest")
webpage <- read_html(x=url)

# Retrieve the table from the HTML source

data <- html_elements(webpage, 'table.wikitable')
data <- html_table(data, header= TRUE)

# Make it a data frame

dead_him <- data %>%
  bind_rows() %>%
  as_tibble()
```

The first instruction simply assigns to a variable (*url*) the URL of the page with the table we wish to read. Then, with function `read_html()` we read the page's HTML source; the first attribute (x) should be a local path or a URL. The result, assigned to variable *webpage*, is in XML format (a structured format often used for web content). Figure 16.2 shows part of the XML file visualized with the RStudio viewer, the main tag `<html>` is on top and includes tag `<head>`, the HTML page's header, and tag `<body>`, with page content.

The following instruction is `html_elements(webpage,'table.wikitable')` with `html_elements()` as the new function, from *rvest v.1.0.0*, replacing the previous one called `html_nodes()`. This is the key step because here we specify the page to inspect (variable *webpage*) and, most of all, the specific HTML element containing the table we want. There are different methods to specify the HTML element, either by the *CSS selector* or an *XPath expression*. We have used a CSS selector, namely `'table.wikitable'`. Let us see how to recognize it. With a web browser (Chrome has been used for the example), open the page corresponding to the URL. Then, you should look for a developer tool for HTML inspection. All modern web browsers provide a tool of this sort, in one way or another, for Chrome it can be found from menu *View-Developer*

Name	Type	Value
<html>	list [2] (S3: xml_document, xr	List of length 2
<head>	list [2] (S3: xml_node)	List of length 2
<body>	list [2] (S3: xml_node)	List of length 2
(xml attributes)	character [3]	'client-nojs vector-feature-l
(attributes)	list [2]	List of length 2
names	character [2]	'node' 'doc'
class	character [2]	'xml_document' 'xml_node'

Figure 16.2 Excerpt of XML representation of a web-scraped HTML page.

(using MacOS, a similar one if Windows is used). From that, select *Inspect Element* or, alternatively, right-click on the page and from the contextual menu there will be again *Inspect Element*. What appears is a standard Chrome tool to inspect the elements of a web page, other browsers, such as Firefox and Bing, have similar ones. Now, let us have a look at Figure 16.3.

On the far left of the menu bar, the one with items like Elements, Console, and Sources, there is a little *icon with an arrow and a square*, by clicking on it, it will turn blue, meaning that we can select page elements just by hovering the mouse on each one of them. When the mouse hovers on an element, it will be highlighted,

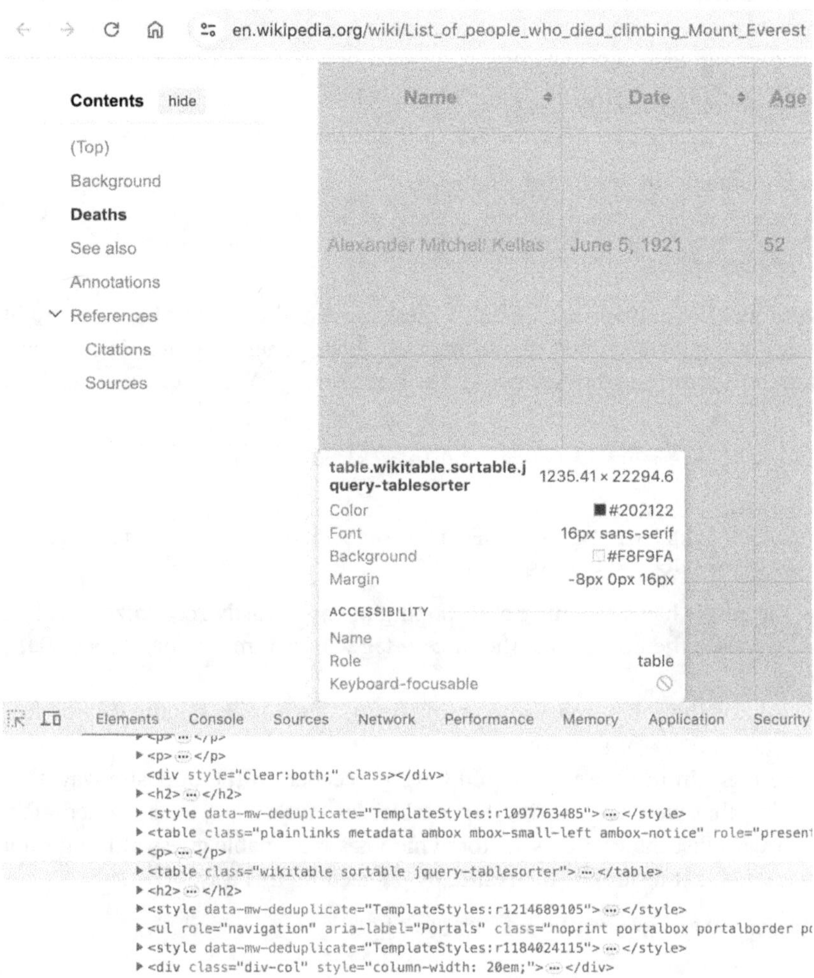

Figure 16.3 Selecting the table element through the Chrome's Inspect Element tool.

and a tooltip will show its properties. In the panel at the bottom (*Elements* menu selected) the corresponding source code is visualized showing HTML tags and elements.

Now the tricky step. What we need to do is to select the HTML *table* element and to do it, a certain amount of patience is required because you will likely end up selecting many other elements before catching the table (try to hover on the table border, that would be easier). At that point, you will see the whole table (and only the table) highlighted, and the corresponding tooltip will give you the required information (Figure 16.3 shows exactly that tooltip). In our case, it states that the CSS selector is `table.wikitable.sortable.jquery-tablesorter`. We are almost done, now we should try selecting with the R code. We try executing on the console (or in a script as well, of course) function `html_elements()` with that selector and look at the result.

```
data <- html_elements(webpage,
             'table.wikitable.sortable.jquery-tablesorter')
```

Checking the result, we find the following:

```
> data
{xml_nodeset (0)}
```

It is empty (`{xml_nodeset (0)}`), meaning that the selector has not caught the table. It should be tuned, try to make it more general by deleting the last part and just leave `'table.wikitable.sortable'`. We check again as done before.

```
data <- html_elements(webpage,'table.wikitable.sortable')
> data
{xml_nodeset (1)}
[1] <table class="wikitable sortable"><tbody>\n<tr>\n<th>Name\n</th>
\n<th>Date\n</th>\n<th align=" ...
```

Now the result has something and looking at it, we easily recognize that it is the table (we see the `table` tag, the `tbody` tag with column names *Name*, *Date*, and so on).

So, we have the table and same result would have been obtained with just `table.wikitable` as selector.

Alternatively, in this case, we could have proceeded in the opposite way, that is, knowing that we were looking for a table, we could have tried immediately to search with just the `table` selector, which is a reasonable guess although not always correct. Let us look at the result, by proceeding this way.

```
> data <- html_elements(webpage,'table')

> data{xml_nodeset (10)}
```

```
 [1] <table class="plainlinks metadata ambox mbox-small-left
     ambox-notice" role="presenta...
 [2] <table class="wikitable sortable"><tbody>\n<tr>\n
     <th>Name\n</th>\n<th>Date\n</th>\...
 [3] <table class="nowraplinks mw-collapsible expanded
     navbox-inner" style="border-...
 [4] <table class="nowraplinks hlist mw-collapsible
     mw-collapsed navbox-inner" style=...
 [5] <table class="nowraplinks navbox-subgroup"
     style="border-spacing:0"><tbody>\n<tr>\...
 ...
[10] <table class="nowraplinks navbox-subgroup"
     style="border-spacing:0"><tbody>\n<tr>\...
```

The result has 10 elements that correspond to the `table` selector (`{xml_nodeset (10)}`), and it is easy to recognize from the list that the right one is the second, `data[2]` (it shows the `tbody` tag, *Name, Date*). We also see that the class is `wikitable sortable`, which could be combined to form the selector `table.wikitable.sortable` that we have found with the first method.

As a third possibility, the *SelectorGadget* tool could be used (https://rvest.tidyverse.org/articles/selectorgadget.html), a Chrome and other browser extension that helps in finding the selector associated to an element of an HTML page. Even in this case, the approach is purely empirical, you should try with the tool until you catch the table. In general, it works well, but in this specific case it turned out to be less easy than the two previous solutions, but anyway, it is worth a try.

One way or another, we put the HTML table into variable *data* and just one more step is left before obtaining a data frame. Function `html_table()` provides the tabular data, then with common R functions `bind_rows()` and `as_tibble()` the data frame corresponding to the original table is ready.

```
data <- html_table(data, header= TRUE)
dead_him <- data %>%
  bind_rows() %>%
  as_tibble()
```

To explain the details, with `html_table()` we already obtain the conversion into an R object, but there is a caveat. If we look at the content of variable *data* or its data type, we recognize it to be of type *list*, rather than of type *dataframe*. It needs a transformation, very easy, to concatenate rows (`bind_rows()`) and convert the data type (`as_tibble()`). Figure 16.4 shows the final R data frame corresponding to the original Wikipedia table.

Name	Date	Age	Expedition	Nationality	Cause of death	Location	Refs
Dorje	June 7, 1922		1922 British Mount Everest expedition	Nepal	Avalanche	Below North Col	[8]
Lhakpa	June 7, 1922		1922 British Mount Everest expedition	Nepal	Avalanche	Below North Col	[8]
Norbu	June 7, 1922		1922 British Mount Everest expediton	Nepal	Avalanche	Below North Col	[8]
Pasang	June 7, 1922		1922 British Mount Everest expedition	Nepal	Avalanche	Below North Col	[8]
Pema	June 7, 1922		1922 British Mount Everest expedition	Nepal	Avalanche	Below North Col	[8]

Figure 16.4 First data frame obtained through web scraping from an HTML page.

For the second table to obtain through web scraping, we proceed in a similar way with just one difference, namely that the web page from The Himalayan Database is dynamically generated with a PHP script from the initial selection of the *Peak Ascent Report* and specifying a certain *Peak ID*. We do not delve into the details of web scraping techniques with dynamic pages, which is needed if you want to systematically web scrape a number of dynamically generated web pages, but we approach the problem in the most trivial way by simply and manually saving locally the resulting HTML page from The Himalayan Database. So, now we have our page as a local resource, rather than accessed with a URL, with the exception of this detail, the procedure is the same as seen before.

This time we look for the right CSS selector by starting with just `table` as a selector. The following is the result we obtain.

```
url2 <- ("datasets/Himalaian_expeditions/
Himalayan Database Expedition Archives of Elizabeth Hawley.html")

webpage2 <- read_html(url2)

data2 <- html_elements(webpage2,'table')

data2
{xml_nodeset (5)}
[1] <table width="100%" border="0" cellspacing="0"
    cellpadding="0"><tbody>\n<tr>\n<td bgcolor="#2F ...
[2] <table width="100%" border="0" cellspacing="0"><tbody><tr>\n
    <td width="15"></td>          <td ...
[3] <table width="100%" height="79%" border="0" cellpadding="10"
    cellspacing="0"><tbody><tr>\n<td ...
[4] <table width="100%" height="100%" border="0" cellpadding="5">
    <tbody><tr>\n<td valign="top">\n< ...
[5] <table id="Peaks" border="1"><tbody>\n<tr>\n
    <th style="width: 40px" align="left"><small> Peak ...
>
```

We find five HTML tables in the page corresponding to selector `table`, and again it is easy to recognize which is the one we are looking for: it is the fifth (i.e., `data2[5]`), having HTML *id* equal to *Peaks*, the first column named *Peak* and so on. An HTML *id* is different from a *class*, that we found in the previous table, but it could be part of a selector as well, it just needs to be prefixed with the sharp symbol #, therefore the more specific selector would have been `'table #Peaks'`. For the example, we use `data2[5]`. It should be converted into an R object with `data2<- html_table(data2[5],header=TRUE)` and transformed from list type to *dataframe* type with `bind_rows()` and `as_tibble()` (see Figure 16.5).

The complete code is available in the *Additional Online Material – Himalayan Database Dashboard, Second version*. Figure 16.6a, Figure 16.6b, and Figure 16.6c show three screenshots, the first for the *Expeditions* tab, the second for the *Summiteers* tab with the table from The Himalayan Database web page, and the third for the *Fatalities* tab with the table from the Wikipedia page.

16.2.3 Shiny Dashboards and Altair Graphics Integration

With the third version of this dashboard, we introduce an advanced improvement, represented by the possibility to integrate interactive Altair graphics into a Shiny dashboard. It is interesting for the excellent quality and features of Altair, but also challenging. Shiny is based on the R environment, while Altair is a Python library,

Peak	Name	Yr/Seas	Date	Time	Citizenship	Sex	Age	Oxy	Dth	Host
EVER	Tenzing Norgay	1953 Spr	May 29	11:30	India	M	39	Y	•	Nepal
EVER	Edmund Percival Hillary	1953 Spr	May 29	11:30	New Zealand	M	33	Y	•	Nepal
EVER	Juerg P. Marmet	1956 Spr	May 23	14:00	Switzerland	M	28	Y	•	Nepal
EVER	Ernst Schmied	1956 Spr	May 23	14:00	Switzerland	M	31	Y	•	Nepal
EVER	Adolf (Dolf) Reist	1956 Spr	May 24	11:00	Switzerland	M	35	Y	•	Nepal
EVER	Hans-Rudolf Von Gunten	1956 Spr	May 24	11:00	Switzerland	M	27	Y	•	Nepal

Figure 16.5 Second data frame obtained through web scraping from an HTML page.

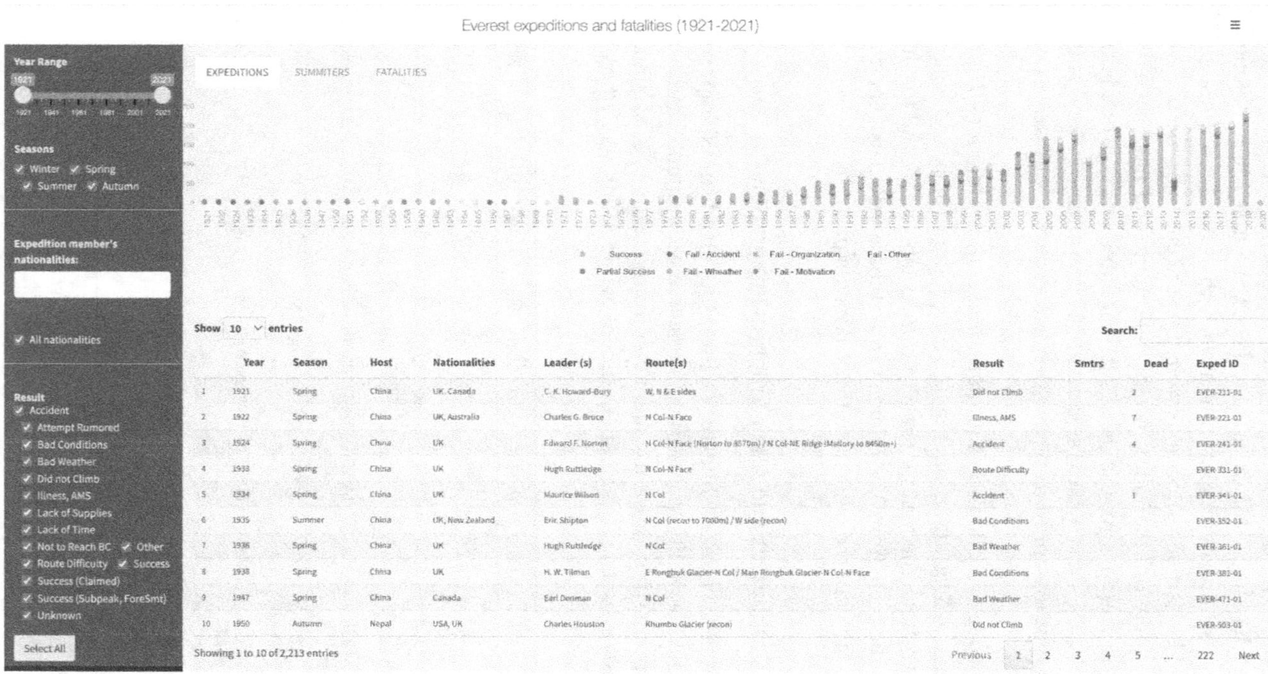

(a)

Figure 16.6 (a) Expeditions tab, default visualization. (b) Summiteers tab, table from The Himalayan Database's web page. (c) Fatalities tab, table from Wikipedia's web page.

(b)

Figure 16.6 (*Continued*)

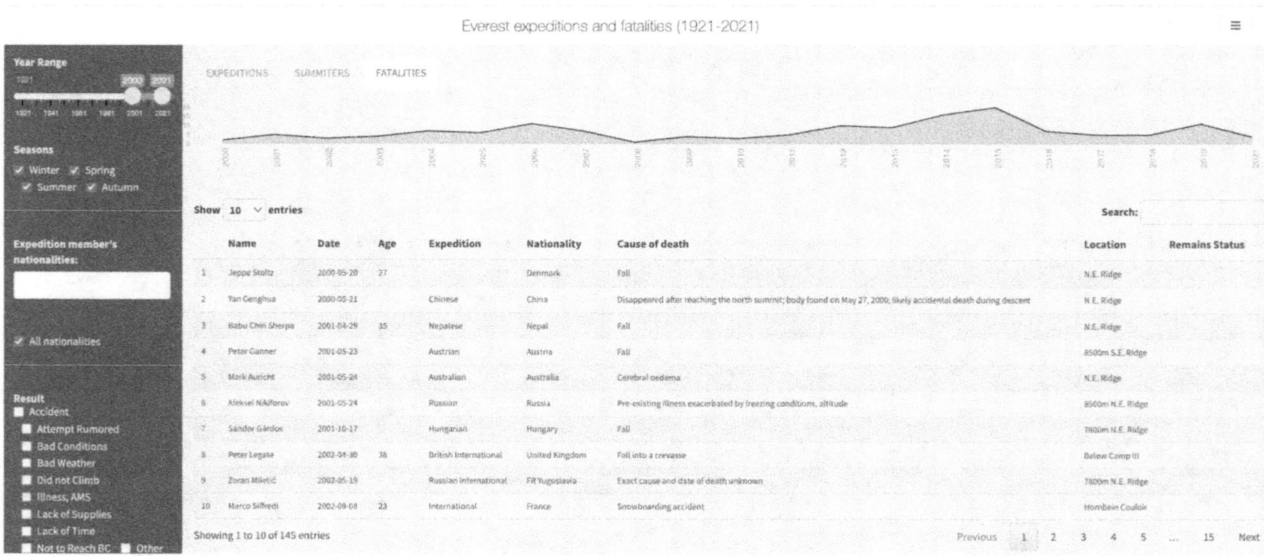

(c)

Figure 16.6 *(Continued)*

truth is that the integrability between R and Python has improved considerably in recent years, but nevertheless it is still a challenging task. So, be prepared to tackle with some difficulties, also due to the fact that the possibility to integrate Altair into Shiny is relatively recent, partially based on novel developments in Vega-Lite, the technology behind Altair, is still not rigorously documented, and with just a few examples available. However, those difficulties being largely predictable, the goal is definitely worth the effort. We proceed step-by-step, as usual.

16.2.4 Altair and *Reticulate*: Installation and Configuration

To start, it is recommended to attentively follow the indications given by the official documentation for the installation (https://vegawidget.github.io/altair/index.html and https://vegawidget.github.io/altair/articles/installation.html). In particular, it is suggested to carefully comply with steps described in *Installation* because it is not sufficient to install the R package *altair* from CRAN, some fundamental operations for using Python functions in an R environment must be executed. To this aim, the R package *reticulate* has been specifically developed, acting as an interface from an R script to the Python execution environment locally installed. Useful is, at least for the initial tests, to create a Python virtual environment by means of *mamba, conda,* or *pip* package managers and assign to it the name used in the Altair documentation (*r-reticulate*), because that same name is the default when the interface between the R frontend and Altair is activated. This way you reduce the configurations to do. The virtual environment should have Python installed as well as all dependencies required by the Python version of package *altair*. If a virtual environment for data science projects is already existing, it might be a good choice to clone it and give to it the name *r-reticulate*. Altair installation into the virtual environment should be executed with the *specific installation function* `altair::install_altair()` *from the R console*. It may happen that an error is raised signaling inconsistencies between versions of some dependencies; all such errors must be fixed before proceeding (for example, at the time of writing, with Altair version 4.2.0, a *downgrade* of Python package *jsonschema* to a version preceding 4.0 was needed).

The final step is to associate *reticulate*, the R interface with Python, with the virtual environment *r-reticulate* just created and configured. The technical documentation suggests to set it by manually editing the configuration file *.Rprofile*. Another possibility is given with the following code, assuming a *mamba* or *conda* virtual environment has been created, it sets the system variable *RETICULATE_PYTHON* to use the *r-reticulate* virtual environment.

```
library(tidyverse)
py_bin <- reticulate::conda_list() %>%
      filter(name == "r-reticulate") %>%
      pull(python)

Sys.setenv(RETICULATE_PYTHON = py_bin)
library(reticulate)
```

There exists a third way, by using RStudio to develop the Shiny dashboard, you likely defined a new R project (if not, it is recommended). In that case, it is possible to specify a local project configuration with menu *Tools – Project Options*. On the sidebar, select *Python* and edit the *Python interpreter* by choosing from tab *Virtual environments* or *Conda environments* (the first if you used *pip*, the second if you used *conda*) the *r-reticulate* virtual environment.

When all installation steps have been completed, it is suggested to test the correct functioning with a simple dashboard. In the next section, one is proposed.

16.2.5 Simple Dashboard for Testing Shiny-Altair Integration

Examples of Shiny dashboards with Altair graphics are quite rare and often they are outdated and no longer working, being based on Altair version 3, but superseded by version 4 that has deprecated some functions previously required and now replaced with the original ones from package *vegawidget*, the one for which Altair acts as an interface.

Here, we present a very simple Shiny dashboard for testing purposes, which integrates an Altair bar plot. The attention points are:

- Usage of functions from package *vegawidget*, replacing the older ones from package *altair* (`vegawidget::vegawidgetOutput()` and `vegawidget::renderVegawidget()`). It is recommended to keep the full syntax with the package notation (`vegawidget::`) in order to avoid conflicts or ambiguities.
- Usage of function `as_vegaspec()` transforming an Altair graphic into *Vega format* (i.e., *vega spec*), which makes it compatible with rendering and output features of package *vegawidget*.

We also recommend not to proceed with the third version of our full dashboard of Himalayan expeditions before having tested the functioning with this simplified dashboard.

```
library(shiny)
library(reticulate)
library(vegawidget)
library(altair)
```

```
# Simple custom data frame
data1 <-
  tibble(
    a= c("A", "B", "C", "D", "E", "F", "G", "H", "I"),
    b =c(56, 33, 12, 22, 98, 65, 25, 16, 76)
  )

# User Interface
ui <- fluidPage(

  titlePanel("Test Dashboard Shiny + Altair"),

  sidebarLayout(
    sidebarPanel(),
    mainPanel(
      # Output vegawidget
      vegawidget::vegawidgetOutput("test_altair")
    )
  )
)

# Server logic
server <- function(input, output) {

  # Altair bar plot e as_vegaspec()
  chart <- alt$Chart(data1)$mark_bar()$encode(
        x= "a",
        y= "b"
      ) %>%
    as_vegaspec()

  # Rendering vegawidget
  output$test_altair <- vegawidget::renderVegawidget(chart)
}

# Run App
shinyApp(ui= ui, server= server)
```

16.3 Third Version: Altair Graphics

With a correct integration between Shiny and Altair, we can finally extend the previous version of our dashboard with static and interactive Altair graphics. Some special adaptation of Altair syntax will be required because originally it has Python syntax, not compliant with an R environment. Two are the main syntactical changes:

- *Dots*: they are the traditional symbols used by Python to concatenate names of libraries, functions, and methods (e.g., `alt.Chart()`, with *alt* as the alias for *altair* library and *Chart()* the Altair function).
  Dots are not compatible with R syntax and are replaced with the dollar symbol **$** (e.g., `alt.Chart()` becomes `alt$Chart()`).
- *Logical conditions* with module *datum*, necessary to identify the source data frame should be rewritten by enclosing them between *quotes*. For example: `.transform_filter(datum.Year<2010)` should be written as `$transform_filter('datum.Year < 2010')`. There is a problem with alphanumeric values, though, that Altair requires to be indicated between quotes. Quotes for logical conditions and quotes for alphanumeric values cannot be the same symbol, otherwise the expression is ambiguous. It is necessary to use different symbols, for example: `.transform_filter(datum.Country == 'United States')` could be rewritten as `$transform_filter("datum.Country == 'United States'")` or, equivalently, `$transform_filter('datum.Country == "United States"')`.

Furthermore, in order to use module *datum* in Python, it is required to import it with `from altair import datum`, a Python directive that R does not recognize. For this, R package *reticulate* comes to help because it is specifically designed to allow running Python commands in an R environment. We could then execute the Python import operation with the following command `py_run_string("from altair import datum")`.

Keeping in mind these caveats, we are able to define Altair graphics for a Shiny dashboard in the same way we have defined the ggplot ones: first, we define the output element in the user interface, then the rendering in the server logic with the Altair script for reading data and creating the plot. Everything with their correct reactive contexts.

Custom functions, as we did for ggplot graphics, are still useful and recommended, helping in managing reactive contexts and enhancing the code organization and readability.

Let us consider the dashboard by starting with the *user interface*. We want to add some Altair graphics to the *Summiteers* tab, which has just the table with expedition members. Four are the Altair graphics that we will create, finally composed into a single one with Altair function `hconcat()` and `vconcat()` or the equivalent symbols of pipe | and ampersand &. The result will be a single graphic in HTML/JSON format.

For this reason, the user interface requires just one output element defined by `vegawidget::vegawidgetOutput`, *climb_altair* is the identifier, and the graphic is placed in the same *fluidRow*, over the table, as we did with previous ggplot graphics in other tabs.

```
tabPanel("SUMMITERS",
         fluidRow(
           br(),
           vegawidget::vegawidgetOutput("climb_altair"),
           p(),hr(),
           column(12, DTOutput("climb"))
         )
),
```

Now the *server logic* starts with graphical rendering. The output element is referred as `output$climb_altair` and for the rendering we use function `vegawidget::renderVegawidget()`. To create the Altair graphics, we define a custom function called `plot_climb()` with three attributes that correspond to the different data frames required by the graphic types that we will produce. Those attributes are *data_climb1()*, *data_climb2()*, and *data_climb3()*, and the corresponding data frames have been prepared with common data wrangling operations.

```
vegawidget::renderVegawidget(plot_climb(
                                  data_climb1(),
                                  data_climb2(),
                                  data_climb3()
                                           )
                              ) -> output$climb_altair
```

We consider now the data frames. They are derived from *climb_him*, the one with data read through web scraping from the web page saved locally from The Himalayan Database.

We start with *data_climb1*. This requires a simple data aggregation with rows grouped for nationality (column *Citizenship*). The number of members for each nationality is counted and values are stored in the new column *Num_summit*. For simplicity, nationalities with less than 100 members are omitted. These data will be used to produce a bar plot having on top of each bar the numerical value.

```
data_climb1 <- reactive(climb_him %>% group_by(Citizenship) %>%
   summarize(Num_summit=n()) %>% filter(Num_summit > 100))
```

It is the turn of *data_climb2()*, just a little more elaborate than the previous one. We separate *Year* from *Season* and convert *Year* into numerical type. Then, we group for name and nationality and count the number of times each name appears. This tells us the number of expeditions every climber has joined. Again, for simplicity, we select those with more than 10 expeditions and sort the list by number of expeditions. This data frame will be used for two bar plots: one for

Nepalese Sherpas, which predictably are by far those with the highest number of expeditions; the other for the non-Nepalese climbers.

```
reactive(climb_him %>%
                 separate('Yr/Seas',
                 into = c('Year','Season'),
                 sep = ' ') %>%
                 mutate(Year= as.integer(Year))%>%
                 group_by(Name, Citizenship) %>%
                 summarize(Num_summit= n()) %>%
                 filter(Num_summit >= 10) %>%
                 arrange(desc(Num_summit))) -> data_climb2
```

Finally, the third data frame *data_climb3()*, this time clearly more elaborate than the others. As before, we separate *Year* from *Season* and convert the data type; then we eliminate rows without a valid value in column *Time* because they refer to seemingly spurious entries always duplicated that would create problems in following operations.

Now the trickiest part. We group by name *without aggregating* (`summarize()` has not been used) and count the number of expeditions for each person. The result of this operation, being not aggregated, has the same size as the original data frame, with the new column *Num_summit* with the same value for all rows referred to the same person (one row for each expedition that a person has joined). With the following transformation, we want to select, *for each person, the row with maximum value and the row with minimum value for column Age*. Basically, we want to obtain, for each person, the first and the last expedition (i.e., this obviously does not apply to persons with just one expedition, but we are not interested in those cases). In order to obtain such selection, seemingly easy, within a piped expression, there is a complication. Functions `slice_max()` and `slice_min()`, commonly used to obtain, for each group of a grouped data frame, the row(s) with highest and the row(s) with lowest value for a certain column, cannot be logically combined to obtain rows satisfying either the `slice_max()` or `slice_min()`. We need another solution unless we want to complicate things by separating the two conditions into distinct selections to be combined afterward. The basic combination of function `filter()` and function `rank()` provides us with an elegant workaround. The form `filter(rank())`, which can be used to obtain the same outcome of `slice_max()` and `slice_min()`, could be expressed as a logical condition, hence could be combined.

Let us see the details. In a grouped data frame, to obtain, for each group, the rows with the *highest* values with respect to a certain column, the following expression could be used `filter(rank(desc(column))<=num)`, with *num* indicating the number of rows with highest values we want to obtain. Conversely, for each group, to obtain rows with the *lowest* values with respect to a certain column, the following form should be used `filter(rank(column)<=num)`. The key is that being both *filter* operations, the *rank* expressions are actually logical conditions, so they could be combined with logical operators. In our case we want the disjunction (i.e., OR) and retrieve just one row for each condition, so to obtain, *for each person, the expedition whose age was the oldest OR the expedition whose age was the youngest*: `(filter(rank(Age)<=1 | rank(desc(Age))<=1))`.

In other words, we obtain, for each person, *the age of the first and the age of the last expedition.*

A last detail remains to be clarified. There is the case of persons who joined more than one expedition at same age (it is rare, obviously, but there are cases). So, for our purpose, we can select just the columns we need and remove duplicated rows.

```
reactive(climb_him %>%
            separate('Yr/Seas',
                     into= c('Year','Season'),
                     sep= ' ') %>%
             mutate(Year=as.integer(Year))%>%
             filter(Time!="") %>%
             group_by(Name) %>%
             mutate(Num_summit=n()) %>%
             filter(rank(Age)<2 |
                    rank(desc(Age))<2) %>%
             arrange(desc(Num_summit),Name) %>%
             select(2,3,7,8,9,10,13) %>%
             distinct()
            ) -> data_climb3
```

16.3.1 Cleveland Plot and Other Graphics

Data frame *data_climb3* just derived, will be used to visualize a *Cleveland plot*, which is an elegant combination of a *scatterplot* and a *line plot* for categorical variables composed by *a pair of values for each category*, such as the maximum and minimum value of common categories like Male/Female, North/South, Left/Right and so on. It is a simple but clever type of graphics with a long history and an intuitive, eye-catching visual effect; it just needs some work to prepare the data.

The server logic is finished, what remains is the definition of the custom function *plot_climb()* for Altair graphics. The complete code is available in the *Additional Online Material*, here we give only the main elements. As already said, the custom function has three parameters corresponding to the data frames.

```
plot_climb <- function(data1, data2, data3) {…}
```

Also, the Altair syntax should be corrected to be compliant with the R environment, so we will have dollar symbols in place of the dot notation. We will define six

`Chart()` plots, that through combinations, will form the four individual graphics, finally assembled into a single one. Here is the list of the four graphics:

Bar plot Nationality/Number of expeditions: the two plots *bar_plot1* and *text* are combined, with the second adding the numerical values on top of the bars. These are static graphics that we have already seen in Chapter 14 and do not present any difficulty. The combination of them specifies some properties.

```
chart1 <- (bar_plot1 + text
)$properties(title='Number of summits by nationality',
             width=400, height=300)
```

Cleveland plot Age/Name: the two plots, *scatter_plot* and *line_plot*, are combined, with the first one that, for each climber (y-axis), draws the two points corresponding to the minimum and maximum age (x-axis), while the second plot draws a line between the two points, creating the typical shape of a Cleveland plot with two points and a line. Some style options have been defined (i.e., *size*, *stroke*) and dynamic tooltips associated to the markers with contextual information (number of expeditions, age, year, and nationality). The two are aligned in a way similar to the previous graphic.

```
chart2 <- (line_plot + scatter_plot
)$properties(title='Top summiters: age at
                    first and at last summit',
             height=300)
```

Bar plots Number of expeditions /Name: these are two distinct bar plots, *bar_plot2* and *bar_plot3*, for Nepalese Sherpas and non-Nepalese climbers. They use the same data frame but a different selection condition, respectively: `$transform_filter("datum.Citizenship=='Nepal'")` and `$transform_filter("datum.Citizenship!='Nepal'")`.

Both have the dynamic tooltip.

To conclude, we consider the final composition of the four graphics, first aligned horizontally in pairs, then vertically for the combined pairs. As a final property, we set the background as transparent, to comply with the dashboard theme. The last step is the transformation of the Altair graphic into *Vega Spec* type.

```
chart <- ( (chart2 | chart1) & (bar_plot2 | bar_plot3)
)$properties(background='transparent')

chart %>% as_vegaspec()
```

The complete code is available in the *Additional Online Material – Himalayan Database Dashboard, Third version*. Figure 16.7 shows tab *Summiteers* with Altair graphics, both static and interactive.

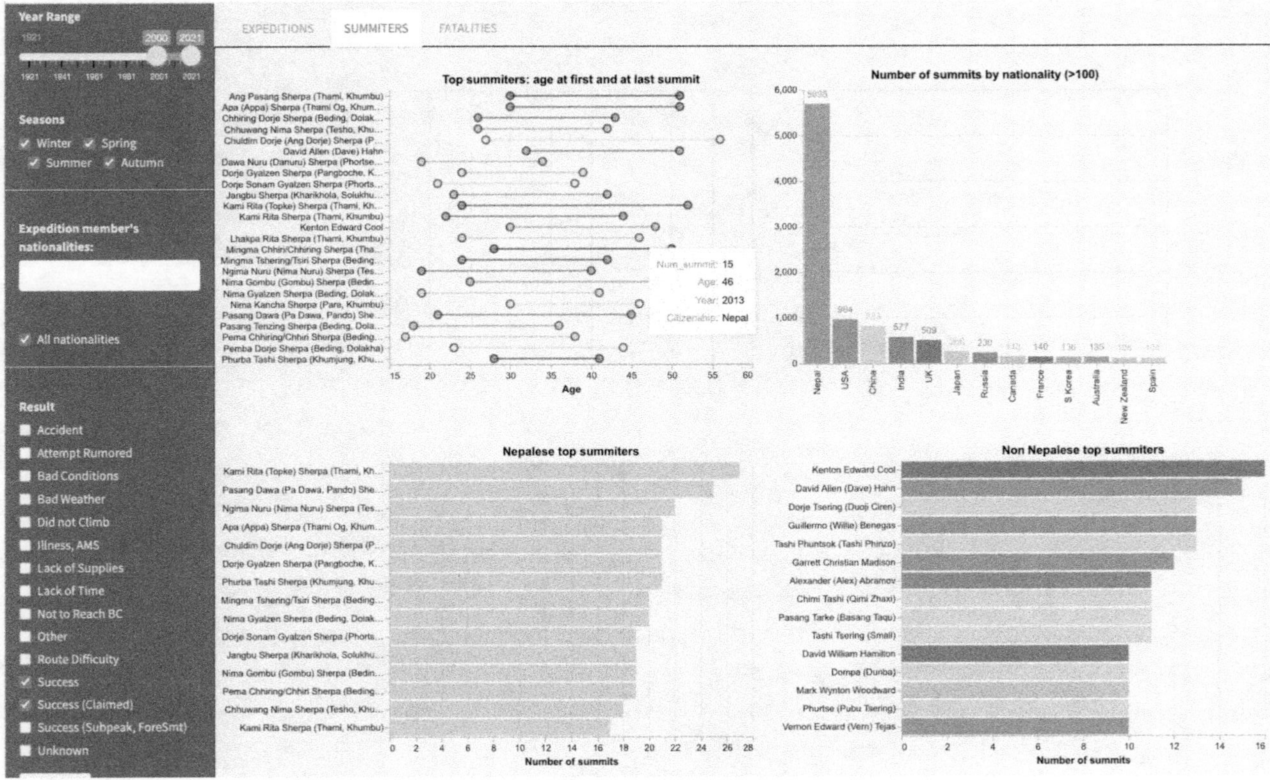

Figure 16.7 Static and interactive Altair graphics in a Shiny dashboard.

17

Plotly Graphics

Plotly is an open-source graphical library offering modern visualization features to Python, (https://plotly.com) for dynamic graphics. It has been subsequently ported to R, although it cannot rival ggplot yet, at least for static graphics. In Python, it has been integrated with an advanced tool for web dashboard development, called *Dash*, which provides the open and free *community edition*, employed for the examples of this book, and the commercial enterprise edition. Plotly syntax, similar to traditional Seaborn, does not follow the grammar of graphics, but is specifically developed for web visualization, it natively offers useful interactive functionalities.

In this book, we will present only a brief summary of Plotly features, they are generally simple, given all what we already have learned with Seaborn, and do not add any particular new skill, but important for us is that Plotly is the reference graphical library for *Dash dashboards*, which we will discuss in the next chapter and represent the real interesting topic to illustrate. Plotly will return in the last Part 4 of the book, when Python geographic maps will be discussed.

Dataset

Tourist/visitor arrivals and tourism expenditure, Open Data from the United Nations (http://data.un.org/), regarding tourist arrivals and expenditure for a set of countries and years. The dataset has been previously introduced.

17.1 Plotly Graphics

Plotly has two main graphical libraries: the most recent *plotly.express* (with standard alias *px*) and *plotly.graph.object* (standard alias *go*), which are largely interchangeable. In the following examples, we will mainly use *plotly.express*, rewriting them with *plotly.graph.object* is straightforward. Let us start from the basics.

Data Visualization in R and Python, First Edition. Marco Cremonini.

Companion website: www.wiley.com/go/Cremonini/DataVisualization1e

```
import pandas as pd
import numpy as np
import plotly.express as px
import plotly.graph_objects as go
import plotly.io as pio
```

We read the United Nations dataset with data about tourists' arrivals and expenditures.

```
df=pd.read_csv("datasets/UN/
      SYB65_176_202209_Tourist-Visitors Arrival and Expenditure.csv",
      thousands=',')
```

	Region/Country/ Area	Country	Year	Series	Value
0	4	Afghanistan	2010	Tourism expenditure	147
1	4	Afghanistan	2018	Tourism expenditure	50
2	4	Afghanistan	2019	Tourism expenditure	85
3	4	Afghanistan	2020	Tourism expenditure	75
4	8	Albania	2010	Tourist/visitor arrivals	2191
	...	...	...	...	...

A few simple preliminary data wrangling operations are needed to prepare the data frame for visualization (i.e., long-form transformation, new column creation with per capita tourist expenditure, removal of rows with missing values).

```
df1= df.pivot(index=['Country','Year'], columns='Series',
             values='Value').reset_index()

df1.columns= ['Country','Year','Expenditure','Arrivals']
df1["Per_capita_Exp(x1000)"]= (df1.Expenditure/df1.Arrivals).\
                              round(3)
df2= df1[~((df1.Expenditure.isna()) | (df1.Arrivals.isna()))]
```

	Country	Year	Expenditure	Arrivals	Per_capita_Exp (x1000)
6	Albania	2010	1778.0	2191.0	0.812
7	Albania	2018	2306.0	5340.0	0.432
8	Albania	2019	2458.0	6128.0	0.401
9	Albania	2020	1243.0	2604.0	0.477
11	Algeria	2005	477.0	1443.0	0.331

	Country	Year	Expenditure	Arrivals	Per_capita_Exp (x1000)
...	...	...	...	...	...
1229	Zimbabwe	2005	99.0	1559.0	0.064
1230	Zimbabwe	2010	135.0	2239.0	0.060
1231	Zimbabwe	2018	191.0	2580.0	0.074
1232	Zimbabwe	2019	285.0	2294.0	0.124
1233	Zimbabwe	2020	66.0	639.0	0.103

17.1.1 Scatterplot

As usual, we start with the scatterplot, the Plotly function is `px.scatter()` having the typical attributes for axes, color, size, and so on. By default, Plotly adds the *interactive tooltip* and the standard *zoom function* of HTML pages. Figure 17.1 shows the first Plotly graphic with the dynamic tooltip, on top-right, icons for the zoom, and other features are visible.

```
# Continuous color scales:
# https://plotly.com/python/colorscales/

scatter1= px.scatter(df2, x="Arrivals",
           y="Expenditure", color="Year",
           size= 'Per_capita_Exp(x1000)', size_max=60,
           color_continuous_scale= px.colors.sequential.Viridis)
scatter1.show()
```

By default, a tooltip shows all values employed as attributes for the graphic. If we want to add variables into the tooltip different than those specified in the graphic definition, we could use attribute `hover_data`. In Figure 17.2, we have added *Country* to the tooltip.

```
# Discrete color palettes:
# https://plotly.com/python/discrete-color/

# Tooltip values have to be strings

df2["Year"]= df2["Year"].astype(str)

scatter2= px.scatter(df2, x="Arrivals", y="Expenditure",
           color="Year", size='Per_capita_Exp(x1000)',
           size_max=60, hover_data=['Country'],
           color_discrete_sequence=px.colors.qualitative.T10)
scatter2.show()
```

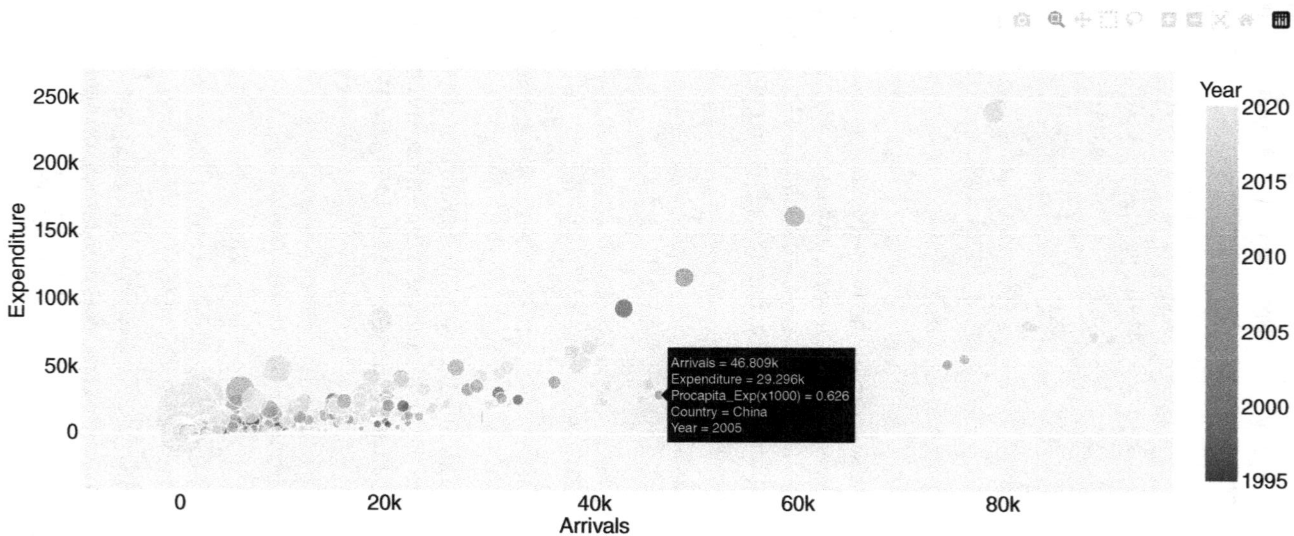

Figure 17.1 Plotly, scatterplot with default dynamic tooltip.

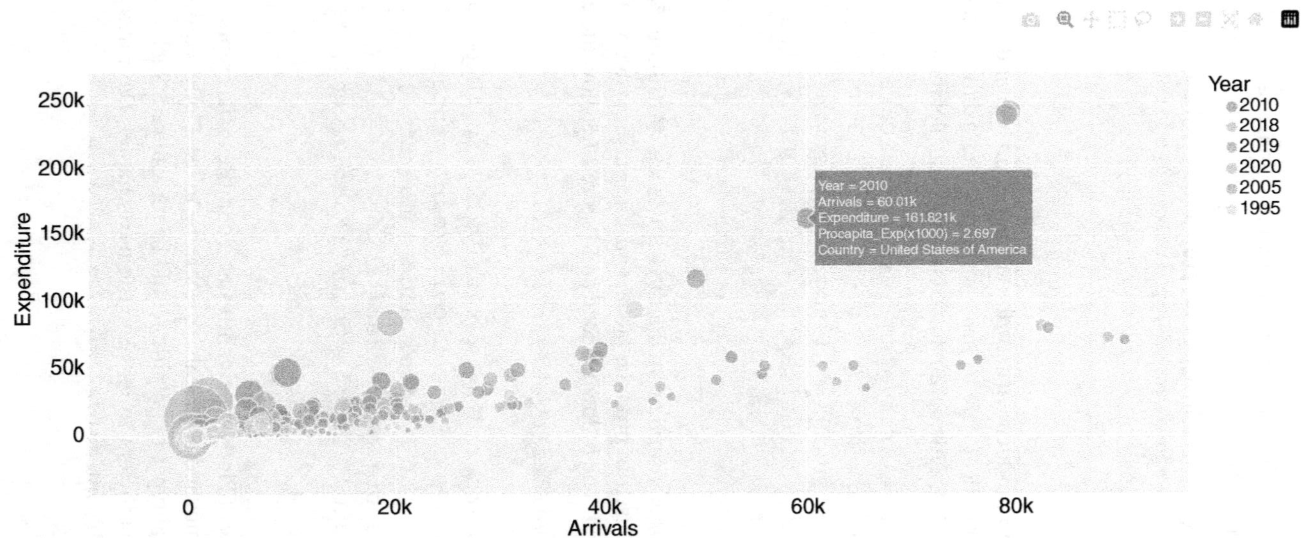

Figure 17.2 Plotly, scatterplot with extended dynamic tooltip.

17.1.2 Line Plot

For the line plot, the Plotly function is px.line() and, again, it has the usual attributes (see Figure 17.3).

```
line1 = px.line(df2, x="Year", y="Arrivals", color="Country",
          color_discrete_sequence= px.colors.qualitative.T10)
line1.show()
```

17.1.3 Marginals

Marginals are easy to produce with attributes marginal_x and marginal_y, which specify the graphical type to place on axis *x* and axis *y*. In the following example and Figure 17.4, a histogram for axis *x* and a rug plot for axis *y* are shown.

```
px.scatter(df2, x="Arrivals", y="Expenditure",
           color="Year", hover_data=['Country'],
           marginal_x="histogram", marginal_y="rug",
           size= 'Per_capita_Exp(x1000)', size_max=60)
```

17.1.4 Facets

We conclude this brief overview of Plotly with facets. Attribute facet_col defines the variable used to produce facets and facet_col_wrap the number of columns of the grid. The following code and Figure 17.5 show the example.

```
df3= df2.sort_values(by="Year")

scatter4= px.scatter(df3, x="Arrivals", y="Expenditure",
                     facet_col="Year", facet_col_wrap=3,
                     hover_data=['Country'])
scatter4.update_traces(marker=
          {"opacity": 0.3, "color":"darkgreen", "size":8})
scatter4.show()
```

This brief overview of Plotly is evidently just a glimpse on its graphic gallery, but equipped with the knowledge of Seaborn, learning to use Plotly requires minimal effort and all classical types of graphics could be reproduced. Such a short introduction is however sufficient to move to the next chapter, *Dash web dashboard*, which is of remarkable interest.

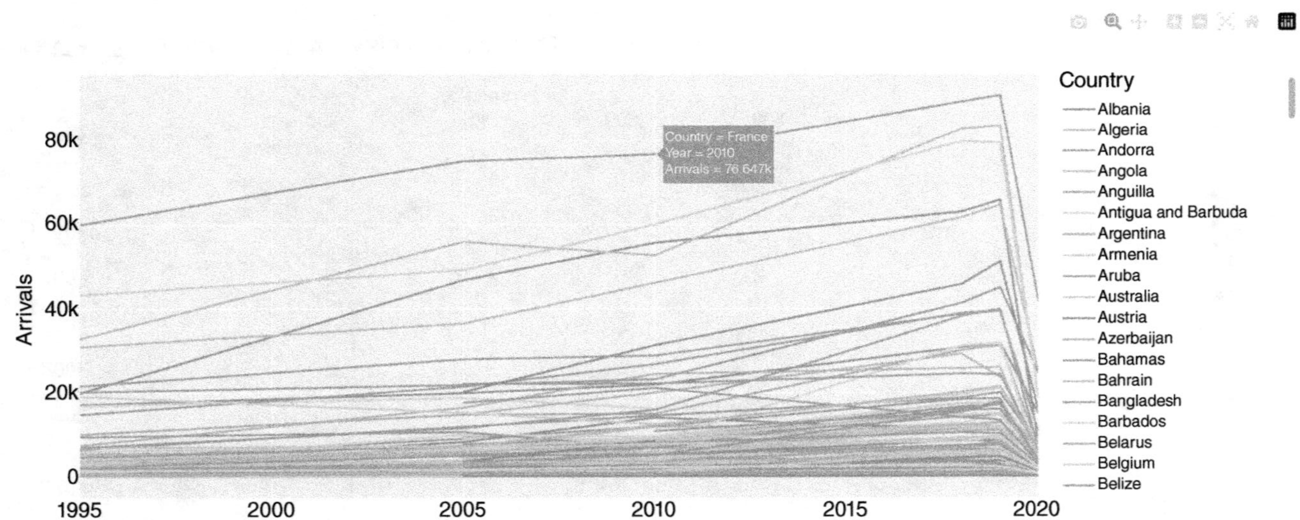

Figure 17.3 Plotly, line plot with tooltip.

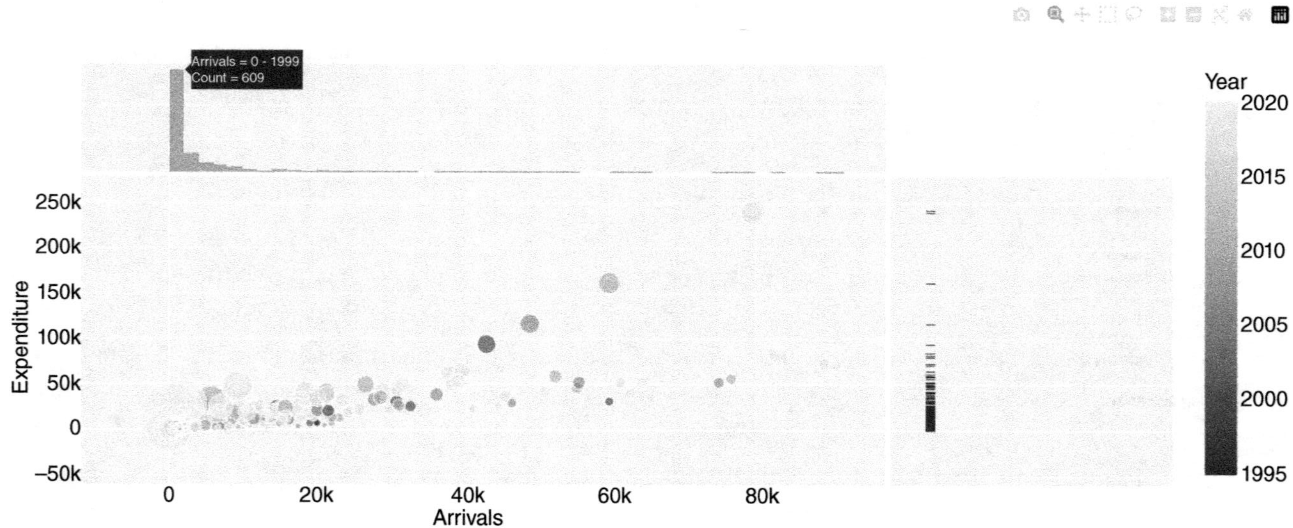

Figure 17.4 Plotly, scatterplot with a histogram and a rug plot as marginals.

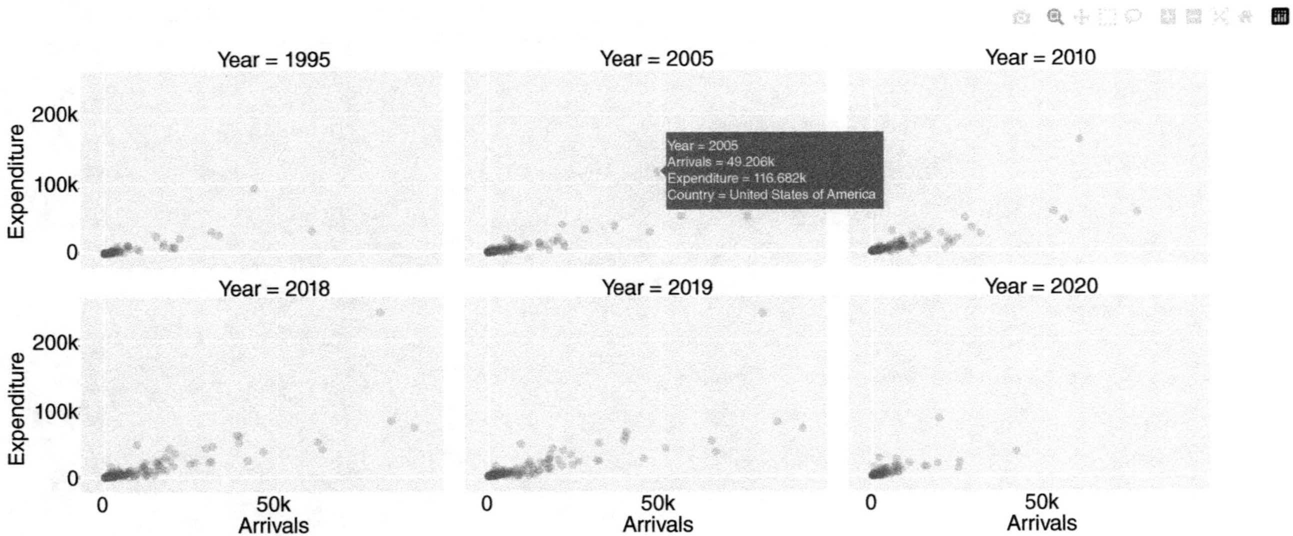

Figure 17.5 Plotly, facet visualization.

18

Dash Dashboards

For developing dashboards with the *Dash framework*, it is recommended using a *Python Interactive Development Environment* (*IDE*). The support for Jupyter Notebook and JupyterLab exists, but there are some differences, and, in general, a Python IDE will serve you much better in this case.

For the Dash installation, the steps described in the official documentation should be carefully followed (https://plotly.com/python/getting-started/).

If JupyterLab is chosen as the development tool, it offers three usage modes: *inline* (dashboard rendering is shown within the notebook), *jupyterlab* (rendering is created in a new tab of JupyterLab), or *external* (a new tab in the predefined web browser is opened and the rendering is presented). Mode *inline* could be used only for truly simple dashboards, other than that it has too many limitations. Mode *jupyterlab* offers more flexibility, but it is an intermediate alternative between the inline and the web browser with not much use. The rendering in the web browser should be chosen as the favorite option, showing the dashboard in its natural environment and permitting mangling with traditional HTML settings and CSS style sheets, instead of just setting inline directives. There also exist (at least at the time of writing) some not-well-documented incompatibilities between the version of the Jupyter library for supporting Dash dashboards (package *jupyter-dash* and its dependencies) and the more recent Python versions (e.g., v.3.10), which may cause problems in the management of the HTTP process that executes the rendering on a web browser. For these reasons, differently from Plotly graphics that are perfectly supported by JupyterLab and Jupyter Notebook, a Dash dashboard development is better developed using a Python IDE, rather than Jupyter tools. Many Python IDEs are available like PyCharm, Spyder, and others, which also provide advanced and useful functionalities for debugging, coloring, and indenting code (relevant to Python), and package management. All examples of this chapter have been developed with *PyCharm Community Edition* and, for

Data Visualization in R and Python, First Edition. Marco Cremonini.

Companion website: www.wiley.com/go/Cremonini/DataVisualization1e

this reason, the corresponding files have extension *.py*. Technical differences with respect to a development with a Jupyter tool are, anyway, just a few:

- Package *jupyter-dash* is no longer required.
- The dashboard is created by running `Dash(__name__)`, instead than `JupyterDash(__name__)`.
- The web application representing the dashboard is executed with no need to specify a mode (e.g., `mode='external'`).

Dataset

In this chapter, we use the same *Tourist/visitor arrivals and tourism expenditure* dataset introduced before.

18.1 Preliminary Operations: Import and Data Wrangling

The following code should come before all excerpts of code that will be presented in this chapter. For brevity, these instructions will not be repeated each time, but they are required to run the examples.

18.1.1 Import of Modules and Submodules

The list of modules and submodules to import is rich and, depending on the IDE of choice, some of them could be preloaded.

```
# NumPy, pandas and Dash
import pandas as pd
import numpy as np
from dash import Dash, dcc, html, Input, Output, dash_table

# Plotly
import plotly.express as px
import plotly.graph_objects as go
import plotly.io as pio

# Dash bootstrap components
import dash_bootstrap_components as dbc
from dash_bootstrap_templates import load_figure_template

# Package lxml (required by pd.read.html())
import lxml

# Inclusion of iframes in HTML pages
pio.renderers.default = "iframe"
```

18.1.2 Data Import and Data-Wrangling Operations

In the following steps of Dash dashboard development, for simplicity, we will keep the same data import and data-wrangling operations to avoid adding unnecessary complexity.

Here is the excerpt of code for data import of the United Nations' dataset and the data-wrangling operations required to prepare the data for visualization.

We also create three local variables, *min_arr*, *max_arr*, and *country_list*, to store the maximum number and minimum number of tourist arrivals, and the country list. We will use them frequently.

```
df= pd.read_csv("datasets/UN/
     SYB65_176_202209_Tourist-Visitors Arrival and Expenditure.csv",
     thousands=',')

df1= df.pivot(index=['Country','Year'],
              columns='Series',
              values='Value').reset_index()
df1.columns= ['Country', 'Year', 'Expenditure','Arrivals']
df1["Per_capita_Exp(x1000)"]=
                    (df1.Expenditure/df1.Arrivals).round(3)

df2= df1[~((df1.Expenditure.isna())|(df1.Arrivals.isna()))]
min_arr= df2.Arrivals.min()
max_arr= df2.Arrivals.max()
country_list= df2.Country.unique()
```

Furthermore, in different versions of Dash dashboards that will be presented, a Plotly graphic will always be included. For simplicity, it will correspond to the second scatterplot showed in previous Chapter 17 (variable *scatter2*). Clearly, the variants are endless, however, for our aim, which is to discuss how to develop and organize a Dash dashboard, using one type of graphics or another is not relevant.

18.2 First Dash Dashboard: Base Elements and Layout Organization

18.2.1 Plotly Graphic

We start with the simplest configuration, which is the visualization of a single Plotly graphic. The dashboard is created with directive `Dash(__name__)`, `app` is the standard name for the resulting object representing the dashboard. With the classical Python dot notation for concatenation, object `app.layout` is assigned to the dashboard page layout. The layout definition largely corresponds to the syntax and organization of an HTML page, only translated into Python syntax. This way, HTML element `<div>`, used to define a page section, becomes function `html.Div()` that requires a list of elements between square brackets. These elements could be HTML elements redefined into Python syntax or Dash elements. In the example, we see that the first element is a header of level H4 (HTML tag <h4>)), here indicated with `html.H4()`, followed by an element `dcc.Graph()`, with `dcc` being the alias of submodule *Dash Core Components*. This element defines a graphic in the layout with attribute `id` as its identifier and `figure` the attribute with the graphical object to include (i.e., in our case the Plotly graphic *scatter2*). The last instruction runs the Dash dashboard locally, it has the form `if __name__ == '__main__': app.run_server()`, with *host* and *port* as optional attributes. As discussed for Shiny dashboard, we see just the local execution; for deploying a Dash dashboard on a production server, we forward the reader to the official Dash documentation.

The result shown in Figure 18.1 does not look impressive, to say the least, it is practically the same as the simple Plotly graphic, nevertheless, the important part is under the hood because this is not just a graphic but a full web application and a Dash dashboard. We will improve it considerably in the remaining of the chapter.

```
app = Dash(__name__)

app.layout = html.Div([
    html.H4('Simple scatterplot'),
    dcc.Graph(
        id= "graph",
        figure= scatter2)
])

if __name__ == '__main__':
    app.run_server(host='127.0.0.1', port=8051)
```

18.2.2 Themes and Widgets

We can now add components, widgets, and, most of all, reactive events to the initial bare dashboard. We start with layout elements.

In order to specify a *Bootswatch theme*, we should use module *Dash Bootstrap Components* (standard alias `dbc`) and its method `dbc.themes`. A list of available themes could be found on Bootswatch's home page (https://bootswatch.com/). We chose a light one (i.e., `dbc.themes.FLATLY`) and specified it in function `Dash()` with attribute `external_stylesheets`.

The following new element is a *widget*, starting with a *slider*, which allows us selecting a range of values for the associated variable, in our case the number of tourist arrivals. The function for the slider widget is `dcc.RangeSlider()`, with an attribute `id` for the identifier and typical slider attributes:

- `min`, `max`, and `step` for the minimum and maximum values, and the minimum step when the slider is moved.
- `value` represents the values shown by default.

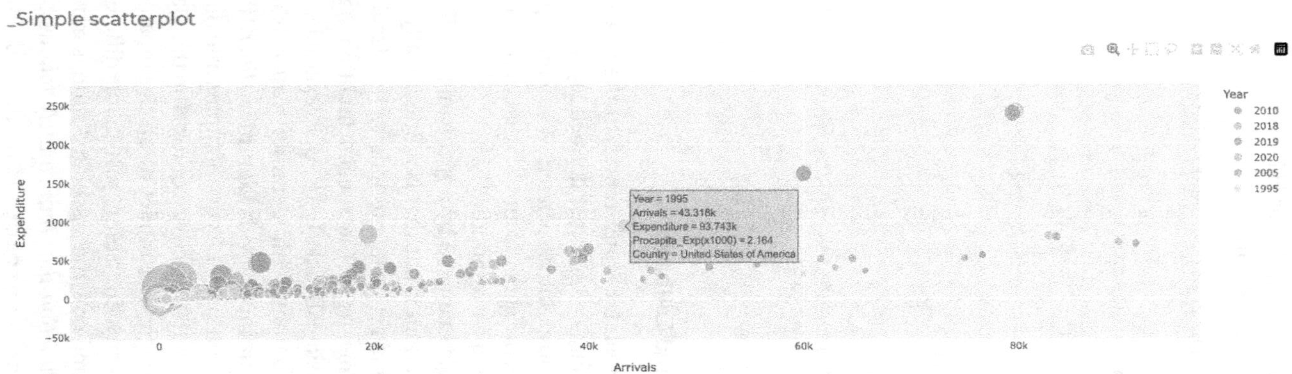

Figure 18.1 Dash dashboard with Plotly graphic.

On top of the slider, we may want to add a text, like a title. We can do this with `html.P()` (again, the Dash translation of HTML tag <p>). All these elements are vertically aligned in the page layout.

```
app= Dash(__name__, external_stylesheets=[dbc.themes.FLATLY])

app.layout= html.Div([
    html.H3('Scatterplot + Slider',
            style={
                'textAlign': 'center',
                'color': 'teal'
            }),
    dcc.Graph(id="scatter"),

    html.P("Tourist arrivals:"),

    dcc.RangeSlider(
        id='slider',
        min= min_arr, max= max_arr, step=5000,
        value= [min_arr, max_arr]
    )
])
```

18.2.3 Reactive Events and Callbacks

Reactive events, as we have seen for Shiny, represent the core of a dashboard, and this holds for Dash too. So far, we have just defined layout elements, and for the slider, in particular, there is no action associated. When the input changes through user interaction, in this case, the slider is moved, that event should be caught, and the dashboard output updated correspondingly.

In Dash, a reactive event is managed by a mechanism called *callback*, namely a function associated to a certain input that is automatically triggered when that input changes, executes some actions, and updates the dashboard. The callback mechanism is defined by means of the special function `@app.callback()` (https://dash.plotly.com/basic-callbacks). In our example, the *callback* will specify that the associated output, with identifier *scatter*, is a graphic (i.e., type `'figure'`) and depends on input, with identifier *slider*, that will pass some numerical values (i.e., type `'value'`). Types of inputs and outputs for a callback are codified in Dash. That is the reactive context for the Dash slider element, which follows the general logic and model of all dashboard's reactive actions, similar to what we have seen with Shiny, just using different constructs. The reactive context is defined, and now the associated actions must be specified. This is provided by *the custom function that immediately follows the callback*. In this case, it is called `update_scatterplot()`; it is a traditional Python custom function, and it is executed when the callback that precedes it is activated.

To recap, the logical flow to manage a Dash reactive event is: the input element is changed, this activates the corresponding callback (`@app.callback()`). The following custom function (e.g., `update_scatterplot()`) is executed and a result is produced, such as the graphic is recreated (e.g., `px.scatter()`) or a table is recalculated. The result is stored in a variable (e.g., `fig` in the example) that is returned, and the dashboard is updated. The following excerpt of code shows the details of the example. Figure 18.2a and Figure 18.2b show two screenshots of the dashboard, the first with default slider values, and the second after having changed the slider input.

```
# Callback definition
# Input type 'value', id 'slider'
# Output type 'figure', id 'scatter'

@app.callback(
    Input("slider", "value"))
    Output("scatter", "figure"),

# Associated custom function

def update_scatterplot(slider_range):
    low, high = slider_range
    mask = (df2['Arrivals'] >= low) & (df2['Arrivals'] <= high)
    fig = px.scatter(df2[mask],
              x="Arrivals", y="Expenditure", color="Year",
              size='Per_capita_Exp(x1000)', size_max=60,
              hover_data=['Country']
              )
    return fig

if __name__ == '__main__':
    app.run_server(port=8051)
```

18.2.4 Data Table

We add a *table* with data. Starting from the layout, we proceed as seen before, first creating the table element, for which a function of module *table* is used, `dash.table.DataTable()` (https://dash.plotly.com/datatable). Let us delve into the details by looking at the definitions presented in the code. The first attribute `data` has the data in *dictionary* format (*dict*), not as data frame, so the data frame has to be transformed. Pandas function `to_dict()` with keyword `records` executes that transformation. The second attribute is `columns`, which is still a *dictionary* this time with column names as values and the index value as keys in dictionary pairs *key:value*. This is the reason for the *for cycle* on column names. Following these two fundamental attributes, the code shows several among the many possible optional features that could be specified for Dash data

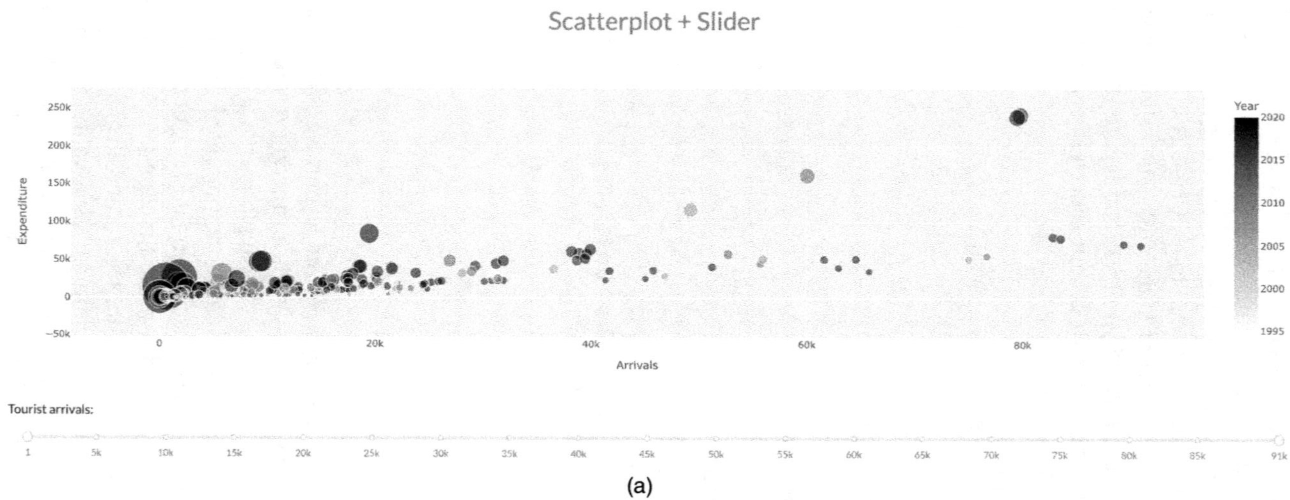

(a)

Figure 18.2 (a) Slider with default range. (b) Slider with modified range (25k–90k).

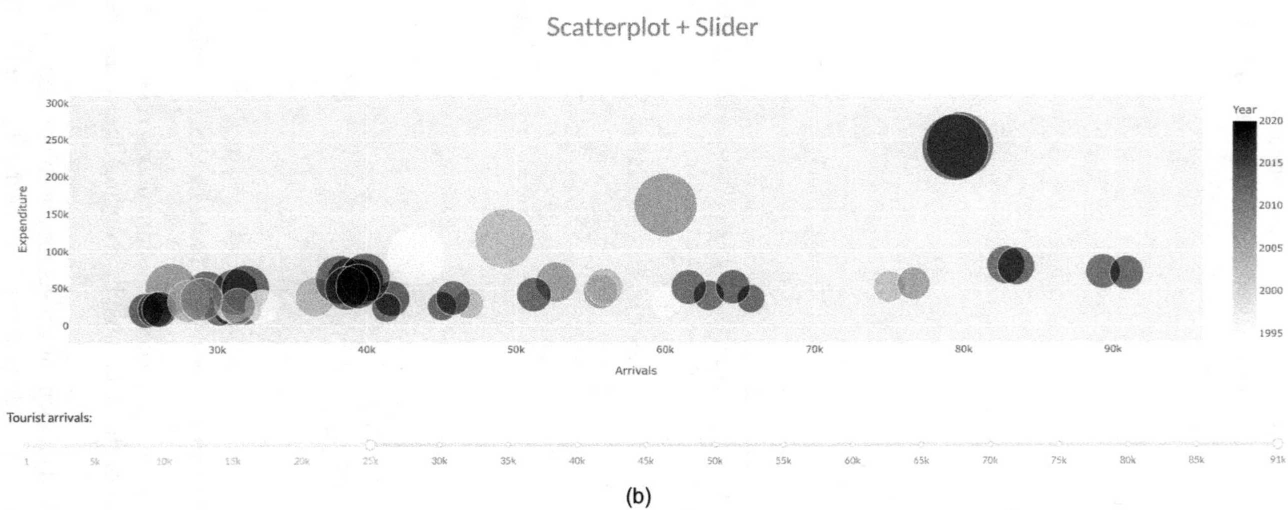

(b)

Figure 18.2 (*Continued*)

tables, such as formatting options, sorting, selection, and so on; in short, features that transform a classical tabular form into an interactive table with features associated to each column. It is suggested to try them all and see the outcome. Figure 18.3 shows the dashboard with the data table.

```
dash_table.DataTable(
    data=df2.to_dict('records'),
    columns=[{'id': c, 'name': c} for c in df2.columns],
    filter_action="native",
    sort_action="native",
    sort_mode="multi",
    column_selectable="single",
    row_selectable="multi",
    row_deletable=True,
    selected_columns=[],
    selected_rows=[],
    page_action="native",
    page_current=0,
    page_size=10,
    style_as_list_view=True,
    style_table={'margin-top': '48px', 'overflowX': 'auto'},
    style_cell={'textAlign': 'left', 'fontSize': 14,
                'font-family': 'sans-serif'},
    style_data={'backgroundColor': 'white'},
    style_data_conditional=[
        {
            'if': {'row_index': 'odd'},
            'backgroundColor': 'rgb(220, 220, 220)',
        }
    ],
    style_header={
        'backgroundColor': 'teal',
        'color': 'white',
        'fontWeight': 'bold'
    }
)
```

18.2.5 Color Palette Selector and Data Table Layout Organization

As a variant of the previous case, we want to introduce a *color palette selector* and also modify the aspect of the data table by reducing its size and centering with respect to page's width.

There is no predefined element or widget for the color palette selector, we have to produce it. First, we need a drop-down input element placed in the layout. We use function `dcc.Dropdown()` with attribute `options` that allows associating

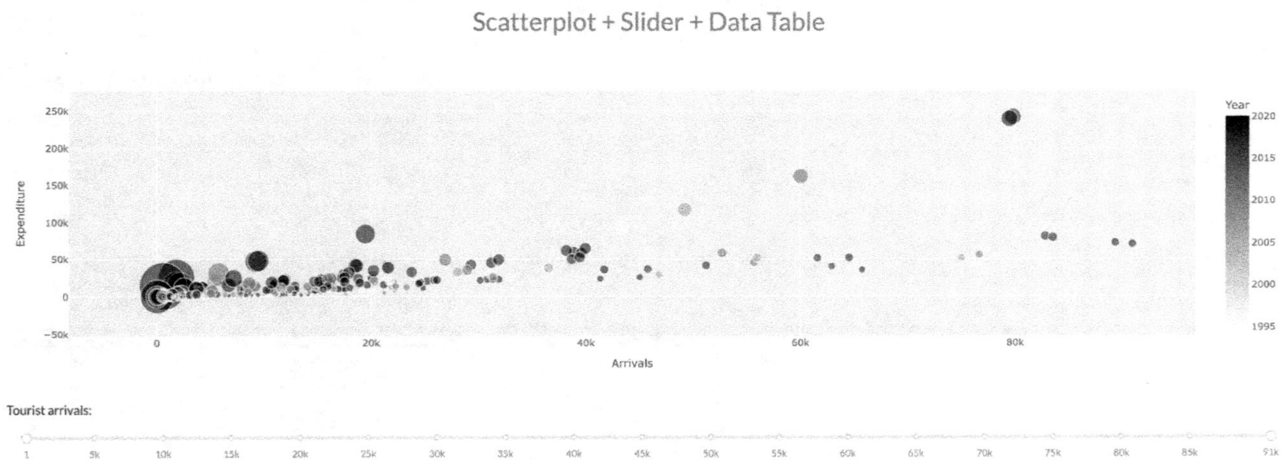

Country	Year	Expenditure	Arrivals	Procapita_Exp(x1000)
	filter data...			
Albania	2010	1778	2191	0.812
Albania	2018	2306	5340	0.432
Albania	2019	2458	6128	0.401
Albania	2020	1243	2604	0.477
Algeria	2005	477	1443	0.331
Algeria	2010	324	2070	0.157
Algeria	2018	197	2657	0.074
Algeria	2019	140	2371	0.059
Algeria	2020	50	591	0.085
Andorra	2019	1910	3090	0.618

1 / 101

(a)

Figure 18.3 (a) Dash, graphic, slider, and data table with interactive features, default visualization. (b) Dash, graphic, slider, and data table with interactive features, slider-modified visualization.

Scatterplot + Slider + Data Table

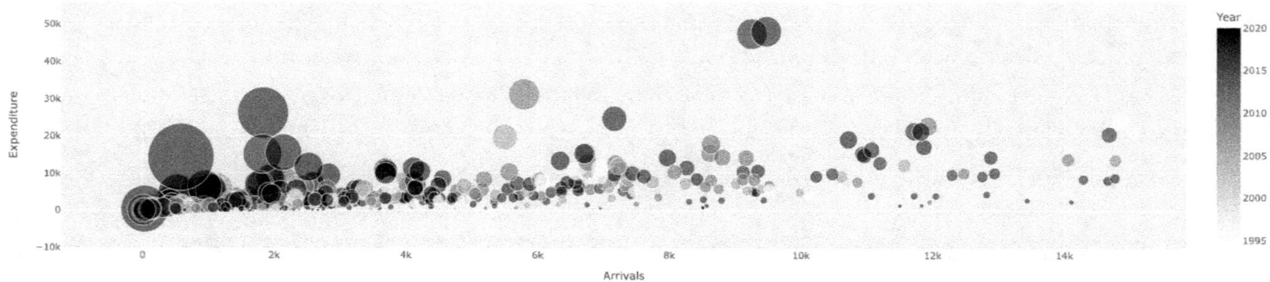

Tourist arrivals:

1 5k 10k 15k 20k 25k 30k 35k 40k 45k 50k 55k 60k 65k 70k 75k 80k 85k 91k

Country	Year	Expenditure	Arrivals	Procapita_Exp(x1000)
	Spain			
Spain	1995	25368	32971	0.769
Spain	2005	51959	55914	0.929
Spain	2010	58348	52677	1.108
Spain	2018	81420	82808	0.983
Spain	2019	79611	83509	0.953
Spain	2020	18352	18933	0.969

(b)

Figure 18.3 (*Continued*)

the list of choices, in our case the list of predefined color palettes. In this case, we could reasonably guess that it exists a function that gives us such list; it does exist: `px.colors.named.colorscales()`, which we could associate to a local variable of the layout.

The drop-down menu with identifier *dropdown* could be placed within an HTML *div* with Dash element `html.Div()`.

```
colorscales= px.colors.named_colorscales()

html.Div([
    html.H4('Interactive color scale'),
    html.P("Select your palette:"),
    dcc.Dropdown(
        id= 'dropdown',
        options= colorscales,
        value= 'viridis'
    ),
]),
```

This is for the layout definition; now it comes with the corresponding reactive action to apply the selected color palette to the graphic. We need to define a callback and the associated custom function. The callback should associate *the input from the drop-down menu to the output represented by the scatterplot graphic.* A callback that takes an input and associates the output to the scatterplot already exists, it is the one defined for the slider. We do not need to create a new one, the one that exists could be customized with an additional input (i.e., `Input("dropdown", "value")`), and the corresponding `update_scatterplot()` custom function modified to handle the two cases: the input from the slider (identifier *slider*) and the input from the drop-down menu (identifier *dropdown*). If the logic is clear, the code is easy to rewrite. The `update_scatterplot()` now has two parameters: *slider_range* with the values from the slider and *scale* with the selected color palette. With *scale,* we can just add the attribute `color_continuous_scale` to the scatterplot to have the graphic produced with the selected palette.

```
# Callback
# input slider and dropdown, both of type value
# output scatter of type figure

@app.callback(
    Output("scatter", "figure"),
    Input("slider", "value"),
    Input("dropdown", "value"))

# Custom function
```

```
def update_scatterplot(slider_range, scale):
    low, high = slider_range
    mask = (df2['Arrivals'] >= low) & (df2['Arrivals'] <= high)
    fig = px.scatter(df2[mask],
                     x="Arrivals", y="Expenditure", color="Year",
                     size='Per_capita_Exp(x1000)', size_max=60,
                          hover_data=['Country'],
                     color_continuous_scale= scale
                     )
    return fig
```

Next, we want to improve the aspect of the data table by reducing its size and centering it with respect to page's width. This tuning might sound trivial but, on the contrary, it is trickier than it should be, and the reason is that there does not exist a specific formatting option to do what we want; if we just reduce table width, it results left aligned, *padding* on the left side could be used to introduce space between the left border and the table, there is a style option for this, but the table will not result correctly centered for all screen resolutions and window sizes. There is a solution, though, by exploiting the virtual 12 columns of the web page. We could create a new virtual row with function `dbc.Row()` and in that row we define three columns with function `dbc.Col()`. In the middle column, we define our data table with the width we wish, the left and right columns, instead, are left empty and of same size. This way the data table will appear centered with respect to the page. An additional detail is that attributes `s/sm/md/lg/xl` are called *breakpoint* in the Bootstrap framework and are used to specify different screen resolutions. Values shown in the following code are the standard ones from the official documentation (https://getbootstrap.com/docs/5.1/layout/breakpoints/). For brevity, all options of the data table defined before have been omitted in this excerpt of code. Figure 18.4a and Figure 18.4b show two screenshots of the dashboard with, on top, the drop-down menu for selecting a color palette, a different color palette applied to the graphic, and the table centered with respect to page's width.

```
dbc.Row(
    [
        dbc.Col(
            html.Div(),
            xs=12, sm=12, md=3, lg=3, xl=3,
        ),
        dbc.Col(
          html.Div(
              dash_table.DataTable(
                  data= df2.to_dict('records'),
                  columns= [{'id': c, 'name': c} for c in
                                 df2.columns],
...             )
          ),
```

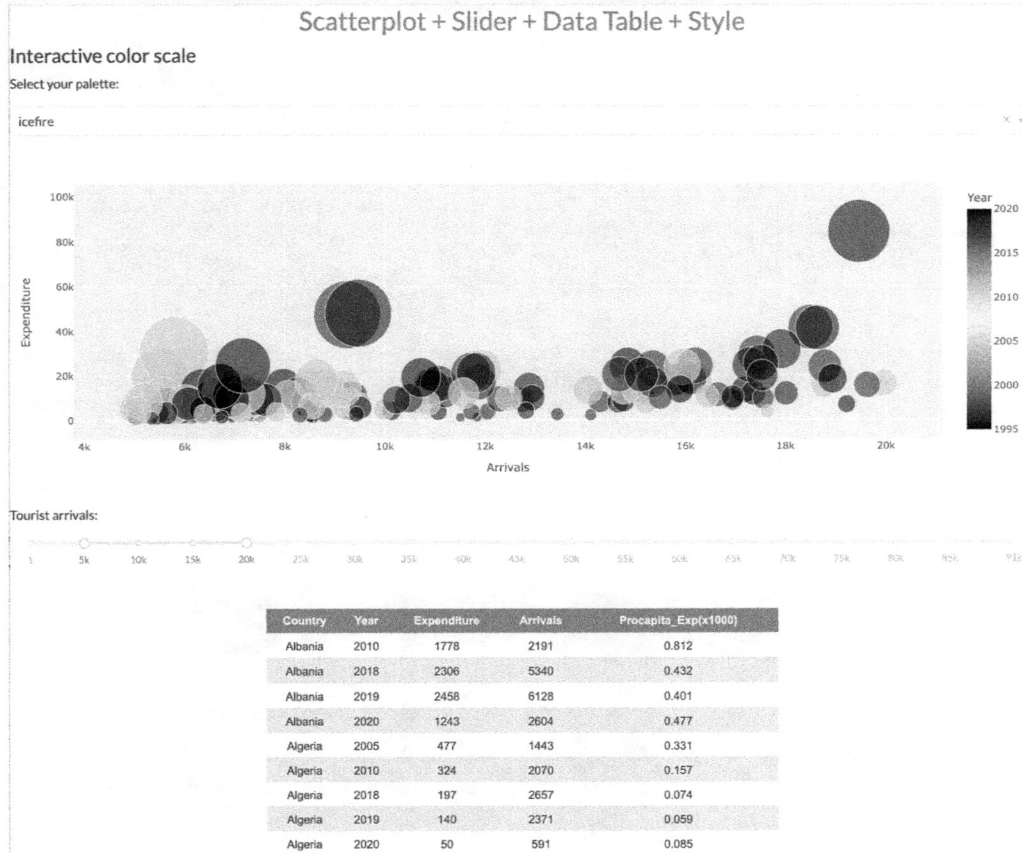

Country	Year	Expenditure	Arrivals	Procapita_Exp(x1000)
Albania	2010	1778	2191	0.812
Albania	2018	2306	5340	0.432
Albania	2019	2458	6128	0.401
Albania	2020	1243	2604	0.477
Algeria	2005	477	1443	0.331
Algeria	2010	324	2070	0.157
Algeria	2018	197	2657	0.074
Algeria	2019	140	2371	0.059
Algeria	2020	50	591	0.085

(a)

Figure 18.4 (a) Color palette selector and centered, resized data table (example 1). (b) Color palette selector and centered, resized data table (example 2).

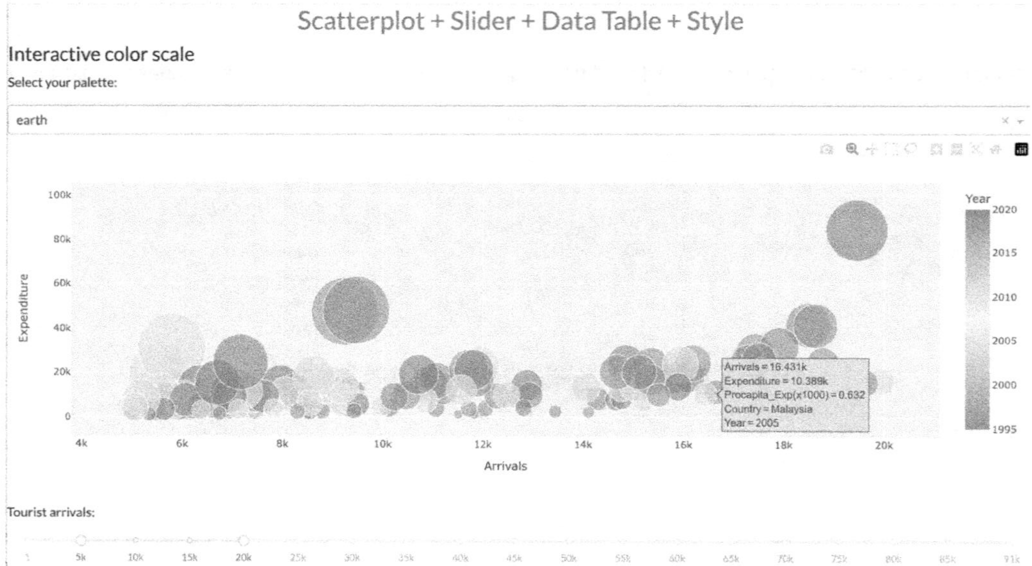

Country	Year	Expenditure	Arrivals	Procapita_Exp(x1000)
Albania	2010	1778	2191	0.812
Albania	2018	2306	5340	0.432
Albania	2019	2458	6128	0.401
Albania	2020	1243	2604	0.477
Algeria	2005	477	1443	0.331
Algeria	2010	324	2070	0.157
Algeria	2018	197	2657	0.074
Algeria	2019	140	2371	0.059
Algeria	2020	50	591	0.085

(b)

Figure 18.4 (*Continued*)

```
          xs=12, sm=12, md=3, lg=3, xl=6,
        ),
        dbc.Col(
            html.Div(),
          xs=12, sm=12, md=3, lg=3, xl=3
      )
  ], className="g-0" # This removes space between columns
)
])
```

18.3 Second Dash Dashboard: Sidebar, Widgets, Themes, and Style Options

With the previous version of the dashboard, we started from scratch with bare graphics and learned how to place some elements in the layout with their corresponding callback with two different inputs. It is still a very easy dashboard, though. Now, we move to the second version with considerably more elements and a more elaborate organization.

The first new step is to add the *sidebar* with some *widgets*.

18.3.1 Sidebar, Multiple Selection, and Checkbox

With the sidebar, we acquire many more possibilities for enriching and improving the dashboard layout organization. Let us first consider a general schema that will be used in following examples; it shows, first, the definition of the sidebar element, then of the main page, one element for each row, then main page's elements are concatenated, and finally the sidebar and the main page are concatenated too, to produce the final layout.

```
# SIDEBAR

sidebar= html.Div(…, style= SIDEBAR_STYLE)

# MAIN PAGE
# First row

content_first_row= dbc.Row(
    [
        dbc.Col(…),
        dbc.Col(…)
  ]

# Second row

content_second_row= dbc.Row(
```

```
    [
        dbc.Col(...),
        dbc.Col(...)
  ]

# Main page: concatenating rows

content= html.Div(
    [
        content_first_row,
        content_second_row,
    ],
    style= CONTENT_STYLE)

# Final layout: concatenating the sidebar and the main page

app.layout= html.Div([sidebar, content])
```

This way, we could modularize the layout organization (`app.layout`) in distinct parts that will be combined together only at the end. This is an important aspect to learn, decomposing the code in modules has many advantages and should always be done, except for very simple cases. As we will see, this also eases applying different style directives to different parts and elements. Specifically, in the schema, *SIDEBAR_STYLE* and *CONTENT_STYLE* are variable names that refer to *CSS inline style directives*, meaning that they are specified into the Python script, rather than defined in a separate CSS style sheet, and they instruct the rendering to apply different style configurations to the sidebar and the main page. The full list of CSS inline directives applied is available in the complete code present in the *Additional Online Material - Second Dash Dashboard.*

With the general layout organization, we can now consider how to define the *sidebar*. It will have some common HTML elements and two widgets: a drop-down menu (function `dcc.Dropdown()`) with identifier *dropdown* and the country list (variable *country_list* has been defined at the very beginning of the chapter) and a *checklist* (function `dcc.Checklist()`) with identifier *checklist*. The checklist selects or deselects the *All countries* checkbox.

```
sidebar = html.Div(
    [
        html.H4('Controls', style= TEXT_STYLE),
        html.Hr(),
        html.P('Countries:', style= TEXT_STYLE),
        dcc.Dropdown(id= "dropdown",
                     options= country_list,
                     value= ['Italy'],
                     multi= True),
        html.Br(),
        dcc.Checklist(id= "checklist",
                      options=[{'label': 'All countries',
```

```
                                  'value': 'AllC'}],
                        value=['AllC']
                        )
    ],
    style=SIDEBAR_STYLE,
)
```

For the elements of the main page, on the first row (*content_first_row*), there is the Plotly graphic and the slider, as seen in the previous version, and on second row (*content_second_row*), we place the data table. With first row *content_first_row*, we also define the relative size. Attribute `md=9` refers to medium-sized screens (the same would have been if we used `width=9`) and it sets a width of nine columns over 12, that is 3/4 of the total width is dedicated to the main page and the remaining 1/4 to the sidebar. This is for the layout.

For reactive actions, we have some changes in callback functions. First, the scatterplot, which in the previous version depended on two inputs, the slider and the color palette, now should depend on three inputs: the *slider* with the number of tourist arrivals, the *drop-down menu* with the country list (the color palette selector is not present in this version), and the *checkbox* to select or deselect the *All countries* option.

For managing the checkbox, we have to modify the callback and the associated custom function, it is an adaptation of logical conditions selecting the rows from the data frame.

The logic is: *if the checkbox is selected*, then all countries should be included, meaning that no row selection is required and the choices from the drop-down menu should be ignored; otherwise, *if the checkbox is not selected*, then only rows corresponding to countries selected through the drop-down menu should be presented. For the slider, only rows corresponding to countries having tourist arrivals included in the selected range will be presented.

This is for the first callback; a second one is now needed because we also want *the data table to be reactive* and reconfigure itself based on input selection from the drop-down menu for country selection and the *All countries* checkbox. The output should be of type `data`. The logic behind the reactive event associated to the data table is equivalent to the one for the scatterplot and depends on the same two inputs. The callback associated to the data table should have its corresponding custom function (`update_table()`) for calculating the table values and the rendering. The following excerpt of code presents the solution: Figure 18.5a and Figure 18.5b are two screenshots showing the result, with the *All countries* option or a list of countries selected.

```
# First callback associated to the scatterplot

@app.callback(
    Output("scatter", "figure"),
```

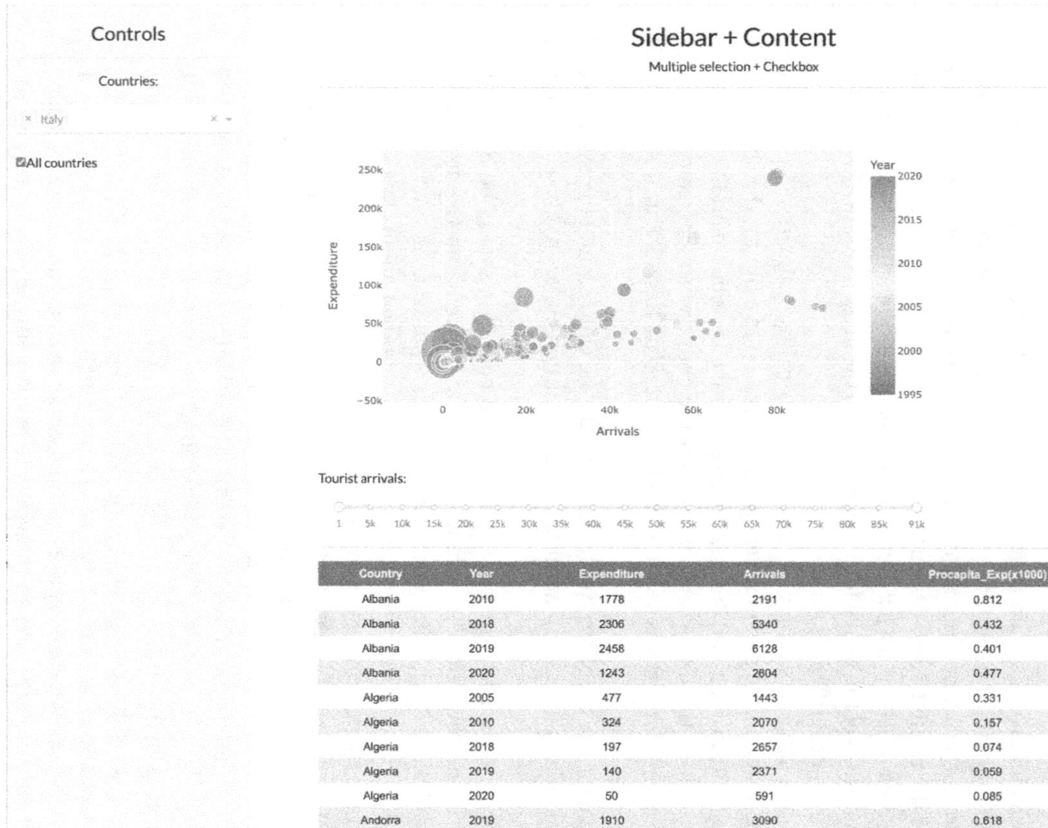

Country	Year	Expenditure	Arrivals	Procapita_Exp(x1000)
Albania	2010	1778	2191	0.812
Albania	2018	2306	5340	0.432
Albania	2019	2458	6128	0.401
Albania	2020	1243	2604	0.477
Algeria	2005	477	1443	0.331
Algeria	2010	324	2070	0.157
Algeria	2018	197	2657	0.074
Algeria	2019	140	2371	0.059
Algeria	2020	50	591	0.085
Andorra	2019	1910	3090	0.618

(a)

Figure 18.5 Sidebar and reactive data table, all country checkbox selected. (b) Sidebar and reactive data table, countries selected from the drop-down menu.

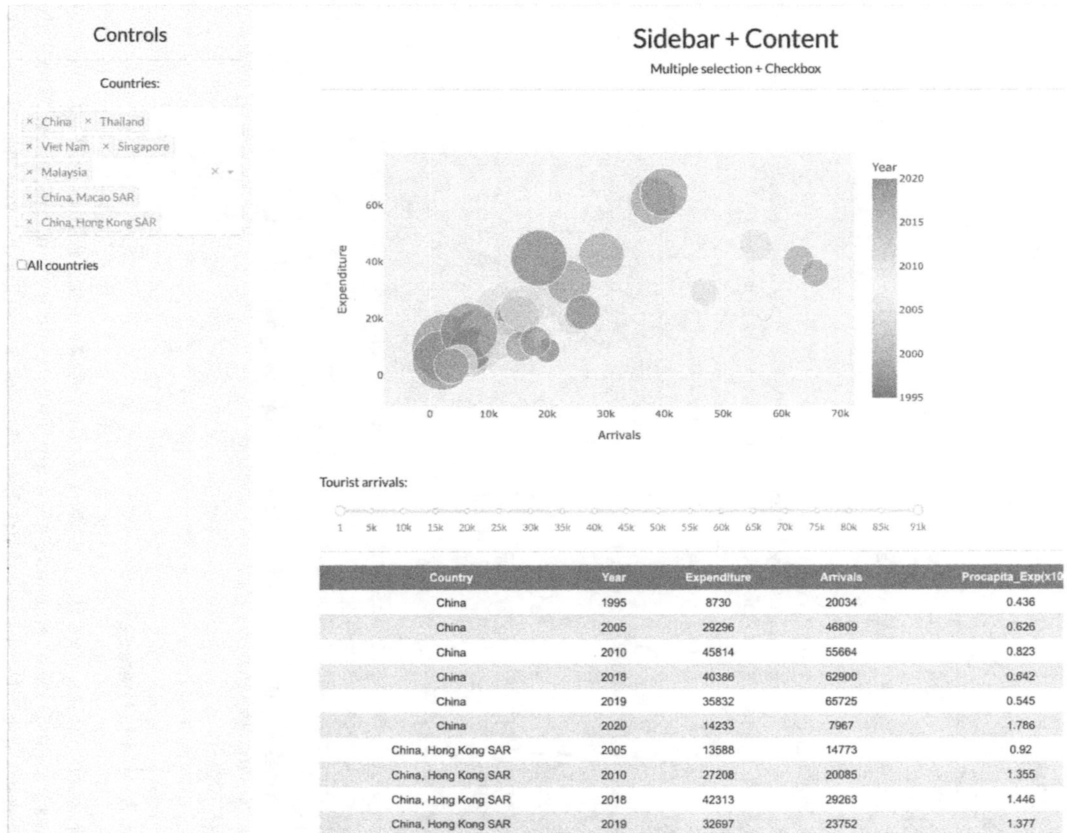

Country	Year	Expenditure	Arrivals	Procapita_Exp(x10
China	1995	8730	20034	0.436
China	2005	29296	46809	0.626
China	2010	45814	55664	0.823
China	2018	40386	62900	0.642
China	2019	35832	65725	0.545
China	2020	14233	7967	1.786
China, Hong Kong SAR	2005	13588	14773	0.92
China, Hong Kong SAR	2010	27208	20085	1.355
China, Hong Kong SAR	2018	42313	29263	1.446
China, Hong Kong SAR	2019	32697	23752	1.377

(b)

Figure 18.5 *(Continued)*

```
    Input("slider", "value"),
    Input("dropdown", "value"),
    Input("checklist", "value"))

# Custom function for the scatterplot

def update_scatterplot(slider_range, dropdown_selection,
                       checkbox_value):
  low, high = slider_range
  if checkbox_value:
     mask= (df2['Arrivals'] >= low) & (df2['Arrivals'] <= high)
  else:
     mask= (df2['Arrivals'] >= low) & (df2['Arrivals'] <= high)
           & (df2['Country'].isin(dropdown_selection))

fig= px.scatter(df2[mask],
         x= "Arrivals", y= "Expenditure", color= "Year",
         size= 'Per_capita_Exp(x1000)', size_max=60,
         hover_data= ['Country'],
         color_continuous_scale= 'geyser')
return fig

# Second callback associated to the data table

@app.callback(
    Output("datatable1", "data"),
    Input("dropdown", "value"),
    Input("checklist", "value"))

# Custom function for the data table

def update_table(dropdown_selection, checkbox_value):
  if checkbox_value:
      mask= (~df2['Country'].isna())
  else:
      mask= (df2['Country'].isin(dropdown_selection))
  data= df2[mask].to_dict('records')
return data
```

18.3.2 Dark Themes

We proceed to improve the dashboard with new functionalities and by applying a *dark theme*. Dark themes are generally less frequent than light ones, especially in corporate environments, but they should be seriously considered because they may offer a visual effect of particular appeal. Choosing between themes has obviously a major subjective component, but an aspect to take into account is that dark themes require more care than light ones to provide a good outcome; a dashboard with a dark theme must have a high graphical quality or better to stick with an easier light one if medium quality is acceptable. With a dark theme, details not carefully crafted are evident at first sight and colors not fully homogenous or ill-chosen give an immediate feeling of carelessness. Light themes are more tolerant of details not perfectly handled and balanced. On the other side, dark themes, when chosen wisely and managed with care, are indeed the more original and eye-catching choice. It is up to you to choose the graphical style of your dashboard.

We produce an example with a dark theme, which is not to be meant as a model for original and personalized dashboards, but as an exercise in curating the visual effect with this type of theme.

A first novelty of this version is the *external CSS style sheet*, whose reference is stated at the beginning of the script. The one referred to is a widely used CSS style sheet also mentioned in the official Dash documentation; many others are available, as well as the possibility to customize a CSS of your own. Technically, to link an external CSS, attribute `external_stylesheets` of function `Dash()` should be used. With the same attribute, we can also select the theme; in this case, the dark theme *SLATE* from Bootswatch. With `load_figure_template('slate')`, the theme is loaded and ready to be applied.

```
dbc_css= "https://cdn.jsdelivr.net/gh/AnnMarieW/
        dash-bootstrap-templates@V1.0.2/dbc.min.css"

app = Dash(__name__, external_stylesheets=[dbc.themes.SLATE,
                                            dbc_css])

load_figure_template("slate")
```

18.3.3 Radio Buttons

We add the *radio button* widget to the dashboard. It is similar to checkboxes, the difference is that radio buttons allow for a unique choice among the available ones. In this case, however, we wish to use radio buttons in a slightly unconventional way, which is *to permit selecting which variables, among those present in the data frame, associate to Cartesian axes of the scatterplot*. Technically, it is easy to do and the result is interesting because this way it is possible to *dynamically reconfigure the definition of the plot and the relation between variables in the graphic*. So, with a single plot, it is possible to have many different combinations of variables on axes. The same could obviously be possible with types of graphics other than the scatterplot.

The radio button definition is placed in the sidebar with function `dcc.RadioItems()`; there will be two radio buttons, one for axis x and the other for axis y of the scatterplot. The first attribute is the list of values to be shown as available choices; in our case, it will be the list of data frame columns (`list(df2.columns)`), a more precise column selection would have been possible, of course. Radio buttons, as all widgets, have also an identifier and possibly a title. It is also possible to associate *inline style directives* to customize the appearance. The details of inline style directives are available in the *Additional Online Material*. We also place some HTML components, such as `html.Hr()`, which is the Dash version of tag <hr> that draws a horizontal line; `html.P()`, which corresponds to tag <p> to insert a text. To insert text, a specific function of *Dash Core Component*, `dcc.Markdown()` is also available, which, as it is easy to guess, lets adding a text in *Markdown format*, with corresponding formatting annotations.

```
html.Hr(),
html.P('Axis:', style=TEXT_STYLE),

dcc.Markdown("'_X Axis:_"'),
dcc.RadioItems(list(df2.columns), 'Arrivals',
               id='radio_X', inputStyle= RADIO_STYLE),
html.Br(),
dcc.Markdown("'_Y Axis:_"'),
dcc.RadioItems(list(df2.columns), 'Expenditure',
               id='radio_Y', inputStyle= RADIO_STYLE)
```

These are the changes in the layout. As we already know well, an interactive input element should correspond to a *callback* to manage the reactive event. In this case, when different variables are selected through radio buttons, the scatterplot has to be reconfigured. A callback for redrawing the scatterplot already exists, so it suffices to modify it. The output now depends on further input elements, the two radio buttons, having identifiers *radioX* and *radioY*, both of type *value*, similar to checkboxes.

The following custom function `update_scatterplot()` should be adapted too, now taking the variable association to axes *x* and *y* from parameters *radio_X* and *radio_Y* passed to the function corresponding to the selections operated on radio buttons.

```
# Callback

@app.callback(
    Output("scatter", "figure"),
    Input("slider", "value"),
    Input("dropdown", "value"),
    Input("checklist", "value"),
    Input("radio_X", "value"),
    Input("radio_Y", "value")
)

# Custom function

def update_scatterplot(slider_range, dropdown_selection,
                       checkbox_value, radio_X, radio_Y):
  low, high = slider_range
  if checkbox_value:
```

```
        mask= (df2['Arrivals'] >= low) & (df2['Arrivals'] <= high)
    else:
        mask= (df2['Arrivals'] >= low) & (df2['Arrivals'] <= high)
              & (df2['Country'].isin(dropdown_selection))

    fig= px.scatter(df2[mask],
             x= radio_X, y= radio_Y, color="Year",
             size='Per_capita_Exp(x1000)', size_max=60,
             hover_data=['Country'],
             color_continuous_scale= px.colors.sequential.gray)

    fig.update_layout(plot_bgcolor='rgba(0, 0, 0, 0)',
                      paper_bgcolor='rgba(0, 0, 0, 0)')
return fig
```

18.3.4 Bar Plot

Proceeding to add elements to the dashboard, it is the turn of a new graphic, a bar plot, this time. In the layout, we should decide where to place it. We choose to have it on the same row of the scatterplot (`dbc.Row()`) by defining a new column (`dbc.Col()`) with the new bar plot, setting the identifier to *bar* and its relative dimension to 1/3 of the row (i.e., *width=4*).

```
content_first_row= dbc.Row(
    [
        dbc.Col([
            dcc.Graph(id= "scatter"),
            ...
        ]),
        dbc.Col([
            dcc.Graph(id= "bar")
        ], width=4)
   ], className="g-0")
```

We want also the bar plot to be a *reactive element*, so we need to define its corresponding callback and the reactive action to be executed. The output element is a graphic, so its type will be *figure*. Regarding the action, we wish to show the relation between tourist arrivals for each year and countries with more tourist influx. The bar plot should be reconfigured based both on the slider values, which allow selecting different ranges of tourist arrivals and on countries selection operated through the drop-down menu or the *All countries* checkbox. So, three are the input elements for the bar plot. The following custom function `update_barplot()` should select the data frame rows to visualize in the bar plot based on the parameters passed corresponding to the three input elements. Some common data-wrangling operations are needed and the bar plot is produced with *plotly.express* function `px.bar()`. The bar plot is of type *stacked* with segments colored based on years, we orient it horizontally for better readability.

A feature that Plotly automatically adds is the *dynamic legend*, which allows for clicking on legend values and shows the corresponding graphical elements highlighted in the plot.

```
# Callback

@app.callback(
    Output("bar", "figure"),
    Input("slider", "value"),
    Input("dropdown", "value"),
    Input("checklist", "value")
)

# Custom function update_barplot()

def update_barplot(slider_range, dropdown_selection,
                   checkbox_value):

  df2["Year"]= df2["Year"].astype(str)
  df2['Country']= df2.Country.str.replace(
                    'United States of America', 'USA')

  low, high = slider_range
  if checkbox_value:
      data= df2.sort_values(by='Arrivals',
                             ascending=False).head(20)
  else:
      mask= df2['Country'].isin(dropdown_selection)
      data= df2[mask].\
             sort_values(by='Arrivals', ascending=False)

# Plotly bar plot

  fig= px.bar(data, x="Arrivals", y="Country", color="Year",
         orientation='h',
         hover_data=["Per_capita_Exp(x1000)"],
         color_discrete_sequence=px.colors.sequential.gray_r,
         labels={"Country": "",
                 "Arrivals": "Total Arrivals"}
            )

  fig.update_layout(plot_bgcolor='rgba(0, 0, 0, 0)',
                    paper_bgcolor='rgba(0, 0, 0, 0)')
return fig
```

18.3.5 Container

The last element we introduce in this version is the *Container*, with function `dbc.Container()` of *Dash Bootstrap Container*, which represents an alternative way of defining the dashboard organization other than the classical `html.Div()`. This approach is not simply possible, in particular when the layout has been defined with functions `dbc.Row()` and `dbc.Col()`, as we did in all examples, but also recommended in the technical documentation (https://dash-bootstrap-components.opensource.faculty.ai/docs/components/layout/). The two alternatives are actually largely interchangeable, except for some very peculiar configurations when one or the other solution could be better because of some specific options made available. In the following code excerpt, we can see how the general organization of the layout composed of sidebar and main page could be rewritten by using the *Container* instead of the HTML *Div*.

```
app.layout = dbc.Container([sidebar, content],
                           fluid=True,
                           className="dbc")


if __name__ == '__main__':
    app.run_server(port='8051')
```

Figure 18.6a shows the default appearance of the dashboard with all elements and the dark theme. Figure 18.6b presents the details of the scatterplot reconfigured according to the selection of radio buttons (Per capita expense on axis *y*) and the dynamic tooltip. Figure 18.6c shows the scatterplot further reconfigured with years on axis *y* and the bar plot adapted according to the selection on the legend (years 2010 and 2018 selected).

18.4 Third Dash Dashboard: Tabs and Web Scraping of HTML Tables

With the third version of our Dash dashboard, we introduce an important element for the layout organization, *tabs*, which allow for producing a multi-page dashboard. We choose another graphical theme from Bootswatch (i.e., *SOLAR*), still *dark* but with a different tint and some colored elements. To populate data used in the second tab, we also exploit a *web scraping technique* to collect data online from HTML tables.

Regarding web scraping techniques, we discussed the context, limitations, and practice in Chapter 16, we forward the reader to that discussion to have a clear understanding of their usage and of potential drawbacks.

18.4.1 Multi-page Organization: Tabs

To introduce tabs, this time we start from the end. The final result we have to achieve, in order to assemble tabs in a correct Dash layout is an organization

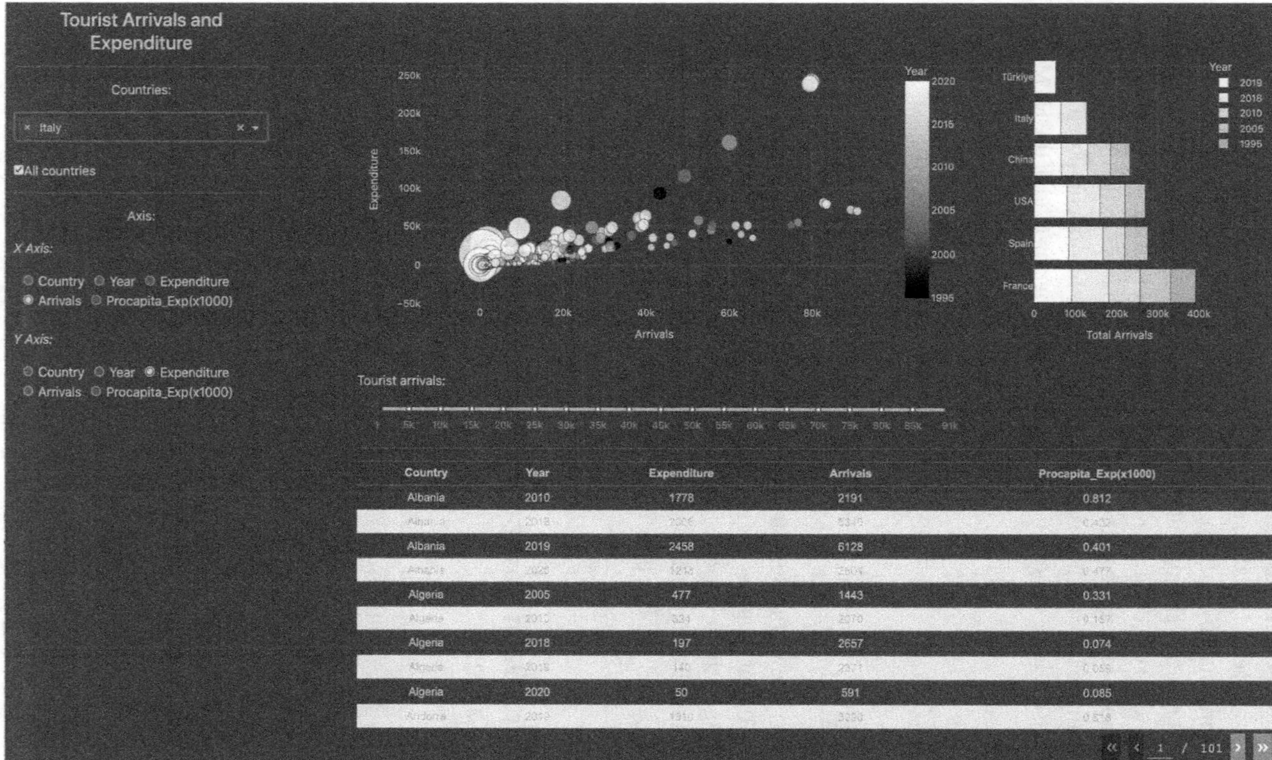

(a)

Figure 18.6 (a) Dash dashboard, default appearance. (b) Detail of the scatterplot reconfigured by changing variable on axis *y*. (c) Scatterplot reconfigured with another variable on axis x and bar plot adapted to selection on the dynamic legend.

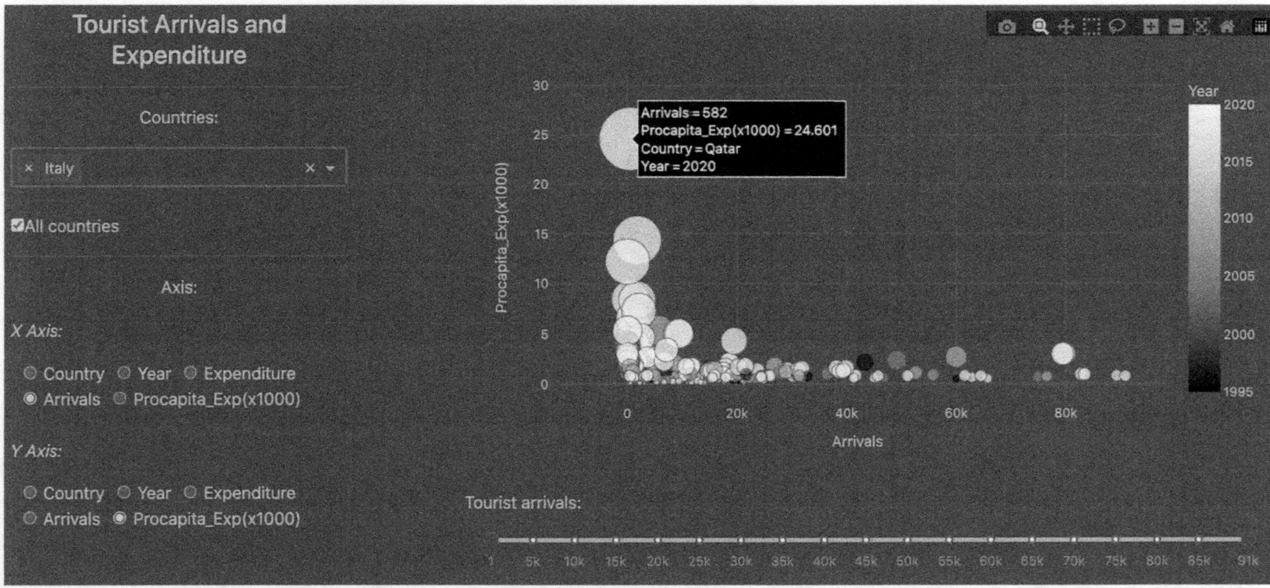

(b)

Figure 18.6 (*Continued*)

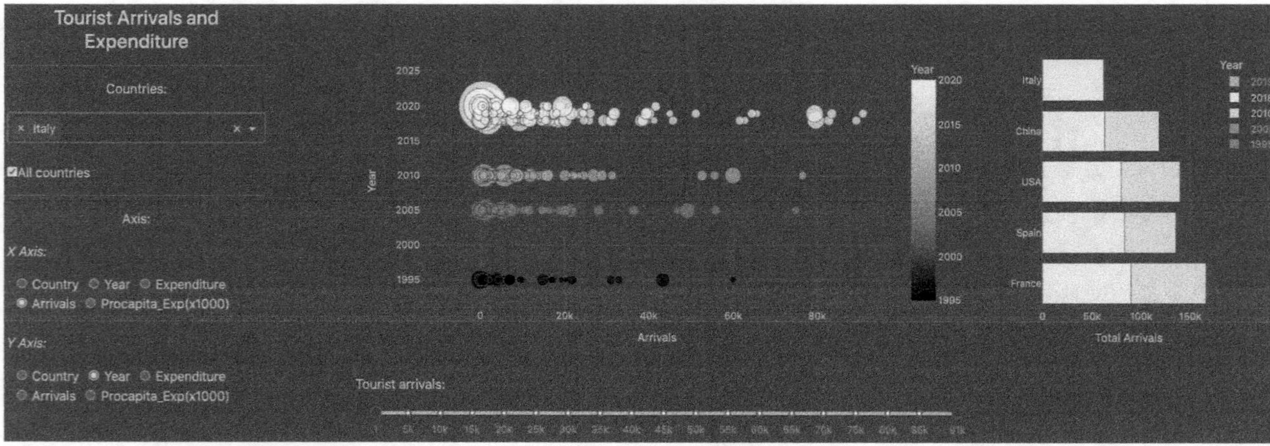

(c)

Figure 18.6 (*Continued*)

similar to what showed in the following excerpt of code. The final *Container* combines the *sidebar* and *tabs* objects, meaning that *tabs are not part of the sidebar and include the main content*, this is the first information we have to know. Moving backward, we should define the *main tab* context. Function `dcc.Tabs()` specifies the general multi-page layout, while *single tabs* are defined with function `dcc.Tab()`. For each tab, the layout is better specified by defining variables (e.g., *content_tab1* and *content_tab2*), for the same reasons we have previously divided the content into a sidebar object, first row, second row, and so on. Such an organization is orderly and clear; it helps to reduce the complexity and to ease the readability and maintenance of the code. It also helps associating different graphical styles to tabs, for example, to differentiate between the one selected and the others.

```
tabs= dcc.Tabs([

  dcc.Tab(label='Countries', children=[
      content_tab1
  ], style= TAB_STYLE, selected_style= TAB_SELECTED_STYLE),

  dcc.Tab(label='Cities', children=[
      content_tab2
  ], style= TAB_STYLE, selected_style= TAB_SELECTED_STYLE)
])

app.layout= dbc.Container([sidebar, tabs],
                          fluid=True,
                          className="dbc")
```

We consider now the organization of a single tab. What follows is referred to as object *content_tab1*. As it is easy to recognize, it reflects the normal layout organization we have used before for the single-page organization of the dashboard; it is composed of rows and columns with corresponding elements. At the end, an HTML *Div* assembles them all. Basically, at single tab level, there is nothing new with respect to what we have already learned.

```
# First row

content_first_row= dbc.Row(
    [
        dbc.Col([
            ...
        ]),
        dbc.Col([
          ...
    ])
```

```
# Second row

content_second_row= dbc.Row(
    [
        dbc.Col(
...     ]
)

# HTML div

content_tab1= html.Div(
    [
        content_first_row_tab1,
        html.Hr(),
        content_second_row_tab1,
    ],
    style= CONTENT_STYLE
)
```

18.4.2 Web Scraping of HTML Tables

Web scraping in Python is very easy, at least for basic cases like collecting an HTML table from a static page. The main function is offered by *pandas* and is `pd.read_html()`, the attribute to specify should be a URL. For example, we read an HTML table contained in the Wikipedia page *List of cities by international visitors* (https://en.wikipedia.org/wiki/List_of_cities_by_international_visitors).

The result is a table that should be prepared to be used in Dash with some data-wrangling operations, which are commented in the following excerpts of code.

```
url= "https://en.wikipedia.org/wiki/
         List_of_cities_by_international_visitors"
dfs= pd.read_html(url)
```

The array *dfs* contains the result and *dfs[0]* is the data frame corresponding to the table. Values of columns *Growth in arrivals (Euromonitor)* have symbol `%` that should be removed to transform them in numerical type. Furthermore, the symbol used as the negative sign is not the minus sign but actually a hyphen, so it should be replaced with the correct symbol; otherwise, it is not recognized as a negative numeric value in the type transformation.

```
dfs[0]['Growth in arrivals (Euromonitor)']=
   dfs[0]['Growth in arrivals (Euromonitor)'].\
   str.replace('%', '')
dfs[0]["Growth in arrivals (Euromonitor)"]=
   dfs[0]["Growth in arrivals (Euromonitor)"].\
   str.replace("[-]", "-", regex=True)
dfs[0]['Growth in arrivals (Euromonitor)']=
    pd.to_numeric(dfs[0]['Growth in arrivals (Euromonitor)'])
```

In addition, some country names have to be aligned to allow the correct selection with those of the drop-down widget with United Nation' touristic data in the sidebar.

```
dfs[0]['Country / Territory']= dfs[0]['Country / Territory'].\
   str.replace('United States', 'United States of America')
dfs[0]['Country / Territory']= dfs[0]['Country / Territory'].\
   str.replace('Turkey', 'Türkiye')
```

For simplicity, the table is presented as a static table, without reactive events associated. It is of course possible to make it reactive in the same way we did with the first data table.

18.4.3 Second Tab's Layout

The second tab is new with respect to the previous dashboard version. We want to place in there two bar plots (*id=bar2* and *id=bar3*) and the data table (*id=datatable2*) produced by web scraping the Wikipedia page. The layout organization presents no difficulties. We have omitted the style options of the data table; they are available in the *Additional Online Material.*

```
# First row

content_first_row_tab2= dbc.Row(
    [
     dbc.Col([
         html.P("Top 20 cities for growth in arrivals (2018)"),
         dcc.Graph(id="bar2"),
     ], width=6),

     dbc.Col([
         html.P("Top 20 cities for arrivals (2018)"),
            dcc.Graph(id="bar3")
        ], width=6)
    ], className="g-0")

# Second row

content_second_row_tab2= dbc.Row(
    [
     dbc.Col(
         html.Div(
             dash_table.DataTable(
                 data=dfs[0].to_dict('records'),
                 id="datatable2",
                 ...
         )
     )
```

```
    ]
)

# Tab's content

content_tab2= html.Div(
    [
     content_first_row_tab2,
     html.Hr(),
     content_second_row_tab2,
    ],
    style= CONTENT_STYLE
)
```

18.4.4 Second Tab's Reactive Events

Finally, we need to specify the reactive actions associated to the bar plots. We want to populate them with data from the table collected from Wikipedia. The description of the two bar plots follows.

Bar plot (id=bar2): with this bar plot, we want to show countries in order of *growth* in tourist arrivals (column *Growth in arrivals [Euromonitor]*). Countries are selected either from the list of the drop-down menu or through the *All countries* checkbox. The logic is that, *if the checkbox is selected*, then all countries are considered and we show the first 20 countries in decreasing order of growth in tourist arrivals; *if the checkbox is not selected*, the countries plotted in the bar plot are those selected with the drop-down menu. We want also to show another graphical effect, bars should be colored differently whether they represent a positive or a negative increment; for this reason, we create the new column *Color* with a textual value. We add the dynamic tooltip with attribute `hover`. Finally, attribute `barplot='relative'` of function `px.bar()` indicates to draw the bar plot relatively to value zero, meaning that bars with positive and negative values take opposite direction. It is a *diverging bar plot*, the one we produce, and Plotly supports it natively. For sake of precision, option `barplot='relative'` is not strictly necessary to specify, being the default, we show it for clarity. Other possible values other than *relative* are *overlay*, when bars of the same group are stacked, and *group* to have bars of same group beside each other.

Bar plot (id=bar3): the second bar plot differs from the first one for the sorting criteria of countries when the *All countries* checkbox is selected. In this case, they are sorted according to the Euromonitor's *ranking* (column *Rank (Euromonitor)*) and the first 20 countries by rank visualized. In the Plotly bar plot, we add attribute `color_discrete_map()` to associate different colors to values *Negative* and *Positive* of column *Color*.

```
# First bar plot: bar2
# Callback

@app.callback(
    Output("bar2", "figure"),
    Input("dropdown", "value"),
    Input("checklist", "value")
)

# Custom function update_barplot2

def update_barplot2(dropdown_selection, checkbox_value):

  temp1= dfs[0].copy(deep=True)
  temp1["Color"]= np.where(temp1["Growth in arrivals
           (Euromonitor)"] < 0, 'Negative', 'Positive')

# Logical conditions for selecting rows

 if checkbox_value:
      data= temp1.sort_values(by='Growth in arrivals
           (Euromonitor)', ascending=False).head(20)
  else:
      mask= temp1['Country / Territory'].\
                      isin(dropdown_selection)
      data= temp1[mask].sort_values(by='Growth in arrivals
            (Euromonitor)', ascending=False)

# Bar plot

  fig= px.bar(data, x="Growth in arrivals (Euromonitor)",
              y="City", barmode='relative',
              orientation='h', color="Color"
              hover_data={'Color': False, 'City': False,
                         "Country / Territory": True,
                         "Arrivals 2018 (Euromonitor)": True},
              labels={"City": ""}
              )

  fig.update_layout(showlegend=False,
                  plot_bgcolor='rgba(0, 0, 0, 0)',
                  paper_bgcolor='rgba(0, 0, 0, 0)')
return fig

# Second bar plot: bar3
# Callback

@app.callback(
    Output("bar3", "figure"),
    Input("dropdown", "value"),
    Input("checklist", "value")
```

```
)

# Custom function update_barplot3

def update_barplot3(dropdown_selection, checkbox_value):

  temp2 = dfs[0].copy(deep=True)
  temp2["Color"]= np.where(temp2["Growth in arrivals
            (Euromonitor)"] < 0, 'Negative', 'Positive')

# Logical conditions for selecting rows

  checkbox_value=1
  if checkbox_value:
      data= temp2.sort_values(by='Rank (Euromonitor)',
                                 ascending=True).head(20)
  else:
      mask= temp2['Country / Territory'].\
                isin(dropdown_selection)
      data= temp2[mask].sort_values(by='Growth in arrivals
            (Euromonitor)', ascending=False)

# Bar plot

  fig= px.bar(data, x="Growth in arrivals (Euromonitor)",
              y="City",
              orientation='h', color="Color",
              color_discrete_map={
                  'Negative': '#ad0a72',
                  'Positive': '#325ea8'
               },
              hover_data={'Color': False, 'City': False,
                          "Country / Territory": True,
                         "Arrivals 2018 (Euromonitor)": True},
              labels={"City": ""}
              )

  fig.update_layout(barmode='relative', showlegend=False,
                    plot_bgcolor='rgba(0, 0, 0, 0)',
                    paper_bgcolor='rgba(0, 0, 0, 0)')
return fig
```

The complete code of this dashboard is available in the *Additional Online Material - Third Dashboard: tab and web scraping of HTML tables*. Figure 18.7a shows the first tab with a selection of countries through the drop-down menu and the corresponding dashboard reconfiguration; Figure 18.7b represents the second tab with the two bar plots populated with the Wikipedia table and the table itself.

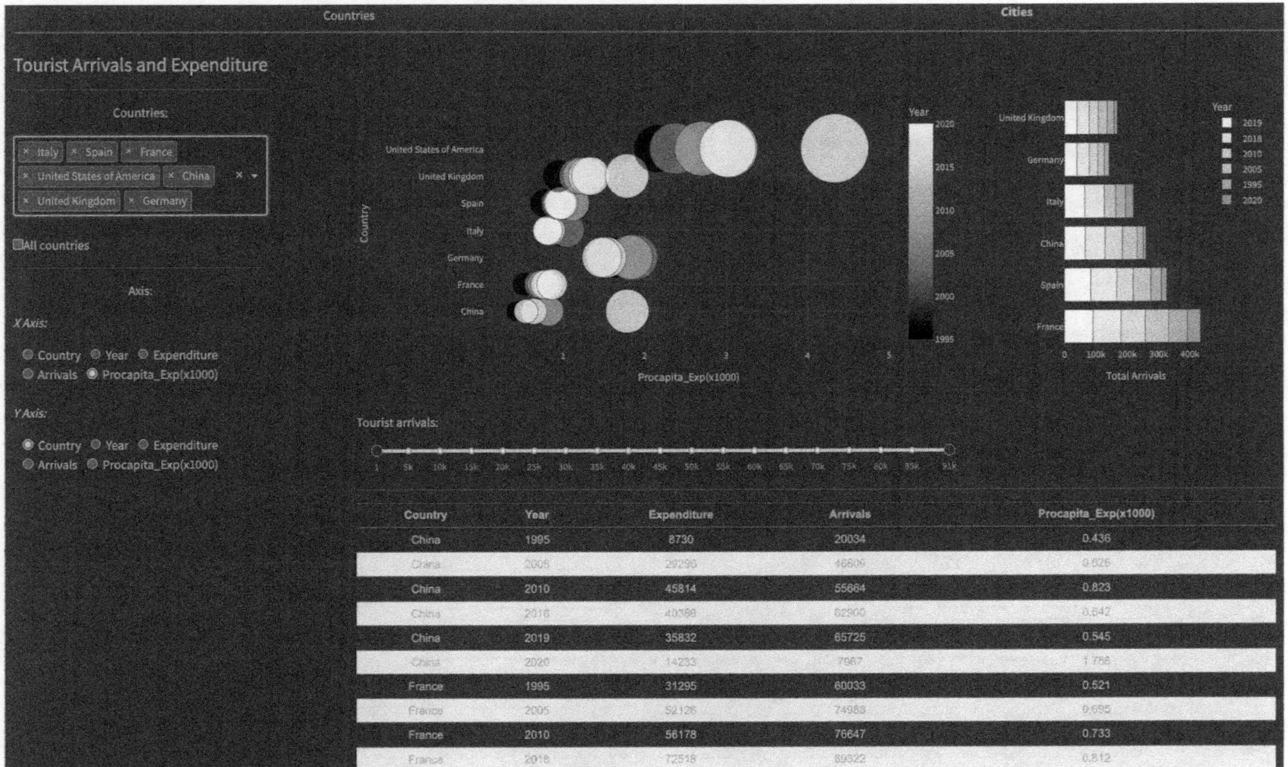

(a)

Figure 18.7 (a) First tab with a selection of countries from the drop-down menu and the corresponding dashboard reconfiguration. (b) Second tab with the two bar plots populated with the Wikipedia table and the table itself.

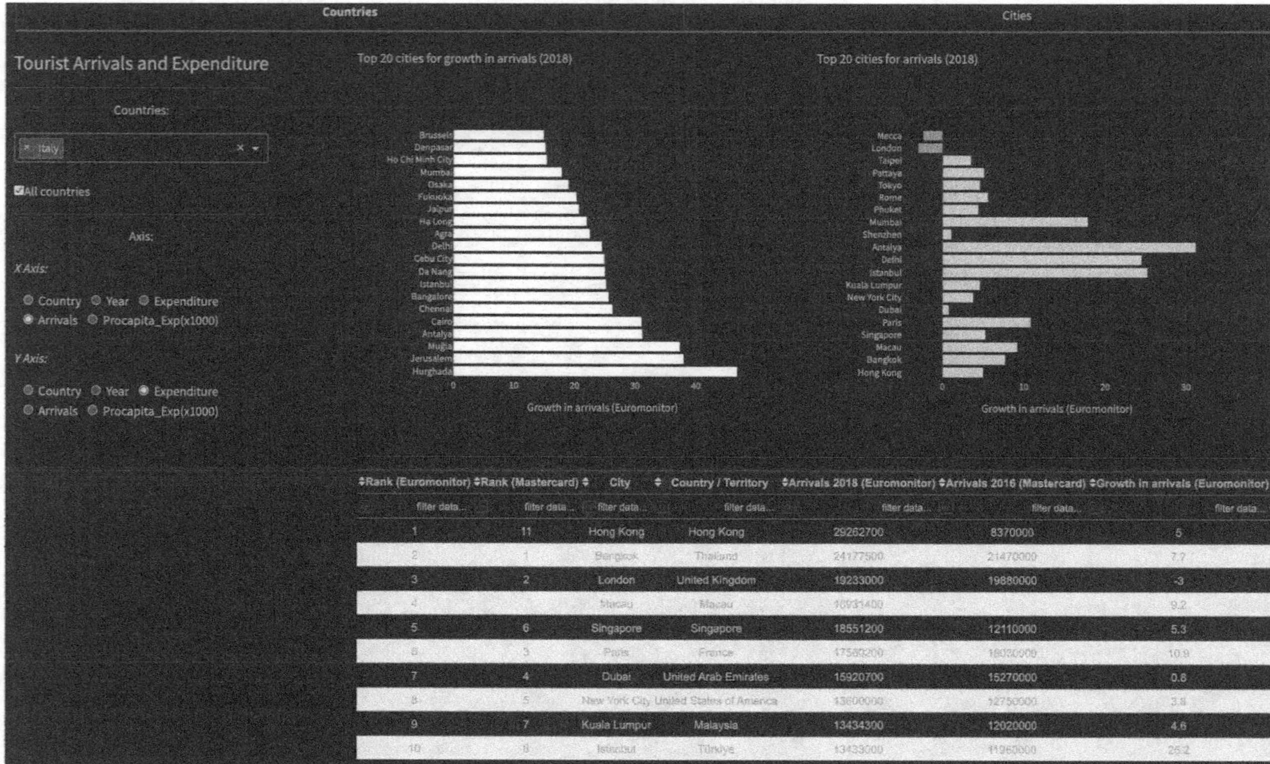

(b)

Figure 18.7 (*Continued*)

18.5 Fourth Dash Dashboard: Light Theme, Custom CSS Style Sheet, and Interactive Altair Graphics

We conclude this presentation of Dash dashboards with the fourth version where we use a *light theme* and associate an *external CSS style sheet* in order to format the dashboard, instead of using inline directives as in previous versions.

This, however, is a small refinement, the real novelty of this version is represented by the integration of *Altair interactive graphics* into the Dash dashboard as *HTML iframe elements*. We already did something similar with a Shiny dashboard by exploiting a specific R package and commenting about the lack of documentation available helping the integration of Altair plots into a Shiny dashboard, given the relative novelty of that possibility. With Dash, despite sharing the common Python environment, the integration of Altair plots into a Dash dashboard is even less documented than for Shiny and, most of all, less supported than in the R environment. That might sound bizarre, but that is what it is. Nevertheless, being poorly documented and not explicitly supported does not mean it cannot be done efficiently and with good results. Altair plots could actually be effectively encapsulated in a Dash dashboard as classical HTML *iframe elements*, with the limitations and difficulties in formatting and configuration that iframes present. Without an official Dash documentation guiding the integration, we may turn to the open community (e.g., StackOverflow) to obtain hints and indications about the way to proceed. Being this the context, you should expect some difficulties and several attempts before figuring out the correct way to do, but the results, once again are worth the effort, with the excellent quality of Altair interactive graphics that could be fruitfully offered in Dash dashboards too.

18.5.1 Light Theme and External CSS Style Sheet

Let us start with the stylistic variations. The Bootswatch theme of choice is *UNITED*, a light theme that we will personalize with custom style directives.

```
dbc_css= "https://cdn.jsdelivr.net/gh/AnnMarieW/
         dash-bootstrap-templates@V1.0.2/dbc.min.css"
app= Dash(__name__,
       external_stylesheets= [dbc.themes.UNITED, dbc_css])
load_figure_template("united")
```

We replace inline style directives defined in *TAB_STYLE* and *TAB_SELECTED_STYLE* used in the previous version with those of the external CSS *tab.css*, which is available in the *Additional Online Material*. Using an external CSS has two main remarkable *advantages*: it permits a *native control* of the HTML graphical configurations, the same way of traditional websites and applications, and it allows for looking at the results of any changes without stopping the dashboard, changing the code of inline directives, and restarting the dashboard, and this is because the style is not defined in the Python script but associated to the web browser and its HTML rendering.

The association with the CSS style sheet (which should be placed in the same directory of dashboard's Python file) is managed by *Dash Core Components* objects; in our case, the specific tab page created with `dcc.Tab()`. Attribute `style` specified in previous versions of the dashboard is no longer needed (in the code it has been commented, for clarity) and replaced with references to CSS classes such as `className='custom-tabs', selected_className='custom-tab--selected')` with *custom-tabs* and *custom-tab—selected* the names of directives defined in the external CSS *tabs.css*. The following excerpt of code shows these references.

```
tabs= dcc.Tabs(
    parent_className='custom-tabs',
    className='custom-tabs-container',
    children=[

# First tab

    dcc.Tab(label='Countries',
            className='custom-tabs',
            selected_className='custom-tab--selected',
            children=[content_tab1]
    ),

# Second tab
# Replaced: style=TAB_STYLE, selected_style=TAB_SELECTED_STYLE),

    dcc.Tab(
        label='Cities',
        className='custom-tabs',
        selected_className='custom-tab--selected',
        children=[content_tab2],
    ),

# Third tab
# Replaced: style=TAB_STYLE, selected_style=TAB_SELECTED_STYLE),

    dcc.Tab(
        label='Altair charts',
        className='custom-tabs',
        selected_className='custom-tab--selected',
        children=[content_tab3],
    )
])
```

```
app.layout= dbc.Container([sidebar, tabs],
                          fluid=True,
                          className="dbc")
```

18.5.2 Altair Graphics

From the previous excerpt of code, you should probably have been noted that a third tab has been defined titled *Altair charts*, it is similar to the others and referred to local variable *content_tab3* for its layout, which is presented in the following explanation.

The organization is already well-known and similar to the other tabs. What changes is the type of output element, now a generic `html.Iframe()`, rather than a graphic, with identifier *altair1* and a preset size expressed with attributes `width` and `height`. This is easy and represents the generic placement of an iframe in a Dash dashboard. The real difficulty is to make an Altair object compatible with a Dash iframe.

```
content_first_row_tab3= dbc.Row(
    [
        dbc.Col([
            html.P("Altair interactive graphics
                    (interactive legend example)"),
            html.Iframe(
                id= 'altair1',
                width="900",
                height="1500"
            )
        ])
    ]
)

content_tab3= html.Div(
    [
        content_first_row_tab3,
    ],
    style= CONTENT_STYLE
)
```

The callback is the trickiest part. Let us start with the definition of input and output parameters. We want Altair graphics to be reactive, as we did with Plotly graphics; otherwise, they will be just simple HTML objects to include in an iframe. For the example, we chose to make Altair graphics reactive to changes in the already defined drop-down menu and *All nations* checkbox, so by changing the selection of those input elements in the sidebar, Altair graphics should be recreated.

The output type has presented the greatest difficulty because it is unusual and, apparently, undocumented. An Altair graphic is not recognized by Dash as an object of type *figure*, like a Plotly graphic. If we write `Output('altair1', 'figure')`, nothing would be visualized in the iframe. What output type is compatible with Dash is not specified in the official documentation (at the time of writing, at least), which just briefly indicates to refer to the Mozilla documentation for HTML 5. No example is provided. Therefore, unless you are specifically skilled with HTML iframes, at first you proceed blindly, just knowing that the layout object is a generic iframe. Therefore, it is not the Dash documentation that would help (although a less succinct note would have been greatly appreciated), but that specific to HTML 5 iframes. There are plenty of examples for iframes in HTML 5, but they always specify attribute `src` with a URL as the source of data. In our case, we have a local Altair object, not a URL to point to an online source of data but trying to refer to it with a local path is inevitably blocked by modern web browsers' security controls. So, we are stuck with the definition of the correct output type for the callback.

The solution comes from a corner of Mozilla's HTML 5 iframe documentation that mentions another option: "Inline HTML to embed, overriding the `src` attribute. If a browser does not support the `srcdoc` attribute, it will fall back to the URL in the `src` attribute." (https://developer.mozilla.org/en-US/docs/Web/HTML/Element/iframe)

"Inline HTML to embed" is exactly what we need, *srcdoc* is the right output type and, with another little help from the community, the correct syntax is found: `srcDoc`.

With the thorniest problem solved, we can define the actions to execute with the custom function `plot_altair()` when the callback is activated. The data frame should be prepared for visualization with common data-wrangling operations (i.e., remove the total of arrivals and revenues for each country, create a new column *Diff_Arr* with arrival differences between years 2018 and 2016, and calculate the percentages in columns *Diff_Arr_percent*).

With the data frame prepared for visualization, Altair graphics could be defined, as a bar plot and a scatterplot. They both are interactive by means of the dynamic legend of the scatterplot allowing for the selection of countries. The selection modifies the colors of markers and bars, highlighting those corresponding to the selected countries and turning transparent those for non-selected countries (In Part 2, we have seen the same example with an Altair scatterplot). In the bar plot, we want a different coloring for bars associated to positive or negative values. Finally, the two charts are vertically aligned, and the background is made *transparent*. Other difficulties have been encountered in sizing the iframe, which is delicate and requires some tests before finding a correct setting. As we were saying at the beginning of this section, integrating Altair graphics into Dash requires patience and several tries. The more elaborate is the layout the more delicate is placing and sizing the iframe; the layout of the example is simple. However, giving a try to Altair is worth the effort because an excellent outcome could be obtained.

```
# Callback

@app.callback(
    Output('altair1', 'srcDoc'),
    Input("dropdown", "value"),
    Input("checklist", "value")
)

# Custom function plot_altair1

def plot_altair1(dropdown_selection, checkbox_value):

# Data wrangling operations

  temp3= dfs[0].copy(deep=True)
  temp3= temp3.rename(columns={"Country / Territory": "Country"})
  temp3= temp3.groupby('Country')\
                [['Arrivals 2018 (Euromonitor)',\
                  'Arrivals 2016 (Mastercard)',\
                  'Income (billions $) (Mastercard)']].\
                agg('sum').reset_index()

  temp3['Diff_Arr']= temp3['Arrivals 2018 (Euromonitor)']- \
                     temp3['Arrivals 2016 (Mastercard)']

  temp3['Diff_Arr_percent']= \
               100*(temp3['Arrivals 2018 (Euromonitor)'] - \
               temp3['Arrivals 2016 (Mastercard)'])/ \
               temp3['Arrivals 2016 (Mastercard)']

# Data selection

  if checkbox_value:
      data= temp3.sort_values(by='Income (billions $) \
                    (Mastercard)', ascending=False).head(20)
  else:
      mask= temp3['Country'].isin(dropdown_selection)
      data= temp3[mask].sort_values(by='Income (billions $) \
                               (Mastercard)', ascending=True)

# ALTAIR CHARTS

    selection= alt.selection_point(fields=['Country'],
                                   bind='legend')
```

```
    change_opacity= alt.condition(selection, alt.value(1.0),
                                              alt.value(0.2))
# Bar plot

    bar_alt= alt.Chart(data).mark_bar().encode(
      y= alt.Y('Country:O', axis=alt.Axis(title='')),
      x= alt.X('Diff_Arr_percent:Q',
         axis= alt.Axis(title='Difference in arrivals (%)')),
         color= alt.condition(alt.datum.Diff_Arr >= 0,
                              alt.value("#325ea8"),
                              alt.value("#ad0a72"),
                                          ),
         opacity= change_opacity,
         tooltip=['Arrivals 2018 (Euromonitor)',
                  'Arrivals 2016 (Mastercard)',
                  'Income (billions $) (Mastercard)']
  ).properties(title='Percent Difference in arrivals 2018-2016')

# Scatterplot

  scatter_alt= alt.Chart(data).mark_circle(size=200).encode(
      y= alt.Y('Arrivals 2018 (Euromonitor)',
               type='quantitative',
               axis=alt.Axis(title='Arrivals')),
      x= alt.X('Income (billions $) (Mastercard)',
               type='quantitative',
               scale= alt.Scale(domain=[0, 60])),
               color= alt.Color('Country:O',
                    scale= alt.Scale(scheme='category20'),
                    legend= alt.Legend(title="Years",
                                       orient="right")),
      opacity= change_opacity,
      tooltip=['Country', 'Arrivals 2018 (Euromonitor)',
               'Income (billions $) (Mastercard)']
  ).add_params(selection
  ).properties(title='Income and arrivals 2018')

# Chart alignment and HTML format

  chart= alt.vconcat(scatter_alt, bar_alt
  ).properties(background='transparent')

  chart.save('iframes/altair_chart.html')

return chart.to_html()
```

The complete code for this dashboard version, together with the external CSS *tab.css*, is available in the *Additional Online Material - Fourth Dashboard: Interactive Altair graphics, custom CSS, and light theme.* Figure 18.8a shows the

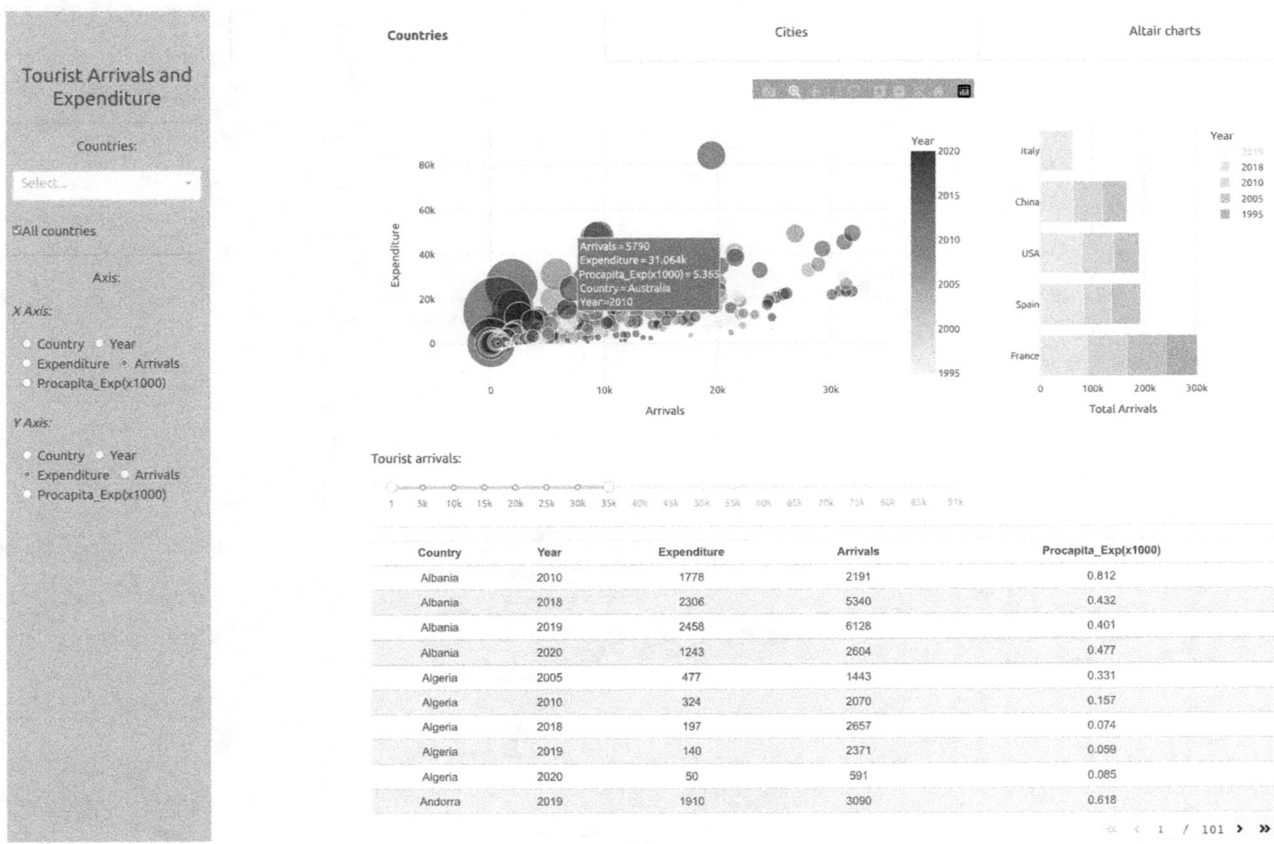

(a)

Figure 18.8 (a) First tab, data table, reactive graphics, and layout. (b) Second tab, bar plots, and data table from web scraping. (c) Third tab, interactive Altair graphics, and default configuration. (d) Third tab, country selection, and reconfigured Altair graphics.

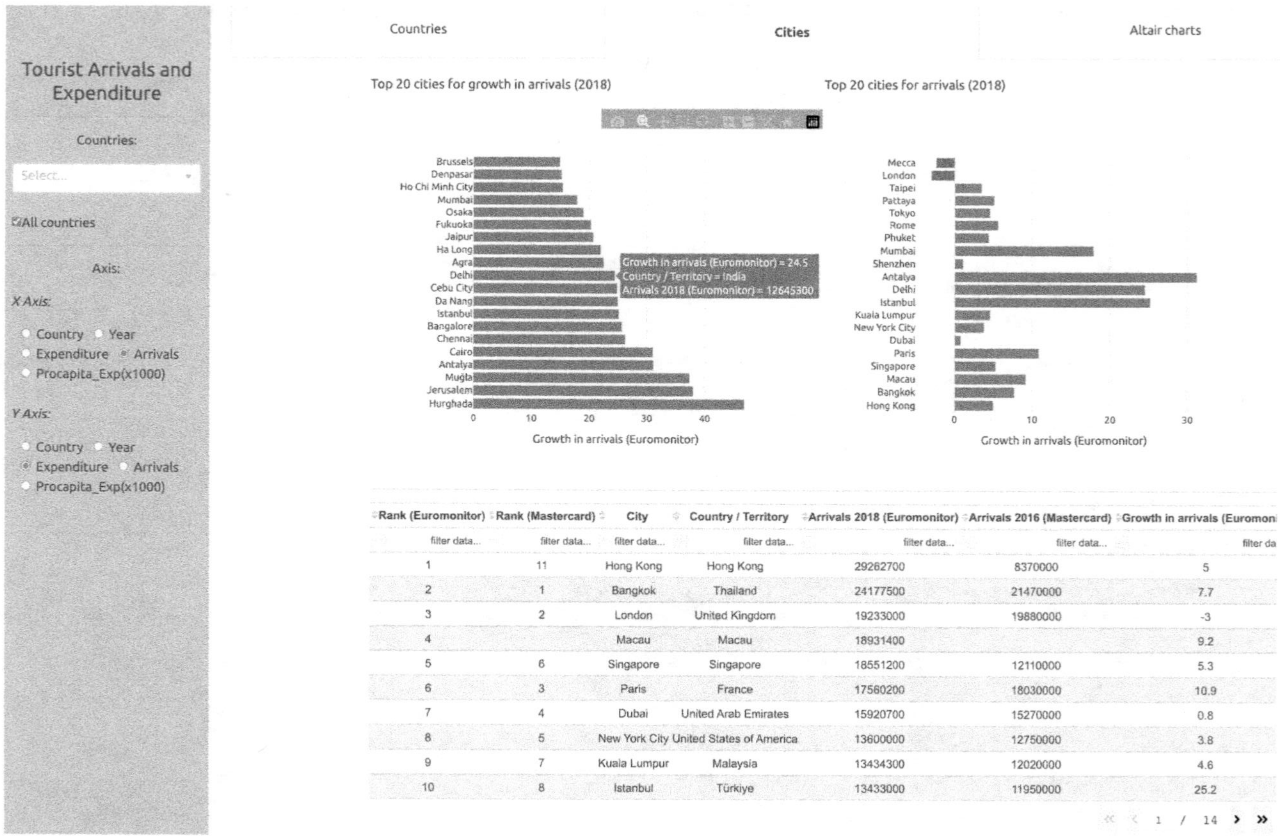

(b)

Figure 18.8 (*Continued*)

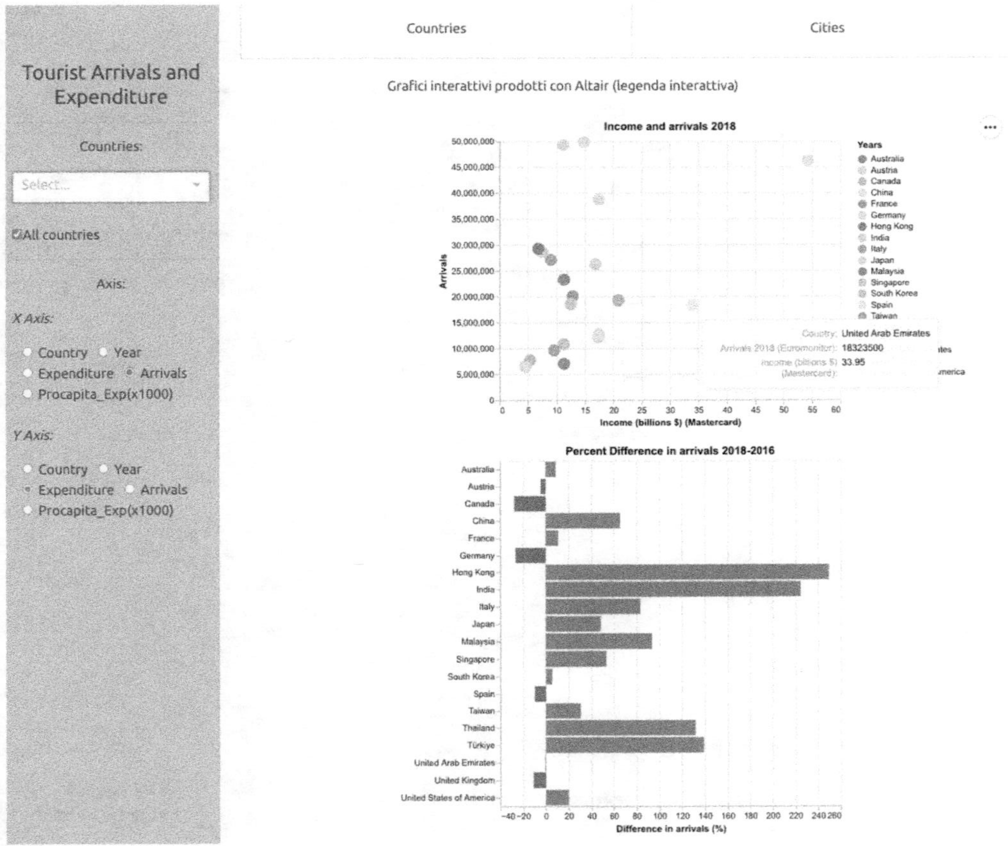

(c)

Figure 18.8 (*Continued*)

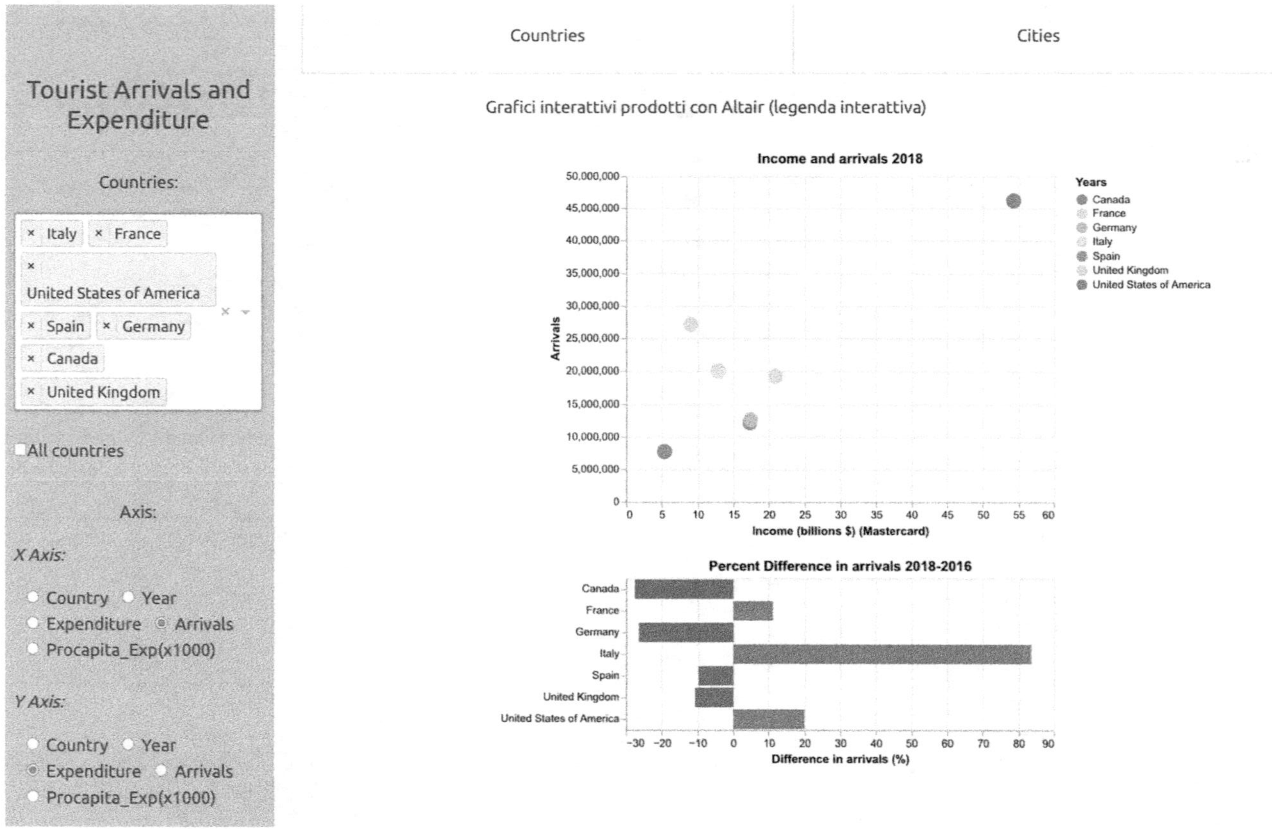

(d)

Figure 18.8 (*Continued*)

first tab with the personalized theme, the scatterplot and bar plot reconfigured according to the slider selection. Figure 18.8b presents the second tab with the two bar plots. Figure 18.8c shows the third tab with default configuration of Altair plots, Figure 18.8d represents the same tab but Altair plots have been reconfigured based on a subset of countries.

Part IV

Spatial Data and Geographic Maps

The visualization of spatial data and geographical maps represents a broad and relatively recent area of data visualization which, for some aspects, is close and sometimes partially overlaps traditional cartography and geographical maps produced with Geographical Information Systems (GISs). In this last part of the book, we introduce the main techniques available in R and Python environments, while cartographic techniques and GISs remain out of the scope, being a technical and scientific sector clearly distinct from data visualization and data science with its own peculiarities, skills, and practices.

With regards to data science and visualization, in recent years *choropleth maps* have become popular on the press, the web, or other publications, including professional and corporate material, and their typical look, with colored regions on a map to indicate differences with respect to a certain phenomenon, should be now familiar to many readers. Choropleth maps are generally easy to produce, both for the diffusion of open and proprietary tools to produce them and for spatial data with geographic information. Tools made available in R and Python, however, permit to work on far more complex and rich geographical representations than choropleth maps, such as managing cartographic *shape files*, creating maps with several layers of geographical information, executing complex operations on spatial data, or introduce interactive widgets in web-based visualizations. In short, R and Python let developers reach high-quality geographical representations by means of relatively recent and advanced tools. The R environment, in particular, which did not provide for advanced features for spatial data until not many years ago, has demonstrated truly remarkable improvements with new and sophisticated features, which rival and often make it better equipped than Python

Data Visualization in R and Python, First Edition. Marco Cremonini.

Companion website: www.wiley.com/go/Cremonini/DataVisualization1e

and many commercial tools, for dealing with spatial data and geographic maps. In short, while until recently, open-source tools from R and Python could not be considered a real alternative for professional projects with spatial data, now they are definitely able to provide state-of-the-art geographical representations and for this reason are widely employed in academia, corporate environments, and are the engines behind some popular online services with geographical features. GIS tools remain of superior level, of course, but in many cases, they are no longer the only possible choice, R and Python are rising even in this very specific and fascinating area.

19

Geographic Maps with R

Dataset/Geodataset

Registry of Domestic Animals (transl. Banca dati dell'Anagrafe Animali d'Affezione), Italian Ministry of Health, data extracted from column *Cani* (transl. Dogs)

(https://www.salute.gov.it/anagcaninapublic_new/AdapterHTTP).

Copyright: Common Criteria CC-BY 3.0

(https://www.salute.gov.it/portale/p5_0.jsp?lingua=italiano&id=50, http://creativecommons.org/licenses/by/3.0/it/legalcode)

Italian Resident Population on 1° January 2022, Italian National Institute of Statistics (ISTAT)

(http://dati.istat.it/Index.aspx?DataSetCode=DCIS_POPRES1)

Copyright: Creative Commons – Attribuzione – versione 3.0 (https://www.istat.it/it/note-legali, http://creativecommons.org/licenses/by/3.0/it/)

Topographic Geodatabase, Technical Chart, Municipality of Venice (https://dati.venezia.it/?q=content/carta-tecnica)

Copyright: Italian Open Data License (IODL)

(https://www.dati.gov.it/content/italian-open-data-license-v20)

Rome Capital – Maps of Municipalities, IPTSAT s.r.l. (http://www.datiopen.it/it/opendata/Municipi_di_Roma_Capitale)

Copyright: Italian Open Data License v2.0 (https://www.dati.gov.it/content/italian-open-data-license-v20)

Rome Open Data, Rome Capital, section *Dataset* (https://dati.comune.roma.it/catalog/it/dataset) and section *Geo Dati* (https://www.comune.roma.it/TERRITORIO/nic-gwt/):

Ville storiche nel territorio di Roma Capitale

(transl. Historical villas in Rome)

(https://dati.comune.roma.it/catalog/dataset/d386)

Data Visualization in R and Python, First Edition. Marco Cremonini.

Companion website: www.wiley.com/go/Cremonini/DataVisualization1e

Strutture ricettive di Roma Capitale nel 2023
(transl. Touristic accommodations in Rome)
(https://dati.comune.roma.it/catalog/dataset/suar2023)
Copyright: Creative Commons Attribution License (cc-by) (https://opendefinition.org/licenses/cc-by/)

SITAR – Rome Archeological Territorial Information System (transl. Sistema Informativo Territoriale Archeologico di Roma), Open Data, ArcheoSITARProject – Ministry of Culture, Special Superintendence of Rome Archaeology, Fine Arts, and Landscape. Data from WebGIS (https://www.archeositarproject.it/piattaforma/webgis/).

Copyright: Creative Commons CC BY-SA 4.0 (https://creativecommons.org/licenses/by-sa/4.0/deed.it)

In this first chapter, we focus on the R environment and consider data from Italian sources, which are rich in geographic data and offer amazing case studies. To start, we consider the simplest example by using data about dog registrations in Italian regions, which will be used for presenting *choropleth maps*, New York City's Open Data has a similar, although richer, dataset that we will use for a more advanced example. With the basis for visualizing spatial data, we will move to more sophisticated tools and geographical datasets, by considering data about two of the most famous and visited cities in the world: Venice and Rome. In both cases, we will use cartographic shape files publicly available from the municipalities, in addition to other geographical datasets.

19.1 Spatial Data

As usual, let us start from the basics with some simple examples. With these, we will produce some rudimental maps, useful for learning the logic and principles of data visualization with spatial data and geographic maps.

For the first example, we use R package *maps* that contains some maps, not particularly updated but handy for a start.

```
library(tidyverse)
library(lubridate)
library(maps)
```

Briefly, we see what package *maps* offers. In package documentation, some maps are mentioned: the world map (name *world*), the US map at state level (name *state*), and at county level (name *county*). Other countries are available, like Italy (name *italy*), France (name *france*), and so on. The main function is `map()`, which, by loading library *maps*, overwrites the usual *map()* from package *purrr*, so be careful if you want to use both functions, you need either to prefix

Figure 19.1 World map from package maps.

the first one as *maps::map()* or the second as *purrr::map()*. Let us look at a first example.

```
map1 <- map("world", boundary=TRUE, interior=TRUE, plot=TRUE)
```

As shown in Figure 19.1, it is a worldview map in Mercator projection (the most common for nautical maps and also for general use). Inspecting object *map1* with common utility functions `class()` and `str()`, we discover that it is of data type *map*, meaning that it is not a generic image but a specific R data type with features associated, in fact, its content is a *list* format with four elements and keys: *x*, *y*, *range*, and *names*. Values of *names* are 1627, much more than the existing countries, meaning that other areas, other than countries, are mapped, for example, main islands and overseas possessions. The other values will be described in a moment. However, important is to know that the R data type *map* has information associated to each territory identified in the map, being countries, states, regions, or anything else that has been mapped.

```
str(map1)
List of 4
$ x : num [1:10671] -69.9 -70.1 -70.1 -69.9 NA ...
$ y : num [1:10671] 12.5 12.5 12.6 12.5 NA ...
$ range: num [1:4] -180 190.3 -85.2 83.6
$ names: chr [1:1627] "Aruba" "Afghanistan" "Angola" ...
```

Let us try another example, this time with attribute `region` to specify a certain territory and two functions: `map.scale()` and `map.axes()`, adding the scale and axes on a map generated with function `map()`.

```
map1 <- map("world", region= "Italy",
    boundary=TRUE, interior=TRUE,
```

```
    plot=TRUE)
map.scale(7, relwidth = 0.15)
map.axes(cex.axis=0.8)
```

Figure 19.2 shows the generated map. This time it is Italy with the scale and axes, whose values are expressed as *longitude North* and *latitude East* degrees. As before, object *map1* is a list and the key *names* has eight values. We can look at them, they correspond to Italy and its major islands. As it will become clear in the following, there is a technical reason for not just mapping the single country as a whole but with its main islands separately, which has to do with the peculiar technique employed to represent planar surfaces as spatial data. For a hint about

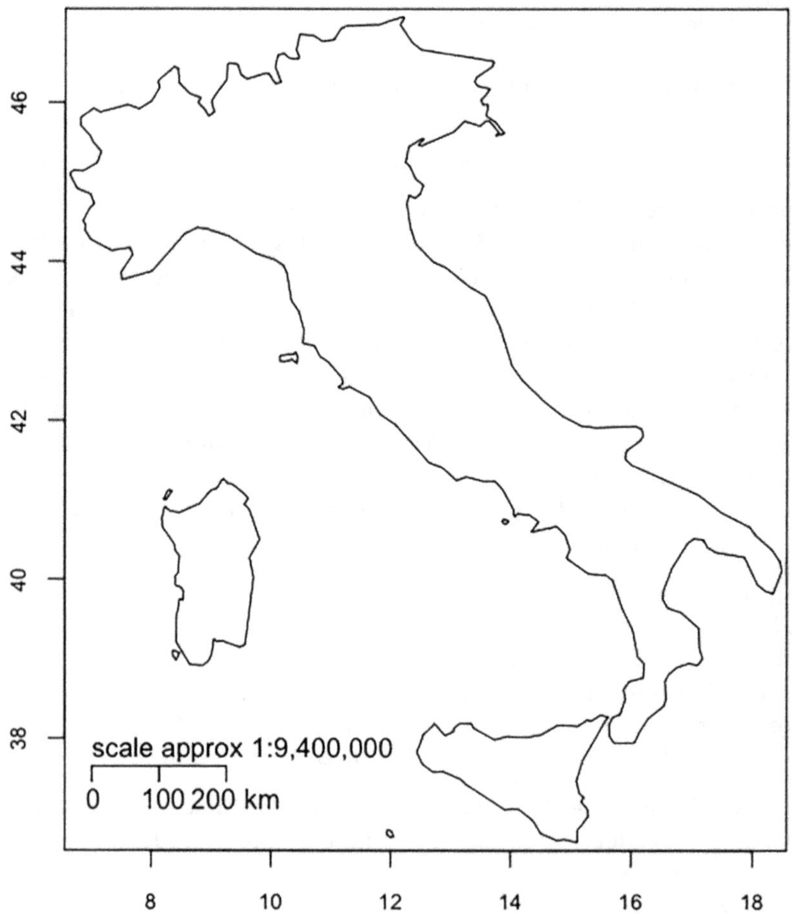

Figure 19.2 Italy's border map.

the reason, a reader could try another country, for example, the United States (i.e., `region='US')`). They will find that also in that case there is one name for the United States, representing the continental region south of Canada, and several for Hawaii, which is an archipelago, but also a distinct name (actually more than just one) for Alaska, which is not an island, but a territory geographically disconnected from the other US states on the continent. The logic should be clear, a geographical region could be represented with spatial data as a unique object only if there is territorial continuity, not if there are disconnected parts. In that case, each disconnected part, to be mapped with spatial data, has to be represented individually, hence the major islands and geographically disconnected regions are separately mapped from the main portion of a country's territory.

```
map1$names
[1] "Italy:Isola di Pantelleria" "Italy:Sicily"
    "Italy:Sant'Antonio" "Italy:Forio"
[5] "Italy:Asinara" "Italy:Sardinia"
    "Italy:Isola d'Elba" "Italy"
```

The list format could be used directly or converted in *dataframe* type. Package *maps* helps with a variant of function *map()* called `map_data()`, which returns a format that can be directly converted into data frame but does not automatically produce the graphic. We will meet again this alternative between the *list* and the *dataframe* data types, both with R and Python (i.e., in Python the R *list* format is called *dictionary* format or *dict*).

```
italy <- map_data("italy") %>% as_tibble()

head(italy)
# A tibble: 6 × 6
   long   lat group order region         subregion
  <dbl> <dbl> <dbl> <int> <chr>          <chr>
1  11.8  46.5     1     1 Bolzano-Bozen <NA>
2  11.8  46.5     1     2 Bolzano-Bozen <NA>
3  11.7  46.5     1     3 Bolzano-Bozen <NA>
4  11.7  46.5     1     4 Bolzano-Bozen <NA>
5  11.7  46.5     1     5 Bolzano-Bozen <NA>
6  11.6  46.5     1     6 Bolzano-Bozen <NA>
```

After the conversion into *tibble* (i.e. a *dataframe* type), we see that the first two columns represent *longitude* and *latitude*. We also see that there is information associated with each row, like the specific region (column *region*) and, possibly a subregion. The excerpt of code shows rows about the Italian province of Bolzano–Bozen, a northern area at the border with Austria. To note is that for such province, there are multiple rows, we can verify the number of rows associated to each Italian province.

```
italy %>% group_by(region) %>% count()

# A tibble: 95 × 2
# Groups:   region [95]
   region          n
   <chr>       <int>
 1 Agrigento     146
 2 Alessandria   105
 3 Ancona         68
 4 Aosta         110
 5 Arezzo        105
# … with 90 more rows
```

From this, we learn that each province, meaning a certain geographical region, same would have been for states or counties in the US, has a different number of rows associated, each row with a pair of longitude and latitude coordinates. What is the meaning of those rows and coordinates? Those coordinates actually refer to the specific way planar surfaces, for example, geographic areas, are represented in such maps, namely through the juxtaposition of small *polygonal elements* that approximate the real shape of a geographic area. Those polygonal elements are not visualized with the map, but they exist and correspond to each single row of the data. This explains why different areas (e.g. Italian provinces) are represented with a different number of rows, it depends on the number of polygons used to approximate the real shape and border of each area. There exist other ways to represent geographic elements, other than with polygons. It depends on their type; if they are not planar surfaces, they could be represented with points or lines. We will see examples.

We can plot the map that corresponds to data frame *italy* with *ggplot* and function `geom_polygon()`. Columns *long* and *lat* will be associated to the Cartesian axes *x* and *y*, while attribute `group` will be assigned to column *group*. Function `geom_polygon()` supports style options like color and linewidth for the borders, as well as color for filling the areas. Graphical theme *theme_void* is the common choice for maps, being devoid of graphical elements, like grids, axes, and so on. Figure 19.3 shows the corresponding map.

The reader could replicate this example with any other country, provided it is present in the *map* package.

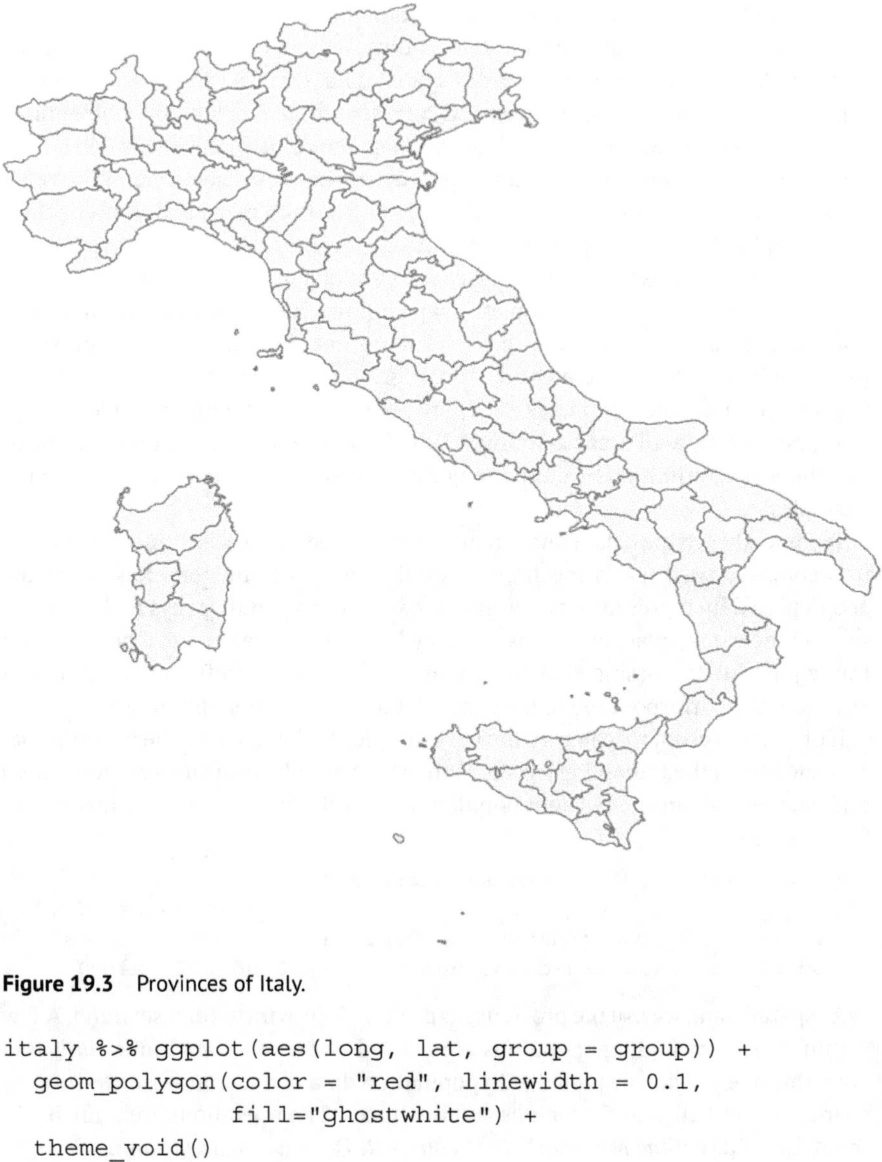

Figure 19.3 Provinces of Italy.

```
italy %>% ggplot(aes(long, lat, group = group)) +
  geom_polygon(color = "red", linewidth = 0.1,
               fill="ghostwhite") +
  theme_void()
```

19.2 Choropleth Maps

What we have seen so far is the basis to start working with spatial data and geographic maps. Now, we want to create our first *choropleth map*. The logic is that we have data about something (e.g. population data) related to territorial areas at a certain granularity (e.g. country, state, county, region, or province) and we need a map with the corresponding areas as spatial data. Or vice versa, we have a map representing certain areas, and we need corresponding data for a phenomenon of interest. Given the two elements, data and map, the result is that areas will be colored to represent data values according to a certain color scale. One of the main reasons for the diffusion of choropleth maps is that both maps at different granularities and data about territorial areas have become more available in recent years, another is that they are eye-catching, easy to understand, and to produce.

The color scale used in choropleth maps follows the same rules of traditional graphs, when a continuous value has to be represented it is normally a continuous palette, when, instead, discrete values are represented, the color palette is discrete, sequential, or classic. Examples widely popular represent with choropleth maps electoral results, with areas assuming the color of the winning coalition or party, income levels, crime rates, ethnic majority, and so on, there are almost infinite examples.

Technically, we have data and a map, and we need to associate one to the other in a coherent way. It is a mechanism similar to data frame join, keys from the geographic data representing areas must match corresponding keys in data representing the same areas. From this, we may have the typical mismatches of a data frame join due to missing elements in one or the other data frame or misspelled keys actually corresponding to the same element but written differently.

If the logic is clear, we can run the first example. As data, we use the Excel dataset extracted from the Italian Registry of Domestic Animals regarding registered dogs and a dataset about the resident population from the Italian National Institute of Statistics (ISTAT).

```
dogs <- read_xlsx("datasets/AnagrafeCanina/
                                     Cani_AnagCanina.xlsx")
istat <- read_excel("datasets/ISTAT-IT/
  Codici-statistici-e-denominazioni-al-30_06_2021.xls")
```

As spatial data, we use the previous map of Italy's provinces (dataset *italy*). A few common data-wrangling operations are needed to prepare data frames *italy* and *dogs*, this one previously joined with population data of data frame *istat*, with data aggregated and aligned for regions and provinces. The operations are available in the *Additional Online Material – Part Four – R: Data-wrangling, Canine Registry*. With the two data frames, data and map, we can execute the inner join operation, which produces a unique data frame with all columns we need for the choropleth map. Here, we join using column *region* for data frame *italy* and column *Region* for data frame *dogs* as keys. Column *Region* represents administrative Italian regions (Note: readers unfamiliar with the administrative distinction between regions and provinces may think about the similar distinction between US states and counties.)

```
italy %>% inner_join(dogs,
            by = join_by(region == Region)) -> italyDogs
```

long	lat	Prov	Region	Pop_Reg	Dogs	Dogs × resident
11.83295	46.50011	Bolzano/Bozen	Trentino–Alto Adige/Südtirol	1 073 574	199 100	0.19
11.81089	46.52784	Bolzano/Bozen	Trentino–Alto Adige/Südtirol	1 073 574	199 100	0.19
11.73068	46.51890	Bolzano/Bozen	Trentino–Alto Adige/Südtirol	1 073 574	199 100	0.19
11.69115	46.52257	Bolzano/Bozen	Trentino–Alto Adige/Südtirol	1 073 574	199100	0.19
…	…	…	…	…	…	…

We can produce the *choropleth map* again with ggplot function `geom_polygon()`, this time defining attribute `fill` as an aesthetic associated to the ratio between dogs and residents (column *Dogs x resident*) (i.e., `fill='Dogs x resident'`). It is a continuous value, so we choose a continuous palette for the area and make borders white. Figure 19.4 shows the result.

```
italyDogs %>% ggplot(aes(long, lat, group= group)) +
  geom_polygon(aes(fill= 'Dogs x resident'),
               colour= alpha("white", 1/2), size= 0.05) +
  scale_fill_viridis_b() +
  labs(fill= "%", title='Residents with dogs (%)') +
  theme_void()
```

We have a choropleth map; we see areas with different colors and the color scale tells us how to make sense of them. The lightest region (yellow in the colored image) at the center of Italy is Umbria and apparently its residents, have a particular love for dogs. Everything looks fine at first sight.

But there is a problem, the visualization is somewhat ambiguous and possibly misleading. What we look at is a map of provinces, not regions – for example, Sardinia and Sicily, the two main islands are regions, but the map shows their provinces – while data are referred to regions because we have joined the data frames with region names as key. What it appears by looking at the choropleth map is that, for example, all provinces of Sardinia have the same ratio of dogs per resident, the same happens for all other provinces of the same region. This is not a truthful information, for sure at province level there are differences, but the visualization is communicating a different information because what it actually tells the observer is that for each region, all its provinces have the same ratio of

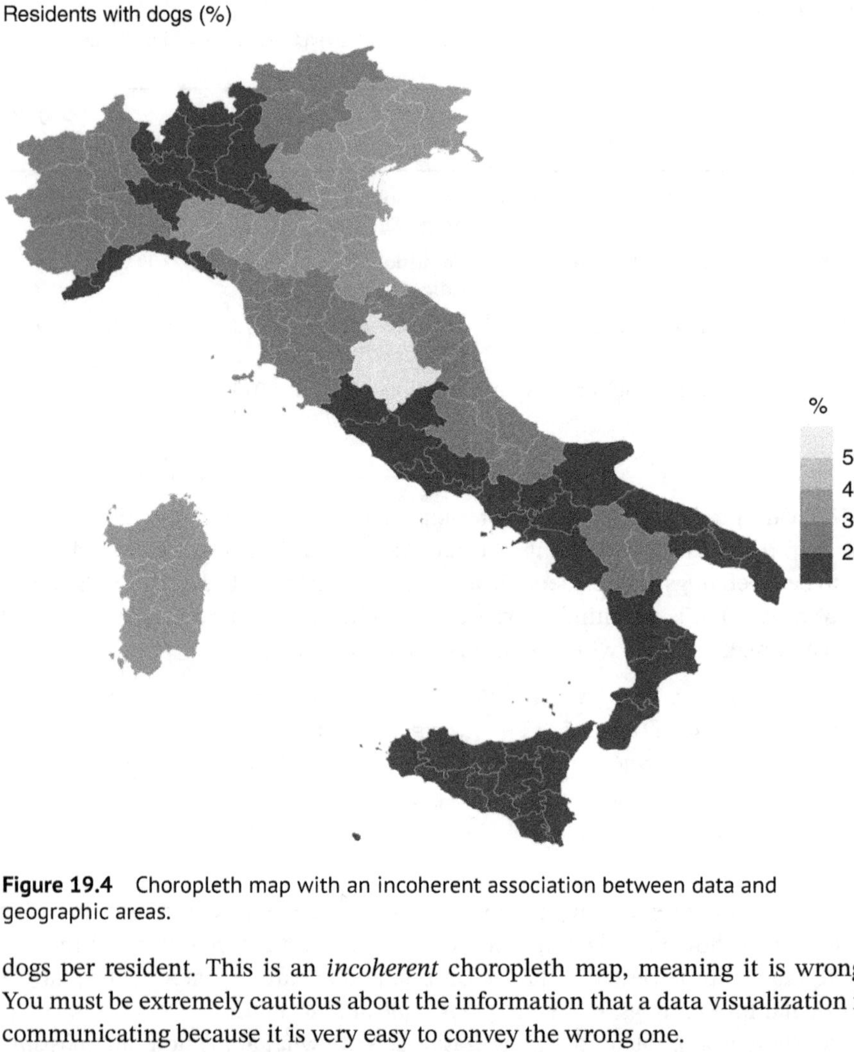

Figure 19.4 Choropleth map with an incoherent association between data and geographic areas.

dogs per resident. This is an *incoherent* choropleth map, meaning it is wrong. You must be extremely cautious about the information that a data visualization is communicating because it is very easy to convey the wrong one.

A correct choropleth map would have used both the map and the data with same granularity, either both at region level or both at province level. We fix it by looking for a map of Italy at regional level, which is very likely to be found freely available.

19.2.1 Eurostat – GISCO: giscoR

Package *giscoR* is a valuable resource for those interested in European geographic data because it represents an application programming interface (API) to Eurostat – the Geographic Information System of the Commission (GISCO), with some local datasets.

It requires package *Simple Features* (*sf*) for several core functionalities to manage standard formats, a key package that we will discuss in detail in next sections. As we will learn, package *sf* is likely the most effective and valuable package among all open-source libraries for supporting spatial data, it is truly outstanding in all respects and definitely worth to be known and used.

> **Note**
>
> *Citation and Source:* Hernangomez D (2023). giscoR: Download Map Data from GISCO API – Eurostat. https://doi.org/10.5281/zenodo.4317946, https://ropengov.github.io/giscoR/

With these two packages, we could use function `gisco_get_nuts()` that allows selecting the so-called *NUTS geometries* (https://ec.europa.eu/eurostat/web/nuts/background/), which are standard representations of geographical areas defined by the European Union for different levels of coarseness. Level 2 (*nuts_level 2*) corresponds to administrative regions, this way we can get the map of the Italian regions. To visualize it (Figure 19.5) we still use ggplot but this time the function should be `geom_sf()` because the map has *sf* format. Alternatively, it would have been possible to use the base R function `plot()` with `st_geometry()`.

```
library(sf)
library(giscoR)

gisco_get_nuts(
  year= 2021, resolution= 20,
  nuts_level= 2, country= "Italy") %>%
  select(NUTS_ID, NAME_LATN)

ggplot() +
  geom_sf(data= nuts2_IT)+
  theme_void() -> nuts2_IT
```

Let us look at the data organization in *sf* format. They are of type *sf* and geographic coordinates are expressed in a column/variable called *geometry*, in our example one geometry element for each Italian region (e.g. Puglia and Basilicata), with *geometry* defined as type *MULTIPOLYGON*, being regions planar surfaces, and each row showing a list of geographic coordinates. This is a different data organization from the case seen before where we had several rows for each area, each one with a single pair of longitude and latitude coordinates, here there is a single row for each area with associated list of coordinates.

Figure 19.5 Regions of Italy.

```
nuts2_IT

Simple feature collection with 21 features and 2 fields
Geometry type: MULTIPOLYGON
Dimension: XY
Bounding box: xmin: 6.630051 ymin: 35.49457
              xmax: 18.51658 ymax: 47.09034
Geodetic CRS: WGS 84
First 10 features: NUTS_ID NAME_LATN geometry
7 ITF4 Puglia MULTIPOLYGON (((15.96243 41ı
8 ITF5 Basilicata MULTIPOLYGON (((16.15755 40…
9 ITF6 Calabria MULTIPOLYGON (((16.62071 40…
10 ITG1 Sicilia MULTIPOLYGON (((15.30001 37…
26 ITF1 Abruzzo MULTIPOLYGON (((14.10346 42…
103 ITF2 Molise MULTIPOLYGON (((14.94085 41…
```

```
105 ITH3 Veneto MULTIPOLYGON (((12.64487 46...
106 ITH4 Friuli-Venezia Giulia MULTIPOLYGON (((13.44023 46...
111 ITH5 Emilia-Romagna MULTIPOLYGON (((9.878123 45...
137 ITI4 Lazio MULTIPOLYGON (((11.84686 42...
```

At first sight, the *sf* data type may look unfamiliar, but actually it is an R data frame, so we can handle it with common operations, such as executing a normal inner join between data frame *nuts2_IT*, for geographic data, and *dogs*. The join key should be region names, which, in *nuts2_IT*, corresponds to column *NAME_LATN*. Then, we can produce the choropleth map again with function `geom_sf()` by filling regions with the color scale corresponding to the ratio between dogs and residents. With the other attributes, we color the borderlines white and set the line width. A little tweak is needed to align the name of an Italian region between the two data frames. Figure 19.6 shows the result that, now, conveys an information coherent and unambiguous.

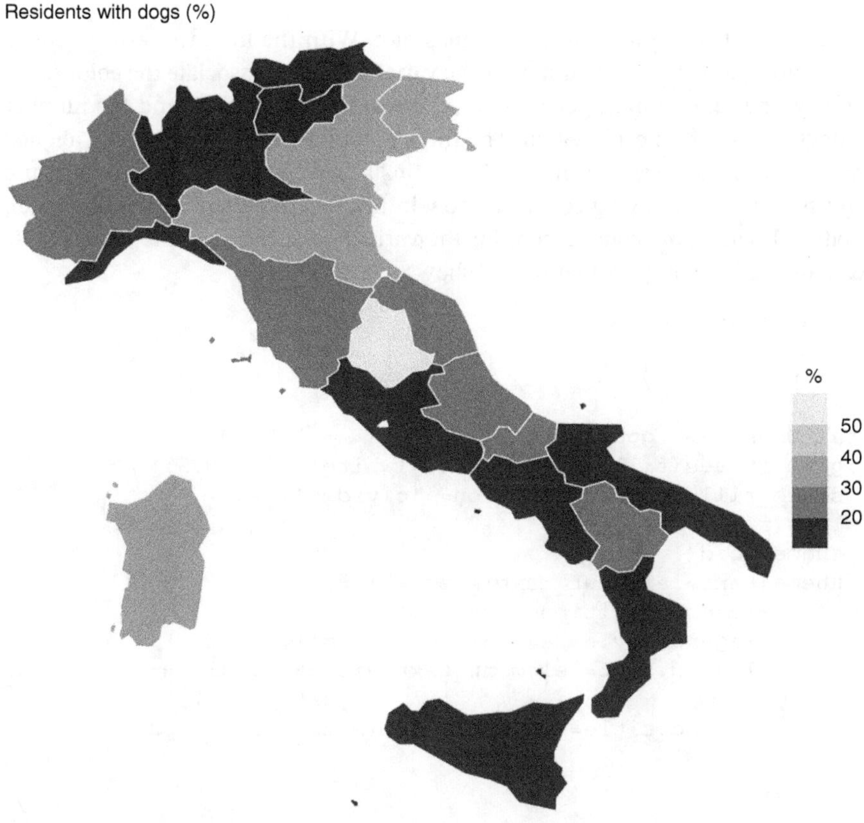

Figure 19.6 Choropleth map with coherent data and geographical areas.

```
nuts2_IT$NAME_LATN = str_replace_all(nuts2_IT$NAME_LATN,
  "Provincia Autonoma di Trento", "Trentino-Alto Adige/Südtirol")
nuts2_IT$NAME_LATN = str_replace_all(nuts2_IT$NAME_LATN,
  "Provincia Autonoma di Bolzano/Bozen", "Trentino-Alto Adige/Südtirol")

nuts2_IT %>% inner_join(dogs,
               by= join_by(NAME_LATN == Region)) -> italyDogs2
italyDogs2 %>% mutate(Dogs_res= 100*`Dogs x resident`) %>%
  ggplot() +
  geom_sf(aes(fill= Dogs_res),
          color='white', linewidth=0.3)+
  scale_fill_viridis_b(option= 'cividis') +
  labs(fill="%", title="Residents with dogs (%)" )+
  theme_void() +
  theme(text= element_text(size=10))
```

19.3 Multiple and Annotated Maps

We consider two variants of the previous plot. With the first, we want to create three choropleth maps that differ for the variable used to associate the color scale, namely: the ratio of dogs per resident, the region's population, and the number of dogs registered in each region. The three graphics will be horizontally aligned by means of package *patchwork* (i.e., *p1|p2|p3*). Legends will be resized and adjusted. In the following code, we show in full just one graphic, the others are produced with same code, except for the variable associated to the *fill* aesthetic (e.g. `aes(fill=Pop)`). Figure 19.7 shows the result.

```
library(patchwork)

... -> p1

italyDogs2 %>% ggplot() +
  geom_sf(aes(fill= Pop), color='white', lwd=0.3)+
  scale_fill_viridis_b(option= 'cividis') +
  labs(fill= "Residents") +
  theme_void() +
  theme(text= element_text(size = 10),
        legend.position= 'bottom',
        legend.key.size= unit(0.4, 'cm'),
        legend.text= element_text(size=6, angle = 90,
                                  vjust = 0.5),
        legend.title= element_text(size=6))  -> p2

...  -> p3

(p1 | p2 | p3)
```

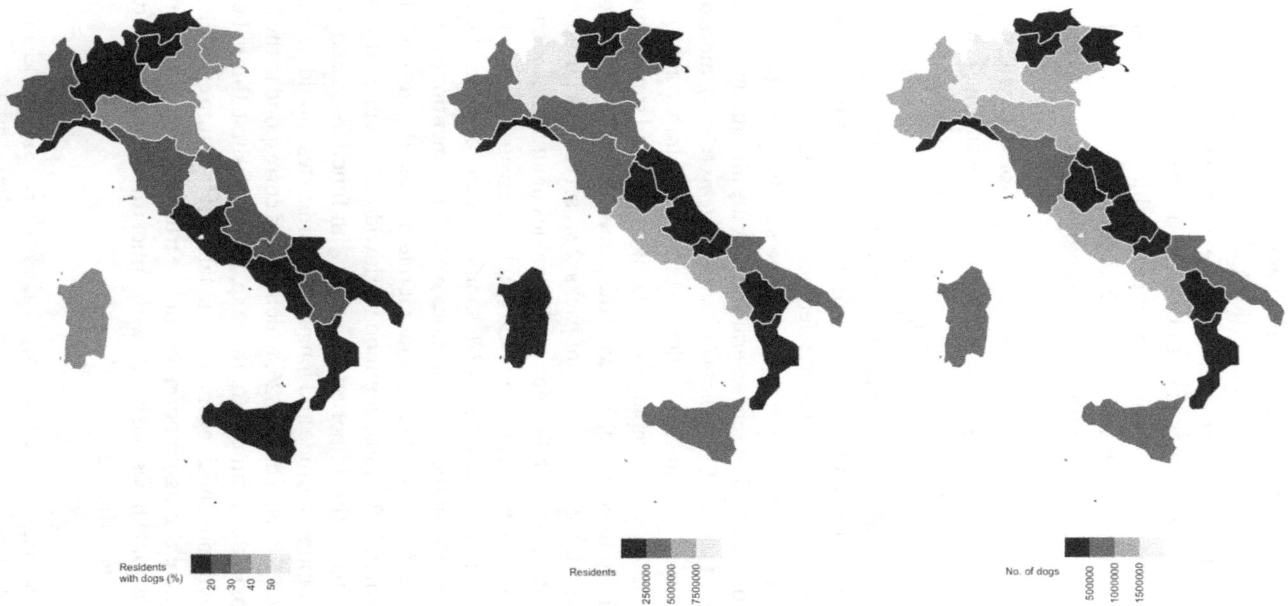

Figure 19.7 Choropleth maps, from left to right: ratio of dogs per resident, region population, and number of dogs registered in each region.

In the second variant, we add *annotations*, meaning graphical and textual elements placed on the choropleth map. These annotations will be of two kinds: *a dot representing the position* of some cities and the corresponding *city name*. These elements should be placed by respecting the correct geolocation of the cities, therefore geographic coordinates have to be used. There is a tiny detail to consider: if the city name is placed on the exact geographic position, it would overlap the dot and the visual result will be unclear, therefore city names should be somewhat displaced in order to not overlap the dot representing the exact city location.

Ggplot function `annotate()` does what we look for; its syntax has a first attribute `geom` specifying the *type of annotation*, in our example, it will be *point* for the dots and *text* for city names; attributes `x` and `y` specify *longitude* and *latitude* of the annotation, then style options follow.

There is a second important element to consider. In order to place the annotations in the correct positions on the map, it is necessary that the map and the annotations share the same coordinate references. That might sound perplexing at first, but the fact is that there is not a unique standard way to define a geographic point on the Earth, there are several and they are all equally effective. More precisely, there exist several *Coordinate Reference Systems* (*CRSs*), more details on CRSs will be discussed in following sections. For now, it is important to learn that to correctly align different geographical objects, like a map and some textual annotations, they all have to be associated with the same CRS, otherwise coordinates will not align. Function `coord_sf()` of package *sf*, serves this purpose because it can specify what CRS to use for interpreting values of attributes `x` and `y` of the annotations. We need to specify attribute `default_crs=sf::st_crs(4326)` telling that for the annotations, *CRS 4326* should be considered as the reference to interpret values of longitude and latitude. We will see mentioned many times in the following this CRS code 4326 because it refers to the *World Geodetic System 1984 (WGS84)*, which is the most common worldwide, although many others are in use as well. To recap this important concept, with function `coord_sf()`, we specify that annotations' latitude and longitude coordinates should be interpreted according to the CRS having code 4326, which should correspond to the CRS associated to the map. In this example, for the map, we just assume this to be the case (actually it is so) without checking map's metadata, but in future examples we will consider cases where this assumption will not be true and further operations will be needed. Figure 19.8 shows the result with annotations, dots, and city names, correctly positioned on the map.

```
p2 +
  annotate(geom="point", x=12.496, y=41.903, color="darkred") +
  annotate(geom="text", x=11.95, y=41.903, label="Rome",
           size=3, color="darkred") +
```

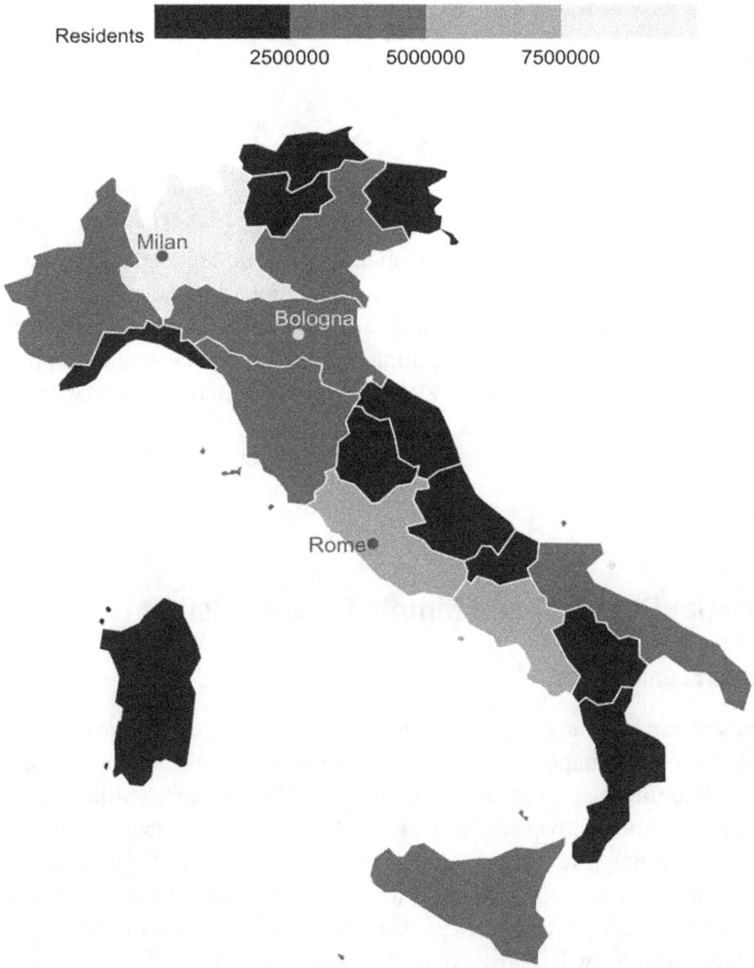

Figure 19.8 Annotated map with dots and city names for Milan, Bologna, and Rome.

```
annotate(geom="point", x=9.190, y=45.464, color="darkred") +
annotate(geom="text", x=9.190, y=45.65, label="Milan",
        size=3, color="darkred") +
annotate(geom="point", x=11.342, y=44.495, color="gold") +
annotate(geom="text", x=11.6, y=44.7, label="Bologna",
        size=3, color="gold") +
coord_sf(default_crs = sf::st_crs(4326)) +
theme(text= element_text(size=12),
      legend.position= 'top',
      legend.key.width= unit(1.5, 'cm'),
```

```
    legend.key.height= unit(0.5, 'cm'),
    legend.text= element_text(size=8, angle=0, vjust=0.5),
    legend.title= element_text(size=8))
```

19.3.1 From ggplot to Plotly Graphics

We introduce a last variant by using package *plotly*. We have already used Plotly in Part 3, here we use a feature of the corresponding R package that automatically transforms a *ggplot* object into a *Plotly* one, meaning it is no longer a static image but an HTML object, this way enriched with the standard interactive features like the *dynamic tooltip*, in this case just limited to the variables associated to ggplot aesthetics, and the *zoom*. In the example, we use one of the ggplot graphics previously created and turn it into a Plotly one with function `ggplotly()` (Figure 19.9).

```
library(plotly)
ggplotly(p1)
```

19.4 Spatial Data (sp) and Simple Features (sf)

19.4.1 Natural Earth

Package *rnaturalearth* is another valuable resource to create geographical visualizations and choropleth maps. In this case too, as well as for *giscoR*, the package provides an API to interface a remote online service, *Natural Earth* (https://www.naturalearthdata.com/), with available datasets of public domain spatial data and maps. The package has a few vector maps already available and, for others, it offers function `ne_download()` that allows for downloading them. An important aspect is that by default it requires package *sp*, the predecessor of package *sf*. We load both because we will analyze their differences.

```
library(sf)
library(sp)
library(rnaturalearth)
```

Both *sp* and *sf* are standard formats in R, easily convertible one into the other. Actually, we have already used them, although without specifically considering their differences. We do it now by using maps from *rnaturalearth* for our examples. Let us start with the more generic among the maps, provided by functions `ne_countries()`, `ne_states()`, and `ne_coastline()`.

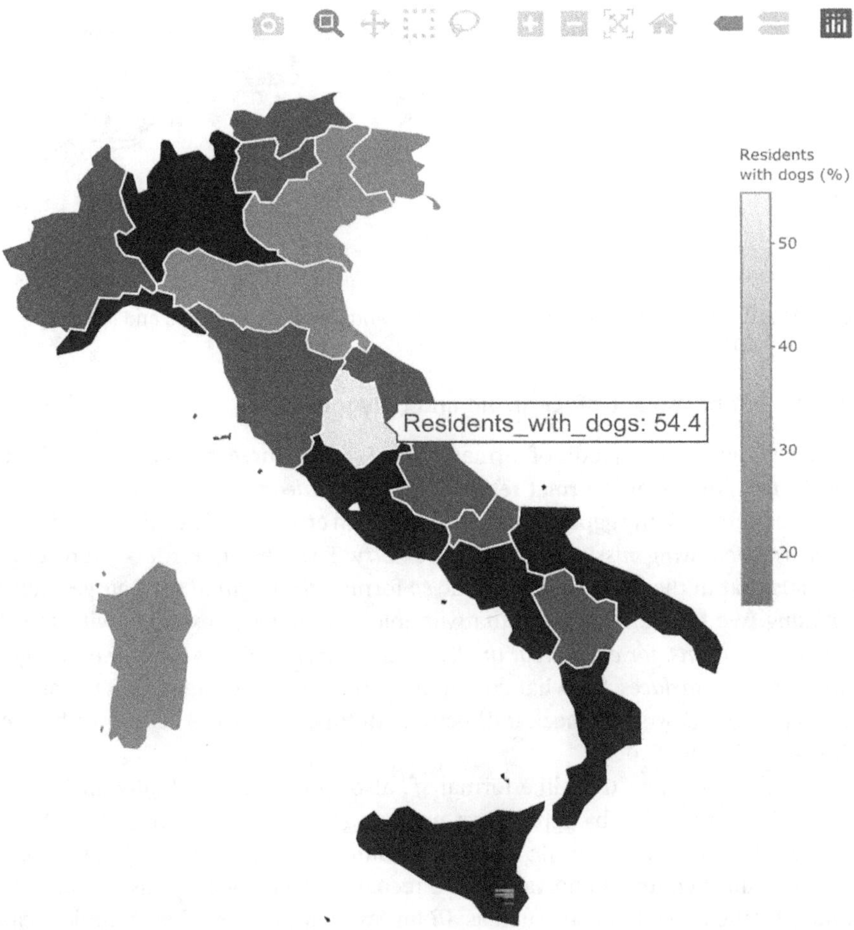

Figure 19.9 ggplot image transformed into a Plotly HTML object.

With the first, we select Sweden and Denmark, and we could specify the scale (i.e., *"small," "medium,"* and *"large"*); with the second there is no option for the scale, just the countries, and with the third the scale could be specified but without selecting a particular region. We use `plot()` function of package *sp* to visualize the maps, Figure 19.10 shows the three maps.

```
sp::plot(ne_countries(country= c("sweden","denmark"),
        scale= "medium"))
sp::plot(ne_states(country= c("sweden","denmark")))
sp::plot(ne_coastline(scale= "medium"))
```

Figure 19.10 Maps from Natural Earth, Sweden and Denmark's borders and regions, coastline world map.

19.4.2 Format sp and sf: Centroid and Polygons

We delve now into the details of formats *sp* and *sf*. The three maps just created are in *sp* format, the default format returned by *rnaturalearth* functions. If we try to visualize them by using ggplot and `geom_sf()` an error would be raised: *'stat_sf()' requires the following missing aesthetics: geometry*. The message error is interesting. It tells us that in the data, namely in the *sp* format, *the required variable geometry is missing*. We have already seen that variable in a previous example with the *sf* format; *it contains, for each area, the list of coordinates of the geometry and polygons for planar surfaces*. So, what does it mean that error message? That format *sp* has no polygons? We can check it directly with function `str()` as shown by the following excerpt of code.

First of all, we note that, like format *sf*, also format *sp* is actually an R data frame, therefore usable by ggplot, just not recognized by function `geom_sf()`, for example, function `geom_polygon()` would have handled it. Then, we see a list of variables/columns and values. We recognize country codes as *alpha2* ISO standards (the two-letter code such as *SE* for Sweden), names of geographic areas (e.g. Norrbotten), Swedish postal codes, and finally latitude and longitude coordinates. Are those polygons coordinates? No, those are a single pair of latitude and longitude coordinates, one pair for each area, so they just identify a specific geographic point, not multiple polygons. What are those coordinates? They represent *the single point that is conventionally used to identify an area* called *centroid of the area*, which represents the geographic center of a planar surface.

```
sw_dk1 <- ne_states(country= c("sweden","denmark"))
str(sw_dk1)

Formal class 'SpatialPolygonsDataFrame' [package "sp"]
  ..@ data :'data.frame': 26 obs. of 121 variables:
...
  .. ..$ iso_a2    : chr [1:26] "SE" "SE" "SE" "SE" ...
...
```

```
  .. ..$ name      : chr [1:26] "Norrbotten" "Västerbotten" ...
...
  .. ..$ postal    : chr [1:26] "NB" "VB" "JA" "KO" ...
...
  .. ..$ latitude  : num [1:26] 66.8 64.7 63.3 60.8 59.8 ...
  .. ..$ longitude : num [1:26] 20.5 18.4 14.5 14.4 13.1 ...
...
  .. ..$ geonunit  : chr [1:26] "Sweden" "Sweden"  ...
...
  .. ..$ name_en   : chr [1:26] "Norrbotten" "Västerbotten" ...
...
```

If we continue looking, we recognize polygons, for each area there is a list of polygons. Therefore, even format *sp* has multiple polygons associated to planar surfaces, just organized differently than in format *sf*, and with no variable *geometry*.

```
  ..@ polygons   :List of 26
.. ..$ :Formal class 'Polygons' [package "sp"] with 5 slots
  .. .. .. ..@ Polygons :List of 10
  .. .. .. .. ..$ :Formal class 'Polygon' [package "sp"]
  .. .. .. .. .. .. ..@ labpt  : num [1:2] 20.1 67
  .. .. .. .. .. .. ..@ area   : num 21.5
  .. .. .. .. .. .. ..@ hole   : logi FALSE
  .. .. .. .. .. .. ..@ ringDir: int 1
  .. .. .. .. .. .. ..@ coords : num [1:663, 1:2] 18.2 18.4 ...
  .. .. .. .. ..$ :Formal class 'Polygon' [package "sp"]
  .. .. .. .. .. .. ..@ labpt  : num [1:2] 22.4 65.4
  .. .. .. .. .. .. ..@ area   : num 0.00273
  .. .. .. .. .. .. ..@ hole   : logi FALSE
  .. .. .. .. .. .. ..@ ringDir: int 1
  .. .. .. .. .. .. ..@ coords : num [1:17, 1:2] 22.4 22.4 ...
  ...
```

19.4.3 Differences Between Format *sp* and Format *sf*

With this understanding of format *sp* and the reason why if we try to visualize an *sp* object with *ggplot()+geom_sf()* we get an error telling us that variable *geometry* is missing, we can look at the same data in *sf* format (https://r-spatial.github.io/sf/articles/sf1.html). Package *rnaturalearth* functions offer attribute `returnclass` that could have two values: *sp*, the default, or *sf*; we use the latter option to have the data in *sf* format.

```
sw_dk2 <- ne_states(country= c("sweden","denmark"),
                    returnclass= "sf")
str(sw_dk2)
Classes 'sf' and 'data.frame':  26 obs. of 122 variables:
...
 $ iso_3166_2: chr  "SE-BD" "SE-AC" "SE-Z" "SE-W" ...
```

```
 $ iso_a2     : chr  "SE" "SE" "SE" "SE" 1
...
 $ name       : chr  "Norrbotten" "Västerbotten" "Jämtland" ...
...
```

As we already know, the *sf* format is an R data frame and the data organization seemingly looks identical to the previous *sp* format, until we catch a tiny difference:

- *sp* data: 'data.frame': 26 obs. of 121 variables
- *sf* data: 'data.frame': 26 obs. of 122 variables

They have the same number of rows (observations) corresponding to geographic areas, but in the *sf* format there is an additional variable. We can check with `names()`.

```
names(ne_states(country= c("sweden","denmark")),
       returnclass="sf")

  [1] "featurecla"..."iso_3166_2"  ...
  ...
[121] "FCLASS_TLC" "geometry"
```

Here it is, column *geometry*. Therefore, the difference between format *sp* and format *sf* is that *sp* has the list of polygon coordinates for each area following the initial data frame variables, whereas *sf* has variable *geometry* that contains, for each area, the list of polygon coordinates. In other terms, the two formats have exactly the same information, just organized differently. This is the reason why they are easily convertible from one into the other, it is just a data reorganization. Transformations from format *sp* to *sf* and vice versa are possible with the following functions of package *sf*:

- from format *sf* to *sp*: `sf::as_Spatial()`
- from format *sp* to *sf*: `sf::st_as_sf()`

We try them with the two objects *sw_dk1* (format *sp*) and *sw_dk2* (format *sf*).

```
# From sp to sf
sw_dk_sf <- sf::st_as_sf(sw_dk1)

# From sf to sp
sw_dk_sp <- sf::as_Spatial(sw_dk2)
```

We verify the resulting data types.

```
str(sw_dk_sf)
Classes 'sf' and 'data.frame':  26 obs. of  122 variables:
...
```

```
str(sw_dk_sp)
Formal class 'SpatialPolygonsDataFrame' [package "sp"] with 5 slots
  ..@ data        :'data.frame': 26 obs. of  121 variables:
...
```

This analysis of formats *sp* and *sf* is important for understanding them clearly, they are both very common, while format *sf* is progressively superseding format *sp*, so it is essential to be able to handle them correctly and transform one into the other if needed.

19.5 Overlaid Graphical Layers

We use now the function of Natural Earth to download new maps, `ne_download()`. The difficulty of the case study increases because we want to produce a result of good quality with several graphical and geographical elements, getting close to what is required for a public presentation or publication. Specifically, we want to show *the map of the main railroad network in Western Europe and highlight some of the busiest railway stations for number of passengers, on yearly base*. Producing the graphic presents some challenges, and we need to make graphical choices in order to have a clear and pleasant visualization. All details need to be carefully crafted.

Let us start with maps that Natural Earth makes available. The list can be read in the package documentation (https://cran.r-project.org/web/packages/rnaturalearth/vignettes/rnaturalearth.html). Two of them interest us: *railroads* and *land*. Not all scales are available, *railroad* has only scale 10. We use format *sf*.

```
rail <- ne_download(scale=10, type="railroads",
                    category="cultural", returnclass="sf")
land <- ne_download(scale=50, type="land",
                    category="physical", returnclass="sf")
```

By executing `ggplot(rail)+geom_sf()` and `ggplot(land)+geom_sf()`, we obtain the maps of Figure 19.11.

They are both world maps, for these ones there is no possibility to select a certain region, it should be cropped from each one of these by specifying the coordinates, again with *sf* function `coord_sf()`. In the following code, Western Europe is selected through `coord_sf()`, CRS 4326 is indicated as the reference coordinate system, and coordinates are defined with attributes `xlim` and `ylim`, which set the boundaries of a rectangle, limiting the area of interest. Then, the ggplot graphic is produced by overlaying the railroad map over the land map. Figure 19.12 shows the result. This map is the basis for working toward our final result; now we have to overlay the other graphical elements referred to the busiest railway stations.

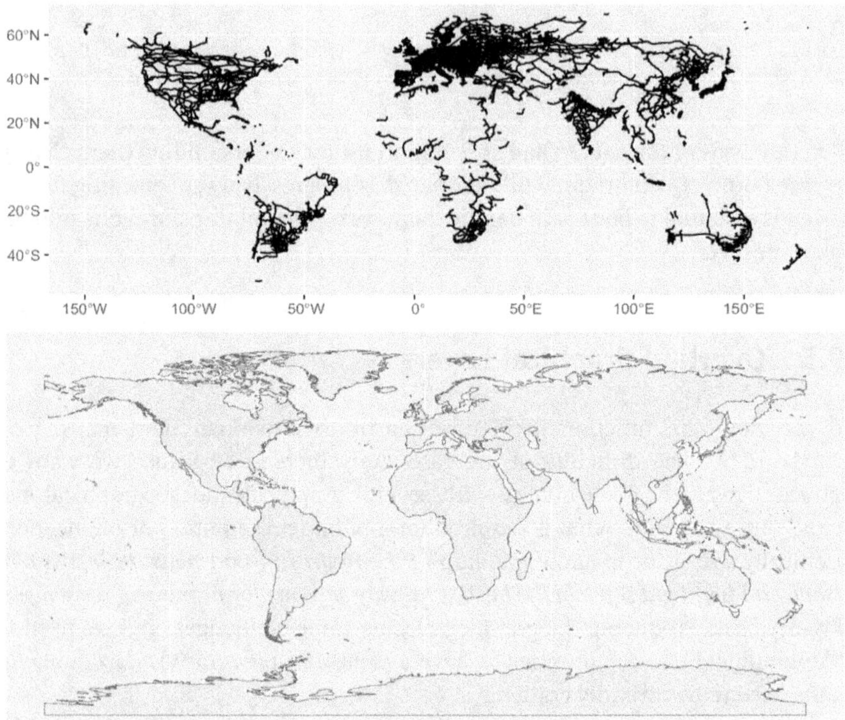

Figure 19.11 Railroad and land maps from Natural Earth.

```
ggplot() +
  geom_sf(data= land) +
  geom_sf(data= rail) +
  coord_sf(
   default_crs= sf::st_crs(4326),
   xlim= c(-10,20),
   ylim= c(35,60)
   )
```

The operations are explained step-by-step in the following, starting with common data-wrangling operations, then graphical elements are added, layer by layer to the ggplot graphic.

STEP 1. First, data on railway stations' number of passengers is needed. There are several possibilities to obtain such data, an easy one is from the Wikipedia page "*List of busiest railway stations in Europe*" (https://en.wikipedia.org/wiki/List_of_busiest_railway_stations_in_Europe). Data are presented in an HTML table

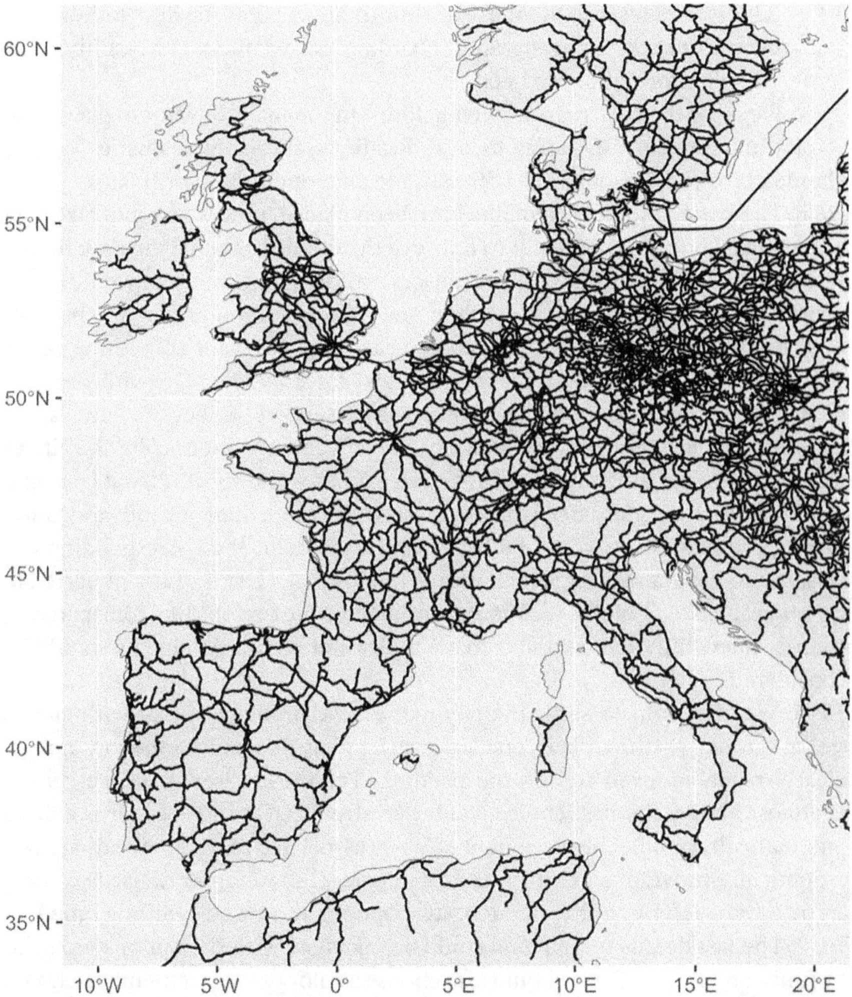

Figure 19.12 Land and railroad maps of Western Europe.

that we read through a *web scraping* technique (as seen in Part 3). Package *rvest* is required, which is included in *tidyverse*. The table needs some tidying because it has two header rows, with simple data-wrangling operations we prepare it.

STEP 2. With the busiest railway stations, we know the corresponding cities and we need their geographic coordinates. The general solution would have been to find a dataset with geographic coordinates of main European cities, but for simplicity we manually built our custom dataset by finding out the coordinates of the first 14 cities with busiest railway stations.

STEP 3. The two datasets, the one with information about busiest railway stations and the one with city geographic coordinates are joined. The resulting data frame has all information we need.

STEP 4. We draw the base map, as seen before. On the map we want to place scatterplot markers corresponding to city's locations, therefore aesthetics *x* and *y* should correspond to columns with latitude and longitude coordinates.

STEP 5. The basic graphical elements have been placed, now we should take care of the visual effect of the result to improve the quality. For instance, we do not just want to design simple dots for railway stations, some of them would result overplotted (i.e., cities with more than one railway station among the busiest) and, in any case, are also not much eye-catching, we want something better than just dots. This could be a good context for a *bubble plot*, with the area of the circle depending on the number of passengers. Then, attribute `size` should be an aesthetic of the scatterplot. Next, we may want to color the circles differently for the different countries, then also attribute `fill` should be a scatterplot aesthetic. Again, since there are cities with more than one railway station among the busiest, it would be better not to overplot the corresponding circles, but to use some jitter, which means that `geom_jitter()` is preferred to `geom_point()`. Finally, we should work with style options like transparency, shapes, linewidth, and colors to create a pleasant result. All details should be considered.

STEP 6. We also want to show the city names, the problem is that with classic `geom_label()` they likely end up overlapping or result somehow not all clearly readable, even tuning the padding. For these cases, package *ggrepel* is almost always the best choice, we have introduced it in Part 1, it is able to automatically handle the placement of labels associated to points avoiding overlapping and providing a clearly readable layout (the function to use is `geom_label_repel()`). In this case too, style options should be carefully tuned.

STEP 7. The last details remain and could be managed with the options provided by function `theme()`, we should also choose a color palette (remember, choose wisely, try several alternatives), set the legend relative to bubble sizes, and hide the one for colors.

The result is a graphic that obviously could be further improved or even created in different ways, but anyhow it is of decent quality, both for the clarity of information and the visual effect. In the following code there is the full script with inline comments; Figure 19.13 follows.

```
library(rvest)
library(ggrepel)

rail <- ne_download(scale=10, type="railroads",
            category="cultural", returnclass="sf")
```

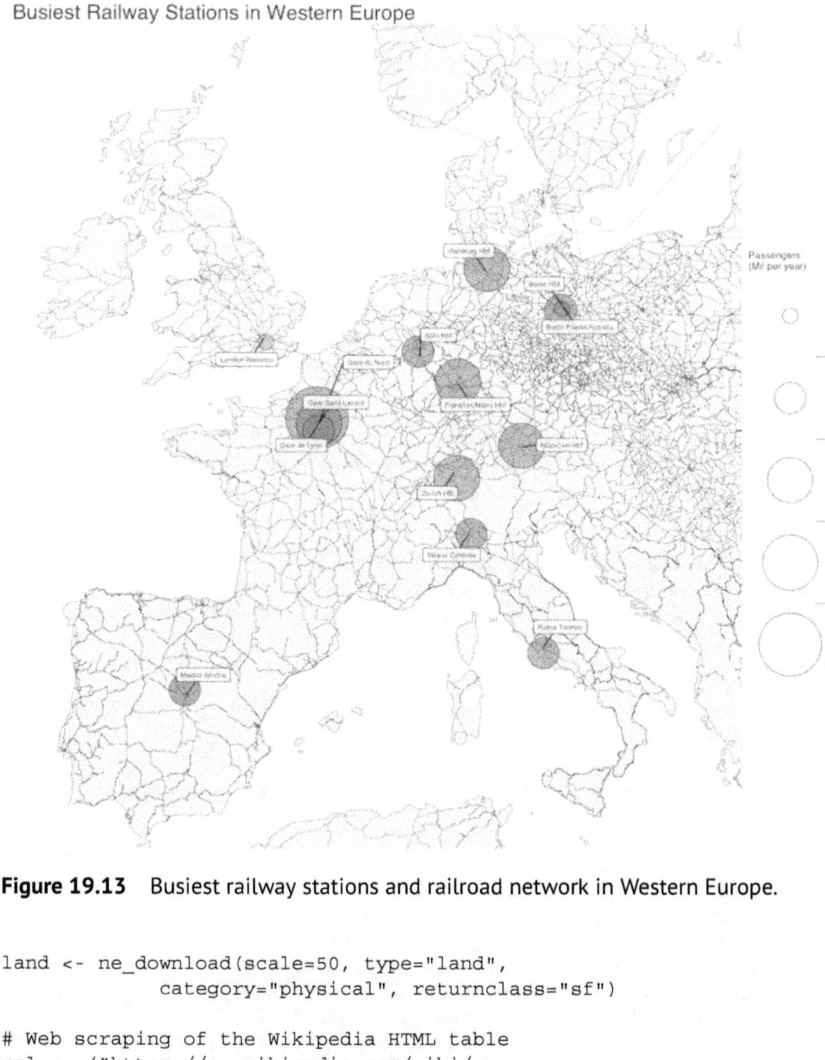

Figure 19.13 Busiest railway stations and railroad network in Western Europe.

```
land <- ne_download(scale=50, type="land",
            category="physical", returnclass="sf")

# Web scraping of the Wikipedia HTML table
url <- ("https://en.wikipedia.org/wiki/
             List_of_busiest_railway_stations_in_Europe")
webpage <- read_html(url)

# Tidying operations on the table
data <- html_elements(webpage, 'table.wikitable')
data <- html_table(data, header=FALSE)
busiest_rail <- data %>%
  bind_rows() %>%
  as_tibble()

# The first row has meanigless values, it is omitted
```

```
busiest_rail <- busiest_rail[2:97,1:8]

# The next first row has column names, we use it to set column names
colnames(busiest_rail)= as.character(unlist(busiest_rail[1,]))

# The first row is now useless and it is omitted
busiest_rail= busiest_rail[-1, ]

# Some passenger total values have notes in square brackets,
#we remove them
busiest_rail$Sum= busiest_rail$Sum %>%
  str_replace_all('\\[[0-9a-z ]+\\]', ") %>%
  as.numeric()

# Data frame with city's geographic coordinates
city <- data.frame(
"RW_St"= c("Gare du Nord", "Hamburg Hbf", 'Frankfurt(Main) Hbf',
'Zürich HB', 'München Hbf', 'Gare de Lyon', "Roma Termini",
'Berlin Hbf', 'Milano Centrale', 'Madrid Atocha', 'Köln Hbf',
'Gare Saint-Lazare', 'Berlin Friedrichstraße',
'London Waterloo'),

"Lon"= c(2.349, 9.993, 8.682, 8.545, 11.576, 2.349, 12.496,
13.404, 9.188, -3.703, 6.953, 2.349, 13.404, -0.118),

"Lat"= c(48.856, 53.551, 50.110, 47.373, 48.137, 48.856,
41.903, 52.520, 45.464, 40.416, 50.935, 48.856, 52.520, 51.509)
)

# Join between the two data frames
busiest_rail %>% left_join(city,
   by= join_by(`Railway station`==RW_St)) -> busiest_rail_geo

# Ggplot graphic
ggplot() +
  geom_sf(data= land, fill="ghostwhite") +
  geom_sf(data= rail, lwd=0.1) +
  geom_jitter(data= head(busiest_rail_geo,15),
         aes(x= Lon, y= Lat, size= Sum, fill= Country),
         color='black', alpha=0.6, shape=21, width=0.1)+
  geom_label_repel(data= head(busiest_rail_geo,15),
         aes(x= Lon, y= Lat, label= `Railway station`),
         size=2.0, alpha =0.85, na.rm = TRUE,
         box.padding = unit(0.75, "lines"))+
  scale_size_binned(range= c(3,25), n.breaks=5,
                   nice.breaks= TRUE)+
  labs(size="Passengers\n(Mil per year)",
       title="Busiest Railway Stations in Western Europe")+
  coord_sf(default_crs= sf::st_crs(4326),
          xlim= c(-10,20),
          ylim= c(35,60)) -> p1

# Style options
```

```
p1 +
  scale_fill_brewer(palette= "Dark2")+
  guides(fill= "none") +
  theme_void() +
  theme(legend.position= 'right',
        legend.text= element_text(size=8, vjust=0.5),
        legend.title= element_text(size=8),
        title= element_text(family= "Helvetica", size=14,
                             color= "darkred"))
```

19.6 Shape Files and GeoJSON Datasets

When the interest in working with maps and geographic data grows, it is inevitable to meet *cartographic* data and *geodatasets* since they are now often made available as open data by municipalities and other public or private subjects. This gets us closer to the world of traditional *cartography*, the best systems in this sector, with a long tradition and a well-earned reputation of quality. These systems are, however, typically not open-source, the best of them at least, and they require specialized skills for handling complex projects, skills that are only partially shared with data science and data visualization.

Tools from data science's open-source environments should not have the pretense of rivaling with those sophisticated and very specialized tools at the level of highly complex projects, but, nevertheless, have become able to handle cartographic data and geodatasets in a good way, certainly at the level of mid-complexity projects, which is almost always adequate for data visualization projects. An example of this excellent qualitative level reached by open-source tools is the availability of native functionalities to handle *cartographic shape files* without requiring format conversions but using them directly. This possibility is not trivial, it means that tools have evolved to support a significant level of complexity of data and formats and are able to perform complex operations on spatial data. For sure, they have reached a level way beyond standard choropleth maps, which is the easy task.

To R packages employed in the previous section, we add a new one called *geojsonsf*, which is an evolution of package *sf* specific for geodatasets in *GeoJSON* format, an open format derived from JSON, which is of type *list* (R) or *dictionary* (Python) and widely used by many Open Data providers (the *shape file* format, older than GeoJSON, is more specific of traditional cartography and typically with geographic data at a very fine level of detail).

```
library(tidyverse)
library(lubridate)
library(sf)
library(sp)
library(geojsonsf)
```

19.7 Venice: Open Data Cartography and Other Maps

In the examples of this section, we look at Venice, one of the most fascinating cities in the world, and we build a case study by using open data of its topology from official sources. In particular, the main source is the Topographic Geodatabase of the Venice Municipality, which is provided as Open Data (*Italian Open Data Licence [IODL]*) and offers several interesting shape files (https://dati.venezia.it/?q=content/carta-tecnica).

As mentioned before, the *shape file* is the traditional cartographic format and the one usually offering more technical and accurate topographic data. Reading shape files in native form has been for long an exclusive feature of specialized GIS tools, therefore the fact that R package *sf* allows for natively reading them through the standard support of a preloaded GIS driver is an outstanding feature. The function to use is `st_read()`. From the cartography of the Venice Municipality, we select some shape files that we will visualize as stacked layers to learn the functionalities of R tools. These are the shape files:

- *Elemento di trasporto su acqua*: *EL_ACQ.shp*
  (Strato01_Viabilita_Mobilita_Trasporti/Tema0103_AltroTrasporto)
  (transl. Waterway transport element)
- *Area di circolazione pedonale*: *AC_PED.shp*
  (Strato01_Viabilita_Mobilita_Trasporti/Tema0101_Strade)
  (transl. Pedestrian circulation area)
- *Linea di costa marina cartografica*: *CS_MAR.shp*
  (Tema0402_AcqueMarine)
  (transl. Coastal marine line)
- *Canale*: *CAN_LAG.shp*
  (Tema0404_ReticoloIdrografico)
  (transl. Hydrographic grid)
- *Ponti*: *PONTE.shp*
  (Strato02_Immobili_Antropizzazioni/Tema0203_OpereInfrastruttureTrasporto)
  (transl. Bridges)
- *Scarpata*: *SCARPT.shp*
  (Strato05_Orografia/Tema0503_FormeTerreno)
  (transl. Escarpments))
- *Aree verdi*: *AR_VRD.shp*
  (Strato06_Vegetazione/Tema0604_VerdeUrbano)
  (transl. Green areas)
- *Numero civico*: *CIVICI.shp*
  (Strato03_ Gestione_viabilita_indirizzi)
  (transl. Civic numbers)

```
waterways= st_read('datasets/Venice/Strato01_Viabilita_Mobilita_
        Trasporti/
        Tema0103_AltroTrasporto/EL_ACQ.shp')
sea= st_read('datasets/Venice/Tema0402_AcqueMarine/CS_MAR.shp')
streets= st_read('datasets/Venice/Strato01_Viabilita_Mobilita_Trasporti/
        Tema0101_Strade/AC_PED.shp')
canals= st_read('datasets/Venice/Tema0404_ReticoloIdrografico/
               CAN_LAG.shp')
bridges= st_read('datasets/Venice/Strato02_Immobili_Antropizzazioni/
       Tema0203_OpereInfrastruttureTrasporto/PONTE.shp')
terrain= st_read('datasets/Venice/Strato05_Orografia/
                Tema0503_FormeTerreno/SCARPT.shp')
green= st_read('datasets/Venice/Strato06_Vegetazione/
              Tema0604_VerdeUrbano/AR_VRD.shp')
civicNo= st_read('datasets/Venice/Strato03_GestioneViabilita_Indirizzi/
        Tema0301_ToponimiNumeriCivici/CIVICO.shp')
```

We have read the shape files, let us look at the content of one of those R objects, for example *waterways*, with the content of *EL_ACQ.shp*.

```
Reading layer `EL_ACQ' from data source
  `datasets/Venezia/Strato01_Viabilita_Mobilita_Trasporti/
Tema0103_AltroTrasporto/EL_ACQ.shp'
  using driver `ESRI Shapefile'
Simple feature collection with 1107 features and 27 fields
Geometry type: MULTILINESTRING
Dimension:     XY
Bounding box:  xmin: 2302196 ymin: 5012733
               xmax: 2326948 ymax: 5047500
CRS:           NA
```

The first information we find is a confirmation that function `st_read()` reads shape file in native form thanks to the *ESRI Shapefile driver* (ESRI is the name of the US company leader in the market of GIS tools with its widely popular *ArcGIS*). The second information is that the object is of type *sf* and that elements of the variable/column *geometry* are of type *MULTILINESTRING* for this shape file, not polygons as it is customary for planar surfaces (i.e., the elements are canals and other waterways, not planar surfaces, they do not have a closed border). This tells us something new: different geographical elements might be represented with different geometries. The last two items are important. The first specifies the *bounding box*, which provides the geographic coordinates of the rectangle that represents the area. The bounding box is defined through the two points corresponding to the extremes of the diagonal of the rectangular area, meaning the bottom-left point (i.e., `xmin` and `ymin`) and the top-right point (i.e., `xmax` and `ymax`). The second important item is the *CRS*, which we already encountered, representing the coordinate system employed for the coordinates of this shape file. In other words, it is the coordinate system that permits to make sense of the coordinate values (e.g. *xmin: 2302196 ymin: 5012733*) that this shape file uses to represent geographic positions. Without knowing which CRS is associated, we simply do not know what latitude *2302196* and longitude *5012733* mean. This is exactly the case of this shape file, there is no indication associated to CRS metadata in the shape file. Is it an error? Is it strange or exceptional? Not at all, on the contrary it is quite common to see shape files with no indication of the CRS. This should not mean that coordinates values have no sense, they are very likely perfectly meaningful and correct according to a certain CRS, it was just not to be stated as metadata in the shape file. But, as it is true for basically every metadata enclosed in digital objects, it might be useful for various functionalities to have it, but it is almost never strictly necessary because, if the metadata is not present, it could be set manually, for example when the file is read, or found in accompanying documentation.

So, not having the CRS specified is not necessarily a problem, it becomes a problem if we are unable to discover which is the CRS when we have to overlay one geographic layer to another because, if the CRSs are not the same, coordinates will be misaligned. In short, the result will be a total mess, same places will not correspond when overlaid. This is why it is so important to clearly understand the role of CRSs, it might not be necessary to know the details of every single CRSs, how the coordinate systems have been defined, their history, and so on, that is a skill of cartographers; but it is mandatory to know the role they have when different topographic layers are overlaid, when the CRS has to be specified, and when a transformation of the coordinate system is necessary to align layers with coordinates from different CRSs.

Let us return to our case study. Since all the *sf* objects produced from reading the shape files have no declared CRS, a possibility is to manually set this information. It is easy with *sf* function `st_set_crs()`, but the real issue is to figure out which CRS should be defined. For this, as it is customary in cartographies, the documentation is very likely to help. In fact, the accompanying information of the Venice Municipality's cartography correctly states it very clearly by specifying the following: *Sistema di riferimento cartografico: Monte Mario/Italy Zone 2 (fuso E) – Datum: Roma 40 – Proiezione: Gauss-Boaga – Fuso: Est (EPSG 3004).* We have left the statement in Italian because that is the original source to look at, but it is easy to recognize that it is specifying the cartographic reference system (i.e., *Sistema di riferimento cartografico*, meaning CRS), and this specific one is called *Monte Mario/Italy Zone 2*, which is very common in Italian cartographic projections (many CRSs in use are similarly based on local topographic references). Important for us is the information provided with *EPSG 3004*, because 3004 is the numeric code of this *Monte Mario* CRS (it could have been easily retrieved with an online search too). So, now we have the information we need and can set the CRS for all those *sf* objects to 3004 with function `st_set_crs()`. In Figure 19.14a,b, the layers for Venice's streets and canals are shown, for now just as single layers with no others overlaid (*Note*: for those that have visited Venice, the topography of these layers might look perplexing, it does not look like the Venice you have seen; the reason is that you likely know just a portion of

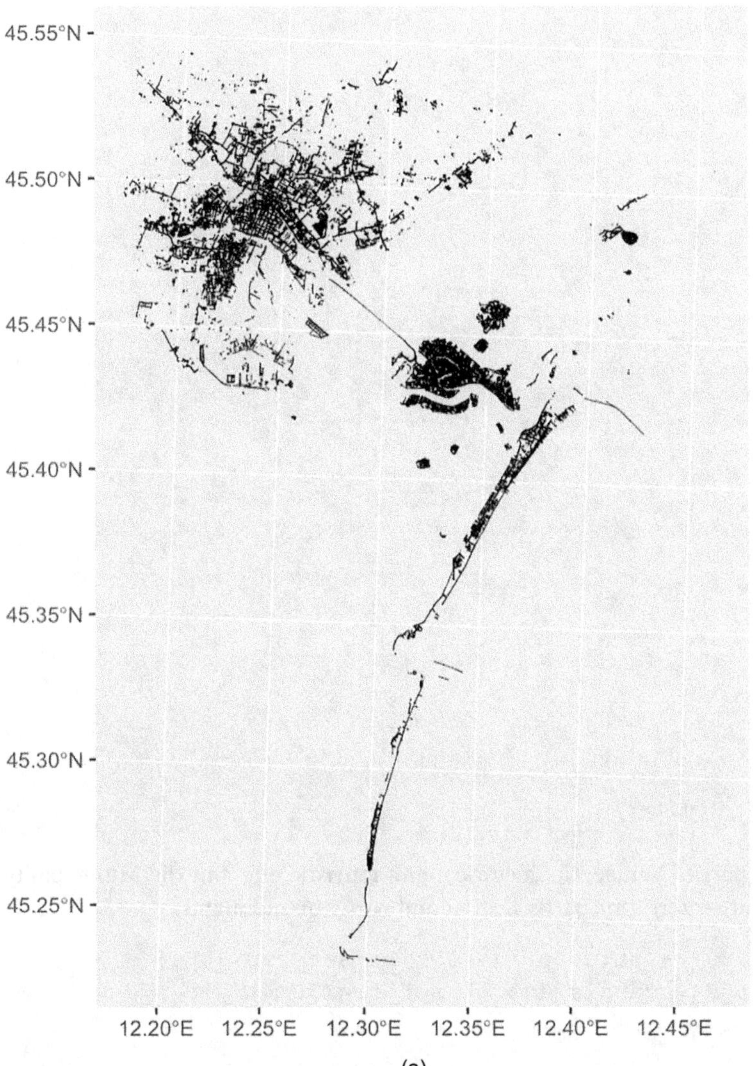

Figure 19.14 (a/b) Venice, streets, and canals cartographic layers.

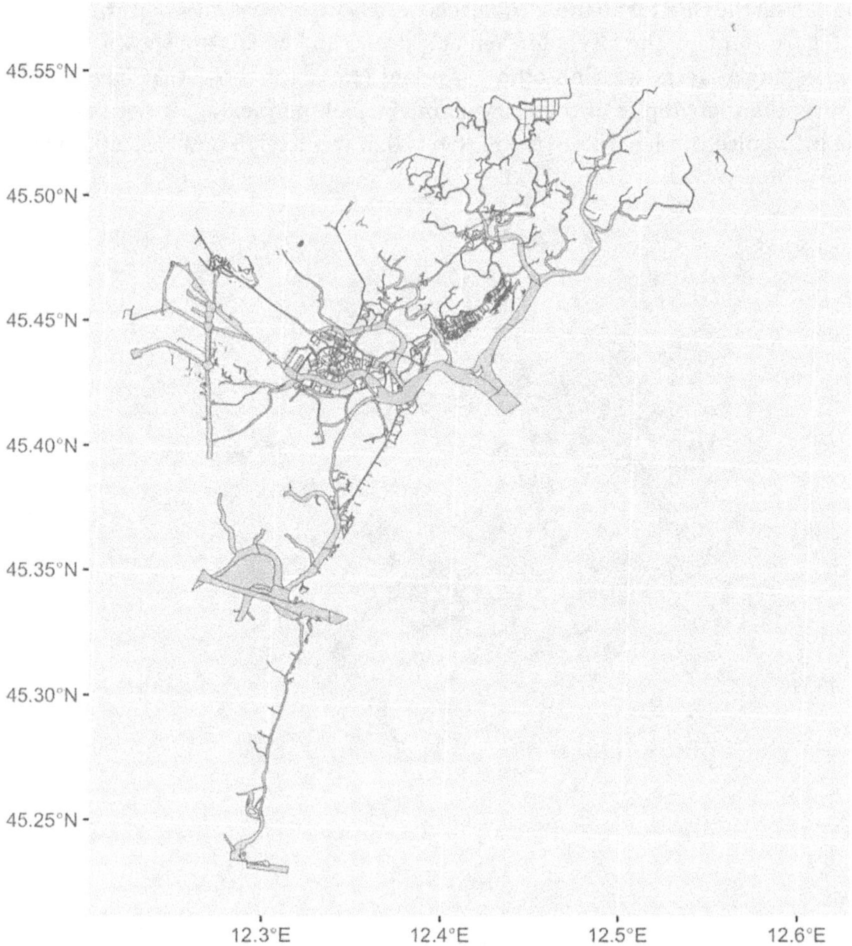

(b)

Figure 19.14 (*Continued*)

the insular part of Venice, the historical and touristic one, but the Municipality includes a larger territory, partly insular and partly on mainland).

```
streets.crs <- streets %>% %>% st_set_crs(3004)
canals.crs <- canals %>% st_set_crs(3004)

ggplot() +
  geom_sf(data= streets.crs, color= "black", lwd=0.1) +
  theme_void() -> plot1
```

```
ggplot() +
  geom_sf(data= canals.crs, fill= "lightblue") +
  theme_void() -> plot2
```

Equally, we do the same for all other *sf* objects.

```
waterways.crs <- waterways %>% st_set_crs(3004)
sea.crs <- sea %>% st_set_crs(3004)
terrain.crs <- terrain %>% %>% st_set_crs(3004)
green.crs <- green %>% %>% st_set_crs(3004)
civicNo.crs <- civicNo %>% %>% st_set_crs(3004)
bridges.crs <- bridges %>% %>% st_set_crs(3004)
```

We add now a non-necessary step that is useful to clearly understand the CRS management: we use a geographical map in *GeoJSON* format, which is a different type of data format than cartographic shape files and has simply the borderline of the Venice Municipality. This is a very common type of map that we have already used in early examples, it is quite common to find it in open format. We get it from *OpenPolis* (https://github.com/openpolis/geojson-italy/tree/master/geojson), an alternative source could have been *Cartography Vector* (https://cartographyvectors.com/map/728-venice). The OpenPolis map is about all Italian municipalities, so we extract just Venice (Italian: Venezia).

For the GeoJSON format, it exists function `geojson_sf()` of package *geojsonsf*, which is the extension of package *sf* to support *GeoJSON* and *TopoJSON* formats (the two have few differences, not relevant for our analysis). Function `geojson_sf()` returns an *sf* object, hence a data frame, from which we can easily extract Venice with a common *filter()*; then we visualize the object with *ggplot()+geom_sf()* (see Figure 19.15)

```
ven_map <- geojsonsf::geojson_sf("datasets/OpenPolis/
                            limits_IT_municipalities.geojson")

ven_map <- filter(ven_map, name == 'Venezia')
ven_map %>% ggplot() + geom_sf()
```

It is a simple map; we look at its characteristics

```
Simple feature collection
Geometry type: MULTIPOLYGON
Dimension:     XY
Bounding box:
xmin: 7.229827 ymin: 44.90396
xmax: 7.973126 ymax: 45.44821
Geodetic CRS:  WGS 84
```

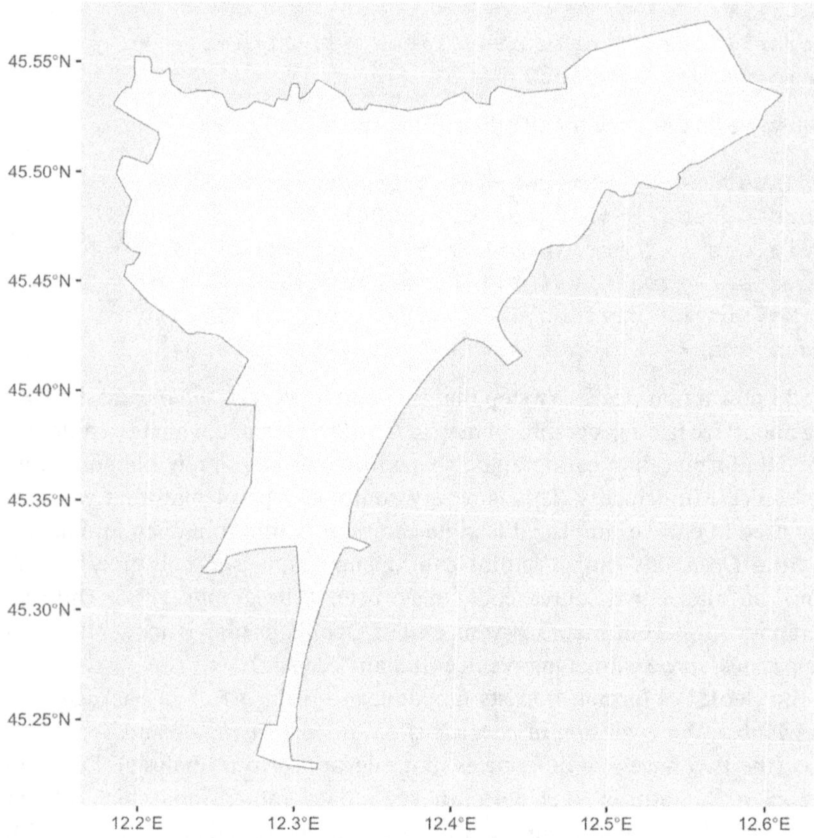

Figure 19.15 Venice municipality border map.

Being a planar surface, it is represented by means of polygons and the associated CRS is specified this time: *WGS 84* is the version. This is one the most common coordinate systems, at least in Western countries, and the bounding box is expressed with the familiar degrees of latitude North and longitude East. Its code is *CRS 4326*, already well-known to us at this point.

So, now we have *sf* objects from the cartographic shape files whose coordinates are expressed according to the Monte Mario reference system and this map with coordinates expressed according to the WGS 84 reference system. These objects cannot be layered one on top of the other because coordinates would not be aligned (you can try, they will not match).

The solution in this case is straightforward: either coordinates expressed as WGS 84 are transformed into Monte Mario coordinates or vice versa the Monte Mario coordinates are transformed into WGS 84. There is no way around it.

This step should be understood clearly. This is a very different situation with respect to the one seen before when we set the CRS that was not specified in *sf* objects. That was simply an operation of writing the value of a metadata inside the *sf* files, we did not touch the coordinates values. Here, instead, we need to *transform coordinate values from one CRS to another*, it is a completely different matter. We need a *coordinates transformation function*:

`st_transform()`. For simplicity, we choose to transform coordinates of the map with the borderline (object *ven_map*) from WGS 84 to Monte Mario, which has CRS code 3004.

```
ve_map.crs <- ven_map %>% st_transform(3004)
```

If we look at the details of object *ve_map.crs*, we recognize that there is one feature because we have extracted just Venice, the geometry is created through polygons and now the CRS is Monte Mario with bounding box coordinates values expressed according to that CRS.

```
Simple feature collection with 1 feature and 18 fields
Geometry type: MULTIPOLYGON
Dimension:     XY
Bounding box:  xmin: 2298936 ymin: 5012153
               xmax: 2332383 ymax: 5050100
Projected CRS: Monte Mario / Italy zone 2
```

Now we can stack these layers, including the map, one on top of the other. Figure 19.16 is realized by overlaying the map, the streets layer, and the canals layer.

```
ggplot() +
  geom_sf(data= ve_map.crs, fill= "ghostwhite") +
  geom_sf(data= steets.crs, color= "gray", lwd=0.1) +
  geom_sf(data= canals.crs, fill= "lightblue") +
  theme_void()
```

The produced map is informative and clearly readable. This first example could be extended in many possible ways, as many as the combinations of stacks of layers allow for. Through our *sf* objects, we can add the marine coastline, bridges, the waterways, the green areas, and the terrain, but many others are available through Venice's cartography.

We make use of another feature of function `coord_sf()` that permits us to define the coordinates of our area of interest, which we can crop from an *sf* object. We focus on the part of Venice that most visitors know better, the historical insular part with ancient palaces, bridges, and iconic canals. We use attributes `xlim` and `ylim` acting the same way as the *bounding box*, meaning the left-bottom and the right-top points of the diagonal of the rectangle of the area of interest. There is

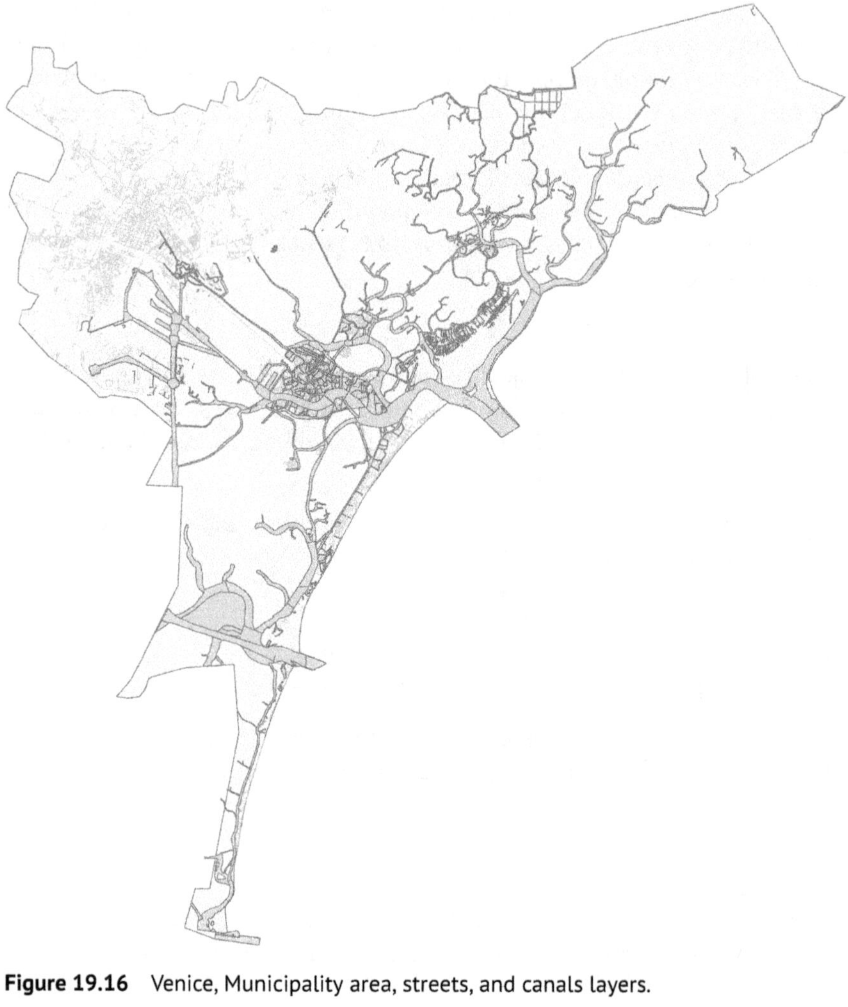

Figure 19.16 Venice, Municipality area, streets, and canals layers.

an additional complication in this example: coordinate values are expressed with Monte Mario CRS, not the common longitude North and latitude East degrees. A couple of steps are needed:

STEP 1. First, we figure out the coordinates for the two points, *xmin, ymin,* and *xmax, ymax*, in the familiar longitude and latitude degrees. We can easily find them by looking at online maps that provide for geographical coordinates of selected locations; otherwise, we can use the map from the GeoJSON file, which is expressed in WGS 84 coordinates, by cropping it with function *coord_sf()* until the desired area is produced.

Figure 19.17 Venice, historical insular part, map with overlaid layers.

STEP 2. Once we have established the coordinates in usual longitude and latitude degrees, they should be converted into the Monte Mario CRS, for example through an online service like https://epsg.io/transform#s_srs=4326&t_srs=3004&x=NaN&y=NaN, where the transformation is set by specifying CRS 4326 for the source and CRS 3004 for the result. This way we can crop all our *sf* objects and overlay them again. It is a little effort for a result that is definitely worthwhile because now Venice appears in its iconic and unmistakable shape (Figure 19.17).

```
ggplot() +
  geom_sf(data=ve_map.crs, fill= "ghostwhite") +
  geom_sf(data=canals.crs, fill= "skyblue2") +
  geom_sf(data=waterways.crs, color= "skyblue2") +
  geom_sf(data=sea.crs, color= "skyblue4") +
  geom_sf(data=bridges.crs, fill= "tomato3") +
  geom_sf(data=streets.crs, color= "gray", lwd=0.1) +

  coord_sf(default_crs = sf::st_crs(3004),
           xlim = c(2308690,2316697),
           ylim = c(5030945,5036255)) +
  theme_void() -> plot2
```

19.7.1 Tiled Web Maps

When geographic data are visualized, it is typical to use a base map, in the previous example we use the simplest one, with just the borderline and the area filled with a color. Many others exist, of different types and visual appearances, from realistic maps of the terrain to political or street maps, with many variations, some particularly original and eye-catching. The use of a base map might have both informative reasons (e.g. showing roads or the orography) or aesthetic, just to obtain a better-looking final result. Typically, the role of base map is realized by so-called *Tiled Web Maps* or, for brevity, *tile maps*.

The name might sound unfamiliar, but everybody knows them: they are the base maps that we look at when we use an online map service like Google Maps, OpenStreetMap, and the like, namely those maps that offer us a zoom feature, usually controlled by a gesture on the touchpad or touchscreen, that let us place markers to set a position and other interactive features. The same tile maps are used for data visualization with the tools we are examining; there is no technical limit to their usage, there is a commercial limit, instead, because an increasing number of tile map providers has transformed the service that they were used to offer freely into a paid subscription one, the most renown example being Google Maps. With commercial providers, an *API key* is required, which is a particular code to specify for downloading the map. The way to obtain an API key depends on the legal terms of the specific commercial service. Nevertheless, a few tile map providers have kept a free option, among them *Stamen* (http://maps.stamen.com/), *OpenStreetMap* (https://wiki.openstreetmap.org/wiki/Tiles), and in a limited way *Carto* (https://carto.com/blog/getting-to-know-positron-and-dark-matter). *Google Maps* offers the possibility to use tile maps freely up to a certain monthly threshold, but even in that case it requires to obtain an API key with a formal contractual subscription. A comment that could be made to this evolution into the commercial realm, is that, on the one hand, the possibility to freely experiment with tile maps has drastically shrunk, on the other, though, this is likely a signal that an increasing professionalization and diffusion of geographic data visualization is now a fact and it is growing.

19.7.1.1 Package ggmap

With a better understanding of the context, we may now turn our attention to package *ggmap* that offers two useful functions: `get_stamenmap()` and `ggmap()`. With the first one, we access the Stamen online server for downloading free maps, while the second is used in place of the *ggplot()* function for creating the graphic. The same package once allowed for the possibility to access maps from Google Maps and OpenStreetMap, but not any longer.

Note

Citation: D. Kahle and H. Wickham. ggmap: Spatial Visualization with ggplot2. The R Journal, 5(1), 144–161. URL http://journal.r-project.org/archive/2013-1/kahle-wickham.pdf

Let us consider a basic example. We can specify the geographic area (variable *mapbound*) in WGS 84 coordinates and with that we download a map among those available from Stamen. Here, we see the example of Venice base map with the two main types of Stamen tile maps: *Terrain* and *Toner*. The second one could be obtained with the following code by replacing `maptype='toner'`. To visualize them, we use `ggmap()`. The difference in the visual effect is evident from Figure 19.18a and Figure 19.18b.

```
library(ggmap)

mapBound <- c(left=12.30, bottom=45.40, right=12.40, top=45.45)
basemap <- get_stamenmap(bbox= mapBound, zoom=13,
                         messaging= FALSE, maptype= 'terrain')
ggmap(basemap) + theme_void()
```

Stamen's free tile maps are not much informative, they serve aesthetic purposes only, as base for other stacked informative layers placed on top of them. A comment on package *ggmap* is that it offers good functionalities but, unfortunately, it suffers from the lack of support of Google Map and OpenStreetMap. It is worth a mention and a try, anyway.

19.7.1.2 Package Leaflet

The R package *leaflet* is technically a *wrapper*, meaning an interface that makes it possible to access functionalities of a different software module, that is the JavaScript library *leaflet.js*, widely adopted for interactive web maps (https://leafletjs.com/) in websites, even very popular ones.

Leaflet has many features, which make it a complete tool for the visualization of interactive geographic maps, not just a library with some useful functions. Therefore, Leaflet is for sure a solution to consider very seriously. A more detailed overview of Leaflet's functionalities will be presented in the final Python's chapter, however, all examples, shown here for R, are fully replicable in Python too, just by adapting the code, with the specific functions being by all means identical because in both environments, R and Python, what is used is a wrapper to the same JavaScript library.

We see a simple example. The function for creating a *leaflet* object is `leaflet()`, which by default downloads tile maps from *OpenStreetMap*.

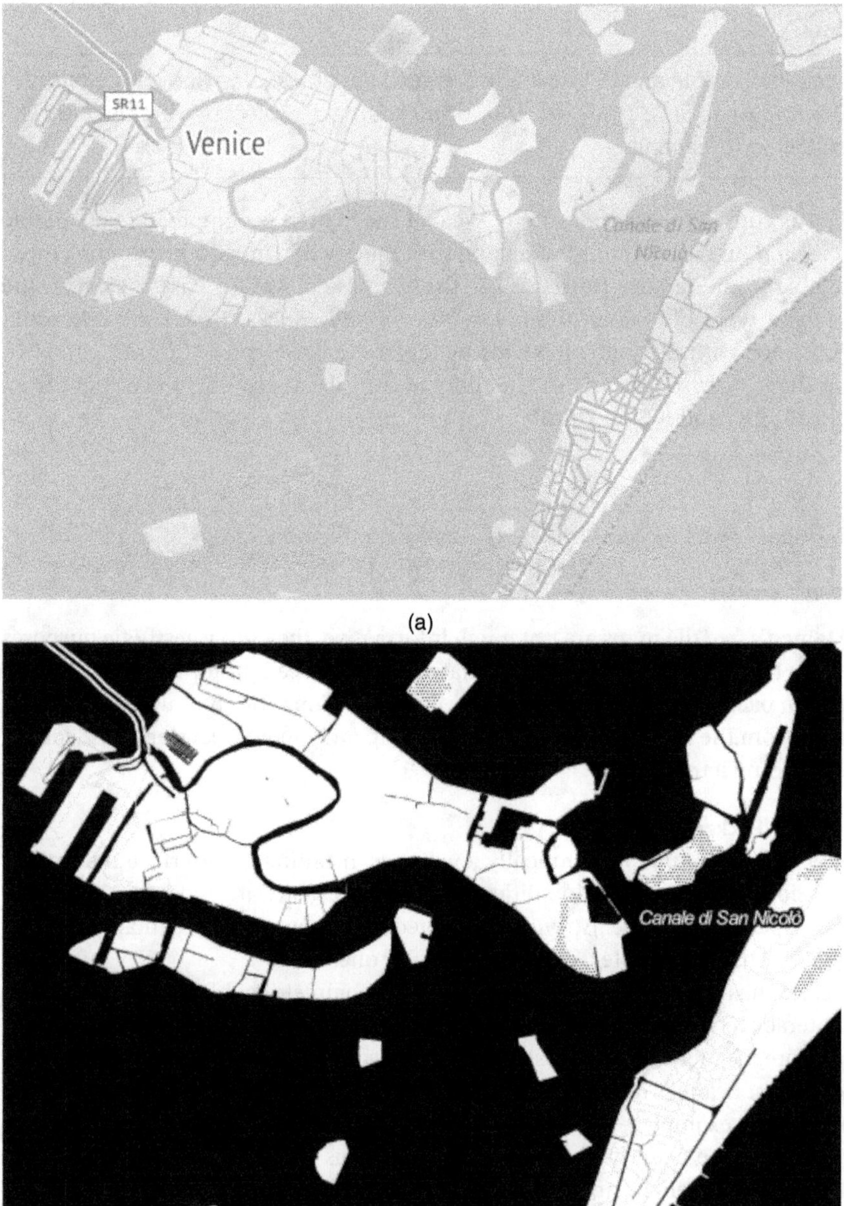

(a)

(b)

Figure 19.18 (a/b) Venice, ggmap, Stamen Terrain, and Toner tiled web maps.

The logic is similar to ggplot, compliant to the *grammar of graphics.* With function `addTiles()`, the first layer made by the tile map is created as the *leaflet* object. Next, we could specify a certain area, otherwise the world map is the default. With function `fitBounds()`, we can define the coordinates of a specific area, i.e., the bonding box, with attributes `lng1`, `lat1` and `lng2`, `lat2` expressed in WSG 84 coordinates as latitude North and longitude East. Finally, in this simple example, we specify the coordinates for the center of the map with function `setView()` (i.e., the ones used correspond to Venice's Ponte di Rialto, transl. the Rialto Bridge) with the zoom level set with attribute `zoom`.

```
library(leaflet)

mapL <- leaflet() %>%
  addTiles() %>%
  fitBounds(lng1= 12.30, lat1= 45.40,
            lng2= 12.40, lat2= 45.45) %>%
  setView(12.3359,45.4380, zoom=14)
mapL
```

The result is a map by OpenStreetMap with more informative content than Stamen maps, which not just serve the purpose of an aesthetically pleasant base map but even alone could provide useful information to the observer. On top of this base map, other graphical elements, such as position markers and dynamic tooltips, could be added. Leaflet offers the zoom feature that lets observing a map in great detail and excellent quality, as Figure 19.19a and Figure 19.19b show.

Other tiled web maps are available, although the actual availability depends on the particular selected area (http://leaflet-extras.github.io/leaflet-providers/preview/index.html). To use them, package *leaflet.providers is required.* In the example, we add Stamen's *Toner* map, Carto's *Positron* map, and ESRI's *WorldImaginery* map. Figure 19.20a, Figure 19.20b, and Figure 19.20c show the corresponding base maps.

```
library(leaflet.providers)

mapL %>% addProviderTiles(providers$Stamen.Toner) -> plot1
mapL %>% addProviderTiles(providers$CartoDB.Positron) -> plot2
mapL %>% addProviderTiles(providers$Esri.WorldImagery) -> plot3
```

19.7.2 Tiled Web Maps and Layers of sf Objects

What we have seen so far are examples with packages ggmap and Leaflet just showing base maps, which for Leaflet could be enriched with graphical elements offered by the package. This is not sufficient, though, because we are working with topographic layers (i.e., cartographic shape files, GeoJSON datasets) for which we have

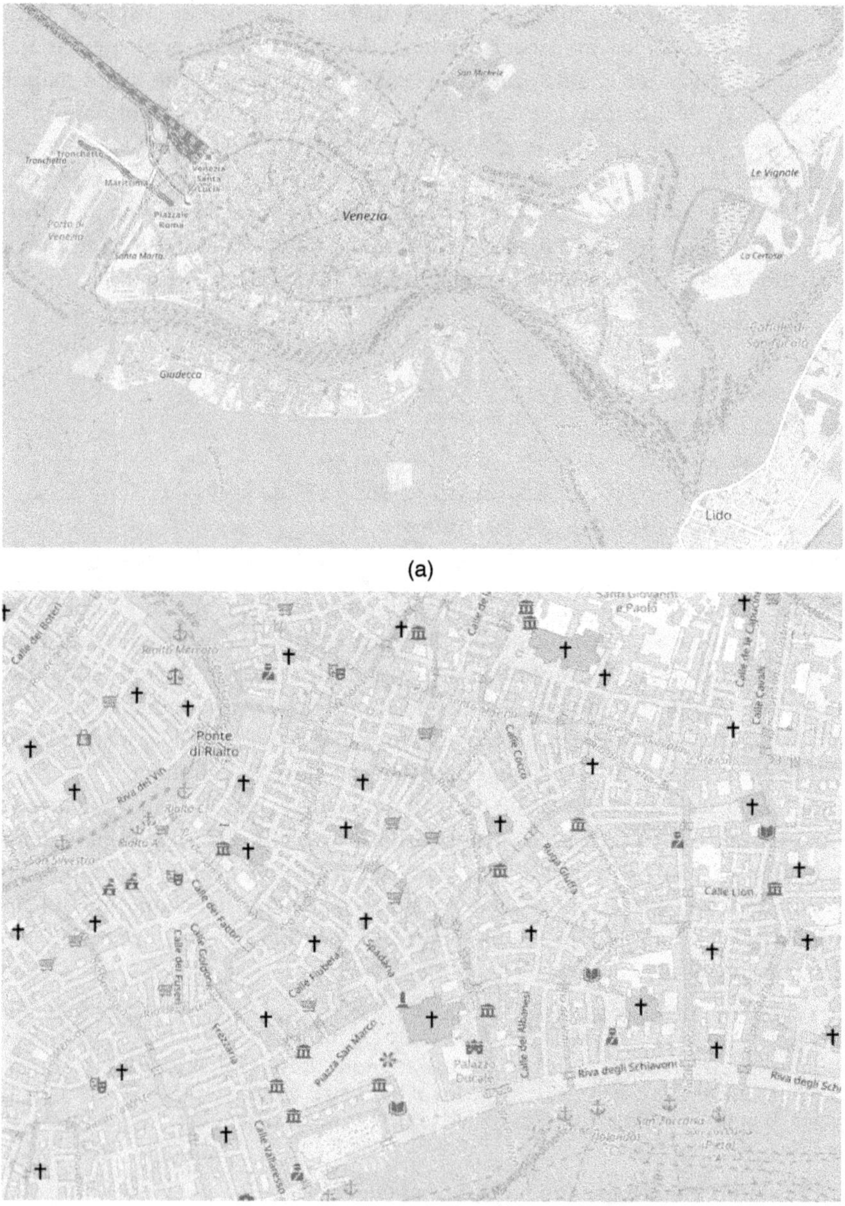

Figure 19.19 Venice, Leaflet base map from OpenStreetMap. (a) Full view. (b) Zoom in.

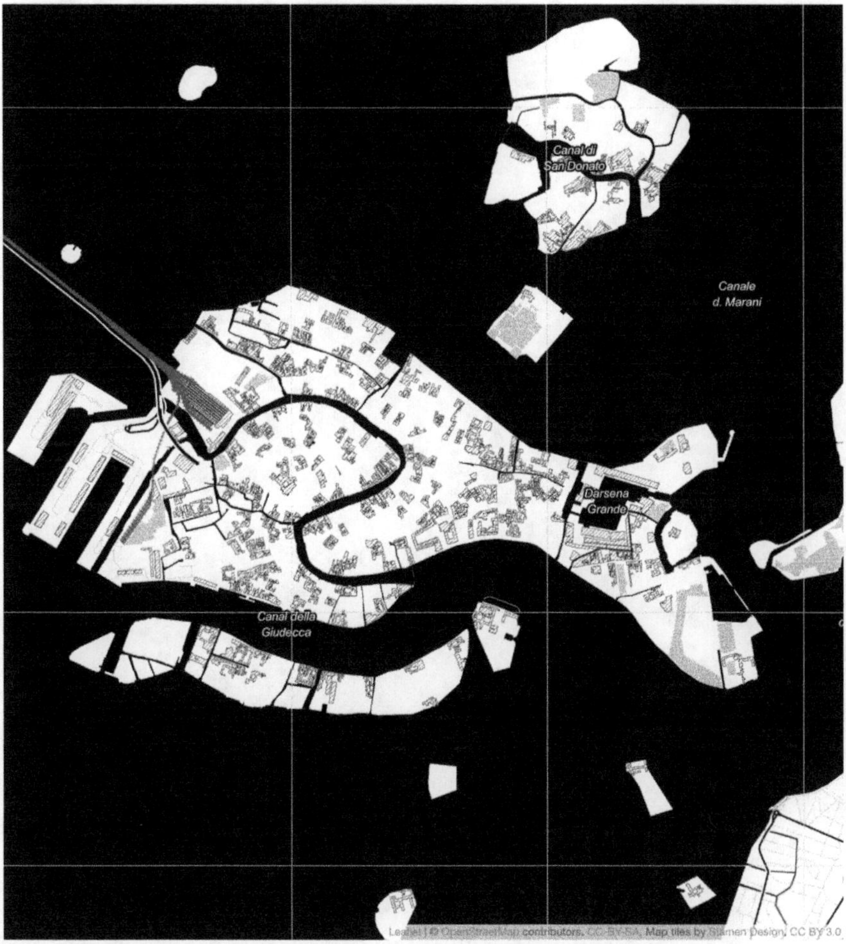

(a)

Figure 19.20 (a/b/c) Venice, Leaflet tile maps from Stamen, Carto, and ESRI.

produced the corresponding *sf* objects and we want to add them to the base map. Let us see how to do that.

19.7.2.1 Tiled Web Maps with ggmap

This case would not create any particular problem if it were not for the complication represented by coordinate systems having different CRSs, as for our case study. Examples available in the documentation are typically presented with the assumption that all layers have same CRS (usually WGS 84), which removes any obstacle. However, reality is always more complicated than didactic examples and,

(b)

Figure 19.20 (*Continued*)

as the adage says, the devil hides in the details. Having layers with different CRSs (i.e., WGS 84 and Monte Mario), we have two main options:

- To convert all coordinates of *sf* objects (i.e., the cartographic layers) defined for the Monte Mario CRS into WGS 84 coordinates, the ones of the base map.
- To convert base map coordinates from WGS 84 to Monte Mario CRS.

Both options have pros and cons, let us start with the first one.

OPTION 1: from Monte Mario to WGS 84 CRS. The main *disadvantage* of this option is that we have several *sf* objects to convert in order to match the

(c)

Figure 19.20 (*Continued*)

coordinates of the single base map object, but the *advantage* is that it is an easy operation to execute. The following excerpt of code shows the repeated coordinate transformations of *sf* objects. Here, we also include the green areas layer, then we use `ggmap(basemap)`, similar to what we would have done with a common ggplot graphics.

```
canals.4326 <- canals.crs %>% st_transform(4326)
streets.4326 <- streets.crs %>% st_transform(4326)
green.4326 <- green.crs %>% st_transform(4326)
bridges.4326 <- bridges.crs %>% st_transform(4326)
```

```
waterways.4326 <- waterways.crs %>% st_transform(4326)
civicNo.4326 <- civicNo.crs %>% st_transform(4326)

ggmap(basemap) +
  geom_sf(data= canals.4326, fill= "skyblue2",
          inherit.aes= FALSE) +
  geom_sf(data= streets.4326, color= "gray", lwd=0.1,
          inherit.aes= FALSE) +
  geom_sf(data= waterways.4326, color= "skyblue2",
          inherit.aes= FALSE) +
  geom_sf(data= bridges.4326, fill= "tomato3",
          inherit.aes= FALSE) +
  geom_sf(data= green.4326, size=0.05, alpha=0.01,
          color= "forestgreen", inherit.aes= FALSE) +
  geom_sf(data= civicNo.4326, color= "darkred",
          inherit.aes= FALSE) +
  coord_sf(default_crs= sf::st_crs(4326),
           xlim= c(12.30,12.40),
           ylim= c(45.40,45.45)) +
  theme_void()
```

OPTION 2: from WGS 84 to Monte Mario CRS. The obvious *advantage* of this solution is that we have just one object whose coordinates should be converted. The *disadvantage* is that the conversion of base map coordinates into a different CRS, for a base map produced with ggmap's `get_stamenmap()`, is not an easy task because the object produced is not of *sf* data type, meaning an R data frame, but a *ggmap* object of type *raster*, namely a *bitmap*, like for example PNG or JPG images. Delving into the details of *raster* images is out of the scope of this book, but we forward the reader to the excellent R package *terra* and its documentation.

For our aims, what we should know is that a standard transformation with function `st_transform()` does not work. In order to perform it correctly there are empirical solutions, though, which work fairly well but are not well-documented, so spending some effort will be necessary. For our case, we choose a solution that proved effective and was proposed by the community, in particular by user *andyteucher* with a post of 2018 (https://stackoverflow.com/questions/47749078/how-to-put-a-geom-sf-produced-map-on-top-of-a-ggmap-produced-raster/50844502#50844502). The idea is to implement a custom function (*ggmap_bbox*) that cleverly manipulates the format of the ggmap object in order to make it compatible with the format expected by package *sf* function `st_transform()`. The following code shows this custom function with the original comments of user *andyteucher*, simply adapted to our case study for converting coordinates from WGS 84 (CRS 4326) to Monte Mario (CRS 3004). As with all custom solutions, it should be chosen only if a standard one of at least equal quality is lacking, but nevertheless it does its job honestly.

```
ggmap_bbox <- function(map) {
  if (!inherits(map, "ggmap")) stop("map must be a ggmap object")

# Extract the bounding box (in lat/lon) from the ggmap
# to a numeric vector, and set the names to
# what sf::st_bbox expects:

  map_bbox <- setNames(unlist(attr(map, "bb")),
                       c("ymin", "xmin", "ymax", "xmax"))

# Convert the bbox to an sf polygon, transform it to 3004,
# and convert back to a bbox (convoluted, but it works)

  bbox_3004 <- st_bbox(st_transform(st_as_sfc(st_bbox(map_bbox,
                        crs = 4326)), 3004))

# Overwrite the bbox of the ggmap object with the
# transformed coordinates

  attr(map, "bb")$ll.lat <- bbox_3004["ymin"]
  attr(map, "bb")$ll.lon <- bbox_3004["xmin"]
  attr(map, "bb")$ur.lat <- bbox_3004["ymax"]
  attr(map, "bb")$ur.lon <- bbox_3004["xmax"]
  map
}

# Use the function:

map <- ggmap_bbox(basemap)
```

With this, the *raster* base map object has been made compliant with function `st_transform()` and then the coordinates converted to the same CRS of cartographic layers, we could now visualize the resulting map. The code is the same presented for *Option 1*, except for the instruction using function `coord_sf()`.

```
ggmap(map) +
 ...
  coord_sf(default_crs = sf::st_crs(3004),
           xlim = c(2308690, 2316697),
           ylim = c(5030945, 5036255)) +
  theme_void()
```

The maps produced are identical for the two solutions, with the exception of a tiny misalignment of the base map with respect to the cartographic layers, introduced with the empirical custom solution, an error that could be corrected with a more precise tuning of parameters of the bounding box, a confirmation that empirical methods should be adopted only when standard methods are not available. Figure 19.21a and Figure 19.21b show two versions of the resulting map with different tiled web maps, OpenStreetMap in the first case and Stamen Toner in the second one, green areas are now visible.

19.7.2.2 Tiled Web Map with Leaflet

Leaflet supports a limited variety of CRSs (https://leafletjs.com/reference.html#crs) so, for our case study, it is more convenient to work with all objects in WGS 84 coordinates, therefore by transforming the cartographic layers from Monte Mario to WGS 84, in the same way seen before. With respect to a previous simple example where we just visualized a Leaflet base map, now we have to add graphical layers on top of it. For this, we have to use Leaflet functions `addPolygons()` and `addPolylines()`, respectively, to add layers with graphical objects with a geometry defined through multi-polygons or multi-lines.

We see two examples. With the first one, we replicate the layered map just produced with *ggmap*. The syntax is intuitive and the result is in HTML format, so we save it with function `save_html()` of package *htmltools*. Being an HTML object, it offers native features like the *zoom*, activated with gestures or clicking on the buttons with + and – symbols. Figure 19.22a and Figure 19.22b show two screenshots of the resulting HTML map, respectively with the Venice full map and a detail by zooming in on Ponte di Rialto (Rialto Bridge) and Piazza San Marco (St. Mark's Square). The tile map is Carto Positron.

```
mapL <- leaflet(width=800, height=800) %>%
  addTiles() %>%
  fitBounds(lng1= 12.30, lat1= 45.40,
            lng2= 12.40, lat2= 45.45) %>%
  setView(12.3359, 45.4380, zoom=14) %>%
  addProviderTiles(providers$CartoDB.Positron) %>%
  addPolygons(data= canals.4326, fill="skyblue3", weight=0.5) %>%
  addPolygons(data= streets.4326, color= "gray", weight=0.5) %>%
  addPolygons(data= bridges.4326, color="tomato", weight=1.5) %>%
  addPolygons(data= green.4326, weight = 0.5, color="forestgreen")

htmltools::save_html(mapL, "Leaflet1.html")
```

In the second example, we introduce a new interactive feature very typical of Leaflet, *dynamic popups* associated to geographic elements (in this case they are popups rather than tooltips, being required to click on the map to show them, not just hovering with the mouse). For simplicity, we use a single cartographic layer (*civicNo.4326*) with as elements the civic numbers corresponding to buildings. This layer will be used for two purposes: to represent the graphical elements on the map, as we have already seen before with other layers, but now also as *the data frame*

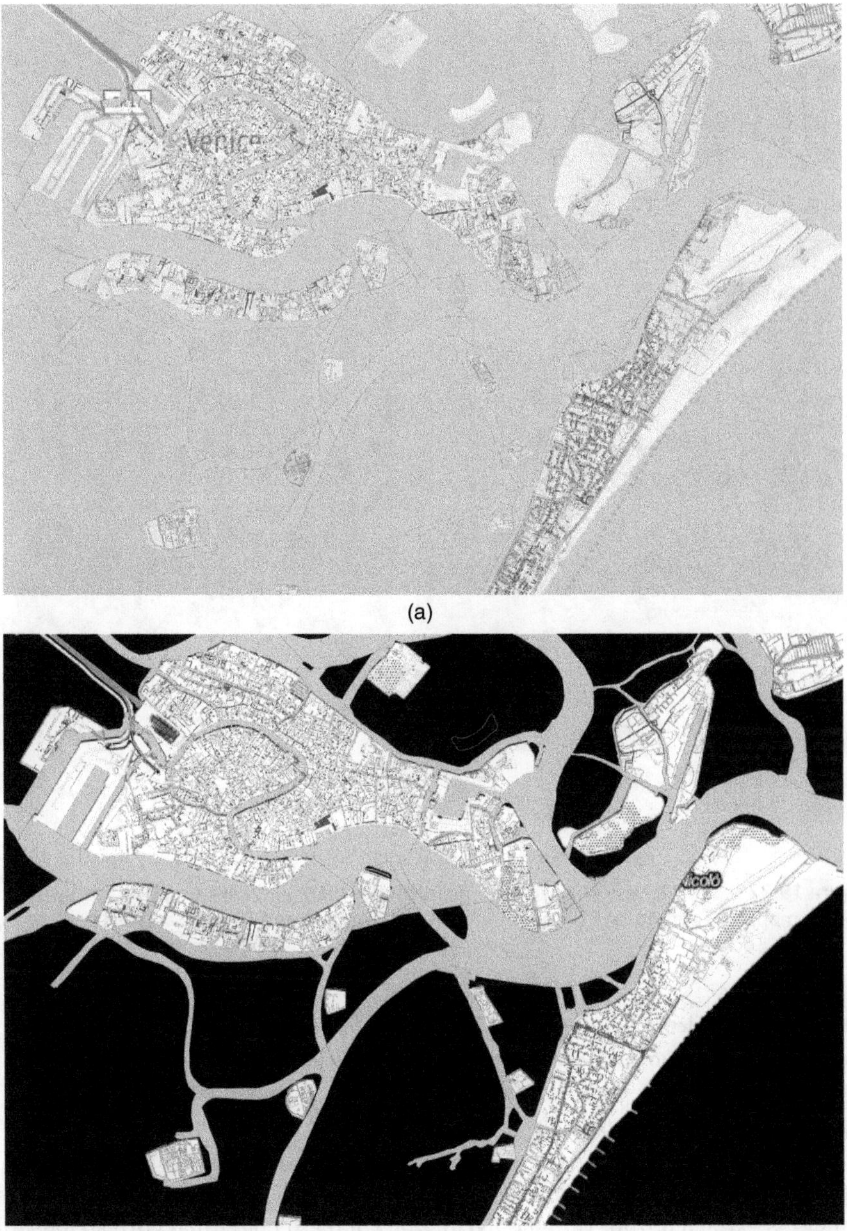

Figure 19.21 Venice, ggmap, tiled web maps with cartographic layers. (a) OpenStreetMap. (b) Stamen Toner.

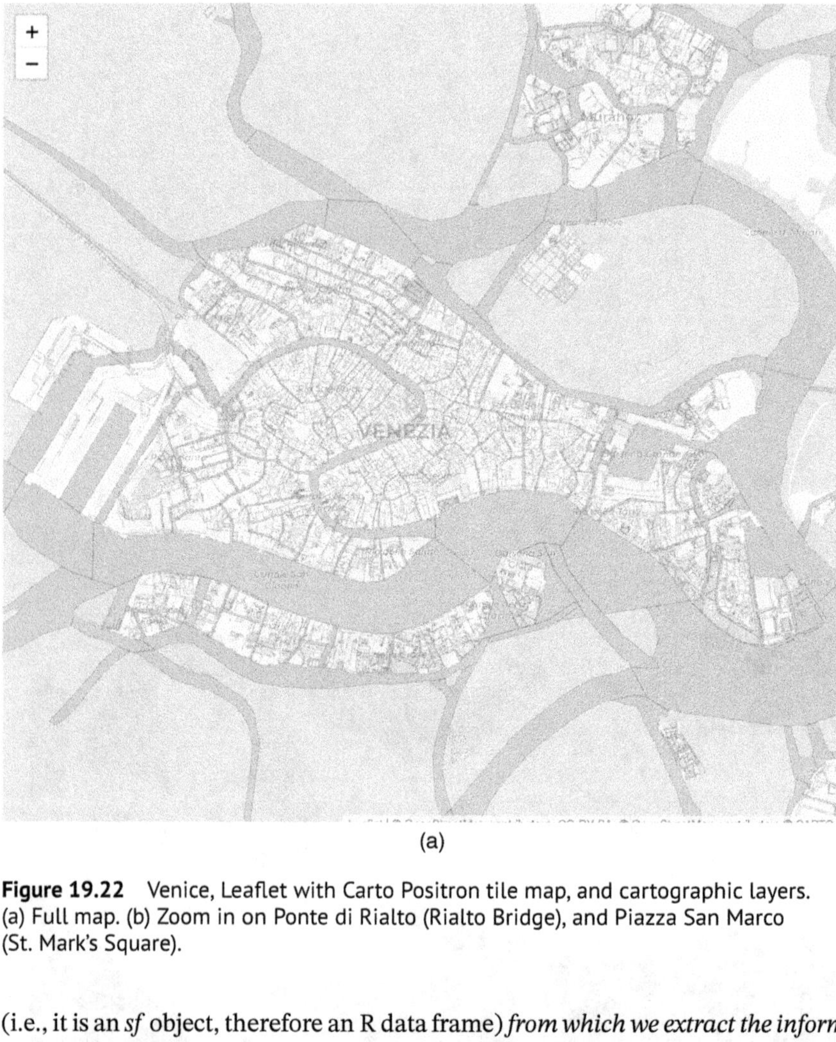

(a)

Figure 19.22 Venice, Leaflet with Carto Positron tile map, and cartographic layers. (a) Full map. (b) Zoom in on Ponte di Rialto (Rialto Bridge), and Piazza San Marco (St. Mark's Square).

(i.e., it is an *sf* object, therefore an R data frame) *from which we extract the information corresponding to each civic number that will be associated to the popups.* This way, each graphical element corresponding to a civic number will become an interactive element that, when clicked, will show the popup with information on that civic number. Technically, in the code is present the following assignment `popup= ~INDIRIZZO` ("indirizzo" means "address" in Italian), meaning that the popup content is extracted from variable *INDIRIZZO of the sf object* that corresponds to the graphical element that has been clicked. Particular attention should be paid to this peculiar syntax that makes use of the *tilde symbol* ~ to declare that *INDIRIZZO* is the name of a variable contained in the same *sf* data of the *geography* (*sf* object *civicNo.4326*), not a local variable. Figure 19.23 shows a screenshot with a popup

(b)

Figure 19.22 (*Continued*)

for St. Mark's Square, all elements shown in red in the original HTML file, or in dark gray on paper, correspond to clickable civic numbers.

```
mapL2 <- leaflet(width=800, height=800) %>%
  addTiles() %>%
  fitBounds(lng1= 12.30, lat1= 45.40,
            lng2= 12.40, lat2= 45.45) %>%
  setView(12.3359, 45.4380, zoom=14) %>%
  addProviderTiles(providers$CartoDB.Positron) %>%
  addPolygons(data= civicNo.4326,
              color= "darkred", weight=1.5,
              popup= ~INDIRIZZO)

htmltools::save_html(mapL2, "Leaflet2.html")
```

Figure 19.23 Venice, Leaflet, civic numbers with dynamic popups associated.

Aesthetically the result is still rough, but nevertheless interesting as a concept because this way we have produced a map of the city with available information, graphically represented and interactive, on all civic numbers, namely all buildings. It is quite easy to imagine a number of possible applications and variants of this basic example, either for touristic, business, or public utility purposes.

Let us see another example, this time with the cartographic layer representing pedestrian areas from *sf* object *streets.crs*, from which we omit missing values. We proceed the same way as in the previous case, with the result shown in Figure 19.24.

```
pedestrianType= c("sidewalk", "traffic island", "arcade",
          "gallery", "steps", "avenue","alley",
          "pedestrian only ", "passageway","other")
```

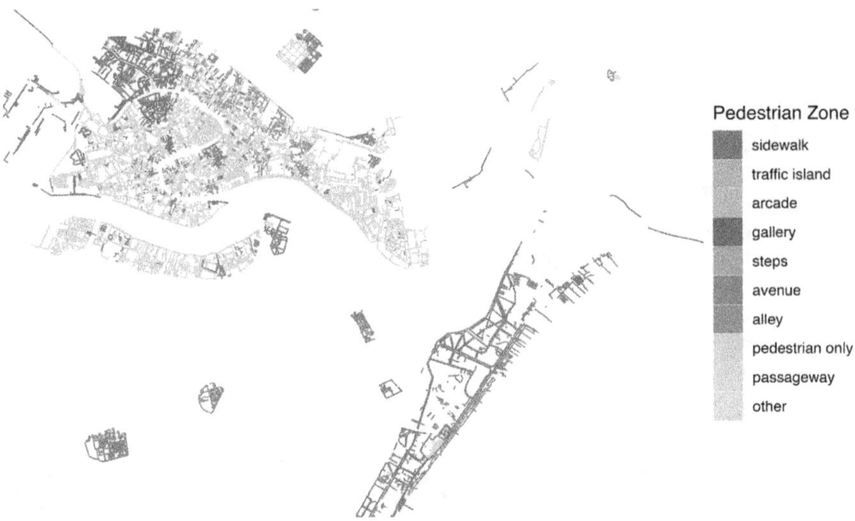

Figure 19.24 Venice, Leaflet, pedestrian areas.

```
ggplot() +
  geom_sf(data= na.omit(street.crs),
          aes(color= AC_PED_ZON,
               fill= AC_PED_ZON), lwd=0.3) +
  labs(color="Pedestrian Zone", fill="Pedestrian Zone") +
  coord_sf(default_crs= sf::st_crs(3004),
           xlim= c(2308690, 2316697),
           ylim= c(5030945, 5036255)) +
  scale_fill_tableau(palette="Color Blind",
                     labels = pedestrianType, direction = +1) +
  scale_color_tableau(palette="Color Blind",
                     labels = pedestrianType, direction = +1) +
  theme_void()
```

19.7.3 Maps with Markers and Annotations

We conclude this section by showing another typical widget of interactive maps: *markers* placed to indicate specific geographic points, in this example enriched with *annotations*. This is the kind of interactive feature for maps where Leaflet shines and is almost unbeatable, but something could be done with ggplot too, we will see both cases. We start with ggplot.

The pin marker comes from a free icon made by Freepik from www.flaticon.com and used by ggplot function `geom_image()` from package *ggimage*. Textual annotations, instead, are produced with function `geom_label_repel()` of package *ggrepel* that we have already used in a previous example. As base map, we use instead a cartographic layer from Venice Municipality and data are simply

Figure 19.25 Venice, ggplot, markers with annotations.

created with a little custom data frame of a few points of interest. The result shown in Figure 19.25 is still aesthetically simple but as a concept once again is interesting and could inspire many applications and variants.

```
library(ggimage)
icon= "./pin.png"

data= data.frame(
  name= c("Guggenheim Museum, Dorsoduro 701-704",
          "Ca d'Oro, Cannaregio 3932",
          "Ca' Foscari University, Dorsoduro 3246",
          "Cinema Palace, Lungomare Guglielmo Marconi"),
  lon= c(45.4308, 45.44065, 45.4345, 45.40579),
  lat= c(12.3315, 12.33413, 12.3264, 12.36719))

ggplot() +
  geom_sf(data= strade.4326, color= "cornsilk3", lwd=0.1) +
  coord_sf(default_crs = sf::st_crs(4326),
           xlim= c(12.30, 12.40), ylim= c(45.40, 45.45)) +
  theme_void() -> plotX2
```

```
plotX2 +
  ggrepel::geom_label_repel(data= data,
                 aes(x= lat, y= lon, label= name),
                 size=2.5, alpha=0.7, na.rm=TRUE,
                 box.padding= unit(0.75, "lines")) +
  ggimage::geom_image(data= data,
                    aes(x= lat, y= lon, image= icon),
                    size=0.05)
```

Finally, we consider the same example by using Leaflet, which will produce a result of much better quality, similar to what we are used to seeing on online maps. We use the same points of interest. Data should be converted into *sf* objects with the transformation function `st_as_sf()` and specifying the CRS. The novelty is represented by Leaflet function `addCircleMarkers()` that adds not just simple marker icons but *circular markers* that dynamically aggregate several close markers in a single visual representation when the map is zoomed out, and again disaggregate into individual markers when the map is zoomed in (attribute `clusterOptions= markerClusterOptions()`). Dynamic popup values are collected from column *name* of the *sf* object with attribute `popup= ~name`, using the particular syntax with the tilde symbol that we explained in the previous example. As tile map, this time we try one with a realistic representation like *Esri.WorldImagery*.

The larger view of Figure 19.26a shows a marker with a popup in the Venice Lido corresponding to the Cinema Palace, another one (red in the original image) corresponding to the Ca' d'Oro on the Canal Grande, an amazing historical Venetian palace, and a third, larger one (green in the original image) with number 2, meaning that it is a dynamically aggregated marker of two single markers (i.e., the Venice Guggenheim Museum and Ca' Foscari University) close to each other, which will be revealed if the map is zoomed in, as in Figure 19.26b.

```
data= data.frame( name= c("Guggenheim Dorsoduro 701-704",
        "Ca d'Oro Cannaregio 3932",
        "Univ. Ca' Foscari Dorsoduro 3246",
        "Palazzo del Cinema Lungomare Guglielmo Marconi"),
  lon= c(45.4308, 45.44065, 45.4345, 45.40579),
  lat= c(12.3315, 12.33413, 12.3264, 12.36719))

data <- data %>%
   sf::st_as_sf(coords= c("lat", "lon"), crs= 4326)

mapL <- leaflet(data, width=800, height=800) %>%
  addProviderTiles(providers$Esri.WorldImagery) %>%
  fitBounds(lng1= 12.30, lat1= 45.40,
```

```
            lng2= 12.40, lat2= 45.45) %>%
  setView(12.3359, 45.4380, zoom=14) %>%
  addCircleMarkers(popup= ~name,
                   radius=10, fillOpacity=0.7,
                   stroke= FALSE, color= 'tomato',
                   clusterOptions=markerClusterOptions())
htmltools::save_html(mapL, "./Fig19.26.html")
```

19.8 Thematic Maps with tmap

R package *tmap* (abbreviated from *thematic map,* https://r-tmap.github.io/tmap/) is a peculiar tool specific for the visualization of spatial data that has quickly gained interest and appreciation for its terrific quality. It conforms to the *grammar of graphics* and is well integrated with package *sf*, this way representing a robust alternative to the use of ggplot/ggmap for geographic maps, or *thematic maps* in tmap parlance. It is definitely worth serious consideration and practical usage in data visualization.

(a)

Figure 19.26 (a) Venice, Leaflet, aggregate circular marker and popup, full view. (b) Venice, Leaflet, disaggregate circular markers and popup, zoom in.

(b)

Figure 19.26 *(Continued)*

Note
Citation: Tennekes M (2018). "tmap: Thematic Maps in R." *Journal of Statistical Software*, **84**(6), 1–39. doi:10.18637/jss.v084.i06.

A potential obstacle to its usage is that, in the past, some installation problems on MacOS have been reported due to some incompatible dependencies, a problem not so rare both in R and Python environments. This problem is the reason of the suggestion to use it preferentially on Windows that is sometimes found online. Contrarily to these comments, the experience of this Author during the book preparation was that the installation of tmap (v. 3.3-3) and its dependencies were flawless on MacOS (Catalina v. 10.15.17), the platform used to develop all the examples. Therefore, the suggestion for MacOS users is not to be discouraged by those comments reporting problems on MacOS and instead to give a try to tmap because it is very likely that everything will be perfectly fine or that dependency problems are easily solvable, as it happens with many other packages, just by installing a different version of the dependency, a requirement that is usually stated in installation message errors.

```
library(tidyverse)
library(tmap)
library(sf)
library(sfheaders)
```

For case studies with tmap, we move from Venice to Rome, obviously another subject rich of suggestions and possibilities for practicing data visualization, also thanks to a good availability of open data. We start from the basic example, the one visualizing a simple map with polygons as the hidden elements to define planar surfaces, in this case toponymy areas of Rome. We use the GeoJSON dataset *Rome Capital – Maps of Municipalities*, which has geographic data of Rome's circumscriptions, and read it with *sf* function `read_sf()`. We obtain an *sf* object from which we can extract two data frames: one for the *neighborhoods* (Italian: *quartieri*), topographic zones typically outside the historical city center, and the second for *districts* (Italian: *rioni*), the historical subdivision of the central area.

For the visualization, the main *tmap* functions are:

- `tm_shape()`: it creates a *tmap* object. The first attribute represents data, which should be either in *sf* format (geometry) or *stars* format (a raster data type that we will not analyze); the second attribute is `name`, which is the title associated to the *legend* when the tmap plot is visualized in *view mode* (more on this in a moment); third attribute is `projection` that specifies the CRS associated to geographic coordinates, by default it assumes the CRS declared in the metadata of the *sf* object; the next attribute is `bbox` that defines the *bounding box*, meaning the size of the map; the following attributes are of lesser importance for our discussion.
- `tm_polygons()`: it draws maps with *polygons* as geometry. It has two variants: `tm_fill()` and `tm_borders()`, respectively to color the internal of each area or just the borderline with a preset color or according to the values of an associated variable (this latter case technically produces a choropleth map). Attribute `title` is the legend's title.
- `tm_layout()`: it permits to configure style options for the map, such as the tiled web map to be used as base maps, colors, margins, and legends. In this case, attribute `title` is the title of the plot.

In the following examples, we also use function `tmap_options()` that allows for the definition of global options for a *tmap* object, such as the maximum number of categories to be visualized in the legend, in order to avoid excessively long and bulky legends. We specify some of the style options, such as title, position, and size of the legend. For uniformity with the following use of Leaflet, we convert all *sf* objects with Monte Mario coordinates into WGS 84.

```
roma <- read_sf('dataset/tmap/Rome/Neighbor/
                   Roma_quartieri.geojson') %>% st_transform(4326)


# 'Quartiere' means 'Neighborhood', 'Rione' is 'District',
# 'Tipologia' is 'Type'

roma %>% filter(TIPOLOGIA == 'Quartiere') -> data1
roma %>% filter(TIPOLOGIA == 'Rione') -> data2

# NEIGHBORHOODS

tm_shape(data1) +
  tmap_options(max.categories=35) +
  tm_polygons("quartiere",
            title='Neighborhoods')+
  tm_layout(legend.position= c("right", "top"),
           title='Rome Neighborhoods',
           title.position= c('left', 'top'),
           legend.width=100)

# DISTRICTS

tm_shape(data2) +
  tmap_options(max.categories=35) +
  tm_polygons("quartiere",
            title='Districts')+
  tm_layout(legend.position= c("right", "top"),
           title='Rome Districts',
           title.position= c('left', 'top'),
           legend.width=100)
```

The result is two simple choropleth maps for Rome's neighborhoods and districts (Figure 19.27a and Figure 19.27b), useful to start familiarizing with tmap syntax.

19.8.1 Static and Interactive Visualizations

A peculiar tmap feature is to have two visualization modes: *static*, called *plot mode*, and *interactive*, called *view mode*. The first is activated by default or explicitly with directive `tmap_mode('plot')` and the second with directive `tmap_mode('view')`.

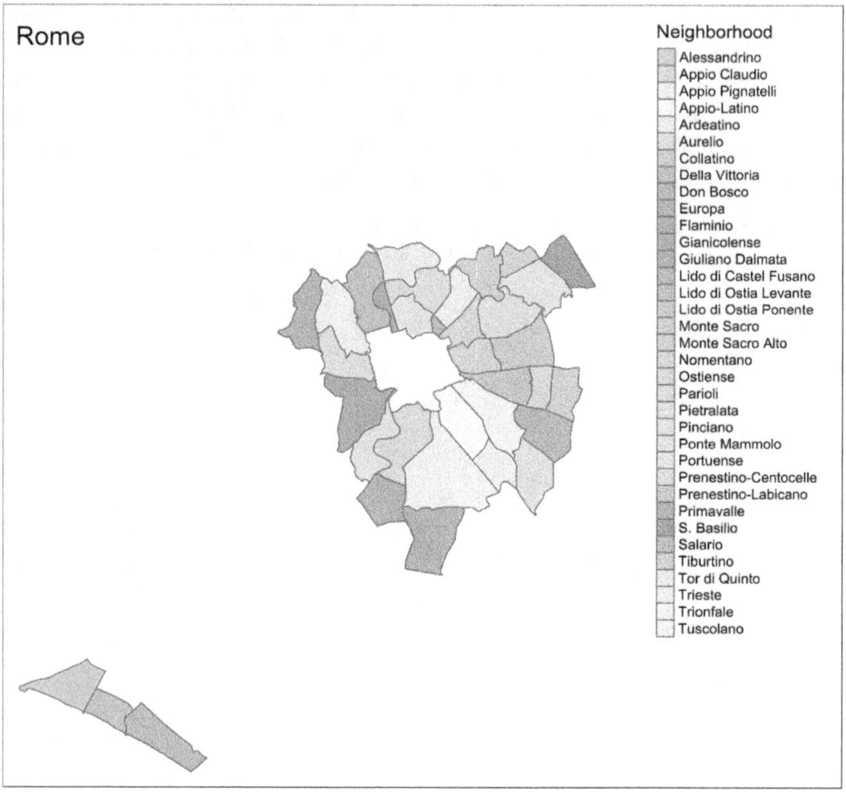

(a)

Figure 19.27 (a/b) Rome, tmap, choropleth maps of neighborhoods and districts.

The difference between the two modes is substantial: for the *plot mode* (static), a map is generated as image file and typically visualized in the RStudio tab *Plots* as customary for ggplot graphics; for the *view mode* (interactive) a map is produced as a *leaflet object*, therefore as an HTML file. The two previous choropleth maps were generated in plot mode.

We read new data in addition to toponymy areas and convert them into WGS 84 coordinates (CRS 4326):

- GeoJSON dataset of Rome's archaeological sites from the *ArcheoSITARProject* Open Data (https://www.archeositarproject.it/en/piattaforma/open-data/).
- Shape file of Rome's historical villas from the *Roma Capital* Open Data.

```
archeo <- read_sf('datasets/Rome/Archeo/Roma_SITAR.geojson') %>%
   st_transform(4326)
villas <- read_sf('datasets/Rome/Villas/Villestoriche_wgs84.shp') %>%
   st_transform(4326)
```

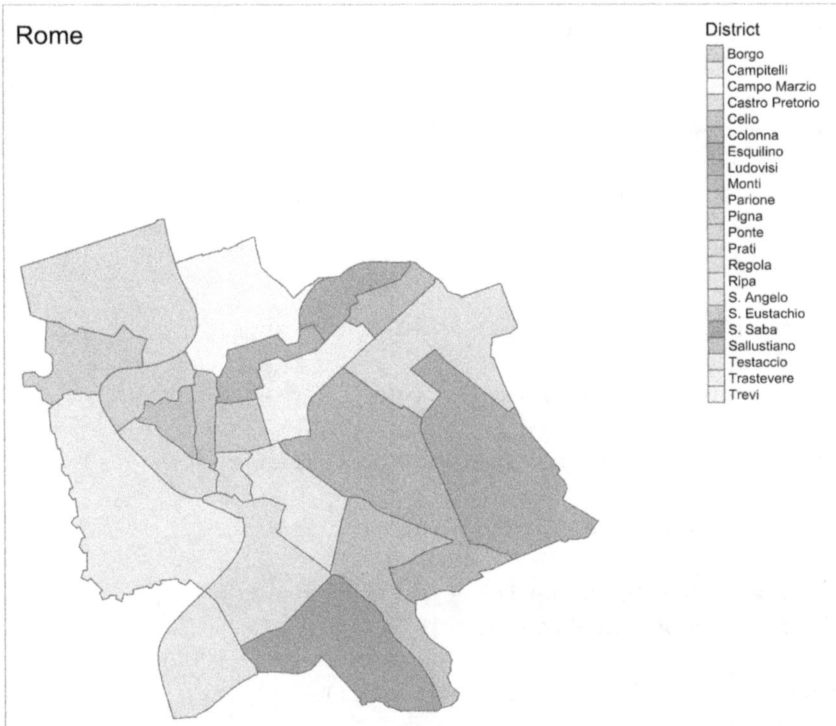

(b)

Figure 19.27 *(Continued)*

We start by considering how to *personalize the bounding box* (the solution presented is adapted from https://www.jla-data.net/eng/adjusting-bounding-box-of-a-tmap-map/). The steps are:

1. Obtain the bounding box of the current *sf* object used as data.
2. Extract bounding box's coordinates *x* and *y* from the geometry of the *sf* object.
3. Modify coordinates *xmin*, *xmax*, *ymin*, *ymax* to define the new bounding box.
4. Transform coordinates *x* and *y* into the *geometry* of the *sf* object with `bbox_new %>% st_as_sfc()`.
5. Save the new bounding box.

```
# bounding box of sf object archeo

bbox_new <- st_bbox(archeo)

# Value range for coordinates x and y
```

```
xrange <- bbox_new$xmax - bbox_new$xmin
yrange <- bbox_new$ymax - bbox_new$ymin

# Define new xmin as xmin - left

bbox_new[1] <- bbox_new[1] - (0.5 * xrange)

# Define new ymin as ymin - bottom

bbox_new[2] <- bbox_new[2] - (0.5 * yrange)

# Define new xmax as xmax - right

bbox_new[3] <- bbox_new[3] + (0.5 * xrange)

# Define new ymax as ymax - top

bbox_new[4] <- bbox_new[4] + (0.5 * yrange)
# Save the new bounding box

bbox_new <- bbox_new %>% st_as_sfc()
```

It is an empirical method, but it works well, and it is easily customizable in order to obtain the desired bounding box. Let us see an example both with the *plot* mode and the *view* mode. We specify a size by using the *sf* object *villas* as the base for the new bounding box (identical to the previous case shown in the code, only different for `bbox_new <- st_bbox(villas)`), then we omit from the data the distant neighborhoods on the marine coast just to have a more compact map and visualize. Figure 19.28a is the static map in *plot mode*, and Figure 19.28b is the HTML map in *view mode*.

```
# Select neighborhoods but omit those on the marine coast

roma %>% filter(TIPOLOGIA == 'Quartiere') %>%
  filter(quartiere != "Lido di Ostia Levante" &
         quartiere != "Lido di Ostia Ponente" &
         quartiere != "Lido di Castel Fusano") -> quart

# Uncomment one of the following two rows to have either
# the static or the interactive visualization
```

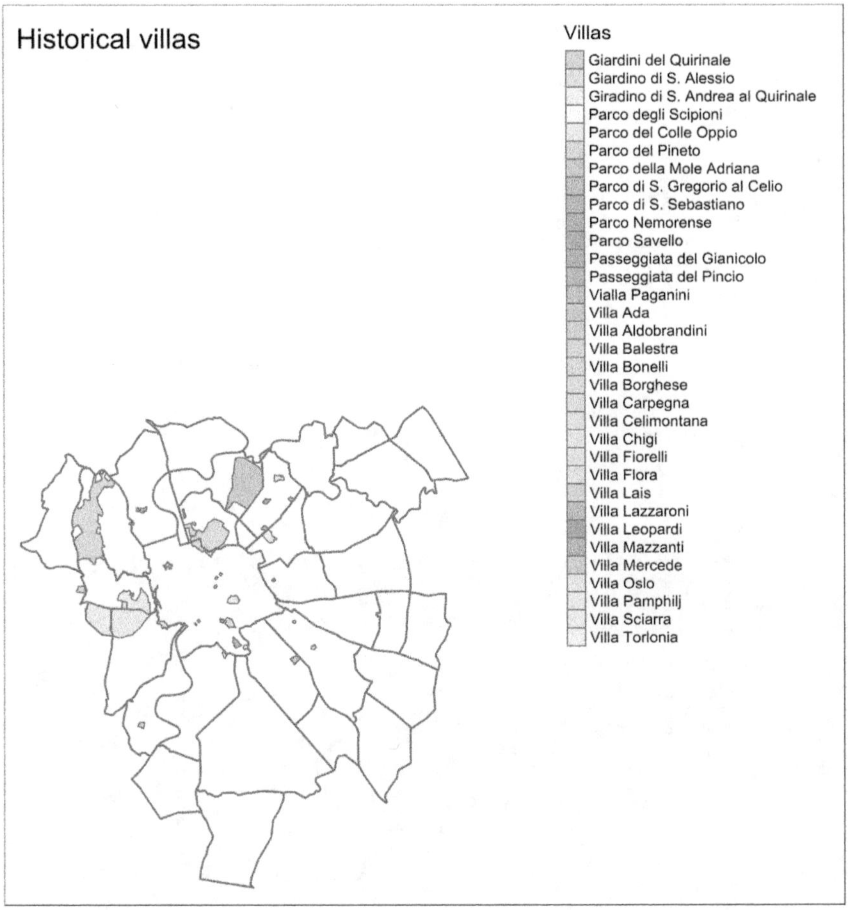

(a)

Figure 19.28 (a) Rome, tmap, historical villas, plot mode (static). (b) Rome, tmap, historical villas, view mode (interactive).

```
# tmap_mode('plot')
# tmap_mode('view')

tm_shape(quart, bbox= bbox_new) +
  tm_borders(col="gray40", lwd=1.5) +
  tm_shape(villas) +
  tm_polygons('Nome', title='Villas')+
  tm_layout(title='Historical villas')
```

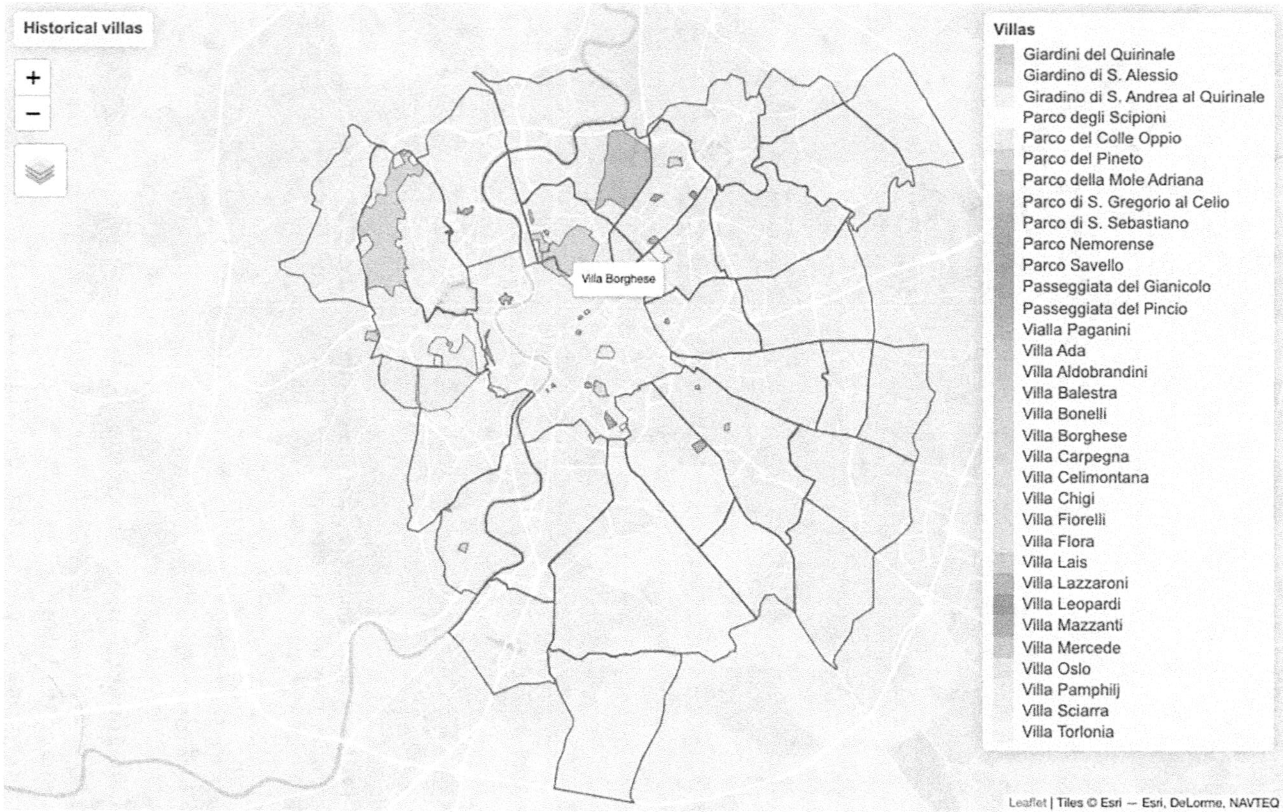

(b)

Figure 19.28 (*Continued*)

19.8.2 Cartographic Layers: Rome's Archaeological Sites

We add data about Rome's *archaeological sites* read from the cartography of the *ArcheoSITARProject*. In this case, the interactive visualization with the HTML page provided by the *view mode* has evident advantages like the zoom feature that permits to zoom in and observe details of archaeological sites and buildings. This mode has indeed a non-negligible computational load, given the fine level of details that the shape file offers. The map is produced by overlaying the archaeological layer on top of the base map of Rome's historical districts of the city center. The code presents two steps, first, the *leaflet* object *map_center* is created with the base map and then the archaeological layer is added to it. Figure 19.29a is a screenshot of the full area without setting a tiled web map, while Figure 19.29b is a second screenshot zooming in on the Colosseum area and with the default Leaflet tiled web map.

```
tmap_mode('view')

# Districts are selected

roma %>% filter(TIPOLOGIA == 'Rione') -> rioni

# New bounding box

bbox_new2 <- st_bbox(rioni)
xrange2 <- bbox_new2$xmax - bbox_new2$xmin
yrange2 <- bbox_new2$ymax - bbox_new2$ymin
bbox_new2[3] <- bbox_new2[3] + (-0.3 * xrange2)
bbox_new2[4] <- bbox_new2[4] + (-0.3 * yrange2)
bbox_new2 <- bbox_new2 %>% st_as_sfc()

# Map of the districs as base map

map_center <- tm_shape(rioni, bbox= bbox_new2) +
  tmap_options(max.categories=111) +
  tm_borders(col= "gray40", lwd=1.5)

# Map of archeologic sites overlaid to the base map

map_center +
  tm_shape(archeo) +
  tm_borders(col= "skyblue3", alpha=0.5) +
  tm_compass(position= c("left", "bottom"), size=2) +
  tm_scale_bar(position= c("left", "bottom"), width=0.15) +
  tm_layout(title= 'City center: archeological sites',
            bg.color= "ghostwhite")
```

(a)

Figure 19.29 (a) Rome, tmap view mode, city center archaeological map with ESRI tiled web map. (b) Rome, tmap view mode, zoom in on the Colosseum area with OpenStreetMap tiled web map.

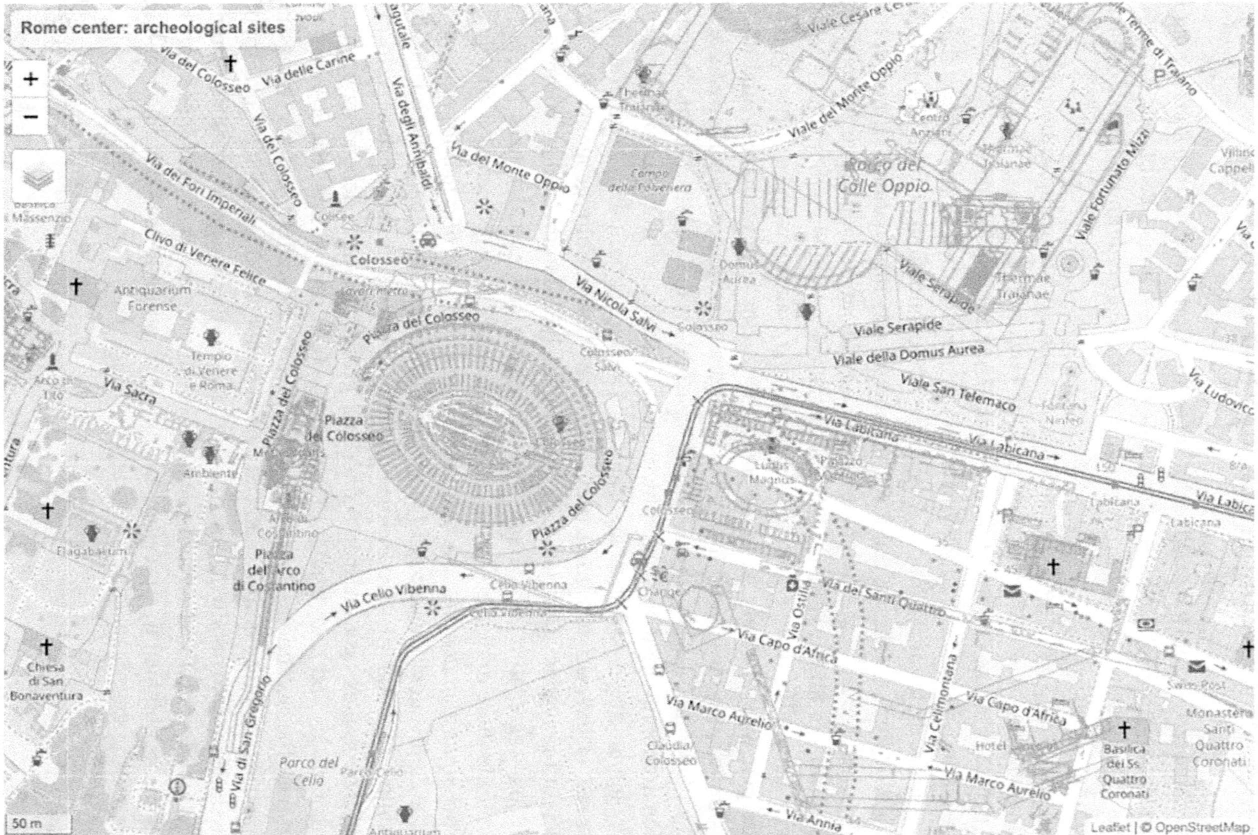

(b)

Figure 19.29 (*Continued*)

19.9 Rome's Accommodations: Intersecting Geometries with Simple Features and tmap

We change type of data to visualize as layer on the map and, still from *Roma Capital* Open Data, we collect the list of accommodations (e.g. hotels, B&Bs, and hostels). It is a CSV geodataset with also two columns for the *latitude* and *longitude* of each accommodation.

We start with a seemingly easy visualization that hides a complication that will lead us to use one of the most awesome and powerful features of the *sf* package and to discuss some important new aspects of handling spatial data.

We want to visualize a *bubble plot* with the areas of the circles proportional to the number of accommodations for each neighborhood and district. The logic is straightforward: we should count the number of accommodations defined in the CSV dataset for each area, neighborhood or district, and create the corresponding bubble plot, as simple as that. With traditional categorical data that would imply just an aggregation with common data-wrangling operations and a normal ggplot scatterplot with attribute `size` as an aesthetic. But here we have spatial data, not simple categories, and things get much more complicated because we have to deal with geometries. So, what we really have to do is to find all accommodations, which are represented by geographic points, which fall within the boundaries of each neighborhood or district area, and then we can count them. In other terms, we need *to intersect two geometries*, which in this case are geographic points and multi-polygons. That task is at a completely different level of complexity than just aggregating data frame rows based on categorical values, orders of magnitude more difficult. As a matter of fact, *intersecting geometries is one of the most computationally intensive and sophisticated features of a tool for managing spatial data*. Luckily, package *sf* again demonstrates its remarkable quality by providing function `st_intersection()`. This is a function that performs a highly complex task on spatial data and geometries and, depending on data characteristics and size, it might take a while (e.g. several minutes or more) to terminate the execution. Data have to be prepared carefully, missing values in geometries should be omitted and CRSs must be aligned. The following excerpt of code shows how to obtain the intersection between the two geometries for accommodations (points) and circumscriptions (multi-polygons), data frame *roma* is the same as obtained in a previous example by reading Rome's circumscriptions dataset.

```
# Read the geodataset of Rome's accomodations
accom <- read_sf('datasets/Rome/Accom/
               StruttureRicettiveRoma2023-02.csv')

accom$latitude %>% as.numeric() -> accom$latitude
accom$longitude %>% as.numeric() -> accom$longitude

# Omit missing values
filter(accom, !(is.na(longitude) |
                is.na(latitude))) -> accom

# Transformation into sf object
st_as_sf(accom, coords= c("longitude", "latitude"),
         crs=4326) -> accom

# Check if the two CRSs are aligned
st_crs(roma) == st_crs(accom) # TRUE

# Select just some columns for simplicity
accom %>% select(1:7) -> accom

# Geometry intersection (might take a while to complete)
intersection <- st_intersection(x= roma, y= accom)
```

With this result (object *intersection*), we can obtain the number of accommodations for each area by aggregating for column *quartiere* (i.e. neighborhood or district) and count them, the result is shown in following table. If the result looks inconspicuous that would be ill-judged because it is actually a true gem of the *sf* package.

```
# Aggregate for neighborhood/district and count the accommo-
dations
int_result <- intersection %>%
  group_by(quartiere) %>% count()

# To show the results, we convent into table and from that
# into data frame, then we sort for number of accommodations
table(intersection$quartiere) -> table1
data.frame(table1) %>% arrange(desc(Freq))
```

Quartiere	Num
Esquilino	1026
Prati	895
Monti	890
Aurelio	880
Castro Pretorio	829
Trionfale	769
Campo Marzio	681
Trastevere	639
...	...

19.9.1 Centroids and Active Geometry

We are a step closer to the bubble plot we want to produce, but there is an important detail to consider that we have not encountered before: in this case, we want to design *a single point for each area* representing the number of accommodations (actually a bubble plot circle, but it is a variant of the basic scatterplot point). Apparently easy, but what is that point? Where are its coordinates in the spatial data? Should we just pick one structure at random for each area and make a bubble circle? Definitely not a wise choice, so how do we pick a single point for each area?

This is the tricky detail that lets us analyze the important concept of *centroid*, already mentioned before, and an important extension to geometries.

First, we analyze the *sf* object *int_result* created with the aggregation from the intersection of geometries and in particular we look at its *geometry* variable/column.

```
Simple feature collection with 114 features and 3 fields
Geometry type: GEOMETRY
Dimension:     XY
Bounding box:  xmin: 12.24941 ymin: 41.69707
               xmax: 12.7894 ymax: 42.12098
Geodetic CRS:  WGS 84
# A tibble: 114 × 4
   IDquartiere quartiere n        geometry
 * <chr>       <chr>     <int>    <MULTIPOINT [°]>
 1 Q01      Flaminio   119 ((12.46649 41.93275), (12.46577 41.9317…
 2 Q02      Parioli     37 ((12.46874 41.93045), (12.46824 41.9311…
 3 Q03      Pinciano    73 ((12.48314 41.92752), (12.48203 41.9263…
 4 Q04      Salario     68 ((12.49965 41.91068), (12.49952 41.9106…
 5 Q05      Nomentano  183 ((12.50502 41.9116), (12.50509 41.91081…
 6 Q06      Tiburtino  198 ((12.51669 41.90625), (12.51975 41.8992…
```

There are 114 rows (features) that correspond to the number of Rome's toponymy areas, and the geometry is of type *MULTIPOINT*, corresponding to the list of coordinates of all accommodations, which are represented by geographic points, for each area.

As a first try, we may think to use *sf* object *int_result* as data for tmap function `tm_shape()` and column *n* as value for the tmap function for bubble plots `tm_bubble()`.

```
tmap_mode("plot")

tm_shape(roma) +
  tm_polygons(col="ghostwhite", lwd=1.0)
  tm_shape(int_result) +
  tm_bubbles(size= 'n', col= "red") +
  tm_layout(frame= FALSE,
            legend.width=0.3,
            legend.position= c('right','bottom'),
            )
```

The result of Figure 19.30 might look nice at first sight, we see little bubbles on the map, but unfortunately it is plain wrong. Pay close attention to what the picture is showing. It is not showing what we were expecting, bubbles are spread all over the areas, and there is no single bubble for each area representing the number of accommodations in there. In this image, bubbles spread over an area correspond to all accommodations and are resized proportionally to the total number of accommodations in that area. This is not what a bubble plot is supposed to look like, this is a mess.

What was the problem? The problem is subtle, and it is that the geometry of *sf* object *int_result* is not the one we need because there is no single representative point for each area in there, instead for each area there is a list of many points, as many as the accommodations in the area. We need *a second geometry with just one representative point for each area*. That point is the *centroid*. The steps we should take are the following ones:

1. Calculate the centroid for each topographic area.
2. Create a second geometry with the centroids only.
3. Reconfigure the *sf* object *int_result* so that the second geometry is used for the map visualization.

Given these steps, two *sf* functions are needed: `sf_centroid()` that calculates the centroid for a geometry, and `sf_geometry()` that permits to reconfigure the geometry in use, which takes the name of *active geometry*. We call *centroid* the new column for the second geometry with centroids.

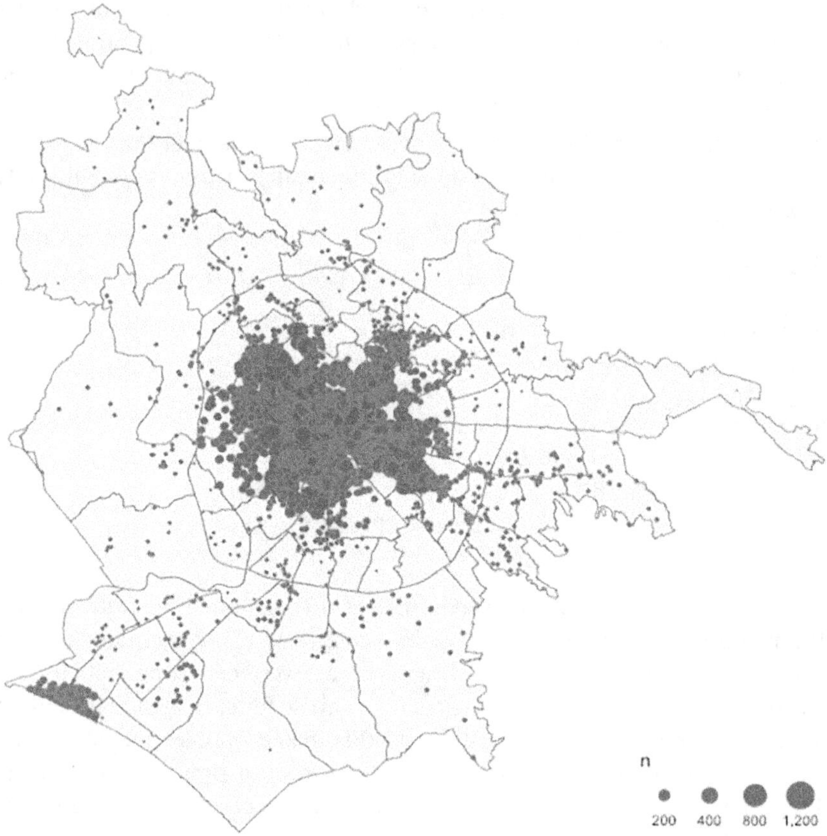

Figure 19.30 Rome, accommodations for topographic area, wrong bubble plot.

```
# We make a copy because the original will be necessary
# in following examples
int_result1= int_result

# The column centroid is created with coordinates of
# centroids for each area
int_result1 %>%
  st_centroid() %>%
  st_geometry() -> int_result1$centroid
```

We look again at the *sf* object, now *int_result1*.

```
Simple feature collection with 114 features and 3 fields
Active geometry column: geometry
Geometry type: GEOMETRY
```

```
Dimension:      XY
Bounding box:   xmin: 12.24941 ymin: 41.69707
                xmax: 12.7894 ymax: 42.12098
Geodetic CRS:   WGS 84
# A tibble: 114 × 5
   quarti…¹ n geometry centroid
 * <chr>     <int> <MULTIPOINT [°]>      <POINT [°]>
 1 Flaminio  119 ((12.46649 41.93275), (1…   (12.46949 41.92139)
 2 Parioli    37 ((12.46874 41.93045), (1…   (12.4853 41.92825)
 3 Pinciano   73 ((12.48314 41.92752), (1…   (12.48585 41.91942)
 4 Salario    68 ((12.49965 41.91068), (1…   (12.501 41.91323)
 5 Nomenta…  183 ((12.50502 41.9116),   (12… (12.51926 41.9123)
```

Two important things happened. The first is that now we have two geometries, respectively for columns *geometry* and *centroid*, the first is of type *MULTIPOINT* being a list of point coordinates, and the second is just *POINT* having the coordinates of a single point for each area. The presence of multiple geometries is not common, but it is not anomalous, a spatial data frame could have more than one geometry for a number of valid reasons.

The second important novelty is that among the initial information, there is a new line (the second one), which reads: *Active geometry column: geometry*, meaning that *an sf object could have multiple geometries, but only one will be active, hence used for visualizations or other operations based on a geometry.*

We have made a step further toward the solution of our problem and the correct bubble plot. Now we know how to pick the single representative point for each area, which is that whose coordinates are written in the *centroid* geometry of the *sf* object.

Here is the final step. We know that just one geometry could be active, and it is column *geometry*, not *centroid*; we should change it. For this, function `st_geometry()` helps again, and it is easy, we just need to instruct it that the new active geometry should be column *centroid*. The following excerpt of code shows the *centroid* column turned into the active geometry and the corresponding metainformation in the *sf* object confirms the change,

```
# Column centroid is set as the new active geometry
st_geometry(int_result1) <- "centroid"

# Checking the sf object confirms the change
int_result1

Simple feature collection with 114 features and 3 fields
Active geometry column: centroid
Geometry type: POINT
…
```

With column *centroid* as the active geometry, the problem is solved, and we can create the bubble plot as we did before. We set the view mode to zoom in on the resulting map and also add the dynamic popup widget.

```
# Column relocation in first position to have
# the neighborhood;s name as the popup title
relocate(roma, quartiere) -> roma
relocate(int_result, quartiere) -> int_result

tmap_mode("view")
tm_shape(roma) +
  tm_polygons(col ="ghostwhite", lwd = 1.0,
              popup.vars=c( "Neighborhood: "="quartiere",
              "Perimeter: "="PERIMETRO", "Area: "="AREA",
              "Neighborhood/Zone: "="TIPOLOGIA")) -> map_roma

map_roma +
  tm_shape(int_result1) +
  tm_bubbles(size = 'n', scale= 0.5, col = "red",
             popup.vars=c("Neighboorhood: "="quartiere",
                          "No. accommodations: "="n")) +
  tm_layout(frame = FALSE,
            title= 'Accommodations',
            title.position = c('center', 'top'),
            ) -> tmap2
tmap2
```

Finally, we have a correct bubble plot, which looks nice and informative. Figure 19.31a and Figure 19.31b show two screenshots of the correct result with the bubbles centered on the centroids of each area. Popups are of two types: one is associated to the topographic areas and shows information about the neighborhood/district (see Figure 19.31a), and the other to bubbles (see Figure 19.31b) showing the name of the area and the number of accommodations.

19.9.2 Quantiles and Custom Legend

In this example, we return to choropleth maps and want to create one by defining categories. The number of accommodations for each area is a continuous variable, the standard method to produce categories from it is to define value ranges, with ranges acting as a categorical variable. Here we chose to divide in *quantiles* the distribution of values, and more specifically we define *deciles*. Therefore, we will have ten ranges of number of accommodations, and each topographic area will fall in one of those ten ranges. The choropleth map is created based on those ten ranges.

Let us consider the steps:

1. Use again the original *sf* object *int_result*, the one with the single geometry, centroids are not useful for this example.

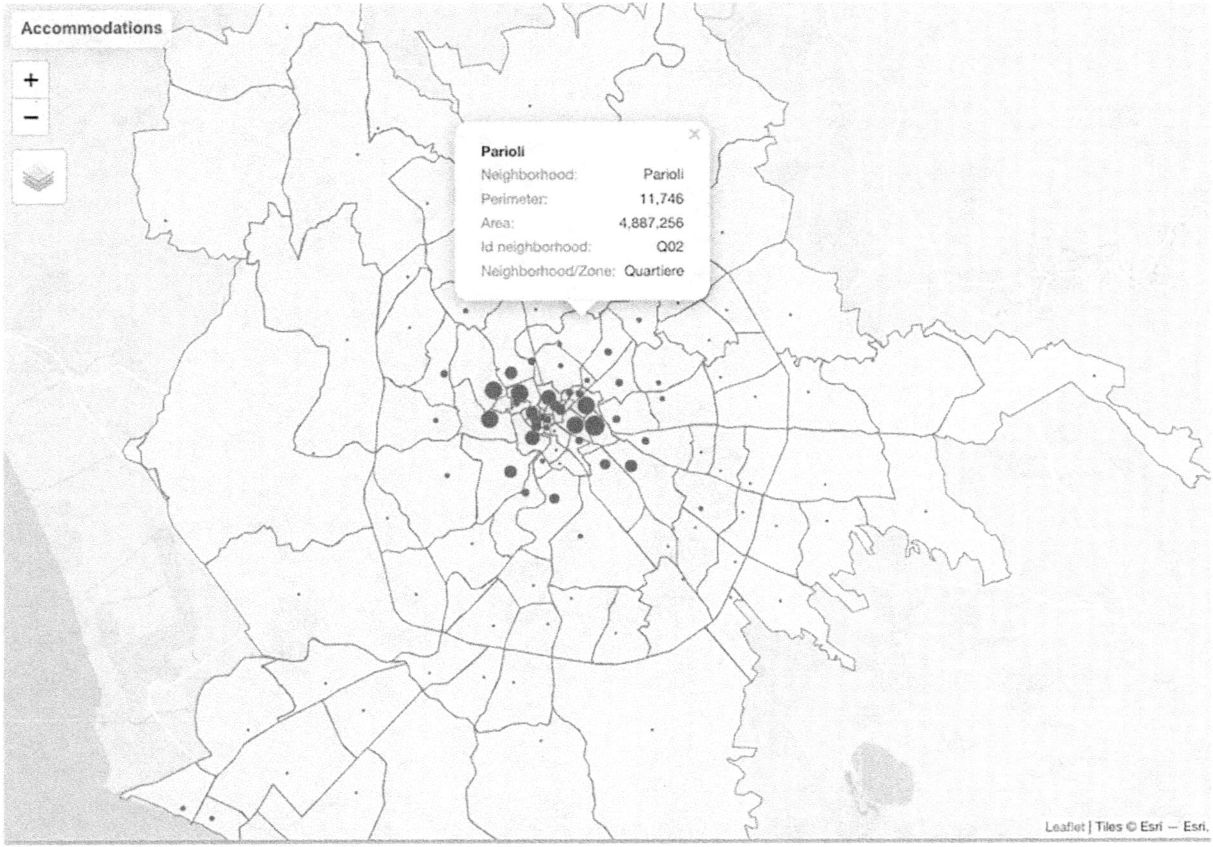

(a)

Figure 19.31 (a) Rome, tmap, full map with bubbles centered on centroids and popups associated to topographic areas. (b) Rome, tmap, detail zooming in with popups associated to bubbles.

(b)

Figure 19.31 (*Continued*)

2. Create the deciles of the distribution with respect to column *n* having the number of accommodations for each area. Function `ntile()` of package *dplyr* included in *tidyverse* does the calculation, it divides in quantiles, to have deciles we specify that they should be 10. As usual for similar functions, the quantiles are automatically calculated trying to have a similar number of items for each one. The new column *decile* in *int_result* will have the index of the corresponding decile for each area.
3. Join the two *sf* objects, it is a *spatial join* so we use function `st_join()`, the map of topographic areas, and *int_result*, in order to have more information regarding the areas.

With these steps, everything would be ready for a visualization, but we want to add a complication to practice with legends and possible tiny details of the final result. What we want to achieve is a legend that for each range specifies a text citing the extremes of the range, such as "from 1 to 4," "from 4 to 10," and so on. Some data-wrangling operations are required to obtain such configuration of the legend because we need to create another new column with the textual labels that correspond to the decile of the area. The logic is as follows:

1. Sort and group areas for decile and, for each group, extract the first and the last row, which corresponds to the minimum and maximum value for that decile.
2. Transform from *sf* object to traditional R *data frame* with `sfheaders::sf_to_df(data, fill = TRUE)`, otherwise some operations cannot be executed.
3. Omit missing values and select only the necessary columns, the decile index, and minimum and maximum values.
4. Create the textual labels for the legend and save the data frame (*cat2*).

With this small data frame with decile index and textual labels for the legend, we can modify the data frame by adding a new column *CAT* with the textual labels, then with another new column *dec2* defined as *factor* type (i.e. categorical) we set factor *levels* corresponding to decile indexes and factor *labels* as the legend labels. It is somewhat tricky, but it is a useful data-wrangling exercise in order to tune that little detail of the legend.

```
# Divide into deciles and execute spatial join
int_result$decile <- ntile(int_result$n, 10)
st_join(roma, int_result, left= TRUE) -> roma_bb

# Ranges of values corresponding to deciles
roma_bb %>% arrange(desc(n)) %>% group_by(decile) %>%
  filter( rank(n, ties.method='first')<2 |
          rank(desc(n), ties.method='first')<2 ) %>%
  sfheaders::sf_to_df(fill= TRUE) %>% select(n,decile) %>%
  distinct(.) %>% filter(!is.na(decile)) %>%
  arrange(decile, n) -> categories
```

```
len1= length(categories$n)

# Create labels for the legend
for (i in seq(1, len1, by= 2)) {
  categories$CAT[i]= paste('from', categories$n[i],
                           'to', categories$n[i+1])
  categories$CAT[i+1]= paste('from', categories$n[i],
                             'to', categories$n[i+1]) }

# Create the data frame with decile indexes and textual labels
rows <- nrow(categories)
odd_rows <- seq_len(rows) %% 2
cat2 <- categories[odd_rows == 1, ] %>% as_tibble()

# Create new column CAT in the data frame with
# textual labels for the legend

roma_bb %>% mutate(CAT= case_when(
    decile == 1 ~ cat2$CAT[1],
    decile == 2 ~ cat2$CAT[2],
    decile == 3 ~ cat2$CAT[3],
    decile == 4 ~ cat2$CAT[4],
    decile == 5 ~ cat2$CAT[5],
    decile == 6 ~ cat2$CAT[6],
    decile == 7 ~ cat2$CAT[7],
    decile == 8 ~ cat2$CAT[8],
    decile == 9 ~ cat2$CAT[9],
    decile == 10 ~ cat2$CAT[10],
    is.na(decile) ~ 'none'
  )) -> roma_bb

# Factorize new column dec2 with levels from decile indexes
# and factor labels from column CAT
roma_bb %>% mutate(dec2= factor(decile, levels= cat2$decile,
                   labels= cat2$CAT, ordered= TRUE)) -> roma_bb2
```

It is ready for visualization. We use function `tm_basemap()` to add a tiled web map from *Leaflet*, here we show results with two of them, others are left commented in the following excerpt of code. Figure 19.32 shows the result.

```
# Column relocation in first position to have
# the neighborhood;s name as the popup title
relocate(roma_bb2,quartiere.x) -> roma_bb2

tmap_mode("view")
map_roma <- tm_shape(roma_bb2) +
#  tm_basemap("Stamen.TerrainBackground") +
#  tm_basemap("OpenTopoMap") +
#  tm_basemap("CartoDB.DarkMatterNoLabels") +
  tm_basemap("Stamen.TonerLite") +
  tm_polygons(col="dec2", palette='-cividis', alpha=0.6,
              colorNA=NULL, title='Accommodations',
```

Figure 19.32 Rome, tmap, quantiles, and custom legend labels.

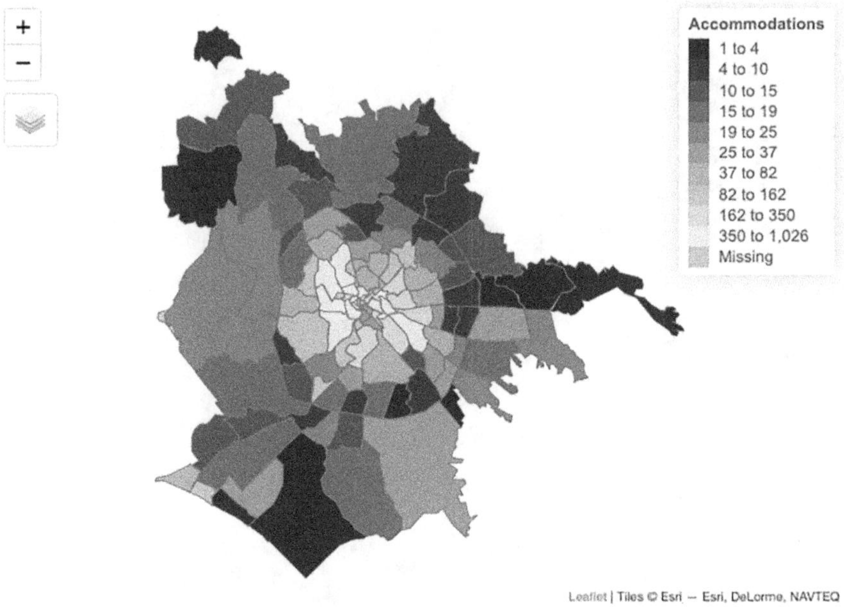

Figure 19.33 Rome, tmap, standard quantile subdivision, and legend labels.

```
             popup.vars=c( "Neighborhood: "="quartiere.x",
                          "No.accomodations: "="n",
                          "Decile: "="decile", "Range: "="dec2"))
map_roma
```

This level of complication is clearly not truly necessary. If such a specific customization of legend labels is not needed, and instead default legend labels are sufficient, then there is a much simpler alternative automatically produced with attribute `style` of function `tm_polygons()`, which takes the number of deciles and does everything on its own.

Figure 19.33 shows a screenshot of the result.

```
temp=int_result

temp$decile <- ntile(temp$n, 10)
st_join(roma, temp,
        left=TRUE) -> roma_bb

map_roma <- tm_shape(roma_bb) +
  tm_polygons(col ="n", title='Accommodations'
              style='quantile', palette='viridis',
              n=10)
map_roma
```

19.9.3 Variants with Points and Popups

We conclude the chapter with two final simple examples, which nevertheless might inspire practical opportunities to exploit the many excellent features of tmap and in general of the visualization of geographic maps.

With the first example, we use a base map of roads (*OpenTopoMap*) and enrich it by overlaying a *transparent layer* of topographic areas (attribute `alpha=0.0`) with a *dynamic popup*. This easy trick makes the tile web map, by all means, an interactive road map with contextual information from the topographic layer. The code and Figure 19.34 just present the name of the area, but it is easy to extend it with further information for the popups.

```
tmap_mode("view")

map_roma <- tm_shape(roma_bb2) +
  tm_polygons(fill=NULL, alpha=0.0, lwd=0.0,
              colorNA=NULL, title='Num. B&B',
              id="quartiere",
              popup.vars=c("Quartiere/Zona"="quartiere",
                           "Tipologia"="TIPOLOGIA")) +
  tm_shape(roma_bb2) +
  tm_borders(col='blue', lwd = 1.5, alpha=0.3) +
  tm_basemap('OpenTopoMap')
  map_roma

  tmap_Roma <- tmap_leaflet(map_roma, mode= "view",
                            show = TRUE) %>%
    setView(12.48, 41.89,zoom=11)
```

The final example extends map information by adding a *layer of points* with function `tm_dots()` corresponding to accommodations in Rome. The result once again is simple but possibly inspiring because it shows Rome's BnBs and hotels associated with dynamic popups. Popups are specifically configured for areas and for dots with information from the associated data frames. The following excerpt of code shows the case of bed and breakfasts visualization; the version with hotels requires simple adaptations (i.e. the initial selection for value "Hotel," the corresponding data frame in function `tm_shape()`, and the title update).

Figure 19.35a shows a screenshot of the full map with *Bed and Breakfasts*, while Figure 19.36a and Figure 19.36b show two screenshots for the *Hotels*, the full map, and a zoom in.

```
# Only Bed and Breakfasts are selected
# Column relocation to first position makes the name
# of the bed and breakfast (BnB) as the popup title
filter(struct2, tipologia=="Bed and Breakfast") %>%
        relocate(denominazione) -> BnB

tmap_mode("view")
map_roma <- tm_shape(roma_bb2) +
```

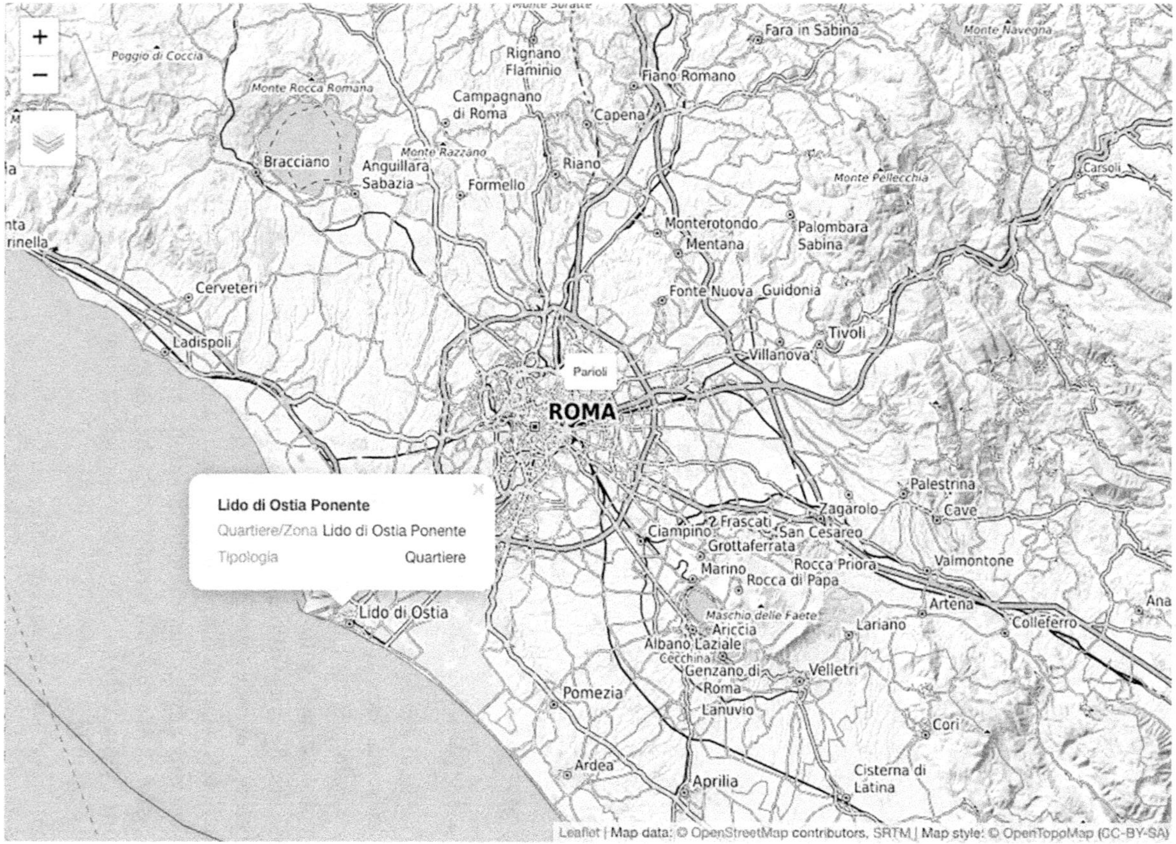

Figure 19.34 Rome region tmap, road map with dynamic popups.

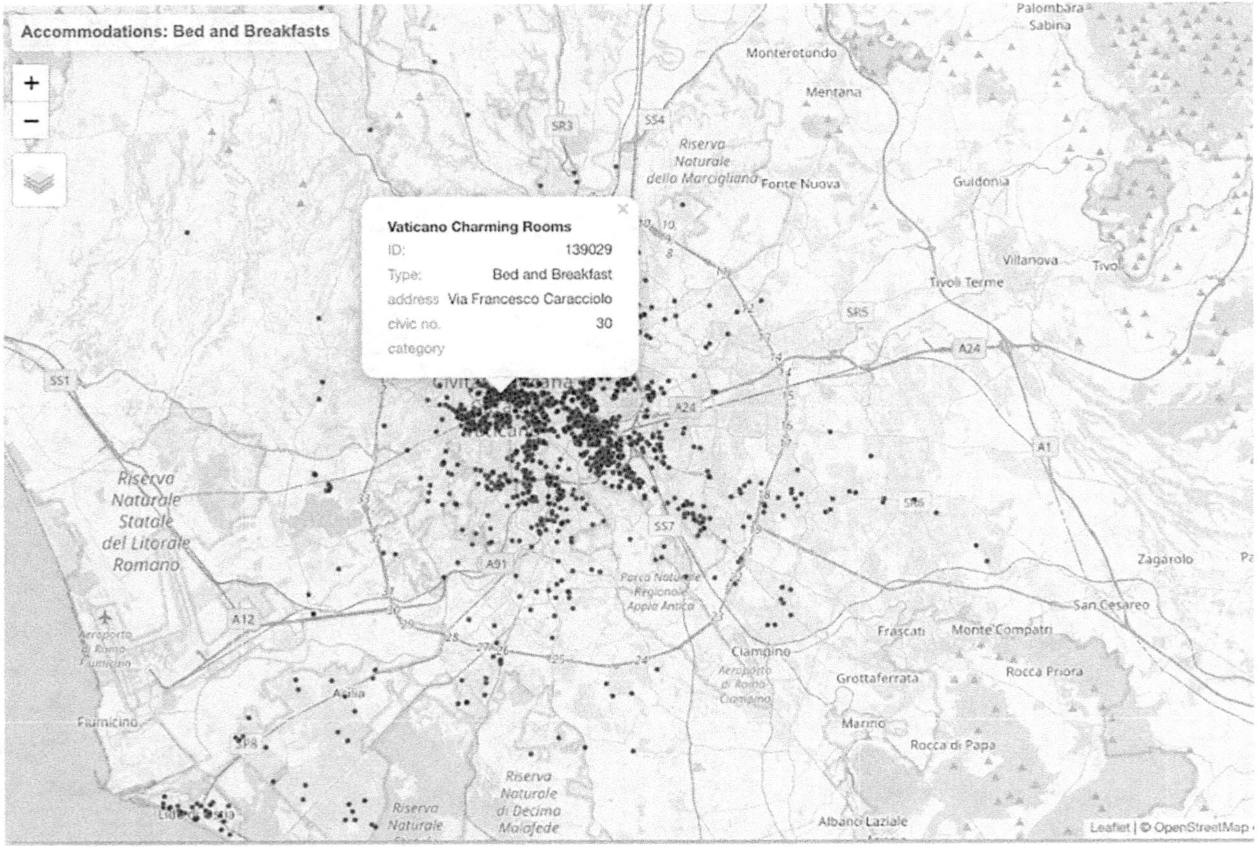

(a)

Figure 19.35 (a) Rome, tmap, Bed and Breakfasts, full map. (b) Rome, tmap, Hotels, full map. (c) Rome, tmap, Hotels, zoom in.

(b)

Figure 19.35 (*Continued*)

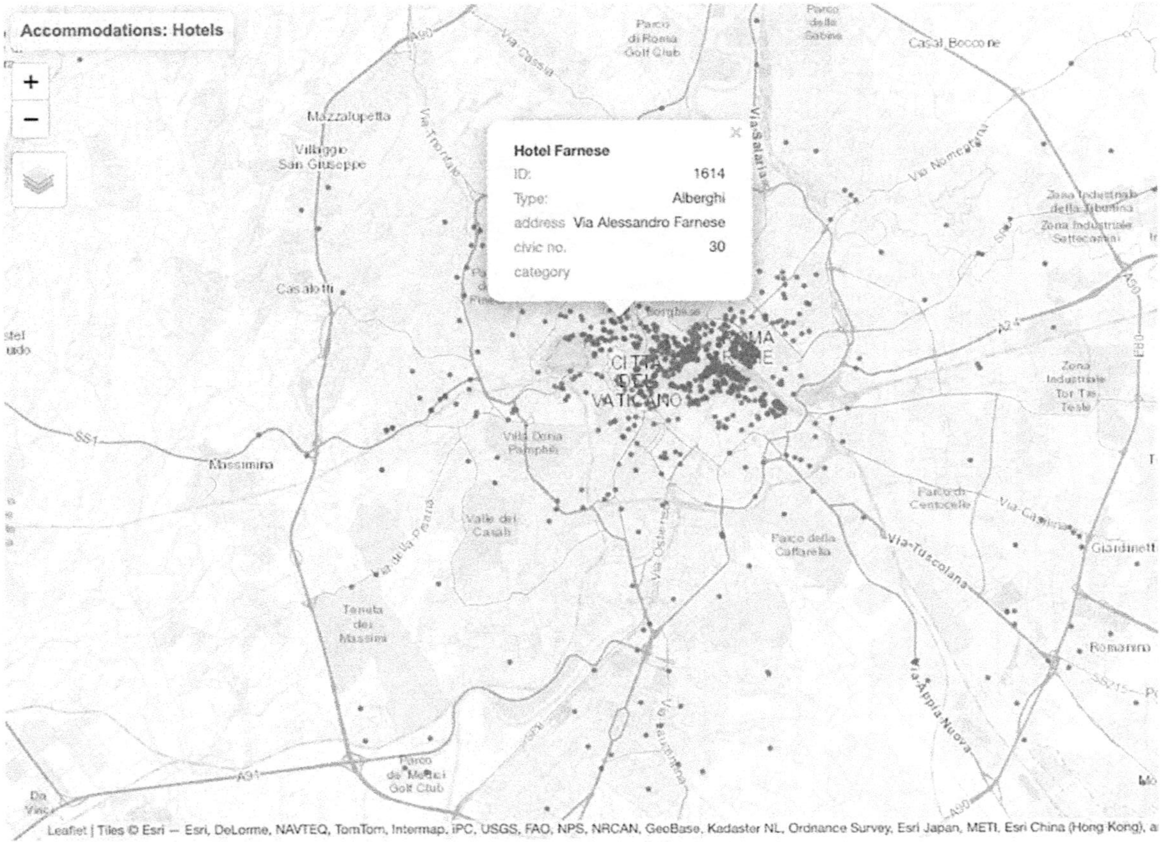

(a)

Figure 19.36 (a) Rome, tmap, hotels, full map. (b) Rome, tmap, hotels, zoom in.

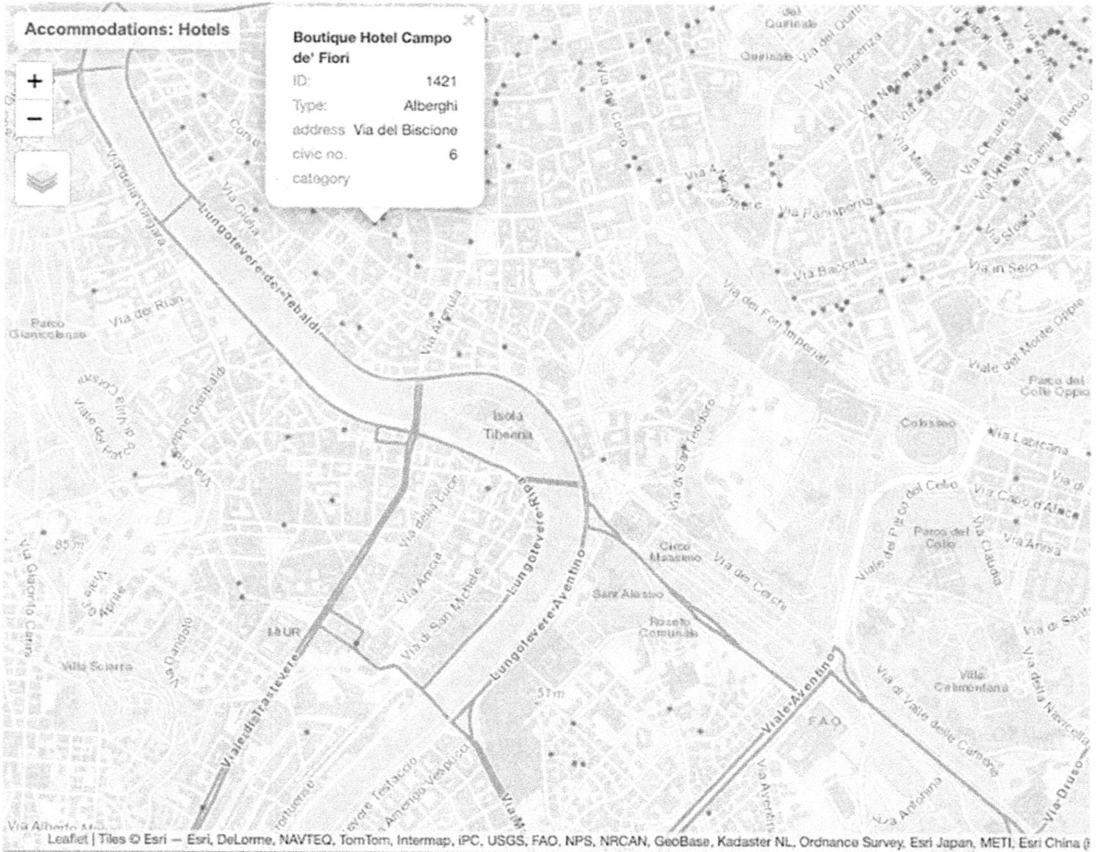

(b)

Figure 19.36 (*Continued*)

```
  tm_fill(fill= NULL, colorNA= NULL, alpha=0.0,
          interactive= FALSE,
          popup.vars=c("Neighborhood: "="quartiere.x",
          "No.accomodations: "="n")) +
  tm_shape(BnB) +

  tm_dots(size=0.02, alpha=0.8, col='darkblue',
          popup.vars=c("ID: "="id", "Type: "="tipologia",
                       "address"="via", "civic no."="civico",
                       "category"="categoria"))+
  tm_layout(frame = FALSE,
            title= 'Accommodations: Bed and Breakfasts,
            title.position = c('center', 'top')
map_roma

tmap_Roma <- tmap_leaflet(map_roma, mode= "view",
                          show= TRUE) %>%
  setView(12.48, 41.89, zoom=14)
tmap_Roma

saveWidget(tmap_Roma, file="...")
```

20

Geographic Maps with Python

Dataset/Geodataset

NYC Open Data (https://opendata.cityofnewyork.us/)

- Modified Zip Code Tabulation Areas (MODZCTA) (https://data.cityofnewyork.us/Health/Modified-Zip-Code-Tabulation-Areas-MODZCTA-/pri4-ifjk)
- *NYC Dog Licensing Dataset* (https://data.cityofnewyork.us/Health/NYC-Dog-Licensing-Dataset/nu7n-tubp)
- *NYC Parks Dog Runs* (https://data.cityofnewyork.us/Recreation/NYC-Parks-Dog-Runs/8nac-uner)
- *NYC Parks Drinking Fountains* (https://data.cityofnewyork.us/Environment/NYC-Parks-Drinking-Fountains/622h-mkfu)
- *Sea Level Rise Maps (2050s 500-year Floodplain)* (https://data.cityofnewyork.us/Environment/Sea-Level-Rise-Maps-2050s-500-year-Floodplain-/qwca-zqw3)
- *Rodent Inspection* (https://data.cityofnewyork.us/Health/Rodent-Inspection/p937-wjvj)
- *Demographic Statistics By Zip Code* (https://data.cityofnewyork.us/City-Government/Demographic-Statistics-By-Zip-Code/kku6-nxdu)
- *Subway Stations* (https://data.cityofnewyork.us/Transportation/Subway-Stations/arq3-7z49)

Copyright: Public domain (https://www.nyc.gov/home/terms-of-use.page)

20.1 New York City: Plotly

To practice with Python geographic maps, we move to New York City, another iconic city like Venice and Rome, and whose *NYC Open Data* represents one of the richest sources of available open data.

As the source for the base map, we choose the territorial division of areas into *Zip Codes*; it is a geodataset in GeoJSON format and the graphical library we will

Data Visualization in R and Python, First Edition. Marco Cremonini.

Companion website: www.wiley.com/go/Cremonini/DataVisualization1e

use is *Plotly*. The following excerpt of code is the usual list of Python libraries to import and the general *load* operation to access the dataset's content.

```
import numpy as np
import pandas as pd
import matplotlib.pyplot as plt
from PIL import Image
import plotly.express as px
import plotly.graph_objects as go
import json

nycgeo= json.load(open('datasets/NYC_opendata/
          Nyc-zip-code-tabulation-areas-polygons.geojson'))
```

The data type resulting from accessing the GeoJSON dataset is of type *dictionary* (*dict* for short), which is the correct data type for Plotly visualizations. We can observe its structure with command `nycgeo.keys()`. It has two keys, *type* and *features*; we can look at the first element of *features*.

```
nycgeo['features'][0]
{'type': 'Feature',
 'id': 0,
 'properties': {'OBJECTID': 1,
  'postalCode': '11372',
  'PO_NAME': 'Jackson Heights',
  'STATE': 'NY',
  'borough': 'Queens',
  'ST_FIPS': '36',
  'CTY_FIPS': '081',
  'BLDGpostalCode': 0,
  'Shape_Leng': 20624.6923165,
  'Shape_Area': 20163283.8744,
  '@id': 'http://nyc.pediacities.com/Resource/PostalCode/11372'},
 'geometry': {'type': 'Polygon',
  'coordinates': [[[-73.86942457284175, 40.74915687096787],
    [-73.89507143240856, 40.74646547081214],
    [-73.89618737867819, 40.74850942518086],
    ...
    [-73.87207046513889, 40.75386200705204],
    [-73.86942457284175, 40.74915687096787]]]}}
```

What we observe represents the standard data structure of GeoJSON datasets, which has the following schema:

```
features:
     |____ id:
     |____ properties:
               |____ <attributes list as key:value>
               |____ geometry:
                          |____ coordinates:
```

Now, we need the data for the first layer to overlay over the base map. We choose the dataset *Dogs Licensing* in NYC; it is a standard CSV dataset.

```
dogs= pd.read_csv('datasets/NYC_opendata/
                  NYC_Dog_Licensing_Dataset.csv')
```

	Animal Name	Animal Gender	Animal BirthYear	Breed Name	ZipCode	LicenseIssue Date
0	Paige	F	2014	American pit bull	10035.0	09/12/2014
1	Yogi	M	2010	Boxer	10465.0	09/12/2014
2	Ali	M	2014	Basenji	10013.0	09/12/2014
3	Queen	F	2013	Akita crossbreed	10013.0	09/12/2014
4	Lola	F	2009	Maltese	10028.0	09/12/2014
...	...	...	...	...	...	...

We will use values of zip codes from column *ZipCode* to associate them with the corresponding zip codes of the areas included in object *nycgeo* read from the GeoJSON dataset, which are stored in element *properties.postalCode*, nested into the *features* element. Before that, we need to prepare data frame *dogs* with some common data-wrangling operations like omitting missing values in column *ZipCode* and transform the data type. Next, we group and aggregate for zip code and count the number of dogs for zip code.

```
dogs= dogs[~dogs.ZipCode.isna()]
dogs.ZipCode= dogs.ZipCode.astype('int64')

dogs_zipcount=
  dogs.groupby(['ZipCode']).size().\
  reset_index(name='counts').\
  sort_values(by='counts', ascending=False)
dogs_zipcount
```

	ZipCode	counts
135	10025	11 439
133	10023	9 164
371	11215	8 829
134	10024	8 826
357	11201	8 757
...	...	...

	ZipCode	counts
400	11274	1
395	11242	1
1	121	1
352	11108	1
783	99508	1

20.1.1 Choropleth Maps: *plotly.express*

As mentioned in Part 3, Plotly has two distinct graphical modules, *plotly.express*, the most recent, and *plotly.graphic.object* (or *plotly go* for short). They have similar features; we will discover that in some cases related to maps (i.e. maps with overlaid layers), *plotly go* is handier. We start with an example of *choropleth map* by using *plotly.express*.

In standard configuration, function `px.choropleth()` by default makes use of the GeoJSON's element `id` to associate geographic data to those of the *pandas* data frame. You may think of it as a kind of join operation with `id` as the join key, which means that element `id` must have correct keys for the join operation. This is not the case of our GeoJSON dataset and pandas data frame because we want to join them based on zip codes, which are not contained in element `id` of the GeoJSON but in element *postalCode* nested into element *properties*. We need to explicitly state it by means of attribute `featureidkey` by specifying the path starting from key *features*, therefore *properties.postalCode*. This is the element with the join key for the GeoJSON, now we need to identify the corresponding column with join key in the pandas data frame *dogs*. We use attribute `locations` to specify column *ZipCode*. We have defined how to associate GeoJSON areas to data frame information, the final step is to state which data frame column has the values to use for the color scale of the choropleth map, in our case column *counts* with the number of licensed dogs for each zip code.

As we discussed when choropleth maps were introduced in the previous chapter, they are generally easy to create. You should take care of preparing the data, have a base map coherent with the granularity of your data, write the values for function's attributes, configure style options, and it is done. It is the same for all graphic libraries. Figure 20.1 shows the result.

```
plt.figure(figsize=(80,80))

fig= px.choropleth(dogs_zipcount, geojson= nycgeo,
                         locations= 'ZipCode', color= 'counts',
```

Figure 20.1 NYC, plotly.express, choropleth map of licensed dogs.

```
                    featureidkey= "properties.postalCode",
                    color_continuous_scale= "Viridis",
                    labels= {'counts':'Dogs Number'}
                          )
fig.update_geos(fitbounds= "locations", visible=False)
fig.update_layout(margin= {"r":0,"t":0,"l":0,"b":0},
                  width=700, height=500)
fig.show()
```

20.1.1.1 Dynamic Tooltips

We modify the data aggregation seen in the previous example to have also the dog's breed (column *BreedName*) as an information, then we count, this time the number of dogs for each breed in every zip code. Finally, we extract, for each zip code, only the breed with the highest number of dogs.

```
a1= dogs.groupby(['ZipCode','BreedName']).size().\
       reset_index(name= 'counts').\
       sort_values(by= 'counts', ascending=False)

dogs_maxbreed= a1.groupby('ZipCode').head(1)
dogs_maxbreed
```

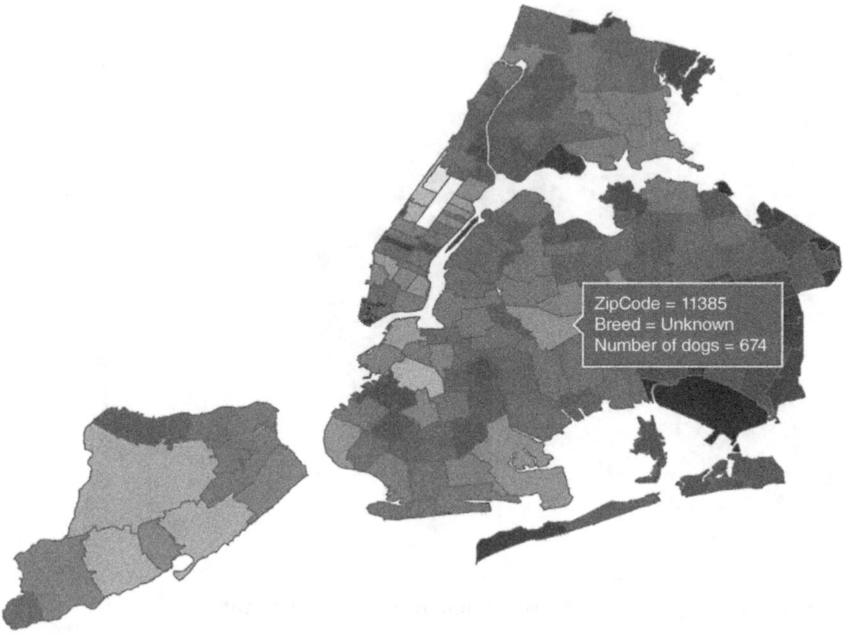

Figure 20.2 NYC, plotly.express, most popular dog breed for zip code.

	ZipCode	BreedName	counts
4 620	10025	Unknown	1 312
4 335	10024	Unknown	946
17 730	11215	Unknown	931
4 061	10023	Unknown	876
10 195	10312	Unknown	842
...	...	...	...

With these data, we could introduce the *dynamic tooltip* feature. It is provided by configuring attribute `hover_data`, assigned with the *list of data frame columns whose values will be shown in tooltips*, and attribute `label` for the *textual labels* to write in the tooltip. Figure 20.2 shows the map.

```
plt.figure(figsize=(80,80))

fig= px.choropleth(dogs_maxbreed, geojson= nycgeo,
             locations= 'ZipCode', color= 'counts',
             featureidkey= "properties.postalCode",
             color_continuous_scale= "Viridis",
```

```
               hover_data=["ZipCode","BreedName","counts"],
               labels={'BreedName':'Breed','counts':'Number of dogs'}
                          )
fig.update_geos(fitbounds= "locations", visible= False)
fig.update_layout(margin= {"r":0,"t":0,"l":0,"b":0},
                  width=1000, height=1000)
fig.show()
```

With the previous data aggregation, the breed that very often appear as the most popular for every zip code is actually the unknown breed, which, probably, is not particularly meaningful information to convey. To improve the result, we could omit dogs with unknown breed. We slightly modify the previous code.

```
dog_breeds= dogs[dogs.BreedName != "Unknown"]

a1= dog_breeds.groupby(['ZipCode','BreedName']).size().\
 reset_index(name='counts').\
 sort_values(by='counts', ascending= False)

dogs_maxbreed= a1.groupby('ZipCode').head(1)
dogs_maxbreed
```

	ZipCode	BreedName	counts
10 106	10312	Shih tzu	591
5 434	10029	Yorkshire terrier	577
10 318	10314	Shih tzu	576
4 477	10025	Labrador retriever	560
4 201	10024	Labrador retriever	459
...	...	...	...

20.1.1.2 Mapbox

With function `choropleth_mapbox()` the aesthetic quality of a choropleth map produced with *plotly.express* could be improved. With that function, we can add a *tiled web map* (attribute `mapbox_style`), a zoom level (attribute `zoom`), the coordinates to center the map (attribute `center`), and others like the transparency (attribute `opacity`) and the map size (attributes `width` and `height`). Figure 20.3 shows the result having omitted dogs with unknown breed and set some style options; the tiled web map is from OpenStreetMap.

```
fig = px.choropleth_mapbox(dogs_maxbreed, geojson= nycgeo,
                  locations= 'ZipCode', color= 'counts',
```

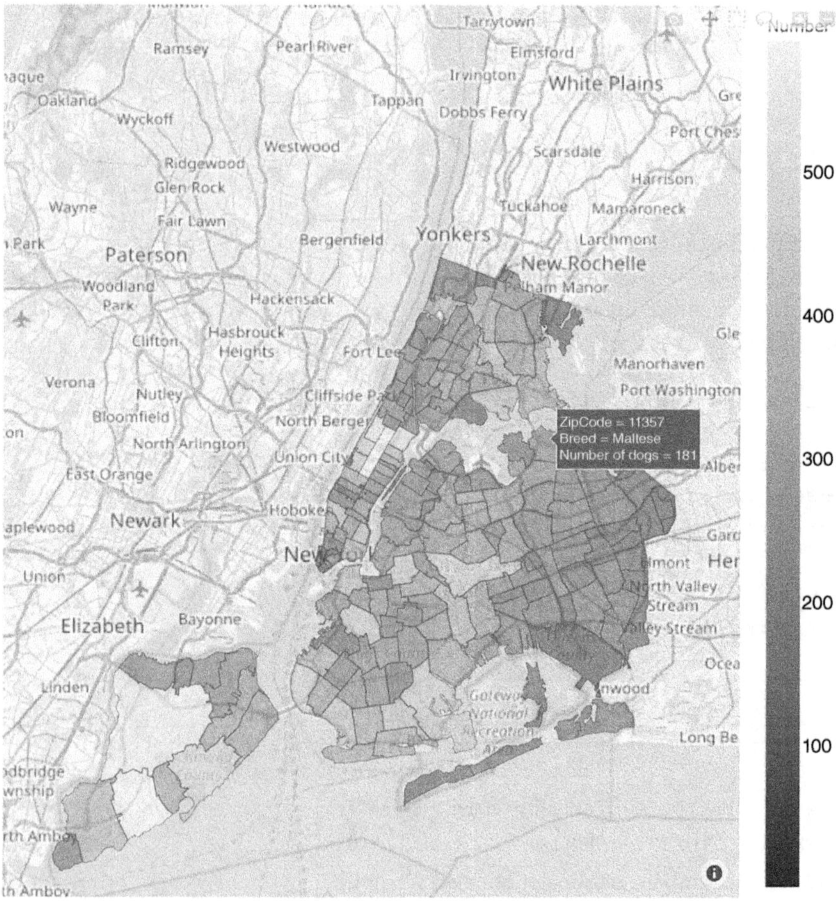

Figure 20.3 NYC, plotly.express, most popular dog breed for zip code, OpenStreetMap tile map, and style options.

```
                featureidkey= "properties.postalCode",
                color_continuous_scale= "Cividis",
                hover_data= ["ZipCode", "BreedName", "counts"],
                labels= {'BreedName':'Breed',
                         'counts':'Dogs Number'},
                mapbox_style= 'open-street-map',
                zoom=9, center= {"lat": 40.7831, "lon": -73.9712},
                opacity=0.6, width=600, height=600
                         )
fig.update_layout(margin={"r":0,"t":0,"l":0,"b":0})
fig.show()
```

20.1.2 Choropleth Maps: plotly.graph_objects (plotly go)

We now turn our attention to the second Plotly module: *plotly.graph_objects* (or *plotly go*). The logic is the same as for *plotly.express*, we should just consider some differences in syntax. The main *plotly go* function to produce a plot is `go.Figure()`, while the specific one for choropleth maps is `go.Choroplethmapbox()`, again with attributes `featureidkey` and `location` to specify the dictionary element used as join key in the GeoJSON and the corresponding data frame column; attribute `z` is for the data frame variable used for the color scale, other attributes have intuitive meaning.

We continue the example seen before and add a more detailed configuration of the dynamic tooltip with attribute `hovertext` that supports very detailed tooltip configurations. For better readability of the code, it is convenient to define a variable (*tooltip* in the following excerpt of code) assigned with the specifics of the layout, which could be composed by a combination of *text*, *columns*, and *HTML elements* (e.g., *
* and *<b>*).

```
tooltip= '<b>Zip Code: </b>'
    + dogs_maxbreed['ZipCode'].astype('str') + '<br>'
    + '<b>Breed: </b>' + dogs_maxbreed['BreedName']
    + '<br>' + '<b>Dogs Number: </b>'
    + dogs_maxbreed['counts'].astype('str')

fig= go.Figure(go.Choroplethmapbox(geojson= nycgeo,
                locations= dogs_maxbreed.ZipCode,
                z= dogs_maxbreed['counts'],
                featureidkey= "properties.postalCode",
                colorscale= "Cividis",
                zmin=0, zmax=600,
                marker_opacity=0.6, marker_line_width=1,
                hovertext= tooltip)
                )

fig.update_layout(mapbox_style= "open-street-map",
        mapbox_zoom=9,
        mapbox_center= {"lat": 40.7831, "lon": -73.9712})

fig.update_layout(margin= {"r":0,"t":0,"l":0,"b":0},
                 width=600, height=600)
fig.show()
```

The resulting map is like that of previous Figure 20.3, however, this way the tooltip content could be carefully customized; we forward the interested reader to the Plotly documentation for an overview of the many possibilities (https://plotly.com/r/hover-text-and-formatting/).

20.1.3 GeoJSON Polygon, Multipolygon, and Missing *id* Element

We want to overly a second layer to the previous map, for that we need a second geodataset from the *NYC Open Data* and choose the one of *Dog Runs Areas*.

```
dogRuns = json.load(open("datasets/NTC_opendata/
                            NYC Parks Dog Runs.geojson"))
```

Let us look at the organization of this GeoJSON, as before we are interested in key *features*.

```
dogRuns['features'][0]
{'type': 'Feature',
 'properties': {'zipcode': '10038',
  'name': 'Fishbridge Garden Dog Run',
  'system': 'M291-DOGAREA0043',
   ...
  'seating': None,
  'councildis': '1',
  'borough': 'M'},
 'geometry': {'type': 'MultiPolygon',
  'coordinates': [[[[-74.0016459156729, 40.70932680472401],
     [-74.00098833771662, 40.70879507039175],
     [-74.00099960334362, 40.70878952584789],
     ...
     [-74.00167338737218, 40.709306008827475],
     [-74.0016459156729, 40.70932680472401]]]]}}
```

It has a different structure than the previous one. First, the geometry now is *Multipolygon* instead of *Polygon*. In short, the difference is that:

- *Polygon* is a planar surface defined by an external border and possibly some internal borders (basically, the shape can have holes).
- *MultiPolygon* is defined by multiple polygons.

Second, *element* `id` *is missing*, which is not a rare case but, nevertheless, does not fully comply with the standard schema for a GeoJSON.

The missing `id` element might or might not be a problem, it depends on what the GeoJSON is used for. For example, in previous examples it would not have been a problem since for the choropleth map, we have specified a key element different than the default `id` by using attribute `featureidkey`. But in this case, the usage is different, we do not use this layer to produce the choropleth map, instead, we want to overlay it on top of the choropleth map to visualize dog runs areas, and to do this the element `id` is required by Plotly, so if it is missing, that is a problem to solve.

The solution is to add it to the GeoJSON file, *one element* `id` *with a unique value for each element of key features*. Therefore, a possible solution (the reference is the Plotly community's comment at https://community.plotly.com/t/possible-bug-plotting-multipolygons-in-scattermapbox/33479/5) is to execute two operations:

1. Go through every element of *features* key and create element `id` (i.e. `df["features"][i]["id"]`), for example with a *for-cycle*.
2. Assign a unique value of type *string* to each element `id`, which could be just the value of the *for-cycle* iterator converted into *string* type (i.e. `str(i)`).

```
for i in range(len(dogRuns["features"])):
    dogRuns["features"][i]["id"]= str(i)
```

By checking with `dogRuns['features'][0]`, we will see the new pair `'id':'0'`, and similarly for all other elements of key *features*. The GeoJSON is now ready to be overlaid as an additional layer.

20.2 Overlaid Layers

Let us start by simply adding the *dog runs* as the single layer over the base map by using *plotly.express*. The main difference with respect to previous examples is the configuration of attribute `locations`, which before was assigned with the data frame column of zip codes, to produce the choropleth map. In general, this attribute should have the list of values to use as keys to create associations with the corresponding GeoJSON elements, which by default are those of the `id` element or could be specified with attribute `featureidkey`.

However, the case we are considering is different, now we do not have a data frame and a GeoJSON to logically join, but just a single GeoJSON, that of dog runs, to place as a layer over another (i.e. the base map). Therefore, attribute `locations` should be assigned with an internal reference to values of the GeoJSON, which should be the list of all elements `id`.

If the logic is clear, the only complication is that the GeoJSON has a *dictionary* data organization, hence we cannot just specify the name (i.e. `id`) of the element as for a data frame column, but they must be explicitly read, for example with an *iteration*. This is why in the following code there is a *for-cycle*, written in the compact form (`[f["id"] for f in dogRuns["features"]]`), as the value of attribute `locations`, it reads all elements `id` nested in the main element `features`.

It may look a little complicated, but that is the price for dealing with *dictionary* structures, however, once the logic is clear the remaining are technicalities.

```
fig= px.choropleth_mapbox(dogRuns, geojson= dogRuns,
         locations= [f["id"] for f in dogRuns["features"]],
         mapbox_style='open-street-map',
         zoom=14, center= {"lat": 40.7831, "lon": -73.9712},
         opacity=1.0, height=600
         )

fig.update_layout(margin= {"r":0,"t":0,"l":0,"b":0},
                width=600, height=600,
                hoverlabel= dict(
                    bgcolor="white", font_size=16,
                    font_family= "Rockwell")
               )
```

The same could be done with *plotly go* with syntax adapted as the only difference. Figure 20.4 shows the map with the *dog runs* overlaid to a base map.

```
figure= go.Figure(
    data= [go.Choroplethmapbox(
        geojson= dogRuns,
        locations= [f["id"] for f in dogRuns["features"]],

# The z attribute in this case sets the number
# of levels in the color scale
        z= [1]*len(dogRuns["features"]),

# This sets the color of the border
        marker= dict(opacity=.8,
                    line= dict(color="blue", width=2)),

# This fills the areas with a color
        colorscale= [[0, "red"], [1, "red"]],

# The color scale is not visualized
        showscale= False
    )],
    layout= go.Layout(
        margin= dict(b=0, t=0, r=0, l=0),
        width=600, height=600,
        mapbox= dict(
            style= "carto-positron",
            zoom=14,
            center_lat= 40.7831,
            center_lon= -73.9712,
        )
    )
)
```

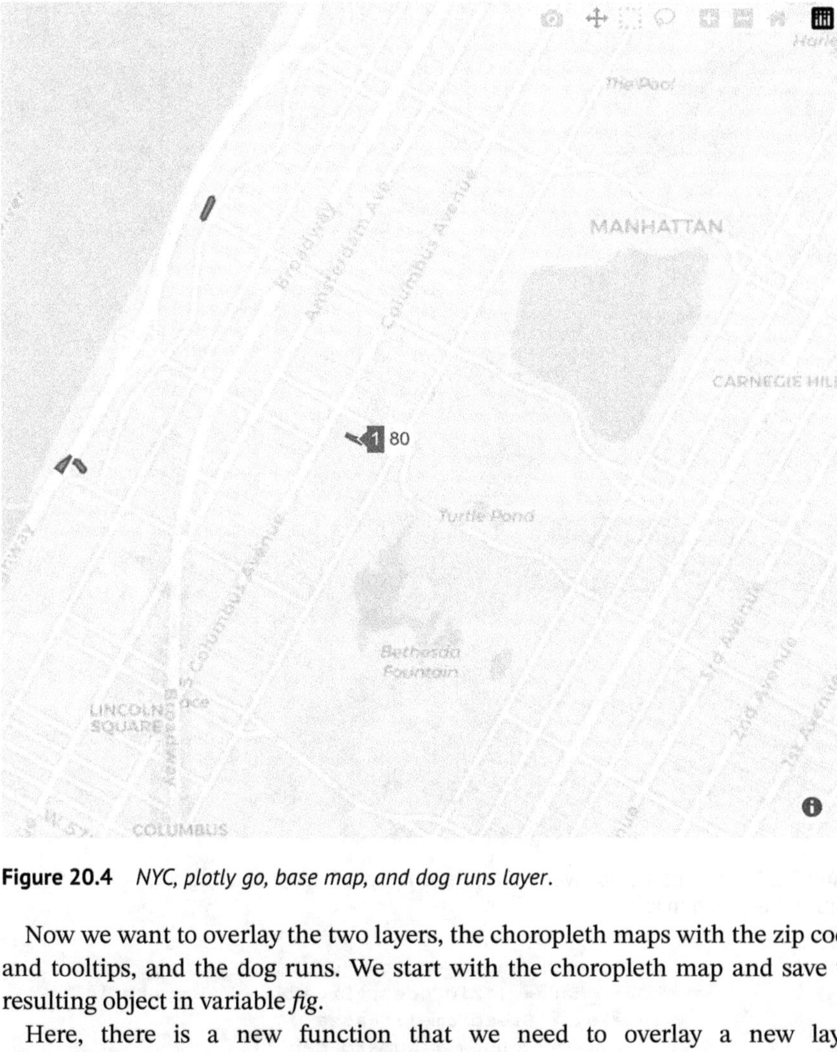

Figure 20.4 *NYC, plotly go, base map, and dog runs layer.*

Now we want to overlay the two layers, the choropleth maps with the zip codes and tooltips, and the dog runs. We start with the choropleth map and save the resulting object in variable *fig*.

Here, there is a new function that we need to overlay a new layer: `add_trace()` of *plotly go*. Using function `add_trace()` is the more general and recommended technique to stack graphical layers on a Plotly map, which makes *plotly go the preferred Plotly module if these type of maps should be produced*. It is also possible with *plotly.express* but it is not that easy and there is basically no reason to use that. The resulting map is shown in Figure 20.5, and the tiled web map is Carto Positron.

```
fig= px.choropleth_mapbox(dogs_maxbreed,
                geojson= nycgeo,
                locations= 'ZipCode', color= 'counts',
                featureidkey= "properties.postalCode",
```

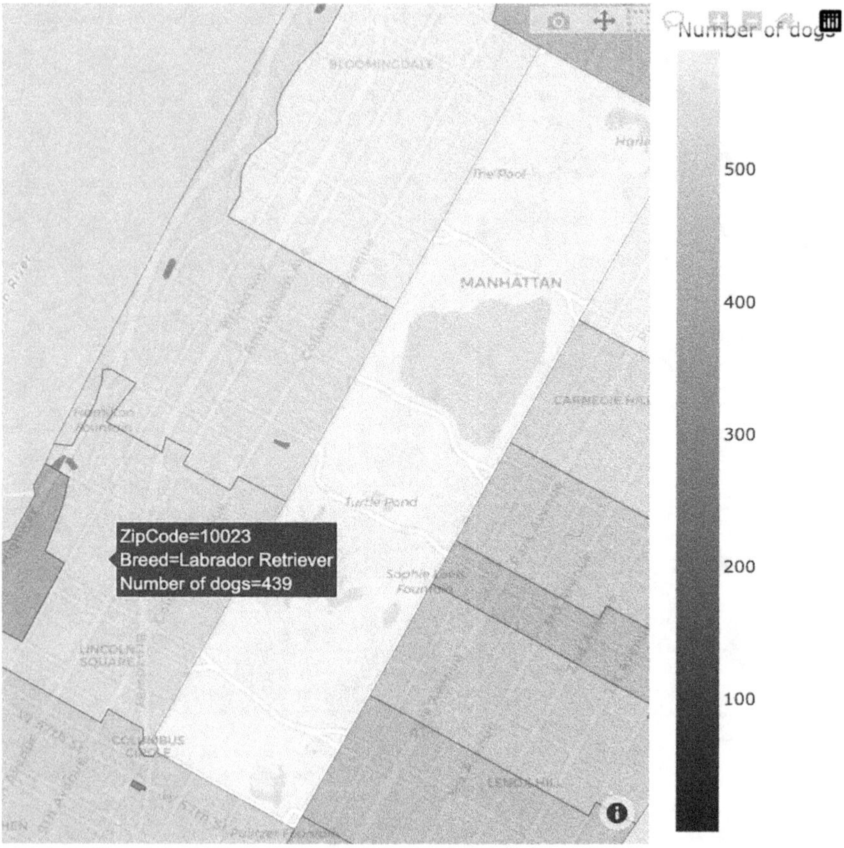

Figure 20.5 NYC, plotly go, overlaid layers, Choropleth map, and dog runs, Carto Positron tiled web map.

```
                    color_continuous_scale= "Cividis",
                    hover_data= ["ZipCode","BreedName","counts"],
                    labels= {'BreedName':'Razza',
                             'counts':'Numero cani'},
                    mapbox_style= 'carto-positron',
                    zoom=13, opacity=0.4,
                    center= {"lat": 40.7831, "lon": -73.9712},
                    width=600, height=600
    )

fig.add_trace(go.Choroplethmapbox(
    geojson= dogRuns,
    locations= [f["id"] for f in dogRuns["features"]],
    z= [1]*len(dogRuns["features"]),
    marker= dict(opacity=0.9, line=dict(color="red", width=2)),
```

```
    colorscale= [[0, "red"], [1, "red"]],
    showscale=False,
   ))

fig.update_layout(margin= {"r":0,"t":0,"l":0,"b":0})
```

20.3 Geopandas: Base Map, Data Frame, and Overlaid Layers

In previous examples, we omitted the presentation of cases that would have been among the most basic ones, such as adding a layer composed of points, because they would have been inexplicably difficult to realize, given the simplicity of the result. This is due to Plotly that does not support well with transformations and combinations of different geometries, for example from a format based on multipolygons to a format with separate attributes for longitude and latitude, or the uneasiness in executing spatial joins based on geographic coordinates. These are all features that we have seen being superbly supported by R package *sf*.

Package *geopandas* represents the best solution currently available to obtain similar functionalities with Python, although some limitations remain and not all functionalities are covered. Historically, it has suffered some installation problems due to the many dependencies that it requires, which could produce conflicts or have misaligned versions. For this reason, in addition to the recommendation to rigorously follow the installation instructions provided by package documentation (https://geopandas.org/en/stable/index.html), it may be safer to create a Python virtual environment with *pip* or *conda* and start with the installation of *geopandas*, so to install all dependencies in a pristine environment, with other packages installed later.

With these potential troubles overcome, the excellent geopandas features turn out to be almost indispensable and play the crucial role that package *sf* has in the R environment. The key concept that geopandas introduces is of *GeoDataFrame*, meaning a pandas data frame format extended to support geographic data through the variable/column *geometry*. Hence, what was a *dictionary* when a GeoJSON was read, with geopandas becomes a *data frame*, with all advantages and simplicity of working with data frames rather than with dictionaries. The main function is `gpd.read_file()`, being `gpd` the standard alias for geopandas. For example, we use the same geodatabases from NYC Open Data of previous sections.

```
import geopandas as gpd

nyc_gpd= gpd.read_file('datasets/NYC_opendata/
nyc-zip-code-tabulation-areas-polygons.geojson')
```

	postalCode	PO_NAME	STATE	borough	geometry
0	11372	Jackson Heights	NY	Queens	Polygon ((−73.86942 40.74916, −73.89507 40.746...
1	11004	Glen Oaks	NY	Queens	Polygon ((−73.71068 40.75004, −73.70869 40.748...
2	11040	New Hyde Park	NY	Queens	Polygon ((−73.70098 40.73890, −73.70309 40.744...
3	11426	Bellerose	NY	Queens	Polygon ((−73.72270 40.75373, −73.72251 40.753...
4	11365	Fresh Meadows	NY	Queens	Polygon ((−73.81089 40.72717, −73.81116 40.728...

We read also the GeoJSON dataset of *dog runs* with geopandas and reproduce the map seen before.

```
dogruns_gpd= gpd.read_file('datasets/NYC_opendata/
                              NYC Parks Dog Runs.geojson')
```

Again, we should add the missing `id` attribute, operation that now is much easier being a traditional data frame column, as values we simply assign sequential numbers.

```
dogruns_gpd= dogruns_gpd.assign(id= range(len(dogruns_gpd)))
```

20.3.1 Extended Dynamic Tooltips

Another remarkable advantage of using geopandas is that we could use for dynamic tooltips and popups *all columns of the GeoDataFrame*, a possibility that before, with a dictionary and a data frame as distinct data structures we did not have.

To produce the *choropleth map*, attribute `geojson` should be set with the *geometry* column of the GeoDataFrame, while attribute `locations` with the column of area identifiers (respectively, *dogruns_gpd.geometry* and *dogruns_gpd.id* in the example). The tooltip can now be extended by specifying the *borough* and the *precinct*. We create the choropleth map using *plotly.express*. Figure 20.6 shows the resulting map by zooming in on a tooltip, the tiled web map is from OpenStreetMap

```
fig= px.choropleth_mapbox(dogruns_gpd,
              geojson= dogruns_gpd.geometry,
              locations= dogruns_gpd.id,
```

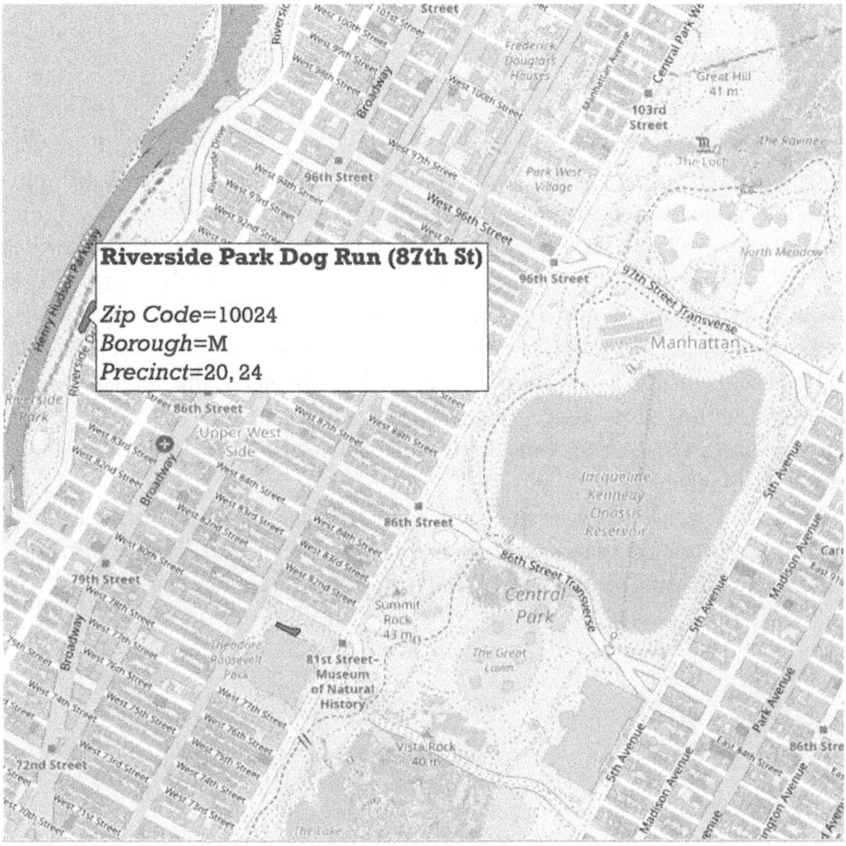

Figure 20.6 NYC, plotly.express and geopandas, dog runs, extended tooltip.

```
                mapbox_style= 'open-street-map',
                hover_name= 'name',
                hover_data= {'id':False, "zipcode":True,
                            "borough":True, "precinct":True},
                labels= {'zipcode':'<i>Zip Code</i>',
                        'borough':'<i>Borough</i>',
                        'precinct':'<i>Precinct</i>'},
                center= {"lat": 40.7831, "lon": -73.9712},
                zoom=14, opacity=1.0,
                width=600, height=600
                )

fig.update_layout(margin= {"r":0,"t":0,"l":0,"b":0},
                  hoverlabel=dict(
```

```
                                    bgcolor="white",
                                    font_size=16,
                                    font_family="Rockwell")
                              )
```

By using *plotly go*, two details need special attention. The first is that function `go.Choroplethmapbox` still requires a dictionary for the `geojson` attribute, not a data frame, therefore assigning it with *dogruns_gpd.geometry* as we did for plotly.express produces an error. The data frame column should be transformed with `eval(dogruns_gpd.geometry.to_json())`, which returns it as dictionary type. The second important detail to take care of is that attribute `locations` by default refers to element `id` of the GeoJSON, but when this element is absent, an alternative solution that works is to refer to the *implicit index* of the *GeoDataFrame* (a reference for this workaround is https://gis.stackexchange.com/questions/424860/problem-plotting-geometries-in-choropleth-map-using-plotly/436649#436649).

With these two tweaks, we can produce the choropleth map by using the GeoDataFrame and configure the tooltip as already seen. Figure 20.7 shows the result, again zooming in on a tooltip and Carto Positron tiled web map.

```
tooltip= '<b>Name: </b>' + dogruns_gpd['name'].astype('str') \
+ '<br>' + '<br>' \
+ '<b>Zip Code: </b>' + dogruns_gpd['zipcode'] \
+ '<br>' \
+ '<b>Department: </b>' + dogruns_gpd['department'].astype('str')

figure= go.Figure(
    data= [go.Choroplethmapbox(
        geojson= eval(dogruns_gpd.geometry.to_json()),
        locations= dogruns_gpd.index,
        z= [1]*len(dogruns_gpd),
        marker= dict(opacity=.8,
                     line= dict(color="blue", width=2)),
        hovertext= tooltip,
        colorscale= [[0, "red"], [1, "red"]],
        showscale= False
    )],

layout= go.Layout(
        margin= dict(b=0, t=0, r=0, l=0),
        width=600, height=600,
        mapbox= dict(
            style= "carto-positron",
            zoom=14,
            center_lat= 40.7831,
            center_lon= -73.9712,
 )))
```

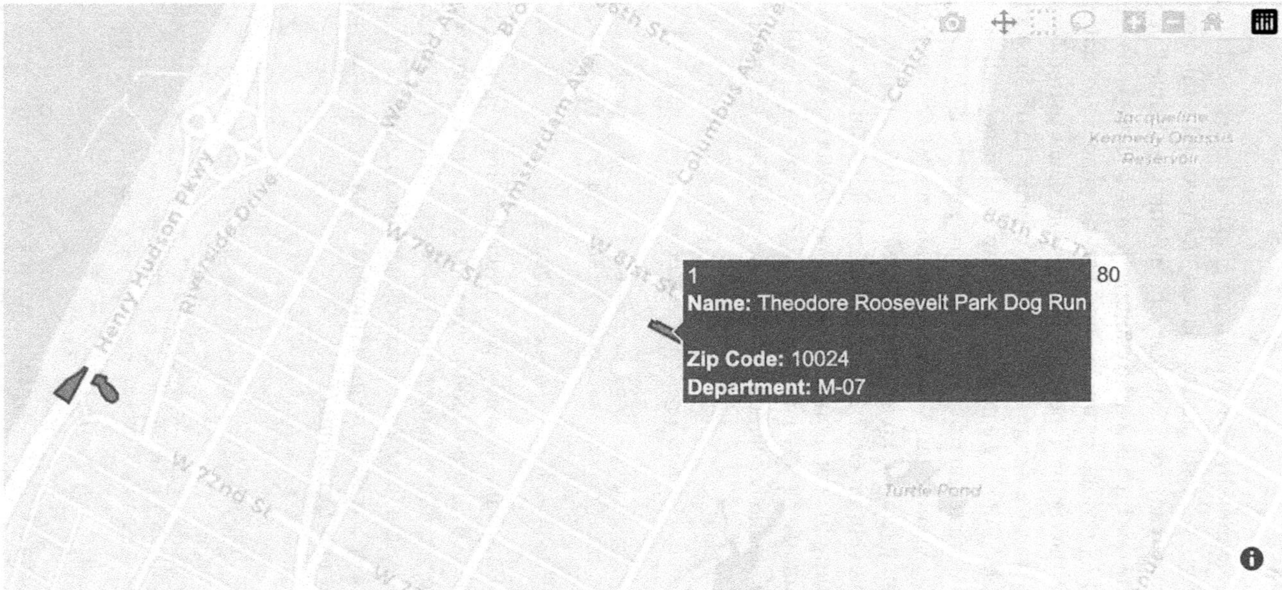

Figure 20.7 NYC, plotly go and geopandas, dog runs, extended tooltip.

20.3.2 Overlaid Layers: Dog Breeds, Dog Runs, and Parks Drinking Fountains

We generalize the example by overlaying more graphical layers, as did before without geopandas. First, we stack just two layers, then we add a third one. We use *plotly go*, which, as already seen, is easier for configuring multiple layers.

We start with the dog breeds for the choropleth map and dog runs area.

Differently from previous examples, we use geopandas, so data from the datasets are of GeoDataFrame type, which lets us join data like traditional pandas data frames. This way, we can prepare the data in order to obtain a single GeoDataFrame with all columns we need for the map and the geometry of polygons. As mentioned, since function `go.Choroplethmapbox` by default makes use of element `id`, being absent in our GeoJSON, we can simply transform into index a data frame column having unique values and refer to it for attribute `location` (i.e. in our example column *OBJECTID* is transformed into an index).

With regard to the join operation, column *ZipCode* of data frame *dogs_maxbreed* and column *postalCode* of GeoDataFrame *nyc_gpd* are the keys, with the caveat that the data types should be aligned, being in one case numerical and in the other strings.

```
nyc_gpd['postalCode']= nyc_gpd['postalCode'].astype('int64')

nycdogs_gpd= nyc_gpd.merge(dogs_maxbreed, left_on='postalCode',
                   right_on='ZipCode').reset_index(inplace=True)

nycdogs_gpd= nycdogs_gpd.set_index('OBJECTID')
```

The single GeoDataFrame is ready, we can produce the map with two layers. First, we define the two different tooltips we will produce by explicitly configuring the layout with text, column names, and HTML elements. The combination of attributes `hovertext` and `hoverinfo` produces the tooltips. As an alternative, attribute `hovertemplate` can be used (more information at https://plotly.com/python/hover-text-and-formatting/).

```
# First tooltip

tooltip1 = '<b>Neighborhood: </b>' + nycdogs_gpd['PO_NAME'] +
'<br>' + '<b>Borough: </b>' + nycdogs_gpd['borough'] +
'<br>' + '<b>Zip Code: </b>' + nycdogs_gpd['ZipCode'].astype('str') +
'<br>' + '<b>Breed: </b>' + nycdogs_gpd['BreedName'] +
'<br>' + '<b>Dogs number: </b>' + nycdogs_gpd['counts'].astype('str')

# Second tooltip

tooltip2 = '<b>Name: </b>' + dogruns_gpd['name'] + '<br>' +
'<br>' + '<b>Zip Code: </b>' + dogruns_gpd['zipcode'].astype('str') +
'<br>' + '<b>Department: </b>' + dogruns_gpd['department']
```

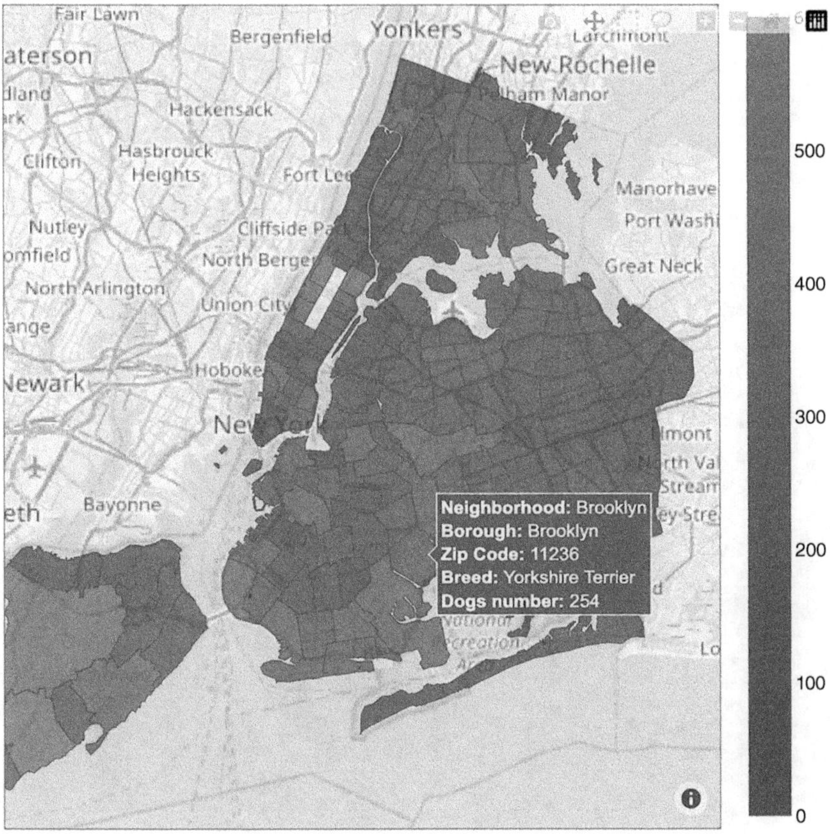

(a)

Figure 20.8 NYC, plotly go and geopandas, dog breeds and dog runs with distinct tooltips; a) full map; b) zoom in.

To create the map, we proceed as seen before. First, the figure is created with function `go.Figure()` and assigned to object *fig*. Then the first layer with the choropleth map is added with function `add_trace()`, next the second layer with the dog runs areas, and finally some style options are configured. Figure 20.8a and Figure 20.8b show two screenshots for the full map with the first tooltip about dog breeds and detail by zooming in a specific zone with the second tooltip for the dog runs.

```
fig= go.Figure()

fig.add_trace(
    go.Choroplethmapbox(
        geojson= eval(nycdogs_gpd.geometry.to_json()),
```

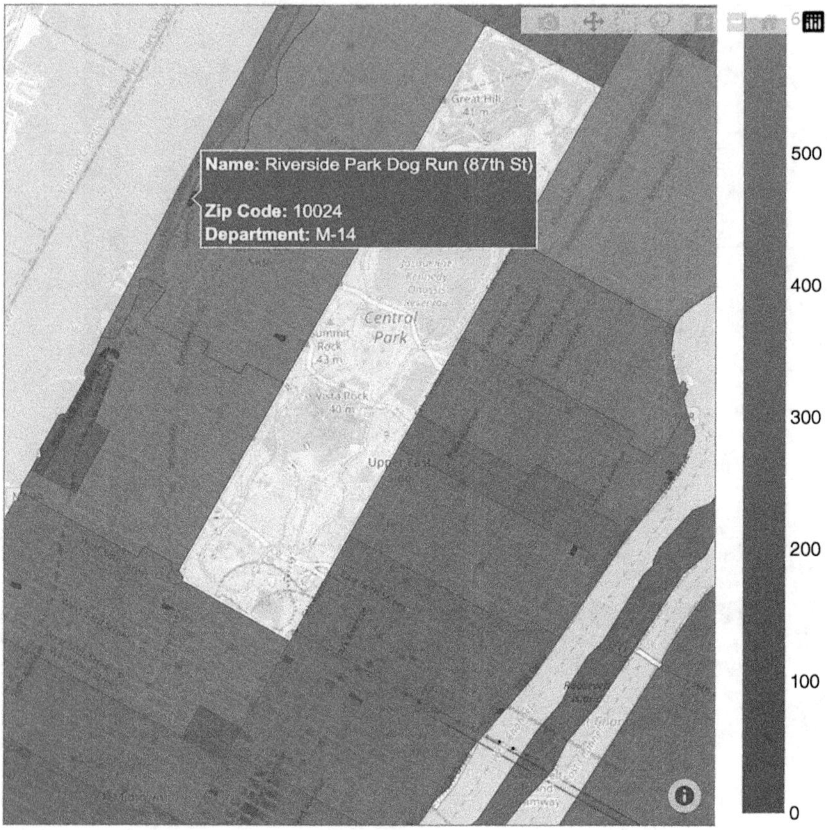

(b)

Figure 20.8 (*Continued*)

```
        locations= nycdogs_gpd.index,
        z= nycdogs_gpd['counts'],
        colorscale= "bluered", zmin=0, zmax=600,
        marker_opacity=0.8, marker_line_width=1,
        hovertext= tooltip1,
        hoverinfo= 'text'
    ))

fig.add_trace(
    go.Choroplethmapbox(
        geojson= eval(dogruns_gpd.geometry.to_json()),
        locations= dogruns_gpd.index,
        z= [1]*len(dogruns_gpd),
        marker= dict(opacity=.8,
        line= dict(color="blue", width=2)),
        hovertext= tooltip2,
```

```
        hoverinfo= 'text',
        colorscale= [[0, "red"], [1, "red"]],
        showscale= False
    ))

fig.update_layout(mapbox_style="open-street-map", mapbox_zoom=9,
                  mapbox_center= {"lat": 40.7831,
                                  "lon": -73.9712},
                  margin= {"r":0,"t":0,"l":0,"b":0},
                  autosize= False, width=600, height=600)
```

We conclude this overview of geographic maps with Plotly and geopandas by adding the third layer to the previous map. Data are from the geodataset of *Parks Drinkable Fountains* and differently from the previous ones it has *Point* as geometry, rather than multipolygons. The difference is that to configure the layer, now we should use *plotly go* function `go.Scattermapbox()` instead of `go.Choroplethmapbox()`. The detail to pay attention to is that for points, it is required to have *distinct columns for latitude and longitude in the GeoDataFrame instead of the geometry column*. A transformation is required because when read by geopandas, the GeoDataFrame has column *geometry*. We proceed step-by-step.

```
fountains_gpd= gpd.read_file('datasets/NYC_opendata/
                             NYC Parks Drinking Fountains.geojson')
```

We have read the GeoJSON and we obtained the GeoDataFrame with column *geometry*. Now we should extract from *geometry* the *longitude* and the *latitude* coordinates and create two new columns (i.e. *lon* and *lat*) with corresponding values. It is easy because we just need methods `x` and `y` applied to column *geometry* to extract the two components, as the following instructions show.

```
fountains_gpd['lon']= fountains_gpd.geometry.x
fountains_gpd['lat']= fountains_gpd.geometry.y
```

	fountain_ty	signname	borough	descr	geometry	lon	lat
0	F High Low	Seth Low Playground/ Bealin Square	B	F High Low, Out in Open	Point (−73.98659 40.60753)	−73.9865	40.6075
1	C	Robert Moses Playground	M	C, In Playground	Point (−73.96863 40.74809)	−73.9686	40.7480
2	D	Chelsea Park	M	D, Under Tree, Near Ballfield	Point (−74.00036 40.75004)	−74.0003	40.7500
3	D	John V. Lindsay East River Park	M	D, Just Outside Playground, Near Ballfield	Point (−73.97290 40.72386)	−73.9729	40.7238

With the two columns for longitude and latitude, we can configure a third tooltip for the drinkable fountains (*tooltip3*) and add the new layer composed of points. Figure 20.9a, Figure 20.9b, Figure 20.9c, and Figure 20.9d show screenshots of the final result with the full map, a detail with tooltip of a drinkable fountain, a detail with tooltip of a dog run area, and a detail with tooltip for the most popular dog breeds in zip codes.

```
tooltip3= '<b>Sign Name: </b>' + fountains_gpd['signname'] + \
'<br>' + '<br>' \
+ '<b>Position: </b>' + fountains_gpd['position']

fig= go.Figure()

fig.add_trace(
    go.Choroplethmapbox(
        geojson= eval(nycdogs_gpd.geometry.to_json()),
```

(a)

Figure 20.9 (a) NYC, plotly go and geopandas, dog breeds, dog run areas, and parks drinkable fountains, full map. (b) NYC, zoom in on a tooltip for a drinkable fountain. (c) NYC, zoom in on a tooltip for a dog run area. (d) NYC, zoom in on a tooltip for the most popular dog breed in a zip code.

(b)

Figure 20.9 (*Continued*)

```
        locations= nycdogs_gpd.index,
        z= nycdogs_gpd['counts'],
        colorscale= "grays", zmin=0, zmax=600,
        marker_opacity=0.8, marker_line_width=1,
        hovertext= tooltip1,
        hoverinfo= 'text'
    ))

fig.add_trace(
    go.Scattermapbox(
        lat= fountains_gpd.lat,
        lon= fountains_gpd.lon,
        mode='markers',
        marker= go.scattermapbox.Marker(
            size=5,
            color= 'orangered',
```

(c)

Figure 20.9 (*Continued*)

```
            opacity=0.7
        ),
        hovertext= tooltip3,
        hoverlabel= dict(bgcolor =
                    ['gray','#00FF00','rgb(252,141,89)']),
        hoverinfo= 'text'
    ))

fig.add_trace(
    go.Choroplethmapbox(
        geojson= eval(dogruns_gpd.geometry.to_json()),
        locations= dogruns_gpd.index,
        z= [1]*len(dogruns_gpd),
        marker= dict(opacity=.8,
                     line=dict(color="blue", width=2)),
```

(d)

Figure 20.9 (*Continued*)

```
        hovertext= tooltip2,
        hoverinfo= 'text',
        colorscale= [[0, "red"], [1, "red"]],
        showscale= False
    ))

fig.update_layout(mapbox_style= "open-street-map",
         mapbox_zoom=9,
         mapbox_center= {"lat": 40.7831, "lon": -73.9712},
         margin= {"r":0,"t":0,"l":0,"b":0},
         autosize= False, width=1000, height=700)
```

20.4 Folium

Folium is a popular Python graphical library for choropleth maps, which could be used as an alternative to Plotly (https://python-visualization.github.io/folium/index.html). It shares with Plotly most of the logic and organization, but the aspect that mostly makes it worth consideration is its tight integration with *Leaflet*, which we already had the opportunity to appreciate in the previous chapter. Like with Plotly, the combination with *geopandas* is worthwhile also with Folium, easing the configuration and extending the possibilities with respect to the only *plotly go* and *plotly.express*.

```
import numpy as np
import pandas as pd
import matplotlib.pyplot as plt
from PIL import Image
import json
import geopandas as gpd
import folium
```

20.4.1 Base Maps, Markers, and Circles

The main Folium *graphical elements* are those already encountered before and basically shared by all modern graphic libraries for spatial data and maps, such as tiled web maps, markers, tooltips, popups, and so on.

To define a base map, Folium has function `folium.Map()` that requires just the coordinates of the center of the map, expressed as latitude and longitude with attribute `location`.

We stay in NYC and choose a point in Central Park, adding a zoom level for the initial visualization (attribute `zoom_start`), and the map size (attributes `width` and `height`). To add a tiled web map there is attribute `tiles` and in case of a commercial tiled web map, a specific attribute for the *API_key* is available. Here we create the base map with the default tiled web map from OpenStreetMap (see Figure 20.10).

```
map1= folium.Map(location=[40.78367, -73.96584,
                    zoom_start=11, width=500,height=500))
```

From this simple base map, it should be noted the default integration with Leaflet, as indicated in the bottom-right footer. To save the map in HTML format, it exists function `save()` (e.g., `map1.save('Map1.html')`).

To add *markers*, a feature imported from Leaflet, function `folium.Marker()` should be used in combination with method `add_to()` needed to add the new element to the base map. It has an intuitive usage showed in the next example.

We choose some popular Manhattan locations to place the corresponding markers and configuring them with style options through attribute `icon` and function `folium.Icon()`, such as the marker's color (attribute `color`) and the specific icon (attribute `icon`), which we get from those freely available by *FontAwesome*

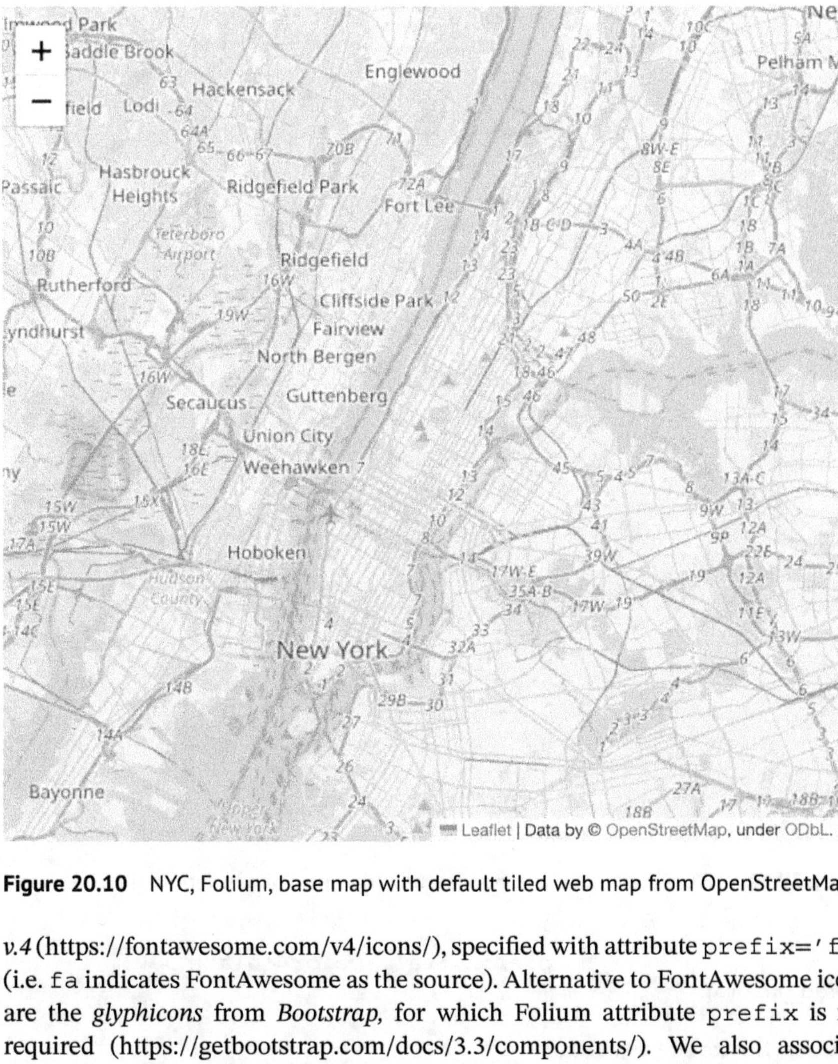

Figure 20.10 NYC, Folium, base map with default tiled web map from OpenStreetMap.

v.4 (https://fontawesome.com/v4/icons/), specified with attribute `prefix='fa'` (i.e. `fa` indicates FontAwesome as the source). Alternative to FontAwesome icons are the *glyphicons* from *Bootstrap,* for which Folium attribute `prefix` is not required (https://getbootstrap.com/docs/3.3/components/). We also associate markers to both popups (attribute `popup`) and tooltips (attribute `tooltip`) to practice and test them.

Figure 20.11 shows the resulting Folium map, this time with Stamen Terrain tiled web map.

```
folium.Marker([40.7116, -74.0132],
     popup= "<i>The World Trade Center and the National \
                September 11th Memorial and Museum</i>",
     tooltip= "Ground Zero",
     icon= folium.Icon(icon="building",
```

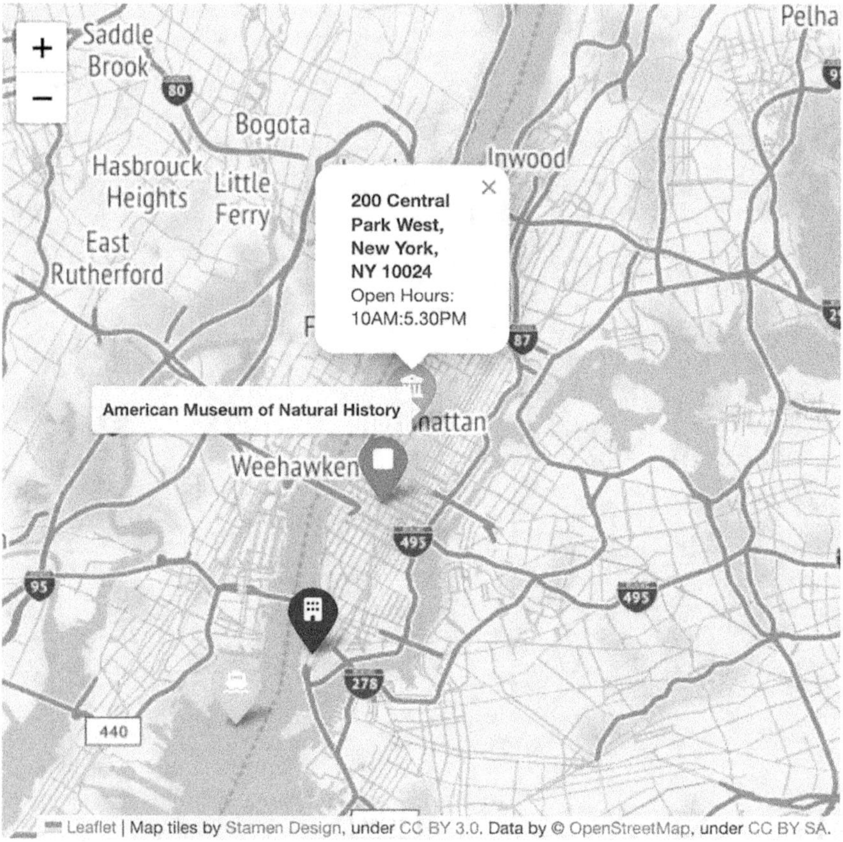

Figure 20.11 NYC, Folium, markers, popups, and tooltips, Stamen Terrain tiled web map.

```
                        prefix='fa', color='black')
).add_to(map1)

folium.Marker([40.6892, -74.0445],
     popup= "<b>The Statue of Liberty is a gift from the \
             people of France</b>",
     tooltip= "<b>Statue of Liberty</b>",
     icon= folium.Icon(color="lightblue",
                         icon='ship', prefix='fa')
).add_to(map1)

folium.Marker([40.7813, -73.9740],
     popup= "<b>200 Central Park West, New York, NY \
             10024</b>" + "<br>" + \
```

```
            "Open Hours: 10AM:5.30PM",
    tooltip= "<b>American Museum of Natural History</b>",
    icon= folium.Icon(icon="institution", prefix='fa')
).add_to(map1)

folium.Marker([40.7580, -73.9855],
              tooltip= "<b>Times Square</b>",
              icon= folium.Icon(icon="square", prefix='fa',
                               color='red')
).add_to(map1)
```

In the same way, circular elements could be added instead of markers, which have two forms: only the border of the circle (function `folium.Circle()`) or a circle including the internal area (function `folium.CircleMarker()`). They act exactly as markers, just with a circular shape.

20.4.2 Advanced Tooltips and Popups

Folium provides for a wide variety of possible configurations for the tooltips, including the possibility to insert in them *Vega/Altair* graphics, tables, and images (see https://nbviewer.org/github/python-visualization/folium/blob/main/examples/Popups.ipynb).

We see an example with an image included in the popups (*Note*: the pictures are free from *Unsplash*, https://unsplash.com/license).

Technically, an image should be included in the popup/tooltip as an *HTML iframe*. To manage the iframe, we use functions from package *branca* (other equivalent solutions are available). Having iframes to manage, we should expect to tackle with common problems and limitations of HTML pages, like for example the *same-origin policy* (https://developer.mozilla.org/en-US/docs/Web/Security/Same-origin_policy) that forbids to load local resources. For this reason, the images included in the popups are directly read online from *Unsplash*. Figure 20.12a and Figure 20.12b show screenshots of the two marker's popups with images.

```
import branca

map2= folium.Map(location=[40.78367, -73.96584],
                 zoom_start=11, width=500,height=500,
                 tiles= 'Stamen Terrain')

# Iframes configuration with image, text, and html tags

# The World Trade Center Memorial

html1= """<div> <img src="https://images.unsplash.com/
```

```
photo-1495954283789-905ff632dca0?ixlib=rb-4.0.3&
ixid=MnwxMjA3fDB8MHxwaG90by1wYWdlfHx8fGVufDB8fHx8&
auto=format&fit=crop&w=774&q=80" \
alt="The World Trade Center and the National September \
11th Memorial and Museum" width=200 height=300 > \
<br/><span>The World Trade Center and the National \
September 11th Memorial and Museum</span> </div>"""

# American Museum of Natural History

html = """<div> <img src="https://images.unsplash.com/
```

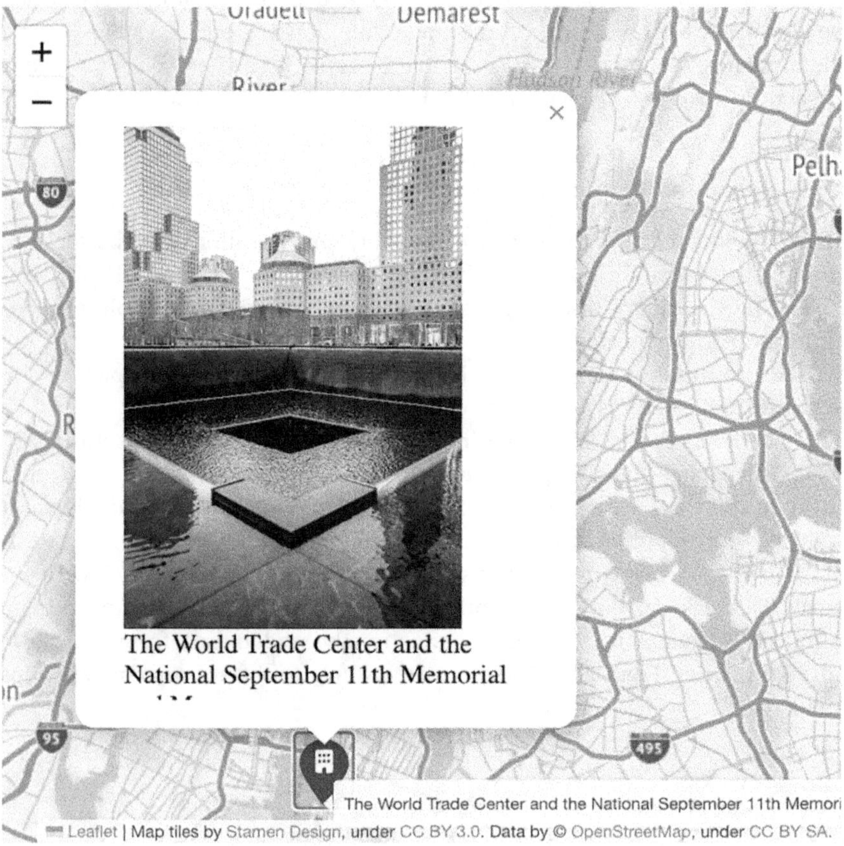

(a)

Figure 20.12 (a/b) NYC, Folium, marker's popups with HTML iframe and image (Redd F / Unsplash.com & Willian Justen de Vasconcellos / Unsplash.com).

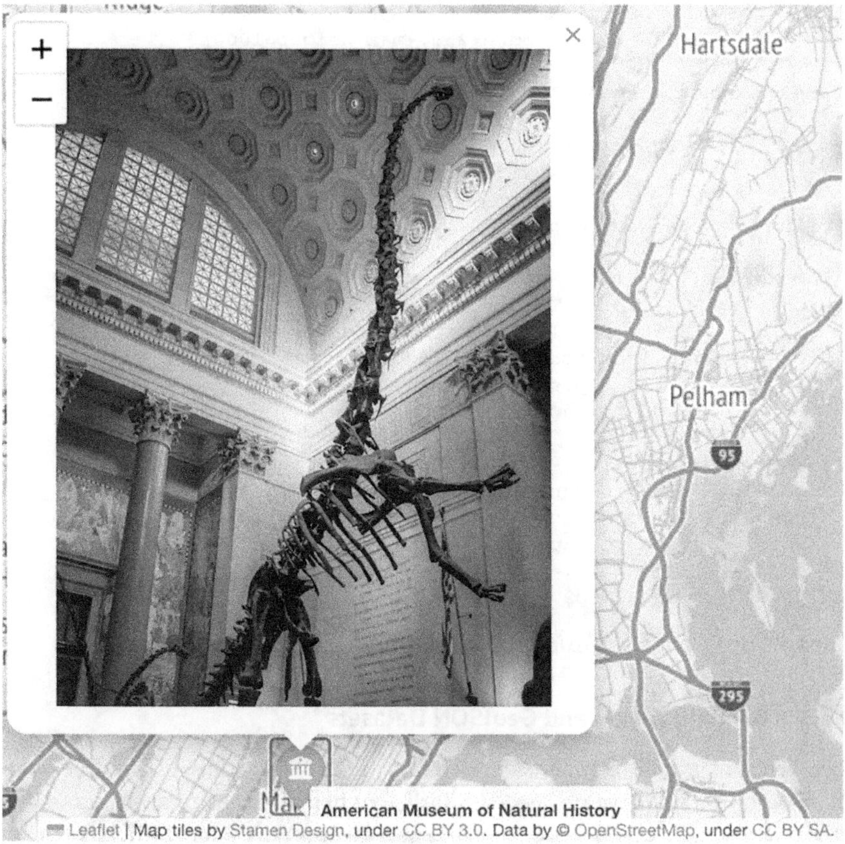

(b)

Figure 20.12 (*Continued*)

```
photo-1647962309326-b77f9732860e?ixlib=rb-4.0.3&
ixid=MnwxMjA3fDB8MHxwaG90by1wYWdlfHx8fGVufDB8fHx8&
auto=format&fit=crop&w=774&q=80" \
alt="American Museum of Natural History" \
width=300 height=500 > \
<br/><span>American Museum of Natural History</span></div>"""

# Iframes definition with functions from library branca

iframe1= branca.element.IFrame(html=html1,
                                width=250, height=350)
```

```
popup1= folium.Popup(iframe1,
                     max_width=250, max_height=1000)

iframe2= branca.element.IFrame(html=html2,
                               width=300, height=400)
popup2= folium.Popup(iframe2,
                      max_width=350, max_height=1000)

# Folium markers with popups

folium.Marker([40.7116, -74.0132], popup= popup1,
    tooltip= "The World Trade Center and the National \
              September 11th Memorial and Museum",
    icon= folium.Icon(icon="building",
                      prefix='fa', color='black')
            ).add_to(map2)

folium.Marker([40.7813, -73.9740], popup= popup2,
    tooltip= "<b>American Museum of Natural History</b>",
    icon= folium.Icon(icon="institution", prefix='fa')
            ).add_to(map2)

#map2.save('./image/map2.html')
```

(Images free from *Unsplash*, https://unsplash.com/license)

20.4.3 Overlaid Layers and GeoJSON Datasets

When layers of graphic elements derived from a GeoJSON dataset should be overlaid on a Folium map, we proceed similarly to what we have done with markers. With function `folium.GeoJson()` the new layer is populated with data from a GeoJSON dataset, and then with method `add_to()` it is overlaid on the map.

With the next example, we add to a base map a layer with elements from the *Sea Level Rise Maps (2050s 500-year Floodplain)* GeoJSON dataset, whose data represent estimates made by FEMA. For the details about the style options, we forward the reader to the official Leaflet documentation (https://leafletjs.com/). Figure 20.13 shows the resulting Folium map.

```
seaRise= json.load(open('datasets/FEMA/
      Sea Level Rise Maps (2050s 500-year Floodplain).geojson'))

map3= folium.Map(location=[40.7831, -73.9712],
                 zoom_start=11, width=500, height=500)

style= {'weight':'1', 'color':'#295499', 'opacity':'0.5'}

folium.GeoJson(seaRise, name="geojson",
              style_function = lambda x: style
              ).add_to(map1)
```

Figure 20.13 NYC, Folium, base map, and GeoJSON layer with FEMA sea level rise estimates.

20.4.4 Choropleth Maps

Creating a choropleth map with Folium is very similar to what we have seen with Plotly. We change the example still using the GeoJSON data set with zip codes, but this time, instead of data about dog licenses, we use data about *Rodent Inspections.*

```
nyc_zip= json.load(open('datasets/NYC_opendata/
          nyc-zip-code-tabulation-areas-polygons.geojson'))
```

From all rodent inspections, we select only those that revealed the presence of rodents (i.e. *Rat Activity*).

```
rats= pd.read_csv('datasets/NYC_opendata/Rodent_Inspection.csv')
rats1= rats[(rats.RESULT == 'Rat Activity')]
```

	STREET_ NAME	ZIP_ CODE	X_ COORD	Y_ COORD	LAT	LONG	BOROUGH	INSPECTION_ DATE
1	NaN	10003	NaN	NaN	NaN	NaN	Manhattan	02/13/2023 01:40:15 PM
9	NaN	10025	NaN	NaN	NaN	NaN	Manhattan	01/27/2020 12:50:35 PM
11	NaN	11237	NaN	NaN	NaN	NaN	Brooklyn	07/22/2021 01:43:11 PM
13	93 Street	NaN	102...	206...	0.0	0.0	Queens	10/29/2019 02:15:25 PM
17	Fordham road	10458	NaN	NaN	NaN	NaN	Bronx	10/14/2022 11:53:12 AM

The data frame should be prepared for visualization by aggregating rows by zip code and counting the number of inspections for each zip code.

```
inspTot= rats1.groupby('ZIP_CODE')[['RESULT']].count().\
      reset_index().sort_values(by= 'RESULT', ascend-
ing= False)

inspTot.ZIP_CODE= inspTot.ZIP_CODE.astype('int64')
```

	ZIP_CODE	RESULT
121	11221	15827
116	11216	15355
74	10457	15093
136	11237	14821
75	10458	13691
...	...	...

We are ready for the visualization. The Folium function to use is `folium.Choropleth()` whose attribute `geo_data` is assigned with the name of the object with geographic data, which has been read from the GeoJSON and is in *dictionary* format. Data to be used for coloring the areas are set with attribute `data` and they are the aggregated results from the rodent inspection dataset. Now the association between the geographic data and the data frame should be configured. On the one side, we need to specify the join key for the data frame. It is declared with attribute `columns`, which has particular semantics: it should be a Python list of two elements, so it requires *square brackets*, where *the first column is the one used as key for the join with the geographic data, the second is the column with values for the color scale* (e.g., `columns= ["ZIP_CODE","RESULT"]`). For the GeoJSON, instead, attribute `key_on` specifies the dictionary element to use as key (e.g., `"feature.properties.postalCode"`, reading the following note is highly recommended).

> **Note**
>
> Pay attention to a *tiny but important detail* of Folium, which is different from Plotly that for a similar attribute implicitly takes element *features* as the root of the JSON hierarchy (e.g., `featureidkey= "properties.postalCode"`), Folium uses the keyword *feature* as the explicit root of the GeoJSON structure (e.g., `key_on= "feature.properties.postalCode"`).
>
> Do not confuse the Folium keyword *feature* with the actual element name *features* of a standard GeoJSON file, otherwise you end up trying to write the second with final 's' and you do not get any data on the map for seemingly incomprehensible reasons.

The remaining attributes are style options with self-explicative names. Finally, method `add_to()` applied to function `folium.LayerControl()` places the layer on the map. Figure 20.14 shows the result.

```
map1= folium.Map(
   location=[40.7831, -73.9712],
   zoom_start=10, width=500,
   height=500)

folium.Choropleth(
    geo_data= nyc_zip,
    name= "choropleth",
    data= inspTot,
    columns= ["ZIP_CODE","RESULT"],
    key_on= "feature.properties.postalCode",
    fill_color="Grays",
    fill_opacity=0.6,
    line_opacity=0.2,
    legend_name="Rat presence",
    ).add_to(map1)

folium.LayerControl().add_to(map1)
```

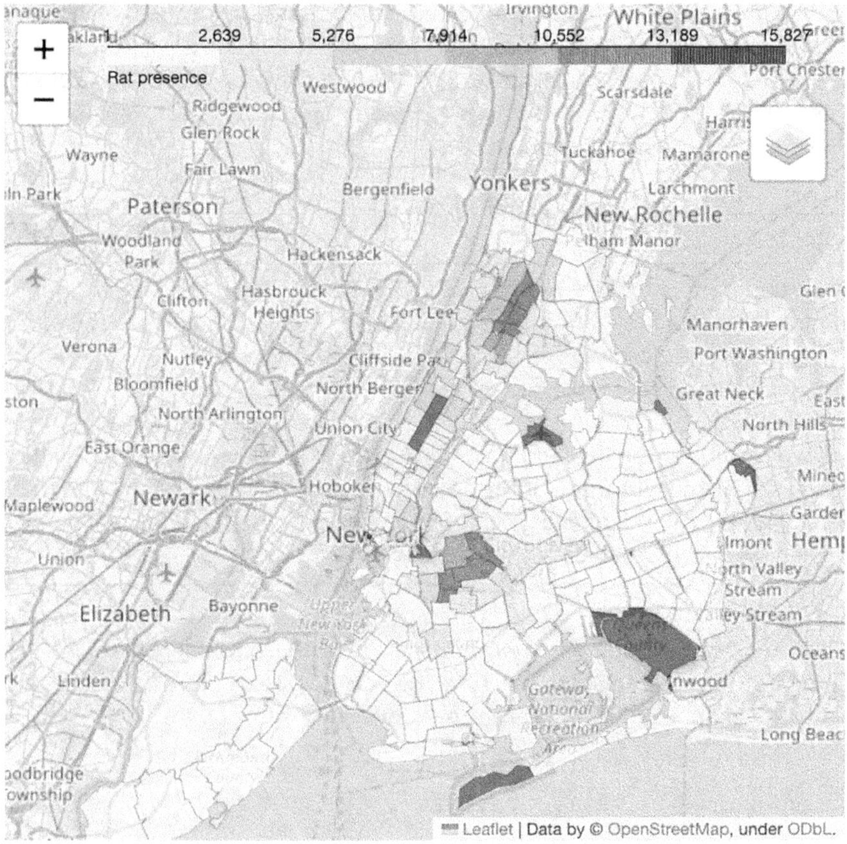

Figure 20.14 NYC, Folium choropleth map, rodent inspections finding rat activity.

20.4.5 Geopandas

Even with *geopandas* the way to proceed in Folium reminds that of Plotly. The geopandas documentation provides the details for using it with Folium (https://geopandas.org/en/stable/gallery/plotting_with_folium.html).

We replicate the previous choropleth map, this time by reading the GeoJSON dataset through *geopandas* and joining the resulting GeoDataFrame with data frame *inspTot* of aggregated data on rodent inspections for zip code. The join operation produces a single GeoDataFrame that we use to produce the choropleth map.

```
nyc_gpd= gpd.read_file('datasets/NYC_opendata/
            nyc-zip-code-tabulation-areas-polygons.geojson',
            driver='GeoJSON')
```

The traditional join between data frames is executed by using *postalCode* and *ZIP_CODE* as join keys. A data type transformation is required to align the data types.

```
nyc_gpd.postalCode= nyc_gpd.postalCode.astype('int64')

nycRats= nyc_gpd.merge(inspTot, left_on='postalCode',
                                right_on='ZIP_CODE')
```

We can produce the choropleth map. The detail to pay attention to, already met with Plotly, is that now we have a single GeoDataFrame, which contains both the *geometry* and the data. In function `folium.Choropleth()`, attribute `geo_data` requires a *dictionary* data format, but now we have a data frame format, hence we cannot just specify the name of the GeoDataFrame (*nycRats*), we have to transform it into a dictionary with method `to_json()` (e.g., `geo_data=nycRats.to_json()`). Attribute `data`, instead, is expecting a data frame, so the GeoDataFrame's name *nycRats* is fine.

We also define a *folium plugin*, in this case a *dynamic popup* with function `GeoJsonPopup()`. To add it, rather than the usual `add_to()` used to overlay layers, a *folium popup* should be added to the map (variable *fig1*) with function `add_child()` (e.g., `fig1.geojson.add_child(popup)`). Being a unique GeoDataFrame, the popup could be configured with all information from its columns. The resulting map is shown in Figure 20.15.

```
from folium.features import GeoJson, GeoJsonTooltip,
                            GeoJsonPopup, LatLngPopup

map1= folium.Map(location=[40.7831, -73.9712],
                 zoom_start=10, width=500,height=500)

fig1= folium.Choropleth(
        geo_data= nycRats.to_json(),
        name= "choropleth",
        data= nycRats,
        columns= ["ZIP_CODE","RESULT"],
        key_on= "feature.properties.ZIP_CODE",
        fill_color= "Reds",
        fill_opacity=0.7, line_opacity=0.2,
        legend_name= "Rat presence",
).add_to(map1)

popup= GeoJsonPopup(
    fields= ["ZIP_CODE", "borough", "PO_NAME", "RESULT"],
    aliases= ["Zip Code: ", "Borough: ", "Neighborhood: ",
              "Num. Inspections: "],
```

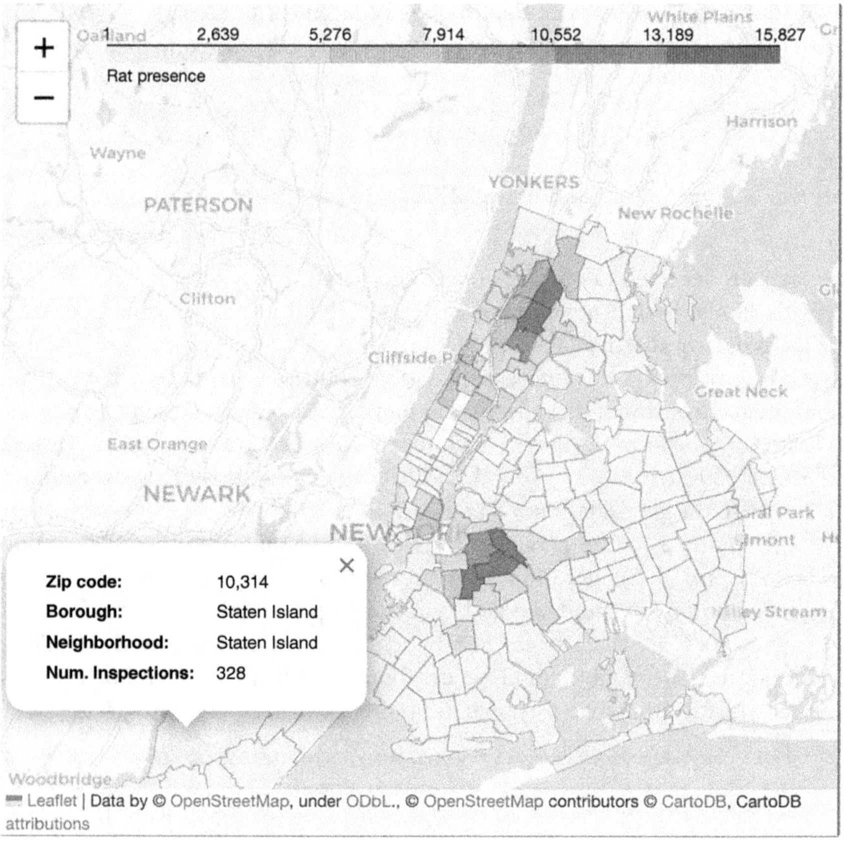

Figure 20.15 NYC, Folium and geopandas, rodent inspections finding rat activity.

```
    localize= True, labels= True,
)
fig1.geojson.add_child(popup)
folium.TileLayer('cartodbpositron').add_to(map1)
```

20.4.6 Folium Heatmap

Folium has several *plugins*, in addition to popups seen in the previous example, for all the details we forward the interested readers to the official documentation (https://python-visualization.github.io/folium/plugins.html). Here we consider the case of *folium heatmaps,* but it is recommended reading the following *note* because the terminology used by Folium could easily mislead.

> **Note**
>
> What *Folium* calls *heatmap* is different from traditional *heatmap* as graphical representations of data in rectangular form. The so-called *folium heatmap*, in other graphical tools (e.g., ggplot, seaborn) is more correctly called *kernel density plot* or *bivariate density plot*.

We should prepare the data frame because the inspections are too many and would produce an unclear result. We select just those made in year 2022 and omit rows with missing values in date or coordinates, or that have value zero.

```
rats1['INSPECTION_DATE']=
        pd.to_datetime(rats1['INSPECTION_DATE'])
rats1= rats1[~rats1['INSPECTION_DATE'].isna()]
rats1['YEAR']=
       rats1['INSPECTION_DATE'].dt.year.astype('Int64')
rats2022= rats1[rats1.YEAR == 2022]

rats2022= rats2022[
   ~rats2022.LATITUDE.isna() & ~rats2022.LONGITUDE.isna() &
   (rats2022.LATITUDE != 0) & (rats2022.LONGITUDE != 0)]
```

The data frame is now ready. We can create the Folium map with function `folium.Map()` setting global elements. Then, we need to subset the data frame by just extracting the two columns for latitude and longitude (e.g., `ratsHeat= rats2022[['LATITUDE','LONGITUDE']]`). This new data frame should be the data for function `plugins.HeatMap()` creating the Folium *heatmap*, which will be finally added to the map as a new layer with method `add_to()`. Style options are also specified for *transparency* and *blur*. Figure 20.16 shows the result, which, as noted, does not look like a heatmap, as usually intended, but a kernel density plot.

```
from folium import plugins

map4= folium.Map(location=[40.7831, -73.9712],
                 tiles="cartodbpositron",
                 zoom_start=10, width=500, height=500)

ratsHeat= rats2022[['LATITUDE','LONGITUDE']]

plugins.HeatMap(ratsHeat,
                min_opacity=0.2, blur=11,
               ).add_to(map4)
```

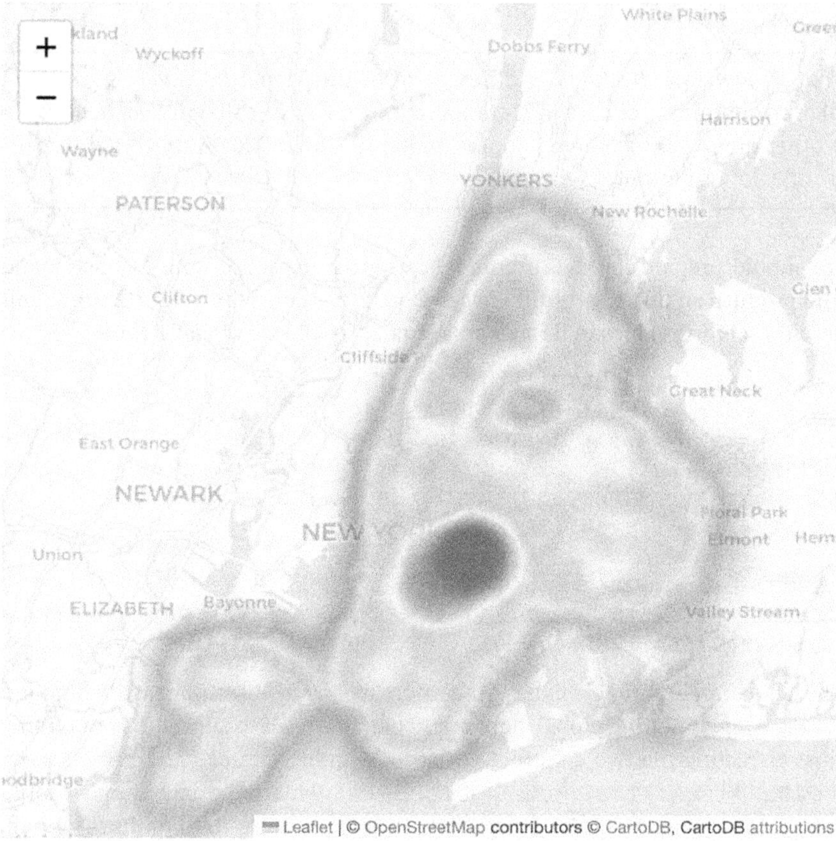

Figure 20.16 NYC, Folium heatmap of rodent inspections with rat activity.

20.5 Altair: Choropleth Map

We conclude Part 4 by mentioning how Altair supports choropleth maps. Currently, Altair supports GeoJSON and GeoDataFrame formats but has limited features for geographic visualizations and spatial data (at least up to version 4.2.2), which makes it not a valid alternative to Plotly or Folium, to remain in the Python environment. Not to mention Leaflet or R with the *sf* package, which are on a completely different qualitative level with respect to what Altair is able to offer. However, it is likely that it will improve in future versions and, for its general graphical quality and clear organization, it deserves to be at least mentioned.

Here, we just see how to produce some standard choropleth maps with Altair.

```
import numpy as np
import pandas as pd
import altair as alt
import geopandas as gpd
import json
```

20.5.1 GeoJSON Maps

To read a GeoJSON dataset, we should employ *geopandas* or read it with base Python method, either way the result could be used in Altair function `alt.Data()`. Let us see this simple example. We start from the GeoJSON with zip codes. Function `alt.Data()`, with attribute `values`, requires a *dictionary* data format, so the base Python method to access a JSON file is fine. It also has attribute `format` that specifies the *root element* in the nested JSON data organization with Altair function `alt.DataFormat()`. For GeoJSON datasets, it will be element *features*.

```
nycgeo= json.load(open('datasets/NYC_opendata/
        nyc-zip-code-tabulation-areas-polygons.geojson'))

data_obj_geojson= alt.Data(values=nycgeo,
                      format=alt.DataFormat(property="features"))
```

Function `mark_geoshape()` is the reference function for visualizing geographic objects. In the following, we just visualize the areas defined by the zip codes (*plot_a*), with no association to a variable for the color scale, then the NYC boroughs (*plot_b*) as a choropleth map by setting attribute `color` with the dictionary element containing borough names (i.e. '*properties.borough*'). Figure 20.17a and Figure 20.17b show the two cases.

```
plot_a= alt.Chart(data_obj_geojson).mark_geoshape(
    fill='ghostwhite', stroke='skyblue')

plot_b= alt.Chart(data_obj_geojson).mark_geoshape(
).encode(color='properties.borough:N')
```

20.5.2 Geopandas: NYC Subway Stations and Demographic Data

Next, we consider *geopandas* that, as usual, make working with geometries easier. In the next example, we use the GeoJSON dataset of *NYC Subway Stations*. Elements have *point* geometry indicating exact locations; therefore, we have to extract latitude and longitude from the GeoJSON *geometry*. We have seen a similar case with Plotly.

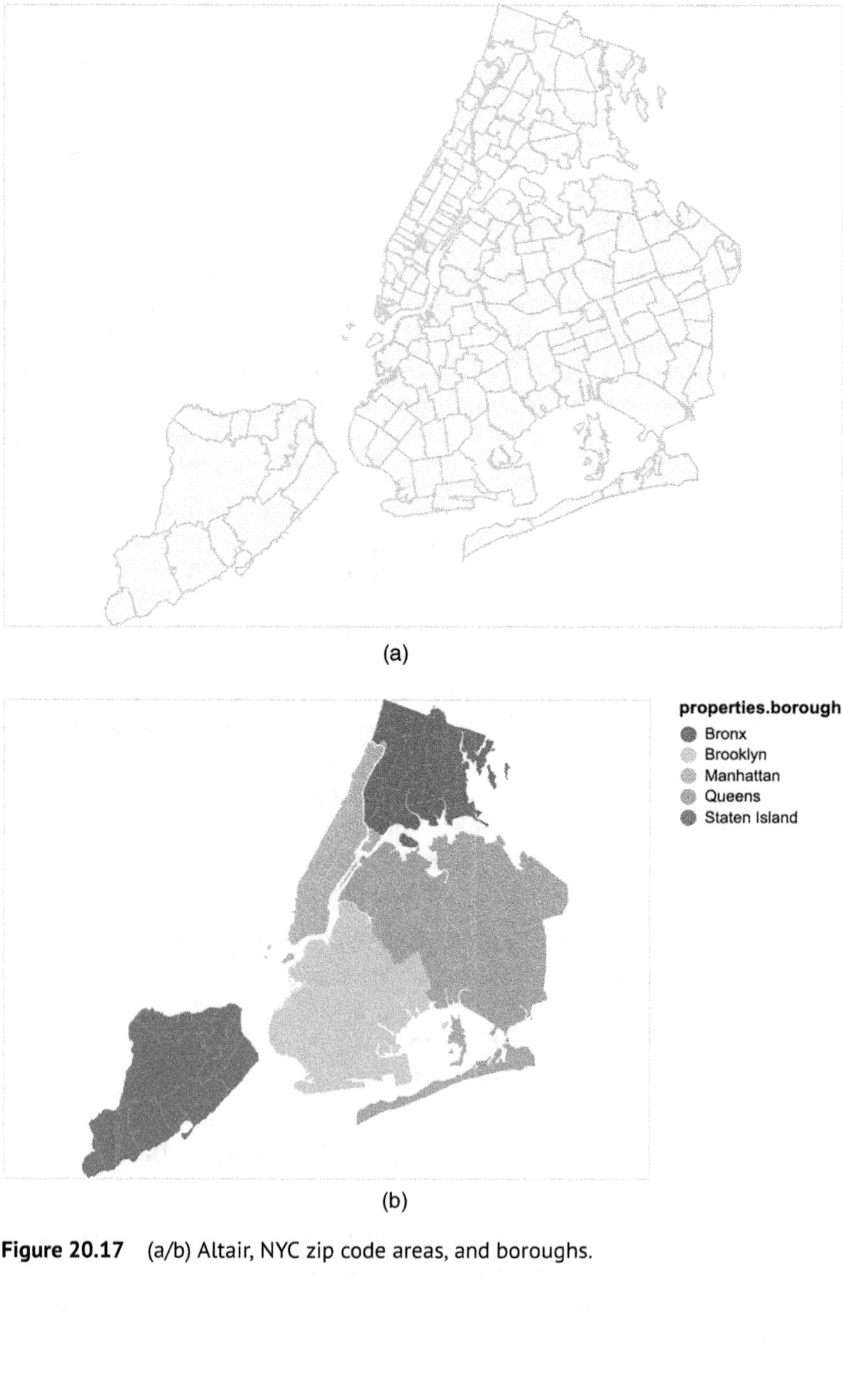

Figure 20.17 (a/b) Altair, NYC zip code areas, and boroughs.

```
stations= gpd.read_file('datasets/NYC_opendata/
                          Subway Stations.geojson')

stations['lon']= stations.geometry.x
stations['lat']= stations.geometry.y
```

	name	line	notes	geometry	lon	lat
0	Astor Pl	4-6-6 Express	4 nights ...	Point (−73.99107 40.73005)	−73.9910	40.7300
1	Canal St	4-6-6 Express	4 nights ...	Point (−74.00019 40.71880)	−74.0001	40.7188
2	50th St	1-2	1 all times ...	Point (−73.98385 40.76173)	−73.9838	40.7617

To create the plot, the syntax is the same as seen in Part 2 for Altair graphics, with the novelty of function `mark_geoshape()` and some geographical attributes like `latitude` and `longitude`. Figure 20.18 shows the NYC map with points corresponding to subway stations.

```
basemap= alt.Chart(data_obj_geojson).mark_geoshape(
    fill= 'ghostwhite',
    stroke= 'skyblue')

points= alt.Chart(stations).mark_circle(
    size=10,
    color= 'darkred'
).encode(
    longitude= 'lon:Q',
    latitude= 'lat:Q',
    tooltip= ['name','line','notes'])

(basemap + points).properties(width= 500, height= 500)
```

To produce a *choropleth map*, we make use of dataset *Demographic Statistics by Zip Code*, from the NYC Open Data.

```
residents = pd.read_csv('datasets/NYC_opendata/
                    Demographic_Statistics_By_Zip_Code.csv')
```

We transform in long form the columns corresponding to four ethnic groups and execute some common data-wrangling operations.

Figure 20.18 Altair, NYC subway stations with popups.

```
etnicGroups= residents.melt(id_vars= 'JURISDICTION NAME',
        value_vars= ['PERCENT HISPANIC LATINO',
                     'PERCENT ASIAN NON HISPANIC',
                     'PERCENT WHITE NON HISPANIC',
                     'PERCENT BLACK NON HISPANIC']).\
        sort_values(by= ['JURISDICTION NAME','value'],
                        ascending= [True,False])

etnicGroups= etnicGroups[~etnicGroups.value.isna()]
etnicGroups.value= 100*etnicGroups.value
```

	JURISDICTION NAME	variable	value
708	10001	Percent Black Non-Hispanic	0.48
0	10001	Percent Hispanic Latino	0.36
236	10001	Percent Asian Non-Hispanic	0.07
472	10001	Percent White Non-Hispanic	0.02
237	10002	Percent Asian Non-Hispanic	0.80
...	...	...	...

Now we read the GeoJSON dataset with *geopandas* and join it with the data frame of ethnic groups just derived.

```
nyc_gpd= gpd.read_file('datasets/NYC_opendata/
            nyc-zip-code-tabulation-areas-polygons.geojson')

nyc_gpd.postalCode= nyc_gpd.postalCode.astype('Int64')

nycEtnies= nyc_gpd.merge(etnicGroups, left_on= 'postalCode',
                                  right_on= 'JURISDICTION NAME',
                                  how= 'inner')
```

We are ready to visualize the choropleth maps corresponding to each ethnic group. Each ethnic group is a subset from the data - —pay attention to the peculiar syntax to execute this selection based on a logical condition in Altair, `chart |= base.transform_filter(datum.variable == etnies)` - and used to produce a choropleth map. Figure 20.19 shows the four choropleth maps horizontally aligned, respectively for Hispanic Latino, Asian Non-Hispanic, White Non-Hispanic, and Black Non-Hispanic.

```
from altair.expr import datum

base= alt.Chart(nycEtnies).mark_geoshape().encode(
        color= alt.Color('value:Q', title="%"),
        tooltip= ['variable:N','postalCode:O', 'value:Q']
).properties(width=200, height=200)

list= ['PERCENT HISPANIC LATINO','PERCENT ASIAN NON HISPANIC',
    'PERCENT WHITE NON HISPANIC','PERCENT BLACK NON HISPANIC']

chart= alt.hconcat()
for etnies in list:
    chart |= base.transform_filter(datum.variable == etnies)
```

Figure 20.19 Altair, choropleth maps for ethnic groups (from left to right: Hispanic Latino, Asian Non-Hispanic, White Non-Hispanic, and Black Non-Hispanic).

Index

Data Visualization in R and Python, First Edition. Marco Cremonini.

Companion website: www.wiley.com/go/Cremonini/DataVisualization1e

b

C

e

m

q

r

S

t

u

www.ingramcontent.com/pod-product-compliance
Lightning Source LLC
LaVergne TN
LVHW020408301125
826457LV00001B/22
* 9 7 8 1 3 9 4 2 8 9 4 8 6 *